THE NEW POLITICS
OF THE
BUDGETARY
PROCESS

Second Edition

AARON WILDAVSKY

University of California, Berkeley

HarperCollins*Publishers*

To the old The Politics of the Budgetary Process,
which did a lot more for me than I did for it.

Sponsoring Editor: Catherine Woods
Project Editor: Donna DeBenedictis
Design Supervisor and Cover Designer: Stacey Agin
Production Manager/Assistant: Willie Lane/Sunaina Sehwani
Compositor: ComCom Division of Haddon Craftsmen, Inc.
Text and Cover Printer/Binder: Malloy Lithographing, Inc.

For permission to use copyrighted material, grateful acknowledgment is made
to the copyright holders on pp. 553–554, which are hereby made part of this
copyright page.

The New Politics of the Budgetary Process, Second Edition
Copyright © 1992 by HarperCollins Publishers Inc.

Library of Congress Cataloging-in-Publication Data
Wildavsky, Aaron B.
    The new politics of the budgetary process / Aaron Wildavsky.—
2nd ed.
        p.   cm.
    Includes bibliographical references and index.
    ISBN 0-673-52179-6
    1. Budget—United States. I. Title.
HJ2051.W483   1991
353.0072'2—dc20   91-18082
                                                        CIP

91 92 93 94   9 8 7 6 5 4 3 2 1

CONTENTS

3 THE DANCE OF THE DOLLARS: CLASSICAL BUDGETING   74

4 THE COLLAPSE OF CONSENSUS   127

5 INSTITUTIONAL MANIFESTATIONS OF BUDGETARY DISSENSUS 174

6 PROCEDURAL MANIFESTATIONS OF BUDGETARY DISSENSUS   224

7 THE POLITICS OF THE ENTITLEMENT PROCESS   272

11 THE DEFICIT   462

12 THE SOLUTION?   482

PREFACE TO THE SECOND EDITION: EXPANDING THE POLITICAL MEANING OF BUDGETING

The first edition of this book was considerably more complex than its older sibling, *The Politics of the Budgetary Process.* The reason was that the process itself had grown more complicated, with much being added and nothing being taken away. The new chapters (Chapters 11 and 12) in this second edition seek to draw lessons about budgeting from the maneuvering around the problem of reducing the deficit. It also seeks to explain the new parts of the budgetary process put in place by the Omnibus Budget Reconciliation Act of 1990 (OBRA). True, this time, a little has been taken away or, like Gramm–Rudman, placed in suspended animation. But much more has been added. Now there are three sequestrations, for instance, instead of one. We could pretend that OBRA doesn't exist. The upside would be that there would be less to learn; the downside, however, would be that for the next five years budgeting would be unintelligible. Are we to study the process that exists or the much simpler one of our distraught imaginings?

Through all the maneuvers, and the maneuvers based on other maneuvers, the same political struggles that animated the first edition of *The New Politics of the Budgetary Process* shine through. There is still deep budgetary dissensus. And these ideological differences about the kind of government and society America ought to have are still being played out through the budget. Only now these conflicts are sharper. Therefore, those who wish to understand politics must acquaint themselves with budgeting if they want to know what is going on.

In *The Politics of the Budgetary Process* I sidestepped the problem of defining "the politics" part by saying that the book was "concerned with budgets as political things" and by focusing on the budget as a record of outcomes and a process of decision making:

> Taken as a whole the federal budget is a representation in monetary terms of governmental activity. If politics is regarded in part as conflict over whose preferences shall prevail in the determination of national policy, then the budget records the outcomes of this struggle. If one asks, "Who gets what the government has to give?" then the answers for a moment in time are recorded in the budget. If one looks at politics as a process by which the government mobilizes resources to meet pressing problems, then the budget is a focus of these efforts. (p 4)

Because what we-the-people decide to politicize is what constitutes "the political" at any one time, this evasion has merit.[1] Enough time has passed and sufficient experience accumulated, however, to begin to put more flesh on the bare bones of politics.

Whether the nation will gain from the political maneuvering that led to the passage of the Omnibus Budget Reconciliation Act of 1990 is an open question. But I have no doubt that the coexistence of a Budget Summit made up of the congressional leaders of both houses of Congress and top officials of the Bush administration and OBRA are good for analysts of political aspects of budgeting. Evaluating the outcomes in these two arenas will enable us to separate those aspects that the national government leadership agreed on in both arenas from those that were altered in OBRA. Thus we can distinguish between the politics that separates elected politicians from the citizenry and the politics of ideology that separates these politicians from each other.

The question of "Who will bear the cost of change?" is of enduring importance. Senior legislators, especially those on appropriations committees, have come to believe that their committees and the agencies for which they are responsible have been getting short shrift. Therefore, they have succeeded in writing into OBRA "hold harmless" provisions that make them more responsible for changes in taxing and spending they initiate but take them off the hook for changes outside of govern-

---

[1]For a discussion of this point in the context of political cultures, see Michael Thompson, Richard Ellis, and Aaron Wildavsky, *Cultural Theory* (Boulder, Colo.: Westview Press, 1990).

ment (war, famine, flood, depression) they feel they cannot control. This withdrawal of responsibility is not as foolish as it sounds. As the continuing debate over the savings and loan collapse indicates, it may be that Americans have been disposed to have government insure them against change (by guaranteeing deposits) while no one worries about who is going to uphold government. Nevertheless, the question of whether it is desirable to have government escape responsibility for what presidents choose to call external changes while citizens must cope with them should be more widely debated than it has been, for it has hardly been discussed at all.

The noticeable speeding up of budgetary reform is convincing evidence that a politics of ideological dissensus is on us. From the Budget Act of 1921 to the Budget Act of 1974 took a little over half a century. Then the act of 1974 was substantially modified as the Gramm–Rudman–Hollings Act (GRH, or Gramm–Rudman in short), with significant new elements added, in 1986, a bare twelve years later. Now OBRA has come a mere four years after Gramm–Rudman. This speed-up, I think, is due to heroic but failing efforts to replace the classical norms of balance, annualarity, and comprehensiveness with new procedures that provide by legislative stipulation what used to be done by informal understandings. The Budget Resolutions of the 1974 act, the deficit-reduction targets of the 1986 act, and the stipulated agreements of the 1990 act (containing, for two years at least, the equivalent of both resolutions and reductions) give legal directions providing overall ceilings, divisions among major programatic areas (i.e., between defense and domestic, entitlement and appropriation), and provide pathways for adjusting to new circumstances. The more precise these instructions become, the more they straitjacket the budgetary process, however, the more fragile they are. With basic differences over policy left standing, these surface to weaken and then destroy the most carefully wrought paper plans. Even now, as I write in mid-March 1991, Republicans are talking about holding off on previously agreed tax increases due to the recession and Democrats are using loosely worded portions of OBRA dealing with supplemental spending to bring in items that would not count against the totals they previously agreed to support.

The expansion of the political agenda to include social issues such as abortion, with its budgetary implications for whether government ought to help poor women afford this choice, should make us aware of the desirability of conceptualizing political values more broadly. The old divisions between left and right, liberal and conservative, were useful at a time when the major political cleavage was between supporters of somewhat larger or somewhat smaller welfare programs. Since both Democrats and Republicans are now divided as well over questions of abortion, of defense, and of prayer in schools, it is desirable to have a way of conceptualizing policy differences that accommodates a wider range of issues. That is why I have introduced cultural language carving the political scene into three unequal parts, namely, egalitarians who believe in diminishing power and resource differences among people, hierarchists who wish to maintain differences with the understanding that the individual parts ought to sacrifice for the collective whole, and individualists who wish to substitute self-regulation for authority. If individualists agree with egalitarians that government ought not to regulate people's personal lives, but disagree with egalitarians about the extent and desirability of regulation of economic activity, the pattern of political conflict we observe should now make better sense. If individualists desire limited economic regulation and hierarchists agree, because they want every person to fulfill the duties of his or her station, yet they disagree about the hierarchists' willingness to intervene in individuals' personal lives, we can understand both the rationale behind their coalition in the Republican party and the precarious nature of that coalition should attention shift from economic to social issues.

From the Budget Summit we learn that Republicans wanted lower taxes, thereby enabling their constituents to hold on to more income, and Democrats wanted higher taxes on higher-income people so as to achieve the more egalitarian objectives on which their party is agreed. From OBRA, which opened up the Summit agreement to legislative preferences after House Republicans defeated the Summit, we learn that rank-and-file Democratic members of Congress are more egalitarian than their leaders. No one who listened to the congressional debates over whether the United States should use armed force to make war in the Persian Gulf, or whether having begun with an air war it should begin a ground war, can have failed to notice that the disagreements were not only about the Persian Gulf itself but also about whether such a war, however successful on its own terms, was a lesser priority than redressing inequalities in American society.

Individual leaders do matter. President Bush's popularity plummeted when he abandoned his promise not to raise taxes, arguing, instead, the greater national need to reduce the deficit. Bush's popularity soared to historic heights when the war ended much sooner and with far fewer casualties than pessimistic forebodings suggested. As Bush stumbled by bringing down on himself maximum disapprobation on the budget, he arose tall during the war when his guidance was both sure and successful. It may be that President Bush's enormous war-gained popularity will confer retrospective validation on his budget-balancing choice, wiping out the fatuity of "read my lips" and replacing it with the vision of "our president doing his best for the country." If the political dissensus theory that animates this book is on the right track, however, the president's personal popularity, except on matters rather directly connected to that war, will not extend to agreement with his less-than-wholly egalitarian views.

If there is now less consensus and more dissensus, how is the budgetary process affected? There should be more disputes over larger amounts that take longer to resolve. And so there have been.

The New Politics of the Budgetary Process was animated by a quite different vision of budgeting as an incremental process. This understanding is reflected in Chapter 3 on ". . . Classical Budgeting" under the straightforward rubric that *"budgeting is incremental."* My major purpose in introducing this term to budgeting was to make readers aware that comprehensive consideration of the budget as a whole, each item compared to all the others, went beyond the possibilities of human calculation. Were it tried, comprehensive calculation would also make agreement on the budget much more difficult. And so, at a time of budgetary dissensus, it has done. The need established by the Budget Act of 1974 to relate total spending to total revenues from the top down has indeed exacerbated conflicts. It does matter greatly when many more major matters are disagreed. Why else would the budget process be so stultified, taking up so much more time and room, often to so little effect?

Consensus means that there is agreement on the budgetary base; when that consensus dissipates, so does incrementalism. Just as the notion of incrementalism depended on the prior existence of a fairly fixed base, which depended on historical continuity, which, in turn, depended on political consensus (see Chapter 3), so budgetary dissensus gravely weakens reliance on the past and opens up policy direction as well as amount of money to change. That is why there is now much more attention to budgeting than before, but by no means more agreement. Just as budgeting was incremental because it was consensual, and consensual because incremental, so dissensual budgeting leads to larger and more rapid changes, which increase disagreement.

Aaron Wildavsky

DEAD ON ARRIVAL?
A PREFACE TO
THE NEW POLITICS OF
THE BUDGETARY PROCESS

Confronted with the vast array of figures in the Budget of the United States, one is likely to think of budgeting as an arid subject, the province of stodgy clerks and dull statisticians. Nothing could be more mistaken.

In introducing the old *Politics of the Budgetary Process* in 1964, I began in all innocence by sharing my most important discovery: Budgeting was interesting. Amazing but true; far from being the preserve of mere technicians, budgeting was the lifeblood of government, the medium through which flowed the essential life-support systems of public policy. No one then seemed to object to being told the obvious.

Today, when budgeting has become the major issue of American national politics, admonitions about its importance, like being told to breathe regularly, have a superfluous air about them—essential but unnecessary. For taxing and spending, resource mobilization and resource allocation, now take up as much or more time on the floors of Congress than all other matters put together. How large government will be, the part it will play in our lives, whether more or less will be done for defense or welfare, how much and what sort of people will pay for services, what kind of society, in sum, we Americans want to have—all these are routinely discussed in budget debates. The importance of conflicts over the size and distribution of the budget—failure to pass a budget on time or at all has become a sign of inability to govern—testifies to the overriding importance of budgeting. Nowadays the State of the Union and the state of the budget have become essentially equivalent.

As the sheer volume of budgeting has risen along with increasingly higher stakes and ever-changing procedures, the need grows apace for an up-to-date account of the new process through which spending decisions are made. As I write (April 1987), there is no contemporary account of how budgets are made. Events have outdistanced all books. Yet I believe a description and analysis of the budgetary process that focused solely on what is happening now would be inadequate, even misleading. Indeed, it is possible to convey an adequate understanding of contemporary budgeting only by comparing it with what has gone before. Since my belief in the indispensability of a historical approach accounts for the organization of the "new" *Politics* and informs its analysis throughout, the reader should know why I have not simply done the best I could with the budget of the day and left it at that.

What is it that no longer exists and is still with us? The substantial changes in budgeting that have taken place in the last twenty years have not really replaced anything; rather, the new has been layered onto the old. There is more of everything—more programs, more money, more debt, more spending devices, more control mechanisms, more participants, more procedures. It is necessary to know about the past because it is still with us. The decentralized, fragmented, legislatively centered budgeting process that stems from its 200-year-old origins still distinguishes the American budgetary process from that of any other democratic nation. The classic dance of the dollars in the appropriations process (memorialized in Richard Fenno's *The Power of the Purse* and my "old" *Politics*) remains: Spending estimates still wend their way from bureaus to departments to the Central Budget Office to the president to the House, Senate, and conference committees, even if some participants have changed roles and new actors are pushing in different directions.

Appreciation of the new depends on distinguishing it from the old. Deciding how much should be spent in toto, how much revenue ought to be raised, and whether a surplus or deficit would be desirable or possible, for instance, seems straightforward. And so it would be anywhere else. But not in America. Not until 1921 did departmental spending estimates go to the Bureau of the Budget (now the Office of Management and Budget) for review before being sent to Congress for consideration. Not until 1974 did Congress commit itself to pass resolutions establishing targets for total spending and revenues. Not until the late 1970s did the president's budget message, which used to set the starting point for congressional action, cease to perform that function; nowadays it is pronounced "dead on arrival."

Here, in the extreme volatility of the budgetary process, we have another reason for taking a historical approach. No one can say whether the Gramm–Rudman–Hollings Emergency Deficit Reduction and Balanced Budget Act of 1985 (GRH) will remain in force (it is now in limbo). It has survived so far not because it is considered desirable but rather because there is no agreement on more sensible alternatives. Whatever happens, GRH's provisions for counting federal credit toward the deficit or, in the Senate, for requiring offsets (new revenues or spending cuts) in order to raise spending beyond the budget resolution, may matter a good deal. It is also possible for the very newest changes to undo the merely new changes; some argue that the 1974 reforms, such as the requirement that Congress make budget resolutions and therefore set up budget committees, make it more difficult to reach agreement. Amid this flux, it seems wise to hold on to a variety of budget procedures, as history has presented them to us, on the chance that practice may well revert back to what it once was.

Whatever form of exposition is adopted, the major omissions of the old *Politics* must be remedied in the new version. Since entitlements (legal obligations on the Treasury to provide people who qualify with stipulated benefits) now amount to just under half of the budget, no book on the subject should neglect it. Yet, aside from an excellent article by Kent Weaver,[1] there is no generic study of entitlements. Nor is there a chapter in a text that can be considered a guide to budgeting for national defense. I shall remedy these lacks here.

This book begins with a discussion of the multiple meanings of bud-

---

[1]Kent Weaver, "Automatic Government: The Politics of Indexation," typescript, 1986.

geting as well as a description of key terms and actors in the process of resource allocation. In order to compare past procedures with contemporary practices, the second chapter surveys the history of budgeting. Here I emphasize the enduring characteristics (from a devotion to budget balance to fragmentation of power) that distinguish America from other nations, and the failing efforts of reformers to provide through the budgetary process the centralized control absent from U.S. politics.

The third chapter on the classical period, roughly 1946 through 1973—now sufficiently remote to wear the patina of time—presents a summary of salient aspects of budgetary calculations and strategies drawn from the old *Politics*. The point made then was that budgeting is so complex—so many items interacting in numerous ways, involving difficult subjects—that budgeters had to simplify by adopting aids to calculation. Certainly the problem of calculation has not gotten any easier; on the contrary, the growth of government (meaning more programs) and the decline of agreement (meaning more closely contested choices) has made figuring out what to do more difficult. The convergence on past agreements that once constituted the base from which calculations proceeded has been eroded; focusing on incremental departures from the base wavers when one cannot agree on where to start: Is it last year's outlays, the president's budget request, the current services budget, the House or Senate budget resolutions, the conference committee recommendation, the continuing resolution, or what? As annual budgeting gives way to continuous revision, agencies cannot be sure of keeping what they were promised nor, given stalemate among the politicians, can they count on getting funds at the stipulated time. Anyone who doubts the increased complexity of the process itself need look only at the Gramm–Rudman–Hollings sequestration procedures (which call for sequential, across-the-board reductions in budget authority when deficit reduction targets are not met) or at the different Senate and House rules for the 302(a) and 302(b) provisions of the 1974 Budget Act, as amended, that, when implemented, shape the rules under which the budget is broken down in Congress. Without such understanding, one cannot tell which subcommittee can handle what items within certain guidelines, or how amendments from the floor can be considered so that it can be known when proposed laws conform to or depart from the agreed spending total—if one exists.

Students of budgeting are safe in studying budgetary calculations, which have merely become more complex; but surely strategies for securing funds must have changed qualitatively. Yes and no. All the old strategies—from the camel's nose to the cultivation of clientele, as the reader will see—are still with us. As is true of the budgetary process itself, new strategies have been grafted on to the old. Strategies based on having the House Appropriations Committee assume the role of guardian of the Treasury, with the Senate acting as an appeals court, have to change when those roles reverse and a newcomer, the budget committees, takes over what is left of guardianship. Participants are bound to have more trouble figuring out the "fair share" for their agency or program when the multiplication of spending sources—loans, loan guarantees, tax preferences, provisions for indexing spending to price changes, annual versus multiyear versus permanent appropriations— makes it so hard to determine who is getting how much. Relationships have to change when the Office of Management and Budget reduces its contacts with agencies in order to conduct continuing negotiations directly with congressional committees.

Chapter 4 provides snapshots of contemporary history that reveal how and why budgetary consensus declined. Entitlements threatened to drive out other spending. Federal credit grew astronomically. Agreements on a balance between revenue and expenditure weakened under the impact of strained economic circumstances and under the theoretical guidance of Keynesian economic doctrine. As economic distress made budget conflicts more severe, other standard practices—agreement on a budgetary base, confining conflicts to incremental departure from that base—began to erode. Reaction to President Nixon's impounding and to Watergate gave Congress reformed procedures under the Budget Act of 1974 but not agreement on how to use them. And the election of Ronald Reagan brought to the fore deep differences over taxation and welfare and defense spending that sharpened budgetary conflict.

The institutional manifestations of this budgetary dissensus, described in the fifth chapter, include transformations in the role of OMB and the appropriations committees and the appearance of the new budget committees. Strategic innovation becomes imperative as agencies and their clientele contemplate new rules of the game. No one and nothing are as they were.

Dissensus, as Chapter 6 shows, brings out both the worst and the best in budgetary procedures. Gimmicks, soft appearances substituting for harsh realities, dismay even those who use them. Across-the-board cuts in GRH substitute for intelligence. Yet there is another side to GRH. When faced with the need to recommend cuts in other programs or tax increases (rather than just asking for more), due to Senate offset provisions, interest-group lobbies begin to engage in previously unheard-of behavior; they become interested in cutting other parts of the budget. Thus an objective that reformers were never able to achieve by exhortation—considering and comparing programs as part of a larger budget—has, for the time being in the Senate, been achieved through the offset mechanism. Were agreement ever reached to limit total spending and to choose the most desired programs within that limit, budget reformers have had a real-life lesson in what to do.

In the seventh and eighth chapters on entitlements, changes in strategies begin to be visible. It is better for program advocates to have funds guaranteed until Congress decides to make a change, than to chance the viscissitudes of the annual appropriations process. It is better for recipients to have their benefits tied to a generous index of rising prices, so that cost of living adjustments are automatic, than to have to ask Congress every year to hold constant the purchasing power of retirees or the unemployed. Unfortunately, such stability for beneficiaries is achieved by risking the instability of government. What is strategically rational for program advocates—indexed permanent entitlements with expanding benefits and beneficiaries—is irrational for budget controllers, who find themselves unable to make large cuts in the relatively small remainder of the budget. Since entitlements make up just under half the budget, freeing them from having to be considered for cuts makes budgeting quite a different game. How to be "entitled" rather than "controllable" is of the strategic essence. Yet there is no budgetary safe harbor. Entitlement status is no guarantee either of rapid growth or of protection against cuts. That is why, in addition to high flyers, I also look at entitlements that failed.

Just as being technically listed as "uncontrollable" in the sense of not being subject to the discipline of annual appropriation does not prevent entitlements from being continuously adjusted, the fact that defense spending takes up the lion's share of "controllable" (i.e., annually appropriated) spending need not signify it will bear the brunt of reductions. But it is large, tempting, and, occasionally, vulnerable.

A chapter on defense spending follows entitlements because it is the second largest type of expenditure. Indeed, with social welfare (mostly entitlements) taking up some 46 percent of total spending, defense 28 percent, and interest on the debt 14 percent, only 12 percent is left for the rest of the budget. These figures constitute the indispensable starting place for any intelligent consideration of contemporary budgeting.

I would be surprised if anyone claims to comprehend fully defense budgeting. Huge dollar figures, long lead times for weapons built out of complex technologies, feast and famine in resources, a rapidly changing world scene, all combine to create confusion. Is there too little oversight or too much micro-management? Are defense managers prevented from doing their best, dragged down by the sheer weight of regulation, or are the services preparing to fight their wars alone so they require much more constraint? All of the above are true under some conditions. As with allegations of "waste, fraud, and abuse" in welfare programs, the general modicum of truth does not tell one where to draw the line between harshness and leniency, initiative and control. If all we care about is having what we need when we need it, and expense is no object, duplication is desirable. Since "how much" affects "what for," the cost influencing the amount and kind of troops and weapons, budgeting is crucial to defense. You tell me: Is it better to learn to live with the faults of defense budgeting, like "goldplating" and "stretchouts," because they are a part of real life and therefore likely to be always with us? Or should we try once again to reform the process, because there has to be a better way? What I can do is explain why every administration complains about the sins of its predecessors and then proceeds to do exactly the same.

The tenth chapter is about proposals for reform of the budgetary process—the line-item veto, constitutional spending limits, statutory balanced budget requirements, and more. The difference between the treatment of reform in the old and new book lies in a much wider perspective. The old *Politics* was virtually bereft of history; although I was astonished at the degree of informal coordination achieved under the old process, I did not pursue its roots in the achievement of balance, annualarity, and comprehensiveness. The new chapter on reform begins with the grave weakening of these norms that once had facilitated coordination of spending and revenue, had lent predictability to budgeting behavior, and had enabled budgeters to minimize their disagreements. Whereas the politics of the old process operated under considerable consensus, so that the importance of agreement on substance was played down, the new politics in a time of dissensus is about grand questions: How much, what for, who pays; in sum, what side are you on? Where before reformers were concerned with improving efficiency and effectiveness in the pursuit of agreed-on objectives, these micro questions (touched on under such designations as performance budgeting, program budgeting, and zero-base budgeting) now have given way to more solemn macro queries: Can we govern? Is there sufficient agreement among the nation's political elites about what kind of society they want in order to do the one thing every government must do—pass its budget? Reforms look quite different if one assumes that changes in political personalities or in budget procedures will produce consensus, rather than fearing that the political visions separating the contestants are too wide to be bridged by anything less than a fundamental change in political alignments. Since I adhere to the latter position, which stresses ideological dissensus, I am less sanguine than others about budgetary cures for political ailments.

Let me put it this way: When there was (mostly) agreement on the base, the old *Politics* stressed conflict over the increments. The new *Politics* stresses the base because it is often disagreed. Conflict is now about fundamentals.

In one respect, neither I nor the budgetary process can go back to where we once were. *The Politics of the Budgetary Process,* circa 1964, has been praised beyond its merits. The budgetary process then was simple; anyone who stumbled on to budgeting could quickly get a grasp of it. Alas, budgeting is no longer so transparent. I have tried to make understandable such previously unheard of subjects as the ability of the federal financing bank to tumble credit off and on the budget, but I cannot guarantee that others will think so. The importance of federal credit is now so manifest—the credit budget, so to speak, being comparable in total to federal spending—that its dimensions cannot fail to impress. After all, credit is money too. So are tax preferences and other forms of resource allocation that do not appear in the budget.

When I first came to the study of budgeting, little preparation was required to understand what was going on. Today you have to know a lot. On the following page, in its entirety, is a letter from two leading Republican representatives to the Democratic Speaker of the House. Can you, the reader, understand what it is about? If not, read on.

Nearly a quarter of a century ago, budgeting was different, and so was I. Closer to students in age (and far closer to them in understanding than my confident prose might suggest), I faced no serious problem of selection; everything I knew about budgeting is in that book. Everything. But no more than the budgetary process can shrug off the accretions of time, can I recapture the days when budgeting meant appropriations and everyone, myself included, took for granted the understandings that made procedures seem so simple. In the old volume, politics was mostly internal to the budgetary process itself. Outside forces figured only through the operations of interest groups and the perceptions of participants as they assessed the political moods of the day. The new volume (in which all is entirely new except for one chapter and a few pages on the nature of budgeting) is much more concerned with the impact of external political forces on the budgetary process. The interests are still there, but they are now joined by ideologies connecting individual programs to the general purposes of government. When budgeting was a side-show, albeit an important one, political stability could be taken for granted. Indeed, that stability made budgeting less vital. The emergence of budgeting center stage signifies its increased dependence on shifting political alignments.

When budgeting operated under a hidden consensus, the subject was

Office of the Republican Leader
United States House of Representatives
Washington, DC 20515

March 24, 1987

The Honorable Jim Wright
Speaker
H-204, The Capitol
Washington, D.C. 20515

Dear Mr. Speaker:

A good many Members of our Budget Committee are apparently willing and anxious now to engage in serious discussions aimed at drafting a Budget Resolution agreeable to the Members of the Democratic and Republican Leaderships.

Such discussions would be a refreshing departure from past practices, and we would welcome them.

We have engaged to date in political give-and-take which seems to be a permanent appendage to the budget process, but as has been the case in the past, the time for such tactics is drawing to a close.

Our Members feel it is important to establish some ground rules or basic understandings prior to such discussions so that neither side is "surprised" by any part of the process or the outcome.

These suggestions have been made to Bill Gray [Dem., PA. Chair, House Budget Committee], but he has felt compelled not to respond. We believe:

1) We must have a Budget proposal submitted by the Committee Majority as a basis for discussion.

2) A final document should contain full and complete reconciliation instructions with full enforcement of those instructions spelled out in the Resolution.

3) That reconciliation package should be brought to the Floor with no new additions to it or incomplete action on the prescribed non-discretionary reductions

4) That the Appropriations subcommittees must be made to comply with their 302b outlay levels, with any failure to comply subject to a point of order. Further, that the so-called "Fazio exception" which allows the Appropriation Committee to bring forward bills which meet their discretionary number even though the Budget Committee outlay ceilings have been breached, must be eliminated.

5) That any omnibus Appropriations bill will be discouraged at all times and that no such bill be brought to the Floor of the House without approval of the bipartisan Leadership for fiscal years 1988 and 1989.

6) That no provision in the Budget Resolution provide for any adjustment in individual or corporate income tax rates.

7) That Gramm–Rudman be corrected to make the automatic sequestration procedure meet any Constitutional challenge.

These stipulations are fundamental to maintaining the integrity of the budget process and would serve as a good foundation for successful negotiations.

It's time you and I and Trent Lott and Tom Foley [Dem. Wash. Majority Whip] got down to business and resolved the differences our two sides have, so that we can get a timetable and come up with something meaningful.

Sincerely,

Robert H. Michel
Republican Leader

Trent Lott
Republican Whip

considered too dull to attract readers. Nine publishers, by my recollection, turned the book down; budgeting was easy to describe but hard to sell. Now that budgeting has acquired some of the interested audience it deserves, the subject unfortunately has become difficult to describe. I hope again to show that the effort to understand is worthwhile. Budget, budget, budget, as members of congress complain, is all we can do unless and until we Americans once again agree on what kind of society and which sort of government we want.

A. W.

ACKNOWLEDGMENTS

Without the extraordinarily favorable reception of the old *The Politics of the Budgetary Process* (Little, Brown and Company, 1964, first edition), I would not have been encouraged to undertake the many studies that have led to this new version. Nor would I have had the material for Chapter 3 on the classical period. Without my collaboration with Carolyn Webber on our *A History of Taxation and Expenditure in the Western World* (Simon and Schuster, 1986), it would not have been possible for me to write the second chapter on the historical development of American budgeting. Without my continuing collaboration with Joseph White on "The Battles of the Budget: From the Last Year of Carter through Gramm–Rudman–Hollings, and Tax Reform," I would not have known enough about contemporary budgeting to write the fourth through the sixth chapters. Without the many papers on entitlements prepared by students in my seminars on budgeting, Chapters 7 and 8 could not have been written. Without the research assistance of Ronald D. Pasquariello, Dean Hammer, and John Gilmore, Chapter 9 on defense budgeting would have been much poorer. Blake Edgar read appropriations hearings so as to supply me with up-to-date versions of budgeting strategies. Readers will benefit by his good taste.

Truly this book, even more than most research, is a collective enterprise. As always, I have benefited from continuing conversation with participants in budgeting. Congressional hearings and GAO reports and the works of scholars have proved invaluable. Far more than in earlier times, I have learned a lot from work by reporters who specialize in budgeting and from periodicals, like the *Congressional Quarterly* and *The National Journal,* that cover the subject. Newsletters—*Inside the Administration* and Stanley Collender's *Federal Budget Report*—and periodic reports from Carol Cox's Committee on a Responsible Federal Budget have helped me understand what is happening as it happens.

After a draft of the manuscript had been completed, I asked Dean Hammer to stand in for all those who did not know about budgeting but wanted to learn. As my lay reader, he helped me simplify my presentation, add material where it was missing, and generally reorganize the manuscript. If I have achieved a level of exposition appropriate to a beginner in the study of budgeting, I owe that to Dean's unremitting efforts to set me straight.

The award for help above and beyond the call of duty goes to colleagues who read the entire manuscript—Naomi Caiden, Mark Kamlet, David Mowery, Jonathan Rauch, James Savage, and Joseph White. They have saved me from many errors and their criticisms have sharpened my perceptions. All of them will have an opportunity in their own work to set the world straight on matters budgetary.

John Ellwood provided a critique of my use of budgetary terms, and Gordon Adams helped improve the chapter on defense. I am grateful to these immensely knowledgeable students of budgeting.

Marie-Anne Seabury edited this book for me with her usual eye for my infelicities. Doris Patton, my secretary, not only typed several drafts of the manuscript impeccably but also prepared research material. No doubt she wondered whether the mountains of note cards would ever diminish. Neither the budget nor budgeting shows any sign of diminishing, so why should studies of the subject decline?

*   *   *

For the first time I am fortunate in having colleagues on the Berkeley campus who are themselves students of budgeting. I am grateful for conversations on the current trends with David Mowery in the Haas School of Business and for a variety of source materials and detailed comments on the last two chapters by John Ellwood in the Graduate School of Public Policy.

Stanley Collender of Price Waterhouse; Robert W. Hartman, Senior Analyst for the Budget Process of the Congressional Budget Office; and Joseph White of the Brookings Institution provided me with detailed comments on Chapters 11 and 12. I am especially grateful to Joe White, who helped me organize these chapters in a more coherent manner. Truly, he has learned more than he was taught. Other reviewers who offered helpful suggestions include: James W. Fossett, State University of New York, Albany; Mark S. Kamlet, Carnegie Mellon University; Alfreda J. McCollough, College of Charleston; Kevin V. Mulcahy, Louisiana State University; David J. Olson, University of Washington; and R. D. Sloan, Jr., University of Colorado, Boulder.

A. W.

THE NEW POLITICS OF THE
BUDGETARY PROCESS

© United Feature Syndicate.

BUDGETING AS CONFLICTING PROMISES

1

THE WORD THAT ORIGINALLY meant a leather bag or pouch used for carrying money has, through the years, taken on a larger meaning. Today we still find etymological traces of the word "budget" when we hear, for example, about the "budget package" put together by Congress and the president. We have come a long way since the days of carrying the budget by hand, though we may regret it. Not only has the pouch expanded considerably, but it has become rather amorphous. No single document represents "the United States budget." The only document that resembles a formal budget is a book representing the president's preferences—his asking price, so to speak. When we hear that this budget is "unrealistic," we learn that many of these preferences are unlikely to be realized. The same can be said of House and Senate budget resolutions specifying how much should be spent in total, and on major programs, as well as how much revenue should be raised. These, too, may be only pious hopes. In the end, we are left with a variety of pieces of legislation—spending through appropriations, entitlements, credit, tax preferences, and more—that taken together constitute the budget.

What do we mean when we speak about the budget? At one level a

1

budget is a prediction. A budget contains words and figures that propose expenditures for certain objects and purposes. The words describe types of expenditures (salaries, equipment, travel) or purposes (preventing war, improving mental health, providing low-income housing), and the figures are attached to each item. Presumably, those who make a budget intend there to be a direct connection between what is written in it and future events. If requests for funds are granted, if they are spent in accordance with instructions, and if the actions involved lead to the desired consequences, then the purposes stated in the document will be achieved. Budgets thus become links between financial resources and human behavior in order to accomplish policy objectives. Only through observation, however, is it possible to determine the degree to which the predictions postulated in budget documents turn out to be correct.

In the most general definition, budgeting is concerned with translating financial resources into human purposes. A budget, therefore, may also be characterized as a series of goals with price tags attached. Since funds are limited and have to be divided in one way or another, the budget becomes a mechanism for making choices among alternative expenditures. When the choices are related to one another so as to achieve desired goals, a budget may be called coordinated. Should it include a detailed specification of how objectives are to be achieved, a budget also may serve as a plan of work for those who assume the task of implementation. If emphasis is placed on achieving the most policy returns for a given sum of money, or on obtaining the desired objectives at the lowest cost, a budget may become an instrument for ensuring efficiency.

There may be a wide gap, however, between the intentions of those who make up a budget and their accomplishments. Although the language of a budget calls for achieving certain goals, through planned expenditures, investigation may reveal that no funds have been spent for these purposes, that the money has been used for other purposes, that quite different goals have been achieved, or that the same goals have been reached in different ways.

Viewed in another light, a budget may be regarded as a contract. Congress and the president promise to supply funds under specified conditions, and the agencies agree to spend the money in ways that have been agreed upon. (When an agency apportions funds to its subunits, it may be said to be making an internal contract.) Whether or not the contract is enforceable, or whether or not the parties actually agree about what the contract purportedly stipulates, is a matter for inquiry. To the extent that a budget is carried out, however, it imposes a set of mutual obligations and controls upon the contracting parties. The word *mutual* should be stressed because it is so easy to assume that control is exercised in a unilateral direction by superiors (congressmen, department heads, and so on) over those formally subordinate to them. But when an appropriations committee approves some expenditures and not others, when it sets down conditions for the expenditure of funds, the committee is also obligating itself to keep its part of the bargain. A department head (to choose another example) who hopes to control the actions of her subordinates must ordinarily follow through on a promise to support some of their requests or else find them trying to undermine her. A budget thus becomes a web of social as well as of legal relationships in which commitments are made by all parties, and where sanctions may be invoked (though not necessarily equally) by all.

The web of interactions involved in allocating resources suggests the manifold difficulties that may arise during the budgetary process. Agreement is difficult because people want different things (or different amounts of the same things). People may also judge the future differently, partly because they prefer different futures, and this will lead them to disagree about what limits (and opportunities) the group faces. In the household, different guesses about next year's food prices and income will justify buying more or less expensive furniture; in government, different guesses and desires about the next year's inflation and revenues will justify buying more or less expensive battleships. Even people who can agree on what to buy may disagree on who should pay for it. The two incomes in a household could contribute equally to the rent, or the rent could be divided proportionately to the incomes. Each person may attempt to pay less by getting others to pay more. But preferences for different ways of life—for more competition, order, or equality—also play a part. Whether one prefers equality of condition or equality of opportunity—the richer subsidizing the poorer or the poorer trying to work their way up, or some combination of the two to maintain social stability—makes a great difference to one's view of desirable public and, therefore, budget policy.

Budgeting in any group is a process in which various people express different desires and make different judgments. In order to construct agreement on a range of items, group members resort to arguments about what is right and just. Now no one makes these values up; they come out of a worldview, an array of preferences about how people ought to live with other people. When these values are not merely ethereal (e.g., brotherhood) but lead to action—more for them, less for us—we see that budgeting is really about opposing and reconciling different ways of life. Sometimes peoples' preferences are dictated by principles (for example, that each should pay according to his ability; or that she who makes the largest contribution should have the most influence). It is hard to tell when people are sincere in invoking principles, for sometimes a principle is just a convenient excuse for a preference that has some other ground. In either case, ideals are invoked in order to persuade others; we have all been involved in arguments where the "principles" seemed to cause more furor than the action (Who will wash the dishes tonight?) would seem to justify. It is one thing, for instance, to argue that defense or social welfare spending is too high; it is another to contend that it would be morally wrong to provide the funds. More or less is easier to compromise than right or wrong. Because it raises questions about how people should relate to each other, budgeting can encompass disputes larger than their seeming subjects.

The desire not to disappoint or anger others makes planning to ensure that promises are kept important. Agreement in advance on spending (the promises in budget legislation) has two advantages: It bypasses continuing negotiation about each purchase, and it allows each member of the group to plan activities with assurance that the others will cooperate. Budgeting is part of the process of cooperative action in which commitments to contribute resources are joined to commitments as to their use. When promises cannot be kept for a year or more, budgeting breaks down.

Always, in the background, questions of authority—Who has the right to decide for whom?—and legitimacy—Do we trust our institutions to act for us?—overlay each choice. "Papa knows best" is different than majority rule or each person making the best deal. The greater the legitimacy accorded institutions, the more disposed are participants to accept outcomes as authoritative. When consent as well as content have to be hammered out on each and every matter, decision making becomes onerous. The process slows down both because many more choices are likely to be contested and because their significance has been enlarged from "how much" and "what for" to "who has the right to decide."

The budgetary process is further complicated by the many different implications for policy in the budget. There is a fiscal policy implication in which the total amount of spending and its deficit or surplus relationship to revenue are designed to stimulate or restrain the economy—to fight unemployment or inflation. The budget is indicative of the role of government; the budget summarizes the balance between public and private sectors of the economy—that is, what proportion of gross national product (GNP) consists of federal government spending—in short, "how much" federal government we have. The distribution of spending in very broad categories describes the kind of government we want: one that emphasizes military might, or protects the middle class, or helps the poor, or builds for the future. The assumptions in budget resolutions, and action on appropriations or entitlements or tax expenditures, also mean that the budget is a package of thousands of specific programs: how much to invest in airport safety; which people, if any, should receive special nutrition benefits; how many F-16s the air force needs.

All these policies are controversial. Some—unemployment versus inflation, the size of government, emphasis on military or social spending—are those that best distinguish Democrats from Republicans, liberals from conservatives. Yet budget politics need not cleave on these lines alone. Not all Republicans are conservatives; many Democrats are not liberals. The choices in budgeting pose tradeoffs that make it hard to predict all choices from party or ideology. Greater military expenditure, without corresponding cuts in social spending, means bigger government and larger deficits; being a conservative or Republican will not tell a congresswoman whether she should prefer budget balance to defense.

Party lines will also be blurred by contradictions between different preferences: Liberals usually like defense contracts for their districts; budget balancers can nevertheless like mortgage subsidies; conservatives can see good in social security or food stamps. Nevertheless, knowing a politician's party is a better guide than any other single factor to predict whether she is likely to vote for larger welfare and less defense.[1]

Just as it is made up of many policies, the budget also has many meanings according to one's institutional position in the government. To the ordinary citizen, budgeting is both mysterious and simple. It is so hard to understand that its complexity may be ignored in resorting to a simple test of virtue: Can the government balance its books or not? Is it in control of itself? For a federal agency—and for the state, local, and semiprivate organizations largely funded by the federal government—the budget is the irrigation system that provides the water without which an agency and its products would parch and wither. Interest groups may see the many steps of budgeting as opportunities or obstacles and budgeting institutions as allies or enemies. Some parts—an appropriations or authorizing subcommittee—may be "captured," but there are too many centers of decision to capture them all. If interest groups can simply try to get more for their favored programs, their strategies may be straightforward; if the budgetary process is arranged so that desires of various groups conflict—more for one of them means less for others—it is harder for each group to figure out what to do.

For the budget and appropriations committees, budgeting is their purpose and their power; their members must work to preserve that power. Since budgeting often encroaches on the turf of authorizing committees, they may view the budgetary process as a threat and an intrusion. For congressmen with strong issue preferences that have been stymied by the relevant authorizing committees (committees whose domain is to recommend programs and activities for congressional approval), budgetary action may provide power. The budget resolutions, appropriations, and occasional debt-ceiling increases are trains that must run, and there may not be time to kick off the stowaways. Appropriations

[1]See James L. Payne, "Voters Aren't So Greedy After All," *Fortune* (August 18, 1986), pp. 91–92.

especially become targets of opportunity for "riders"—opposition to abortion and military aid to Central American forces, for example. Budget resolutions provide chances for votes on issues that might not otherwise reach the floor (e.g., public works funding or increases in veterans' benefits). For partisans, particularly leaders, of the Democratic and Republican parties, the totals for big programs in the budget resolutions measure their party's influence on the course of American government; short of the actual organization of the two houses (election of the Speaker, committee assignments), no other action is potentially of as great moment to the party leadership. The battle of the budget is the test of generalship. The ability of the parties to stay together in the final encounter (apart from the vote to organize the houses along partisan lines) is now their ultimate test of cohesion.

To those congressmen who identify with the institution—and this, depending upon the issue and challenge, ranges from a few to all of them—budgeting is a test of Congress. Can Congress choose, can it enforce its will? In short, can Congress govern? The president asks the same questions, slightly changed: "Can I govern the agencies? Can I govern Congress? Can I govern responsibly and maintain public support?" Both president and Congress must ask, "Do we make policy or do the policies control us?" And, "Can any of us control events?"

The complexity of the federal budgetary process—the large numbers of wide-ranging yet uncertain consequences—reveals that the purposes of budgets are as varied as the purposes of the people who make them. One budget may be designed to coordinate diverse activities so that they complement one another in the achievement of common goals. Another budget may be put together primarily to discipline subordinate officials within a government agency by reducing amounts for their salaries and pet projects. And a third budget may be directed essentially to mobilizing the support of clientele groups who benefit by the services the agency provides. Nothing is gained, therefore, by insisting that a budget is only one of these things when it might be any or all of them or many other kinds of things as well.[2] One may, however, adopt a particular view

[2]A good discussion of the nature and variety of budgets may be found throughout Jesse Burkhead's *Government Budgeting* (New York: Wiley, 1956). See also the illuminating comments in Frederick C. Mosher, *Program Budgeting: Theory and Practice, with Particu-*

of the budget as most useful for the purposes he has in mind. Without claiming to have found the only right perspective, or to have exhausted the subject in any way, I would like to propose a conception that seems useful in talking about the budgetary process as a phenomenon of human behavior in a governmental setting.

Taken as a whole, the federal budget is a representation in monetary terms of governmental activity. If politics is regarded in part as conflict over whose preferences shall prevail in the determination of national policy, then the budget records the outcomes of this struggle. If one asks, "Who gets what the government has to give?" then the answers for a moment in time are recorded in the budget. If one looks at politics as a process by which the government mobilizes resources to meet pressing problems, then the budget is a focus of these efforts.

The size and shape of the budget is a matter of serious contention in our political life. Presidents, political parties, administrators, congressmen, interest groups, and interested citizens vie with one another to have their preferences recorded in the budget. The victories and defeats, the compromises and the bargains, the realms of agreement and the spheres of conflict in regard to the role of national government in our society all appear in the budget. In the most integral sense, budgeting— that is, attempts to allocate scarce financial resources through political processes in order to realize disparate visions of the good life—lies at the heart of the political process. That there are visions of the good life enables people to make commitments to one another through the budget; that these visions conflict means that not all such promises can be kept.

BUDGETS ARE CONFLICTING COMMITMENTS

Our government makes different commitments to people and to other units of government, and these commitments take varied forms. All the

lar Reference to the U.S. Department of the Army (Chicago: Public Administration Service, 1954), pp. 1–18.

commitments ultimately are shaped by law (and therefore by Congress, the president, and the courts). Some of these laws, *appropriations acts,* constitute permission for agencies of the government (e.g., the FBI or National Institutes of Health) to either spend or contract to spend specific amounts of money during the coming year or years. Other laws, such as the 1935 Social Security Act with its numerous amendments, contain promises to individuals that the government will pay specific sums to those who meet certain criteria. These laws, frequently called *entitlements,* differ from appropriations acts in four crucial ways:

1. Entitlements do not specify spending totals. Total spending under these programs, such as Unemployment Compensation, is simply the sum of the legislatively mandated payments to individuals. Administering agencies may withdraw from the Treasury whatever funds the law and the situation require.

2. Since totals are not legally mandated, they can be "guesstimated" but cannot be known in advance. Actual figures will depend on the number of people who qualify for the program and the amounts to which they are entitled. Payments for Unemployment Compensation, for example, depend upon both the number of unemployed and their previous base earnings, neither of which can be known exactly in advance. Not only are totals not directly chosen, they can only be known in retrospect.

3. The authority to spend is not limited in time. Rather than being authorized for use in the coming fiscal year, funding is available so long as a program exists; no ending date is established.

4. Unlike the relationship of other agencies to the budget process, the process for creating and amending these programs does not, in any meaningful way, involve House and Senate Appropriations Committees.

"Once enacted," a Government Accounting Office report summarizes the differences, "entitlement legislation may automatically authorize an administrative agency to spend the funds for making the prescribed payments without advance appropriations from the Congress, thereby effectively relinquishing congressional control through the normal appropriations process."[3] The differences between appropriated and entitlement spending mean that legal authority for spending is the product of decisions taken by different kinds of committees at different times. Entitlements proposed by legislative committees have been adopted and amended separately over the years. The appropriations acts themselves, recommended by a separate set of committees, moreover, are not all considered at the same time. Every year there are at least thirteen of them, each considered by a different subcommittee of the appropriations committees in the House and Senate, often at somewhat different times.

There is also a combination of these two commitments: the *appropriated entitlement.* As in the case of Aid to Families with Dependent Children, authority to make payments is enacted in the authorizing statute, but Congress must also make an annual grant of spending authority in an appropriations bill.

Among the most important misunderstandings about federal government appropriations is the belief that they ordinarily enumerate the specific projects on which money will be spent. They may, but they often do not. Instead, money is appropriated in lump sums for general purposes with particular projects listed in conference committee reports or the reports of House or Senate Appropriations subcommittees.

The nomenclature of budgeting adds to the difficulty in understanding the process. Laws that commit the government to spend money create *budget authority.* Budget authority (BA) is just what it sounds like: authority granted to some agent of the government to spend money. When the money is spent, it is called an *outlay.* Outlays cannot be made without budget authority.

The federal government cannot provide money to individuals or other units of government unless Congress gives legal authority to do so. This authority is defined in most cases (although not in all cases, as with loans

---

[3]Report to the Congress by the Comptroller General of the United States, "What Can Be Done to Check the Growth of Federal Entitlement and Indexed Spending," March 3, 1981, PAD-81-21, p. 10.

and loan guarantees) as budget authority. The statutes that grant budget authority are of two general types: appropriations bills and "backdoor authority," which occurs outside the normal appropriations process. The most common forms of backdoor authority are borrowing authority, contract authority, and entitlements.

Appropriated funds are not necessarily all spent in a given year; the acts provide budget authority, but each year's outlays (i.e., actual spending) result from a combination of this year's and previous years' authority. For example, an appropriation may allow the Urban Mass Transit Administration (UMTA) to commit $200 million for a rapid transit extension in Chicago. This budget authority allows UMTA to enter into an obligation (i.e., contract) to spend that money. The money will, however, actually be outlaid (spent) over a period of years as the extension is built and material, labor, and design paid for.

In retrospect, outlays or actual expenditure for a given fiscal year are known. In prospect, they can only be estimated. Jonathan Rauch says it well: "Where Congress is concerned, budget authority is law, and therefore solid; outlays are staff estimates of the probable effect of the law, and thus are slippery."[4]

This difference between budget authority and outlays is a primary source of confusion for people who follow federal budgeting. Congress votes on BA, but each year's spending, and thus fiscal policy and the deficit, depends on outlays. Congressmen have some idea about the size of outlays that will result from their votes on BA, but, as we will see, the estimates can be controversial. What they vote on—authority— therefore, is not quite what they fight about—outlays. The distinction between budget authority and outlays allows all sorts of tricks, traps, and maneuvers, some of them inadvertent. Why, then, does it exist?

This situation results from the nature of many federal programs and the problems in administering them because of the size of the federal government. In our early history, the size that mattered was geography. Before the telegraph and the locomotive, communications were much slower. The federal government did not do very much, but what it did often took place a long way from Washington. Federal agents—customs officials from Boston to New Orleans; postmasters or army units spread from the Northwest territories to Florida—could not possibly be directed closely from the center. Slow communications meant that in the War of 1812 the Battle of New Orleans was fought weeks after peace had been made. In those days the government had to let its agents incur costs as they came along; then auditors would check the records in slow and excruciating detail. Congress provided authority to spend and under the Treasury Department chiefly controlled the honesty and frugality of actual outlays through its accounting system. Smaller local governments could vote on annual outlays directly because their work was closer at hand, and errors could be corrected if necessary by getting the legislature, say, a city council, together for a special meeting. Gathering Congress was more difficult. The kind of annual focus on outlays that concerns us now was impractical, at least for much of the nineteenth century.[5]

Later, change from a focus on budget authority to one on outlays was inhibited by established congressional routine and the nature of many federal activities. The organizational structure of federalism had become important. An organization that does its own work, like an individual spending only on himself, can change spending plans more easily than can one that works through obligations to others. The federal government has always done a lot of its work through others; contractors carried mail through Panama or built dams; in later years, state and local governments received federal funds for everything from law enforcement to caring for the poor. Working through third parties meant that federal planners had less idea of how work would be scheduled, while recipients of money needed some guarantees about federal action for their own planning. The organizational complexity, the layers of federal

[5]See Leonard D. White's histories, *The Federalists* (New York: Macmillan, 1961), *The Jeffersonians* (New York: Macmillan, 1951), and *The Jacksonians* (New York: Macmillan, 1956). See also Frederick C. Mosher, *The GAO: The Quest for Accountability in American Government* (Boulder, Colo.: Westview Press, 1979); and James Sterling Young, *The Washington Community, 1802–1828* (New York: Columbia University Press, 1966).

administration, therefore, encouraged a system in which funds were committed annually but their use was not restricted to a strict annual schedule.

In short, Congress' focus on budget authority rather than outlays arises chiefly from the difficulties of managing federal activities. Those difficulties in turn inhibit control of the deficit. The annual *balance sheet*—the outlays—is not the same as *commitments*—the budget authority.

Among outlays based on entitlements, outlays based on previous years' appropriations, and outlays voted and spent that year, each year's spending is based on commitments made at different times. In fiscal 1980, according to the Office of Management and Budget, only 27.3 percent of outlays were determined by the appropriations process for that year. In addition to interest on the debt and prior year's authority, most of the rest was made up of entitlements, and these in turn were largely composed of payments to individuals. Government has gotten good at writing checks.

TAX PREFERENCES

What is true of spending is more true of taxing: Tax law is an accretion of years of decisions. Like entitlements, tax law is open-ended in that individuals are obligated to contribute according to various criteria, rather than the government's being guaranteed some sum of revenue. Revenue may be influenced and estimated but, in these circumstances, not decreed. When economic or demographic conditions change—how many people at which incomes fit into certain categories—revenues rise or fall accordingly.

Tax legislation is handled by the House Committee on Ways and Means and the Senate Committee on Finance. These committees also have jurisdiction over many entitlement programs, such as Unemployment Compensation and the massive Old Age, Survivors, Disability and Health Insurance (OASDHI) system. OASDHI includes the old age pensions we normally call social security, disability pensions, and medicare, the largest programs in the budget. The tax committees have jurisdiction over these entitlements because, by their design, these programs directly relate taxes to benefits. People earn the right to benefits by contributing to the system, thereby making the program look like insurance (you pay premiums to insure against the risk of being old, sick, or unemployed). The contributions are earmarked for trust funds, and benefits are paid out of each program's fund.

Such contributions are taxes: If you meet the criteria for paying them, but fail to do so and are caught, you may go to jail. While payments to individuals in some of these programs, like medicare, have little to do with the amounts contributed (and the Treasury is obligated to make up any shortfall through its general revenues), the trust-fund financing device requires that decisions about benefits be linked to financing. That link is accomplished institutionally by giving the revenue committees jurisdiction over benefit levels as well. The insurance (real or hypothetical) mechanism of these programs also deepens their character as obligations that may not be changed: People have paid for their benefits. Of course, people also have paid for appropriated programs, but in the social insurance programs, recipients can argue that they individually contributed for the specific purpose of personal insurance.

The committees have another type of spending jurisdiction—"tax preferences." These provisions of the law reduce taxpayers' liability to the government so long as they are engaged in some activity that the government wishes to encourage. Tax preferences are used to encourage certain industries or to promote widely desired individual goods (the tax deduction for mortgage interest encourages the construction industry as well as home ownership). Also they may be justified in terms of the wider national interest (credits for energy exploration serving to reduce dependence on foreign oil). Those who do not like tax preferences call them "loopholes," "gimmicks," or "tax expenditures." The metaphor suggests money escaping, or being diverted from its intended use, and is misleading. Such loopholes are passed by Congress and are as intended as any other legislation (although, as with other legislation, there may be unintended consequences, so that a group that was not originally supposed to receive tax preferences is able to qualify). The mortgage interest deduction and the nontaxation of employee health benefits (which, after all, are equivalent to income) are examples of tax decisions that involve many billions of dollars and major social policies. Because tax preferences affect many groups, the tax committees are petitioned for aid by a huge array of constituencies, all trying to get something out of a given tax bill.

Tax preferences and entitlements are similar in that it is hard to imagine either of them being subject to substantial annual review. In each case, large numbers of people make commitments on the basis of government policy—to invest under certain depreciation rules; to save at a certain rate because social security exists. Entitlements in particular involve commitments that politicians view as substantially different from those made by appropriations; the consequences will come up in Chapter 7. Our discussion so far should establish that taxing may look like spending, and spending may be many different things.

For most of American history, as in the old *Politics*, appropriations were what people meant when they spoke about the budget. We can understand this if we review some of the power stakes in appropriations.

APPROPRIATIONS: THE POWER OF CONGRESS AND POWER WITHIN CONGRESS

Americans have long feared oppression by the political executive. Congressmen have long seen themselves as the bulwark against such oppression. The public, judging from opinion polls, trusts Congress no more than the presidency; but congressmen still see themselves in a protective role. Their major weapon is the "power of the purse"—the fact that, as the Constitution states, "No money shall be drawn from the Treasury, but in consequence of Appropriations made by law." The power of the purse is, then, a legislative power in that no money may be spent without the granting of budget authority by Congress.

The process of annually appropriating funds for federal agencies is intended to enforce dependence upon Congress of those agencies' officers. Unless an agency justifies itself each year, it risks losing funding. If the agency behaves in ways that upset Congress, it has an annual opportunity to bring the agency into line through threats or actual changes in appropriations. The agency does not have the advantage of delay, as it would if Congress needed to legislate a change because funding was permanent or multiyear unless otherwise altered. Unlike entitlement funding, annual appropriations mean that delay will cause funding to run out and the agency's activities to cease. Appropriations acts are privileged in floor consideration because congressmen do not ordinarily want maneuvering or logjams to shut down programs.

The House Appropriations Committee, being larger in number but with fewer duties (and therefore more specialized), has always paid more attention to detail than has its Senate counterpart. Not all details are incorporated into the annual act or report, but intensive review enables members and staff of the appropriate House subcommittee to judge whether an agency is using the money as Congress intended, or as its members intend, rather than in the political interests of the current administration or the desires of administrators.

The appropriations process is in part a response to the very problem of designing expenditure controls in a system full of advocates. We may ask why budget oversight, just like the rest of oversight, is not left to the authorizing committees—those, such as Armed Services or House Energy and Commerce, which write the legislation that creates, and gives power to, the agencies. The answer is that they do not have budget powers because Congress does not trust them to control themselves. Congressmen believe that members of the authorizing committees have very strong incentives to ally with the agencies they authorize. By looking at the job of a congressman, we can understand both this belief and why congressmen act on it by regulating themselves.

Congressmen, as Richard Fenno emphasizes in his *Congressmen in Committees,* have multiple goals: They want to make good policy, have personal power, keep Congress strong (their power depends on the institution's), make voters happy, and please people who can influence voters (by giving money or publicity or other campaign help). The congressional committee system helps congressmen pursue all of these goals, but with some drawbacks for budgeting.[6]

The committee system divides the labor—of attending to the facts, and of assessing the group preferences involved in hundreds of policy issues—because the average member can develop expertise only in a tiny portion of policy matters. But he can look to the committees for guidance on other legislation; and he expects others to look to him for guidance in his own field, where he has power and the attendant chance to make policy.

Committees do not always get their way. They cannot push through Congress legislation that a majority finds obnoxious; committees that persist in trying (e.g., House Education and Labor in recent years) risk losing the benefits of deference from their colleagues. Other congressmen, however, rarely are familiar with the details of legislation in a committee's jurisdiction and therefore may not even know that they do not like it. There is a large gray area in which a committee will have discretion.

Further, legislation needs committee approval to reach the floor. Therefore, the committees have a virtual veto over, and largely shape, policy initiatives in their areas. While it is possible to bypass committees through such devices as a discharge petition, the immense effort, as well as hard feelings, discourage most efforts. Hence those concerned— farmers and the USDA for agriculture, the Federal Communications Commission and broadcasters for Energy and Commerce, for example—greatly value influence on those committee members.

Often congressmen sit on a committee because they bring to Congress a special interest in that subject. Sometimes the clientele served can provide helpful support (or damaging opposition) for reelection. Members may seek to do the most good, however conceived, and that may well mean doing good for those people and in that policy area over which, as committee members, they have the greatest influence. Interest groups encourage such attention, whatever its origin, with campaign

[6]See Richard F. Fenno, Jr., *Congressmen in Committees* (Boston: Little, Brown and Company, 1973).

assistance; agencies respond to policy suggestions even if not incorporated in legislation; and over time there develops a mutually supportive, three-point relationship among committee members, interest groups, and agencies. These alliances have been called *iron triangles,* and critical observers hold that these bonds cannot be broken by outsiders. Actually these triangles are of widely varying strength (as a study of entitlements will show).

When the House Ways and Means Committee and the Senate Finance Committee report legislation on social security and Unemployment Compensation, they may simultaneously be spending and supporting that spending with revenues. When legislative committees authorize spending without specific revenues, as in entitlements such as kidney dialysis, other congressmen fear this spending may be excessive. Since members of individual legislative and appropriations committees do not know the needs of other committees as well, and since they are particularly aware of and concerned by needs in their own areas, congressmen fear that each of their committees will ask for more funding than they, as a body, are willing to support. The total requested may be more than congressmen are willing to vote in taxes.

All congressmen care about the relation of spending to taxing, and so do voters; congressmen fear the consequences, both for their own reelection and for the institution, if they continually spend more than they can raise. For that reason the appropriations committees were constituted with extensive powers. Congressmen on authorizing committees delegated to congressmen on appropriations committees the power (subject to floor votes) to limit spending. Thus the appropriations committees are in an inherently adversarial relation with the rest of Congress. They are protected by confidence in their discretion; when they are believed to have overstepped their bounds, they might lose their power (as happened in both House and Senate in the last quarter of the nineteenth century). The late nineteenth century experience, however, was not deemed a success, and since 1921 the appropriations committees have been among the more powerful in Congress.

Budgetary policy is determined by both authorizing and appropriating legislation. Louis Fisher has described the standard model of the relationship:

As a general principle, authorizing committees are responsible for recommending programs and activities to be approved by Congress. The committees establish program objectives and frequently set dollar ceilings on the amounts that can be appropriated. Once this authorization stage is complete, the Appropriations Committees recommend the actual level of "budget authority," allowing federal agencies to enter into obligations. This, of course, is an idealized model. Actual congressional operation is substantially different.[7]

And it is different because appropriations now fund substantially less than half the budget.

The old authorizing-appropriating dichotomy no longer works so neatly. The old relationship does not apply, mostly because presidents and Congresses have wanted to spend more by guaranteeing payments to individuals. Appropriations acts are so complicated, moreover, that the appropriations subcommittees develop substantial independence from the parent committee, thus limiting the potential to trade off spending among the activities funded by the acts. The authorizing committees, unsurprisingly, sometimes resist and try to reverse appropriations committee action on the floor. Almost always this is done to increase spending.

The boundaries between authorizing and appropriating decisions are hard to maintain in practice. A decision not to fund an activity, or to fund it under certain conditions (e.g., abortions allowed only in case of rape or serious threat to the life of the mother), looks much like a policy decision. Unfortunately, the many possibilities for undermining appropriations and authorizations exacerbate power struggles among committees. They also create incentives to complicate appropriations legislation with floor amendments ("riders" that the authorizing committees would disapprove); appropriations, which must pass, thus may be held hostage.

Yet the appropriations process has been and is meaningful: Appropriations committees derived power from the special advantages granted to legislation on the floor; placement on the committee, for many years, of congressmen from fairly safe districts; and the influence of powerful chairmen, in the years when chairmen had great formal powers over

[7]Louis Fisher, "The Authorization-Appropriation Process in Congress: Formal Rules and Informal Practices," *Catholic University Law Review,* Vol. 29, No. 5 (1979), pp. 52–105.

committees (which lasted until the mid-1970s). Most important, the role of the committee was accepted both by its own members and by other members of each house. Since anybody could spend, committee members for many years found both virtue and power in limiting expenditure.

The appropriations committees exemplify the American practice of opposing ambition with ambition, of functioning under the checks and balances so eloquently justified in *The Federalist.* The ambition of those committees to restrain spending counters that of the authorizers to increase it; the results vary. In a wider sense, House, Senate, and president all check each other. When they were thought not to check each other enough, a new layer of committees, called budget committees, was added to help safeguard the treasury. Once that happened, something obvious, yet unexpected, occurred: The appropriations committees withdrew from their previous positions as guardians of the treasury. Support for committee norms gave way in part to self-expression by members. For some members, program advocacy became the main purpose. For others, still adhering to notions of helping improve the management of federal program efficiency remained important but holding down spending did not.

Despite these changes in ideology and perceived self-interest, the appropriations committees remain important. For one thing, the growth of government to a trillion dollars a year means that the two-fifths going through the appropriations committees represents big money. Put another way, although the proportion of the whole passing through the appropriations process has declined, the absolute amount is still far larger than the total budget for all but the last two decades. For another thing, as social security has been placed politically out of reach, and other entitlements get harder to decrease, appropriations become a large part of what is up for grabs in the short term. But we run ahead of our story.

The mutual checking of House and Senate is easily overlooked, but hard to overemphasize. These bodies represent people in different ways; their members deal with different political facts (campaigning every six years instead of every two changes members' perspectives immensely);

their budget committees are of different sizes (causing different patterns of division of labor, the Senate being less detail and more debate oriented). The leadership and members of the two bodies depend on each other very little, and neither will accept leadership from the other. Independent and different, the two houses frequently support different policies. In appropriations or tax bills, as on any other, disagreement must be resolved by bargaining on conference committees, in which delegates from each house work out a package of provisions that can be supported by both. What emerges from conference, if anything, may be quite different from what either house wanted. Members of the House, anticipating conference, build coalitions and take positions with one eye always on the Senate. Senators may vote for more defense spending than they really want, establishing a bargaining position to take to conference. House members may vote for a program that wins constituency support, even if they dislike it, calculating that Senate nonsupport will allow dropping the proposal in conference. An interest group, defeated in the House, will work to prevail in the Senate and then in conference. So does the president.

The bicameral system complicates legislation, assuring that many votes will be taken before a final decision is made. It provides numerous opportunities for bargaining. Until a bill emerges from conference and gains final approval, not only its fate but its provisions may be uncertain. Because it is hard to distinguish between maneuver and preference, interpretation of congressional action is difficult. Even after a bill is passed, the president might veto it. Of course, if all the president gets a crack at is a single omnibus bill for the whole government, a continuing resolution, it is not easy to veto that.

THE PRESIDENT IS BOTH RIVAL OF AND PARTNER OF CONGRESS

The president has the first and last moves in the budget process. He can both check and use Congress, and it can both check and use him.

The last move is the veto—a bludgeon where a scalpel might be more apt. Rarely will a president dislike more than a small part of an appropriations bill, the bulk of which funds relatively uncontroversial and long-standing activities. Therefore, the veto of an appropriation act becomes part of a game of chicken; neither the president nor the act's supporters in Congress want to be blamed for shutting down federal activities in a dispute over details. The president—if only because members of his own party do not want to see him lose—usually can find enough support in at least one house to sustain the veto. He also holds the high ground in a public mudslinging contest with Congress: The president commands more media attention; as the only nationally elected official, he can claim to represent the national interest better than any set of congressional leaders; and Congress is less popular with voters than even the most unpopular president. For these reasons the president is likely to win a veto battle, with Congress having to pass a new bill that suits the chief executive.

Yet the relationship has its own dynamic. Congressmen do not like a pattern of vetoes and may unite to defend their institutional power against a president who overdoes it. Presidents do not like to lose, especially because losses reduce the White House's credibility. Anticipated reaction—the side that expects to lose giving in—is the usual rule. When the president fails to heed the signals, as with the Women's, Infants, and Children's program, he can ask for less and end up having to spend more (see Chapter 8). In essence, both president and Congress have good reason to avoid a public veto fight, in which one or the other may be embarrassed, programs that each values be hurt, and much time be wasted. The veto, therefore, gives the president a loud voice in the bargaining over spending and tax legislation; its threat is more important than its use.

The Constitution, through the veto, gave the president a voice in bargaining; Congress gave him the right to set many of the terms. The Budget and Accounting Act of 1921 created the Bureau of the Budget. The Bureau, in a couple of steps, became the Office of Management and Budget (OMB), located in the Executive Office of the president. OMB prepares, and the president submits to Congress, a budget for each fiscal year. (Each fiscal year runs from October 1 of the previous calendar year to September 30 of the same numbered calendar year; thus fiscal 1986 began October 1, 1985, and ended September 30, 1986.) The president's budget is submitted at the beginning of the congressional session at which appropriations for that fiscal year must be made (e.g., January of 1985 for fiscal 1986).

The president's budget is a combination of proposals for legislation and predictions of events. It suggests amounts of budget authority for various line items (e.g., salaries and expenses) for each agency, which will be considered by the appropriations committees. The president's budget estimates outlays both from last year's actual spending and from the combination of old and new budget authority. It predicts the performance of the economy and, from that, the revenues and expenditures that will be produced by current tax and entitlement law. Estimated interest rates (which, at times, are difficult to predict) determine estimates of the government's debt-service costs. These proposals and estimates are summed to a bottom line: surplus (quite unlikely) or deficit (now quite large). The deficit, along with total spending and revenues, are the most publicized aspects of the president's proposal and must be justified both to himself and to others as good policy and good politics.

In the past the only way to affect the totals was to affect the components. The budgetary process worked by adding together spending and revenues as they emerged in separate actions, though with informal understanding of what the totals would be. The Gramm–Rudman–Hollings deficit reduction process, as we will see, would, if followed, work the other way—from totals to parts. Outlays would have to fit within prespecified deficit reduction targets.

In preparing his budget, the president faces the problem of matching preferences over programs with preferences about overall spending, taxing, and borrowing. In the past, since agencies limited their spending bids, the first step was to ask them what they needed or wanted. Budget examiners at OMB analyzed detailed agency submissions, searching for the best places to make cuts, if needed. Their judgments were based both on rules of thumb (cut new elements or reduce ineffective programs) and on a sense of the administration's attitude toward each program. While OMB was examining, the president's economic advisors—the Secretary of the Treasury, Chairman of the Council of Economic Advisors, Director of OMB, and others—prepared estimates of economic performance and arguments in support of particular tax and spending levels. But that was then. Nowadays, with presidential preferences starting out at much lower totals, the OMB sends out advice on the level of permissible spending. Sometimes this advice includes "give backs," that is, previously allowed funds that must be returned. This is not to say that the OMB previously existed only as a passive repository of departmental requests. The OMB did provide spending guidelines in the past, but the extent and focus of this involvement has changed dramatically.

Normally the totals suggested mean spending at a lower level than the total of the agency submissions to OMB. How the president resolves that mismatch depends on the economic situation, his own policy preferences, his management style, and how other political actors, such as commentators, congressmen, and interest groups, are expected to respond. Whatever politico-economic judgments are made, decisions on individual programs may be reconciled with preferred totals by:

1. Changing appropriations requests for the agencies either by presidential command through OMB or by placing supporters in charge of agencies. This method has a distinct advantage; Congress has to enact *some* appropriation and therefore must confront the president's proposal and justify different action.

2. Recommending changes in the laws governing entitlements. Congress need not act at all. Thus the president cannot force the Committee on Ways and Means to report out medicare changes. But Congress may choose to act by limiting eligibility, reducing payments, or limiting cost of living increases.

3. Recommending tax changes. Tax hikes are usually political poison; politicians do not want to be seen sponsoring them. Hikes, therefore, tend to be disguised as loophole closing, reform, "revenue enhancement," or are called "temporary" surcharges.

4. Changing the economic projections to make the tax and spending estimates come closer together. In the past, economic projections were made only by the White House. Now the House and Senate budget committees and the Congressional Budget Office join in the act. Former budget director David Stockman's admitted juggling of the numbers is unusual only in its notoriety. This tactic if done too often or too blatantly, however, may cause Congress to ignore the president's budget altogether. But it has an advantage: The administration need not propose to hurt anyone. Since economic forecasting is a highly uncertain art, the economists in any event are quite probably wrong. Use of this tactic requires that the president care more about fiscal appearances than consequences. After all, the budget and the economy will be there again next year.

5. Deciding that the totals are not so bad after all. Ronald Reagan did that with his deficits, but so did Jimmy Carter and many other presidents. When Congress decides that the appearance of meeting the Gramm–Rudman–Hollings deficit reduction targets is better than the havoc caused by the necessary cuts, it is doing the same sort of thing. Problems are bad only if their solutions are not worse.

However the president defines his problem, his budget is issued with great fanfare. The budget documents include detailed justifications of his choices. Agency heads are expected to argue for the president's proposals even if they had requested larger funds.

The obvious questions are: Why did Congress establish this procedure? How much effect does it have on what Congress does? The main advantage to Congress is that this procedure gives the president primary responsibility for proposing cuts. The president can impose his priorities on the executive branch in a way that is impossible for any part of Congress, since the executive is in principle (and, in part, in fact) a hierarchy; Congress is anything but. A president can create a package that the noncentralized appropriations committees would have a hard time doing. Congressmen can then respond to his package of programs, changing it where it differs too much from their own priorities or where constituency pressures are great, and letting the president take the blame for other decisions.

Often the price of power is blame; this gives both president and congressmen reason to duck responsibility in budget politics. The process was once flexible enough for congressmen to act if they felt it necessary. They could beat up on agencies in hearings, showing these agencies did not deserve increases. They could ask leading questions at appropriation hearings, enabling agency heads to establish for the record why higher spending might be justified. They could pick and choose among presidential requests, raising popular ones (the National Institutes of Health) and cutting unpopular ones (foreign aid). By cutting here and increasing there, appropriations committees could expand some programs while staying below the president's total. Congressmen who disliked the committees' actions could blame them or fight for changes on the floor.

These partly cooperative and partly conflicting relationships existed within a general framework of informal understandings: The budget would be balanced, the level of taxing and spending would not grow rapidly, and agreements on the amount and distribution of public monies would be maintained. The understandings and agreements that underlay the old budgetary order, however, have been undermined, as I shall show, thus raising in a more acute form the question of which of the many promises that make up the budget will be maintained.

CONFLICTING PROMISES: THE MULTIPLE MEANINGS OF BUDGETARY CONTROL

Thus far I have sought to describe what is meant by the budget and to depict the various actors and procedures involved. Underlying the discussion has been the question of who is in control. As might be expected, the question of control raises a host of difficult issues.

The word "control" may usefully be considered a synonym for "cause" or "power": One controls events by making them come out as intended, against opposition. Budgetary control involves conflict among people who want different outcomes and who attempt to exert power in order to make the size and distribution of spending different than it might otherwise have been. To say that "the budget is out of control," therefore (to invoke the most common public statement), implies a whole series of failed relationships among participants that relate to intentions and outcomes. Inability to specify these relationships makes control (over what, by whom, under which circumstances) a murky subject. Consequently, the information content of most statements about budgetary control is near zero or even negative. Before readers delve into the history of budgeting, they may wish to consider various useful ways of thinking about common questions of control.

Who is to do the controlling? Is it the general population, interest groups, Congress as a whole, appropriations committees alone, the president, agency heads, political parties, or some combination of the above? If it is the general public one has in mind, then certain considerations—well-known to students of democracy but rarely applied to the process of budgeting—must be taken into account. There may well be no general opinion on most matters of budgeting. Politics in general, let alone expenditure in particular, is far from being at the forefront of citizen consciousness; that is one good reason for electing representatives. Indeed, whatever opinion the citizenry holds may be but a shallow reflection of what they have learned from their politicians and parties. Even supposing there are definite opinions, these cannot be directly applied to the budget. For, in the absence of referenda, people vote for or try to influence their representatives. Now, since these representatives deal with many nonbudgetary matters, voting against a candidate solely on budgetary grounds may be unwise. Hence it is possible that citizens may actually vote for people whose budgetary preferences they oppose.[8]

The advent of public-opinion polling, however, has made it possible

[8]See, by inference, Robert A. Dahl, *A Preface to Democratic Theory* (Chicago: The University of Chicago Press, 1956).

to ask whether citizen preferences do or do not generally accord with those expressed in consecutive budgets. In a rough and ready way, government does not appear to have departed too far from the people. A good illustration would be the presidency of Ronald Reagan. The best evidence[9] suggests that most people thought welfare spending was too high and defense spending too low in 1980. Opinion on the level of taxation was mixed, but there was widespread sentiment that the tax code was biased in favor of those already well-off. The Reagan administration moved spending in the direction desired by the electorate and then some. By 1984, polls revealed that the general public wanted more welfare and less defense spending than Reagan. Congress followed these wishes. In the discussion of clever maneuvering around the budget, it is well to note that shifting political alignments, which come from elections, remain by far the largest determinant of outcomes. The ultimate power remains with the people. But if the people are divided, as we often are, and are too far away to exert direct control, that task belongs to officeholders.

Who has power over the budget does not tell us whether or not the budget is under control. That is to say, we need to develop criteria to judge the prospect of budget control or, for that matter, of knowing what it would mean to be in or out of control. Actually, two approaches are commonly proposed. The first of these is to look at the apparent agreement on, but failure to achieve, budget balance. Surely, it is said, the government budget must be out of control if Congress cannot keep its continuously reiterated commitment to budget balance. It is true that huge majorities in Congress say they want balance. It is probably true that they mean what they say. But that truth is not the only truth because reducing the deficit is not the only goal that is important to congressmen. Some want to reduce welfare spending while others wish to raise taxes. Only a minority cares more about balance than about other policies. The majority supports balance but not to the extent of giving up other preferences.

[9]See J. Merrill Shanks and Warren Miller, "Policy Direction and Performance Evaluation: Complementary Explanations of the Reagan Elections." Presented to the Annual Meeting of the American Political Science Association, New Orleans, Aug. 29–Sept. 1, 1985.

A second criterion for viewing the budget as out of control is that appropriations committees no longer make annual decisions on anything like most of the budget. These "relatively uncontrollable" expenditures, to use government parlance, essentially are estimates of spending that cannot be changed without altering the statute that authorized the expenditure. As the General Accounting Office puts it:

> From the perspective of the Office of Management and Budget (OMB), the spending in any 1 year for a program that is determined by existing statute, contract, or other obligation is considered relatively uncontrollable and is so classified. OMB also treats the legislative and judicial budgets as uncontrollable; the Congress, on the other hand, regards these budgets as alterable. Under OMB's general rules, the President's budget, submitted on January 15, 1981, reported that about 76 percent of the budget is now relatively uncontrollable.[10]

Thus, relatively uncontrollable spending includes not only entitlements but also obligations incurred and contracts signed in prior years. There are also immutable or fixed costs, such as interest on the debt or a variety of loans to which the credit of the United States is pledged. Only an unthinkable default can alter these expenditures. Looked at another way, much of the rest of the budget is tied up in salaries for soldiers and civilians, operating expenses, data collection, and other items not easy or desirable to change at a moment's notice.

Is it true, then, that the budget becomes uncontrollable because the appropriations committees cannot cover most of it every year? I think not. Taxes generally continue in force until changed, yet few claim they are out of control; this is because, at any time, Congress can alter them. The same is true of entitlements.

There is some utility to the relatively controllable and relatively uncontrollable dichotomy. The observer is sensitized to certain important facts: The relative uncontrollables are growing; the portion passing through the appropriations committees is declining; most controllables are in the defense budget; and it may be more difficult to change a law than to alter an appropriation.

Yet to identify controllability with appropriations and uncontrollabil-

---

[10]Report to the Congress by the Comptroller General of the United States, "What Can Be Done to Check the Growth of Federal Entitlement and Indexed Spending?" p. 10.

ity with entitlements also can be misleading. The distinction between controllable and uncontrollable expenditures "indicates *how* budget items may be changed."[11] Appropriations are seen as easier targets for change because Congress must act on them annually, but they are not necessarily more flexible. Congress can cut the Coast Guard, the Bureau of Labor Statistics, and the Federal Aviation Administration somewhat but not a great deal; after all, people need to be rescued, unemployment statistics are vital, and safety in the air is a legitimate concern. Since entitlements occupy a large budgetary space, moreover, they can actually offer more tempting targets—and these targets are hit every year, albeit not every one or to the same extent. The Omnibus Reconciliation Act of 1981, for instance, raised the level at which the states would start paying extended benefits for Unemployment Compensation. And states toughened eligibility requirements.[12] Further, since many appropriations are sacrosanct while most entitlements are frequently adjusted— through changes in eligibility, indexing against inflation, taxation of benefits, and a host of other devices—to speak of the former as controllable and the latter as uncontrollable is somewhat inaccurate.[13]

The truth of the matter is that the 75 percent figure for uncontrollables significantly underestimates the proportion of the budget that is politically subject to change at any one time.[14] As discussion of classical budgeting will make clear, a good 90 to 95 percent of total spending is locked in as a consequence of past commitments and present promises. Here, in commitments to others, lies the insight we have been seeking into the apparent decline of controllability.

Congress wants to keep more expensive promises to a more extensive body of people (a phenomenon that sometimes goes under the name of the welfare state) than it did in the past. Consequently, though Congress

[11]Lance LeLoup, "Discretion in National Budgeting: Controlling the Controllables," *Policy Analysis,* Vol. 4, No. 4 (Fall 1978), pp. 455–75; quote on p. 456, italics in original.
[12]Kent Weaver, "Controlling Entitlements," in John E. Chubb and Paul E. Peterson, eds., *The New Direction in American Politics* (Washington, D.C.: The Brookings Institute, 1985), p. 321.
[13]For an excellent discussion, see LeLoup, "Discretion in National Budgeting."
[14]Martha Derthick, *Uncontrollable Spending for Social Services Grants* (Washington, D.C.: The Brookings Institute, 1975).

could renege on its promises all at once, it does not want to do so. Whether this reluctance stems from fear of retribution at the polls from those who lose a portion of social security payments, or from abandoning a moral commitment, as with kidney dialysis, or, more likely, from some combination of motives, Congress is torn between two kinds of contradictory promises: to certain beneficiaries in particular, or to people in general, in regard to budget balance. This conflict is resolved in the usual way by backing and filling, that is, by doing something that seems to satisfy each promise. With rare exceptions, such as revenue sharing, Congress keeps most commitments while making marginal moves toward budget balance. Just as political parties under pressure from rival factions move first "left" and then "right," and just as appropriations members used to satisfy committee norms by cutting the president's budget and constituency demands, by granting more money than in the previous year, Congress keeps its promises by modifying them.

For good reasons, this policy flexibility has been rendered more difficult in recent years. Automatic protection of entitlement against price rises makes sense in many ways. Needy beneficiaries no longer have to chase declining purchasing power. Politicians are no longer tempted to make up for inflation by election year benefit increases. Promises to the sick and elderly are kept with a minimum of fuss. Idyllic, isn't it? Well, the trouble is that as government absorbs the shock of price increases, it also loses the flexibility to respond to other changes—such as huge deficits that themselves stem in part from another set of promises, to provide tax cuts and to protect people against facing higher tax brackets because of inflation. It is neither right for people to pay more taxes while their purchasing power remains the same and government collects more from inflation, nor for government to have to spend more through indexing entitlements while simultaneously collecting less from income taxes. A "right" for one side obviously makes a "wrong" for the other.

Promises today conflict in other ways unknown to practitioners of budgeting until after the Second World War. The Employment Act of 1946 made the federal government responsible for keeping people at work. That promise, in keeping with the principles of Keynesian economics, was deemed to require varying the deficit or (rarely) surplus to suit the needs of the economy. While fiscal policy called for varying the rate of spending, however, the promise of entitlement policy was to keep the value of benefits constant. If government often resembles a contortionist, this is because it promises, in effect, to move simultaneously in two opposite directions.

Thus far I have looked at conflicting promises as residing between governmental actors and between government and citizens. But there is a different dilemma that occurs in budgeting—the conflict between individual and collective rationality. What makes sense to pursue individually may appear undesirable when these individual actions are viewed from a more general perspective. We see this conflict in budgeting: A desire for more programs conflicts with spending control.

Often, it is revealed with a certain amount of cynicism that members of Congress will vote for spending increases for specific programs and then turn around and vote for deficit reduction measures. But to focus solely on Congress is to investigate only part of the issue. Polling data, for example, suggest that the public is similarly ambivalent. While a large majority of citizens favor a balanced budget, they do not want higher taxes and they support most programs most of the time.

In trying to understand this dilemma, it is important to examine both attitudes and the structure of opportunity. There is little doubt that increasing program expenditures is compelling for congressional participants and the electorate alike. Each of us has particular programs that benefit us or aid someone we know, or we may view particular governmental activities as essential to the community or the nation. But the structure of the political system does not permit us to choose which programs we want and discard the rest; rather the political system works toward the exchange of benefits. To get what we want necessitates our acceptance of programs other people want, programs to which we may be either indifferent or averse. Within Congress, this is exemplified by the bill that becomes laden with a multiplicity of programs designed to muster widespread support.

What we desire in particular (more programs) turns out not to be what we desire in general—less total spending and lower taxes. The trouble is that while incentives exist to expand programs, few incentives exist to control the totals. The voter is rarely presented with the choices spelled out and usually does not have the opportunity to place limits on totals (whether that be taxes or program expenditures). Members of Congress, while having the opportunity to see budget totals, do not have a corresponding incentive to control these totals. Whether because of a perception by members of Congress that cuts will alienate voters or because of an inability to agree on what programs should be cut, the fact remains that even with the new focus on totals (brought about by the Congressional Budget and Impoundment Control Act of 1974), the incentives to cut remain weak.

For government to keep its promises requires not only a will but a way. Agreement on budget policy satisfies only governmental actors; no internal agreements can guarantee that external forces—wars, the weather, what have you—won't interfere with the best-laid plans. Resilient response is made more difficult, however, because governmental resources are now dedicated in advance to so many good causes. Alice Rivlin, former head of the Congressional Budget Office, observed that

> Spending is no longer growing for the old pork barrel, log-rolling reasons. Prospective spending growth is concentrated in a small number of programs with very broad popular support (primarily defense, pensions, and medical benefits), and revenues after the tax changes in 1981 and 1982 are simply not growing fast enough to close the gap, even if the economy continues to improve. This is not a procedural problem, it is simply a question of wanting more government services than there are revenues to pay for them and having to make some hard choices to bring the two sides of the budget closer together.[15]

I am not suggesting that controlling the budget implies that it must be balanced or that domestic and/or defense spending must be held down. Rather, control goes more to the roots of governmental will. For there to be control, there must be a conjuncture of purposes; the promises government makes to others must coincide with its own budgetary plans. As it now stands, the promise of balancing the budget conflicts with all the other commitments government makes and would like to keep.

We are more likely than our predecessors to suspect that "the budget

[15]Alice M. Rivlin, "Reform of the Budget Process," *The American Economic Review*, Vol. 74, No. 2 (May 1984), pp. 133–37; quote on p. 137.

is out of control" because there are so many more knowledgeable people around to tell us so. In olden times, reaching back through the 1950s, public officials and a few politicians on appropriations committees were the only budget experts. And they rarely quit their jobs or were removed from office. The monopoly of expertise and security of tenure that Max Weber listed as defining characteristics of modern bureaucracy applied to this tiny cadre of political administrators. No longer. Every area of public policy has layers of experts who once served in office or who soon expect to do so. They are in the think-tanks, the universities, state and local governments, foundations, research centers, and the big consulting and accounting firms. In effect, there are rival teams out there in the hinterlands. Second guessing becomes a sophisticated art when there are so many informed people to do it. With the loss of their former near-monopoly of information, public officials find it increasingly difficult to keep deficits from being publicized. Whether we are talking about welfare or defense, super-fund or the trade deficit, very little can be kept from public scrutiny. More and more people now know where the dollars are buried.

The existence of a loyal opposition in parliamentary democracies guarantees a string of criticism against existing governmental policy. But such criticism tends to be quite general. The only people who know much are civil servants who now work for the other side or who are silenced by official secrets acts. The existence of rival teams of policy analysis in the United States, with no commitment to governing but with superior sources of information, by contrast, guarantees that there will be numerous and quite specific allegations of unwise or improper budgeting. Too much is being spent for X, not enough for Y. Error rates (the wrong people receiving welfare payments) or cost overruns (the wrong people profiting from defense) are exposed. Needy populations, the emergence of children as the largest category of poor people, or unmet technological needs that, if neglected, promise to ruin American competitiveness are heard of every day. Criticism has been institutionalized, but support has not. The remarkable devices used in the Omnibus Budget Reconciliation Act of 1990 to leave congressional appropriators free of fault if external circumstances make their budget plans go awry, as we will see in Chapter 12, have their roots in a criticism so constant that legislators despair of being thought to have acted wisely no matter what they do. The task of control, of coordinating commitments, is so difficult because of the many different meanings the budget has for different people, hence the conflicting criticisms leveled against a particular budget. In the past these variegated desires were held together by certain common concerns: a balanced budget, avoidance of rapidly rising spending or taxing, and a broad agreement on the distribution of expenditures. The collapse of these premises of the old budgetary order, an issue I will deal with in later parts of the book, has loosened the strictures that constrained these many desires. Because the new order is being built on the scaffolding of the old—not so much replacing as adding to it—I begin the next chapter with the historical origins of American budgeting, origins that still affect what is done today.

BUDGETS AS STRUGGLES FOR POWER: A HISTORICAL PERSPECTIVE

2

FEW TRUISMS OF AMERICAN POLITICAL THOUGHT are more hoary than this: The power of the purse is the heart of legislative authority and thus an essential check on the executive branch. An executive establishment freed from dependence for funds upon the legislature (and hence the public) would be a law unto itself and ultimately a despotism. Those who made the American Revolution concluded from experience in Britain and the colonies that a free people had to keep its governors on a tight fiscal leash. The insistence on that principle helped make America's budgetary experience unique. From the earliest days of American government, budget decisions were treated as a struggle for power.

From the middle of the seventeenth century to today, America's difference from rather than similarity to Europe in most fiscal matters is striking. It would be hard to invent a country whose budgetary behavior could be so much at odds with that of European nations.[1] Revenue, expenditure, and debt per capita have been markedly lower in the United States. Where European budgets have been unitary, with expenditures and revenues considered together, American budgets have been fragmentary, each agency submitting spending proposals separately and with revenue considered entirely apart from outlays. Where Europeans have considered budgetary balance a technical, financial matter of ability to raise revenue to support spending, Americans, from the beginning, have considered balance a question of political philosophy: Who shall rule over whom? Where all European nations have stressed the financial power of the executive, America has stressed the financial power of the legislature, albeit in the form of a legislative committee called the cabinet.

COLONIAL ORIGINS OF THE LEGISLATIVE BUDGET

Colonial expenditures were simple in nature. Care of the poor, insane, sick, or otherwise indigent was a local responsibility. Public works were few and scattered. Highways were short and rough, and courthouses, though sometimes gilded with a handsome facade, were small. Judges were few and did not require many helpers. No colonial navy existed and the army—except in the period of the great Indian wars, or during the war with France for control of the North American continent—was composed of local militia. Legislatures met only for short periods, and payment, if received, was small. Colonial executive departments were tiny, and officials were often paid by fees rather than from general revenues. Royal governors alone received substantial salaries.

The extraordinary effort of colonial legislatures to control executives by limiting their expenditures, the duration for which they could be paid, and the objects for which the money could be spent, gives this

[1]For a more detailed study, see Carolyn Webber and Aaron Wildavsky, "Balanced Regimes, Balanced Budgets: Why America Was So Different," Chapter 7 in *A History of Taxation and Expenditure in the Western World* (New York: Simon and Schuster, 1986).

period its peculiar stamp. If the colonies belonged to England, and if the colonists were English subjects, then it was their duty to support royal governors. Since the colonists wanted British protection but not British rule, however, they freely used the English tradition of denying supply in order to force compliance with the legislative will. The commonplace view, assiduously peddled by colonists in the prerevolutionary period, was that if the English king were only reasonable they would love him; but that truism is not supported by financial fact.

Merely to say that royal governors were kept amenable to colonists' desires does not do justice to "Yankee" ingenuity in devising financial restraints.[2] Connecticut may have been extreme in making the salary of the governor and other important executives dependent upon semi-annual appropriations, but it was common colonial practice to vote salaries annually. It might be thought that indirect taxes, excises, and import duties would stand until changed, but these were often reenacted yearly. Royal governors were allowed no permanent sources of revenue that might make them "uppity."[3] And that was only the beginning: Appropriations were specified for object and amount; extremely long appropriation clauses prescribed exactly what could and what could not be done and for how much. The requirement that all unexpected balances revert immediately to the treasury added insult to injury.

Even so, it might be thought that once an appropriation was voted, a royal executive could proceed to spend the money for the purpose stipulated. Several colonies, however, went so far as to elect independent treasurers that precluded the governors from managing their own finances. Other legislatures insisted that no payment might be made without their specific consent, thus giving colonists control over the disbursement of public funds. And when an emergency arose that everyone felt should justify a special appropriation, colonial assemblies might well appoint special commissioners accountable to them rather than to the governor. Should such measures prove too loose, there were still

[2]See Robert C. Tucker and David C. Hendrickson, *The Fall of the First British Empire: Origins of the War of American Independence* (Baltimore/London: Johns Hopkins University Press, 1982), pp. 152–59, 174–75, 406–10.

[3]Charles Bullock, "The Finances of the United States from 1775–1789 with Special Reference to the Budget," *Bulletin of the University of Wisconsin*, Vol. 1, 1894–1896, Frederick Turner, ed. (Madison: University of Wisconsin Press, 1897), pp. 217, 225.

others: Revenues were segregated by voting taxes for exceedingly narrow purposes (such as the building of a fort or of a lighthouse or the salary of a governor), always with the added clause that once the purpose had been accomplished, that money could be spent for "no other use or purpose whatsoever."[4] Colonial assemblies also reduced the salary of royal officials; they stipulated the precise name of the person who was to do the work and made these officials legally accountable for all funds expended without the most direct and specific legislative act. If the character of a government be known by its finances, America was already "independent" in every respect except name.[5]

When it came to doing sums, everyone understood what was at stake: Royal governors and their supporters desperately wanted a civil list of appointments and perquisites independent of the funds supplied by legislatures; the colonists wanted to create uncertainty, parsimony, and narrowness so as to bend royal governors to their will. To the English, it seemed only reasonable for the colonists to pay for the support of the royal government that was acknowledged in name. The Stamp Act, duties on tea, and other impositions on colonists were a parliamentary effort to provide independent sources of income for English officials in America. Power, not money, was the issue. As put by a contemporary commenting on the colonial government of New York:

> It will be seen that the democratick branch of the colonial government had placed the governor, and almost every other office, in a state of dependence upon its votes and measures. Not a single shilling could be withdrawn from the treasury, but by legislative consent. This was particularly galling to the lieutenant governor. It had stripped him of that executive patronage and influence, which was deemed by him so essential to the support of his administration. In truth, it was a great step towards that independence which was afterwards obtained.[6]

Even this brief background should help the modern reader appreciate the colonists' insistence on legislative direction of finance. From their perspective, a war for independence from a distant hierarch would be perverse if it replaced an English king with a new authority, all the more hateful for being closer to home.

[4]*Ibid.*, pp. 216–19.
[5]*Ibid.*, pp. 219–21.
[6]*Ibid.*, p. 218.

After the Revolution, Americans found that it was hard to run a government that lacked authority. If they wanted action, they had to give the executive leeway. The Constitutional Convention was called into being by those attempting to create a more energetic government than existed under the Articles of Confederation—one with direct coercive power over individuals. Nevertheless, supporters of legislative power were represented, and their influence helped make American budgeting exceptional in the weakness of its presidents. For Roger Sherman, as for many others, an independent executive was "the very essence of tyranny. . . ." The legislature was "the depository of the supreme will of the society." Edmund Randolph of Virginia went so far as to suggest that there be three executives, one each from the major regions of the country.[7] That the United States should have a chief executive at all was by no means a foregone conclusion.

Alexander Hamilton always saw political power behind financial power. He believed it necessary to fund state debts incurred during the Revolutionary War not only to establish strong credit, but also as a means of attaching the people who would be paid to the purposes of government.[8] From the outset of his term as Secretary of the Treasury, he wrote Congress that Americans had to learn "to distinguish between oppression and the necessary exercise of lawful authority."[9] Hamilton's interest in levying taxes other than tariffs and in enforcing the exercise of the taxing power in the case of an excise tax on whiskey had as much to do with his desire to strengthen government as it did with the need to raise money.

If the Constitution had settled the battle over establishment of a stronger central government, within which there would be a single, potent chief executive, then the position of department heads as agents of that power should have been readily established. Not so.

Immediately upon Hamilton's appointment there arose a clamor,

[7]Leonard D. White, *The Federalists: A Study in Administrative History* (New York: Macmillan, 1961), p. 14.

[8]William J. Shultz and M. R. Caine, *Financial Development of the United States* (New York: Prentice-Hall, 1937), p. 100.

[9]Dall W. Forsythe, *Taxation and Political Change in the Young Nation 1781–1883* (New York: Columbia University Press, 1977), pp. 44–45.

unfathomable outside the United States, that a powerful Secretary of the Treasury, by giving his opinion to Congress, might overawe or otherwise influence that body in an undesirable manner.[10] "The Secretary seemed to take the whole government upon his shoulders," William Findley of western Pennsylvania said in a speech, "and to consider all the great interest thereof to be committed to his providence. His report spoke the language of Frederick of Prussia, or some other despotic prince, who had all the political powers vested in himself—not the language of a dependent Secretary, under a free and well-ordered Government."[11] Hamilton's side thought such fears were nonsense. "Our proceedings smell of anarchy . . . ," staunch Federalist Fisher Ames of Massachusetts declared. "The heads of departments are head clerks. Instead of being . . . the organs of the executive power . . . they are precluded of late even from communication with the House by reports." Having ordained that ministers shall be dumb, Ames concluded, "we forbid them to explain themselves by signs."[12]

The law establishing the Treasury Department merely said that the Secretary was supposed to send departmental estimates to Congress; the law did not say that the Secretary was to revise these estimates or, if he did, whether anybody had to pay attention. Over time, an informal understanding developed that though the Secretary might interest himself in estimates, his sole duty was to collect them, and send them, without comment, to Congress. Though there is evidence of a secretary questioning this or that estimate and of occasional intervention by a president, the trend was to make appropriations without participation of the president or the Secretary of the Treasury.

Since the strong executive was part of their platform, the Federalist Party preferred "lump-sum" appropriations for each specified purpose—say, customs collection or a navy—which would give administrators as much leeway as possible. Favoring economic stringency and distrusting the executive—the one reinforcing the other—the Republican Party sought specific, line-item appropriations—for personnel, maintenance,

[10]Shultz and Caine, *Financial Development,* pp. 93–94.
[11]White, *The Federalists,* p. 70.
[12]*Ibid.,* p. 94.

supplies, on and on—that would limit department heads to exactly what Congress had commanded.[13]

What could Congress do? Plenty. It could itemize appropriations in excruciating detail; it could seek to apportion funds by the month or quarter so that agencies did not run out of money before the end of the fiscal year—potential deficiencies that might lead to requests for supplementary funds to carry out essential functions; it could limit transfers from one line-item to another and recapture unexpended funds, or at least it could try. Congress could and did specify the number of employees, their exact remuneration, and sometimes their names. One of the many budget reform acts forbade all departments, except State, to spend more than $100 on newspapers; denied funds for commissions of inquiry, except courts-martial; refused extra allowances and additional clerks; insisted upon detailed reporting about the expenditure of contingency funds; prohibited the purchase of engravings, pictures, books, or periodicals other than by written order of head of department; and set the maximum amount that could be paid to the Dragoman of Constantinople. Whether it was known then that committees of experts always recommend spending more on their favorite subject is not clear, but Congress did respond to President Tyler's appointment of three people to investigate public works in Washington, D.C., by denying them supplies.[14]

Congress became used to specifying line-items of expenditure in stultifying detail. Senator Lewis Cass wanted to authorize the navy to install the best possible condenser for its ships, for instance, but he protested against the legislative requirement for a specific type of condenser. Another Congress terminated one employee in the Corps of Engineers and specified that his duties be performed by a different, particular person. Protesting the demoralizing effect of this detailed specification on the army, President Buchanan declared in 1850 that "officers might then be found . . . besieging the halls of Congress for the purpose of obtaining special and choice places by legislative enactment."[15]

---

[13]*Ibid.*, p. 324.
[14]Leonard D. White, *The Jacksonians: A Study in Administrative History 1829–1861* (New York: Macmillan, 1954), pp. 126–27.
[15]*Ibid.*, pp. 138–40.

Despite continuous legislative effort to narrow administrative leeway, Congress could not control everything. The army and the navy, insisting they could not be held to specific line-items, did get their way.[16] The legislated sanctions against executive offices for overspending, unauthorized transfers, or other violations of the innumerable prohibitions were not invoked; no doubt enforcement was not possible.[17] Most departmental appropriations soon became regular and customary as to both content and amount. Whether or not a new annual appropriations bill was passed, Congress did renew allocations in more or less the same manner year after year; social stability had produced agreement on a budgetary base.

An easy way around specific appropriations was to transfer sums from one purpose to another. The Act of 1820 allowed the president to make only certain transfers; all others were forbidden. But, when Congress became overburdened with requests for change and discovered it could not monitor even a small proportion of transactions, it tried to legalize prevailing practices. Funds for forts could be moved from one stockade to another, as could appropriations for naval forces from branch to branch, and postal funds from here to there. Departments kept appropriated funds from lapsing by finding ways to spend at the end of the fiscal year. When, in 1842, department heads received authority to transfer surplus funds from one item to some other (always excepting, of course, funds for newspapers, which in those days were party organs), the battle against transfers had been lost.[18]

Those who can redefine financial terms generally also can get their way. What, for instance, was a surplus? In the 1850s, the attorney general declared that the term "unexpended" actually meant an "unobligated" appropriation, which thus reserved such a balance for future executive discretion. But by then the Civil War had come and with it disinterest in expenditure control.[19]

[16]*Ibid.*, p. 131.
[17]*Ibid.*, p. 141; and Albert S. Bolles, *A Financial History of the United States, 1774–89* (New York: Appleton, 1879), pp. 539–40.
[18]White, *The Jacksonians*, pp. 133–34.
[19]*Ibid.*, pp. 134–35.

A REVOLUTIONARY COALITION: AGREEMENT ON THE NORM OF BUDGET BALANCE

The winning side of the American Revolution represented three social orders: a weak social hierarchy that wanted to replace the English king with a native variety better suited to colonial conditions, emerging individualistic market men who wanted to control their own commerce, and the heirs of a continental republican tradition that stressed small, egalitarian voluntary associations.[20]

The balanced budget, at low levels except in wartime, was the crucial compromise that allowed these three social orders to coexist. Of course, unlike the signing of the Declaration of Independence, the compromise was not made in a single day, nor was there a formal declaration. The informal understanding, however, lasted for a century and a half until it unraveled in the 1960s.

What was this understanding that arose out of such diverse interests? How was it verified and enforced? And what was in it for everyone concerned? To answer these questions, we must first examine the positions of the groups involved.

The Federalists and their successors, a coalition of social hierarchs and economic individualists, sought to promote social order through deficit finance, first by making internal improvements and second by the financial arrangements arising out of the resulting debt. President John Quincy Adams avidly sought appropriations for rivers and harbors, lighthouses, beacons, piers, and, most of all, roads. Adams' major effort had been to use the surplus to provide a "permanent and regular system . . . of . . . internal improvements" so that "the surface of the whole Union would have been checkered with railroads and canals. . . ."[21] During this time, a House committee on Roads and Canals and a Civil Engineer Corps as part of the Army Corps of Engineers was established. Grants of public lands were routinely made to new states to encourage them to

---

[20]J. G. Pocock, *The Political Works of James Harrington* (Cambridge, Mass.: Cambridge University Press, 1977).

[21]Leonard D. White, *The Jeffersonians: A Study in Administrative History 1801–1829* (New York: Macmillan, 1951), p. 483.

build roads and canals, and "Rivers and Harbors" appropriations—that (in)famous "Pork Barrel" legislation, in which it was alleged (with good reason) that congressmen dipped their hands to get goodies for their districts, much as the boys at the country store did around the barrel of real pork—had their beginning.[22]

The program of the market men allied with the hierarchy of the Whig Party consisted of federally funded internal improvements that were closely connected to the debt and the tariff. Besides encouraging the growth of industry, the tariff provided surplus revenues to expand roads, canals, and other facilities that today go under the general rubric of infrastructure. The debt also increased money in circulation, thus aiding industry, as well as tying its holders to the central government. Put another way, all these devices gave the federal government and those who controlled it a role to play.

The rationale for internal improvements was to bind the nation together. The parts were to sacrifice for the whole by paying taxes to help the nation grow. Whigs used a version of the public goods argument on behalf of a national whole greater than the sum of its parts. As Henry Clay said,

> In regard to internal improvements, it does not follow, that they will always be constructed whenever they will afford a competent dividend upon the capital invested. . . . In a new country, the condition of society may be ripe for public works long before there is, in the hands of individuals, the necessary capital to effect them. . . . The aggregate benefit resulting to the whole society, from a public improvement, may be such as to justify the investment of capital in its execution. . . .[23]

One can almost hear modern proponents of governmental provision of public works speak of its social benefits exceeding its economic costs.

But the Federalists and Whigs had to contend with the republican believers in small egalitarian communities who threatened to withdraw consent to union unless the size and scope of the central government and benefits to capital were severely limited.

[22]Margaret G. Myers, *A Financial History of the United States* (New York: Columbia University Press, 1970), pp. 108–109.

[23]William Letwin, ed., *A Documentary History of American Economic Policy Since 1789* (New York: W. W. Norton, 1972), p. 63.

The opposition to debt was not opposition to business or to private markets per se. Most farmers were, in effect, small businessmen. On the contrary, market competition was in high repute, provided only that it was truly competitive, that is, uncontaminated by artificial restraints imposed by the central government. Nor was government itself the object of vilification. State governments were encouraged to do the very thing denied to the central government. Why this hostility toward central government?

"This measure," Jefferson wrote, referring to federal assumption of state debts, "produced the most bitter and angry contest ever known in Congress before or since the Union of the States." This was so, Jefferson argued, because the debt acted "as a machine for the corruption of the legislature. . . ."[24] By corruption, Jefferson meant the perversion of judgment caused by giving men who had a financial stake in the debt a special interest in, and an enhanced capacity for, undermining the independent judgment of Congress. In the first instance, then, opposition to the debt was grounded in its direct political consequences. To inhibit the formation of a class with direct financial interest in government activity, funded by the government's interest payments, Jeffersonians meant to pay off its debts and to keep the central government small so it would not accumulate still more.

Jeffersonian Democratic–Republican thought, reflecting the anti-Federalist fear of strong centralized government, called for small agricultural communities in which an educated electorate, not far from one another in economic status and geographic distance, would handle their affairs on a face-to-face basis. If the government were to grow too large, and if substantial inequality of resources developed, Jeffersonians believed, then personal liberty would be endangered. The Jacksonians, two decades after them, believed exactly that.

The widespread belief among Jacksonians was that government was giving someone opportunities at the expense of someone else. It was felt that payment of interest on the national debt was reverse redistribution

---

[24]Adrienne Koch and William Peder, *The Life and Selected Writings of Thomas Jefferson* (New York: Modern Library, 1944), p. 123.

of income from poor to rich people. This was true, Jacksonians believed, because the debt (and interest on it) depleted the limited capital fund from which wages were drawn. If such capital were transferred into private hands, productivity would increase and wages would go up as well. Jacksonians believed that a weak central government, at the very least, would not add artificial to natural inequality and thereby would preserve representative government. At best, in the land of opportunity that was America, individuals free to fend for themselves would thrive. Individuals would be allowed, indeed encouraged, to keep all gain that resulted from the unfettered use of their own talents. But everything artificial and unnatural, everything the federal government might attempt to impose on man in his free state, such as charters, franchises, banks, and debt, was anathema.

Allied with a protective tariff that produced ever-larger sums, President Polk believed that "the operation and necessary effect of the whole system [of internal improvements] would encourage large and extravagant expenditures, and thereby to increase the public patronage, and maintain a rich and splendid government at the expense of a taxed and impoverished people."[25] Favoring the common man, to Jacksonian individualists, meant promoting individual or state, not central, government enterprise.[26]

It would be difficult to overstate the Democrats' distrust of debt during the years leading up to the Civil War. "I place economy among the first and most important of republican virtues," Jefferson wrote, "and public debt as the greatest of the dangers to be feared."[27] Realizing that the debt remaining from the War of 1812 might be retired during his administration, Andrew Jackson waxed lyric: "We shall then exhibit the rare example of a great nation, abounding in all the means of happiness and security, altogether free from debt."[28] Then, from the wellsprings of abundance, surfaced the specter of a corresponding evil—

[25]Lewis H. Kimmel, *Federal Budget and Fiscal Policy 1789–1958* (Washington, D.C.: The Brookings Institution, 1959), pp. 31–32.
[26]*Ibid.*, p. 19; and White, *The Jeffersonians*, p. 483.
[27]Kimmel, *Federal Budget and Fiscal Policy*, p. 14.
[28]*Ibid.*, pp. 19–20.

"The unnecessary accumulation of public revenue," as Andrew Jackson called what would seem wonderful but impossible today, a surplus. Why should this cornucopia be an embarrassment? Because, as President Van Buren argued in his last annual message, it "would foster national extravagance" which, when it inevitably became a habit, would encourage rapid accumulation of a larger and more onerous debt. (A recent parallel would be the huge debts of the 1980s incurred by the suddenly oil-rich nations of the 1970s.) One hundred and forty years ago the ancestors of our Democrats were arguing that unless revenues were limited, government would get hooked on spending.[29]

The struggle over the debt in the early American republic raised the same question—How should Americans govern themselves?—as it does today. Then, as now, all believed in self-government; but they located leadership and virtue in different institutional arrangements. For the Jeffersonians and Jacksonians (coalitions including both economic individualists and social egalitarians), virtue resided in participation by public-spirited citizens who were continuously active in their local communities. Free government was within reach of the common man, provided only that he possessed sufficient resources to compete and that central government did not corrupt him through special privilege. Avoiding debt had become associated with democracy itself. The rivals of this Democratic–Republican party, first Federalists and then Whigs, who combined their economic individualism with a strong element of social hierarchy, located virtue within national elites who would act out of a desire to excel, and who would restrain both themselves and the passions of those less qualified to rule. The two sides disagreed about the potential and purposes of government, the nature and dangers of rule.

Egalitarian republicans were able to place limits on central government. And the supporters of social hierarchy obtained a larger role for collective concerns, provided they were able to gather sufficient revenue. No order of society got everything it wanted, but all got something. The belief, widely espoused in the Jacksonian era, that equality of opportunity

[29]*Ibid.*, pp. 21–22.

TABLE 2-1

Federal Expenditures, Fiscal Years 1800, 1825, 1850, and 1860
(in millions of dollars)

	1800	*1825*	*1850*	*1860*
Civil & miscellaneous	1.3	2.7	14.9	28.0*
War Department	2.6	3.7	9.4	16.4
Navy Department	3.4	3.1	7.9	11.5
Indians	—	0.7	1.6	2.9
Pensions	0.1	1.3	1.9	1.1
Interest	3.4	4.4	3.8	3.2

*Includes postal deficit of $9.9 million.

would lead to equality of result (i.e., that pure market relations would achieve egalitarian objectives) helped cement this cultural union.

What could be more optimistic than the belief that liberty and equality could be made compatible, and what could be more exceptional than the view, anchored in an alliance between individualists and egalitarians, that class conflict was not inevitable in America? How could we know? One optimistic sign was the balanced budget.

The dollars and cents embodiment of the national consensus on balanced budgets at low levels of revenue and expenditure was the small size of the federal government. The era before the Civil War remained a time of tiny government. Between 1800 and 1860, as Table 2-1 shows, federal expenditures rose from about 11 to 63 million dollars in total. More than half were military expenditures. The general category of "Civil & Miscellaneous" included a substantial amount for the postal deficit, thus covering everything except defense, pensions, Indians, and interest on the debt. Kimmel is correct in concluding "that federal expenditures made little or no contribution to the level of living. Only a minor portion of Civil and miscellaneous expenditures were for developmental purposes. . . ."[30]

[30]*Ibid.*, p. 57.

The doctrine of the balanced budget—a doctrine that became so powerful over time that terrible things were supposed to happen should its boundaries be violated—was far more than an economic theory. It meant (and, to many people, still means) that things are all right. The "balance" referred to was not only between revenue and expenditure but also between social orders. If the competing cultures that make up American life are in balance, meaning that they still accept the legitimacy of their uneasy alliance, all is indeed well in the new world.

THE DECLINE OF CONGRESSIONAL CONTROL: CIVIL WAR THROUGH WORLD WAR II

The written law often follows from the law of necessity. Public officials who believe an act to be essential may undertake it without legislative warrant, appealing to Congress to approve their conduct retroactively. The strongest proponent of this view was undoubtedly Abraham Lincoln. As the nation split into irreconcilable factions, Lincoln took the position that whatever was required for national defense had to be approved. On grounds that there was then "no adequate and effective organization for the public defense," he justified ordering the Treasury to advance $2 million to a variety of private agents to provide requisitions for the military:

> Congress had indefinitely adjourned. There was not time to convene them. It became necessary for me to choose, whether, using only the existing means, agencies, and processes which Congress had provided, I should let the Government fall at once into ruin or whether availing myself of the broader powers conferred by the Constitution in cases of insurrection, I would make an effort to save it, with all its blessings, for the present age and for posterity.... The several Departments of the Government at that time contained so large a number of disloyal persons that it would have been impossible to provide safely through official agents only for the performance of the duties thus confided to citizens favorably known for their ability, loyalty, and patriotism.[31]

[31]Lucius W. Wilmerding, Jr., *The Spending Power: A History of the Efforts of Congress to Central Expenditures* (New Haven, Conn.: Yale University Press, 1943), p. 14.

The higher law was one thing and low-down behavior another; investigations provided ample evidence of abuse of contract power during the war.[32]

Performance being more important than protocol during the war, Congress legally authorized all that it had been denying for the past century: lump-sum appropriations, spending in excess of authorizations and appropriations, transfers, revolving funds perpetuated by reimbursements, and more.[33] After the war, Congress tried hard to take back these grants of authority.

When, because funds were inadequate, transfers failed to produce necessary moneys, departments could and did resort to the tactic of the coercive deficiency. What could Congress do if the money for an essential service were to run out before the end of the fiscal year, other than to pass a supplemental appropriation? As deficiencies before the Civil War rose to something like 10 percent of total spending, there were doomsayers aplenty who could claim that congressional control over spending had ended. Congress did demand to be informed of an emergency leading to a waiver of required apportionments, but by the time the waiver was reported there was no effective remedy.[34] Establishment of the Bureau of the Budget in 1921 and the "Anti-Deficiency Act" in its various forms eventually limited the use of coercive deficiencies, but they are still with us.

From time to time, departments used unexpended balances for purposes not previously contemplated in congressional statutes. In 1869 Congress reiterated that funds should be spent only for authorized purposes, for the Secretary of the Navy had begun to rebuild the service with balances accumulated over ten years.[35] It was not the first instance of administrative discretion. In President Jackson's term, during the 1830s, the Congressional Committee on Public Expenditures had expressed amazement at finding "a Naval force springing up amongst us,

[32]Albert S. Bolles, *The Financial History of the United States from 1861 to 1885* (New York: Appleton, 1886), p. 231.
[33]Wilmerding, *Spending Power*, p. 154.
[34]*Ibid.*, pp. 137–47.
[35]Bolles, *Financial History of the United States from 1861 to 1865*, pp. 530–31.

controlled by the Secretary of the Treasury, accountable to no one but him, expended at will by him, supported by him out of the revenue before it gets to the Treasury, and may cost the country whatever he shall direct."[36]

The Civil War acted as a catalyst for the president to wrest from Congress some discretion over spending. The war also resulted in a structural transformation of the congressional budgetary process. For the first 75 years of the republic (from 1789 to 1864), revenue and expenditure matters in the House of Representatives were handled by its Committee on Ways and Means (and in the Senate by the Finance Committee). But, as Louis Fisher points out, "The magnitude of war finances after 1861 proved to be too great a strain on the legislative structure."[37] Largely in response to the Ways and Means Committee being overworked, the House in 1865 and the Senate in 1867 carved a Committee on Appropriations out of the old single committee. This dual committee system—one for taxes, the other for spending—lasted until 1885.[38]

The new Appropriations Committee "embodied a balance between the need for some financial expertise with the aversion to placing too many institutional resources in the hands of one individual."[39] The arrangement allowed for unified control of spending in one committee. Yet, the Appropriations Committee did not have authority to control all spending—the size of pensions and other permanent appropriations (together constituting over half the budget) were determined by other committees.[40]

By and large, members of Congress appeared content with the new arrangement. Collaboration occurred between the Ways and Means

[36]White, *The Jacksonians*, p. 138.

[37]Louis Fisher, *President and Congress* (New York: Free Press, 1972), p. 92.

[38]E. E. Naylor, *The Federal Budget System in Operation* (Washington: Hayworth Printing, 1941), pp. 20–21.

[39]Charles Haines Stewart III, *The Politics of Structural Reform: Reforming Budgetary Structure in the House, 1865–1921*, Dissertation, Stanford University, August 1985, p. 139.

[40]*Ibid.*, pp. 139–40.

and the Appropriations Committees and there was consensus in Congress that Civil War spending and waste needed to be curtailed and that war profiteering had been widespread. Additionally, Congress was too preoccupied with Reconstruction to get caught up in other domestic issues.[41]

In the succeeding years, the House Appropriations Committee came under attack for amassing too much control over other committees' programs, primarily through Appropriations control over reporting bills out. As the smooth flow of patronage was threatened by the Appropriations Committee, members of Congress reacted in 1885 by giving a number of spending bills to the substantive legislative committees made up of spending advocates. Congress first stripped Appropriations of constituency-oriented legislation (rivers and harbors spending, agriculture) and then moved to more general items (army, navy, diplomacy, post office, and Indian affairs). By these acts, more than half of the total appropriations, including the most controversial items, were effectively removed from the Appropriations Committee's jurisdiction.[42]

These changes became "a symbol of dysfunctional fragmentation in Congress and of waste and mismanagement, and would serve as a rallying point in the creation of an executive budget focused around presidential leadership."[43] Actually, the escalation of spending after 1885 was less the result of decentralization (spending rates increased at fairly equal rates for bills outside Appropriations control compared to bills under Appropriations jurisdiction) and more the consequence of an acceleration of visible spending, including army and navy reform and the rebuilding of southern productive centers destroyed during the war, in response to two decades of neglect.[44]

The leading budget reformer before World War I, Frederick A. Cleveland, excoriated the chairmen of these spending committees as

[41]*Ibid.*, p. 140.
[42]Richard F. Fenno, *The Power of the Purse: Appropriations Politics in Congress* (Boston: Little, Brown, 1966), p. 43.
[43]Stewart, *Politics of Structural Reform*, p. 211.
[44]*Ibid.*, p. 215.

functionalized, bureaucratic, feudal lords [who] did not look to their titular
superior, the leader chosen by and responsible to the nation, for powers
and policies. They looked to irresponsible committees. And because of the
independence that was thus given, each chief built around himself a
bureaucratic wall that even the constitutional Chief Executive himself
could not get over. . . .[45]

Cleveland's theme, bureaucratic feudalism, reveals the emergent pattern
of budgeting. Close relationships were developing among chiefs of governmental bureaus, their clientele, and the chairmen and ranking members of the congressional appropriations committees. Today we call
these relationships "iron triangles." In reading the complaints of numerous other reformers about lack of coordination,[46] I conclude that a norm
of reciprocity existed. In voting on appropriations outside their area of
specialization, members of each committee must have been deferring to
the judgment of all the others.

"The estimates are nearly always inflated by the officers who prepare
them," wrote reformer Arthur Buck, "either intentionally or as a result
of super-abundant enthusiasm for their work; . . . this, it seems, is to be
expected."[47] To Buck, the administrative bureau's role in budgeting
ought not to have been, but actually was, to advocate higher spending.
The House Appropriations Committee was supposed to cut these estimates, but the Senate would then act as an appeals court to give the
money back. "Appropriations bills generally provide for an expenditure
considerably less than that called for by the estimate," Woodrow Wilson observed, "as returned from the Senate they usually propose grants
of many additional millions, having been brought by that less sensitive
body up almost, if not quite, to the figures of the estimate."[48]

The representative who said that the Appropriations Committee
treats "every executive officer as if he were a suspicious character, and
he treats us as if we were a lot of numbskulls who know nothing about

[45]Frederick A. Cleveland, "Leadership and Criticism," *Proceedings of the Academy of
Political Science,* Vol. 8 (1918–20), p. 31.

[46]Woodrow Wilson, *Congressional Government: A Study in American Politics* (Boston:
Houghton Mifflin, 1892), pp. 136–37.

[47]A. E. Buck, *Public Budgeting* (New York: Harper, 1929), p. 339.

[48]Wilson, *Congressional Government,* p. 156.

the needs of the service"[49] was putting his finger on the slowly developing role of the Appropriations Committee as a "watchdog of the Treasury" or defender of the public purse. "You may think my business is
to make appropriations," said Joseph Cannon, a powerful former
Speaker of the House and chairman of the Appropriations Committee,
"but it is not. It is to prevent their being made."[50] Presumably, the
committee performed the watchdog role by cutting the spending estimate, and it performed the advocacy role (as defenders of activities and
bureaus under its care) by raising spending above the prior year.

In 1894 Congress passed and President Cleveland signed the first
income tax bill. Its strongest proponents argued that this tax would be
paid for by "wealth, not want"; the time had come to "put more tax
upon what men have, less on what they need."[51] Opponents argued that
the income tax was a tax on "mind and energy," taking from the "thrifty
and enterprising" to give to "the shiftless and the sluggard."[52] In the
political conditions of the 1890s, the kind of incidence and taxation was
far more important than the amount.

The Supreme Court ruled the progressive aspects of income tax
unconstitutional in *Pollock* v. *Farmers Loan and Trust Co.* (157 U.S.,
429) in 1895. The federal government was in deficit 11 of the 21 years
from 1894 through 1914. What to do? Faced with revenue shortfalls,
Presidents Roosevelt (in his 1906 annual message) and Taft (accepting
the Republican nomination in 1908) both endorsed the idea of an
income tax. But the Supreme Court was a large barrier. In 1908 the
Democrats called for a constitutional amendment to allow the tax, and
in 1909, under substantial pressure, Taft agreed. The amendment sped
through Congress with little debate in 1909[53] and was ratified in 1913.
The income tax subsequently enacted was, however, extremely small.
And any prospect that it could handle budget shortfalls was eliminated
when America entered World War I. Income-tax revenues were greatly

[49]Wilmerding, *Spending Power*, pp. 151–52.
[50]Fenno, *Power of the Purse*, p. 99.
[51]Edwin R. A. Seligman, *The Income Tax* (New York: Macmillan, 1921), p. 497.
[52]*Ibid.*, p. 500.
[53]*Ibid.*, pp. 590–96.

expanded, but failed by a large amount to match wartime spending. In the three years from 1917 through 1919, federal debt grew from $1.2 billion to $25.5 billion.[54]

Coping with that massive debt, retrenching from wartime to peace-time expenditures, and responding to the new public awareness of bud-getary issues resulting from a direct tax (rather than hidden taxes such as tariffs) posed a major challenge. Congressmen searched for ways to meet the goal of spending reduction as quickly yet painlessly (for them) as possible. As usually happens when problems arise, people were waiting with pet solutions. The appropriations committees wanted their power back. The president and a group of Progressive reformers wanted an executive budget. Congress moved to create an executive budget, but also to strengthen itself.

THE EXECUTIVE BUDGET MOVEMENT

Reformers are not radicals; those who left their imprint upon Ameri-can budgeting between the Civil War and 1920 were not opposed to American social structure or to competitive markets, nor were they proponents of income redistribution. A political force unique in this most unusual of nations, reformers were the establishment's antiestab-lishment—critical of the fragmented way politicians did things—and also the anti-anti-market, who opposed threats by corporate trusts to limit competition. To lessen the "irresponsible power" of party bosses and chairmen of congressional standing committees, the budgetary re-formers wanted a visible and democratically accountable Chief Execu-tive served by experts dedicated to the public interest. The experts, whose ideas and attitudes matched the reformers', would be the instru-ments of change.

The people of the United States had a deep attachment to the Constitution and to the separation between executive and legislative

[54]Historical Statistics of the United States, Colonial Times to 1970, Part 2; U.S. Department of Commerce, Bureau of the Census, pp. 1104, 07–08, 14–15, 21–22, 24–25, 49.

branches it embodied. Yet it was precisely this separation (or at least the form it took in America) that the reformers opposed. "The business of national government has become so huge and so complex," Nicholas Murray Butler wrote in 1918, "that the sharp separation of the executive and the legislative powers to which we have been accustomed for 140 years is distinctly disadvantageous."[55] Woodrow Wilson, extending his criticism to the other great division of power, that between states and the federal government, had earlier concluded: "It is, therefore, manifestly a radical defect in our federal system that it parcels out power and confuses responsibility as it does."[56]

The budgetary practice to which the reformers most objected was the timeworn one of itemization of spending, known today as the line-item budget. Itemization was wasteful and, worst of all, did not allow for executive discretion. President Taft's Commission on Economy and Efficiency argued that because government did not trust its officers, "judgments which can be made wisely only at the time that a specific thing is to be done are attempted to be made by a Congress composed of hundreds of Members from six months to a year and a half beforehand on the recommendation of a committee which at most can have but a limited experience or fund of information as a basis for their thinking."[57] The principle of deference to expertise was thus twice denied by Congress, once to the Chief Executive and then again to his subordinates.

The piecemeal process by which budgets were put together—each committee recommending appropriations for the agencies and purposes under its control, and the houses of Congress acting on them one at a time—was singled out for special condemnation. Because of this fragmentation, no formal attention was given to total spending. "In the United States," as Charles Wallace Collins put it, "no one knows in advance of action, what the government proposes to spend for the coming year. This can be arrived at only at or near the close of the

---

[55]Nicholas M. Butler, "Executive Responsibility and a National Budget," *Proceedings of the Academy of Political Science,* Vol. 8 (1918–20), p. 46.

[56]Wilson, *Congressional Government,* p. 284.

[57]Quoted in Wilmerding, *Spending Power,* p. 150.

session by summing up the various bills which have been acted on."[58]

Reformers had no concept of informal coordination and never thought to ask whether all concerned might not have had a pretty good idea of where they were, and were likely to end up. It was chiefly the form of the budget, and what it represented, to which they objected: "no standard classifications . . . of expenditures according to their character and object . . . no uniform scheme of expenditure documents calling for the recording of expenditure data in accordance with any general information plan . . . no budgetary message, no proper scheme of summary, analytical and comparative tables. . . ." In short, nothing in the United States appropriations process remotely resembled budgeting in the executive-centered governments of Europe.[59]

So much for what the reformers were against; what were they for? Hierarchy, known to them as "executive leadership," is the best short answer. Leadership would purify politics. This was Woodrow Wilson's theory, and his practice as president.[60] Wilson was ready with both diagnosis and remedy: "This feature of disintegration of leadership runs . . . through all our legislation; but it is manifestly of much more serious consequence in financial administration than in the direction of other concerns of government." Budgets must be "under the management of a single body; only when all financial arrangements are based upon schemes prepared by a few men of trained minds and accordant principles, who can act with easy agreement and with perfect confidence in each other" will budgets make sense.[61] The major premise of executive leadership led also to its important corollary: executive discretion by reliance on experts. It is important to understand that the reformers believed their recommendations derived from scientific principles. Often they referred to "the science of budgetmaking,"[62] or said they

[58]Charles Wallace Collins, *The National Budget System* (New York: Macmillan, 1917), p. 3.

[59]William Franklin Willoughby, *The Problem of a National Budget* (New York: Appleton, 1918), pp. 56–57.

[60]Arthur Macmahon, "Woodrow Wilson: Political Leader and Administrator," in Earl Latham, ed., *The Philosophy and Policies of Woodrow Wilson* (Chicago: University of Chicago Press, 1958), pp. 100–22; reference is to page 113.

[61]Wilson, *Congressional Government,* pp. 180–81.

[62]Charles Beard, "Prefatory Note," *Municipal Research,* No. 88 (August 1917) (New York: Bureau of Municipal Research), p. iii.

were subjecting budgetary problems "to scientific analysis."[63] Their assumption was that the goals or objectives of budgeting were agreed so that only the details of administrative execution were left to be considered.

The policy–administration dichotomy—in which political choices are made through general legislative enactments, and administrative choices are limited to technical implementation of these larger and prior decisions—was an essential postulate of budget reformers. They held that if administrators also were to make large and therefore political choices, the principle of neutral competence—which justified civil-service reform and the important role reformers wished to give to experts—would be undermined. Their text was Frank J. Goodnow's *Politics and Administration.* Goodnow believed that the two primary functions of government were to determine the will of the people and to execute that will. Though, as Dwight Waldo observes, Goodnow was far from making the distinction exclusive (seeing better than his followers the interpretation of the two functions), when taken up by less sophisticated acolytes Goodnow's ideas generated the doctrine of a strict separation between the two.[64] This dichotomy legitimizes taking power from the legislature and giving it to the executive—and, ultimately, to the executive's expert administrators, the reformers themselves.

The reformers' recommendation to adopt business practices manifestly did not mean approval of bidding and bargaining among legislature and executive. Rather, they adopted from big business its internal organization, that is, its hierarchical structure, which served to solidify the distinction between policy and administration that the reformers wished to make.

The reformers' budgetary principle of principles was reiterated like a litany: "There must be established a national budget prepared and recommended by the Chief Executive."[65]

If the proposals were adopted, how did the reformers picture themselves (or people like them) as participants in the budgetary process?

[63]Willoughby, *Problem of a National Budget,* p. 55.
[64]Dwight Waldo, *The Administrative State* (New York: Ronald Press, 1948), pp. 105–107.
[65]Butler, "Executive Responsibility," p. 49.

They had already been instrumental in staffing commissions to recommend the proposed reforms. These same men aimed to become part of the expert staff of the executive—mayor, governor, or president—whose task would be formulating the budget. As A. E. Buck said so succinctly, "budget-making requires special staff assistance . . . to . . . assist the executive. . . ."[66] By extending this function to other governmental purposes, budget experts could easily become a general administrative staff supporting the Executive. When one recognizes that presidents of the United States up to Franklin D. Roosevelt's time were assisted at most by a few clerks, these were far-reaching proposals.

A simile—be like Britain—justified recommendations for budget hierarchy in the United States. The only way Parliament could alter the budget was to change the government. "If one looks for the secret of . . . the English system," Willoughby comments, "it must be found in . . . the clear distinction . . . between legislative and administrative powers. . . . No proposals for . . . expenditure . . . shall be made . . . except . . . by the cabinet acting as the custodian of the administrative powers of government. . . ."[67]

Because the British Chancellor of the Exchequer and Department of the Treasury are responsible for both expenditure and revenue, the reformers believed that these would be taken up at the time and that, therefore, comprehensive and simultaneous consideration would be given to the relative desirability of spending versus taxing.[68] Whether this formal unity would make any difference, either to the totals or to the division of expenditures among departments, was not a subject for discussion by reformers who already knew the answer.

Agency personnel were to be completely subservient to budgetary decisions of the president. Replying to the charge that it would be difficult for agency heads to support estimates changed by the president, Cleveland and Buck claimed:

> This is a reason of no substance whatever. The heads of departments are and should be loyal to the Administration, and should . . . support the view

[66]A. E. Buck, "The Development of the Budget Idea in the United States," *Annals of the American Academy of Political and Social Science*, Vol. LXIII (May 1924), p. 36.
[67]Willoughby, *Problem of a National Budget*, pp. 59–60.
[68]*Ibid.*, p. 405.

which the President has adopted . . . in respect to the budget. They will have no difficulty in so doing. If any head of a department does, then his place is not in the Cabinet.[69]

If the president fires a dissident department head, said the reformers, the difficulty disappears. Apparently it never occurred to them that heads of spending departments might speak privately with legislators or, if wide-ranging differences arose, that presidents might not be able to maintain dominance over the cabinet. In those days cabinet members represented party factions; asking a cabinet member to step down therefore had significant political costs.

The reformers insisted that, having gained executive approval, every spending proposal would ipso facto represent the national view. Charles Wallace Collins insisted:

> After the budget is presented to the legislature there can be no "log-rolling" . . . to secure funds. . . . A locality deserving a post office building would have to gain the sanction of the Post Office Department. After an examination of all of the facts the Department would come to a decision. Should it be favorable . . . the department would have further to gain the assent of the Treasury before the item . . . could be put into the estimates. . . . Both the Department and the Treasury would look at the matter from the national point of view.[70]

In Lewis Carroll's *Through the Looking Glass,* the Red Queen tells Alice, in the same manner, that anything she says three times is true.

At the time, the reformers' position was effectively criticized by Edward A. Fitzpatrick in his *Budget Making in a Democracy* (1918). His views are interesting because they embody the stance of the expert administrator who does not aspire to be a staff assistant to the Chief Executive. Fitzpatrick looked at the political implications of the president amassing such budgetary power. "Are we to have a one-man government? That," Fitzpatrick told his readers, "is the fundamental question in back of the executive budget propaganda."[71]

As for the much-vaunted British example, cabinet government, he

[69]Frederick A. Cleveland and Arthur E. Buck, *The Budget and Responsible Government* (New York: Macmillan, 1920), pp. xviii–xix.

[70]Collins, *National Budget System,* p. 41.

[71]Edward Augustus Fitzpatrick, *Budget Making in a Democracy* (New York: Macmillan, 1918), p. 55.

said, was not government by one person, but by a committee of the legislature, a parliament with the ultimate right to dismiss its cabinet.[72] *"Do those who are proposing the executive budget also propose the legislative recall of the executive?"*[73] This is what the British Parliament does and that is what a business board of directors does when it loses confidence in management. Fitzpatrick, however, insisted such action is impossible under presidential government with its fixed terms.[74] Reformers, Fitzpatrick contended acidly, should tell the people they want to make a fundamental change in the American form of government, and not camouflage the issues "under the name of 'executive budget.' "[75]

To promote the idea of a federal executive budget, President William Howard Taft set up a Commission on Economy and Efficiency. The commission's tone was set by its chairman, Frederick A. Cleveland, then director of the New York Bureau of Municipal Research, and by other noted budget reformers appointed with him, including Frank J. Goodnow and W. F. Willoughby.[76] The commission's basic task, accepted by Taft in its entirety, was that the president would submit spending estimates to Congress and would assume responsibility for them.[77] The commission's major report, "The Need for a National Budget," completed in 1912, was followed by "A Budget for the Fiscal Year 1914," in which President Taft, at the commission's instigation, submitted the kind of budget document he thought appropriate for the Chief Executive as top administrator.[78] It rejected the prevailing narrow view of economy—of spending merely the minimum. Instead, the President (like earlier advocates of internal improvements) stated that he wanted the government to operate economically in order to do more for the people with available resources.[79] Power for presidents and their advisors

[72]*Ibid.*, pp. 50–51, 59.
[73]*Ibid.*, p. 54.
[74]*Ibid.*, p. 5.
[75]*Ibid.*, p. 292.
[76]Naylor, *Federal Budget System in Operation*, pp. 23–24.
[77]Cleveland, "Leadership and Criticism," p. 33.
[78]Naylor, *Federal Budget System in Operation*, p. 24.
[79]Wilmerding, *Spending Power*, p. 151; and Jesse Burkhead, *Government Budgeting* (New York: Wiley, 1956), p. 119.

was sublimated under a rubric with which it was difficult to argue: efficiency.

Congress was of a different mind altogether. Expressing fear of the Executive's usurpation of power (in language harking back to the early days of the republic), Congress passed a law requiring department heads charged with preparing estimates to do what they had always done: to send estimates directly to congressional appropriations committees.[80] And department heads responded to these contradictory directives by preparing one set as Congress specified, and another as directed by the president. As business conditions improved and passage of the Sixteenth Amendment in 1913 permitted a graduated income tax, thus raising revenue, pressures for change in the budget system diminished.

Nothing was done to establish an executive budget until after the First World War.[81] In 1916, chambers of commerce all over the country voted almost unanimously for the introduction of a national executive budget. The Republican party platform that year criticized Democrats for their "shameless raids on the Treasury" and their opposition to President Taft's proposal for "a simple, business-like budget system." To these Republicans, reform meant lower taxes.

The desire for fiscal prudence, both against the growing debt and for a balanced budget, reasserted itself with a vengeance after the war. World War I had been fought largely on borrowed money. From 1914 to 1918, the government's role in directing economic activity expanded enormously. There was a new public concern that the profligate habits of wartime would carry over into peacetime civilian life. The Victory Liberty Loan Act of 1919 established a sinking fund to reduce the debt, which was cut a third by the end of the 1920s. Wilson's Secretary of the Treasury, Carter Glass, pointed out the "grave danger that the extraordinary success of the Treasury in financing the stupendous war expenditures may lead to a riot of public expenditures after the war, the consequences of which could only be disastrous." His successor under President Harding (1921–1923), David F. Huston, similarly observed

---

[80]Naylor, *Federal Budget System in Operation*, pp. 24–25.
[81]Burkhead, *Government Budgeting*, pp. 20–21.

that "we have demobilized many groups, but we have not demobilized those whose gaze is concentrated on the Treasury."[82]

, The end of World War I saw renewed interest in a national executive budget; between 1918 and 1921, the reformers presented proposals to congressional committees. Once again reformers criticized the federal expenditure process: There was overlap among substantive committees, and hence duplication of effort; there was no comprehensive consideration of revenues and expenditures; the consequence of bureaucratic rivalry was waste. In short, according to Representative Good of Iowa (chairman of the House Select Committee on the Budget System in 1919), "the estimates are a patchwork and not a structure." He thought "a great deal of the time of the committees of Congress is taken up in exploding the visionary schemes of bureau chiefs for which no administration would be willing to stand responsible."[83] He did not explain why these schemes were approved if no one supported them.

In the name of managing the huge national debt, the Budget and Accounting Act of 1921 made the major changes budget reformers had long supported. Departments sent spending estimates to the president through a new institution, the Bureau of the Budget, and the Chief Executive had total control over the Budget Bureau. Henceforth no appropriation could be considered unless first reviewed by the president and the two appropriations committees. "Review," however, was a far cry from the near-absolute control exercised by European cabinets.

No stronger statement of the spirit of legislative supremacy, or of its practical consequences, can be found than in the House report commenting on the Budget and Accounting Act of 1921. The only executive aspect of that act, the House insisted, was that the president would henceforth be held responsible for the agency estimates he submitted. After that, the budget was still legislative all the way. Members of Congress could still move his proposed numbers up, down, or sideways by ignoring them entirely. If anyone doubted that the president's budget was just his set of recommendations, the Committee Report sought to disabuse them:

[82]Kimmel, *Federal Budget and Fiscal Policy,* p. 88.
[83]Fritz Morstein Marx, "The Bureau of the Budget: Its Evolution and Present Role," *American Political Science Review,* Vol. 39, No. 4 (August 1945), pp. 653–84.

It will doubtless be claimed by some that this is an Executive budget and that the duty of making appropriations is a legislative rather than Executive prerogative. The plan outlined does provide for an Executive initiation of the budget, but the President's responsibility ends when he has prepared the budget and transmitted it to Congress. To that extent, and to that extent alone, does the plan provide for an Executive budget, but the proposed law does not change in the slightest degree the duty of Congress to make the minutest examination of the budget and to adopt the budget only to the extent that it is found to be economical. If the estimates contained in the President's budget are too large, it will be the duty of Congress to reduce them. If in the opinion of Congress the estimates of expenditures are not sufficient, it will be within the power of Congress to increase them. The bill does not in the slightest degree give the Executive any greater power than he now has over the consideration of appropriations by Congress.[84]

If Congress were to give the president the power to propose, it wanted also to ensure its power to dispose, and then to oversee the execution of its decisions. It created the Bureau of the Budget and the Executive Budget process, but checked the president in two ways. In 1920 the House, and the Senate in 1922, restored their former powers to the appropriations committees, thus providing an institutional counter-weight to the centralized executive process. In addition, Congress removed from the Treasury the power to audit and account for expenditures (where it had resided since 1789) and lodged it in a General Accounting Office (GAO) outside of the president's control. The Comptroller of the Treasury was replaced by a new official, the Comptroller General of the United States. He had a single, 15-year term and could be replaced only by a joint resolution of both houses of Congress, signed by the president.

What remained to be decided was the function of the newly created Budget Bureau within the executive branch. Its first head, General Charles G. Dawes, a student and practitioner of administration, insisted that the offices not be in the Treasury Building, but outside it, and near the White House (Dawes wanted to insulate the bureau from inter-

---

[84]House Report No. 14, 67th Congress, 1st Session, 6–7 (1921), cited in Louis Fisher, "The Item Veto: The Risks of Emulating the States." Prepared for delivery at the Annual Meeting of the American Political Science Association, New Orleans, August 29–31, 1985, p. 6.

departmental squabbles).[85] He insisted on his right to call department heads into conference; President Warren Harding wisely suggested that such conferences be held in the White House Cabinet Room (instead of in the Budget Director's office), to emphasize the Chief Executive's commanding role in budget decisions.[86]

The 1920s witnessed a major assault on federal spending. Led by General Dawes, his successors, and businessmen whom Dawes brought into government (often working for "a dollar a year"), the bureau zealously pursued efficiency. Its accomplishments provoked panegyrics. Martin Madden, chairman of the House Committee on Appropriations, wrote as if the promised land had been reached: "One noticeable feature has been the . . . self-sacrificing of local interests in favor of the common good. When one recalls the former days when appropriations were sought with avidity for local projects . . . it is appropriate to commend the change from local to national attitude."[87]

An economy mood prevailed. The reconstitution of the appropriations committees and the Budget and Accounting Act of 1921 reflected overwhelming agreement on a balanced budget at a restricted level of spending. That consensus enabled the system to work with little friction. Far from exceeding revenues, spending had to fit within them, and then some, to permit deficit reduction. Through the 1920s, conveniently a time of plenty when Congress was receiving few petitions for help anyway, the debt was steadily reduced.

Good times and an overriding goal consensus nurtured the new system. Speaking at the tenth regular meeting of the Business Organization of the Government, Director Lord, second head of the Bureau of the Budget, exclaimed, "We still follow you, Mr. President, singing the old and tried battle song, economy with efficiency, one and inseparable. May we continue to sing it until in a noble paean of praise it heralds the day when taxes cease to be burdensome and serve what is a grateful

[85]See Charles G. Dawes, *The First Year of the Budget of the United States* (New York: Harper, 1923).

[86]*Ibid.*, p. 29.

[87]Quoted in William Franklin Willoughby, *The National Budget System with Suggestions for Its Improvement* (Baltimore: Johns Hopkins, 1927), pp. 287–88.

expression of our appreciation of the numberless privileges and bound-less blessings we enjoy in this most favored Nation of the earth."[88] Director Lord accordingly founded various clubs to hold expenditures down, such as the Two-Percent Personnel Club (to cut personnel spending in that amount per year), a Correspondence Club to save money on messages, and so on. He also established the Loyal Order of Woodpeckers "whose persistent tapping away at waste will make cheerful music in government offices and workshops during the coming year. . . ."[89] Honest.

Creation of the Budget Bureau, however, did not work instant wonders. True, the new procedures gathered spending proposals into a single budget document that when presented to Congress, symbolized presidential authority. But creation of a new executive layer in the budget process did not modify the separation of powers nor alter the federal system. After all, European cabinets, even when majorities were tied to party discipline, often did not limit spending.

Then came the market crash of 1929, followed by the Great Depression of the 1930s. Federal revenues were cut in half (1930: $4.06 billion; 1932: $1.92 billion); state and local revenues plummeted; demands for relief soared. State and local funds ran out; people turned to Washington.

The depression marked both a beginning of using variable expenditure as an instrument of economic stabilization and a subsequent end to the primacy of the balanced budget. The great budgetary equation had been fundamentally reoriented. The emphasis shifted from matching spending and revenue at the lowest possible level to manipulation of the difference between them.

THE DEMISE OF THE BALANCED BUDGET

Though his administration urged a variety of methods to enhance business activity as the depression began, President Herbert Hoover insisted

---

[88]Kimmel, *Federal Budget and Fiscal Policy,* p. 96.
[89]*Ibid.,* p. 97.

that "we cannot squander ourselves into prosperity." To Hoover, a balanced budget was the "very keystone of recovery" without which the depression would continue indefinitely. He stressed lowering federal expenditures and, if that failed, raising taxes.[90]

The Democratic opposition firmly shared his opinion that achieving a balanced budget was essential to ending the depression.[91] The new president, Franklin D. Roosevelt, was so concerned about the near $1.6 billion deficit—"A deficit so great that it makes us catch our breath"— that he promised during his campaign and then in his inaugural address to make a balanced budget top priority.

Though just a cloud on the horizon at first, the federal government's goal of achieving a balanced budget during a depression soon came under attack. Progressive publicists, such as Waddill Catchings and William Trufant Foster, wrote against the idea of a negative state that relied on the private sector to generate income and employment; instead they advocated maintaining employment through long-range public works. Though new debt would be created, the additional economic activity and increased revenue would make repayment of the debt easier than would an ongoing depression. "We must conquer the depression by collective action," Foster insisted in 1932. "This necessarily means the leadership of the federal government—the only agency which represents all of us. . . . We must abandon our policy of defeatism, our worship of the budget, our false economy program. . . . Instead, we must collectively put into use enough currency and credit to restore the community price level of 1928."[92]

By the early 1930s, a number of Americans in the Democratic party began to seek a rationale for encouraging the government to expand public works and thus increase employment. They found this rationale in the work of economist John Maynard Keynes and introduced his thought to key figures, including President Roosevelt.[93] Building on

---

[90]Kimmel, *Federal Budget and Fiscal Policy,* p. 160; Joseph Dorfman, *The Economic Mind in American Civilization 1918–1933* (New York: Viking Press, 1959), pp. 610–16.
[91]Kimmel, *Federal Budget and Fiscal Policy,* p. 148.
[92]*Ibid.,* p. 155.
[93]For Felix Frankfurter's efforts in this direction, see H. N. Hirsch, *The Enigma of Felix Frankfurter* (New York: Basic Books, 1981), p. 113.

ideas advanced in 1931 by his collaborator R. F. Kahn, Keynes argued that it was appropriate, in a deflationary period when vast economic resources went unused, for the government to create deficits as a means of expanding demand. When economic activity was slow, government should step in to speed it up; when the economy overheated and inflation resulted, government could decrease spending. In short, raising and lowering the deficit would become a prime means of economic control. The important point, however, is not the practice of Keynesian doctrine—any student of politics knows that it would be much easier to raise than to lower spending—but that it provided a strong intellectual rationale for doing what many people wanted. At long last, politicians could combine spending with virtue. But not without inner doubt.

The New Deal in the United States never was a coherent set of measures. Rather it comprised ad hoc answers to immediate crises.[94] Roosevelt's presidential campaign platform held that the cause of the depression lay within the American economy and hence could be cured only through domestic action. Accordingly, Roosevelt's program (presented to Congress in the famous first Hundred Days) aimed at relief, recovery, and reform. Barely established in Washington, Roosevelt offered proposals to reestablish public confidence in the banking system, to achieve a balanced budget by cutting government spending, to revive agriculture through an increase in farm incomes, to assist industry by creating a system of price codes, and to institute a program of public works. Specifically, Roosevelt sought to bring output in line with consumer demand by limiting production and reducing government spending.

During those first Hundred Days, the House of Representatives passed the Economy Bill, which halved the pensions of disabled war veterans, reduced congressional salaries as well as those of all federal employees, and curtailed other federal expenditures. The Economy Bill was designed to balance spending with revenue, which, since two-thirds of it was based on individual and corporate income taxes, had declined

[94]Jim Potter, *The American Economy between the World Wars* (New York: Wiley, 1974), p. 113.

by nearly a half between 1930 and 1933. This bill increased hardships among pensioners and, by curtailing government expenditure, reduced individual purchasing power.

Clearly, Roosevelt was no believer in the desirability of deficits. Indeed, when Keynes conferred with Roosevelt in Washington in 1935, the two apparently did not agree. Roosevelt maintained his balanced budget preferences; throughout the 1930s, he viewed current spending as pump priming. After an overwhelming victory in the 1936 election, Roosevelt tried to cut spending in 1937 to balance the budget, but a sharp upturn in unemployment in 1938 forced him to abandon this effort.[95]

"The New Economics" (as Keynes' theory was soon labeled) and the old balanced-budget norm clashed head-on. As newly converted Keynesians began to propose deliberately unbalanced budgets, some sympathetic observers—who advocated government spending to revive the economy and thus relieve human misery—foresaw that it might be difficult to turn off the tap after citizens in democracies became accustomed to benefits provided by central government.[96]

As the debate over balance or imbalance grew hotter in the late 1930s, sober voices pointed to the likely outcome once the bastions of the balanced budget were breached. A *New York Times* editorial on December 27, 1938, maintained:

> There is one objective standard that everyone understands clearly—Federal budgets "annually balanced." Once we depart from that, except under the sheerest necessity, we are adrift on the seas of confusion, for all sorts of ingenious reasons are invented for not going back, and the vested interest in keeping the new situation is enormous. . . . To enable a legislator to vote for appropriation bills and at the same time avoid voting for increases in taxes is to provide him with the politician's paradise.[97]

Extrapolating from the depressed economies of the late 1930s, one doomsayer contended "There is a real and very great danger that a

[95]Robert Lekachman, *The Age of Keynes* (New York: McGraw-Hill, 1966), pp. 122–23.

[96]Harvey Stephen Perloff, *Modern Budget Policies: A Study of the Budget Process in Present-Day Society,* Ph.D. dissertation submitted to the Departments of Government and Economics, Harvard University, December 1, 1939, p. 140.

[97]*Ibid.*, pp. 139–40.

democracy may spend itself to death, as it were, once it departs from a balanced budget."[98] Obviously, this specter has not been realized. However, the critics were right in one respect: There was to be no law of budgetary gravity; spending proved to be an escalator that went only one way—up.

A look at federal income and expenditure between 1929 and 1939 gives some sense of government's growth and its expanded role in the economy. In 1929, federal expenditure was $3.3 billion; in 1939, $8.9 billion. While federal spending increased by 170 percent, there was only a 25 percent increase in federal revenues (from $4.0 billion in 1929 to $5.0 billion in 1939). Federal expenditure as a percentage of gross national product (GNP), moreover, tripled (from 3.2 percent in 1929 to 9.7 percent in 1939) whereas federal revenue as a percent of GNP during the same period did not even double (from 3.9 to 5.5 percent).

The enduring legacy of the New Deal was acceptance by the American public of the doctrine that the federal government has ultimate responsibility for the economy. After the Second World War this legacy was institutionalized in the Full Employment Act of 1946, which created the Council of Economic Advisers.

After the Second World War (during which budget balance was, of course, impossible), the norm of balance see-sawed, but generally remained strong through the Truman and Eisenhower administrations. Both presidents, while recognizing government responsibility for economic performance, saw a balanced budget as economically desirable. As President Truman remarked in his memoirs, "There is nothing sacred about the pay-as-you-go idea so far as I am concerned except that it represents the soundest principle of financing that I know."[99] Eisenhower believed that the primary economic problem was inflation, so he "responded to recessions cautiously and turned quickly to the anti-inflationary policy of budget-balancing when economic revival was in sight." While there was some opposition to the policy, "in general it

---

[98]Dan Throop Smith, "An Analysis of Changes in Federal Finances, July 1930–June 1938," *Review of Economic Statistics,* Vol. 20 (November 1938), pp. 149–60; cited in Perloff, *Modern Budget Policies,* p. 140.

[99]Harry S Truman, *Years of Trial and Hope,* in *Memoirs by Harry S. Truman,* 2 Vols. (Garden City, N.Y.: Doubleday & Co., 1956), 2:41 quoted in Herbert Stein, *The Fiscal Revolution in America* (Chicago: University of Chicago Press, 1969), p. 207.

commanded a great deal of bipartisan support and reflected the common view of the nation's economic problem."[100] Many congressmen, like most of the public, saw balance "as a symbol and test of discipline and responsibility in government."[101]

Of particular importance to the continued adherence to a balanced budget during this time was the existence in Congress of a conservative coalition: an alliance between conservative Republicans and conservative Democrats, mostly from the South. The coalition was held together by basic policy agreement on limited government and was facilitated by joint meetings among the leaders. "On one occasion, so close did House conservatives work together, that John Taber (R-N.Y.), a leading conservative on the Appropriations Committee, lent ["Judge"] Smith [D-Va., a leading spokesman for southern Democrats in the House] one of his staff men to assist Judge in finding ways of reducing federal expenditures."[102]

This bipartisan group could muster substantial support for limiting spending at the committee level and on the floor. Representative Joe Martin, House Republican leader from 1939–1959, spoke of his ability to raise votes across party lines: "In any case when an issue of spending or of new powers for the President came along, I would go to Representative Howard W. Smith of Virginia, for example, and say, 'Howard, see if you can't get me a few Democratic votes here.' Or I would seek out Representative Eugene Cox of Georgia, and ask, 'Gene, why don't you and John Ranken and some of your men get me some votes for this?' "[103] Throughout the 1940s and into the late 1950s, the conservative coalition was able to win at least 70 percent of the votes in both Houses.[104]

In the 1960s balance became partisan in a way that it had not been

[100]Herbert Stein, *The Fiscal Revolution in America* (Chicago: University of Chicago Press, 1969), p. 284.

[101]Everett Ladd, "Americans' Hate Affair with Deficits," *Fortune*, June 14, 1982, pp. 77–84.

[102]John F. Manley, "The Conservative Coalition in Congress," *American Behavioral Scientist*, Vol. 17, No. 2 (November/December 1973), pp. 223–48; quote p. 232.

[103]*Ibid.*, p. 232.

[104]*Ibid.*, p. 239.

since before the Civil War, only now the Democrats were the skeptics. Balance was a conservative position used by lower-spending Republicans as a weapon against the higher-spending liberal Democrats. Since the dominant theory of economic management was Keynesian economics, the norm of balance also conflicted with the widespread desire that the government ensure a healthy economy. The balanced-budget norm could no longer constrain and coordinate decisions as it had in the past.

The struggle for power that has marked the budget process since colonial times has taken on a new dimension: As government has faced outward toward society—to alleviate poverty, encourage medical care, cope with the consequences of unemployment—its budgetary procedures, previously reflecting an orientation toward internal control, have become more concerned with relating spending to revenue than with the substance of spending itself. Consensus as to governmental responsibility was joined to a decline of the balanced-budget norm.

Under Keynesian doctrine, as understood and practiced at the time, the idea was to balance the economy at full employment (accepting between 3 and 5 percent of "frictional" unemployment), not necessarily to balance the budget. To the extent that relationships between participants in budgeting depended on belief in balance—since revenue limits expenditure, no spending agency can grow faster than the economy without taking unfair advantage of the others—the pillars of spending control were severely shaken. So long as there was more for everyone, so good. If (or, rather, when, in view of historical experience) the rate of economic growth declined, however, the participants in budgeting would have to agree on their fair share of a more limited pie without the support provided by consensus on budget balance. Before we can understand how operating under conditions of ideological dissensus affects budgeting, we need to understand how ideological consensus, when it existed, moved budgeting along a more incremental path.

THE DANCE OF
THE DOLLARS:
CLASSICAL
BUDGETING*

3

WARS ARE CATALYSTS OF CHANGE. The United States emerged from the Second World War determined not to reexperience the depression of the 1930s. Its central government, being victorious, enjoyed an enhanced respect. The task assigned was to maintain prosperity by managing the economy; how far government should go was a matter of controversy, but that it should act was accepted. Along with that consensus came an expanded importance for the Executive Office of the President, including the Bureau of the Budget (BOB). From an inspector of agency budget estimates, the BOB had become the keeper of the president's program; it shaped the policies of a given presidency, cleared proposed legislation with spending implications (i.e., almost everything), helped enforce presidential priorities within the executive branch, and stood up for them before Congress. Now it was the BOB's pruning of agency estimates, delivered as the president's budget, that provided the accepted starting point for the congressional budget process.

Although there was a lot of doubt and soul searching about the place

*This chapter is largely a summary of the sections on "Strategies and Calculation" in the 1964 edition of *The Politics of the Budgetary Process.*

74

of the United States as a (perhaps the) major international power after the war, internationalism won out over isolationism. There was no turning back.

The budgetary consequences for postwar America were profound. War had accustomed the nation to hitherto unheard of levels of taxation; while these went down considerably, they never fell to prewar levels. Domestic spending rose not only for veterans (the G.I. Bill put many through school) but also for social purposes. Unemployment Compensation, for instance, stood as a hedge against adversity and also provided what were called built-in stabilizers, so that, following Keynesian doctrine, spending rose as the economy declined. After the roller-coaster of rapid demobilization was followed by the buildup after the Korean War, the defense budget had stabilized at levels much higher than the prewar period. By 1955 defense constituted over two-fifths of total spending while social welfare programs, including social security, were about one-fifth. The economy began to grow. By keeping defense stable in constant dollars (adjusted for inflation and without raising tax rates) domestic spending began to rise in the late 1960s and early 1970s with the advent of new and expanded welfare programs, such as medicare for the elderly and medicaid for the poor. Government grew painlessly. Though President Kennedy cut taxes to stimulate the economy in the early 1960s and President Johnson rejected the advice of the Council of Economic Advisers to raise them during the Vietnam War in the mid-1960s, revenue and expenditures remained close, with small, albeit growing, deficits. No great sacrifices—substantial tax increases or large spending cuts—were seen to be necessary. Incremental advance was the order of these times.

The inherited practices and understandings of the budgetary process were widely accepted. The budget was to be balanced except in wartime (the old exception) or in depression (the new exception). Existing levels of taxation were not lightly to be altered, hence spending had to stay within hailing distance of revenue. Inflation was anathema, even at levels of 3 or 5 percent; but spending could be cut and taxes raised to deal with that threat to stability. The annual budget was sacrosanct; appropriations bills were to be passed on time and to last the entire year. Multiyear and supplemental appropriations were frowned upon, barely acceptable for special reasons, intolerable as standard practice. Just as earmarked funds were disfavored on the idea that all revenue should go to the central treasury, so as to give maximum flexibility to government, expenditures were expected to pass through the annual appropriations process. Classical budgeting, we see in retrospect, was premised upon agreement on the size, scope, and distribution of expenditure. Conflict was confined to the margins, a little more there, a little less there. We will understand the present better by seeing how different it is from the past.

What follows is written in the present tense so as to retain a sense of immediacy. The reader should be aware, however, as the following chapters attest, that much of what follows belongs to a bygone era. Calculations remain complex, even more so, but the roles and strategies of the participants and the budgetary process itself have been markedly altered. Imagine a long discussion of strategies for budgeting in discretionary accounts that makes no mention of the budget resolution, which is now the main locus of decision-making activity for many of these accounts; imagine speaking of the House Appropriations Committee as a place devoted to looking for cuts and more cuts, at a time when it spends a great deal more energy looking for ways to avoid cuts called for by the budget committees and the administration; imagine a discussion that treats agencies as the advocates in the process of budgeting, and that discusses at length how they maneuver for advantage in making budget requests, when it is now often OMB that is writing the requests and when agencies are routinely sent up to defend budgets that they loath; imagine statements that Senate appropriations view their House counterparts as unreasonable tightwads; and so on. This chapter is about the routine business of a bygone age.

CALCULATIONS

Participants in budgeting operate in an environment that imposes severe constraints on what they can do. Neither the opportunities they seize upon nor the disabilities they suffer are wholly, perhaps not even largely, within their control. Though perceptions of reality differ somewhat, and views of what is desirable differ more, budgetary actors accept certain elementary facts of life to which they must adjust.

Everyone is aware of the structural conditions of political life—such as the separation of powers, the division of labor within appropriations committees, and the customary separation between appropriations and substantive legislative committees. All participants face the usual overt political factors involving group pressures, relationships between congressmen and their constituents, political party conflicts, executive-legislative cooperation and rivalry, interagency disputes, and the like. Participants soon come to know the rules of the budgetary game, which specify the roles they must play and the kinds of moves that are more or less permissible. It would be hard indeed to ignore the contemporary climate of opinion—a spending or cutting mood—as when a rise in defense spending becomes obvious after a provocation (such as the invasion of South Korea by North Korea), or when a rise in unemployment demands creating jobs. Trends in the growth of national-welfare programs and increasing federal responsibility for a host of services are unlikely to be reversed. The participants take these conditions as "given" to a considerable extent and so must we if we expect to understand why they act as they do.

In this section, we will approach budgeting from the standpoint of the participants to see how they perceive their environment and make the calculations upon which their decisions depend. By "calculation" I mean the series of related factors (manifestly including perceptions of power relationships) that budgetary actors take into account in determining the choice of competing alternatives. Calculation involves a study of how problems arise and are identified; how they are broken down into manageable dimensions; how they relate to one another; how determinations are made of what is relevant; and how the actions of others are given consideration.

Complexity

One cannot hope to understand why people behave as they do unless one has some idea about how they make their calculations, and calculations are far from neutral. "Who gets what and how much" in politics depends on how calculations are made. Different methods of calculation often result in different decisions.

Budgeting is complex, both because there are many interrelated items and because these often pose technical difficulties. Suppose that you were a congressman or a Budget Bureau official interested in the leukemia research program and you wondered how the money was being spent. By looking at the National Cancer Institute's budgetary presentation you would discover that X amount is being spent on a project studying "factors and mechanics concerned in hemopoiesis," but that much less is being put into "a study of the relationship of neutralizing antibodies for the Rouse sarcoma virus to resistance and susceptibility for visceral lymphomatosis." Could you tell whether too much is being spent on one as compared to the other, or whether either project serves any useful purpose? You might sympathize with congressman Melvin Laird (R-Wis.), member of the Defense Appropriation Subcommittee, who plaintively cried, "A lot of things go on in this subcommittee that I cannot understand." It is not surprising, therefore, that congressmen express dismay at the difficulties of understanding technical subjects. Representative Jensen has a granddaughter who is reputed by him to have read "all the stuff she can get on nuclear science. . . . And . . . she just stumps me. I say, 'Jennifer, for Heaven's sake. I can't answer that.' 'Well,' she says, 'You are on the Atomic Energy Commission Committee, Grandpa.' 'Yes,' he replies, 'But I am not schooled in the art.' " When Representative Preston (D-Ga.), chairman of the Congress and Related Agencies Appropriations Subcommittee, says "I cannot recall any project of any size that has ever been presented to this committee—that came out in the end like the witnesses testified it would be at the outset," the problem is not always one of self-interested bureaucrats estimating on the low side, but of not knowing how to do better.

Endless time and unlimited ability to calculate might help. But time is in short supply, the human mind can encompass just so much, and the number of budgetary items may be huge. "We might as well be frank," stated the chairman of the Defense Appropriations Subcommittee, Representative George Mahan (D-Tex.), "no human being regardless of his position and . . . capacity could possibly be completely familiar with all the items of appropriations contained in this defense bill. . . ." But decisions have to be made. "There is a saying around the Pentagon," former defense comptroller McNeil informs us, "that . . . there is only one person in the United States who can force a decision, and that is the Government Printer [when the budget must go to the press]."[1]

Aside from the complexity of individual budgetary programs, there remains the imposing problem of making comparisons among different programs—how much highways are worth as compared to recreation facilities, national defense, and schools—that have different values for different people. No common denominator among these functions has been developed. No matter how hard they try, therefore, officials discover that they cannot find an objective method of judging priorities among programs. How, then, do budget officials go about meeting their staggering burden of calculation?

Aids to Calculation

The ways in which the appropriations committees go about making budgetary calculations are affected by their central position in the congressional system. Their power to make budgetary decisions is in a sense rooted in their ability to help keep the system going by meeting the needs of other congressmen. Appropriations must be voted each year if the government is to continue to function. (The experience of the Fourth French Republic, in which the practice of voting "twelfths" [one month's appropriations] because of inability to agree sapped the stability of the regime, is instructive on this point.) To put together budgets running into the billions of dollars and involving innumerable different activities is a gargantuan task. "This [House Appropriations] Committee is no place for a man who doesn't work," a member said. "They have to be hardworking. It isn't just a job; it's a way of life."[2] But sheer effort

[1]Subcommittee on National Policy Machinery, Committee on Government Operations, *The Budget and the Policy Process*, U.S. Senate, 87th Congress, First Session, 1961 (hereafter cited as *Jackson Committee Hearings*), p. 1061.

[2]Richard F. Fenno, Jr., "The House Appropriations Committee as a Political System: The Problem of Integration." *The American Political Science Review*, Vol. 56 (June 1962), p. 314.

is not enough. The committees must reduce the enormous burden of calculation involved in budgeting, in order to reach the necessary decisions. Otherwise, the necessity for decision might propel them into making random or wholly capricious choices that would throw governmental operations out of kilter. Nor could Congress as a whole shoulder the burden. Most congressmen are busy with other things; they can hardly hope to become knowledgeable in more than a few areas of budgeting, if that. Unless they are to abdicate their powers, some way of reducing their information costs must be found. The way congressmen have adapted is to accept the verdict of the appropriations committees most of the time and to intervene just often enough to keep the committees (roughly) in line.

Budgeting is consensual. There must be agreement on the general direction of public policy, at least on most past policies, or Congress would be swamped with difficult choices. Past policies would have to be renegotiated every year, a time-consuming and enervating process. Simultaneously, new programs are sure to engender controversy; without agreement that keeps the past mostly out of contention, it becomes harder to deal with the present. Consensus on policies need not be total; conflict is ever-present. Yet if disagreement encompasses too many policies, aids to calculation will not work well.

Budgeting is historical. One way of dealing with a problem of huge magnitude is to make rough guesses while letting experience accumulate. When the consequences of various actions become apparent, it is then possible to make modifications to avoid the difficulties. This is the rationale implicit in McNeil's statement justifying the absence of a ceiling on expenditures at the beginning of the Korean War.

> There was no long background in the United States, with 150 years of peak and valley experience, as to what carrying on a high level of defense year in and year out for a long period would cost, or what was involved. I think a very good start was made in listing everything that anyone could think they needed . . . knowing full well, however . . . that if you overbought certain engines or trucks, it could be balanced out the following year. That method was used for a year or two and then sufficient experience had been

gained . . . to know that . . . defense would cost in the neighborhood of $35 to $40 billion.[3]

Since members of Congress usually serve for several years before getting on appropriations committees, and since they are expected to serve an apprenticeship before making themselves heard, the more influential among them typically have long years of experience in dealing with their specialties. They have absorbed the meaning of many past moves and are prepared to apply the results of previous calculations to present circumstances. In this way the magnitude of any one decision at any one time is reduced, and with it the burden of calculation.

A line-item budgetary form facilitates this historical approach. Instead of focusing on various programs as a whole, the committees usually can concentrate on changes in various items—personnel, equipment, maintenance, specific activities—which make up the program. ". . . we will take an awfully long look when we come to the part of your budget that adds 5 additional people to the agency," Representative Jensen assured the Fish and Wildlife Service in 1960. By keeping categories constant over a number of years, and by requiring that the previous and present year's figures be placed in adjacent columns, calculations made in the past need not be gone over again completely. And though members know that the agency is involved in various programs, the line-item form enables them to concentrate on the less divisive issue of how much for each item.

Yet the past is not a foolproof guide to the future. Because so many actions are being undertaken at the same time, it is hard to disentangle the effects of one particular action compared to others. Consequently, disputes may arise about the benefits of continued support for an item. Ultimately reliance on a theory of cause and effect to provide guidance as to what is expected to happen becomes necessary.

Budgeting is fragmented. Budgets are made in fragments. Agencies develop budgetary requests based on their specialized needs. These requests are then channeled to any number of the multiple levels of specialization within Congress—the House and Senate appropriations

[3]*Jackson Committee Hearings*, p. 1075.

committees, their subcommittees, the subject areas within these sub-committees, the Senate Appropriation Committee appeals procedure, the Conference Committee, and the authorizations functions of the substantive committees and their specialized subcommittees. Even the subcommittees do not deal with all items in the budget but will pay special attention to instances of increases or decreases over the previous year. In this way, it might be said, subcommittees deal with a fragment of a fragment of the whole.

The Senate differs somewhat in that there is considerable overlap of membership between substantive and appropriations subcommittees and that outsiders from substantive subcommittees are welcome at hearings. The Senate, however, does add another level of consideration. The applicable decision-rule in most cases is that the most specialized member or members carry the day.

Fragmentation is further increased by the Senate Appropriations Committee, which concentrates on items that are appealed from House decisions. The senators, therefore, often deal with a fragment of what is already (through House action) a fragment of a fragment.

Budgeting is incremental.   The largest determining factor of this year's budget is last year's. Most of each budget is a product of previous decisions. The budget may be conceived of as an iceberg; by far the largest part lies below the surface, outside the control of anyone. Many items are standard, simply reenacted every year unless there is a special reason to challenge them. Long-range commitments have been made, and this year's share is scooped out of the total and included as part of the annual budget. The expenses of mandatory programs (entitlements), such as price supports or veterans' pensions, must be met. Some ongoing programs that appear to be satisfactory are no longer challenged. Agencies are going concerns and a minimum must be spent on housekeeping (though this item is particularly vulnerable to attack because it does not appear to involve a reduction in services or benefits). Powerful political support makes including other activities inevitable. The convergence of expectations on what must be included, for example, shows up in Representative Daniel Flood's (D-Pa.) comments on the census of business, which had been in trouble in previous years: "There is no longer any doubt that this is built right into our system any more." At any one time, after past commitments are paid for, a rather small percentage—seldom larger than 30 percent, often smaller than 5—is within the realm of anybody's (including congressional and Budget Bureau) discretion as a practical matter.

Budgeting is incremental, not comprehensive. The beginning of wisdom about an agency budget is that it is almost never actively reviewed as a whole every year, in the sense of reconsidering the value of all existing programs as compared to all possible alternatives. Instead, it is based on last year's budget with special attention given to a narrow range of increases or decreases. General agreement on past budgetary decisions combined with years of accumulated experience and specialization allows those who make the budget to be concerned with relatively small increments to an existing base. Their attention is focused on a small number of items over which the budgetary battle is fought. As Representative W. F. Norrel (D-Ark.), chairman of the Special Legislative Appropriations Subcommittee, declared, ". . . most of our time is spent in talking about the changes in the bill which we will have next year from the one we had this year, the reductions made, and the increases made. That which is not changed has very little, if anything, said about it."[4] Political reality, budget officials say, restricts attention to items they can do something about—a few new programs and possible cuts in old ones.

Senate practice too is undoubtedly incremental. "It has been the policy of our [appropriations] committee," Senator Thomas reported, "to consider only items that are in controversy. When the House has included an item, and no question has been raised about it, the Senate Committee passes it over on the theory that it is satisfactory, and for that reason the hearings as a rule do not include testimony for or against items contained in the House bill."

Budgeting is simplified. Another way of handling complexity is to see how actions on simpler items can be indices for more complicated ones.

---

[4]The Committee on Rules, U.S. House of Representatives, *To Create a Joint Committee on the Budget,* 82nd Congress, 2nd Session, 1952, p. 61.

Instead of dealing directly with the cost of a huge new installation, for example, congressmen may look at how personnel and administrative costs, or real estate transactions with which they have some familiarity, are handled. If these items are treated properly, then they may feel better able to trust administrators with the larger ones. The reader may have heard of this practice under some such title as "straining at gnats." And no doubt this is so often what it is; unable to handle the more complex problems, congressmen throw in the towel and retreat to the simpler ones. But I want to point out here that this practice sometimes may be valid if it is used as a testing device, and if there is a reasonable carryover between the competence shown in handling simple versus complex situations.

Budgeting is social.   Participants take clues from how others behave. They try to read character to reach programs. This method calls for looking at the administrative officials responsible rather than at the subject matter. To see if they are competent and reliable, officials can be questioned on a point here and there, a difficulty in this or that. One senior congressman reported that he followed an administrator's testimony to probe for weaknesses, looking for "strain in voice or manner," "covert glances," and so on.[5] Also, if an official can get people to go along, and if too many others do not complain too long and loud, then he may take the fact of agreement on something as his measure of success.

Budgeting is "satisficing."   Calculations may be simplified by lowering one's sights. Although they do not use Herbert Simon's vocabulary, budget officials do not try to maximize but, instead, they "satisfice" (satisfy and suffice).[6] Which is to say that the budgeters do not try for the best of all possible worlds (whatever that might be) but, in their own words, try to "get by," to "come out all right," to "avoid trouble," to

---

[5]L. Dwaine Marvick, *Congressional Appropriation Politics*, Ph.D. Dissertation, Columbia University, 1952, p. 297.

[6]Herbert, Simon, *Models of Man* (New York: Wiley, 1957); see also Jerome S. Bruner, Jacqueline J. Goodnow, and George A. Austin, *A Study of Thinking* (New York: Wiley, 1956), for a fascinating discussion of strategies of concept attainment useful for dealing with the problem of complexity.

"avoid the worst." And since the budget comes up every year, and deals largely with piecemeal adjustment, this is one way to correct glaring weaknesses as they arise.

Budgeting is treated as if it were nonprogrammatic.   This statement does not mean that appropriations committee people do not care about programs; they do. Nor does it mean that they do not fight for or against some programs; they do. What it does mean is that, given considerable agreement on policy, appropriations committees see most of their work as marginal monetary adjustments to existing programs so that the question of the ultimate desirability of most programs arises only once in a while. "A disagreement on money isn't like a legislative program . . . ," one member said in a typical statement, "it's a matter of money rather than a difference in philosophy." An appropriations committee member explains how disagreements are handled in the mark-up session when members retire behind closed doors to work out their recommendations. (Nowadays many such sessions are open.) "If there's agreement, we go right along. If there's a lot of controversy we put the item aside and go on. Then, after a day or two, we may have a list of ten controversial items. We give and take and pound them down till we get agreement."[7] Obviously, they do not feel too strongly about each item or they could not agree so readily.

Budgeting is repetitive.   Decision making in budgeting is carried on with the knowledge that few problems have to be "solved" once and for all. Everyone knows that a problem may be dealt with over and over again. Hence considerations that a congressman neglects one year may be taken up another year, or in a supplementary action during the same year. Problems are not so much solved as they are worn down by repeated attacks until they are no longer pressing or have been superseded by other problems. Problem-succession, not problem solving, best describes what happens.

Budgeting is sequential.   The appropriations committees do not try to handle every problem at once. On the contrary, they do not deal with

[7]Simon, *Models of Man.*

many problems in a particular year, and those they do encounter are dealt with mostly in different places and at different times. Many decisions made in previous years are allowed to stand or to vary slightly without question. Then committees divide up subjects for more intensive inquiry among subcommittees and their specialists. Over the years, subcommittees center now on one and then on another problem. When budgetary decisions made by one subcommittee adversely affect those of another, the difficulty is handled by "fire-truck tactics," that is, by dealing with each problem in turn in whatever jurisdiction it appears. Difficulties are overcome not so much by central coordination or planning as by a cybernetic approach—attacking each manifestation in the different centers of decision in sequence.[8]

The Conference Committee carries on the process of sequential calculation by concentrating on the items of difference between Senate and House. To facilitate give and take, bargaining is carried on in great secrecy. Failure of the Conference Committee to reach agreement on many items would disrupt the entire legislative process, especially since their deliberations frequently take place at the tail end of the session. Horse-trading is one way to secure agreement: Referring to a Conference Committee session on the United States Information Agency, Representative Frederic Coudert (R-N.Y.) reported that the House agreed to raise its figure and "in return the Senate yielded on these little things. . . . When you have different things in dispute the two [subcommittee] chairmen [Representative John Rooney and Senator Kilgore] just trade them off, back and forth."

Another way of reaching agreement has been described by T. C. Schelling[9] as the presence of a prominent solution. Given the necessity for arriving at agreement and inability to decide what it should be, the conferees may split the difference and choose the highest, or the lowest,

---

[8]The methods of calculation described here are similar to those attributed to social scientists by David Braybrooke and Charles E. Lindblom in their *A Strategy of Decision* (New York: Free Press, 1963), and to private firms by Richard Cyert and James March in their *A Behavioral Theory of the Firm* (Englewood Cliffs, N.J.: Prentice-Hall, 1963).

[9]See Thomas C. Schelling, *The Strategy of Conflict* (Cambridge, Mass.: Harvard University Press, 1960).

amount for each item. Inevitably, there is a premium on raising or lowering amounts voted in the House or Senate so as to leave room for "concessions" to the other side. That there is room for compromise signifies that the participants were originally not that far apart.

These aids ease the burden of calculations that are necessary for the development of a budget. Because attention is focused on the increment rather than on the relative value of a particular program compared to others, aids to calculation also serve to moderate conflict. The specialized and apparently nonprogrammatic character of decisions enhances the appearance of the budgetary process as technical. Since decisions are simplified and are made in different arenas at different times, the chance that severe conflict will converge is reduced.

FAIR SHARE AND BASE

Time and again participants in the budgetary process speak of achieving an estimate of what is the "fair share" of the total budget for an agency. "None of this happened suddenly," a man who helps make the budget informed me. "We never go from $500 to $800 million or anything like that. This [the agency's] total is a product of many years of negotiations in order to work out a fair share of the budget for the agency."

At this point it is necessary to distinguish *fair share* from another concept, *the base.* The base is the general expectation that programs will be carried on at close to the going level of expenditures. Having a project included in the agency's base thus means more than just getting it in the budget for a particular year. It means the expectation that the expenditure will continue, that it is accepted as part of what will be done, and, therefore, that it will normally not be subjected to intensive scrutiny. (The word *base,* incidentally, is part of the common parlance of officials engaged in budgeting and it would make no sense if experience led them to expect wide fluctuations from year to year, rather than additions to or subtractions from some relatively steady point.) Fair share means not only the base an agency has established but also the expectation that the agency will receive some proportion of funds, if any, which are to be increased over or decreased below the base of the other governmental agencies. Fair share, then, reflects a convergence of expectations on roughly how much an agency is to receive in comparison to others.

The absence of a base, or an agreement on fair shares, makes it much harder to calculate what the agency or program should get. That happens when an agency or program is new or when rapid shifts of sentiment toward it take place. A Senate Appropriations Committee report on the United States Information Agency demonstrates the problem. "Unlike the State Department," the report reads, "the USIA does not have a fixed, historic structure which sets a floor or ceiling on the amount of money which should be expended. Furthermore, its role must necessarily vary with the times. Therefore the issue of how much should be spent is not a matter of fixed obligations but a matter of judgment. . . ."

When times are tough, the base is subject to debate and adjustment. The base may be defined as the "current estimate" (existing spending level of an agency), or next year's anticipated cost of maintaining programs at current levels of service (particularly important in inflationary times). In the fiscal 1957 budgetary planning cycle, for example, $457 million of the $1160 million the Budget Bureau cut from agency requests was the result of different estimates of the effects of economic and demographic factors.[10] "In especially tight years," Kamlet and Mowery find, "the size of each agency's budgetary increment is small or nonexistent; an agency can only increase its budgetary allowances by increasing its base." In these times the Budget Bureau will attempt to employ a narrow definition of what constitutes the base, and agencies will disagree.[11]

[10]Mark S. Kamlet and David C. Mowery, "The Budgetary Base in Federal Resource Allocation," *American Journal of Political Science*, Vol. 24, No. 4 (November 1980), pp. 806–21.
[11]*Ibid.*, pp. 817–18.

THE AGENCY: ROLES AND PERSPECTIVES

Agency people are expected to be advocates of increased appropriations. "You may blame the War Department for a great many things," General Douglas MacArthur said in 1935, ". . . but you cannot blame us for not asking for money. That is one fault to which we plead not guilty." A classic statement of this role was made in 1939 by William A. Jump, a celebrated budget officer for the Department of Agriculture, who wrote that in budgeting

> . . . there inevitably are severe differences of judgment as to whether funds should be provided for a given purpose and, if so, in what amount. . . .
>
> It is at this stage that the departmental budget officer becomes an advocate or special pleader of the cause he represents. His position in representing the department then is analogous to that of an attorney for his client. In such circumstances, departmental budget officers put up the strongest and most effective fight of which they are capable to obtain . . . funds. . . . No apologies are offered for a vigorous position, or even an occasional showing of teeth, if circumstances seem to require it. The [national political] system is one of checks and balances, and the Federal machinery for combating and deflating departmental concepts of what is necessary is so extensive and at times so difficult of persuasion that unless departmental representatives proceed to present their viewpoint in a vigorous and tenacious manner, objectives which are essential . . . to the public welfare might, for the time being at least, be submerged by some purely budgetary objective . . . rather than served thereby. At this point the departmental budget officer proceeds on the principle that the government exists to serve the needs of a great people and not primarily for the purpose of creating a model budget system.[12]

Jump justifies playing the advocate's role partly on the grounds that other participants have counter-roles that necessitate a strong push from the departmental side.

Appropriations committee members tend to view budget officials as

---

[12]W. A. Jump, "Budgetary and Financial Administration in an Operating Department of the Federal Government." Paper delivered at the conference of the Governmental Research Association, September 8, 1939, p. 5. See also the psychological portrait in Robert Walker, "William A. Jump: The Staff Officer As a Personality," *Public Administration Review*, Vol. 14 (Autumn 1954), pp. 233–46.

people with vested interests in raising appropriations. This position is generally accepted as natural and inevitable for administrators. As Assistant Chief Thayer of the Forest Service put it, "Mr. Chairman, you would not think that it would be proper for me to be in charge of this work and not be enthusiastic about it and not think that I ought to have a lot more money, would you? I have been in it for thirty years, and I believe in it." At times this attitude may lead to cynicism and perhaps annoyance on the part of House Appropriations Committee members: "When you have sat on the Committee, you see that these bureaus are always asking for more money—always up, never down. They want to build up their organization. You reach the point—I have—where it sickens you, where you rebel against it."[13] Yet if agencies did not advocate, Congress would have a harder time figuring out what they needed and wanted.

DECIDING HOW MUCH TO ASK FOR

With appropriations always falling short of desires, how much of what they would like to get do agencies ask for from the Budget Bureau and Congress? (The Bureau of Budget [BOB] became the Office of Management and Budget [OMB] in 1970. For reasons of clarity, I will refer to the Budget Bureau when discussing classical budgeting.) The simplest approach would be to add up the costs of all worthwhile projects and submit the total. This simple addition rarely is done, partly because everyone knows there would not be enough resources to go around. With revenues fixed in the short run, asking for a lot more would mean taking these sums from other agencies and programs; this would not be popular. Largely, however, the reason is strategic. If an agency continually submits requests far above what it actually gets, the Budget Bureau and the appropriations committees lose confidence in it and automatically cut large chunks before looking at the budget in detail. It becomes much harder to justify even items with top priority because no one trusts

[13]Fenno, "House Appropriations Committee as a Political System," p. 320.

an agency that repeatedly comes in too high. Yet it is unrealistic for an administrator not to make some allowance for the inevitable cuts that others will make.

The verb "pad" is not too crass to describe what goes on; administrators realize that in predicting needs there is a reasonable range within which a decision can fall, and they just follow ordinary prudence in coming out with an estimate near the top. "If you do not do this," an official told me rather vehemently, "you get cut and you'll soon find that you are up to your ass in alligators."

Budgeting goes on in a world of reciprocal expectations that lead to self-fulfilling prophecies; agencies are expected to pad their requests to guard against cuts. As Representative Jamie Whitten (D-Miss.), Chairman of the Appropriations Subcommittee on Agriculture (who is still with us) put it, "If you deal with the Department [of Agriculture] long enough and learn that they scale down each time, the bureau or agency can take that into consideration and build up the original figures." The Budget Bureau is expected to cut, partly because of its interest in protecting the president's program, and partly because it believes that agencies are likely to pad. Appropriations committees are expected to cut to fulfill their roles, and because they know that the agency has already allowed for just this action. Cuts may be made in the House in the expectation that the Senate will replace them. Congressmen get headlines for suggesting large cuts, but they often do not follow through for they know that the amounts will have to be restored by supplemental appropriations. Things may get to the point where members of the appropriations committees talk to agency officials off the record and ask where they can make a cut that will have to be restored later.

Whether disposed to pad or not, the agency finds that it must allow for cuts, and the cycle begins again as these prophecies confirm themselves. We have seen that an agency's budget is chiefly a product of past decisions. Beyond this is an area of discretion in which budget people want to get all they can, but cannot get all they want. Asking for too much may prejudice their chances, so it soon becomes apparent that the ability to estimate "what will go" (a phrase of budget officials) is a crucial aspect of budgeting.

Participants look out for, and receive, signals from the Executive Branch, Congress, clientele groups, and also their own organizations; in this way they arrive at a composite estimate of how much to ask for in the light of what they can expect to get. After an administration has been in office for a while, agency personnel have a background of actions and informal contacts to tell them how its various programs are regarded, especially for the preceding year. They also keep up with public announcements and private reports about how tough the president is going to be in regard to new expenditures. Formal word comes in the shape of a policy letter from the Budget Bureau, which usually has some statement on how closely this year's budget should resemble the last one. The impression made by this letter may be strengthened or weakened by reports of remarks made in cabinet meetings or by statements from those high up in the administration. If the president's science advisor speaks favorably of a particular program, his comments may offset tough remarks by the Director of the Budget. And, together, all these are seen in the light of the agency's experience in day-to-day dealings with the Budget Bureau staff, whose attitudes and nuances of behavior may speak more eloquently than any public statements as to administration intentions.

A major factor for agencies to consider is the interest of specialized publics in particular programs. Periodic reports from the field on the demand for services may serve as a general indicator. Top officials may travel and see at first hand just how enthusiastic the field personnel are about new programs. How detailed and concrete are their examples of public reaction? Agencies also may have advisory committees and use newspaper clipping services to provide information on the intentions of the interests concerned. The affected interests ordinarily lose no time in beating a path to the agency's door and presenting data about public support. When the agency begins to notice connections between the activities of supporting interests and calls from congressmen, it has a pretty good idea of the support for a program.

Since there is much continuity of both agency and personnel and the committees and staffs in Congress, there is a rich history on which to base predictions. Agency officials are continuously engaged in "feeling the pulse" of Congress; likes and dislikes of influential congressmen are well charted. Hearings on last year's budget are perused for indications of attitudes on specific programs, particularly on items that may get the agency into trouble. If the committee chairman lets it be known that not enough is being done in a certain area, the agency knows that a program there will meet with sympathetic consideration. For example, should a congressmen inform an agency that "We have heard Sam Rayburn and some of the other most distinguished members of Congress, urging us to bring up these 11 organized watersheds more rapidly . . . ," the agency might well take the hint and ask for more. Overall congressional support may be indicated by debates on votes or amendments or new legislation. Finally, continuous contacts with appropriations committee staff leaves agency people with definite feelings about what is likely to go over with the committee.

It would take a real dullard to disregard the indicators in examples taken from House Appropriations hearings:

> Representative O'Brien (1947, Census Bureau): I have just come back from Chicago and . . . the people of this nation are complaining about the spending of the Government's money, and they want to know when we are going to quit. . . . I do not know why you ask for these additional employees. . . . I have never been against anything you wanted. . . . It is now time to stop it. That is all I have to say.
> Representative Thomas (1952, Housing and Home Finance Agency): Keep up your research. We want to admonish you to do that. We are not going to give you all of the money you think you ought to have. We are going to keep you going over a period of years because we know that you are going to come up with something that will save John Q. Public many millions of dollars.
> Representative Flood (1957, Weather Bureau): Do you need dollars? . . . Can you "crash" weather observation? . . . You told Mr. Thomas that you do not have [the necessary equipment]. . . . The mood of the House is that they do not want to quibble about that [cost of equipment].

O'Brien's comments might be interpreted to signal a "go slow, be careful" approach; Thomas's statements might indicate "be sure to include this in moderately rising amounts"; and Flood's strongly suggests "you can get virtually anything you ask for that is remotely reasonable."

Last—but certainly not least—agencies also study the national political situation in deciding how much to try to get. Are there political reasons for increasing or decreasing spending? Is control over the national government split between the parties, with the result that there will be competition for support of particular programs or for holding the line? Do certain elements in Congress want to force presidential vetoes, or will the threat of veto result in program changes more favorable to the president?

From time to time agencies are affected by emergent problems, current events that no one could have predicted but that will radically alter budgetary prospects for particular programs. A change in missile technology, a drought, a new plant disease, a social problem may drastically improve the prospects for some programs. The agency or interest group that can exploit the recognized needs arising from these events or generate such recognition is in an excellent position to expand support for its budget. When the rather sluggish Weather Bureau failed to respond immediately to the opportunities created by a series of climatic disasters in the middle 1950s, the aptly named Representative Flood was impelled to comment at an appropriations hearing: "Your Weather Bureau is looked upon by the people and has been for 100 years as a collection of old men on an island some place, and nobody ever heard of you until the last couple of years. Now you have become adults, and everybody is excited. If you do not take advantage of it you are not well advised."

DECIDING HOW MUCH TO SPEND

Deciding how much to ask for may be a big problem; but sometimes it is equally hard for an agency to figure out precisely how much to spend. If an agency has a substantial carryover, the Budget Bureau and especially the appropriations committees may take this as a sign that the agency does not need as much as it received and may cut off that amount in the future. The practice of penalizing carryovers leads to a last-minute flurry of spending in the fourth quarter of the year despite the Budget Bureau apportionment of quarterly allotments. But you can't win. The agency that comes out exactly even is likely to be suspected of spending its limit without considering the need for economy. Coming out even seems just too neat to be true. "It must seem strange," a representative told the army, "that you are always able to consume everything you have purchased for that specific period." The hapless agency that runs out of funds, on the other hand, may well be accused of using the tactic of coercive deficiency, of trying to compel Congress to appropriate more funds on the grounds that a vital activity will otherwise suffer. Most agency budget people try to end up with a little amount in reserve for most programs, but with an occasional deficit permitted in programs to which they are quite certain that funds will have to be restored.

Since agencies are likely to lose funds they carry over, however, their incentive is to spend up to the limit. Agencies are acutely aware that the reputation they have built up can help or hinder them greatly in matters of this kind. The agency with a reputation for economy may be praised for turning funds back and not get cut the following year, whereas the agency deemed to be prodigal may get slashed on the grounds it must not have needed the money in the first place.

DEPARTMENT VERSUS BUREAU

The term *agency* has been used thus far to signify either a bureau or a department, and most of the considerations do apply with equal force to departments and bureaus. Now it will be useful to make a distinction between departments and their component units, the bureaus, in discussing the special problems that departments face in deciding how much to try to get for bureaus under their jurisdiction. Let us assume that the department Secretary and her staff have managed to work out some notion of the Secretary's policy preferences, and it so happens that these preferences run counter to those of a bureau. Problems of influence immediately arise.[14] The most obvious is that some bureaus may have considerable support in Congress and can thus override departments. Still, the Secretary and her staff might well decide to push their own preferences anyway, if that were all that had to be considered. One difficulty, however, is that a record of a department recommending far less than Congress appropriates (and a bureau wants) may lead to a general disregard of what the Secretary proposes. Why pay attention if she is obviously a loser? Another difficulty is that if department officials need bureau support in other matters, they may find that hostility over deep cuts can interfere with the necessary good relations. So the department often finds it wise to temper its preferences with a strong dose of calculations as to what would be acceptable to the other participants.

Considerations such as these involve the various departments (whether they know it or not) in resolving a basic question of political theory: Shall each bureau ask for what it wants or shall priority go to the total departmental situation in making requests? (Put in a different way, the question might be phrased: Is it best for each interest to pursue its own advantage or shall each seek a solution it believes is in the interest of all?) "One of my most difficult tasks," a budget official asserted, "is finding out what these bureau people really want so I will know how to deal and bargain and oppose them if I have to. Many [bureaus] won't speak up. I don't want them to tell me what's good for the department. That's the Secretary's job and my job and his staff's too. But it is difficult to divide the pie if you don't know for sure how much of a piece each one really wants." Of course, if every bureau just shoots for the moon, the total reaches an astronomical figure and that is not much help. Except in years when there are exceedingly powerful reasons for keeping budget totals down, the approach preferred by most department officials is a modified version of "tell us what you really want."

---

[14]See Herbert A. Simon, Donald Smithburg, and Victor Thompson, "The Struggle for Existence," in *Public Administration* (New York: Knopf, 1950), pp. 381–422.

The usual practice is for a high department official to lay the whole budget before the bureau heads to show them why they cannot get any more than their limited share, despite the fact that the programs are eminently deserving. Some budget officials are extremely talented at cutting without getting the blame.

THE BUREAU OF THE BUDGET: ROLES AND PERSPECTIVES

The dominant role of the Bureau of the Budget, in form and in fact, is to help the president carry out his purpose,[15] and its orientation, therefore, depends on that of the Chief Executive. His concerns about the relative priorities of domestic and foreign policy programs, his beliefs about the desirability of a balanced budget, and his preferences in various other areas determine a good deal of what the Bureau tries to do. Ideally, a meeting of the various executive policy decision streams—domestic and defense budgeting, and fiscal policy, which are represented by the president with advisors from the White House, National Security Council, Defense Department, Council of Economic Advisers, Treasury, and Budget Bureau—will produce a "target total" for outlays and promote a rough indication of domestic and military priorities. A decision on target total outlays serves as the basis for the Budget Bureau to develop agency ceilings. Thus the Bureau finds itself trying to get appropriations from Congress for presidential programs and, at times, prodding agencies to come in with new or enlarged programs to meet the president's desires. Yet the BOB is also responsible for establishing

[15]See Fritz Morstein Marx, "The Bureau of the Budget: Its Evolution and Present Role, II," *American Political Science Review*, Vol. 39 (October 1945), pp. 869–98; Richard Neustadt, "Presidency and Legislation: The Growth of Central Clearance," *American Political Science Review*, Vol. 48 (September 1954), pp. 641–71; Arthur Maas, "In Accord with the Program of the President?" in Carl Friedrich and Kenneth Galbraith, eds., *Public Policy*, Vol. 4 (Cambridge, Mass.: Graduate School of Public Administration, 1954), pp. 77–93; Frederick J. Lawton, "Legislative-Executive Relationships in Budgeting as Viewed by the Executive," *Public Administration Review*, Vol. 13 (Summer 1953), pp. 169–76; and Aaron Wildavsky, *Dixon-Yates: A Study in Power Politics* (New Haven: Yale University Press, 1962), p. 64.

agency ceilings based on the target total outlays. Thus BOB ordinarily gives less weight to advocating presidential programs than to keeping them within bounds, particularly since everyone already expects the agencies to perform the functions of advocacy. That can be seen in the responses of Budget Director Maurice Stans to a question on the role of the Bureau:

> Mr. Tufts: Did you conceive it as part of your job as Director to advise the President, then, whether departmental programs were adequate for what you call great purposes?
>
> Mr. Stans: I considered it our responsibility to do that just as much as to indicate that programs were excessive or unnecessary.
>
> I might say that the occasions for us to make recommendations along that line were very much less frequent because the agencies themselves did a pretty good job in asking for all the things that they thought they could effectively carry out.[16]

This top-down approach to budgeting (i.e., the establishment of boundaries by setting budgetary totals) contrasts with the bottom-up incremental development of budgetary totals reflected in congressional decision making.

There are, of course, always some people in the Budget Bureau who identify more closely with an agency or program than do others, or who develop policy preferences independent of the president. They have a creative urge. ("I don't like to think of myself as a red-pencil man.") They see themselves as doing the right thing by pursuing policies in the public interest, and they may convince themselves that the president would support them if only he had the time and inclination to go into the matter as deeply as they had. They would rarely resist a direct presidential command, but these are few at any one time and ordinarily leave much room for interpretation. The role adopted by its budget examiners is important to an agency even if the general orientation of the Budget Bureau is different.

Even within the same administration, different budget directors can have an impact of their own on Budget Bureau decisions. Some directors have much better relationships with the president than others; they get

---

[16]*Jackson Committee Hearings*, pp. 1104–1111.

in to see him more often and without going through subordinates; he backs them up more frequently on appeals from the agencies. In bargaining on recommendations, a budget director who is close to the president has an important advantage since he knows how much leeway he has within the Chief Executive's desires.

Should the president turn down an appeal, the agency and its supporters may seek to discover how much of an increase they can get from Congress without risking a presidential veto, or strong opposition. The president really cannot insist on precise and strict limitation of funds. If he says $500 million, he can hardly object to $503 or probably $510 million, and the agency may seek the highest point in this game.

Congressmen are ambivalent about the Bureau of the Budget; essentially they regard it as a necessary evil. The ambivalence comes through, for example, when a member of the House Appropriations Committee, at one time, with a trace of contempt calls Bureau officials a bunch of bureaucrats who think they are making the budget, but on another occasion reviles them for not having done enough. Or, further, the Bureau may be regarded as a rival for control of appropriations. Representative Flood (talking as a member of the Defense Appropriations Subcommittee) dramatized this feeling when he said, "Mr. Secretary [of Defense] . . . you are a very important man in the Government . . . but you are a minor deity, believe me, compared to the Director of the Budget. He is the Poo-Bah of this town. . . . I feel so strongly about it and many members of the committee and Congress, that we think the Bureau of the Budget as it is now set up should be ripped out altogether."

Every agency and its officials have to decide what kind of relationship to maintain with the Budget Bureau and particularly with its examiners. Since no examiner can know everything, the agency may decide to provide only the data specifically requested. More and more, however, one sees a tendency actually to heap data on the examiners all the time, not merely when they ask. Why? First, abundant information helps the examiners to defend the agency's viewpoint competently at Budget Bureau meetings when agency personnel is not represented. Second, well-informed examiners may become converted into advocates of particular programs. Third, the examiners' knowledge can be turned to advantage by getting them to secure administration assistance in clearing up some difficulty. The associated disadvantage, of course, is that examiners "get to know where the bodies are buried this way," as one budget officer put it. "But," he continued in words echoed by many others, "you can't hide serious weaknesses for very long anyway, and so the advantages far outweigh the disadvantages."

Agency people agree that Budget Bureau support is worth having if you can get it without sacrificing too much in Congress. Given the congressional propensity to cut, what the Budget Bureau proposes for an agency is likely to be the upper limit. (What was true in the classical period, I remind the reader, is not necessarily true now.) In addition, there are multitudes of small items that Congress would not ordinarily investigate but that might have trouble getting funded if Bureau approval were lacking.

Agencies recognize two basic limitations on Budget Bureau influence. The most serious handicap under which the Budget Bureau labors is not so much that Congress may raise its proposed spending (though this is obviously important) but that the BOB cannot guarantee a cooperating agency will receive the amount it has recommended.[17] Agencies that could depend on receiving what the Budget Bureau recommended would have much greater incentive to cooperate.

A second limitation of the Bureau is that its actions are often constrained by its perceptions of how Congress will view agency requests. Everyone knows that agencies make end runs around the Bureau to gain support from Congress. Yet if agencies do so too often, the Budget Bureau finds that its own prestige has declined. Hence the Bureau frequently accepts consistent congressional action as a guide. (During Ronald Reagan's presidency, this rule was honored more in the breach.) A close eye is kept on congressional action for the preceding year before the Bureau sets an agency's total for the next one. The Bureau must also be wary of particular programs favored by Congress.

---

[17]See the first edition, *The Politics of the Budgetary Process* (Boston: Little, Brown, 1964), p. 41.

Suppose an agency must choose between two alternatives, one favored by congressmen, another by the Budget Bureau. The strategy probably would be to side with Congress because its record with Congress determines how an agency is viewed and treated both by the Budget Bureau and the department.

THE APPROPRIATIONS COMMITTEES: ROLES AND PERSPECTIVES

When Representative Preston asked, "Is there anything fantastic about this 18th Decennial Census that . . . we should know about as guardians of the taxpayer's money?" he was acting out one of the prevailing roles played by members of the House Appropriations Committee. As guardians of the public purse, committee members are expected to cast a skeptical eye on the blandishments of a bureaucracy ever anxious to increase its dominion by increasing its appropriations. After one administrator spoke of the wonderful things accomplished by research in forestry, Representative Clarence Cannon struck the proper note by replying, "All these Government researchers every year come in here and outline . . . great progress that has been made in the various industries and claim credit for them where it would have gone ahead if they had not been in existence, and you are no exception to that rule."

There is perhaps something romantic here—a concept of the sheriff warding off the mob; of Horatio at the bridge; or of the unappreciated but faithful servant who guards his master's fortune against the pernicious schemes of wasteful relatives. Fenno quotes a veteran committee member as saying that "No subcommittee of which I have been a member has ever reported out a bill without a cut in the budget. I'm proud of that record."[18] Among typical comments, Representative John Rooney (D-N.Y.), who was chairman of the Senate, Justice, Commerce, and Judiciary Appropriations Subcommittee, said, "I am questioning you for the taxpayer. I approach [the budget] with the idea that it can

[18]Fenno, "House Appropriations Committee as a Political System," pp. 311–12.

be cut. It's an asking price." And another committee member says, "Here we look at the bright side. We see a reduction." In order to make an objective check on the effectiveness of this orientation, Fenno examined the appropriations histories of 37 bureaus concerned with domestic policies from 1947 to 1959 and discovered that the committee reduced the estimates it received 77.2 percent of that time.[19]

The role of guardianship is reinforced by the House leadership, which deliberately chooses committee members from safe districts who can therefore afford to say "no."

It cannot be emphasized too often that we are describing the most generally accepted role, and not the only one that guides all committee members in all situations. Some members identify completely with an agency or its programs. "To me forestry has become a religion . . . ," said Representative Walter Horan. In a profound violation of House Committee norms, he took his protest against his own appropriations subcommittee to the Senate hearings, declaring that "The items are totally inadequate and I do not care particularly which way *we* get them, but *we* do need funds" (emphasis supplied). At times, then, the feeling of having served a great cause may create a sense of identification with an agency or program that overwhelms other considerations. Witness the poignant remarks Representative Anderson addressed to the Administrator of the Soil Conservation Service:

> You know every man serving in Congress hopes to leave his imprint in some small way upon work in which he is interested.
>
> The activities of our Government and the responsibilities are so vast that we are fortunate if we leave Congress even after twenty or thirty years and have our name attached even in a slight degree to something really worthwhile, and I am proud of the fact that sixteen years ago, gentlemen, I was fighting to increase in this very room the money set aside for soil conservation operations.

To get credit for cutting, by contrast, requires an institutional milieu in which people are honored for being negative.

In the case of local constituency interests, the deviation from guardianship of the budget is exceedingly powerful because it touches on the

[19]*Ibid.*, p. 312.

most basic relationship a congressman may have—that with the people who elect him and might conceivably defeat him—and because congressmen are prone to take on faith another of their roles as defender of constituency interests. Where their constituencies are affected, appropriations committee members use all the vast leverage over men and money their positions give them to secure favorable outcomes. Representative John Rooney engaged in a battle royal to keep a Department of Commerce office in New York City so that his constituents would not lose their jobs. An Assistant Secretary of Commerce had the temerity to suggest that this was not exactly an example of ideal administration, and Rooney lit into him: "Do you mean that employees of long standing, who, for instance, live right in my Congressional district . . . have no right to . . . raise their voices to prevent the loss of jobs . . .? Were any of the employees who came to this committee from that New York office penalized . . .?" "I can assure you that was not done, Mr. Congressman," said the Assistant Secretary. Then there was Representative Ivor Fenton's tenacious campaign to have an anthracite laboratory located in Schuylkill Haven instead of Hazleton, Pennsylvania. Fenton said that he got no action until he got on the Appropriations Committee. At that time he accused the Secretary of the Interior of "the cheapest kind of politics" and decided "that no funds now available for the laboratory be obligated until this matter is clarified to the satisfaction of the Appropriations Committee." The funds were denied. In the other chamber, Senator Meyers spoke of "exceptional energy on the part of one of the subcommittee members in seeking to establish some sort of political plot to locate the laboratory in a district other than his." The law that was passed specified that the laboratory had to be built in Schuylkill Haven. In another skirmish, a little arm-twisting was applied by Senator Lyndon Johnson in order to make certain that a prison was built in the right place. "I sure would hate to put in this money to build a prison in Congressman Grey's district and Senator Dirksen's state in Illinois and find out that they got it in X, Y, Z, somewhere."

Tough as they may be when cutting the budgets of their agencies, appropriations committee members, once having made a decision, generally defend the agencies against further cuts on the floor. In an exchange with a member of the Appropriations Committee, Representative Clarence Brown (R-Ohio) complained that when an amendment is offered "to reduce an appropriations item, the Appropriations Committee stands like a stone wall most of the time, saying 'No, you mustn't touch this.' "[20] This kind of action is in part self-interest. The power of appropriations subcommittees would be diminished if their recommendations were successfully challenged very often. Members believe that the House would "run wild" if "orderly procedure"—that is, acceptance of committee recommendations—were not followed. But the role of defender also has its roots in the respect for expertise and specialization in Congress, and in the ensuing belief that members who have not studied the subject should not exercise a deciding voice without the presence of overriding considerations. An appeal to the norm of specialization is usually sufficient to block an attempt to reduce appropriations. Appropriations Committee members, as McKellar cried on one occasion, had "worked almost like slaves on the bill. . . . Here at the last moment comes an amendment offered by a Senator who has not taken part in any hearings." That senator lost.

A member of the Senate Appropriations Committee is likely to view himself as the responsible legislator who sees to it that the irrepressible lower House does not do too much damage either to constituency or to national interests. And though members of the House Appropriations Committee tend to view their opposite members in the Senate as frivolous spendthrifts of the public purse, senators reverse the compliment by regarding their brethren in the other chamber as niggardly and jealous types who do not care what happens to "essential" programs so long as they can show that they have made cuts. Senator Mundt expressed this feeling in 1957 when he said, in regard to a Bureau of Indian Affairs appropriation, "I think it is important to have in the record . . . that the House finds no fault with the program of construction. They just failed to provide the money. The need is there and it is our responsibility to meet that need." House members would say that there is also

---

[20]House Government Operations Subcommittee, *Improving Federal Budgeting and Appropriations,* 85th Congress, 1st Session, 1957, p. 139.

a need for restraint. The difference in perspective between the two committees was illustrated by Senator Dirksen, who used to glory in his role as tough guardian of the purse. Referring to a House action to reduce from ten to six the number of employees in an office, Dirksen said, "It was great, good fun when I was on the House Appropriations Committee to cut four [positions]. Too often you discover that the six positions depend in large measure on the four. You just wasted the money for the six. I would rather give you nothing or whatever it takes to do a good job." These words—"I . . . give you"—speak volumes.

The senators are rather painfully aware of the House committee's preeminence in the field of appropriations; they know that they cannot hope to match the time and thoroughness that the House body devotes to screening requests. For this reason, Senate members put a high value on having agencies carry appeals to it. "We all know," said Senator Richard Russell (D-Ga.), Chairman of the Agriculture Appropriations Subcommittee, "that almost since the inception of the Government, the Senate Appropriations Committee has served as an appeal body and has heard requests . . . that deal principally with items that have been changed or reduced or eliminated by the House of Representatives." Senators value their ability to disagree on disputed items as a means of maintaining influence in crucial areas, while experiencing the least possible strain on their time and energy. This dominant Senate function as responsible appeals court depends upon agency advocacy and House committee guardianship.

Keenly aware of the particular roles adopted by members of the House and Senate appropriations subcommittees who deal with their programs, the predominant view that agency officials have of these legislators is that they are very powerful: "They can do you a world of good and they can cut your throat." "These men, notably the Chairman, can murder you and also make things easy." As long as they do not violate widespread and intense preferences among fellow legislators, committee and subcommittee chairmen can do much to reward or punish agencies and their personnel without much fear of being contradicted. *Newsweek* (April 7, 1958) quotes a State Department official as saying, "Let's face it. When Rooney whistles, we've just got to dance." Another investigator reports that "one otherwise articulate official was so unstrung after testifying that he offered his resignation as soon as he returned to his office. Another was caught by his wife arguing with an imaginary Rooney."[21]

Although it appears that agency personnel are more dependent on committee staff than vice versa, the relationship is by no means a one-way proposition. The staff man knows that he can do a more effective job if he has the cooperation of the budget officer. After all, much of the staff's work depends on securing information from the agency about current programs and the possible effects of various changes. The staff may be blamed for not informing congressmen of changes in agency plans and expenditures. And when complex problems arise, the agency actually may do the work for the staff. Mutual dependence is the order of the day, and both sides generally regard harmonious contacts as prerequisites to doing their best work. Yet mutual dependence is, of necessity, tinged with the realization that committee staff and budget officers do represent different organizations, whose roles are not always compatible.

STRATEGIES

How do agencies—the advocates in the process of budgeting—go about trying to get what they want? What strategies are used under which circumstances? What are some counter-strategies used by other participants?

Budgetary strategies are actions by governmental agencies intended to maintain or increase their available funds. Strategies are the links between the intentions and perceptions of budget officials, and the political system that both imposes restraints and creates opportunities for them.

Strategic moves take place in a rapidly changing environment in

---

[21]Peter Wyden, "The Man Who Frightens Bureaucrats," *Saturday Evening Post* (January 31, 1959), p. 87.

which no one is quite certain how things will turn out and in which new goals constantly emerge. In this context of uncertainty, choice among existing strategies must be based on intuition and hunch—on an "educated guess"—as well as on firm knowledge. Assuming a normal capacity to learn, however, experience should eventually provide a more reliable guide than sheer guesswork.

Be a Good Politician

What really counts in helping an agency get the appropriations it desires? Long service in Washington has convinced many high agency officials that some things count a great deal and others only a little. Although they are well aware that it is desirable to have technical data to support requests, budget officials commonly derogate the importance of the formal aspects of their work. As several informants put it in almost identical words, "It's not what's in your estimates but how good a politician you are that matters."

Being a good politician, these officials say, requires essentially three things: cultivation of an active clientele, the development of confidence among other governmental officials, and skill in following strategies that exploit one's opportunities to the maximum. Doing good work is viewed as part of being a good politician.

Clientele

Find a clientele. For most agencies, locating a clientele is no problem at all; the groups interested in their activities are all too present. But some agencies find this a difficult problem, demanding extraordinary measures to solve. Men and women incarcerated in federal prisons, for instance, are hardly an ideal clientele. And the rest of society cares only to the extent of keeping these people locked up. So the Bureau of Prisons tries to create special interest in its activities by inviting congressmen to see what is going on. "I wish, Mr. Bow, you would come and visit us at one of these prison places when you have the time. . . . I am sure you would enjoy it." The United States Information Agency faced a similar problem—partly explaining its mendicant status—because its work is all abroad rather than directly benefiting people at home. Things got so bad that the USIA sought to organize our country's ambassadors to foreign nations into an interest group, to vouch for the good job USIA said it was doing.

Serve your clientele. For an agency that has a large and strategically placed clientele, the most effective strategy is to serve those who are in a position to help the agency. "If we deliver this kind of service," an administrator declared, "other things are secondary and automatic." His agency made a point of organizing clientele groups in various locations, priming them to engage in approved projects, serving them well, and encouraging them to inform their congressmen of their reaction. Informing one's clientele of the full extent of the benefits they receive may increase the intensity with which they support the agency's request.

Expand your clientele. In order to secure substantial funds from Congress for domestic purposes, it is ordinarily necessary to develop fairly wide interest in the program. This is what Representative Whitten did when he became a member of the Appropriations Committee and discovered that soil conservation in various watersheds had been authorized, but that little money had been forthcoming: "Living in the watersheds . . . I began to check . . . and I found that all these watersheds were in a particular region, which meant there was no general interest in the Congress in this type of program. . . . It led me to go before the Democratic platform committee in 1952 and urge them to write into the platform a plank on watershed protection. And they did." As a result, Whitten was able to call on more general support from Democrats as well as to increase appropriations for Soil Conservation Service watersheds.

Concentrate on individual constituencies. After the Census Bureau had made an unsuccessful bid to establish a national housing survey, Representative Sidney Yates (D-Ill.) gave the bureau a useful hint. The proposed survey "is so general," Yates said, "as to be almost useless to the people of a particular community. . . . This would help someone like Armstrong Cork, who can sell its product anywhere in the country . . . but will it help the construction industry in a particular area to know whether or not it faces a shortage of customers?" Later, the Bureau submitted a new program that called for a detailed enumeration of metropolitan districts with a sample survey of other areas to get a national total. The New National Housing Inventory—endorsed by mortgage holding associations, the construction material industry, and federal and state housing agencies—received enthusiastic support in Congress where Representative Preston exclaimed, "This certainly represents a lot of imaginative thinking on your part. . . ." In another case, the National Science Foundation made headway with a program of summer mathematics institutes not only because the idea was excellent but also because the institutes were spread around the country, where they became part of a constituency interest congressmen are supposed to protect.

Secure feedback. Almost everybody claims that their projects are immensely popular and benefit lots of people. But how can elected officials find this out? Only by hearing from constituents. The agency can do a lot to ensure that its clientele responds by informing them that it is vital to contact congressmen and by telling them, if necessary, how to go about it. In fact, the agency may organize its clientele in the first place, and then offer to fulfill the demand it has helped to create. Policies create clients just as clients can create policies. Indeed, congressmen often urge administrators to make a show of their clientele: Senator Wherry: "Do you have letters or evidence from small operators . . . that need your service that you can introduce into the record. . . . Is that not the test on how much demand there is for your services?" When feedback is absent or limited, congressmen tend to assume no one cares and they need not bother with the appropriation: "A dozen or more complaints do not impress me very much. . . . We cut this out last spring and we did not hear any wild howls of distress. . . ."

Guarding the treasury may be all right but it becomes uncomfortable when cuts return to haunt a congressman. This is made clear in Representative Clevenger's (R-Ohio) tale of woe:

> I do not want to economize on the Weather Bureau. I never did. I do want an economical administration. . . . I have been blamed for hurri-

cane Hazel. My neighbor, who lived across the road from me for 30 years, printed in his paper that I was to blame for $500 million in damage and 200 lives. . . . His kids grew up on my porch and yet he prints that on the first page and it is not "maybe." I just "am." He goes back to stories that related to cuts that I made when I was chairman of the Committee.

Most agencies maintain publicity offices (under a variety of titles) whose job is to inform interest parties and the general public of the good things the agency is doing, thus creating a favorable climate of opinion. Congressmen who do not like an agency and/or its programs may raise objections to this self-glorification, but those who favor the agency consider it desirable.

End-runs. When political considerations attach to the idea of a balanced budget, an administration may seek appropriations policies that minimize the short-run impact on the budget, even though total expense may be greater over a period of years. In the Dixon–Yates case (1954–1956) a proposed TVA power plant was rejected partly because it involved large immediate capital outlays. The private power plant that was accepted was to involve much larger expenditures over a 25-year period, but this spending, spread out over time, would have had comparatively little impact.[22]

When clientele are absent or weak there are some techniques for making expenditures so that they either do not appear in the budget or appear much later on. The International Monetary Fund may be given a Treasury note to be used at some future date when IMF needs money. Buildings for public use may be constructed by private organizations so that the rent paid is, in the short run, much lower than an initial capital expenditure would have appeared. (In the 1980s the military tried to take that approach to its housing.) An agency and its supporters who fear hostile appropriations committee action may seek authorization to spend directly from the Treasury to avoid direct encounter with the normal budgetary process. This action is bitterly opposed as backdoor spending, especially in the House Appropriations Committee.

[22]See the author's *Dixon-Yates: A Study in Power Politics.*

Confidence

The sheer mass of budgetary matters means that some people have got to trust others because only rarely can they check up on things. "It is impossible for any person to understand in detail the purposes for which $70 billion are requested," Senator Thomas declared in regard to the defense budget. "The committee [recall this is way back when] must take some things on faith." If we add to this the idea of budgeting by increments (where large areas of the budget are exempt from serious questions each year), committee members will treat an agency much better if they feel that its officials will not deceive them.

Administrative officials unanimously agree that they must, as a bare minimum, enjoy the confidence of appropriations committee members and their staff. "If you have the confidence of your subcommittee your life is much easier and you can do your department good; if you don't have confidence you can't accomplish much and you are always in trouble." How do agency personnel seek to establish this confidence?

Be what they think they are. Confidence is achieved by gearing one's behavior to fit the expectations of committee people. Essentially, the desired qualities will appear to be projections of the committee members' images of themselves. Bureaucrats are expected to be masters of detail—hard-working, frank, self-effacing people devoted to their work, who are tight with the taxpayer's money, recognize a political necessity when they see one, and keep congressmen informed. Where Representative Clevenger speaks dourly of how "fewer trips to the coffee shop . . . help make money in most of the departments . . .," Rooney flips to the other side of the coin to speak favorably of calling the Census Bureau late at night and finding its employees "on the job far later than usual closing hours." An administrator is highly praised because "he always knows his detail and his work. He is short, concise, and to the point. He does not waste any words. I hope when it comes to the economy in your laundry soap it is as great as his economy in words."

To be considered aboveboard, a fair and square shooter, a frank person is highly desirable. After an official admitted that one item had been so far down on the priority list that it had not been discussed with him, Senator Cordon remarked, "All right, I can understand that. Your frankness is refreshing." An administrator like Val Peterson, head of the Federal Civil Defense Agency, will take pains to stress that "There is nothing introduced here that is in the field of legerdemain at all. . . . I want . . . to throw the cards on the table." Agency people soon catch on to an economy motif: "I have already been under attack . . . for being too tight with this money . . .," Petersen said, "I went through it [a field hospital] very carefully myself to be sure there were no plush items in it, nothing goldplated or fancy."

If and when a subcommittee drops the most customary role and becomes an outright advocate of a program, as with the Polaris missile system, the budget official is expected to shoot for the moon; he will be criticized if he emphasizes petty economies instead of pushing his projects. Interior Appropriations Subcommittee Chairman Michael Kirwan (D-Ohio) and ranking Republican Jensen complained, for example, that the Bureau of Land Management did not ask for enough money for soil conservation. "It is only a drop in the bucket," Kirwan said, "they are afraid to come in." "This committee has pounded for the seven years I know of," Jensen responded, "trying to get them to come in with greater amounts for soil conservation and they pay no attention to it." The norm of opposing waste may even be invoked for spending, as when Kirwan proclaimed that "It is a big waste and loss of money for the U.S. Government when only $6 million is requested for the management of fish and wildlife." In 1948 the head of the Cancer Institute was admonished in no uncertain terms: "The sky is the limit . . . and you come in with a little amount of $5,500,000." It is not so much what administrators do but how they meet the particular subcommittee's or chairman's expectations that counts.

Play it straight!   Everyone agrees that the most important requirement for confidence, at least in a negative sense, it to be aboveboard. As Rooney once said, "There's only two things that get me mad. One is harebrained schemes; the other is when they don't play it straight." A lie, an attempt to blatantly cover up some misdeed, a tricky move of any kind, can lead to an irreparable loss of confidence. A typical comment by an administrator states, "It doesn't pay to try to put something over on them [committee members] because if you get caught, you might as well pack your bags and leave Washington." And the chances of getting caught are considerable because interested committeemen and their staffs have much experience and many sources of information.

Administrators believe that punishments for failure to establish confidence are greater than the rewards for achieving it. But at times they do slip up, and then the roof falls in. When Congress limited the amount of funds that could be spent on personnel, a bureau apparently evaded this limitation in 1952 by subcontracting out a plan to private investors. The House Subcommittee was furious:

> Representative Jensen: It certainly is going to take a house-cleaning . . . of . . . all people who are responsible for this kind of business.
> Official: We are going to do it, Mr. Chairman.
> Representative Jensen: I do not mean "maybe." That is the most disgraceful showing that I have seen of any department.
> Official: I am awfully sorry.

A committee that feels that it has been misled can take endless punitive actions. Senator Carl Hayden (D-Ariz.), Chairman of the Senate Appropriations Committee, spoke at one time when a bureau received a lump-sum appropriation as an experiment. "Next year . . . the committee felt outraged that certain actions had been taken, not indicated in the hearings before them. Then we proceeded to earmark the bill from one end to the other. We just tied it up in knots to show that it was the Congress, after all, that dictated policy."

Integrity. The positive side of the confidence relationship is to make it known that the agency official is a man of high integrity who can be trusted. He must not only give but must also appear to give reliable information. Agency people must keep confidences and not get a congressman into trouble by what they say or do—willing to take blame (but never credit). Like a brand name, a budget official's reputation comes to be worth a good deal in negotiation. This is called "Ivory Soap value," that is, 99 and 44/100% pure.

If you are believed to have integrity, then you get by more easily.

> Rooney: Mr Andretta [Justice Department], this is strictly a crystal ball operation; is it?
> Andretta: That is right.
> Rooney: Matter of an expert guess?
> Andretta: An expert guess. . . .
> Rooney: We have come to depend upon your guesswork and it is better than some other guesswork I have seen.

A good index of confidence is an agency official's ability to secure emergency funds on short notice with skimpy hearings. No doubt Andretta's achievement was related to his frequent informal contact with Rooney.

> Rooney: I am one who believes we should keep in close contact with one another so we understand one another's problems.
> Andretta: I agree.
> Rooney: You very often get in touch with us during the course of the year when you do not have a budget pending, to keep us acquainted with what is going on.
> Andretta: Exactly. . . .

When columnist Peter Edson editorially asked why the Peace Corps waltzed so successfully through appropriations, compared to the difficult times had by the State Department and the Agency for International Development, he concluded that Sargent Shriver, head of the Corps, "has tried to establish congressional confidence in him and his agency. Of the 537 members of Congress, he has called on at least 450 in their offices."

An agency that enjoys good relations with subcommittee staff has an easier time in Congress than it might otherwise. The agency finds that more reliance is placed on its figures, more credence is given to its claims, and more opportunities are provided to secure its demands. Thus one budget officer who received information that a million-dollar item had been casually dropped from a bill was able to arrange with his source of information on the staff to have the item put back for reconsideration.

On the other hand, asked if they would consider refusing to talk to committee staff, agency officials uniformly declared that such a stance would be tantamount to cutting their own throats. A staff person whose nose is out of joint can do harm to an agency by expressing distrust of its competence or integrity.

I'd love to help you but. . . . Where the administrators' notion of what is proper conflicts with that of a congressman with whom he needs to maintain friendly relations, there is no perfect way out of the difficulty. Most officials try to turn the congressman down by suggesting that their hands are tied, that something may be done in the future, or by stressing some other project on which they are agreed. After Representative William Natcher (D-Ky.) spoke for the second time of his desire for a project in his district, Don Williams of the Soil Conservation Service complimented him for his interest in watershed activity in Kentucky but was "sorry that some of the projects that were proposed would not qualify under the . . . law . . . but . . . they are highly desirable."

Congressional Committee Hearings

Play the game. The Bureau of the Budget lays down the rule that members of the Executive Branch are not to challenge the Executive Budget. But everyone knows that administrative officials want more for their agencies and—in league with supporting congressmen—sometimes are in a position to get it. On such occasions the result is a ritual that any reader of appropriations hearings will recognize. The agency official is asked whether or not he supports the amounts in the president's budget and he says "yes" in such a way that it sounds like yes but that everyone realizes means "no." His manner may communicate a marked lack of enthusiasm or he may be just too enthusiastic to be true. A committee member will then ask how much the agency originally requested from the Budget Bureau. There follows an apparent refusal to answer, in the form of a protestation of loyalty to the Chief Executive. Under duress, however, and amidst reminders of congressional prerogatives, the agency man will cite the figures. Could he usefully spend the money? he is asked. Of course he could. The presumption that the agency would not have asked for more money if it did not need it is made explicit. Then comes another defense of the administration's position by the agency, which, however, puts up feeble opposition to congressional demands for increases.

When the game is played according to the rules, the administrator has a proper rejoinder available. Senator Allen Ellender (D-La.), member of the Defense Appropriations Subcommittee, asked Admiral Burke how the House committee ever got the idea that the navy wanted nine Polaris submarines when the Budget Bureau allowed only two. "Did you ever give [that number] to them?" "No, sir," the Admiral replied, "however, let me amplify that. This number was brought out under specific questioning by the Defense Subcommittee of the House. We had recommended to the Secretary of Defense that there be nine."

It works: The problem of effectiveness.   Apart from overwhelming public support, there is nothing that succeeds better than tangible accomplishment. The Polaris does fire and hit a target with reasonable accuracy; a range-reseeding project does make the grass grow again. Congressional interpretation of accomplishments as being worthwhile depends on what criteria of effectiveness agencies use and on how tough Congress permits them to be. An antiballistic missile defense may excel if it is supposed to knock down only a few enemy missiles; ABMs may be utterly inadequate if they are expected to destroy all or most missiles. There is great temptation for agencies to devise a criterion that will enable a project's supporters to say that it works. At the same time, opponents of a project may unfairly propose criteria that cannot be met. And there are times when reasonable people disagree over criteria. We hope and pray to avoid nuclear war. But if it comes, what criteria should a civil-defense program have to meet? If one argues that it must save everyone, then no program can show results. Suppose, however, that one is willing to accept much less—say half or a third or a fifth of the population. Then everything would depend on estimates that surely could be improved upon, but which nobody can really claim to be reliable—as to likely levels of attack, patterns of wind and radiation, and a multitude of other factors.

Avoid extreme claims that can be disproved.   A desire to show direct results may boomerang because of the very absurdity of the claim. Such is the unhappy tale of the State Department official who refused to admit that money spent on a Chinese-language program would necessarily have a deferred payoff in view of the fact that the United States then had no formal diplomatic relations with Communist China—and thus few places to send its Chinese-speaking officers:

> Representative Rooney: I find a gentleman here, an FSO-6. He got an A in Chinese and you assigned him to London.
> Mr. X: Yes sir. That officer will have opportunities in London—not as many as he would have in Hong Kong, for example—
> Representative Rooney: What will he do? Spend his time in China-town?
> Mr. X: No, sir. There will be opportunities in dealing with officers in the British Foreign Office who are concerned with Far Eastern affairs. . . .
> Representative Rooney: So instead of speaking English to one another, they will sit in the London office and talk Chinese?
> Mr. X: Yes, sir.
> Representative Rooney: Is that not fantastic?
> Mr. X: No, sir. They are anxious to keep up their practice. . . .

Strategies Designed to Capitalize on the Fragmentation of Power in National Politics

The separation of powers and the internal divisions of labor within Congress and the Executive Branch present numerous opportunities for program advocates (including both agency personnel and congressmen) to play one center of power off against another.

Compensation.   Program supporters who have superior access to one house of Congress may seek to raise the program's grant in one house to allow for bargaining with the other. If they can get their way or arrange to split the difference in the Conference Committee, they are that much ahead. A congressman may ask the agency for the lowest addition that would make a project possible so he will know how far he can go in conference. Thus Senator Pat McCarran (D-Nev.) told the Census Bureau that he "just wanted to see . . . how much we could lose in the conference, and still give some assistance to be of value."

Cross fire.   Although the presence of differing interests and degrees of confidence in House and Senate may give an agency room to maneuver, this may also subject it to a withering cross fire from which there is no immediate escape. Take a controversy over grazing fees on public lands: The House was for increases, and the Senate was opposed. When Representative Malcolm Tarver (D-Ga.) asked the Forest Service whether anything could be done to expedite a study of the fee situation, the following exchange ensued:

> Forest Service official: I guess you really ought to try to get the Senate to go along with you. The Senate told us not to and you told us to do it; so that we are between two fires.
> Representative Tarver: I was wondering whether there was some place in this appropriation where we would make a substantial cut for the purpose of impressing upon you the desirability of making this study.

Both ends against the middle.   The separation between appropriations and substantive committees creates another opportunity to exploit differences between dual authorities. Appropriations committees often refuse funds for projects authorized by substantive committees. And substantive committees, with or without agency backing, sometimes seek to exert influence over appropriations committees. As the classical period ebbed, substantive committees greatly increased their use of annual rather than multiyear or permanent authorizations. A familiar tactic is the calling of hearings by substantive committees to dramatize the contention that an authorized program is being underfinanced or not financed at all. Knowing that the appropriations committees have the final say, substantive committees can afford to authorize any project they deem good without too much concern for its financial implications. Also, appropriations committees sometimes seek to write legislation into appropriations bills; this effort may lead to a conflict with the substantive committee that spills over onto the floor of the houses of Congress.

Agencies stand to gain by exploiting such conflicts to their own advantage. They can try to use an authorization as a club over the head of the appropriations committees by pointing to a substantive committee as their source of commitment for funds. In seeking an increase for fishery research, for example, the Fish and Wildlife Service declared that it "came about through direction of a Congressional Committee. . . . The [substantive] committee directed that hereafter the department should include this item for their appropriations." This strategy does not create much difficulty in the Senate, where some members of the substantive committees are likely also to sit on the Appropriations Committee. But House members do not like it at all—though a member may from time to time brag about how he got through a pet appropriation without a real authorization—and they are quick to remind administrators of their prerogatives.

> State Department official: I believe the legislation includes a specific amount of $8,000.
> Representative Rooney: We would not be discussing this at all if the legislation did not permit such a thing as entertainment, but never lose sight of the fact that Appropriations Committees are the saucers that cool the legislative tea. Just because you have an authorization does not mean a thing to us. . . .
> State Department official: I understand, sir.

Cut the popular program.   No one should assume that most agencies engage in perpetual feasting. There is always the specter of cuts. A major strategy in resisting cuts is to make them in such a way that they have to be restored. Rather than cut the national office's administrative expenses, for instance, an agency might cut down the handling of applications from citizens—in full realization that the ensuing discontent would be bound to get back to congressmen, who then would have to restore the funds. When the National Institutes of Health wanted funds for a new, struggling institute, it would cut one or all of the popular institutes. The committee, upset that heart, cancer, or mental health had been cut, would replace the funds.

Cut less-visible items.   Counter-strategies are available to legislators. Many congressmen feel a need to cut an agency's requests somewhere. Yet the same congressman may be sympathetic to the agency's program or feel obliged to support it because people in his constituency are believed to want it. Where, then, can cuts be made? In those places that do not appear to directly involve program activities. The department office or general administrative expenses, for example, may be cut without appearing to affect any specific desirable program. This fits in well with a general suspicion current in society that bureaucrats are wasteful. Housekeeping activities may also suffer since it often appears that they can be put off another year and they do not seem directly connected with programs. Yet deferred maintenance may turn out to cost more in the end. But cutting here enables the congressman to meet conflicting pressures for the time being.

All or nothing.   This tactic is to assert that if a cut is made the entire program will have to be scrapped. "Reducing the fund to $50,000 would reduce it too much for us to carry forward the work. We have to request the restoration . . . ," said the Bureau of Mines. The danger is that Congress may take the hint and cut out the whole program. So this strategy must be employed with care, and only in connection with a program that is most unlikely to be abolished.

Shift the blame.   A widespread strategy is to get the other party to make the difficult decisions of cutting down on requests, thus shifting the onus for the cuts. He who must take the blame may not be willing to make the cut. Everyone knows that many agencies raise their budgetary requests (among other reasons) in order to show their supporting interests that they are working hard but are being thwarted by the president. So the Budget Bureau is disposed to cut. The most frustrating aspect of this activity is that when an agency's budget is squeezed it is often not the "wasteful" things that come out; priorities within the agency and Congress vary greatly and some lengendary, obsolete facility may survive long after more essential activities have disappeared. Thus the Budget Bureau may be caught between a desire to make the agency responsible for cuts and the need to insist that cuts be made in certain places rather than others.

They made me.   Congressmen have developed their own strategies for making cuts without taking full responsibility. Just as budget officials say that "circumstances" have compelled them to ask for increases, so do congressmen assert that "outside forces"—a climate of opinion against spending, strong views of influential colleagues, presidential opposition, attempts by the other party to make spending an issue, an overriding need to balance the budget—leave them with little choice. Representative Mahon spoke in this vein about the army's construction activities: "Day before yesterday one of the most influential members of the House of Representatives stopped me in the corridor and asked me how the hearings were progressing. He is a great friend of the military forces and the cause of national defense. He said to me, 'George, heretofore I have stayed with you on military appropriations, but this year I am going to vote to cut, and to cut deep, because the military people are wasting so much money.'" This strategy has a corollary: If a subcommittee is not sure what to cut but feels pressure, it may make the cut and let the agency's protests reveal what the agency is really unwilling to give up.

The transfer. One way of moving ahead while appearing to stand still is to keep appropriations for particular categories constant so that no change seems to be made although various past expenditures, no longer being made, have been replaced with others. Items may be transferred from one category to another so that no particular one stands out as being too far out of line. If a committee or the Budget Bureau is concerned over increases in administrative expenses, ways may be found of transferring these expenditures to other items by including them as part of less suspect costs. Some agencies include administrative expenses under each program instead of under the administrative category.

Congressmen realize how dependent they are on a historical and comparative approach to budgeting and try to keep the categories constant from one year to the next. Their dependence on consistency helps account for the insistence of appropriations committee members that budgetary forms not be changed too often.

The camel's nose. A large program may be started by an apparently insignificant sum. The agency then claims that (1) this has now become part of its base and that (2) it would be terrible to lose the money already spent by not going ahead and finishing the job. As Representative Rooney observed, "This may be only $250 but this is the camel's nose.

These things never get out of a budget. They manage to stay and grow." Congress has tried to counter this strategy by passing legislation requiring a total estimate for a project before any part can be authorized. But estimates are subject to change and a small sum one year rarely seems imposing even if a large amount is postulated for the future.

In arguing against a change in accounting procedures, Representative Mahon sketched the strategic implications:

> I believe it was last year that we appropriated $1 million, just a little $1 million to start a public works project of the Army Engineers which is to cost $1 billion. Why, if I go to Congressman Kilgore and say, "Listen, Joe, we have been colleagues for a long time, can't you vote for this little $1 million for my area to help me and my people?"
>
> Well, Joe, I am sure he would do whatever was right and proper, but it might be something tempting, particularly if I had voted for a million-dollar project for Joe on a former occasion to vote for my proposal. But if I go up to Joe and I say, "Listen, Joe, I want you to vote for this project, it costs a billion dollars over a period of years, and if you start it, it is going to be completed."[23]

A foot in the door. The desire of budget officials to keep items in the budget, even if they are small and underfinanced, is readily explained once it is understood that they may one day serve to launch full-blown programs when conditions are more favorable. Research projects are often not terminated when they have either proven successful or have failed; a small item concerning applicability of the research is retained in the budget so that if the agency wishes to resume it has a foot in the door.

Just for now. "Is there anything more permanent than a temporary agency of the Government?" Representative John Phillips (R-Calif.) wanted to know. His colleague, Mr. Thomas, spoke with some asperity of a temporary activity that had begun four years ago. "Of course, [the agency] said it would take them about two years to clear it up and then they would be off the payroll. Since then I think you have added 30 [people] to this group." A temporary adjustment to a passing situation

---

[23]*Improving Federal Budget and Appropriations,* House Subcommittee on Government Operations, 85th Congress, 1st Session, pp. 132–33.

results in an emergency appropriation for a fixed period, which then turns out to be a permanent expenditure.

The commitment. Although expenditures may rise and requests for money may increase, an agency can hardly be blamed if it had no choice. As one official put it, "The increases are in every case presented as either related to commitments . . . or other uncontrollable factors."

A favorite strategy is to lay down long-range goals for an existing program, which the agency can use to show that its requirements are not being met. The very statement that there are X acres not yet under soil conservation practices or so many Indian children who need schooling may serve to create an implied commitment to meet the demand. The NIH and its congressional allies go one step further by speaking of "moral obligations" for continuing projects mounting up to tens of millions of dollars.

It pays for itself; it makes a profit. An increase may not seem like one if it can be shown that the increase brings in revenue equal to or greater than the cost. Although government is presumably not conducted for profit, the delight congressmen take in finding an activity that returns money to the Treasury is indicated by the frequency with which they use this fact to praise administrators and to support programs they prefer. Senator Dworshak told the Fish and Wildlife Service that "when you return money like that [$1 million from seal furs] back in, you should be proud of it and have the record show it." Not to be outdone, J. Edgar Hoover pointed out that the FBI had recovered $73 million more through its investigation activities over a ten-year period than it had received in appropriations.

The crisis. There comes a time, however, when it is necessary to admit that a new program is in the offing or that substantial increases in existing ones are desired. This situation calls for a special campaign in which three techniques—the crisis, salesmanship, and advertising—are often called into play. The purpose is to generate extraordinary support so that the agency or program does not merely inch ahead but secures sizable new appropriations.

Events do not have meaning in themselves; they are given meaning by observers. The agency in a position to meet a crisis, as TVA was by supplying huge amounts of power to nuclear-energy installations, can greatly increase its appropriations. And, soon after a jet plane had crashed because of contact with a flock of starlings, the Fish and Wild-life Service was able to obtain funds for research into the habits of these birds. There is also a borderline area of discretion in which crisis may be made to appear more critical. A number of agency officials are famous in budgetary circles for their ability to embellish or make use of crisis. By publicizing a situation, dramatizing it effectively, and perhaps asking for emergency appropriations, an agency may maneuver itself into a position of responsibility for large new programs.

Salesmanship runs the gamut from a cops-and-robbers appeal— "agents of our [Narcotics Bureau] . . . engaged in a 45-minute gun battle with Mexican smugglers"—to the "agony sessions" at NIH hearings. Who could resist Senator Hill's plea:

> As we begin today's hearings on appropriations . . . we take notice of the passing of . . . John Foster Dulles [who] fell victim to the most dreaded killer of our time, cancer.
>
> Cancer, that most ancient and accursed scourge of mankind, has . . . robbed the U.S. Senate of some of its greatest leaders: Robert A. Taft, Arthur Vandenberg, Kenneth Wherry, Brian McMahon, and Matthew Neely. What more fitting . . . memorial . . . could there be than a high resolve . . . to re-double our research efforts against the monstrous killer which . . . will claim the lives of 250,000 more Americans before this year has ended? . . . We are very happy to have with us our colleague, Senator Neuberger. . . . [then dying of cancer]

The impact on a congressman of many vivid descriptions of disease is described by Representative Scrivner:

> A week ago, Mr. Chairman, after this hearing about cancer, I went home and checked all the little skin flecks and felt for bumps and bruises. I lay awake that night and could have convinced myself I had cancer. And then more recently I lay awake listening to my heart after hearing the heart-trouble talk. I listened to see if it went too fast or if it was too weak or if it was irregular or whether it was pumping too hard. . . . And here I am listening to all this mental health talk . . . and I wonder what I am going to dream about tonight.

Who would vote against appropriations for medical research after being subjected to this treatment?

The crisis strategy is well known to appropriations committee members. Rooney begins exclaiming, "That is the magic word this year, Africa. That is the gimmick that is really giving the taxpayer the business." His colleague obligingly responds with "It is taking the place of sputnik." And Rooney comes back with, "Every year it is something different." But this does not mean that congressmen are immune. They recognize the signs of the times.

In the classical era of American national budgeting, that quarter century between the end of World War II and the early 1970s, there was a recognizable budgetary process, almost a budgetary minuet. Conflict was routinized and confined by informal understandings. These understandings, supported by the norm of balance, reinforced by agreement on the general lines of public policy and an expansive economic climate, led to budgetary incrementalism. Since there was agreement on most programs, these constituted a base that was generally considered untouchable. For the most part, differences centered upon small departures from the base, rather than the program itself. By focusing upon remedial measures, by usually dealing with difficulties as they revealed themselves, and by making repeated attacks upon problems in different forums—within agencies, between agencies and the OMB, in House and Senate subcommittees—those problems could be factored down into small and manageable components. Calculation was improved and conflict limited by this incremental, remedial, and serial approach.

Just enough central control had been grafted on to historical budgeting—the process remained focused on the legislature and fragmented within that—to create a semblance of order. Indeed, my first reaction to classical budgeting was a sense of wonder of how much coordination actually was achieved without a central coordinator. Revenue and expenditure were approximately equivalent. Decisions were made on time. Deference was shown to informed judgment. Evident political self-interest was both accommodated—congressmen were expected to vote their district—and limited: The leadership populated appropriations committees with people from safe districts; the president could be expected to impound overspending by prearrangement; spending considered unwise could be voted for and then allowed to die. Though there were complaints about insufficient analysis, followed by efforts to introduce more systematic intelligence, moderation remained the order of the day. Improving analysis of choices on individual programs was the great hope; no one thought of directly deciding total revenue and expenditure. No one then, just twenty years ago, dreamed of making decisions on total spending and taxing.

The disintegration of the budgetary base—to disputes over the starting point as well as to the end in view—caught budgeters unawares. With all of Congress involved in many more spending decisions, but without being able to agree on them, the annual budget is no longer made on time or nearly as binding as it once was. From the time of historical budgeting, when it did not exist, to classical budgeting where it set the agenda, to dissensual budgeting in which it is ignored, the president's budget has lost its veneer of authority. The BOB-OMB has become much less of an agency controller and much more of a congressional bargainer. The original roles of advocacy, guardianship, and appeals have been transformed: Advocacy (on welfare) has moved to the House and (on defense) to the president; guardianship has gone to the budget committees; the only appeals court is the Conference Committee. In sum, the continuing resolution replaces the annual budget.

It is not, I remind the reader, that historical and classical budgeting are gone. They have not been replaced so much as built upon by new edifices (budget committees) and complicated by new practices (reconciliation procedures). And no sooner had Congress adapted to the procedures of the Budget Act of 1974 than they were altered by the Gramm–Rudman law in 1986, which in turn was altered by OBRA in 1990. Thus the hapless student of budgeting is faced with new procedures modified by still newer ones that are altered again within a few years. What has happened? Why has it happened? To these questions we now turn.

THE COLLAPSE OF CONSENSUS

4

We're a very divided committee, with some very conservative Republicans and very liberal Democrats. I always had to find different members for each coalition.

—a congressman

Any book that says the appropriations committee sees its job as to cut the President's budget would just be wrong. They may see their job as to rearrange priorities but to stay within the total. But on this subcommittee the pressure's all upward.

—a committee staffer

SHORTLY AFTER THE STANDARD ACCOUNTS of classical budgeting were published in the early 1960s—Richard Fenno's *The Power of the Purse* and the first edition of my *Politics of the Budgetary Process*—that process began to collapse. What Allen Schick in *Congress and Money* calls the "Seven Year Budget War" lasted from 1966 to 1973. It ended with what he calls "The Congressional Budget Treaty of 1974," which Congress called the Congressional Budget and Impoundment Control Act of 1974 (the Budget Act). The new act, like the Gramm–Rudman–Hollings bill of 1985, did not abolish the old process; it heaped new relationships and institutions atop, and also layered them among, the old ones.

In retrospect, the pattern is clear; Congress and presidents have trouble agreeing. More time is being spent on budgeting to less effect. The difficulties are attributed variously to recalcitrant personalities, hard economic times, or defects in the process. The personalities, the time, and the process change but to no avail. Maybe better times, new leaders, different procedures will break the stalemate. Everything and nothing changes. The central question remains: What has caused the budgetary process to become so unsatisfactory?

THE GROWTH OF ENTITLEMENTS

Entitlement spending grew swiftly from 1960 to 1974. In part, entitlements grew from the need to keep old promises; as more and more people reached retirement age, the promised social security or civil service retirement pensions cost the government more. Entitlements grew also from the making of new promises—medical care to the aged (medicare), nutrition to the impoverished (food stamps)—and by the increasing costs of big, old programs (social security).

New efforts to preserve old promises were particularly important. Benefits promised in specific dollar amounts, such as pensions based on earnings, lost as inflation devalued their dollar worth. As a result Congress had to raise pension benefits frequently. By the early 1970s—in part to keep the promises solid, and in part to prevent congressmen from voting over-adjustments on highly popular programs—Congress began indexing major benefit systems.

Entitlement spending grew faster than did other spending. Thus an increasing portion of federal spending could not be determined by the appropriations process. By "uncontrollable," of course, OMB did not mean beyond human control. Congress could, at any time, reduce spending or cancel the entire program. It is just that entitlement spending could not be controlled through the appropriations process.

A lot more could (and should) be said about entitlements (see Chapters 7 and 8). They grew partly at the expense of defense, which remained relatively stable in constant dollars but declined greatly as a proportion of total spending (see Chapter 9). With defense and economic growth used up as a means of funding social welfare programs, the question was, Where else might the money come from? A quick answer was federal credit. More was going on to raise spending in ways that did not appear directly or fully in the budget. One way was the use of tax preferences to do things, such as subsidizing home ownership, that could have been done through the appropriations process. Another way, which I shall emphasize here, was the extraordinary growth of federal credit.

NOW YOU SEE IT, NOW YOU DON'T: FEDERAL CREDIT

In 1987 the amount of federally assisted, outstanding credit was over a trillion dollars, marginally more than total federal spending (see Table 4-1). While the credit figure is an accumulated total and the spending is a single year's commitments, I use the more dramatic comparison because many people are not aware (ask and see) how large federal credit has become. Credit has become a major instrument of public policy. What does this development portend?

Without doubt, credit is an important way to increase federal spending; it vastly expands the scope and extent of federal influence. Credit is also a flexible instrument that helps implement diverse public policies—from rural electrification to student loans to increasing the volume of exports. Given the desire to subsidize certain activities, the instruments used—loans, guarantees, refinancing through the Federal Financing Bank (FFB)—may be an efficient mode of accomplishing that result. Subsidization of such favored borrowers, however, may well decrease the growth of the economy by diverting resources from more to less productive uses. These debt instruments also make the desired activities budgetarily more attractive; either they do not show up in the budget at all or they appear at a much lower amount than they would if they came in the form of appropriations. By the same token, credit instrumentalities raise federal spending and its reach far beyond what would take place in their absence, partly by obfuscating accountability. Credit instruments make it difficult to determine how much is being

TABLE 4-1

Summary of Outstanding Federal and Federally Assisted Credit[1]
(billions of current dollars)

Year	Direct loans on-budget	Direct loans off-budget	Guaran-teed loans	Government sponsored enterprise loans	Total
1974	$ 46.1	$ 15.4	$180.4	$ 43.8	$ 285.7
1975	49.8	24.4	189.0	43.5	306.7
1976	64.2	21.6	200.7	54.0	340.5
1977	68.2	32.7	214.5	71.8	387.2
1978	76.5	43.9	226.1	93.8	440.3
1979	83.0	57.5	264.6	123.0	528.1
1980	91.7	72.3	299.2	151.0	614.2
1981	91.3	93.7	309.1	182.3	676.4
1982	100.2	107.6	331.2	225.6	764.6
1983	105.0	118.0	363.8	261.2	848.0
1984*	103.7	128.8	393.6	301.0	927.1
1985*	101.5	139.3	428.1	343.9	1012.8
*Est.					

[1]Table from Clifford M. Hardin and Arthur T. Denzau, "Closing the Back Door on Federal Spending: Better Management of Federal Credit," Formal Publication #64, September 1984, Center for the Study of American Business, Washington University, St. Louis, Missouri.

Source: Special Analysis F., *Budget of the United States Government, FY 1985*, and earlier special analyses; and *Mid-Session Review of the 1985 Budget.*

spent by whom for what purpose and with what consequences. Though the formal responsibility of the federal government for increasing national debt seems diminished, because much of this debt does not show up in the budget as proposed by the president or enacted by Congress— since the resources are provided directly by the federal treasury—the debt itself does go up. Though the actual operations of federally assisted credit are hard to believe (especially the shell games through which debt on budget is passed through the Federal Financing Bank so that, voila!, it goes off-budget), a tour through the interstices of these operations does help explain why credit is an important mechanism for funding public policy.

Backdoor Spending: Borrowing Authority

Big changes often come from small beginnings. The authority of federal agencies to borrow money through the Treasury is not an ancient practice; it dates back only to 1932 when, after bills to create a Reconstruction Finance Corporation (RFC) were on the way to passage, the Treasury Department recommended that in addition to being able to borrow from the general public, RFC should also be able to borrow from the Treasury so as to avoid interfering with its own debt issues.[2] In the next few years, once the precedent had been set at a time when antidepression measures were paramount, borrowing from the Treasury was extended to housing authorities, the Tennessee Valley Authority, and the Commodity Credit Corporation.

From this beginning in 1932 to mid-1965, funds going through the then-normal appropriations committee amounted to nearly $2 trillion while authorization to borrow amounted to $106.6 billion or 5.4 percent of spending by appropriations, a small proportion. Of this borrowing authorization, the appropriations committees provided $12.7 billion while $93.9 billion came directly from the Treasury. These direct drafts came to be called treasury budgeting or, more popularly, *backdoor financing,* on the grounds that these sums had been obtained by bypassing the appropriations process.[3]

Gradually five types of borrowing authority came into being—or, as the Treasury Department called it, "the authority to expend from public debt receipts." The amounts can be definite, that is, have a ceiling, or indefinite, that is, of unlimited duration, limited to one specified fiscal

[2]Sun Kil Kim, "The Politics of a Congressional Budgetary Process 'Backdoor Spending,'" *Western Political Quarterly,* Vol. 21 (December 1968), pp. 606–23; especially pp. 607–609.
[3]*Ibid.,* p. 609.

year or to no fiscal year. By contrast, borrowing through the appropriations process is far more constrained, nonrevolving, available only in
specified fiscal years, and with fixed ceilings.[4] Revolving funds can use
repayments to sponsor still more borrowing ad infinitum.

From an institutional and partisan point of view, the backdoor (or
"Treasury financing," as Hubert Humphrey termed it, being famous for
suggesting that young men ought to have two mortgages to encourage
their ambition) method was favored by the more liberal Senate in the
1950s and early 1960s while the more conservative House, fearing invasion of its prized power of the purse, unsuccessfully resisted the device.
Appropriations Committee members disliked most the fact that the
Senate would pass additional credit authorizations in what Appropriations considered violation of the constitutional provision requiring that
money bills originate in the House. The granting of such "special favors," Chairman Clarence Cannon thundered, had made the Senate
into "the dominant body of Congress."[5] Supporters would argue that
programs would be more effective if funded by loans available over the
long term, while opponents responded that all such matters should go
through the appropriations process where, of course, requests were certain to be treated less generously. "The debate over 'backdoor spending,'"
Sun Kim concluded, "is a contingent battle over the programs themselves."[6]

The Federal Financing Bank

Whenever economists and efficiency experts meet up with politicians,
watch out! During the 1960s and early 1970s, the proliferation of federal
credit offerings (by 1972 such issues appeared in financial markets three
out of every five days) caused concern about the efficiency of these
operations. Coming from everywhere, without order or expertise, federal
credit offerings were often badly placed, wrongly sized, and poorly publicized, so that rates of interest were considerably higher than ordinary

[4]*Ibid.*, p. 607.
[5]*Ibid.*, pp. 617–18.
[6]*Ibid.*, p. 622.

treasury securities. In order, it said, to reduce costs of administration and of interest, the Treasury Department proposed in 1973 (and in 1975 the government began) the Federal Financing Bank (FFB), a small unit "within the Treasury that would centralize the issuance of federal securities, thereby eliminating underwriting fees and securing other such economies. That did happen. But Paul Volcker, then Undersecretary for Monetary Affairs, promised that the FFB would not be "a device to remove programs from the federal budget. . . . The Bank would in no way affect the existing budget treatment of federal credit programs."[7] But that promise was not kept.

It has been well said in ecology that no act does only one thing. Nowhere is that more true than of the FFB. It did indeed cut the micro costs of borrowing. Despite its small one-eighth of a percent loan fee, FFB brings in far more than it spends. Loan costs to agencies went down considerably. Everybody wins, right? Wrong again, for the costs of federal credit depend on whether it is desirable to expand loan guarantees. The question of "efficiency for what" is always pertinent. Were it true that the less done the better, then inefficiency might well leave the nation better off. As James Bickley put it, "The very success of the FFB's operation may have also contributed to the rapid growth of federal credit assistance. Agencies can more easily and quickly provide credit assistance through the FFB. Lower interest costs to recipients have expanded some programs, particularly those credit programs without a dollar limit."[8] If loan guarantees are a good thing, the FFB is great, but, if not, doing a bad thing more efficiently is worse than not doing it at all.

At the outset, it is important to understand that the size of the Bank's holdings are not limited by statute nor are its disbursements and receipts included within budget totals nor is there any limit on its outlays (that is, the excess of loans over receipts).

There are four basic types of FFB operations whose effects on the

---

[7]James M. Bickley, "The Federal Financing Bank: Assessments of Its Effectiveness and Budgetary Status," *Public Budgeting and Finance*, Vol. 5, No. 4 (Winter 1985), pp. 51–63; quote on p. 51.

[8]*Ibid.*, p. 57.

federal budget need to be distinguished. In what might be called "replacement borrowing," agencies that are "on-budget," that is, in the budget, borrow from FFB as a substitute for the public financial markets. No change there except easier access and lower cost of funds. In "operational borrowing," agencies already "off-budget" use the Bank to finance their activities. Since this borrowing would not otherwise have appeared in the budget, the only change is again lower cost and easier access. There are, however, two methods of changing on-budget to off-budget loans that deserve scrutiny.

When a loan is sold by an on-budget agency to the FFB, which is off-budget, by sleight of accounting the same status is conferred on that loan. The agency retains title to the loan, continues to service it, and remains responsible for defaults. In some way that may make sense to accountants, it is the assets in the loans but not the loans themselves that are sold. Now a lot changes. For one thing, the loan no longer is added to the deficit attributable to the federal budget though it does, until repaid, add to total government borrowing. Since these "loan assets," as they are conventionally called, belong to the Bank while the sponsoring agency still has the title, the agency can use these presumed assets as, in effect, collateral for additional loans. Easy as pie.

The fourth category, which might be termed a "second party loan," occurs when a federal agency, providing a guarantee, directs the FFB to issue a loan to a nonfederal borrower. Though the agency is responsible for any defaults, the loan is, with the speed of a single transaction, converted into off-budget status.[9]

It should come as no surprise, therefore, that FFB on-budget agency debt from 1975 to 1984 declined from 41.2 to 20.2 percent while loan assets went from 0.3 to 43.7 percent and its second party guaranteed debt rose from 16.6 to 35.3 percent.[10] While this debt does count toward whatever overall debt limit Congress established, it does not count in the federal deficit. And that—enabling agencies to borrow more on behalf of their clients while keeping the formal deficit down—is apparently the purpose of these transactions.

[9]*Ibid.*, pp. 54–55.
[10]*Ibid.*, p. 55.

How much, we may ask, following the medieval philosophers, is a loan guarantee worth? Defaults are counted as outlays. But the difference between the cost in private markets and the rate at which the FFB-cum-Treasury can borrow is not. And that difference is real money amounting to billions over a large volume of transactions. Guaranteed loans get priority, which is also worth something. In 1982, for example, new direct loans of $44 billion and loan guarantees amounting to $78 billion were given by the federal government. Total cash disbursements were $15.3 billion, but only $4.8 billion was noted in budget accounts. It would not be excessive, though there is no agreement here, to estimate the cost of the subsidy at over $20 billion, albeit not in one year.[11] Thus the size of the deficit is distorted in two ways, one by moving nearly 80 percent of loan transactions off-budget and the other by providing a substantial but unaccounted-for interest rate subsidy. Whatever opportunity there might be, moreover, for comparing the relative desirability of different loans—say, Rural Electrification Administration versus Farmers' Home Administration versus the Foreign Military Sales Program, to mention three of the largest—or to evaluate them in the context of on-budget spending programs is lost or made more difficult.

How did it happen that in 1981 the Farmers' Home Administration (FHA) granted over $9 billion in new loans while the federal budget, implying that repayments must have exceeded new disbursements, listed a new reduction of outstanding loans to the tune of $900 million? All FHA did was sell $7 billion of its new on-budget loans to the FFB, thereby moving them off-budget, thus lowering the federal deficit (though not, to be sure, the unified national debt) by that amount.[12] Repayments on budget did, in an accounting sense, exceed disbursements on budget, but it was not quite what it seemed.

By 1983, FHA had extended $25 billion in loans (How easily one learns to deal in billions!) through the Agricultural Credit Insurance Fund (ACIF), $4.4 billion of which were delinquent. After numerous

---

[11]Marvin Phaup, "Accounting for Federal Credit: A Better Way," *Public Budgeting and Finance*, Vol. 5, No. 3 (Autumn 1985), pp. 29–39; figures from p. 30.

[12]Thomas J. DiLorenzo, "Putting Off-Budget Federal Spending Back on the Books," *The Backgrounder*, No. 406, Heritage Foundation, January 30, 1985, p. 3.

foreclosures, delinquencies grew to $5.7 billion in 1984. I mention this not to remind readers of hard times on the farm but to make a point about creative accounting. In the pattern to which we have been accustomed, ACIF borrows against the loans it has made through FFB (the so-called loan assets), greatly expanding its portfolio. How, then, did ACIF pay FFB back if the default rate is so high? It used repayments on good loans to pay the interest on defaulted loans.[13] This accounting house of cards would eventually collapse but not yet. In the fiscal 1986 budget, despite stated intentions otherwise, after President Reagan vetoed a $100 million program, he eventually approved a three-year $490 million FHA interest rate subsidy. "The program was pushed," the *National Journal* reported, "by Senator Edward Zorinsky, D. Neb., who received a commitment from the Administration not to oppose it last May [1985] when he provided the lone Democratic vote for the Senate Budget Resolution. The bill passed only with Vice President George Bush casting a tie-breaking vote."[14] When this infusion runs out, the credit will still be good because of the general understanding that in the end the federal government will make everything whole. Indeed, the some $2 billion in loans that FFB has financed for Community Development Bloc Grants are arranged so that full repayment can come about only through appropriation. "The government gets repaid," Representative Bill Gradison neatly sums up, "only by repaying itself."[15]

Why not put an end to creative accounting by placing all FFB loans on-budget? "Right now we deal with Congress and FFB to finance our programs," the president of the National Rural Electric Cooperatives said. "If we are put on budget, we will also have to deal with OMB."[16] The Rural Electrification and Telephone Revolving Fund (RETRF) needs all the help it can get. Created in 1973 under a Republican administration, the funds provide loans for 35 years at 5 percent interest

[13]Hardin and Denzau, "Closing the Back Door on Federal Spending," p. 8.

[14]*The National Journal,* January 11, 1986, p. 63.

[15]Bill Gradison, "Accountability and the 'Off-Budget' Deficit," *Wall Street Journal,* May 15, 1984.

[16]Darwin G. Johnson, "Comments" on Robert Hartman, "Issues in Budget Accounting," in Gregory B. Mills and John L. Palmer, *Federal Budget Policy in the 1980s* (Washington, D.C.: Urban Institute Press, 1984), pp. 448–56; quote on p. 451.

2 percent for hardship cases. Its $7.9 billion endowment funds were mostly composed of old loans bearing a 2 percent interest rate whose repayment (interest only until 1993, principal thereafter) was to go to the Treasury until the entire amount had been paid off. Since these payments amounted merely to $314 million while new disbursements were twice that sum, the rural fund made up the difference by reducing its cash on hand, borrowing short-term notes from the Treasury, and issuing Certificates of Beneficial Ownership to FFB, for which the rate was one-eighth percent plus the rate of long-term treasury debt, then around 13 percent. Clearly, with defaults on the rise, repayment would be difficult. So legislation has been introduced that would, according to a CBO estimate, increase costs to the federal government by $10.4 billion over a quarter century. Among the many mechanisms proposed, one would allow the funds to refinance these Certificates if interest rates decline (though not if they rise), and another would count the $7.9 billion debt as equity for the Treasury, requiring no payment of interest. Although the value over time of going from the loan interest of 5 percent to zero would, properly discounted, be about $2 billion, it would appear in the budget only as a decline in estimated receipts.[17]

What was the Tennessee Valley Authority to do when it accumulated excess inventories of nuclear fuel due to a slowdown in plant construction? I won't go into the leaseback arrangement to "sell" the fuel and buy it back as needed; presumably that made TVA's balance sheet look better. First TVA thought of borrowing $1 billion from private lenders, through a subsidiary, to buy back the fuel. The Treasury suggested FFB. So TVA arranged a $2 billion line of credit, thereby saving over $20 million a year in interest costs without having to pay the usual substantial commitment fee for the right to use the remaining balance. This loan was larger than the New York City and Chrysler loans without the attendant publicity and with much less security.[18]

The importance of being off-budget, to go to my final example, is

[17]Phaup, "Accounting for Federal Credit," p. 33.

[18]Clifford M. Hardin and Arthur T. Denzau, "The Unrestrained Growth of Federal Credit Programs," Formal Publication 45, December 1981, Center for the Study of American Business, Washington University, St. Louis, p. 14.

illustrated by the consequences of losing that opportunity. The Rail Passenger Service Act of 1970 gave the Department of Transportation the authority to guarantee loans for Amtrak. Under a maximum loan authority of $900 million, Amtrak borrowed $850 million from FFB. By 1976 Congress was paying interest but not principal and the relevant members indicated that the debt should be brought on-budget. By 1980 the General Accounting Office had become concerned that this debt was unlikely to be repaid and should therefore be recognized by being brought on-budget. Though no cash would be involved (since the Treasury had already issued notes and bonds to give Amtrak the money), a direct congressional appropriation of $850 million would clear the books, and the federal deficit would increase by that amount (but not the national debt, because the loans already were counted as part of it). After being defeated on two suggestions for remaining off-budget, Amtrak borrowed the $850 million directly from the Treasury (not FFB) so the sum went on-budget.[19]

What should be done? If Treasury borrowing costs little or nothing, for instance, why should not every loan in the United States receive at least a federal guarantee, thereby reducing interest rates for everyone? Aside from removing risk from all activities by private parties, thus abolishing capitalism, there would be no point in that kind of borrowing for all. The whole point is to be a preferred borrower, to do better than others. If everyone is a preferred borrower, however, then no one is. Indeed, as soon as the Treasury took on all individual debt, it would become a less worthy borrower because it would have less ability to repay, thus increasing the interest cost of servicing the debt.

The federal government is now beginning to exert greater control over its credit. OMB regularly provides an appendix to the president's budget that tries to account for all governmental credit. In fiscal year 1981, for the first time nonbinding targets for federal credit were made part of congressional budget resolutions. In the following two years these targets were disaggregated to functional levels, tied to the same appropriations subcommittees that consider regular spending. Where formerly the

[19]Hardin and Denzau, "Closing the Back Door on Federal Spending," p. 9.

Defense Department used FFB to place guaranteed loans for arms purchases off-budget, Congress decided in 1984 that in the future such loans will appear on-budget. Finally, and most important, the Gramm–Rudman–Hollings bill of 1985 (GRH) included a section reforming budgetary procedure that places the FFB on-budget. If GRH is not repealed, a major reform will have taken place.

A remaining question is whether the actual cost of guaranteed loans is reflected in the budget. The higher the imputed cost that shows up in the budget, the less the incentive to use guaranteed loans, whether it is the Reagan administration's placement of the oil reserve off-budget to reduce the federal deficit or any other use. Using the cash paid out in loans minus cash received in payments as a measure of cost tells only part of the story. The economic cost of a direct loan is not only the cash outlay but also the value of the loan if it had been received from a private lender. This calculation assumes the private market to be the standard of value. Were that universally acknowledged, there would be little reason to grant government loans. For loan guarantees, the market cost is the difference between the premium required to get the guarantee, if any, and the charges made by an insurance company for the same pledge. Now if private insurance were available at the same price, again there would be no reason to go to government. This is another way of raising the ancient question of the appropriate discount (or interest rate) to be charged for governmental credit. Presumably, government enters in order to act differently than the markets.

The plot thickens. Proposals surface to sell loans and guarantees to private lenders. While there might well be considerable loss from face value, the large amounts involved (CBO estimates $95 billion in cash for $225 billion in direct loans) would help reduce the short-term deficit.[20]

There is yet another side to this story. The House Budget Committee, operating under a Democratic majority, points out that sales of loan assets would reduce deficits in the short term, but not in the long term; the cash that comes in early from sales would be offset by lower future

[20]*Ibid.*, p. 15.

payments, thereby increasing deficits in these out years. On the other hand, cash now, according to accepted discounting principles, is worth more than cash later as loans are repaid. Nor would there be less government competition in the loan markets because the volume of loans would remain unchanged. Similarly, fiscal policy would be unaffected because national savings would not change. The basic question behind the Reagan administration's proposal to privatize the loan debt is not the one-time $30 billion return but rather, as HBC put it, "the role of government." The question remains "whether the federal government or the private sector should provide certain services to citizens." I agree. But there also may be information effects—the size of the subsidy would be highlighted—and incentive effects—agencies would be charged these costs.

From the standpoint of budgeting as resource allocation, it would help if the cost of loans were attributable to the agencies that sponsor them, so these could be compared to other expenditures. If sales of loan assets were treated as debt financing (equivalent to other agency debt, as Hartman suggests), agencies would have to be billed for them.[21] Very rapidly a sense of appropriate risk would grow because loan costs would be real dollars fungible with others that might be available for agency programs.

It would also help if the costs incurred, however calculated, were charged to the agency at the time they were made so as to assure careful consideration in the here and now rather than in some vague future. Thus the accumulation of hidden costs, loans worth far less than their face value, would be diminished. Selling loans on the open market as they are made would accomplish this purpose.

A cautionary note is in order. Many federal activities other than loans—for example, regulations on the private sector, conflicting monetary activities (the Federal Reserve may be restricting strong borrowers while the FFB is lending to weak ones), tax provisions—influence the economy. Comparing the relative worth of these activities is beyond the capabilities of existing theory or practice. One could say that is why we need politics.

[21] *Ibid.*

No miracles are in sight. "No matter what budget concept is chosen," Darwin Johnson tells us, "there will always be program advocates—in Congress, the administration, and special-interest groups—working to devise ways to increase program activity without reflecting that activity in the budget."[22] There are also program opponents who would like to decrease these activities by making them appear larger than they are in the budget. Recent steps to increase surveillance and control of credit are overdue. But this will not end the use of credit for strategic purposes.

Entitlements and credit alone, however, cannot explain dissatisfaction with the old budget process. The accompanying deficits alone could not have united a broad bipartisan majority behind the Budget and Impoundment Act of 1974; for that Congress needed Richard Nixon to give high-spending liberals reason to back budget reform.

PRIORITIES

The division of roles among the president and Congress, OMB, and the appropriations committees was weakening simultaneously with the growth of entitlements. The system could work only so long as conflict about both totals and relative priorities was kept within negotiable bounds. In 1960 most government programs had either been around long enough for their existence and scope to be taken for granted (the New Deal ended 20 years earlier) or, if recent, had been endorsed by both Democratic and Republican administrations in the course of passage. Even though Congress was Democratic and the administration Republican, or vice versa, there was broad agreement about the existence or size of programs: Government was to limit itself to the existing tax take. During the 1960s, however, and especially after the 1964 landslide election, Congress became more Democratic and northern liberals dominated the Democratic party. Lyndon Johnson's Great Society created many new programs and agencies.

Republican Richard Nixon was nothing if not flexible. In his first term (1968–1972) he approved or allowed large spending increases, especially,

[22]Johnson, "Comments" on Hartman, p. 456.

as in housing, where the costs did not show up immediately. When spending was popular, despite contrary rhetoric, he spent. Faced with the consequences of past commitments, including those of his own administration, buoyed by a large electoral victory in 1973, Nixon returned to his long-standing convictions, determined in his second term to rein in spending.

Northern liberals had created many new programs and agencies to heal social ills that ranged from inadequate medical care for the aged to poverty in the mountains of West Virginia. To most Democrats these programs, many of which included implicit promises of more to come, were the new base. To Richard Nixon, most Republicans, and many southern Democrats, these programs were bad ideas at worst or, at best, nice sentiments that could not be afforded. These attitudes toward spending commitments were reversed when the spending was for the military. Particularly after Nixon took office and they were no longer constrained by loyalty to their Democratic president, congressional liberals thought the levels of spending generated by what they considered a stupid and immoral war in Vietnam could hardly be claimed as an inviolable "base." Conservatives thought new domestic welfare programs were equally illegitimate. The result was a series of debilitating battles over budget priorities. Richard Nixon used his budget powers to challenge congressional priorities. He proposed some funding levels far below what majorities in Congress expected. Then when the appropriations committees responded by raising the allocations, Nixon refused to spend the money. He impounded the funds.

IMPOUNDMENT

It had always been understood that if money were appropriated for a purpose that turned out to be unnecessary, or if the funds could not be spent usefully and immediately, the executive did not have to spend it, so long as most concerned members of Congress concurred. Indeed, they might want the president to do what was necessary when it was nonpolitic for congressmen to do so. Thus impounding based on taccit consent was an informal safety valve for keeping spending under control. Congress would not have to vote to repeal the funding (since that was troublesome); the president, through OMB and the Treasury, would merely refuse to release the funds to the affected agency. And of course the decision would come too late for the agency to protest effectively. Nixon tried to change this tradition of informal understandings in special cases to a general presidential prerogative. He would spend only what he chose to. After other efforts to shape appropriations through vetoes and lobbying had failed, and after the 1972 election had, he claimed, given him a mandate, Nixon resorted to impoundment en masse. As Allen Schick wrote,

> Far from administrative routine, Nixon's impoundments in late 1972 and 1973 were designed to rewrite national policy at the expense of congressional power and intent. Rather than the deferment of expenses, Nixon's aim was the cancellation of unwanted programs. . . . When Nixon impounded for policy reasons, he in effect told Congress, "I don't care what you appropriate; I will decide what will be spent."[23]

The policy stakes in Nixon's impoundments may have been striking enough, but the political stakes were decisive. Save during a major war, no president had ever asserted his primacy over Congress so bluntly. If Nixon could get away with massive impoundments, what could he not do? If the power of the purse could be defied, what was left for Congress?

The power of the purse had to be protected in 1974 as in 1774—but in 1974 for the opposite reason. The world had been stood on its head. For two centuries Congress had defined the threat as an executive that wanted to spend too much. Since the days of royal governors and their civil lists, the legislature's problem had been to restrain the executive by limiting its funds. Now it faced a chief executive who wanted to spend too little, and who defied the legislature (or, as Congress saw it, the people) by refusing funds for the bureaucracy. The challenge to Congress was as great, but its meaning to the public and the possible remedies now had to be very different.

[23]Allen Schick, *Congress and Money* (Washington, D.C.: Urban Institute, 1980), pp. 46, 48.

A division of labor and sharing of power in budgeting requires shared notions of what is accepted, and thus not subject to dispute—that is, controversy must be limited to the margins, and battles once settled must not be continually refought, lest the system collapse. Much of the legitimacy of OMB and the president depends on a belief that they too concur in Congress's base, that they merely adjust it by judging the technical aspects of programs and the management needs of agencies. If, instead, the president's preferences differ and if his budget becomes mainly an attack on programs he does not like, its use to Congress is drastically reduced. The appropriations committees' power similarly depends on their not going overboard and using that power to change policy beyond the will of Congress. If they overstep their bounds, Congress will revolt. If the appropriations committees had gone along with Nixon, they would have been overridden in their parent houses. When, instead, they conformed to congressional intent, Nixon, by impounding, tried to short-circuit the entire appropriations process. Congress had to respond.

REVISITING THE RULES OF THE GAME

As agreement about priorities diminished, attitudes toward budget totals also changed. Total revenue and expenditure became both more controversial and more important. To the old conflicts over marginally "how much" was intertwined the potentially more divisive question of totally "what for."

Until the mid-1960s, attitudes toward total spending could be summarized by a few simple statements:

1. Deficits are bad. Borrowing has to be paid for later, gives financiers too much power (if you are liberal), and diverts money from productive use in the private economy (if you are conservative). The public views debt as bad for the government in the same way as for the household: a burden for the future, an indicator of poor

management, and a sign that the country is in trouble. Charles Murphy, former special counsel to President Harry Truman, typified this attitude at this time when he pointed out that Truman had "an unmistakable belief in the virtues of a balanced budget." A decade after leaving office, Truman responded to Kennedy's tax cut by suggesting that taxes should be reduced until the budget was balanced.[24]

2. Spending helps people in need and is therefore good, except that it must be paid for. Of course, some spending is better than others.

3. Taxes are necessary but unpalatable. Responsibility for tax hikes is dangerous. Avoid across-the-board tax increases by the "silent tax" of bracket creep or by selective, marginal changes that are difficult to oppose. Hope that economic growth will create a dividend in enhanced revenues so that part can fund higher spending and part can keep income tax rates stable or even reduced.

These rather contradictory premises fit with a set of decision rules for congressmen designed to make calculations simple, conflicts manageable, and public policy predictable:

1. Do what you did last year if that worked out O.K. Change only at the margins so you can easily change back again.

2. Budgets should be balanced, or if not, as close as possible, and should look like they are getting closer.

3. If you have room to increase spending, do not increase it to an extent that would require tax increases or borrowing.

4. If none of the above is possible, something unpleasant must be done. To minimize political cost, make the president propose a solution first. If his solution is tolerable, adopt it and blame him for what unhappiness does result (congressmen with different constituencies will blame him for different consequences). If a seem-

[24]Remarks of the Honorable Charles S. Murphy at the Harry S. Truman Library, April 1, 1967.

ingly more popular solution can be found, adopt it and take the credit. Reaction to the president's proposal can be used to gauge the political pressures.

ECONOMIC ACTIVISM

These premises and decision rules were challenged by the Keynesian revolution in macroeconomics. The simplified Keynesian premise is:

The goal of policy should be to balance not the budget, but the economy. The government should adopt the levels of spending, taxing, and borrowing that will produce acceptable levels of GNP, inflation, and unemployment.

Keynesianism was as much a political as an economic revolution. Keynes pointed to a theoretical way out of the strictures of classical economics (although through actual experimentation several European countries had arrived at Keynesian solutions without benefit of Keynes). No longer did government have to raise taxes and cut spending in times of recession. Politicians could finally justify what they had long desired to do, namely, do something (spend) to help people (and, in turn, benefit the economy) in a time of crisis. Thus Keynesianism destroys old premise 1, that deficits are bad. Sometimes deficits are necessary to stimulate the economy. In an obvious way, this makes budgeting much easier. Constraints are loosened, especially when the economy declines, which automatically reduces revenues and increases both entitlement costs and thus the deficit. Keynesian theory says that deficits are desired precisely when unemployment rises, which is certainly convenient, if not largely unavoidable. There are, however, hidden costs to the Keynesian perspective.

In most of Europe and the United States, after the initial fear of postwar depression proved unfounded, rapid economic growth in stable economies was expected to continue indefinitely. The Keynesian doctrine of economic stabilization by means of counter-cyclical spending triumphed everywhere. So powerful was this faith in the feasibility of economic fine-tuning and of its potential for sustaining economic stability that few if any mainstream advisors to governments in those days considered the possibility of having to make cuts in spending. The political difficulty of cutting was still recognized, but, expecting the expansion to go on indefinitely, no one worried much about reductions or how to implement them.

Keynesian economics posed a powerful threat to the balanced budget norm, since it allowed politicians, experts, and other participants to justify deficits—but only to each other. What V. O. Key called the political stratum—politicians, the press, bureaucrats, experts, group leaders—came to adopt, or at least respect, Keynesianism. Even that elite was divided because Republicans saw Keynes' beliefs as an invitation to government interference with the private realm (they called it "the market") in which they were dominant. Labor embraced Keynesian economics precisely because it justified interference with the private sector (which they called "the corporations"). Yet the public never abandoned the norm of balance. A 1982 Roper poll showed that 80 percent of Americans still described themselves as "conservatives" on budget balance more than on any other issue listed (see Figure 4-1).

FIGURE 4-1

Percent of Americans Describing Themselves as Conservatives on . . .

Deficit Spending				
Homosexuality				
Whites Dating Blacks				
People Smoking Marijuana				
Harsh Penalties for Convicted Criminals				
Couples Living Together Without Being Married				
Having National Health Insurance for All				
Women Being in Traditional Male Occupations				
0	25	50	75	100%

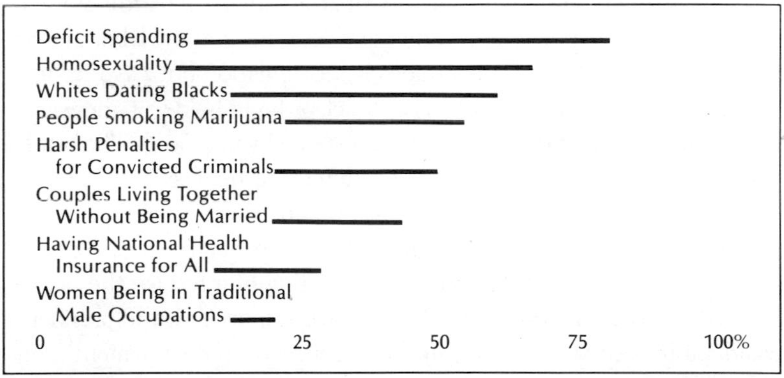

Source: Everett Ladd, "Americans' Hate Affair with Deficits," *Fortune,* June 14, 1982, p. 77.

As Keynesianism developed through years of political use, old premises 2 and 3 also were revised. When times are good, according to Keynes, spending should be limited and taxation increased to keep the economy from overheating. Put in terms of political appearance, "Times are good so we should do less because citizens can afford to pay (their real income is rising) and they won't notice." Instructions to reduce benefits people are already enjoying, however, are not attractive. Consequently, in both good times and bad, despite Keynesian doctrine, spending kept going up.

Less obviously, the Keynesian perspective calls the first decision rule into question. What "worked," which means what was politically acceptable last year, cannot be assumed to work this year, since the perceived needs of the economy may have changed. When politicians assume responsibility for managing the economy, and the economy changes faster than party coalitions, the political task becomes complicated.

The president's role also becomes more troublesome to congressmen, for budget totals become more important. Keynesian economics would see a tradeoff between unemployment and inflation; a healthy economy is defined in terms of some balance of the two evils (hopefully both at low levels). Unfortunately, politicians may not see eye to eye on the proper balance; some politicians (usually Democratic) are more worried by unemployment, others (usually Republican) are more fearful of inflation. The choice depends on whether one's constituents are labor unions (which can defend in their contracts against inflation but have trouble defending against unemployment) or stock or bond holders (who worry less about unemployment but can be clobbered by inflation). The tradeoff therefore hits at the fundamental difference between Democratic and Republican constituencies. When a Republican president must deal with a Democratic Congress, congressmen, in allowing the president the first move, do not necessarily succeed in getting him to take the blame for going in the direction that Congress wishes; instead, the president could push them in a direction—say, choosing unemployment over inflation—where they would not choose to go. And at that particular time, before the Congressional Budget and Impoundment Control Act of 1974, the appropriations process gave Congress no way to articulate a coherent alternative.

When budget totals become a tool of economic policy, then those totals, not just the spending programs within them, become a subject of major constituency conflict. Politicans can be blamed if the economy runs into trouble, for proper fiscal policy would presumably have kept the economy healthy. This responsibility is dangerous enough if politicians are actually able to direct the economy. In the last half of the 1970s, acceptance of Keynesian premises did establish political responsibilities while the policy theory it represented turned out to be less useful than expected.

The stagflation of the 1970s, when unemployment and inflation rose together, could not be solved within the Keynesian framework. Perhaps the causes were outside of the framework, or perhaps the fiscal tools available were too blunt for the job. Possibly, as Robert Eisner argues, failure to measure the proper level of deficits, due to inflation and the lack of a capital budget, gave the wrong signals.[25] The community of economists, businessmen, and labor leaders, however, persisted in demanding the "proper" macroeconomic adjustments. Even the revolt against Keynesianism in the form of supply-side economics (basically, much lower marginal tax rates to increase incentives for economic activism) presumed that there was a proper economic policy that would save the country if misguided politicians would only see the light.

Yet the public never abandoned the old premises. Deficits remained unpopular, spending for programs appreciated, and taxes difficult to justify. Macroeconomic activism added a new layer of expectations and responsibilities to budgeting without eliminating the old concerns.

In 1974 not all of these consequences were clear. After President Nixon engaged in a spate of impounding, and as his authority declined precipitously during Watergate, Congress had both the motivation and the capacity to exert control. Whether what was bad for Nixon would be good for his adversaries was another matter. In any event, the Budget Act was an attempt to reassert Congress's role.

[25]See Robert Eisner, *How Real Is the Federal Deficit?* (New York: Free Press, 1986).

THE BUDGET ACT: MORE CHECKS, MORE BALANCES, BUT NOT MORE CONTROL

Another word is in order about that elusive concept called control. By itself it is a synonym for power. But power over people is not necessarily the same as power over events. Controlling the president is not necessarily the equivalent of control over the budget, and neither necessarily adds up to control over the economy. While Congress in general did want more power over presidents and did wish to relate expenditure more closely to revenue, it was not in agreement about whether expenditures per se were too high, or revenues were too low, or, if so, which parts should be raised or lowered. The question of whether Congress could achieve self-control, making at least the budget come out as it wished, was solved at a formal level: It could command itself to do right. Whether Congress was sufficiently in agreement to obey its own command was the question. If Congress was agreed on the desirability of making big choices on total spending and taxing but disagreed about the content of these decisions—both "how much" and "what for"—Congress would get not control but stultification.

The old procedures were controlling neither spending nor the president. Yet new procedures would shift power within Congress and therefore would meet resistance. Decisions about totals would need to be converted into decisions on programs. The taxing and spending committees would have to be both coordinated and coerced. Any procedure that could do all that, however, would put great power in someone's hands. Historically congressmen have been unwilling to give that power to any of their number.

The solution, of course, was compromise. Nothing was taken away (hence the need for chapters on historical, classical, and entitlement budgeting). Following the traditions of the American political system, Congress created new committees above and beside the appropriations and tax committees, adding to the system of checks and balances.

Impoundment Again

A new procedure was created that formalized the impoundment process. If the president wishes not to spend appropriated funds, he can propose a rescission; if he wishes only to delay spending, he must propose a deferral. For a rescission to take effect, both houses must pass a bill approving the change within 45 legislative days of its proposal. If they do not do so, the money must be spent as originally appropriated. A deferral takes effect automatically but cannot last longer than through the end of the fiscal year. Either house can reject the deferral with a vote specifically disapproving it. This procedure exploits the difficulty of congressional action. By requiring positive action in both houses, the more serious policy change (rescission) is made unlikely. The lesser change (deferral) is allowed to occur, but either house can choose by majority vote to enforce the appropriation legislation.

If the president fails to spend the money but does not report to Congress, the Comptroller General (who, as head of the General Accounting Office, monitors the executive for Congress) reports the action himself. His report has the same legal effect as the president's proposal of a rescission or a deferral. If presidents ignore congressional disapproval, the Comptroller General can bring a civil action in the courts. Presidents can, of course, choose to provoke a constitutional crisis. Because they must live with Congress, they are unlikely to do so. Because they are increasingly at odds with Congress, presidents are tempted to take back with one hand (impoundment) what they cannot gain with the other (the congressional budget process).

CBO

The 1974 Act also created a new staff institution, the Congressional Budget Office (CBO), budget committees in each house, and new budget procedures.

The CBO was set up to provide a congressional counterpart to the OMB and the president's economic staff, the Council of Economic

Advisers (CEA). Much of budgeting, such as projection of entitlement costs, involves technical analysis. It is fairly easy to rig the numbers, and congressmen did not believe that the presidential staff would be above such activity. In fact, they did not even believe that congressional committee staffs would be much more reliable. The CBO was to provide a bastion of neutral analysis, loyal to the institution of Congress, rather than to committees or to parties. Its director, with extensive authority over the office, is appointed jointly by the Speaker of the House and Senate President Pro Tem for a four-year term.

In a development that reminds us that our institutions can work well, the CBO, under Dr. Alice Rivlin, won a reputation for both competence and neutrality. While its reports have not always been popular, its technical work has been credible. CBO became a modest actor in budgeting, greatly reducing congressional dependence upon the president's experts. Its success was made most evident when, in 1983, the succession of Alice Rivlin by Rudolf Penner—of a moderate Democrat by a moderate Republican—was accomplished without conflict and without obvious change in CBO behavior.

Because estimates of future spending cannot be made with certainty, there are bound to be errors. CBO, no more immune than anyone else, also may make overoptimistic or overpessimistic assumptions about economic growth, inflation, unemployment, and other matters—such as the value of the dollar or the price of oil or interest rates—that confound expectations. That is why Director Penner has suggested using the average of the last five years' economic performance rather than prognostications as the basis for budgeting. In regard to estimates of individual programs and agencies, however, CBO probably has less reason to compound lack of knowledge with a policy or partisan bias than have agencies or the OMB. In its first few years, especially, CBO's estimates proved more accurate. Since OMB and agency estimators do not wish to be thought of as incompetent or worse, they have reason to move closer to CBO by prior consultation. In short, the existence of competition in estimation has led to modest improvements in accuracy. Evidence suggests that executive long-range economic forecasts tend to be more optimistic than CBO projections, though the accuracy of both forecasts is similar.[26]

CBO and impoundment control easily found their places in the congressional process. Budget committees, and the new budgeting schedule, however, have worked far less well.

SBC

The Senate Budget Committee (SBC) was established in 1974 with sixteen members, to be chosen by the party caucuses and to serve indefinitely. The House Budget Committee (HBC) was structured in an unusual manner. Five of its members were to come from the Appropriations Committee and five from Ways and Means. One was a member of the Democratic leadership and one from the Republican leadership. The other thirteen members were appointed through the usual House procedures (this discussion is in the past tense because of changes in details, but not in the basic design, in later years). The committee is a mixture, therefore, of regular members and representatives of power centers within the House. In addition, membership is rotating, rather than permanent; no member could then serve on the Budget Committee for more than four years (now six) out of every ten. Rotation decreases the chance that budget members will become isolated or parochial in their viewpoints, and helps the committee to gain information from other committees. Rotation also ensures that power will not be hoarded by a small group of representatives, even if HBC itself becomes powerful.

Scheduling

The new schedule both added new steps and changed the timing of old ones. Previously, Congress convened in early January, the president

[26]Mark S. Kamlet, David C. Mowery, Tsai-Tsu Su, "Whom Do You Trust? An Analysis of Executive and Congressional Economic Forecasts," *Journal of Policy Analysis and Management*, Vol. 6, No. 3 (1987), pp. 365–84.

submitted his budget in late January, and Congress had to adopt appropriations acts by July 1, when the next fiscal year began. Appropriation and authorization legislation created logjams; often an appropriation could not be made because some part of the act was annually authorized and the authorization had not yet passed (e.g., as in military procurement). Frequently, appropriations were delayed past July 1, forcing Congress to pass a continuing resolution (CR). A CR provides funding for agencies lacking appropriations for some short period of time at the rates authorized during the previous year. Its need was minimized for a short while, however, by changing the fiscal year's start to October 1. This calendar change gave Congress three extra months to perform all its old tasks and to pass the new budget resolutions.

Resolutions

These budget resolutions were the centerpiece of the new process. The first resolution, originally to be passed by May 15 (now April 15), was intended to set targets for other committees, and Congress as a whole, to meet. It included recommended levels for budget authority, outlays, revenues, that year's deficit or surplus, and the resulting total public debt. The first resolution also recommends totals for spending divided into a small number of budget functions. These are the same categories of programs into which the president's budget is divided—such as Function 150, "International Affairs," or Function 350, "Agriculture." The resolution is a formal reply to the president's proposal. Budget committee staff and members tend to have rather detailed ideas of how the functional totals translate into committee jurisdictions and report those to the committees as required by Section 302 of the Budget Act. For much of this time there were nineteen functions. These divisions match the president's budget, but not Congress' committee structure. Consequently, there arose the need to "crosswalk" between the nineteen categories in the president's budget and those used by the thirteen congressional subcommittees.

The first resolution is assembled on the basis of a wide range of information. HBC and SBC are to have available a Current Services

Budget prepared by OMB to show the cost of continuing services at the current level (including changes in prices). The president's budget provides another basis for comparison, analysis, and, in its appendices, argument. CBO analyzes the president's budget and its deviations from current policy. By March 15 (now February 15) committees with jurisdiction over spending and/or taxing legislation are to submit to the budget committees views and estimates that tell the budget committees what members on other committees would like to do.

The budget committees, meanwhile, hold hearings to discuss the president's economic policy and projections, as well as other aspects of his budget. With the president's proposal, their colleagues' views and estimates, and much technical analysis in hand, HBC and SBC then craft their versions of the First Resolution. Procedures in passing that resolution are much like those for any other bill except that since the resolution is a rule for Congress, it does not need the president's signature. Neither does it have the force of law or appropriated funds. Disagreements between House and Senate must be resolved in conference.

As designed by the Budget Act, the First Resolution is more than, less than, but much like the president's budget. It resembles the president's budget in being only a recommendation, something to which action will be compared. It is less than the president's budget because it is less detailed; aggregated only at the functional level, it contains only very general guidance and standards for comparison. The First Resolution is more than the president's budget because it is the product of a lengthy process of discussion and accommodation within Congress; it is therefore more likely to reflect what Congress will actually do. And it is, again, much like the president's budget in being, in its estimates of revenue and debt and entitlement spending, dependent upon predictions of the future course of the economy.

After passing the First Resolution, Congress was to go about its business of authorizing and appropriating. By the Monday after Labor Day, the regular authorizing and appropriating legislation—the laws that actually commit funds—should have passed. The budget committees in late summer would have held hearings to review the latest data about the economy and the actions taken or expected to be taken by the rest of Congress. This information was to be used to decide whether the targets from the First Resolution need adjustment. HBC and SBC then reported out versions of the Second Concurrent Resolution on the budget. The Second Resolution had the same components as the first, except that the Second Resolution's total was supposed to be binding. Thus any legislation considered after passage of the Second Resolution, which would cause limits in that resolution to be breached, could be objected to and ruled out of order.

Reconciliation

If the limits in the First Resolution could not be met, due to legislation passed before the Second Resolution is adopted, reconciliation instructions could be included in the resolution. These would order the relevant committees to report legislation that reconciles spending or taxing to the budget totals. When authorizations as well as appropriations are reconciled, the flow of funds is stopped at the source. In other words, reconciliation is a form of coercion wielded by the budget committees. Reconciliation legislation is to be packaged by the budget committees without substantive change and enacted by September 25.

Complexity

The budget resolutions added a new layer of activity to what was already a complicated process. Appropriations already were conditioned by authorizations. Now both were to be based on budget resolutions, which in turn were derived from estimated authorizations and appropriations. All this instruction and advice among different parts of Congress were to be coordinated by provisions of the Budget Act. Authorization bills were to be reported by May 15, enabling the appropriations committees to work with both the reports and the First Resolution as guidelines. No act making budgetary commitments—appropriating funds, creating a new entitlement, or changing taxes—could be considered on the floor before adoption of that resolution. Special procedures expanded both the appropriations committees' ability to question entitlement growth, and their control over various other types of "backdoor" spending. CBO reports, required by the act, provided information for decision making at specified times. These assorted provisions were meant to relate action on programs to action on the totals. The budget committees, presumably, were to do the coordinating. But could they?

A Congressional Budget, or Merely More Budgeting?

In form, therefore, the 1974 act created a budget: Congress would look at programs, think about totals, choose a relationship between spending and revenue, and bring the two together. Entitlement spending would be confronted while considering the totals. New entitlement spending would be analyzed by CBO and delayed by provisions in the schedule, thus getting a longer, harder look than it had before. Established entitlements might be adjusted during reconciliation. The budget resolutions would enable congressional majorities to respond directly to the president's budget, asserting their own functional priorities and fiscal goals. The process of adopting resolutions would focus attention on these questions—the relative sizes of revenue and expenditures and their effects on the economy—far more explicitly than had been done in the past; and voting would force congressmen to take stands in a way not previously required. Hearings and CBO analyses would generate information; resolutions would occasion debate; debate would inform congressmen and the public about the choices made. The procedures relating taxing and spending to the size of the budget would force congressmen to take the totals seriously.

All that was possible; yet, instead of creating a budget, the new procedures might merely create more budgeting. Budget resolutions might just represent extra stages of bargaining, rather than decision making that controlled other decisions. The "new" budget might commit no one to anything. Worse, the extra stages, new actors, and larger questions might undermine the hallmarks of the older budgeting—ease of calculation and diminution of disagreement.

The new budget process was a form of government of congressmen, by congressmen, for congressmen. It created rules for Congress, but any majority can change such procedures. Legislation in the House and Senate often is considered under rules tailored to the occasion; amendment of those rules on the floor is common enough. Congressmen would follow the budget act's rules only if they wanted to do so; they would want to do so only if they valued the process itself more than they valued what they would lose if they obeyed the act.

THE BUDGET PROCESS, 1975–1979: THE STRUGGLE TO RELATE TOTALS TO DETAIL

At stake was power and policy: power within Congress, the power of Congress in regard to the executive branch, and congressional power over programs. If Congress disagreed over policy, however, its members would find that power over one another had a different institutional significance than power vis-à-vis the presidency.

Members of the budget committees had a power stake in making the process work. Unless budget resolutions influenced taxing and spending action, HBC and SBC members would gain nothing from membership. Appropriations committee members objected to their loss of power, of course, but they also had reason to go along with the process. Before 1974, deficits were blamed on them; the new process made it possible to direct attention toward the authorizing, in particular the tax, committees. Members of these other committees were threatened by the Budget Act, which could undermine their committees' independence and ability to serve constituents. Because only a minority of congressmen serve on budget and appropriations committees, enforcement of budget totals required either that they be satisfactory to other congressmen and their roles as committee members, or that other roles and allegiances (to party, to a president, to a constituency, or to an ideology) override congressmen's loyalties as committee members. The budget committees therefore tried both to create resolutions that stepped on very few toes and to mobilize those other loyalties to pass and enforce resolutions on the floor of their respective houses.

In the Senate, budget committee chairman Edmund Muskie

(D-Maine) and ranking minority member Henry Bellmon (R-Okla.) worked to develop resolutions that could command substantial bipartisan support. They then united in defense of the recommendations on the floor. In the House, the resolutions became partisan documents. Republicans continually opposed them on the ground that taxing and spending were too high. Democrats were forced to seek resolutions that could carry without Republican votes. In mobilizing Democratic majorities, party leaders became key actors in that process. Only the Speaker and his lieutenants could (sometimes) muster the Democratic troops. The Democratic House resolutions and bipartisan Senate plans were often difficult to compromise in conference.

By 1980 budget process observers and participants were engaged in a running debate as to whether these resolutions, and the entire process, were having any, and if so what, effect on spending and taxing policy. I cannot rerun history to see what would have happened without the process and therefore cannot settle the debate. I can, however, discuss the effects of various parts of the process, which will help us understand what took place.

The views and estimates submitted by the committees to HBC and SBC on March 15 tended to turn into wish lists. Requests averaged about 10 percent higher for spending than actually were approved. Because the budget committees had so many alternate sources of information, they fortunately did not have to depend on the March 15 reports for technical data. Instead, both the formal reports and informal contracts among committee staffs made budget drafters aware of how much conflict might be expected in considering alternative spending levels. HBC and SBC therefore had enough information of two types for their purposes. They had estimates of the program base—what was spent last year, which obligations existed, and how the expected performance of the economy would influence program costs. This information might not be accurate, for some of it was unknowable, but budget members would be as informed as anyone else. They also knew, normally, what kinds of changes would be proposed by various participants, such as the president and the authorizing committees, and could judge the political force of those proposals. Of course, HBC and SBC members could be surprised by events or a presidential change of mind (e.g., the invasion of Afghanistan and Carter's response). In general, however, if HBC or SBC could not reconcile preferences about programs and totals, it was not due to lack of either technical or political information.

A far greater difficulty was the potential that the First Resolution, however nicely calibrated, would be ignored at other steps of the process. First Resolution totals for the functions—spending, taxing, etc.—were only targets, but, as it turned out, they were moving targets. This occurred despite HBC and SBC efforts to get their parent houses to judge legislation according to its closeness to budget targets.

The stakes, and difficulty, of such challenges were highlighted in the first year of the process (1975 for fiscal 1976). Senator Muskie, whose chairmanship of the Senate Budget Committee gave him the incentive to keep spending within the limits of his committee's resolution, challenged authorization legislation for both military procurement and the school lunch program, therefore showing he had no policy axe to grind. In each case he was able to force changes in the legislation, but in doing so he risked a backlash, which materialized a year later, from members whose policies were threatened by reduced spending.

The military procurement example was particularly interesting: Bernard Asbell described the confrontation on the Senate floor between Muskie and John Stennis (D-Miss.), chairman of the Armed Services Committee:

> Stennis . . . turns to what really galls him and other chairmen. Going into conference committee, pitting the strength of the Senate against the strength of the House, trying to return to your colleagues with the prestige of victory or at least a workable compromise, is difficult enough. But now comes this new complication, not only a crippling one, but a demeaning one, as chairmen see it. After going through the torments of compromise, a chairman must go on bended knee to a fellow chairman—indeed, the chairman of a mere babe among committees, the Budget Committee—to ask meekly, "Will this compromise be all right? Do you approve of the new figure?"[27]

[27]Bernard Asbell, *The Senate Nobody Knows* (Garden City, N.Y.: Doubleday, 1978), p. 273.

The power stakes were not simply those of John Stennis, but the interests of all senators who liked the conference compromise on defense procurement.

The military procurement bill would not in itself cause the allocation for the national defense function to be exceeded. While this annual authorization gives committees fairly close guidance as to the level of spending desired by other congressmen, the appropriation might come in lower. Further, the function includes more than military procurement—operations and maintenance, for example. Therefore Muskie was really arguing that the authorization for procurement would influence appropriations, and those appropriations, joined to the likely action on other parts of the defense function, would cause the function's limits in the defense resolution to be exceeded. On the one hand, he was quite likely right. On the other hand, the great temptation in this circumstance is for senators to say that they will cross that bridge when they come to it. It is difficult to determine when the totals are threatened and when to take a stand.

Against all these considerations, Muskie had one powerful argument: "Now if the view of all Senators is that expressed by the distinguished chairman—that the numbers that are within the budget go out the window when his committee walks to the conference—we have got nowhere to go."[28] The Senate would be going nowhere in its budget enterprise. This time the Senate backed Muskie, 48–42. His argument, however, had weaknesses; after all, whatever the Senate votes for is the Senate's preference. So long as they voted for that bill, while aware of its effect on the budget, senators could be said to be trading off program and fiscal policy values. Muskie needed to establish a precedent, directing committees to compare their legislation to the first budget resolution. But, as he and other congressmen knew, he could not hope to win all direct confrontations.

What was the purpose of the Budget Act? Did the design enable Congress to work its will? If so, whatever that will turned out to be, was

it in accord with the reformed budget process? Was the process supposed to allow Congress to keep total spending lower than it otherwise
would have been? Why else go to all this trouble, if but to do what
Congress does naturally—spend?

Within this context of mutual uncertainty, HBC and SBC worked
to accommodate other congressional actors, and they tried to avoid
direct confrontations with budget committees. The terms of accommodation depended in part upon who was trying to change the status quo.
The budgeters could more easily resist new legislation, by publicizing its
cost or nonconformance to the resolution, than they could force the
passage of a change that would cut spending or increase revenue. It is
easier to stop people from acting than to make them do something,
especially if the action is complicated, requires cooperation, and involves
congressmen. Proponents of legislation, who had strong incentives to
avoid complications on the floor (delay can be deadly), tried to adapt
bills to satisfy the budget committees. But the budget committees could
do little to urge, say, Ways and Means to report out medicare reforms.
In between these two extremes were legislative changes that seemed so
pressing to so many congressmen that, if budget committees got in the
way of passage, they might be regarded as pests and brushed aside—as
happened whenever they tried to reduce the rate of increase in social
security. In general, if the First Resolution assumed either legislative
changes to programs or funding below what had been Congress's habit,
the First Resolution had to be adjusted upwards.

ECONOMIC MANAGEMENT

One of the major aims of budget reform was to connect more closely
attempts to manage the economy with the expenditure process. And it
does appear that members of budget committees have taken the trouble
to learn more about the relationship between levels of spending and the
condition of the economy. One difficulty is that not much is known;
another is that ability to apply what little is known is strictly limited.

Economic management (or fiscal policy, as it is called) requires a notion of what level of expenditure is appropriate either to stimulate or depress economic activity. Commitments of the past make up the largest part of the budget, however, and it is difficult, either legally or politically, to alter them drastically. Considerations of desirable defense and domestic expenditures compete of necessity with optimal fiscal policy, assuming anyone knows what that should be. Among the many constraints within which the makers of fiscal policy operate, the least understood are those imposed by time and by targeting.

Take time: There is a fallacy that assumes that fiscal policy goes into effect at the time it is made. If we are talking about expenditures, that assumption cannot be correct. The most important time, usually, for bringing fiscal considerations to bear on budgetary totals is during the spring preview conducted by OMB in April. Suppose this is done in April. (Nowadays all this timing is way off, but we will pretend there is a schedule for relating economic forecasts to spending projections. In this make-believe way we can at least look at how this relationship is supposed to work.) The fiscal policy total is considered along with other matters, and OMB establishes and passes down a budgetary target to the spending agencies. For the moment, suppose that this total is not challenged by agencies nor revised by the president but goes directly into his budget in the winter. Even if these contrary-to-fact conditions are met, Congress will not finish acting on appropriations bills until almost a year later in the fall of the next calendar year. Spending agencies will take several months to act on this legislation; the impact of these expenditures, then, will not begin to be felt until the winter of the following year. Thus about two years elapse before the thoughts that went into fiscal policy are reflected in real budgetary behavior. By that time, to be sure, conditions may have markedly changed so that what seemed appropriate then is now inappropriate.

The two years can be shortened to eighteen months by postponing or modifying fiscal policy decisions until November or December. This alternative, however, sacrifices the benefit of considering fiscal policy in the ceilings initially set by OMB. Renegotiating all the bargains of the prior six months in a few weeks in late November and December is an experience that most participants will try to avoid. By late fall, fiscal policy can be adjusted but the entire orchestral arrangement (insofar as budgetary totals are concerned) is likely to have been settled earlier or not at all. Fall fiscal policy is even tighter than what was already an extremely constrained situation the previous spring.

The existence of unprecedented rates of inflation in the mid-1970s, followed by extraordinarily high interest rates in the late 1970s, coming together with multi-hundred-billion-dollar deficits in the early 1980s, and topped off by the largest unemployment rate since the Great Depression have highlighted congressional responsibilities for economic management. But no budget committee can do this alone. Reducing the deficit, for instance, requires a package deal about taxation and domestic and defense spending that can be achieved only by concerted action among congressional committees, backed up or led by the formal leadership, and supported by the president. If this agreement is lacking, congressmen will only end up fooling themselves: There are any number of innovative ways that Congress can circumvent its own will. Congressional efforts at economic management have been stymied both because of doubt over effective policy and inability to act together to enforce whatever set of actions is deemed desirable.

DOES THE BUDGETARY PROCESS HAVE A
PRO-SPENDING BIAS?

The Budget Act of 1974 expressed Congress's desire to enhance its own power of the purse by granting it the ability to visibly relate revenue and expenditure. Since the broad coalition supporting the Act included both high and low spenders, however, the new process was not designed to favor either side. On the one hand, the mere existence of budget committees raised another possible impediment to higher spending; on the other hand, the need for these committees to maintain collegial relations with tax and spending committees, as well as to remain subject to the will of Congress, meant that budget committees had to subordinate themselves to the widespread desires for higher spending. The evidence from Allen Schick's *Congress and Money* is conclusive:

In almost a hundred interviews with Members of Congress and staffers, no one expressed the view that the allocations in budget resolution had been knowingly set below legislative expectations. "We got all that we needed," one committee staff director exulted. The chief clerk of an Appropriations subcommittee complained, however, that the target figure in the resolution was too high: "We were faced with pressure to spend up to the full budget allocation. It's almost as if the Budget Committee bent over backwards to give Appropriations all that it wanted and then some."[29]

All internal incentives work to raise expenditures. Who, for instance, would take the lead in reducing expenditures? Each sector of policy, including the people in Congress who care most about it, naturally is concerned with its own internal development. Those who favor radical restructuring of programs soon discover that this is exceedingly difficult to do without sweetening the pot. More money makes it easier to settle internal quarrels. The price of policy change is program expansion.[30] Like all others who wish to be influential, budget committees can afford to lose only a few times, for if it becomes obvious that budget committees are likely to lose, no one need pay attention to them.

The HBC's difficulties in enforcing reductions, to no one's surprise, have come from advocates of increased spending. In regard to a bill to extend unemployment compensation benefits, for example, Ways and Means required a waiver of a provision in the Budget Act that forbids passage of spending legislation before a budget resolution has been passed for the year in which spending is to occur. When HBC opposed the waiver, Representative Corman, in charge of the bill, let loose a blast:

> I think the Budget Committee was trying to tell the Ways and Means Committee that it doesn't have much power any more. The whole game up here is power, and the staff of the Budget Committee would like to see the committee have a veto over all the other congressional committees.[31]

Or consider the case of highway spending, when both the Appropriations and the Budget committees wanted to put a $2.2 billion cap on

[29]Schick, *Congress and Money*, p. 313.

[30]For example, see Aaron Wildavsky, *Speaking Truth to Power* (Boston: Little, Brown, 1979), Chapter 4, "Coordination Without a Coordinator," pp. 86–107.

[31]*National Journal*, September 25, 1976, pp. 1349–50.

state spending. Although the chairman of the Public Works and Transportation Subcommittee on Surface Transportation offered a successful amendment on the House floor to remove the ceiling, the Budget Committee tried to reinstate the ceiling in the final version in conference committee. No one would accuse Chairman Howard of undue restraint when he vented his feelings:

> The Committee on the Budget, through its chairman and ranking minority member, has taken it upon itself to advise the House conferees to run up the white flag and surrender—or perhaps betray might be a more appropriate word—the expressed will of the House. In all my years in the House of Representatives, I cannot recall a more arrogant reach for power than this attempt to sell out our own conference stand and reverse the majority decision of the House.[32]

Controlling expenditure will not necessarily matter much unless revenue also is adjusted. Bringing resource allocation together with resource mobilization is, after all, the major purpose of the budget reform. This requires the cooperation (read, to some extent, subordination) of revenue committees.

It is in the Senate that the clash between the Budget and Finance committees has been most severe. Chairman Muskie of SBC was interested in the big picture. As he told the Senate, the Budget Committee "is not a line-item committee."[33] Tax preferences cause so much loss of revenue and, indeed, are so much an alternative form of accomplishing the same purpose as expenditures, Muskie felt, that to ignore them would be to nullify efforts at budget control. In colorful language, he raised and answered the rhetorical question:

> Are we supposed to meet each March to propose a congressional budget and then retire to the cloakroom until the fall, when it is too late to advise the Senate of the implications of its tax and spending decisions? And then pop back out like some unwelcome jack-in-the-box each fall to shout, "Surprise! You've blown the budget."? Hardly.[34]

Not to be outdone, Senator Russell Long, chairman of the Committee on Finance, retorted, "The chairman of the Budget Committee cannot

[32]*Ibid.*, p. 1350.
[33]*Ibid.*, pp. 1348–49.
[34]*Ibid.*, p. 1347.

find anything small enough for the Finance Committee to decide anything about."[35] Back at the House, an HBC staff member expressed dismay at such direct confrontation, saying, "We're aware that we'll get killed if we take on other committees head to head. All we have to work with is the good will of other committees."[36]

Public spending could be described as engaging in a game of reverse musical chairs—when the music stops, there are extra chairs to fill. The golden rule of agencies and program advocates is that each may do unto the other as the other does unto it while there still is more for both. But never, never shall one agency or program break the chain by taking resources from another; to "beggar thy neighbor" is *verboten*. Extraordinary programs, with special appeal, may go up so long as others do not go down. Even when defense spending in the 1970s declined as a proportion of total spending, defense retained the same constant dollar amount it had had since 1955. There is, in the language of evolution, selection "up" but not "out."

How were these happy accommodations possible? Because the public sector was able to solve its internal problems by absorbing the growth of the private sector. But when that easy avenue was blocked by economic decline, the necessity for resource subtraction, as well as resource addition, was brought home.

The budget reform was designed to help Congress relate obligations to income by setting targets for total expenditures. Senator Muskie said of legislators' simultaneously voting for more spending and lower budget deficits, "We just can't make the system work with that kind of philosophy."[37] Yet Joel Havemann has reported several instances of congressmen engaging in this sort of behavior on the grounds, as one put it, "That's the beauty of the budget process. You can vote for all your favorite programs, and then vote against the deficit."[38] What, then, has

[35] *Ibid.*, p. 1348.
[36] *Ibid.*
[37] See Aaron Wildavsky, "Ask Not What Budgeting Does to Society but What Society Does to Budgeting." Introduction to the second edition of *National Journal Reprints* (Washington, D.C., 1977), p. 4.
[38] *Ibid.* See Mark S. Kamlet, David Mowery, and Gregory Fischer, "Modelling Budgetary Tradeoffs: An Analysis of Congressional Macrobudgetary Priorities, the Impact of the Congressional Budget Act, and the Reagan Counterrevolution." Paper prepared for the Midwest Political Science Association Meetings, Chicago, Illinois, April 22, 1983; and

happened to congressional efforts to engage in economic management?

To increase spending, no coordination is necessary; program advocates already want to do that. To decrease spending, coordination is essential. Without spending ceilings that require choice among programs, budgeting by addition rather than subtraction remains common practice.

Once it becomes commonly understood that limits are elastic, no one has sufficient incentive to abide by them. In Denmark, for instance, governments have not abided by the limits they presumably imposed on themselves. Why not? Christensen explains:

> . . . that for the public sector there is no such thing as resource scarcity. Even if resources may be scarce in the sense that demand for public expenditure always exceeds the resources available, a normal political response to this kind of resource scarcity has been to expand the total amount of resources available for public sector purposes. In other words, if resources are scarce in the public sector, they have to be made so politically. . . . Such processes should . . . make it politically possible to repudiate claims for supplementary appropriations which exceed the official limits for public sector growth. . . . Nothing like that happens.[39]

Reagan's tax cuts and deficits provided those limits.

POLARIZATION: CLASSICAL BUDGETING WITHERS WITHOUT QUITE DISAPPEARING

President Reagan wanted to accompany his tax cuts with deep slashes in domestic spending. In this he failed. He did, however, achieve a substantial ($30 billion) cut in 1981 that holds a lesson for students of budgeting. When congressmen are urged to cut desired programs, they are reluctant to do so not only on substantive grounds but also because they have good reason to believe that others will take up the resulting slack and add the savings to quite different programs. The point of this

Louis Fisher, "In Dubious Battle? Congress and the Budget," *The Brookings Bulletin,* Vol. 17 (Spring 1981), pp. 6–10.

[39]Jorgen Gronnegard Christensen, "Growth by Exception: Or the Vain Attempt to Impose Resource Scarcity on the Danish Public Sector," *Journal of Public Policy,* Vol. 2 (May 1982), p. 140.

story is that it is not worthwhile for anyone to cut unless others also must do so. After all, the advantage of the cuts, if any, lies in cumulating them so as to make a substantial impact on the deficit. The reconciliation procedure provided in the Budget Act of 1974 was invoked to create that incentive to cut. By requiring a vote on all cuts taken together, rather than one at a time as usual (so a large cumulative cut would emerge), participants could see that there was some point in sacrifice.

Suppose you and I agree to cut out our preferred programs in the common interest of debt reduction. That would do no good unless everybody else did the same. If our loss is someone else's spending gain, why should we play this game? This point emerges from a study of the great tax reform of 1986. When congressmen are asked to give up various tax preferences one at a time, they resist because there is no way to get everybody in the act. By aggregating the revenue saved from the reduction of tax preferences into a large-enough amount to afford large-scale tax relief, however, the gordian knot of tax reform was cut. Lower tax rates could be exchanged for fewer and smaller tax preferences. Package deals have become part and parcel of budgetary negotiations.

But deals of any kind require people who agree sufficiently to come to a compromise. Increasingly it became clear that compromise on the budget would be difficult to obtain. The president wanted higher defense spending, much lower domestic spending, and no tax increases. The opposition wanted higher taxes, lower defense spending, and higher domestic spending than did the president. Each insisted that their preferred programs were not up for negotiation. The result was stalemate. From 1982 on, the budgetary process slowed down. Individual appropriations were delayed. Continuing resolutions came to replace the ordinary budget process. Dissensus was the order of the day.

By 1982 it became clear that the old appropriations process was not long for this world. It had been ailing for quite a while, as its lifeblood—spending control—oozed away to other committees, especially taxing committees. In the 1970s the appropriations committees had moved away from their role as guardians of the Treasury.[40] A combination of appointing advocates to appropriations and the existence of budget

[40]Schick, *Congress and Money*.

committees did the trick. With more liberal Democratic members and more conservative Republicans, the policy distance among members grew, thereby reducing internal cohesion. And as budget committees were placed over appropriations committees, the spending committees tended to regard their recommendations not as likely to be final but rather as opening bids in a sequence of negotiations. Like the executive spending agencies, therefore, appropriations subcommittees tended to pad their favorite programs so as to leave room for cutting by budget committees and by action on the floor.

New patterns began to emerge. Neither the guardian norm nor spending control had totally disappeared. Indeed, spending control was what made appropriations decisions worth contesting. But appropriations politics became vastly more centralized—a contest not only among committees and agencies, but also among OMB and congressional leaders, whose differences were not so much about individual programs as about spending totals or about the largest possible divisions—domestic versus defense—within them.

Little in Congress is completely original; heirs to old practices tend to bear some resemblance to their parents. So it was with appropriations. Committees continued to write bills and party leaders within the committees still had important roles in bargaining and in floor maneuvers. Many programmatic differences (especially on defense) were worked out in committee. In small matters, the attention to district interests, which critics of all political persuasions find so unseemly, remained. So did the unusual nonpartisanship of House appropriations staff, especially compared to the partisan rancor in the House budget committee. Most important, the appropriations committees still held the role of translating program preferences into the line-item language of appropriations acts. Therefore they maintained a crucial position in the process of program funding.

It is equally true that dominant features of the new system existed in embryo, or on occasion, before 1981. Supplemental appropriations and continuing resolutions were nothing new,[41] and the barriers between

[41]Louis Fisher, "The Authorization–Appropriation Process in Congress: Formal Rules and Informal Practices," *Catholic University Law Review*, Vol. 29, No. 1 (Fall 1979), pp. 52–105.

authorization and appropriation politics already had been diminishing for quite a while.[42] But the relationship among all these parts of the process changed drastically as the broad sweep of partisan budget politics, reflecting deep division over public policy, took primacy over the management of agencies and distribution of benefits through appropriations oversight. The new policy partisanship did not so much displace the old as subsume it.

BUDGETING FOR THE EXECUTIVE OFFICE OF THE PRESIDENT

In contrast to the battles over appropriatons for domestic and military spending, the budget for the Executive Office of the President (EOP) for the most part remains untouched and little noticed. While the amount (approximately $100 million for FY87) is not that large when compared to other budget categories, I do not believe this quiescence can be attributed solely to the size of the expenditure. After all, Congress has become involved in budgetary disputes over much smaller items.

History provides the backdrop for congressional neglect of this budget category. From the beginning of the republic, Congress has refused to direct how the president must spend the funds appropriated for his personal expenses. At the same time early Congresses were specifying exceedingly small line items of expenditures, these same Congresses also voted a lump-sum compensation for the president (rather than distinguishing between presidential salary and expenses).

This tradition of comity, the willingness of Congress to let the president have the funds he requests for his own staff, so long as he does not question what it spends on itself, continues into the present (interrupted only briefly during Watergate). The consequence, according to John Hart, of "comity between the legislative and executive branches of government has rendered the appropriations process impotent as a tool of fiscal oversight of the presidential branch."[43] Although Congress is

---

[42]Fisher, "In Dubious Battle," pp. 6–10.
[43]John Hart, *The Presidential Branch*, typescript, p. 241.

better informed now about the EOP than it was in the 1950s and 1960s, Congress still makes little effort to question what the funds are being used for, to investigate whether the requested expenses are necessary, or to oversee how the money is actually spent.

Until 1978, most funds for White House staff were appropriated without being authorized. In 1978 the White House Personnel Authorization-Employment Act authorized EOP staff levels. But the act still does not indicate who does what in the White House, thus clouding attempts by Congress to exercise effective oversight.

In the age of dissensus, however, everything is potentially controversial. While the EOP has thus far remained immune from the budgetary debate, suggestions have been made that indicate that Congress has an eye on the executive. As an apparent slap at President Reagan, the House initially cut requested FY85 funds for the Office of Administration and for salaries and expenses for the White House and the OMB (although most of the funding was later restored). Representative Levitas (D-Ga.) exclaimed that the cuts were an effort to show the president that "charity and spending cuts should begin at home."[44]

BUDGETING FOR CONGRESS

Just as Congress pays little attention to the budget for the presidential branch, so presidents rarely clash with Congress over funds for the legislative branch. "Although the president makes a legislative branch budget request, Congress writes the figures and the administration includes them in the budget without comment."[45]

Unlike the budget for the EOP, the legislative budget is significantly larger. The $1.6 billion appropriated for 1987 includes $307.6 million for Senate operations, $463.9 million for House operations, and $103.1 million for joint items (franking [free mail] being the largest item in this account). Legislative appropriations also fund other congressional opera-

[44]Congressional Quarterly Weekly Report, July 7, 1984, p. 1652.
[45]Congressional Quarterly Weekly Report, June 30, 1984, p. 1591.

tions, such as the Office of Technology Assessment and the Congressional Budget Office, and provide money for related agencies, such as the Library of Congress and the General Accounting Office.

The calm between the executive and legislative branches is not reflective of the budget process within the legislature. Unlike the drafting of the budget for the EOP, the development of legislative appropriations is acrimonious. Significant partisan attacks occur during markup. Republicans charge Democrats with waste and patronage while Democrats in turn attack Republicans for making the process into a political sideshow. But controversy also cuts across partisan lines, especially where the franking privilege is concerned. Franking, which allows members of Congress to send out mail without postage, thus reaching their constituents at low costs to themselves, has increased from $61.9 million in 1980 to an estimated $144.5 million in 1986. Despite efforts in the past to restrain franking, it has become "one of the most cherished privileges in Congress, defended jealously by both Republicans and Democrats."[46]

As an indication of the level of conflict over legislative funding, between 1979 and 1985 the Senate never passed the funding bill. Rather, operations were funded through continuing resolutions. In this era of budget cutting, we would expect increased conflict over limited dollars as Congress comes under increasing pressure to show restraint. Cuts mandated by Gramm–Rudman–Hollings have already forced Congress to decrease staff, staff salaries, and restrict printing and distribution of congressional documents.

The tradition of comity was broached, however, when Reagan proposed a 10 percent across-the-board cut in legislative funding in 1985. Representative Vic Fazio, Chairman of the House Appropriations Legislative Subcommittee, expressed his dismay at Reagan's proposal: "That's an unprecedented break with comity between the branches. We usually get back whatever we send over."[47] Such are the uncertainties that dissensus brings to even the most inviolate spheres.

---

[46]*Congressional Quarterly Weekly Report,* October 19, 1985, p. 2109.
[47]*Congressional Quarterly Weekly Report,* February 9, 1985, p. 248.

INSTITUTIONAL MANIFESTATIONS OF BUDGETARY DISSENSUS

5

THE BATTLES OVER THE BUDGET that have been waged from the end of the 1970s until today are remarkable. Neither in American history nor in contemporary budgeting in other industrial democracies do we see their like. Disagreement over the size or scope or content of budgets has been a frequent occurrence before and after the founding of the American republic, but not all of these at once. Never have budget battles been pursued for so long. The only period of comparable intensity is far in our past. I refer to the largely successful efforts of colonial legislatures to hamstring royal governors by keeping them on the shortest possible string. And we know what happened: The colonists' refusal to pay taxes as well as to grant sufficient supplies to the governors were indeed an indicator of profound polarization, leading to the Revolution. Even then, however, the budget did not take up everyone's time; and budgets, albeit unsatisfactory to the king's men, were passed.

Inability to reduce spending is certainly not unique to the United States; virtually all industrial democracies suffer from that disease. Raising taxes, however, is not generally the problem, though most of these other industrial nations willingly do so because they simply are not rich enough to pay for all they want. By contrast, the United States could raise revenue but is divided over whether it should. The other democracies agree on objectives; they just lack the means; America has the means but differs over the ends. And that difference matters more because the separation of powers institutionalizes these differences by giving the opposing sides independent platforms from which to carry on their struggle.

None of the other nations with which we compare ourselves experienced prolonged difficulty in agreeing on a budget, or fought essentially the same issues over and over again with the same high intensity and as little conclusiveness as have Americans. By any measure—time, intensity, dissensus, historical or contemporary comparison—the budgetary battles of our time are extraordinary. It is not surprising, therefore, that the institutions and practices concerned with budgeting have undergone substantial change.

OMB IN AN ERA OF PERENNIAL BUDGETING

As governing and budgeting became equivalent in the late 1970s and the 1980s, the part played by the Office of Management and Budget (OMB) was bound to be more important than it had been. No matter who was (or is) the director of the budget, the rise of budget resolutions, continuous resolutions, reconciliation, the deficit, the strategic centrality of negotiations over the size and composition of taxing and spending, the ensuing stalemate (and hence the extraordinary degree to which budgeting crowds out other issues)—any, or all, of these would have made OMB more pivotal. David Stockman, a man of exceptional force and talent, and President Reagan's Director of the Budget from 1981 to 1985, speeded up the transformation of OMB from an agency-centered to a congressionally centered presidential adviser-cum-negotiator. Stockman also gave this change an enhanced centralized slant. But under circumstances in which the budget dominated policy making, no one could have prevented OMB from being a key player.

In order to separate cause from effect—OMB as prime mover from OMB as responding to larger trends—we must make a nuanced interpretation of its part in these events. Since its establishment in 1921, when it was cutting small sums, to its revitalization in the late 1930s—and again after the Second World War as presidential staff agency with a cutting bias—OMB (then the Bureau of the Budget) has counted itself (and has been considered by others) to be powerful. Without money of its own, without authority except what the president lends it, and without a large staff (around 200 examiners being the norm), OMB has long been an elite unit. It is one of the best places to be. Service there counts high for promotion elsewhere. The sense of service to the president, upon whose backing all depends, coupled with a belief that this central staff has a national (rather than parochial) viewpoint, has long created a strong esprit de corps.

While it is true that the BOB (and later OMB) participated in a process of budgeting from below (bureau requests, departmental review, submission to and revision by the Director's Review, recommendation to the president, limited agency appeal, final president's budget, congressional validation by use of this budget as its starting point), this was not the whole truth. At least since World War II, when Keynesian doctrines were dominant, BOB–OMB also has worked from the top down.[1] Considerations of fiscal policy, involving the effects of total expenditure and revenue on the economy, mattered. Presidents Truman and Eisenhower believed in (and, to a considerable extent, achieved) balanced budgets. Deeply concerned about inflation, they applied strong downward, or carefully controlled upward, pressure on spending. Although their formulas differed—Truman took revenues, subtracted desirable domestic spending, and left the remainder for defense; Eisenhower subtracted desirable defense from revenues, reserving the rest for domestic purposes—their goals of price and employment stability, reinforced by balanced budgets, were similar. President Kennedy used tax cuts to get a sluggish economy moving without the pain of significant inflation or large deficits.

The usual practice was for OMB to conduct a Spring Preview in

[1]David C. Mowery, Mark S. Kamlet, and John P. Crecine, "Presidential Management of Budgetary and Fiscal Policymaking," *Political Science Quarterly,* Vol. 95, No. 1 (Fall 1980), pp. 395–425.

which likely spending demands (estimated by OMB staff) were compared to expected revenues; then both were manipulated to achieve
desired effects on the economy. Agency spending bids, therefore, were
made in a controlled context. Because agencies were told how high they
could go, they could accurately translate administration intentions into
a loose (ask for more) or tight (keep what you've got) budget request.
Agencies could appeal to the president or make an end-run to Congress.
But such attempts had to be limited not only because they might fail
but also because, given limited time and attention, extra political efforts
were better reserved for the most important issues. On run-of-the-mill
stuff, the guts of agency activities, OMB recommendations were likely
to be final.

There is now a pronounced difference. Working largely top down is
not the same as working largely bottom up. Once budget examiners used
to examine; they went into detail on programs, made field visits, and
otherwise kept track of agency programs. Some still do; many do not.
Now most examiners deal with aggregates, with total agency spending.
Within that total, agencies are freer to spend as they wish (subject, of
course, to congressional constraints and clientele demands). The price
of this enhanced discretion is increased uncertainty. There may be not
only less money but its flow also may be interrupted by delay, deferrals,
rescissions, the latest continuous round of negotiations, stalemate followed by continuing resolutions, on and on. Budgetary planning is not
easy. The decline of the annual budget, early decisions good for a year,
is but the other side of the coin of continuous budgeting.

Differences in quantity, if they are large enough, may become differences in quality. BOB–OMB always had relations with Congress. There
were always appropriations committees. Since these committees were
even more important then than they are today (taking up a larger share
of the budget), the director and his chief aides, including top civil
servants specializing in public works and other matters of interest to
these legislators, had frequent contact with appropriations committees.
Failure to pass appropriations on time or the need for supplementals or
raising the debt ceiling required OMB to arrange a policy position for
the Executive Branch. The difference today lies in the increased fre-

quency of contacts, the institutional arrangements facilitating them, and the character of the interactions.

Today totals dominate all discussion. How much, not what for, is the first question. Nor can there be much room for analysis when the only question of allocation is how much for welfare and how much for defense. Escaping from macro choices over total taxing and spending, moreover, is hardly possible when the Budget Act of 1974 requires an annual resolution to do just that, a requirement reinforced by the establishment of congressional budget committees whose main assignment this is.

"The creation of the budget committees," Bruce Johnson writes, "gave the OMB its own committees to work through. OMB became a client of the budget committees—perhaps their chief client—like the Veterans Administration is a client of the Veterans committees. A similarity of purpose grew, and staff-to-staff contacts developed. The budget committees became a window through which the OMB could view and influence Congress."[2] Given the assumed role of the Senate Budget Committee as spokesman for responsible finance—that is, deficit reduction through increased control over budget authority—it is a natural ally of OMB. OMB also becomes a window through which SBC can obtain information about executive office discussion, and thus leverage in trying to influence executive policies. When the Executive Office of the President reaches out to external constituencies, by the same token, SBC reaches in. For what is going on in Congress then becomes a part of White House deliberation.

Partisanship and ideology also influence executive–legislative relationships. The informal cooperation between SBC and OMB depended in part on the fact that from 1981 to 1986 the Senate was Republican while the House was Democratic. It remains to be seen whether this symbiosis will continue under a Democratically controlled Senate. As policy differences between moderate Senate Republicans and the more conserva-

---

[2]Bruce Johnson, "The Increasing Role of the Office of Management and Budget in the Congressional Budget Process." Paper prepared for the Fifth Annual Research Conference of Association for Public Policy Analysis and Management, Philadelphia, October 21–22, 1983, p. 6.

tive Reagan administration deepened, moreover, it became more difficult for OMB and SBC to maintain informal cooperation. OMB and SBC became antagonists, but the early reasons for their cooperation remain and may well reassert themselves.

The existence of the Congressional Budget Office (CBO) has been the scene for another mixed-motive game. Unlike the old days, OMB no longer has carte blanche in manipulating agency estimates. Should events prove CBO's spending estimates more accurate in too many instances, OMB's reputation suffers. Over time, therefore, the staffs of the two agencies have come closer together. This regard is furthered by the substantial presence in both organizations of economists (the two heads of CBO have been economists) with similar perspectives about how to value governmental programs. This does not mean that the two organizations harmoniously coexist. Much of President Reagan's first term was marked by strenuous disagreement between the OMB and CBO over economic assumptions and deficit projections.

Changes in attention (the financial markets, other governments, and congressional budget committees observe total spending) and in process (continuous budgeting) have made the central budget agency more important. Bruce Johnson has it just right.

> To respond immediately to changing financial market reactions to the Federal budget, the Executive branch has to be able to change the budget quickly. Only the OMB can perform this function for the Executive branch. The fine-tuning of fiscal policy is now occurring every 3 to 6 months when it used to be an annual affair.
>
> Not only is the Executive branch, under the guidance of the OMB, formally changing its budget requests to Congress more frequently, but *implicit* Administration budget policy is changing almost monthly as a result of compromises struck with Congress. . . . Each time a new "bipartisan compromise" is announced by the President, the Administration's internal budget estimates change (although for public consumption they may just receive an asterisk to show they are out of date). Various deals are also struck with Congress as the appropriations bills wind their way through committee floor and conference action. OMB is the only Executive branch agency able to sum the totals of all the give and take of the Congressional process to see where the budget estimates are going. The importance of budget "scorekeeping"—keeping track of all these deals—

has been increased by the emphasis on budget projections and their importance to the financial community. For this reason alone, the OMB has
assumed a leading role in negotiating budget and fiscal policy adjustments
with Congress.[3]

Had total spending not become all-important, neither would OMB. It
is the concentration on totals, combined with the requirement for annual budget resolutions, together with the possibility of invoking reconciliation, and, so long as it lasts, the necessity of avoiding or following
Gramm–Rudman–Hollings sequestration procedure, that make the central budget agency so central. When one budgets all the time, budgeters
may indeed get more tired, but also they become more important.

Though any specific starting point must be arbitrary, the entry of
OMB into congressional negotiations may be traced to the time of
James T. McIntyre, Jr., President Carter's budget director, who gradually recognized the need for stronger contact with Congress. He increased his liaison staff from two to six.[4] When Carter submitted his
last full budget, the fact that it had a (what, in retrospect, looks like a
tiny) $16 billion deficit so discomforted the financial markets and con-
gressional leaders, already down on the president, that it was withdrawn. After a week of negotiation with Democratic party leaders,
McIntyre helped resubmit a new budget. In order to implement the
deficit-reduction package (the first of many to follow), McIntyre made
novel use of the then-dormant reconciliation procedure. Given the
short time available, McIntyre, instead of going through the authorizations, appropriations, and finance committees, dealt only with top
party and committee leaders.

As Carter began to squeeze the budget in FY80, OMB took a more
active role in lobbying Congress for the president's preferences. The
budget negotiations of March 1980 and subsequent continuing resolution difficulties increased the relative influence of OMB. David
Mathiasen, deputy assistant director for budget review at OMB, has
noted that more important than the package of cuts in 1980 was "the

---

[3]*Ibid.*, pp. 7–8.
[4]Jonathan Rauch, "Stockman's Quiet Revolution at OMB May Leave Indelible Mark
on Agency," *National Journal*, Vol. 7, No. 21 (May 25, 1985), p. 1213.

way in which this revision took place. Traditionally the American budget has been developed by the executive and presented to the Congress and the public without formal discussions or negotiations. . . . In contrast, the 1981 budget revisions were literally negotiated between executive branch representatives (primarily the Office of Management and Budget and the White House) and the leadership in both houses of the Congress."[5] The emphasis should be on *negotiating* spending legislation.

The 1980 (fiscal 1981) budget battles therefore foreshadowed a situation in which detailed examination of agency performance and estimates by appropriations committee members would have less influence on spending decisions. When "how much" matters more than "what for," agencies and appropriations subcommittees matter less than the actors (presidents and congressional leaders) who negotiate about totals. When these legislative leaders vary from time to time, however, according to who can craft the necessary compromise, the process becomes less predictable. The combination of more intractable problems with more numerous and diverse participants spells trouble.

Stockman institutionalized the ad hoc developments of 1980 and took them a giant step further. He sent a list of proposals for cuts, with accompanying explanations, to Capitol Hill, following them up with personal visits to assess reaction. Earlier, under the Ford administration in the mid-1970s, Director James Lynn had used similar advocacy papers, and Carter's director, McIntyre, had sometimes utilized the requirement under the Budget Impoundment and Control Act for narrative statements explaining how actions met "national needs" to sell the budget. Stockman provided the all-time hard sell. He was able to gauge support from reactions to his proposals, all the while making program supporters feel lucky to get by with cuts that, though modest by Stockman's standards, were considerably larger than agencies otherwise would have contemplated.[6]

Stockman changed OMB's focus from the examining and assembling

---

[5]"Recent Developments in the Composition and Formulation of the United States Federal Budget," *Public Budgeting and Finance* (Autumn 1983), p. 107.

[6]Bruce Johnson, "From Analyst to Negotiator: The OMB's New Role," *Journal of Policy Analysis and Management,* Vol. 3, No. 4 (1984), p. 507.

of agency requests to that of lobbying the administration budget through Congress. Budget examiners spent far less time in the field getting to know their agencies. Instead, staff was dedicated to tracking budget action through the multiple stages of the congressional process—resolutions were tracked from budget committees to the floor and into conference, out again into appropriations subcommittee and full committee markups, to reappearance on the floor in a continuing resolution, then again in a regular appropriations bill, seemingly settled only to pop up again in markup on a supplemental. To facilitate this tracking, Stockman ordered the development of a computer system that aggregated budget items by both budget function categories and committee jurisdictions, allowing him to trace the spending implications of action at all levels. He also increased the size of the OMB unit that was tracking spending legislation through Congress. Stockman could afford to take this course because there was nothing that he really needed to know about the agencies. For at least a few years he could get by on previous analysis by OMB, the extensive literature produced by GAO, CBO, and the think tanks, and his own preferences about what government should and should not do. Ideology provided a substitute for information. The new OMB approach, Hale Champion commented, therefore "almost excluded cabinet departments and agencies from the formulation of the budget."[7]

Since Stockman (and the president) were interested in achieving a preferred set of cuts, not in using the budget to finance agencies, OMB also moved away from the norm of annual budgeting. The annual budget served many needs, but its primary purpose was to regularize the funding, and therefore functioning, of government agencies. Funded for a year in advance, an agency would be able to plan and coordinate its activities. Since in many cases the administration either did not care about these agency functions or was convinced it knew a better (and, not coincidentally, cheaper) way to do the job, in 1981 and 1982 Stockman discarded the norm of annualarity, proposing instead large rescis-

[7]*Federal Budget Policy in the 1980s,* Urban Institute, p. 292. Also see Hugh Heclo, "Executive Budget Making," in Gregory B. Mills and John L. Palmer, eds., *Federal Budget Policy in the 1980s* (Washington, D.C.: Urban Institute Press, 1984).

sions—administratively imposed cuts of previously approved appropriations. Basically the budget was under continuous negotiation so that even a place in the formal budget did not guarantee funding at the once-agreed level. Federal agencies, therefore, were whipsawed back and forth, torn between hope and fear that their allocations would be changed during the year. Predictability of spending flows, and whatever short-term planning went with it, were lost.

OMB also gave up its role as protector of agencies against sudden and unreasonable reductions. The place of agencies in the new appropriations process was both precarious and peculiar. Both their budget authority and staffing levels (also partially controlled through that process) were unpredictable. Many agencies were running reduction-in-force (RIF) operations, which were designed to reduce employment while maintaining civil service preferences and protections against political bias. RIFs and a twist called RIF exercises—in which procedures were war-gamed in a drill to determine who would land where in the game of civil-service musical chairs—were spreading fear and chaos in agencies far out of proportion to actual layoffs.

There is no doubt that Stockman was knowledgeable. That matters, partly because information is the medium through which policy is negotiated. It is important as well that staff, allies, and adversaries be made aware that they are dealing with someone who is factually smart. Whether Stockman was also institutionally smart—able to create and sustain social relationships that facilitated his goals—was less certain.

After the congressional elections of 1982 increased Democratic majorities in the House and discomfited the Republican majority in the Senate, reconciliation no longer seemed a viable option to the administration. Nor—considering the liberal Democratic majority in the House and the moderate Republican party Senate majority, which wanted higher taxes and lower defense spending—was Reagan likely to get acceptable budget resolutions. Therefore, Bruce Johnson explains,

> In the absence of a budget resolution acceptable to the president, the director of the OMB attempted to impose presidential budget targets on the various appropriation bills. Because of the implicit and sometimes explicit threat of a presidential veto, the OMB was successful in exerting

such influence in an area of decision normally reserved for an agency and its appropriation subcommittees. Thus, although the process of budget resolution and reconciliation was near collapse in 1983, the OMB continued to be active in the appropriation process, attempting to sell pieces of the president's budget to Congress in that forum.[8]

One might well say that OMB became the president's lobbyist in Congress.

Within OMB, the realization was growing that the budgetary game had undergone decisive changes. Resolutions did not carry enforcement powers; they could not be counted on to pass; if they did, they often were not enforced. Failing to agree meant only that the real play was in a continuing resolution. Besides, appropriations committees could work without a resolution. Authorizations mattered for entitlements but big ones were unbudgeable and little ones didn't move much. Not much point in talking to authorizers when there are no new programs.

Discovering by 1984 that it could not get authorizations down far enough to bite, OMB concentrated almost entirely on discretionary appropriations and, within that, on the 302(b) allocations under which appropriations committees divided the amount they received from budget committees. Like the old joke about the man who looks for his collar button under the street lamp rather than where he lost it—because the light is better there—OMB concentrated on the pieces of the budget it could do something about. This focus on appropriations accounted for the bulk of time Director Stockman spent negotiating with committee members as well as tracking bills. Before deals could be struck on appropriations, it was necessary to estimate how much they were worth and where the bill was located in the process.

OMB expanded its handful of bill trackers to thirteen, one for each of the major committees. Trackers infiltrated hearings, got data whenever they could, and immediately prepared letters to all concerned on Capitol Hill about whether they thought savings were real or illusory. Keeping score is serious business. But why is it necessary?

The appropriations committees can transfer funds from an entitlement to a discretionary account. This maneuver has the effect of increas-

[8]Johnson, "From Analyst to Negotiator," p. 504.

ing discretionary spending while often creating a shortfall in the entitlement, a shortfall that has to be made good in the future. Two examples are transfers of $39 million to the Agriculture Extension Service from food stamps and $66 million from the CCC (Commodity Credit Corporation) reimbursement for prior year losses to the Conservation Service. OMB's bill trackers do not treat such transfers as savings, but the appropriations committees may use them to fit within the budget resolution.[9]

OMB scores as increases in spending transfers from unobligated balances in one account, say, Small Business Administration disaster funds, unlikely to be used, to other accounts, say salary and expenses, that will be used. The amount may be the same—$100 million for the Coast Guard—but the account may differ—a transfer from the navy. Since conflicts occur over the size of defense, OMB wants to charge the amount to domestic, not to defense.

OMB wants to show the amounts authorized in a fiscal year even if they are not spent in that year. Advance appropriations, to be spent in future years, no further action required, and appropriations deferred because they lack authorization, although funds are likely to be provided in a supplemental or continuing resolution, are not scored in that year by Appropriations but they are scored by OMB. Reasonable people might disagree. Similarly, where supplements are routinely provided, as for fire fighting, or discretionary activities are purposely underfunded in OMB's opinion, it will score the funds as if they had been fully appropriated. There are also occasional adjustments, such as provisions for savings—pay reductions or delayed repayments of loans—that never materialize, which OMB scores as spending.

Among the most important and most controversial scoring choices is the distinction OMB makes (and would like appropriations committees to make) between discretionary and entitlement programs. A cut in appropriations for a discretionary program is indeed a cut. But an apparent reduction in spending for an entitlement "not accompanied," in OMB's words, "by language in appropriations bills to reduce the statu-

[9]OMB, "OMB's Scoring of Appropriations Bills," March 4, 1986.

tory spending requirements are not scored by OMB as reductions." No doubt there will be disagreement on OMB's promised list of what it considers discretionary versus mandatory for that too would affect scoring.

This emphasis on scoring, reinforced by a cadre of OMB bill trackers, testifies to the importance of the deficit, hence the significance of progress toward reduction and the temptation to appear to be saving more or less depending on the political needs of the moment. For their part, appropriations people figure OMB is cheating when it tells them to cut entitlements that are outside their jurisdiction.

As OMB improved its congressional intelligence, thus being able to intervene in the right subcommittees at the right time, it sought further to streamline its task by combining consideration of appropriations hitherto dealt with separately. The development of continuing resolutions, from stopgap funding to program changes with future spending implications, provided OMB with another point of entry.[10] OMB was monitoring spending not only in agencies but also in Congress. Would the role of salesman to Congress of spending cuts, the OMB staff wondered, interfere with its tradition of neutral competence and general repository of wisdom about the value of programs?

The director's use of budget examiners as personal staff or, better still, as research assistants, became well known. According to a civil servant, "It's not uncommon to be called over there—boom, boom—and have him say, 'OK, I've prepared this presentation, I want you to check it and fill in the numbers.' And he'll say, bring it back tomorrow."[11] Not everyone cares for this kind of spot-research role. Observers worry that OMB's stature as an institution to serve presidents and the Executive branch over the long term may decline while its political clout temporarily increases. Hugh Heclo, for instance, is troubled "that the capacity for loyal independence . . . may have diminished over time."[12] Heclo quotes an OMB division director: "He [Stockman] bangs on you for

[10]Johnson, "From Analyst to Negotiator," and "Increasing Role of the Office of Management and Budget."
[11]Rauch, "Stockman's Quiet Revolution," p. 1215.
[12]Interview quoted in Rauch, "Stockman's Quiet Revolution."

information on the day that he needs it. He doesn't think about how to strengthen the agency's general ability to provide what is wanted. He gets what he wants when he wants it and wherever he can. He doesn't say to himself, I'd better get an organization and process in motion to be able to supply what is needed."[13]

There are, as usual, two sides to this story. OMB had become somewhat demoralized due to low morale in the Carter administration in general, and to disregard of administration recommendations in particular. There is nothing better for restoring high spirits than having a respected director who is on the winning side. OMB under Stockman was an important and exciting place for those staff members to be. His kudos became theirs. The director could not be expected to overcome presidential opposition to raising taxes or cutting defense; that was part of the old and continuing role of presidential servant. But their director was a key member of the White House legislative strategy group. He was bright, more than living up to their self-image as being the smarter service. Such strokes made up for a lot.

So far as loss of agency supervision was concerned, it was compensated for by greater OMB influence with Congress. True, examiners whose predecessors had once spent the slow summer months nosing around agencies could no longer do so. Yet, if they were honest with themselves, they knew that the old ways had started to crumble with the new requirements of the 1974 budget reform. Phenomena like budget resolutions, running totals, even reconciliation, had not been invented, only intensified, by David Stockman. The Central Budget Management System, which records existing spending-decision and projects alternatives, was inevitable in that era of conflict over totals and panic over deficits. Whatever else might be attributed to or blamed on Stockman, he was only a reflection, albeit bigger than life, of conflicts that had deep roots in the nation's political life. When he left, dissensus would remain.

Depending on one's political philosophy, the politicization of OMB began either with its predecessors (BOB as linchpin of big government under Franklin Roosevelt) or with the Reorganization Plan Number 2

[13]Heclo, "Executive Budget Making."

in 1970 under President Nixon, which established a new strata of four Program Associate Directors who were political appointees. President Carter's creation of a new Executive Associate Director for Budget to supervise the earlier four only intensified this practice. Politicization is bipartisan. It may be that more OMB staff than in the past, not just its political appointees, will move with a change of administration. Heclo is rightly interested in maintaining the ethos of OMB, that "It was not a place to be just another bureaucrat. It was a place to work for the presidency broadly understood."[14] But if the presidency is no longer "broadly understood" in the sense of presidential preferences being widely agreed, the politicization of those who serve presidents may be unavoidable.

In a polarized political environment the significance of significance, as it were, also changes. Is it significant to understand the effects on programs of changes in funding? Surely. But it may be deemed more significant to understand the implications of different programs for the size of government. If the Budget Review Division, where the big budget totals are put together, has become the place in OMB where bright young people try to go, as Heclo informs us,[15] that may be because they know where the action is. Unless and until there is consensus rather than dissensus over the size and composition of government, the division that deals with totals is where the action will continue to be.

ROLE REVERSAL

With agencies under repeated attacks, appropriations committees had to come to their defense. Committee members of both parties objected to the repeated cuts on programmatic grounds but also, and more important, because rescissions were presidential challenges to the power of Congress and to its appropriations committees. Yet the politically

[14]*Ibid.*
[15] *Ibid.*, p. 283.

appointed heads of the agencies, and their immediate civil service subordinates, formally supported most of these OMB decisions. In appropriations hearings, agency heads continually cited the need for budget restraint, or the administration's philosophy, as the reason for cuts. There were some cases in which the positions taken probably did reflect the views of the senior civil servants involved. But, generally, civil servants were testifying in obedience to the desires of their political superiors; they had to worry about the consequences for their careers of defying those superiors. This hierarchical control, as well as placement of ideological Reaganauts in policy-making positions, left agencies in the peculiar position of publicly endorsing their own suffering. The peculiarity was not that agencies had never been in such a position before—they surely had—but that saying "yes" and meaning "no" had become the standard position.

Although thus formally neutralized, civil servants could, of course, feed information secretly to the appropriations staffs. Then, in hearings, committee members would try to establish for the record that the justifications for many reductions were, in their view, insupportable. Congressmen also used hearings to inform the administration that it was stirring up hornets' nests that were best left undisturbed. A good example of a number of these themes—skepticism about agency justifications; agency leaders squirming to justify reductions; congressmen furious about the short life span of agreements with the administration; the adverse effects on agency operations; and the disregard for Congress—is provided by a Senate hearing on compensatory education and programs for special populations. Ms. Harrison, for the Department of Education, claimed that state and local governments can, and will, find cheaper ways to do things, or pick up the slack, in response to reductions in federal aid. In the circumstances of 1982 this argument won little support, since state and local governments themselves were slashing programs because of their own recessionary fiscal crisis. Mark Andrews (R-N. Dak.) was skeptical on principle:

> Ms. Harrison: Despite these cuts we do not expect a drastic reduction in the number of disadvantaged students served. However, we are projecting a lower per project cost. We also expect that State and local govern-

ments will seek more cost-effective ways of serving these students in order to offset the decreased Federal contribution. . . .

Senator Andrews: You know the impression you give us on the other side of the bench when you come up with a statement like that is that somehow or another you have found a magic way of doing exactly the same thing that has been done years ago for two-thirds of the cost. Have your people somehow or another found a way to spend in essence two-thirds of the money and have exactly the same amount of success?[16]

Clearly, Senator Andrews and his committee were not convinced. Shortly thereafter the majority whip, Senator Stevens (R-Alaska), and department representatives crossed swords over the use of rescissions. The agency argument that entitlement overruns required discretionary reductions did not win praise.

Senator Stevens: I'm greatly concerned with the 1982 rescission concept. It seems to me that [the grant recipients] have been led to believe they had money for 1982, and now you come and say there is no money for 1982. . . .

Ms. Harrison: I can only respond that this is consistent with our position in September 1981 relating to those programs. In fact, if you look at a program like the Follow Through program, that program has been proposed for phaseout and abolishment by successive administrations. These grantees are well aware of the fact that there has never been any guarantee of the money.

Senator Stevens: But successive Congresses have disagreed. So it looks like what you are telling us is that this year you are not going to spend the money in spite of the action of Congress last year. The President signed that bill last year.

Ms. Harrison: That's why we are proposing a rescission. . . .

Senator Stevens: I think the Department is just buying itself a fight. . . . There is a de facto breaking of a commitment as far as the government is concerned to those people, because you are putting us in a position of fighting the fiscal year 1982 battle again, the battle that you lost last year.

Mr. Jones: . . . In order to stay within our budget mark, we needed to stay with the President's budget request because of the nearly $1 billion supplemental request for the guaranteed student loan. So, if you subtract the supplemental from the rescission—

[16]Hearings before a Subcommittee of the Committee on Appropriations of the U.S. Senate on Departments of Labor, Health and Human Services, Education, and Related Agencies, Appropriations for FY1983, Part IV, pp. 100, 105.

> Senator Stevens: . . . What you are saying is that you are going to take
> the increasing entitlements out of discretionary funding, which you can't.
> You people are not reading Congress correctly if you think you are going
> to get away with this.[17]

No, they would not. Far more important, the principle followed—the
president's budgetary base was what he recommended last year, not
what Congress voted and he signed—signalled a radical change in the
president's role.

The Reagan administration's proposals were likely to put agency
heads in a tough spot because congressmen expected agencies to defend
their own missions. Responses of bureaucrats and political appointees
varied with their inclinations and their circumstances. Senate appropriations chairman Mark Hatfield, for example (explaining that "I happen
to be a bibliophile"), came to the defense of federal aid for libraries.
(Such aid was commonly used by conservatives as a prima facie case of
the federal government taking on what was clearly a local responsibility.
If local libraries were a federal responsibility, they argued, what wasn't?)
Testifying on behalf of their own elimination, agency representatives
insisted that states and local governments would pick up the slack. "You
and I know," Hatfield countered, "that library services are usually some
of the first to be cut or reduced in community services." Having declared
that he had their support(!), the senator then told his witnesses he would
take the matter up with the president.[18]

The observer of budgeting who overslept the 1970s, though possibly
surprised by the intransigence, nevertheless would still recognize the
classic motives. The voice might be the voice of Republican Senator
Norris Cotton ("You will forgive me, but you will not forget the Norris
Cotton Cancer Center up in Hanover, will you? That will be the only
memorial I will leave after 28 years in Congress"[19]) but the body might
be any one of a legion of legislators. An official of the National Cancer
Institute, anxious like his predecessors to follow the strategy of "spend
to save," contends that ". . . each annual cohort of patients brings into

[17]*Ibid.*, pp. 142–43.
[18]*Ibid.*, pp. 176–81.
[19]Quoted in Scott Stofel, student paper on "Budgetary Strategies."

the national economy about $3 billion. Federal revenues from their earnings is in the range of $500 million a year. So in just a cost effectiveness consideration, the program has been very productive."[20]

The "all or nothing" strategy is also alive and well. While the head of the Federal Aviation Administration (FAA) joined the Reagan administration in rallying "around to help reduce the deficit" in 1985, he was careful to point out that his agency was "a carefully woven organization designed to function as a whole."[21] Everyone knows that seamless garments should not be cut.

Voices calling for "fair shares" could still be heard. Amtrak, the government owned and operated railroad, had its reputation damaged by studies showing that every passenger cost the government $35. Without quite denying the allegation, Amtrak insisted it was "misleading and unfair" because, taking into account tax expenditures, airline passengers were subsidized even more heavily.[22]

Though our Rip-Van-budgeter might not see many differences in kind, he could not help but observe considerable differences in degree. There are many more programs whose futures are threatened by the kind of criticism that Democratic Senator Lawton Chiles called "widespread reports of fraud and abuse in CETA (Comprehensive Employee Training Administration) that have created a public attitude that threatens the very existence of the program." Democratic liberal David Obey told the CETA administrator

> You are asking for a lot of money for CETA: I think I have been a strong supporter of it in the past. But, frankly, at home, all I hear about CETA are complaints. . . . And I never hear the Federal Government getting any credit and most of the local people I talk to think the program is screwed up and I am beginning to agree with them. Do you have any evidence that the program is working, is performing the goals that we have set for it?

On the defensive, a CETA official pointed out, not unreasonably, that changing the course of a program was like "changing the direction of

[20]*Ibid.*

[21]Clifton Von Kann Testifying in Hearings before a Subcommittee of the Committee on Appropriations, Subcommittee on the Department of Transportation and Related Agencies, Appropriations, for FY1986, House of Representatives, 99th Congress, 1st Session, Part 5, April 3, 1985, p. 322.

[22]W. Graham Clayton, Jr., *ibid.*, Part 8, May 2, 1985, pp. 384–85.

a supertanker," it took time. "I think . . . ," Senator Chiles responded, "this tanker is about to be bombarded; it won't be on the high seas anymore if you don't get something done to change it." And when the senator asked for the number of people employed in the program and was given "a number more than 100,000 over," his reaction to the "false figure you gave us" was "you don't have any credibility." When Senator Warren Magnuson, then a power in the Senate, as well as chair of the Appropriations Committee, said, in regard to a request for funds that had been granted but had not been used, "You should originally have been more candid," CETA's days were numbered.

Unusual in the extreme in classical budgeting, but common during the Reagan administration, was to present cuts that looked less severe than they actually were. The Environmental Protection Agency's (EPA) press release stated that "When comparing EPA's 1981 operating and superfund budget of $1.43 billion and 10,621 work years, the President's proposal for next year represents a 2% reduction in spending." While the statement was true as far as it went, the EPA budget included $200 million for the superfund, an item that did not exist when the 1981 budget was adopted. If superfund spending is excluded, EPA's operating budget would have represented a cut of 12 percent in 1982.[23]

One relationship that has not changed is congressional dislike of presidential interference in their pet programs. Usually, it is easier just to blame OMB. Here is Representative William Scherle's complaint in 1974: "I am about as much of a conservative as anybody you will ever meet. . . . My objection to what they [OMB staffers] have done is the way they have established their priorities. I know what is good and what is bad a lot more than they do in a lot of the agencies."[24]

There are many more instances of appropriations committee members acting as program advocates than there used to be. Most often administrators show quiet appreciation. If legislators insist that the National Park Service acquire new space, using that to justify more money for maintenance, officials will play along with the "squeezed to

[23]Lawrence Mosher, "Will EPA's Budget Cuts Make It More Efficient or Less Effective?" *National Journal*, No. 33 (August 15, 1981), p. 1468.

[24]House, Hearings before the Agriculture, Environmental and Consumer Protection Subcommittee, 93rd Congress, Vol. 3, p. 766.

the wall" strategy. Explaining why NPS could not "take a cut," an NPS official gave his "personal feeling . . . that the Park Service is stretched about as thin as it can be manpowerwise and financially, given the new areas and responsibilities that have been added in the last several years."[25] So far, so much the same. As legislators have rushed to protect programs, however, their administrators have begun to fear being crushed by a too-loving embrace. Asked in 1984 what was the biggest obstacle to the improvement of Amtrak's financial position, its chairman, Graham Claytor, Jr., claimed that "the single biggest threat is that Congress will legislate reverals of management decisions that we make not to run trains that are going to cost a lot of money, or not to do cost saving things that we have undertaken to do, or not to do re-routes because there's local opposition."[26] Between those who liked them too little and those who loved them too much, federal administrators were caught between a rock and a hard place.

Hearings turned into forums for attacks on the administration that had little to do with budgets, but a lot to do with disagreement over policy. Observers witnessed the strange spectacle of agency representatives and congressmen trading barbs—hardly a model for how to get funds from guardians of the public purse. Here, for instance, David Obey was trying to score points on Occupational Health and Safety Administration (OSHA) Director Thorne Auchter, who responded in kind:

> Mr. Auchter: If I could respond to your question.
> Mr. Obey: But you are not responding.
> Mr. Auchter: But I would if you would let me get to it.
> Mr. Obey: You are giving a non answer to a question.
> Mr. Auchter: I am giving you a much better answer than the question that you asked.

Appropriations hearings became the site of policy wars between the administration and House Democrats. Often congressmen elicited information they could use to justify their positions. In one case—person-

[25]House, Hearings before the Appropriations Subcommittee for the Department of Interior and Related Agencies, 96th Congress, 2nd Session, p. 599.
[26]J61, A6, 98th Congress, #23, Part 5, House, AMTRAK, 3/29/84, p. 871.

nel levels for the National Park Service—Representative Sidney Yates (D-Ill.) established that what was really at stake was an administration preference for "contracting out" federal personnel needs, thereby reducing direct federal employment:

> Mr. Yates: It is almost like a yo-yo, because last year you added 300 employees. What is it, the Secretary giveth and the Secretary taketh away, blessed be the name of the Secretary? [Secretary of the Interior Watt was known for his religiosity.] . . . Your figures . . . do show that rather than paying $5,732,400 in employee salaries, you are going to contract that work out. . . . Let me ask somebody who operates a park. What is the advantage? Is it better to have your employees on hand, or to contract the work out? Which would you rather do?
>
> Mr. Dickenson [Russell Dickenson, Director of the National Park Service]: I have to tell you in all candor that as an experienced manager there really is no substitute to having the flexibility that comes from Federal employees. But the thrust of the Administration right now is to move into the contractor field. Therefore, we are adhering to that instruction.

The defense subcommittees on appropriations and the substantive Armed Services Committees had self-selected members with a bias toward the military. But the full Appropriations Committee in the House was more liberal than its authorizing counterpart; hence it was concerned about leaving room for social programs. The late House subcommittee chairman Joseph Addabbo was a solid liberal whose committee staff was far more suspicious of the military than was its counterpart at Armed Services. As a result, House appropriations and Addabbo were the military's most dangerous domestic adversaries, and their exchanges reflected that relationship. This excerpt from testimony on the FY82 supplemental captures the flavor of that antagonism:

> Mr. Addabbo: My spies got a copy of a memorandum to the chief of Naval Operations written by the Chief of Navy Legislature Affairs dated July 9, 1981. It was stated that: "Appropriation members and their staffs are not as thoroughly briefed and informed as their authorization counterparts." How did the Navy arrive at that conclusion? [The Navy's man made a properly deferential denial.] . . . I think they meant our staff and the members of the Appropriations Committee are not [as] brainwashed as the authorizing committee members.

If liberals were watching defense to create room for domestic spending, the conservative Reagan administration, to be sure, was attempting its own end-runs around authorizing committees in the domestic policy arena. Thus the administration's FY82 education rescissions included legislation that changed the rules on guaranteed student loans. Though such legislation was clearly out of order in an appropriations bill, that route was still more promising than going through the House Education and Labor Committee. This zeroing out of programs was a slightly more formally acceptable way to legislate through appropriations, but only slightly.

> Mr. Yates: Tell me about the historic preservation fund. Has Congress repealed the basic legislation for which you are eliminating all funds?
> Mr. Dickerson: No, sir, the Congress has not.
> Mr. Yates: Why are you eliminating the funds then?

Budget fights took so much time that little was left for floor action on authorizations. Since the widely differing positions of the administration and the authorizing committees made agreement on legislation difficult, the committees tried to hitch rides on the appropriations process, particularly the continuing resolutions, as well as to exploit reconciliation. Representative Silvio Conte expressed the appropriators' discomfort with the result. "Personally," he told the House, "I am not at all comfortable dealing with issues such as steel import licenses and the International Coffee Agreement. But," he added, "the facts of life are that when the legislative committees are not able, for whatever reason to resolve highly controversial issues, Congress will find some other way, which is usually appropriation bills."[27]

The authorization impasses further confused appropriations. In housing, for example, the administration proposed defunding programs that already existed in order to fund programs that had yet to be authorized. House Subcommittee Chair Edward Boland (D-Mass.) pointed out that the relevant authorizing committee was not about to pass the new proposal, so HUD in fact was asking for no money for anything. That was not satisfactory. When the HUD bill was passed, the committee

---

[27]*Congressional Record,* October 1, 1982, p. H8360.

ended up by postponing a decision, promising that the funds eventually authorized for whatever subsidized housing program emerged would keep total HUD funding within budget guidelines. At the end of the year, with no authorizing legislation agreed, the appropriators funded the old program, even though its authorization had lapsed. Job training, sewer grants, and transportation were other instances in which authorizing delays forced appropriators out of their usual schedule. Even when they were on schedule, however, they began to find their work undone by a new spate of impoundments.

DEFERRAL AND RESCISSION REDUX

In form (and, occasionally, in fact) the budget process as reformed in 1974 does (or could) work. Congress could attack deficits and any other problem of priorities through its resolution and reconciliation procedures. Given a determined majority in favor of a particular policy, Congress has all the necessary tools to implement its desires. The trouble so far has been the lack of majorities. Individual appropriations often do pass with substantial majorities, but these majorities differ among the thirteen appropriations bills, and the budget resolutions that are designed to tie them together have even less support. Indeed, the fact that budget resolutions require a majority of majorities—a majority comprehensive enough to integrate all other majorities—stultifies the process.

The lack of support for a central, comprehensive approach to budgeting does not come from lack of opportunity. Budget resolutions operating through budget committees give Congress an opportunity to work out a central solution. Party leadership and party caucuses are now routinely involved in budget negotiation. So is the president. What is missing, as throughout most of American history, is an agreement at the center on a solution that would be validated by legislative majorities.

The power of Congress as an institution is at odds with the power of congressmen as a collection of individuals. Congress is internally conflicted between getting its way on programs versus prevailing on totals. A more centralized procedure works, through resolutions, to get at total spending, taxing, and deficits. Budget committees and party caucuses and leaders are made important, individual legislators less so. Making (or, better still, reversing) budget decisions on the floor through shifting majorities, a decentralized approach, makes individuals more important but central leadership much less so.

Deep dissensus has led both the president and ad hoc congressional majorities to attempt to impose their will unilaterally. The provisions of the Gramm–Rudman–Hollings Act restricting presidential flexibility on defense spending illustrate the congressional effort. The struggle over the impoundment of funds reveals presidential efforts to gain by executive action what Congress will not give through its budgetary process.

Presidents can try to act on their own. They can try to forbid agencies from making requests for programs presidents want eliminated or reduced. They can reorganize units and categories so as to make it more difficult for affected interests to figure out where their money is and, therefore, how much they are being cut.[28] Presidents can impose hiring freezes and otherwise try to reduce what they consider unnecessary personnel. Their most direct approach, however, is to refuse to spend funds Congress has appropriated.

In the past, impounding was based on tacit consent; either the president's staff persuaded the committees involved, or committees indicated they would not mind too much if the money were not spent. When the Reagan administration found itself unable to persuade Congress, and as it failed to get approval for an item veto, it tried to achieve similar results by a delay or a refusal to spend. Then the courts entered the fray by calling the impounding procedure into question.

Under the act of 1974, designed to limit the president's powers, presidents can stop spending, provided that within 45 days *both* houses of Congress give their consent to this rescission. Alternatively, presidents can delay spending to the end of the fiscal year, unless the Senate *or* the House voted to override the deferral. In 1983, however *(Immigration and Naturalization Service* v. *Chadha),* the Supreme Court de-

---

[28]See Irene Rubin, *Shrinking the Federal Government: The Effect of Cutbacks on Five Federal Agencies* (New York: Longman, 1985), inter alia.

clared a legislative veto by one house an unconstitutional violation of the separation of powers. As things stand, Congress cannot overturn a deferral without passing a law to that effect. And the situation surrounding rescissions (Were they constitutional?) was confused. Thus the president could use impounding as a de facto item veto. He could wait, thus delaying spending; he could postpone until the end of the fiscal year when it might be too late for Congress to act; he could attempt to straddle the fiscal years, combining a future cut with a past deferral. "What's at stake," Democratic Representative Bruce A. Morrison explained in regard to the struggle over appropriations with a deferral, "is how many bites of the apple the President gets in the appropriations process."[29] The other view, expressed by Budget Director Miller, in testifying before Congress, was that "You took a risk in utilizing the one-house veto. Well, you rolled the dice and the President won."[30] However, as life would have it, other courts have temporarily taken the president's deferral power away.

Miller's talk was hardly the stuff to smooth already ruffled feathers in an era of budgetary dissensus. Miller cast away an agreement reached between former OMB Director David Stockman and the Appropriations Committee chairmen that OMB would not consider amendments disapproving individual deferrals to appropriations bills as grounds for a presidential veto. When Reagan used deferrals in several programs that Congress had explicitly told him to continue, Congress responded with outrage. Although the administration suggested that the deferrals were no different than deferrals in prior years, Congress felt Reagan was attempting "to an unprecedented extent . . . to implement his controversial policy goals" through this method.[31]

Efforts to distinguish between deferring spending for management efficiency and for policy impoundments foundered in a spate of accusations. Irene Rubin tells a typical story:

> In fiscal year 1983, just after the new reauthorization legislation was passed, the administration requested a deferral of expenditures for UMTA

[29]Jonathan Rauch, "Power of the Purse," *National Journal*, May 24, 1986, p. 1261.
[30]*Ibid.*, p. 1259.
[31]*National Journal*, May 24, 1986, p. 1060.

(Urban Mass Transportation Administration) of $229 million. It was not clear whether this was a technical deferral or a policy deferral because the president opposed the program, particularly parts of the new reauthorization act.

UMTA Administrator Teele presented to a congressional committee the administration's argument that the deferral was technical, based on the startup of the new gas tax trust fund. He stated that the original estimates of revenue to be produced were too high, and when the administration got the revised estimates, it asked to defer the difference between congressionally authorized spending levels and the revised amount expected to come into the trust fund.

Congressmen argued back that other trust funds were not treated in that way, that actual expenses would be paid out later when the money was present, and that the administration was in effect keeping spending way below congressionally authorized levels. Congressmen interpreted the requested deferral in light of the proposed budget reductions for 1984 and decided that the administration was still trying to implement its program of phasing out operating assistance.[32]

Unless there is agreement on the frame of reference, technical (or management) deferrals cannot be distinguished from changes in policy. The only real distinction is between programs you approve of and the ones you don't.

Congress could subject deferrals to the same procedures as rescissions so they would be nullified if Congress failed to approve them. But that would increase its workload at a time when congressmen already are sick of doing nothing but budgeting.

There's the rub: Agreement on the broad outlines of the budget—how much, what for—facilitates compromise on the details. Knowing they are headed in the same direction, participants can talk about better ways to get there. Divided as they stand, however, disagreement over policy turns in on itself in two directions: Technical management questions become policy disputes, and policy differences become converted into disputes about who has the authority to decide. While it is true that there can be no fast line between means and ends, techniques and objectives, converting every question of fact into one of value expands

---

[32]Rubin, *Shrinking the Federal Government,* p. 133.

the scope and intensity of conflict. The same is true of the old policy–administration dichotomy. It is quite wrong to imagine that Congress makes only broad policy choices while the executive branch merely implements the legislative will. If there is no difference between policy and administration at all, however—so that an administrative regulation is equivalent to a congressional statute—relationships between the branches of government would become chaotic. And that, just that, as the controversy over impoundment reveals, is beginning to happen to budgeting.

There was dissensus at every stage of the budgetary process, disagreement over policy compounded by differences over process. Deals on appropriations totals had to stretch across a variety of bills and stages of the process. Each stage's agreement required trust that all parties would perform as promised at the next stage. Of course if everybody really were reliable, they would have delivered on the spot. In fact, agreements on defense between the administration and parts of Congress kept unraveling, while at the same time antagonists ceaselessly looked for ways to make up lost ground on domestic spending. Every agreement between the Republican administration and the Democratic House eventually collapsed under charges that the legislators had not provided sufficient cuts in social programs or that the executive branch had spent too much on defense or that both had distorted the budgetary base.

THE GREAT EXCEPTION: CENTRALIZED PROCEDURE/DECENTRALIZED CONGRESS

Once upon a time, which may yet come again, program expansion came largely from agencies and their clientele. The main exceptions were FDR's Hundred Days in the early 1930s and LBJ's Great Society in the mid-1960s; then even OMB was pressed into service as a midwife of spending programs. Otherwise, agencies proposed and OMB disposed by rejection or modification. With the cutting role at the forefront, however, not only the Executive Branch but also Congress has evolved far more centralized budgetary procedures. The difference is that centralization fits the structure of authority in the Executive Branch but not in Congress.

Why has Congress, an institution noted for the dispersion of power among its members, adopted budgetary procedures that require (or at least imply) a concentration of power? How have the new procedures, beginning with the Congressional Budget Act of 1974, interacted with controversies over the size and composition of revenue and expenditures come to produce the creeping stalemate that provoked Gramm–Rudman–Hollings? These questions are easier to state than to answer. The coexistence of dispersion and concentration of power is both confusing and suggestive, confusing because trends move in opposite directions, suggestive because precisely the effort to move in different directions is what causes the disarray of which we are all aware. No easy task here. Before attempting to disentangle these intersecting knots, we must first see how they were tied. Complexity before simplicity. The anomaly is well put by John Ellwood:

> The procedures used by Congress to make economic and budget policy since 1974 are the great exception in an overall trend toward the decline of central and aggregating institutions and the resulting dispersal of power and accountability. During the same era when congressional scholars pointed to the decline of political parties, the seniority system, the power of committee chairmen, and such guardians as the House Appropriations Committee and to the rise of subcommittee government, autonomous legislators, and the power of iron triangles and issue networks, the Congressional Budget and Impoundment Act of 1974 created new procedures and institutions that reflected a more centralized and integrated decision making process than had previously been used to make economic and budget policy.[33]

During the early 1970s, the norms of participatory democracy had their way in Congress. Power was dispersed from committee chairs (no longer guaranteed by seniority) to a proliferation of subcommittees (all commit-

---

[33]John W. Ellwood, "The Great Exception: The Congressional Budget Process in an Age of Decentralization," in Lawrence Dodd and Bruce Oppenheimer, eds., *Congress Reconsidered*, 3rd ed. (Washington, D.C.: CQ Press, 1985).

tees had to have them) and new staff. Democrats did the most; under a subcommittee "bill of rights," the prerogative of determining the number, budget, size, and jurisdiction of subcommittees was transferred from the chairs of standing committees to the caucus of the majority party. The Democratic caucus also had the right to elect subcommittee chairs. From 1967 to 1980 the personal staffs of representatives rose from 4,051 to 7,376, an 82 percent increase, while in the Senate the increase was 114 percent (1,749 to 3,746). During the decade of the 1970s, Senate standing committee staff rose 88 percent (635 to 1,191). Not to be outdone, House staffs went up 173 percent (702 to 1,917).[34]

Whereas in earlier times, subcommittee members might be chosen with an eye toward countering constituency influences, now they mostly select themselves. "What we find," a staff member told Allen Schick, "is that the city and inner-city guys are all on Labor-HEW, all of the hawkish guys go to Defense, and the big (full) committee chairman no longer has the power to take a guy who has a defense interest and say, 'you serve on the Agriculture subcommittee and do the public some good.' "[35]

No wonder individual legislators had more clout. No longer under the thumb of seniority, loaded with staff, they could express many more preferences with less personal expertise than in the past. The tendency to behave as individual political entrepreneurs, often running against Congress as an institution, was strengthened by a greater ability to intervene in more areas of policy and thus serve larger numbers of constituents or by their own visions of desirable public policy. While Democratic chairs had more reason to stand close to their party cohorts, it was not just the Speaker and the whips but the entire caucus (which could not be expected to act very often) to whom they were beholden. Members could act with impunity on individual programs, providing their overall voting record was roughly in line. What were members of Congress using their newly found freedom for?

[34]Ellwood, "Great Exception," pp. 4–5 of typescript.
[35]*Ibid.*, pp. 5–6. Quote from Schick is in his *Congress and Money* (Urban Institute Press, 1980), p. 432.

Annual Authorizations

With increasing rapidity, from the 1950s until the present time, permanent or multiyear spending authorizations have been giving away to the annual kind. (Before 1950, there were only two; three were passed in the 1950s, seven in the 1960s, sixteen in the 1970s, several more so far in the 1980s.)[36] One reason for this trend toward annual authorization was to exert better or more frequent control over administrative agencies; another was to increase influence over appropriations subcommittees. The funding preferences of authorizing committees are no secret: By and large, they want higher spending. While reducing authorizations is an effective way of cutting spending over the next few years, raising authorizations may be ineffective if the appropriations committees refuse to recommend the necessary budget authority. By repeating those requests on an annual basis, authorzing committees create more numerous opportunities to lobby for them; this lobbying also serves as a means of influencing the actions of agencies. On the one hand, annual authorizations are a pain to administrators who have to keep testifying. On the other hand, since the result is more likely to be higher than lower future spending, there is some recompense for this inconvenience.

When annual authorizations were first applied to the National Space Agency (NASA), Louis Fisher informs us, the practice was defended as necessary to control a new and growing agency: "But the authorizing committees understood that legislative action by them each year would put pressure on the Appropriations Committees to fund the agency at more generous levels. Senator Lyndon Johnson argued that the procedure would assist NASA officials in guiding their budget through the Appropriations Committees."[37] That is why the House Appropriations Committee, supported by Republican Representative (and, later, president) Gerald Ford, voted 34 to 14 against annual authorization in 1959, while the House Science and Astronautics Committee voted unanimously in favor. In the late 1970s, to look at another field of policy, the

[36]See Louis Fisher, "Annual Authorizations: Durable Roadblocks to Biennial Budgeting," typescript, n.d.
[37]*Ibid.*, p. 29.

Carter administration, like its predecessors, wanted to abolish the U.S. Travel Service as an unnecessary activity. In order to keep the agency alive, the Senate suggested annual authorization, and the House followed suit. The agency now is called the Travel and Tourism Administration.[38]

With two sets of hearings—appropriations and authorizations—scheduled each year in each house, the opportunities for interaction on spending between administrators and legislators, as well as among legislators, expand greatly. So do the opportunities for delay. The complexity of the joint authorizing-appropriations process, moreover, lends itself to further maneuver.

Let us suppose you are a president who wants to do two things at once—things that more simple-minded folk think are incompatible: simultaneously reduce and increase spending. Like a Lyndon Johnson, you may wish to keep outlays (the actual disbursement of funds in a single year) from exceeding a stipulated amount while preparing the way for higher spending in the future. Thus Johnson recommended higher authority that would increase spending only in future years. This exchange also has the virtue of making immediate cuts more palatable to agencies who can look forward to better times in the future. Side payments, decreasing outlays in return for increased authority, were largely absent only in fiscal 1980 and 1981 when reconciliations of authority was adopted in the first budget resolution.[39]

Eventually, of course, the aptly named "buck" has to stop somewhere. Budget committees, especially in the Senate where deficit reductions have been taken as their goal, find the appropriations-authority tradeoff fatal. Unless they can get support for limiting authority, budget committees will be unable either to hold down multiyear spending or to use the reconciliation process effectively. No sense in fighting on outlays this year only to have the funds reappear in those infamous out years.

If you cannot get the appropriations committees to go along with your spending request, what can you do? Try to raise spending on the floor.

[38]*Ibid.*, p. 30.
[39]Mark S. Kamlet and David C. Mowery, "Contradictions of Congressional Budget Reform: Problem of Congressional Emulation of Executive Branch," typescript, 1984.

ROLLED ON THE FLOOR

During the heyday of the Appropriations Committee, its members prided themselves on the high (over 95 percent) proportion of recommendations that were accepted by the House. Being "rolled on the floor" was a mark of ineptitude or disgrace. It meant that members were out of touch, that they had not performed their political function of anticipating and, therefore, failed to ward off opposition before it occurred. Why, if they were to get rolled often, the most knowledgeable and (more important) the most responsible members might lose control so that budgeting and chaos became equivalent terms.[40] What they feared has now come about.

In the twenty years following 1963, the number of amendments offered annually to appropriations acts rose continuously, from 120 to 433. The average number of amendments per bill went up from 2.5 to 9.2. Where the number of amendments approved by the House (more accurately, the Committee of the Whole) remained at roughly 25 percent until the mid-1970s, by the end of the decade it had gone to 43.3, after 1980 rising to over 50 percent. Looking more precisely at the success rate of contested amendments, these went from a high of 30 percent in the 1960s to the 1980s average of just under half.[41] Evidently, as Stanley Bach concludes,

> Increases in the number of amendments proposed in recent years, and increases in the percentage of winning amendments, suggest that the Committee has had increasing difficulty in accommodating to the preferences of the House and in anticipating and settling potential controversies in advance. In turn, this may reflect decreasing sensitivity and acumen among Committee and subcommittee leaders, a decline in adherence to such norms as reciprocity and comity, or the increasing divisiveness and

[40]cf. Richard F. Fenno, *The Power of the Purse: Appropriations Politics in Congress* (Boston: Little, Brown, 1966).

[41]The data come from Stanley Bach, "Representatives and Committees on the Floor: Amendments to Appropriations Bills in the House of Representatives, 1963–1982." Paper prepared for 1985 Annual Meeting of the American Political Science Association, New Orleans, August 29–September 1, 1985.

controversy within the House as a whole over spending policies and priorities.[42]

Incomplete explanations for the growth of victorious amendments to appropriation bills are easy to find. There are more subcommittees with more members. Access to meetings is far more open while interest in activities is more widely spread. After all, government has grown larger, programs have broader impacts (defense, housing, and unemployment programs occur almost everywhere), legislators have more staff, and they are more interested in making a name for themselves in a number of areas rather than just in one. Congressional centers of expertise, such as CRS and CBO, offer help in tracking the status and effects of appropriations, as does a generation of informed legislators. All this is persuasive. Congressmen offer more amendments because there is more to amend, more interest in amending it, and more of a chance to be successful.

There are now fewer sanctions than in the past for stepping out of line by challenging committee recommendations. Chairmen are no longer powerful enough to control the outcomes. The growing partisanship over budgetary matters has increased the likelihood that subcommittee members will visibly disagree; choosing among various majority and minority reports, consequently, is less a violation of the norms of reciprocity than it once would have been. Party leaders and committee chairs can do little to invoke sanctions. Assignments are difficult to deny, since now there are many more to go around. Staff is plentiful; so are subcommittee positions. Inded, because congressmen serve on more subcommittees, they are less liable to assign overriding importance to a single amendment or to be challenged on one of their recommendations. Short of the ultimate sanction—reading a legislator out of the party, which is only a last resort—the publicity and perhaps even the power go to those who act and speak up.

Consideration of the merits may also lead legislators to try to overturn subcommittee judgments. Because there are many more pro-

[42]*Ibid.*, pp. 24–25.

grams and expertise is more widely shared, there is less reason to believe that subcommittees know more than other congressmen. Since turnover on subcommittees also has risen, there is less reason to defer to expertise.

BUDGETING PENETRATES CONGRESS

Votes on budget resolutions and major spending items have become more partisan even though members of appropriations and budget committees are not more partisan than the House as a whole.[43] The basic reason for this is that differences over the budget have increasingly come to define differences between the parties.

A good indicator of this noteworthy development is the growing importance of votes on budgeting in Congress. Before the Budget Act of 1974, votes on budgeting—taxes, appropriations, debt ceilings— represented less than one-third of votes on all matters. To add in votes on authorizations—including entitlements, the fastest growing portion of the budget, as well as the new budget resolutions and reconciliation— produces a startling result: Ellwood's account shows that from 1982 to 1984, half of floor votes in the House and two-thirds (!) in the Senate were concerned with budgeting.[44] It took some thirty-odd roll calls for the Senate to pass its resolution in 1985. If one saw budgetary matters as irrelevant to political parties, there would be little left about which parties could be relevant.

An indirect indicator of the ever-growing importance of budgeting is the workload of the Congressional Budget Office. CBO produces estimates of the likely cost of almost every bill that requires expenditure.

---

[43]On the House Budget Committee, see John W. Ellwood and James A. Thurber, "The New Congressional Budget Process: The Hows and Why of House-Senate Differences," in Lawrence Dodd and Bruce Oppenheimer, eds, *Congress Reconsidered* (New York: Praeger, 1977), pp. 163–92.

[44]John W. Ellwood, "Providing Policy Analysis to U.S. Congress: The Case of the Congressional Budget Office." Paper prepared for 1984 Annual Meetings of the Association for Public Policy Analysis and Management, New Orleans, October 18–21, 1984.

As the markup of legislation proceeds, it gives informal input on estimates. But that is not all. CBO is also required to issue periodic scorekeeping reports on the degree to which outlays and authorizations stay within the budget resolutions. So far, so simple—until it turned out that the Senate and House committees want different scores. As Ellwood informs us,

> The more conservative Senate Budget Committee wanted CBO to emphasize the extent to which the Senate would exceed the targets of budget resolutions should it enact all of the legislation it was considering. The more liberal House Budget Committee wanted to emphasize the additional spending that was possible before the House reached the targets or ceilings and floors of budget resolutions.
>
> Although there was no disagreement as to CBO's numbers it quickly became evident that the two budget committees could not reach a compromise. So the inevitable happened, CBO provided the numbers for two documents, one in the Senate format one in the House format.[45]

All along the way, CBO alters its estimates to keep up with the president's budget, committee changes, budget resolutions, floor amendments, and the like. Cross-tabulations are then made between these estimates in order to relate one to the others, if desired. The important consequence is not that CBO succeeds in keeping all this straight, which it does, but that Congress, as it decomposes itself into subcommittees, is dealing with different budgetary bases.

Because it takes so much time in so many places, the budget displaces whatever else Congress would be doing. The number of places increases because Congress wants to exert greater control over its budget, including the relationship between taxing and spending. Therefore it establishes HBC, SBC, and CBO. The time increases not only because there are more actors but also because each must, in effect, negotiate with the others and with the president. In addition to more participants, there are also larger choices—annual budget resolutions, continuing resolutions, and reconciliations—that either were not made before or, if they were, were made far less frequently.

[45]*Ibid,* p. 10.

Whether one says "It is Congress, therefore it budgets," or, "It budgets, therefore it must be Congress," the conclusion is the same: Congress and budgeting are becoming synonymous.

One might think that with so much time and effort devoted to budgeting Congress would get better at it. In a sense, this is true. There is much more understanding of spending, taxing, and the relationship between them in Congress. But understanding does not agreement make. Indeed, the more that people fundamentally in disagreement know about the consequences of their actions, the better become their reasons for opposing one another. Disagreement has spread not only to present policies but also to past policies; from an agreed base to what that base ought to be; from where the budget should go, to where it is.

THE SHIFTING BUDGETARY BASE

In days of old, budgeting had far fewer participants. Though the rule was sometimes honored in the breach, the president's budget was the acknowledged starting point for congressional considerations. Most disputes about initial requests were resolved within the executive branch—albeit in anticipation of congressional action. Nowadays differences that would have been resolved within the executive spill over into Congress. Why?

It is easy to forget the obvious. The power of the purse belongs to Congress. Presidents have previously acknowledged that fact by the ancient rule of anticipated reaction; the presidential role was to both acknowledge and alter incrementally the prior years' congressional action. By this act of acquiescence, presidents provided a convenient starting point, not far from last year's congressional action, so as to maintain continuity in budgeting. When in President Reagan's time, however, the president's desires were far from congressional majorities on taxes, defense, and welfare, his budgets were routinely pronounced "dead on arrival." The president's base has become his own preferences.

According to the Budget Act of 1974, reconciliation was to be used near the end of the budgetary process in order to bring what Congress had voted on individual items into line with the Second Resolution. The Budget Act of 1974 introduced new layers of actors and rules to an already complex environment. As the budget process became increasingly important, budget negotiations moved from the budget committees to extra-committee groups. "Members do not defer to the decisions of autonomous, well-integrated committees, as they would in a committee-centered budget system," John Ellwood informs us. "Instead, the policy decisions conveyed by budget resolutions are the result of direct negotiations among large numbers of members that produce a majority coalition in favor of a single budget policy."[46] Now reconciliation is attached to the First Resolution in an effort to provide advance protection for the resolution. Reconciliation has been transformed, Allen Schick informs us, "from a means of reviewing decisions made during the current year into a process for revising legislation (mostly entitlements and revenue laws) enacted in previous years."[47] Reconciliation, therefore, especially reconciliation of budget authority, represents a permanent institutional attack on the budgetary base.

The budget both reflects and justifies the existing political order. Its boundaries guard that order. This is the social significance of the budgetary base, the bulk of which is protected from serious scrutiny, so it will remain unchallenged.[48] Inside the base, except for small additions or subtractions, all is protected; outside the base, everything is up for grabs. On the stability of the budgetary base, therefore, rests the stability of ongoing government programs. An across-the-board attack on the budgetary base is equivalent to a radical restructuring of spending priorities. Governments, therefore, seek to invest major items of expenditures with some sort of sanctity; "entitlement" is but a stronger method of guarding one's borders. Breaching the base is equivalent to opening up to

[46]*Ibid.*, pp. 35–36.

[47]Allen Schick, "The Evolution of Congressional Budgeting," in Allen Schick, ed., *Crisis in the Budget Process* (Washington, D.C.: American Enterprise Institute, 1986), p. 13.

[48]See Aaron Wildavsky, *The Politics of the Budgetary Process*, 4th ed. (Boston: Little, Brown, 1984), pp. 16–18, 102–108, 231–33, for discussion of the budgetary base.

renegotiation the boundaries of past political contracts. The fundamental priorities of the regime—who will receive how much for which purposes—are in danger of being turned upside down.

Way back then, the budgetary base—the residue of past agreements not normally opened up for reconsideration—was approximated by the amounts in the prior year's budget. Recommending small changes, depending on presidential desires for economic management as well as preferences on a few programs, the president's proposed budget was an acceptable further approximation of the base. Not now. Kamlet and Mowery pronounce the last rites:

> . . . agreement within Congress on the definition of the budgetary base no longer exists. Both the House and Senate Budget Committees frequently have employed a definition of the budgetary base that differs from the one utilized in the Appropriations Committess. This practice has created severe problems in the compatibility of budget resolutions and appropriations actions. Moreover, the House and Sente Budget Committees themselves frequently use different definitions of the budgetary base, with disastrous consequences for the conference committees charged with the development of a joint budget resolution.[49]

Whether or not the president's budget is pronounced unsuitable, unworthy of further use, a mere historical curiosity, or even if it is closer to certain congressional desires, it no longer serves as the base. Instead, Congress, through its budget committees, uses either the CBO's current-services budget or the House or Senate budget resolutions, or some combination thereof, depending on the programs in question.

Since playing the budgetary game in Congress now requires a respectable deficit-reduction number—deficit cuts, not the total deficit, are the focus of attention—obfuscation of the base may be a deliberate move to overestimate how much will be cut. Manipulating baselines enables legislators to meet the twin imperatives of helping clients by saving programs and helping the economy by cutting deficits. "The baselines have an important political advantage," Schick tells us. "They depict

[49]Mark S. Kamlet and David C. Mowery, "The First Decade of the Congressional Budget Act: Legislative Imitation and Adaptation in Budgeting," *Policy Sciences*, Vol. 18, No. 4 (December 1985), pp. 313–34; quote on page 320.

rising expenditures as budget cutbacks. Between fiscal 1981 (when reconciliation was first applied) and fiscal 1986, medicare has climbed from $39 billion to an estimated $67 billion. Yet Congress has taken credit for almost $25 billion in medicare cutbacks during these years."[50] Like the youngster in my childhood experience who would save the candy store from being robbed by deciding not to do it, "savings" are not calculated as reductions from last year's outlay but from a hypothetical baseline—an estimation of what future spending would have been without the action in question. Baselines, therefore, are man-made, depending on predictions of price changes and participation rates. Suppose a $100 billion increase is projected; would a mere $80 billion increase lead to a $20 billion "saving"? Like the man who "saves" $50 by buying the $100 hat (that he didn't have to have) at a half-off sale?

The disappearance of an agreed base is both a symptom and a cause of disagreement over the amount and distribution of expenditures and revenues. It is a symptom because disagreement must be running deep if participants cannot agree where to begin, no less than where to end. It is a cause of further disagreement because policy differences are exacerbated by quarreling over the proper place to start.

Disagreement over the budgetary base, by delaying the budget, causes the same kind of repetitive budgeting—remaking the budget throughout the year—that sounds the death knell for the annual budget. A budget officer told Irene Rubin, in regard to 1981, that "we did a budget each month practically—one in August, one in September, one in October, and one in December. All told, there were five or more revisions of the budget. Probably all agencies did the same thing."[51]

If, due to a combination of resource scarcity and ideological differences, decisions are made more difficult, we can better understand the unhappy predominance of budget issues in Congress. Kamlet and Mowery are among many others who observe that "debates within Congress over budgetary matters have become increasingly strident over the past

---

[50]Allen Schick, "Controlling the 'Uncontrollables': Budgeting for Health Care in an Age of Mega-Deficits." Paper prepared for AEI Pew Fellows Conference, November 1985, pp. 25–26.

[51]Rubin, *Shrinking the Federal Government*, p. 91.

ten years, particularly in the House, and the norm of mutual accommodation now seems much less universal. . . . There may be many other
factors responsible for this decline in accommodative behavior, including greater ideological differences within and among the House, the
Senate, and the White House than in previous years."[52] Why are these
differences so difficult to resolve?

THE FISCALIZATION OF THE POLICY DEBATE

Another sign (and further cause) of polarization is what Robert Reischauer has called "the fiscalization of the public policy debate." Few
programs are considered solely on their substantive or political merits.
Rather, it is asked, to what degree do programs contribute to the deficit?
Do they fit within the latest congressional budget resolution or the
president's budget? How fast would defense or welfare grow? The substantive question, however—What is being bought with the money?—
increasingly is shunted aside. One reason for emphasizing the aggregate
amounts is that these are what matter for purposes of macroeconomic
management.

Efforts at economic management by the federal government, however, have largely disappeared in fact, though not in form. Automatic
stabilizers, such as Unemployment Compensation, still operate. But the
doctrinal basis is gone. President Reagan's policy is to reduce income tax
rates as low as possible. When the economy does well, rates would be
cut because they can be; and when the economy does badly, rates would
be cut as a necessary stimulus. Presumably, tax cuts are good for all
seasons.

Despite hard times, however, Democrats would like to increase taxes
in order to reduce the deficit and prevent the compounding of interest
on the debt that will force out future spending. In good times, taxes
should be increased because the extra can be used to fund more programs. With the major parties committed politically to tax decreases or

[52]Kamlet and Mowery, "Contradictions of Congressional Budget Reform."

increases, irrespective of economic circumstances, there is not much room for adjustment. Ideology has replaced economic "fine-tuning" with Johnny one-note.

The reconversion of Democrats to budget balance—for the good of the economy, for ammunition against Republican deficit makers, for preventing interest on the debt from driving out their preferred programs—has made it difficult for Democrats to use the Keynesian approach to the size of deficits in order to manage the economy. So long as Gramm–Rudman–Hollings remains in force, moreover, budget balance is national policy. Tax reform has, for the time being, ruled out the use of new or enlarged tax preferences for social purposes. Thus Democrats are temporarily without the major instruments of policy—fiscal manipulation, tax preferences—they have relied on in the past.

A second reason for looking closer at totals is that with the growth of government it becomes difficult to gain attention for small programs that amount to "only" a few billion apiece. But the most important reason is that in a period of ideological polarization, quantities come to stand for qualities.

Fiscalization of the policy debate is a crude but effective way of accounting for wins, losses, and ties. To the extent that bigger is deemed better for some and worse for others, more for welfare or less for defense, higher or lower tax rates, these sum up the political struggle. Where observers once thought that confining conflict to amounts would make it easier to reconcile differences as a matter of a little more or a little less, fiscalization has come to have the opposite effect. By aggregating totals and converting them into signs of who is ahead or behind, budgeting becomes a conflict of principles that is difficult to resolve.

Conservative Republicans insist that the budget be moved toward balance by sharp reductions in domestic spending while defense is increased—and all without new taxes. Liberal Democrats agree on balance but only by cutting defense while maintaining domestic programs, preferably aided by new taxes on business or high-income individuals. Conservative Democrats and moderate Republicans together insist first and foremost on balance, the sooner the better, however it is arrived at; they contemplate defense and domestic cuts as well as tax increases. Everyone, it seems, is for balance but not on the same terms. No perspective commands a majority. What to do?

The prospects for agreement would be better if balance were regarded as a prudential virtue, to be achieved or approximated over time, with no strict timetable so long as it was increasing. Lower interest rates might reduce the cost of refinancing the debt, and sustained economic growth might bring in higher revenues. Combined with somewhat lower expectations (Would not a deficit of only $100 billion be supportable as the economy expands?), the deficit becomes manageable. Reasonable, yes; politic, no.

For the deficit has become both an obsession and a weapon. Controlling the deficit has become a "metaphor for governing."[53] On the political extremes, the deficit is a stick with which (take your pick) to beat liberals for excessive domestic spending or conservatives for excessive defense spending. Precisely because those at the extreme poles correctly suspect each other of insincerity and know each other to be vulnerable, both types speak as if possessed of the one true religion. How better to beat the other side than by spewing forth what former Supreme Court Justice Thomas Reed Powell called a "parade of horribles" about the catastrophic consequences of deficits? In this, extremists are gladly joined by the party of responsibility because this is the one belief (and weapon) that they genuinely share. So the fiscal responsibles trot out streams of the nation's economists who swear that (even without actual hard evidence) it is in the nature of things, or plain common sense, that awful events—depression, inflation, higher interest rates, the fall of civilization as we know it—are just over the horizon. This may or may not be true in the long run. Short-run cries of catastrophe, such as those contained in David Stockman's *The Triumph of Politics,* have not yet been borne out. But it is certain that any adverse economic circumstances will be blamed on deficits, so, whatever else happens, it is necessary to disassociate oneself from their contaminating influence. In sum, the deficit has become a means of holding adversaries accountable for adversity without oneself being responsible.

[53]Symposium on Budget Balance: Do Deficits Matter? New York City, January 9–11, 1986, p. 161.

In an insightful discussion of how legislators think about economic management, Steven Schier sets the conceptual stage for congressional action:

> The pursuit of a credible deficit reduction goal has become a major event of American "high politics" involving Congressional, administration and business leaders. The first step for the committees in this dance is the targeting of a credible deficit reduction goal. Cues are disseminated at hearings and in the press from national business leaders (such as Henry Kaufman of Wall Street) and economists (such as Alan Greenspan, Charles Schultze and Herbert Stein) and administration economic policy-makers. . . .
>
> Decisions about specific functions also require majority members to consider how likely potential cuts are to pass on the floor. Prospects for floor success are enhanced by achieving a respectable deficit number and arranging carefully the treatment of particular priorities in the resolution. The central dynamic in resolution formulation is the balancing of deficit reduction with a politically acceptable treatment of priorities. The deficit number itself is of political concern to committee members. Important national figures have flagged the issue, and attentive constituents are aware as well. Achieving a responsible deficit target thus becomes a crucial exercise in political credibility for the committee. Members have learned in a general way the substantive economic reasons for a deficit reduction goal, and unmistakably perceive the issue's political cachet.
>
> The final product, then, is ideally a resolution that (1) achieves a credible deficit or deficit reduction number, (2) satisfies the substantive priorities and institutional interests of the majority party members on the committee, and (3) on these grounds is passable on the floor. By the mid-eighties, the process of working toward this product had become quite partisan in both of the Budget Committees. This reflects the exercise of "high politics" in which political parties duel for political credit and blame over the deficit issue. Since the issue dominates the domestic agenda, divided party rule of Congress encourages a partisan battle for credit and blame within the committees. . . .
>
> One House Democrat described the sequence of decisionmaking in this way: "First you have to look at the overall number—the deficit. Then you have to look at the big pieces—revenues, entitlements, defense—and ask yourself what can I get from these? Then you look for vulnerable items, those both politically and substantively vulnerable. The question here is: who should I go after? Finally—and all resolutions have this to some degree—there's the bullshit list, specious assumptions about user fees,

contracting out, and the strategic petroleum reserve. The focus in all this is to keep the overall choices in line with a credible deficit or deficit reduction number."[54]

To be taken seriously as a deficit reducer-cum-dragon-slayer, it is necessary to arrive at a credible number, viz. a number that would make a dent in the deficit, thereby imposing pain, but not so much as to make the number politically unfeasible and the process that sustains it untenable.

A tall order. Indeed, an impossible one until the policy complexion of Congress and of the presidency changes, so that one of the three prevailing views can garner a majority. The impossibility of doing what everyone claims is essential explains a number of otherwise puzzling features of the battle of the budget.

LEADER, LEADER, WHO'S THE LEADER?

The people who provide the crucial deficit reduction number differ from one year to the next. Sometimes the budget committees make it; most often, they do not. Neither does the president nor the formal congressional leadership. President Reagan and Speaker O'Neill, the elder statesmen, served as lodestars; their agreement gave permission to people on their right and left respectively to follow suit. But by refusing permission the president and the Speaker were better at stopping what they didn't like than in getting what they wanted because, like other would-be leaders, they lacked majorities. Thus the budgetary stalemate offers up opportunities for political entrepreneurship. Anyone who can figure out (or guess) what sorts of alliances—around which combination of policy priorities—might emerge victorious has an opportunity to try.

The coalition that emerges may not, in fact, be a product of foresight but of random perturbation. Perhaps the order to which alternatives are considered, and ruled out, leaves the remaining possibilities in an inadvertently superior position. Perhaps a package fits for reasons unknown.

---

[54]Steven E. Schier, "Thinking about the Macroeconomy: The House and Senate Budget Committees in the 1980s." Paper prepared for 1985 Annual Meeting of APSA, New Orleans, August 29–September 1, 1985, pp. 15, 21–22.

In any event, since the participants cannot figure out beforehand "what will go," and thus uncertainty rules the congressional roost, we can see why the winning combination (and hence the victorious combiner) cannot be known in advance. Exciting, sure, but enervating as well, for many combinations must be assembled before one is chosen.

Why, if Congress agrees that deficit reduction is so vital, does it not come to agreement? The primary answer is that deficit reduction means different things to the contending forces. One prefers the budget to be balanced at high levels of revenue and expenditure, the other at low levels. Each has a different solution as to who shall pay and who receive. The secondary answer is that in the absence of immediate and evident crisis, where the evil plausibly can be attributed to the deficit, the adversaries are unwilling to give up policy preferences and unable to persuade one another. Only the party of responsibility sees the danger as immediate and cares more about balance than about its other preferences. And it lacks a majority.

The demand for balance does not come from an aroused citizenry. While ordinarily balance is preferable to imbalance, the general public, aware that economic times are pretty good, has no desire to make large sacrifices—large tax increases or spending cuts—on behalf of balance. Deficit panic is an elite phenomenon.

While the American people, insofar as is known from the polls, dislike the growing deficit, they do not, by and large, think it disastrous enough to justify extreme measures. As Peggy Richardson, a worker at a Nissan plant told a small panel put together by the *Wall Street Journal,* "I feel like the government doesn't need to go off in a panic. . . . I don't think the deficit is a here-and-now crisis that has to be solved over night."

A good part of the problem is that the public, as reflected by their politicians, is divided over what to do. Yes, a *Journal*/NBC news poll shows that the deficit is second only to nuclear war, with 31 percent saying it is the nation's most serious problem. But no, across-the-board slashes under GRH are opposed by 72 percent. Yes, spending should be cut, but no, not on medicare (86 percent) or the Small Business Administration (69 percent); and the public is evenly split on mass transit, defense (51 percent against, 45 percent for), a tax on gasoline, income taxes, on down the line of deficit-reducing measures. When asked whether they were willing to have their income taxes raised, 40 percent of those polled were willing compared to 56 percent who were not. A national sales tax fared better (52 percent for, 44 percent opposed) but the margin is too small to be decisive. And among those in favor of GRH, few think it will actually succeed.[55]

Apparently the general public, though firmly opposed to large deficits, is unwilling to contemplate extreme measures to eliminate it overnight. Deficit panic would not occur, I think, unless there were (1) polarization among political elites; (2) lack of trust in institutions to bridge this gap; and hence fear that the government would be unable to control itself.

What can be done when there is no majority behind deficit reduction policies, and yet the demand among participants for balance becomes obsessive? A budget has to be passed to keep government going; yet because there is no agreement, the annual, drag-out struggle is conducted amid accusations that the other side (or sides) is hypocritical in that it really doesn't care about balance. Grave mutterings—first whispers, then shouts—say that the public interest is being abandoned to (shudder) private interests. Somehow, before real reductions take place or taxes are raised, apparent devotion to budget balance must be made compatible with continuation of spending policies. Reconciling the irreconcilable depends on the rules under which spending proposals are voted on in Congress.

WHAT A DIFFERENCE A RULE MAKES:
302(b)s AND THE FAZIO RULE

Rules for considering spending differ in instructive ways in the House and Senate. Their budget committees report out and their members

[55]Ellen Hume, "Ambivalent Voters: Americans See Deficit As a Disease, but They Balk at Proposed Cures," *Wall Street Journal,* February 11, 1986, pp. 1, 28.

vote on budget resolutions containing two numbers, a total for budget authority and a total for outlays. Moving between the two numbers creates possibilities for strategic interplay. The budget committees generally wish to come out with the highest possible deficit reduction number. Therefore they tend to estimate less in outlays than is likely to be obtained from a given amount of authority. This conversion factor going from authority to outlays creates difficulties for the appropriations committees. Before I can show why this difficulty occurs, and how the two chambers differ in handling it, we must consider how the appropriations committees divide the totals given to them in budget resolutions among their subcommittees.

In the Senate, totals for outlays and authority are handed down to the Appropriations Committee under Section 302(a) of the Budget Act of 1974. In the House, by contrast, a further distinction is made between mandatory and discretionary accounts. The definitions are to some extent arbitrary, but in the main they distinguish between entitlements, like provision for civil service retirement, that go up or down by a preset formula, and annual appropriations. Now we are ready for a little exercise without which contemporary budgeting cannot be fully understood. Suppose a subcommittee handles a bill for its functions amounting to $106 billion of which $76 billion is mandatory and $30 billion is discretionary. Suppose unemployment rises so that the mandatory part of this bill goes up to $9 billion. What happens then? Is the subcommittee held to its $106 billion total, thus requiring a cut of $9 billion from its discretionary funds? Or will it be allowed to claim that it (or, better still, its programs) should not be held responsible for the consequences of external forces beyond the subcommittee's control? Shall the rule be, as some legislators would wish, that a ceiling is a ceiling, so if spending goes up in part of a subcommittee's jurisdiction, it has to find the money in another account? That would hold down spending. Or should the rule be that worthy programs should not be penalized for excesses in others especially in mandatory items? That rule would increase spending.

The Senate follows the low-spending rule: Spending control is subject to a point of order to enforce the 302(b) provisions of the 1974 budget act, which are enforceable at the subcommittee level for budget authority, credit authority, entitlement authority, and outlays. Each subcommittee can be kept within its own allocation of outlays or authority by a point of order. This is a vital difference. Why it is vital helps us understand the importance of procedures.

In the House the Fazio rule means that subcommittees cannot be subject to points of order if their proposals are within the total spending allowed under the 302(b) allocations *for discretionary budget authority.* Therefore, if an appropriations subcommittee spends beyond the amount allocated to it by the House budget resolution, there is no procedure for stopping it until total approved spending goes beyond the ceiling specified. The Fazio rule enables the House Appropriations Committee and its subcommittees to ignore the effects of misestimation of mandatory spending on overall allocations. If you give us a target we can meet, a House staffer said, we will. But "If you get us clobbered because Rosty [the chairman of the Ways and Means Committee] said screw you [by failing to reduce mandatory items or raise revenues] then appropriations will just ignore the process."[56] A point of order stopping consideration of an appropriations bill will not lie (i.e., remain in force) if that bill exceeds the total outlays assigned to that jurisdiction. The bill is still in compliance with House rules if discretionary spending is within the limits set out in the House budget resolution.

A participant helps us place this story in a broader context:

> This administration under Stockman . . . would fight on the resolutions and then . . . try to use these to constrain the size and composition of individual appropriations bills. I saw my job as telling them that only the formal targets were constraints. Anything we wanted to do with these constraints were our prerogatives.
>
> I have always resisted use of the budget process to determine the contents of appropriations bills. Until 1980 that was an adversary process between us and House Budget Committee. Under Reagan it has also been an adversary process with the administration. They did not try to work at the subcommittee level with us, but would wait until we got to the floor

[56]Interview, February 25, 1986, Washington, D.C.

and then sandbag us with positions based on implications within the budget resolution.

[But the budget resolution denies the priorities in the president's budget, so why is it practical to use the president's budget as a standard?]

It's not practical if they don't then change it. Say our request was $7 billion, and the benchmark off the resolution is $7.5 billion. I want the administration to change their request. I don't want to look at resolution assumptions. *That takes away the most important thing an Appropriations member has: influence on the amount of money for a program in an appropriations bill* [emphasis supplied]. If he's dealing with OMB he has two numbers, OMB and ours, and can bargain between them. I don't know how many times I said to Stockman, amend your request. I want to deal with *you*, not the Budget Committee.

I think he did tremendous damage to the influence of the president. He turned the president's budget into a joke. The number-specific on a program in the president's budget no longer means anything. Whereas before it was the most important part of the process.[57]

The intersection of process, purpose, and personality could not be better illustrated. The purpose was to gain power while avoiding responsibility for the deficit.

The use of gimmicks to raise spending while appearing not to do so is inherent in the mixed motives that necessarily accompany budgeting. Where promises are limited, and thus may be fulfilled through playing by the rules, gimmickry declines. When promises are too large in relationship to available resources, gimmickry, as we will now see, grows to epidemic proportions.

[57]Interview, May 2, 1986, Washington, D.C.

PROCEDURAL
MANIFESTATIONS
OF BUDGETARY
DISSENSUS

6

INCREASED ATTENTION TO TOTAL SPENDING led, as we know, to increased White House attention to budgeting in Congress. The president's budget message was written with a view toward gaining bargaining advantage with Congress. When that did not pay off, Budget Director Stockman tried reconciliation through budget resolutions, and when that petered out, he intervened directly with the spending committees. "These serial negotiations," Hugh Heclo shrewdly observed, "often had the effect in turn of undercutting the budget committees and their comprehensive process. In 1981 David Stockman had been the prime mover in a national budget process of epic scale. But in 1984 he was mainly in the role of chief damage control officer fighting a defensive, rearguard action throughout the congressional committee system."[1]

Like Jimmy Carter, Congress was "puzzled and irritated by the fact

[1]Hugh Heclo, "Executive Budget Making," in Gregory B. Mills and John L. Palmer, eds., *Federal Budget Policy in the 1980s* (Washington, D.C.: Urban Institute Press, 1984), pp. 255–91; quote on p. 276.

that the choices were [are] so brutal. He [and they] grew to hate the budget process."[2] Always, however, Congress resolves to do better.

R AND R: RESOLUTION AND RECONCILIATION

It used to be said of Latin America that what was needed was a law stating that all the other laws be enforced. In this respect, budget resolutions may be said to represent the Latin Americanization of federal budgeting. For these resolutions do indeed resolve to enforce all the other actions that Congress claims it is undertaking to balance the budget or control spending or achieve some other worthy purpose.

The low congressional morale caused by delays in budgeting is nothing compared to the feelings of administrators who must live with them. "After a quarter century in this business," sighed the Chief Budget Officer of the Department of Housing and Urban Development, Albert Kliman, "I have never before been in the middle of January where I didn't know what the [budget] numbers are. . . . That bothers my professional pride." Among the items to be sacrificed is after-hours heating, which is more sacrifice than usual because of all the evening meetings required to cope with the cuts.[3]

The Second Resolution, as contemplated in the act of 1974, was the one that was supposed to be binding. The First Resolution, to be passed in May, was to be tentative, setting the process in motion with a general sense of revenue and spending goals. The work of the tax and spending committees was to proceed until September when the Second Resolution would, if necessary, reconcile the whole to the parts. "The idea of waiting until September to make strategic budget decisions and still have time to translate them into detailed appropriations and tax laws before the first of October," Alice Rivlin insisted, "is patently absurd."[4] But why? Why couldn't Congress either ratify committee decisions or

---

[2]W. Bowman Cutter, "The Battle of the Budget," *The Atlantic*, Vol. 247, No. 3 (March 1981), p. 64.

[3]Joan S. Lubin, "Bureaucracies Budget Officers Are Beleaguered by Spending Curbs in the Gramm–Rudman Law," *Wall Street Journal*, January 23, 1986.

[4]Alice M. Rivlin, "The Political Economy of Budget Choices: A View from Congress." Paper presented at AEA meeting, December 29, 1981.

shape them at the margins during the month of September before the fiscal year begins on October 1st? Were there informal understandings about the size and shape of the budget, codified in the form of a First Resolution, committee recommendations would bear a family resemblance to that resolution. Only modest adjustments would then be required to arrive at the second and final resolution. In the early years after 1974, something like this did happen as the budget committees, by anticipation, made room for spending desires. Spending discipline was not evident but then neither had it been before.

Two things happened to make the Second Resolution unsatisfactory. One was that it exerted too little control, the other that it exerted too much. Control was insufficient in that even when economic conditions changed and ideas about public policy moved toward lesser spending, such views were difficult to translate into practice. The concentration of benefits made potential losers far more aware and better organized than taxpayers whose costs were widely dispersed. Nor, since the First Resolution was not binding, was it possible to apportion sacrifices, for reductions on the First Resolution might well be made up on the Second. By giving in in advance, congressional program advocates got nothing except to watch others spend what had once been their money. As everyone learned quickly to open with higher bids, without being able to accommodate the totals to which the bids added up, the new budget process proved flawed. From 1979 on, the Second Resolution required either big cuts (in the $30 billion range) if it were to live up to the First, or admitting large deficits. The solution in essence was to strengthen the First Resolution with the reconciliation procedure and other protections. Year after year, therefore, the Second Resolution fell into disuse. A 1981 rule provided that if the Second Resolution had not been passed by October, the First Resolution would become final.

Reconciliation procedures did not feature prominently in the Budget Act of 1974. Originally, reconciliation was to be applied to spending bills after they had passed in order to bring them within the budget resolution's totals. While under fire in fiscal 1981 for tolerating a deficit during rampaging inflation, the budget committees rediscovered their "elastic clause," a hitherto obscure provision of the budget act permitting them to install "any other procedure which is considered appropriate." By then, the necessity of using Third Resolutions to accommodate excesses in the Second (necessary because of overages on the First) persuaded budget committee members that they needed a device to make the First Resolution stick. For this reason reconciliation was made part of the First Resolution in the Carter administration.[5]

With their elastic clauses in hand, the budget committees, led by the Senate, expanded into trying multiyear controls. Spending targets, beginning in 1978, were to be made for five years at a time. Containing allotments for both revenue and spending, these budget resolutions propounded targets not only for the next fiscal year but for the two succeeding ones. The budget committees were willing, but it turned out that congressional flesh was weak. So new devices to assist self-control were added.

The enrollment of bills, that is, putting bills into official form so as to be in shape to send to the president for consideration, was subject to deferral if subcommittees spending threatened to exceed their functional allocations. The original bulwark against exceeding budget limits—the point of order raised against legislation that went over the budget resolution—formerly had been available only after the Second (binding) Resolution, including its ceiling on outlays and total budget authority as well as its floor on revenues, had been passed. And there was no way of compelling committees or subcommittees to keep to those mandated limits. Scorekeeping and early-warning reports only emphasized the helplessness of budget committees. So they invented deferred enrollment. No legislation that reduced revenues by more than $100 million or exceeded the functional Section 302 totals specified in the resolutions could be "enrolled."

So far the threat of deferral has proved stronger than its use. A minor reason is that some committees, knowing they are over their allotments, choose to wait until the start of the next fiscal year on October 1st when deferral lapses. This sort of hide-and-seek suggests

[5]Jean Peters, "Reconciliation 1982: What Happened?" *PS*, Vol. 14, No. 4 (Fall 1981), pp. 732–36.

the major reason: Congress has been deferring many bills until after the fiscal year.[6]

GLOBAL RESOLUTIONS AND THE RISE
OF PARTISANSHIP

A notable accompaniment of the concentration on budget resolutions— total taxing and spending—has been an increase in partisanship. As Schick reminds us, "Since 1975, the two parties have been polarized on budget policy. Twenty resolutions [not every one passed] have wended their way through the House over the past decade; on every one of these, a majority of Democrats have been on one side and a majority of Republicans on the other."[7]

Votes on resolutions are far more partisan than votes on individual programs. Ellwood shows that in the House from 1975 to 1984, the Rice Cohesion Index of partisanship (the tendency of Democrats and Republicans to vote on party lines) was 69 (on a scale of 100) on budget resolutions and reconciliation but on individual items just 53. In the Senate, the Index was 15 points higher, that is, more partisan, on votes relating to the whole budget rather than on its parts. Moreover, partisanship has been growing. The average cohesion score in the House on resolutions and reconciliation increased from 60 during the period 1975 to 1979 to 69 in the next four years. In the same two periods in the Senate, cohesion rose fro 40 to 61. Cohesion on appropriations shows similar increases, though from a lower level.[8]

Why has partisanship over the budget increased so sharply? Ellwood suggests that "the movement toward a coordinated, top-down decision making process is one explanation. In the appropriations process mem-

[6]Robert Reischauer, "Mickey Mouse or Superman? The Congressional Budget Process during the Reagan Administration." Paper presented to APPAm, October 20–22, 1983, Philadelphia, p. 3.

[7]Allen Schick, "The Evolution of Congressional Budgeting," in Allen Schick, ed., *Crisis in the Budget Process* (Washington, D.C.: American Enterprise Institute, 1986), p. 35.

[8]John W. Ellwood, "The Great Exception: The Congressional Budget Process in an Age of Decentralization," in Lawrence Dodd and Bruce Oppenheimer, eds., *Congress Reconsidered*, 3rd ed. (Washington, D.C.: CQ Press, 1985).

bers are cross-pressured. They have an individual and party commitment to increases or decreases in expenditures, revenues and deficits; but they also want to serve their constituencies and interest groups. In such a situation they are more likely to abandon their ideological and party position."[9] The difference in the type of issue—parts versus the whole budget—may well account for the higher scores on global issues but it does not serve to explain the general rise in partisanship.

Louis Fisher of the Congressional Research Service, an astute observer of budgeting, argues that changes in the form of budgeting are responsible for the rise not only in partisanship but also in the intensity of conflict. According to Fisher:

> Increasing the size of a legislative vehicle—from an appropriations bill to a budget resolution—magnifies the scope of legislative conflict and creates the need for additional concessions to Members. The likelihood is that it will cost more to build a majority. . . .
>
> Paradoxically, it appears that Members could redistribute budgetary priorities more easily under a fragmented system. They could trim the defense appropriations bill and add to the Labor-HEW appropriations bill, without ever taking money explicitly from one department and giving it to another. The budget process of 1974, Schick explains, may have complicated the congressional process because it focuses attention on budget priorities, especially by moving money from one functional category to another. Yet Members are reluctant to vote on amendments that transfer funds between categories. They prefer to do this implicitly and by indirection. The ironic result is that congress did more reordering of budgetary priorities 'before it had a budget process than it has since.'[10]

In this view, inserting centralized procedures into a decentralized institution has diminished Congress's capacity to cope with conflict.

Perhaps. It is possible also that congressional insistence on trying (and sometimes failing) to make global decisions is not so much a cause as a consequence of the prior existence of larger policy differences. When Congress was better at resolving differences, it was also true that those differences were narrower. Conflict resolution took place in the climate of

[9]*Ibid.*, p. 44.

[10]Louis Fisher, "The Congressional Budget Act: Does It Have a Spending Bias?" Paper delivered at Conference on the Congressional Budget Process, Carl Albert Congressional Research and Studies Center, University of Oklahoma, Norman, February 12–13, 1982, pp. 21–22.

informal understandings about the tolerable limits of taxation and the extent of permissible spending; budget balance, that is, provided strong guidelines. Once that agreement collapsed, Congress and the president were left with the shell—balance the budget—but not with agreement to do it through higher taxes or lower spending, nor whether domestic or defense programs should bear the brunt. The proliferation of spending devices had made control not only more difficult but also more uncertain because it is hard to gauge the comparative cost of different programs funded in different ways. "Fair shares" are more difficult to determine when there is also disagreement about what agencies and programs are actually receiving. If Congress were to go back to pre-1974 procedures, deficits would be blamed on antiquated procedures that proscribed direct confrontation of global revenue and spending. If for no other reason than their immense size, welfare and defense programs still would be controversial. Turning the clock back is possible only if one also can re-create the conditions that facilitated consensual decision making.

"In the current environment," Robert Reischauer comes closer to the problem, "the nation and its budget process may be capable of handling a fight over the relative distribution of spending benefits and tax burdens but they are not capable of taking on both fights at once."[11] The difficulty of reaching agreement is certainly multiplied by the intersection of these two global issues. But why are they considered part and parcel of the same conflict? Spending issues might be ameliorated, no doubt, if there were more ample revenues. And tax questions would be easier to answer if more revenue were not necessary. Yet how can revenue and expenditure ever be kept separate when each depends so vitally on the other? Only in America, as the saying goes, have the two sides of the budgetary coin historically been kept separate. The overriding reason revenue and expenditure did not meet up at the same time and the same place with the same set of officials is not that they could not have agreed but rather that they would have agreed only too well. Revenue was limited by common consent which, except in wartime, changed only gradually. Expenditure was expected to (and mostly did) fit within that revenue. No formal instructions

---

[11]Reischauer, "Mickey Mouse," p. 48.

were needed. Now we need such formal instructions because agreement is lacking—has not Congress voted any number of times to balance the budget? But rules in the midst of disagreement are very hard to enforce.

To the extent that taxing and spending are viewed as essentially the same, or as similar issues, disagreement is intensified. One set of issues then cannot be resolved while the other remains open. The more comprehensive the agreement required (not only because there are global resolutions but because the issues are linked in the minds and hearts of participants), the harder it is to achieve.

How might such an overarching disagreement be resolved, if at all? Electoral change just might create the necessary majorities. The citizenry as well as politicians, however, are divided. Polls show that large majorities of the general public oppose reductions in welfare programs and increases in taxes. Small majorities or pluralities oppose additional cuts in defense.[12] Alternatively, the contending parties might agree on equality of sacrifice. Unfortunately, it is precisely over equality that they so deeply disagree.

A general rule is that to cross-cut cleavages is to reduce the intensity of conflict. Legislators who oppose each other on some issues know that they will need one another's support on a different type of issue. Therefore, they moderate their positions. Budgetary polarization may be explained (or, at least, described) by exactly the opposite phenomenon: self-reinforcing, hence ever-deepening, cleavages. The same people who oppose each other on one kind of issue now tend, more than before, to oppose each other on other issues as well.

Consider in this context the bipartisan foreign policy that developed after the Second World War. While Republicans and Democrats differed over welfare issues, they came closer together on foreign policy. Their agreements modified their disagreements. But not now, not, at least, to the same extent. For most of those who wish to maintain or add to welfare spending wish to decrease spending on defense—and vice versa. Nor is that all. The social issues—school prayer, abortion, women's rights, affirmative action, parental versus children's rights—

[12] *Wall Street Journal,* October 24, 1986.

tend to move in the same direction, with conservatives and liberals taking opposite positions. Of course, there are issues—the social safety net, equal pay for equal work—on which widespread agreement does exist. But those still leave plenty of room for these three major cleavages (welfare, defense, and social issues) to reinforce one another.

Why, we should ask, are these seemingly disparate matters increasingly being treated as one? Social issues raise questions of traditional authority. Going one way implies support for authorities (parents, professionals, governments) to enforce traditional social norms; going the other way gives those formerly subject to authority—women, children, gays, and lesbians—the freedom to choose as they wish. In a word, these are issues of equality.

Relating equality/inequality to social-welfare spending is easy, involving as it does the redistribution of financial resources from richer to poorer people. Does defense fit in? It need not, of course. Defense spending may be considered on its merits, the external danger related to the internal cost. Yet defense might also, depending on the perceptual frame brought to it, be perceived in part as an egalitarian issue. If defense were viewed either as in competition with spending on welfare, or if the United States were seen as trying to exert control over poorer and weaker nations (say, in Central America), defense could be considered as antiegalitarian.

One can believe in a strong defense and yet feel the current buildup has been excessive. After all, the actual relation of defense spending to national security is as tenuous as welfare spending is to personal development. Yet those for whom defense of the nation is part and parcel of the preservation of its market institutions have come to view lower taxes and higher defense spending as mutually supportive.

In analyzing a national poll of citizens, Arthur Sanders found that "party identification is significant for almost every variable. Democrats are likely to favor more spending in just about every area than are Republicans. The one exception, not surprisingly, is military spending, where the Republicans are more supportive of expenditures."[13] There

[13]Arthur Sanders, "Public Attitudes on Public Spending." Paper prepared for the 1984 Annual Meeting of the American Political Science Association, Washington, D.C., August 30–September 2, 1984, p. 8.

is a strong and positive connection between a desire for deficit reduction and increased military spending:

> [T]hose whose first priority is lower taxes or lower spending are more likely to prefer cuts in welfare, aid to cities, and food stamps. . . . Interestingly, those desiring a lower deficit or lower taxes as a first economic priority were significantly more supportive of military spending than those with other economic priorities. In fact, these were the most important contributors to views on military spending. . . . Thus, a strategy keyed to lowering the deficit which focused on military spending is unlikely to be well received. Those most concerned with the broader economic issue of the deficit are not the same people who want less military spending. In fact, just the opposite is true.[14]

Investigation into the question of whether congressmen must vote for higher spending in order to get reelected comes up with a negative conclusion: Legislators may think so but their perceptions are mistaken.[15] (Of course, were this relationship held uniformly, no fiscal conservative could ever get elected.) Every test so far devised suggests that spending in general or within a district does not help an officeholder. High spenders, even if they occupy marginal seats, fare no better at the polls than low spenders. Congressmen who announce their retirement do not change their pattern of voting or vote differently than those who continue to run for office. Members from safe districts do not systematically vote for lower spending. But, at least on domestic issues, Republicans vote for less and Democrats for more.[16] My guess is that the movement of Republicans to the South and of southern conservatives to the Republican party has made the major parties more internally cohesive. By the same token, however, this development has driven the parties further apart on the budget. While everyone will say, with self-satisfaction, that they favor a balanced budget, the parties differ dramatically on how this should be done. Balance at lower levels is quite different than balance of taxing and spending at high levels. The mix between defense and domestic, even the distribution between welfare

---

[14]*Ibid.*, p. 9.

[15]Paul Feldman and James Jandrow, "Congressional Elections and Local Federal Spending," *American Journal of Political Science,* Vol. 28, No. 1 (February 1984), pp. 147–64.

[16]James L. Payne, "Why They Spend," typescript, 1986.

and infrastructure (science, roads, education), are matters of contro-versy. With the major parties divided on the size and allocation of the budget, it is not so surprising that agreements to disagree have become far more common; their name is Continuing Resolutions (CRs).

CONTINUING, OMNIBUS RESOLUTIONS

Continuing Resolutions, which provide interim funding, are old hat. Where in the past they were exceptional, nowadays they have become routine. What is more, CRs have become longer; between 1975 and 1984 they grew from 5 pages to an average of 100 pages. Length grows with function. Where before CRs were applied only to a few programs or agencies, now they may cover most of them. Where before simple language would do—merely stating the agency would be funded at the lowest level passed by House or Senate, or a committee thereof—now entire appropriations bills are included.

"[T]he growth of continuing resolutions," Robert Keith and Ed-ward Davis correctly conclude, "appears to be directly related to the growing inability to enact some regular appropriations bills on time or at all."[17] True, but not true enough. If time were the major difficulty, pushing back the fiscal year, together with abandoning the Second Resolution, should have alleviated it. If time mattered most, CRs would be shorter, not longer. On the contrary, the complexity of CRs is a strong indicator of dissensus; CRs carry on the struggle over spending in another guise. The overwhelming detail can only be meant to commit the parties to specified spending. Thus we learn that by incorporation CRs now commonly include references to authoriz-ing legislation whose sponsors were otherwise unable to have them passed on their own merits. The more continuous Continuing Resolu-tions become, the more they testify to a breakdown of what had been ordinary modes of accommodation.

The culmination of the Continuing Resolution occurred in 1986.

[17]Robert Keith and Edward Davis, "Congress and Continuing Appropriations: New Variations on an Old Theme," *Public Budgeting and Finance*, Vol. 5, No. 1 (Spring 1985).

Instead of using CR for only a few appropriations bills, the CR packaged all 13 bills in an Omnibus Appropriations Act. No, Congress wasn't kidding; the act included all regular appropriations bills and a lot more (from Pentagon procurement rules to transferring Washington's airports to local control). To vote "no" or to veto meant closing down government. To vote "yes" meant voting in ignorance. "Either vote is irresponsible," Representative Henry Hyde (R-Ill.) expostulated, "and any process that puts you in that kind of a position is an abomination." Congress was following the football adage, "When in doubt, punt." Angered, Hyde said "We kick on signal. It's a disgrace."[18]

An omnibus CR does obfuscate responsibility. It is not easy to say who voted for or against what. Perhaps budget analyst Stanley Collender, author of a national newsletter on the budget, is right when he argues that

> The President and Congress, the House and Senate, and the two major political parties have fundamentally different fiscal policy agendas—and fundamental differences of opinion over budget priorities. These very real differences are frustrating efforts to resolve the deficit problem. Elected officials, unable to compromise their differences and solve the problem, are seeking ways to avoid accountability [19]

Collender also observes that the CR approach, by focusing on total expenditures, may make it less necessary to struggle over individual programs. The chairman of the Senate Appropriations Committee, liberal Republican Mark Hatfield, was on target when, according to a *National Journal* summary, he anticipated ending up with an omnibus CR "because it would be very hard to get President Reagan to sign separate bills while congressional and White House priorities are so different."[20]

One could argue, as some legislators do, that the omnibus approach works better than the regular process; appropriations passed on October 17, 1986, whereas in prior years some lingered until November or December.[21]

---

[18]Jonathan Rauch, "One Big, Big Bill," *National Journal*, November 1, 1986, p. 2654.
[19]Committee for a Responsible Federal Budget memo, October 20, 1986, p. 3.
[20]Rauch, "Big, Big Bill."
[21]*Ibid.*

When conflicts are of long standing, the CR is the ultimate weapon. It is now possible for the entire texts of appropiations bills that would otherwise face special difficulties on the floor to be folded into an omnibus CR. In this way foreign aid has been partially protected from congressmen who want to shift funds to domestic spending.

Although a CR gives committee chairs power over subcommittees, because the chair is in charge, it is hard to see why so few members protest unless they are seeking leverage against the president. Continuing Resolutions do vitiate the veto power. While the president, through OMB, has ample oportunity to express his preferences, it is not easy for him, in effect, to veto the government. Whereas President Reagan vetoed a bill for several executive agencies in 1985 because it contained $900 million more spending than he wanted; for instance, he signed a CR for only $115 million less.

Representative Neal Smith (D-Iowa) summed up the main advantage: "It [the CR] permits both sides to be forced to compromise."[22] That is why Representative David Obey, a House leader on budget reform, suggested to the Democratic caucus it would be better to embrace the inevitable by acting from the beginning as if an omnibus appropriation had become the normal mode of budgeting. Obey's proposal was turned down in caucus 53 to 176, but members expect it to come up again.[23]

WHY BUDGET DECISIONS HAVE BECOME SO DIFFICULT

In order to understand why budget issues have become so hard to resolve, recourse to the Thompson–Tuden matrix (Figure 6-1), in which degrees of agreement on objectives and knowledge of how to attain them are related to each other, may be helpful.

When there is agreement on objectives of policy as well as on the means to achieve them, decisions are programmed; that is to say, ac-

[22]Stephen Gettinger, "Congress Returns to Tackle Biggest-Ever 'CR,' " *Congressional Quarterly,* September 6, 1986, pp. 2059–63.
[23]*Ibid.*

FIGURE 6-1
Thompson–Tuden Matrix.

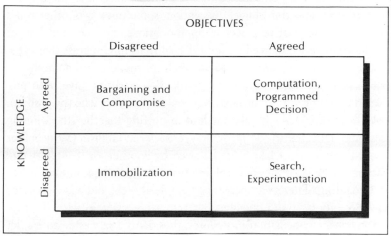

cepted formulas are used to compute solutions. Agreement on objectives but disagreement on the means for achieving them leads to search and experimentation in pursuit of new knowledge. Disagreement on objectives but knowledge of how to achieve various ones propels the political system into bargaining and compromise over the objectives of participants. Dissensus, disagreement over both ends and means, leads to immobilization.

From the end of the Second World War until the late 1960s, the budgetary process was stable. Though there were efforts to alter its form, such as program and performance budgeting, these were largely concerned with improving the efficiency and effectiveness of existing programs. Hence we can conclude that there was general agreement on ends, give or take a few percent and a few programs, but some dissatisfaction with the means of achieving them. While efforts to improve efficiency continued, the Budget Reform Act of 1974 focused attention on the substance of the budget—how much in total, how divided among major programs, who should pay. From the mid-1970s onward, the reformed process worked in a manner of speaking—decisions were made—but the procedures did not work in quite the same way in any two consecutive years. Sometimes the president's budget message provided the starting point, sometimes it didn't. Sometimes there was a first, second, and third budget resolution, sometimes two, other times only one. The relative power of appropriations, finance, and budget committees varied markedly. And the coalitions in Congress that eventually made the crucial choices—so much for defense and domestic, so much in total, reallocation of tax burdens—could not have been predicted from one year to the next. Nor could anyone say who (by position, role, or ideology) would take the lead in putting together the winning coalition. Uncertainty, delay, disarray, crisis, even fatalism (Why bother if each heroic effort had to be followed by another, or if interest rate increases wiped out the effects of months of struggle?) became hallmarks of budgeting. There was increasing complexity (the old appropriations and tax processes still operated but they were overlaid with the new resolutions, reconciliation procedures, presidential sequester orders, let alone credit and tax expenditure budgets) but there was not clarity. What did all this mean?

I recall hearing it said about a father of eleven children that he was always one child over being adequate. Perhaps the simplest explanation of budgetary dissensus is that the demands made on Congress, together with its self-imposed requirements, always remained one step above congressional capacity to manage. In the dramatic rise of government spending from the mid-1960s through the 1970s, there was nothing intrinsic that had to lead to overloading the budgetary process. Even the decline in economic growth, though it undoubtedly made decisions more difficult (there being less to go around), was no insuperable obstacle. Indeed, the Budget Reform Act enabled Congress, were it so inclined, to relate revenue to expenditure—either raising taxes or reducing expenditures so as to arrive at totals it thought appropriate. And Congress did try. The rate of increase in spending did slow down. New entitlements, and other forms of spending that had hitherto escaped the appropriations process, were made more difficult to achieve. If rates were not raised, "bracket creep" increased the tax take in an inflationary period. While deficits continued, they did not represent as large a proportion of national product.

At the same time, however, Congress had placed itself in the position of having to take global positions unique in American budgetary history. It did have to establish total spending and revenue and divide these totals by major substantive categories. Whereas before such choices were best described as outcomes or resultants—known only by adding up choices made on an item-by-item or program-by-program basis through a maze of semi-independent committees and subcommittees— now Congress had to operate as a collective body. Of course, such choices could be (and were) obfuscated by setting totals high or by appearing to stay within them while knowing additional sums would be required. As long as most legislators believed that they had come close enough, that deficits of a certain range were acceptable, even desirable, they could persuade themselves that government was not only appearing to be, but actually was, coping.

The villainous "stagflation," that hitherto unheard-of, simultaneous occurrence of inflation plus unemployment, was to change all that. Stagflation undermined congressional (especially Democratic) confidence in Keynesian methods of managing the economy. "Fine-tuning" was out. Instead of the widespread consensus based on positive postwar economic performance, doubt grew not only about whether deficits were desirable but also about whether there was any right way to proceed. The knowledge portion of our matrix had been undermined.

The broad agreement on economic management was not total. Always there were market individualists—supporters of a smaller government that would intervene less in economic activity. What was new in the 1970s was that they had developed ideas—monetarism, supply-side economics—at variance with the by-then conventional Keynesian wisdom. For a time it was hard for individualists to argue with economic success. Stagflation brought them to the fore. At the same time, the Democratic party was demoralized as the Carter administration sought to fight inflation through recession. Consequently, as the matrix suggests, when there is disagreement over the causal relationships, the general public and political elites were disposed to try something new.

Enter Ronald Reagan. Attention has been focused on his efforts to reduce domestic spending. He and his administration tried in their first term but they were only modestly successful. Had they cut more, however, nothing would have prevented Democrats from raising spending later. Too little attention has been devoted to the important ways in which Reagan made it harder to budget in the old ways. The Kemp–Roth income-tax cuts wiped out several years of resources otherwise available for incremental program increases and deficit reductions. Indexation of tax brackets took away revenue increases that would otherwise have come about without requiring legislative action. Increases in defense spending left less room for maintenance of domestic programs or deficit reduction. Taken together, these Reagan-inspired changes made hard choices by Congress more necessary but also more difficult. For such changes foreclosed the most important actions—quiet revenue and spending increases—that participants in budgeting might, in earlier times, have used to come to an accommodation.

The visible presence of Ronald Reagan brought to the surface a phenomenon that had been going on for at least two decades—an increasing polarization of elites. The conservative majority of the Republican party and the liberal majority of the Democratic party were further from each other in the 1980s than they had been in earlier decades. The main cleavage was over how far government should go in reducing social and economic inequalities. It was easy to draw such a conclusion in a time of diminishing fiscal resources, sizable defense increases, and cuts in many social programs.

Let us suppose that there was general agreement on budget balance. One way to proceed would be to raise revenues and/or reduce expenditures. But Democrats want to maintain or increase domestic spending while Republicans wish to cut taxes and increase defense spending. No room there. Another way would be to cut all spending (except interest on the debt) across the board, thus avoiding disputes over distributive issues. But if Democrats insist on not cutting welfare programs and Republicans refuse to touch defense, the scope for cuts would be small. When there are big things neither side will give up, the scope for compromise is much diminished.

Thus disagreement over the desired levels of spending and taxing became intertwined with differences over how benefits and burdens should be distributed. The "objectives" dimension of our matrix now joins "knowledge" as disagreed.

If decisions on taxing and spending could be disaggregated, it might be possible to find shifting majorities on this or that alternative. That is exactly how things were done from the mid-1970s through the early 1980s. But Congress increasingly denied itself that option. The result, consequently, of having to confront the issues—the size and composition of taxing and spending—all at once is the creeping stalemate that characterizes budgeting today. As the creators of the Thompson–Tuden matrix wrote, "the most likely action in this situation . . . is the decision not to face the issue,"[24] otherwise observed as delay, obfuscation, continuing resolutions, and other manifestations of dissensus. Instructive evidence of what happens when there is neither agreement nor trust is the proliferation of budgetary gimmicks, the use of deceptive procedures.

GIMMICKS

When relations among participants in budgeting are relatively stable and trustworthy, based on long-term convergence over objectives, the use of gimmicks—appearances costumed as realities—have their amusing aspects. Taking a cut that is actually an increase because an inappropriate base has been used, or because lost funds will have to be restored, the ancient Washington Monument ploy (named after impossible proposals to close down this American shrine) may be treated with wry amusement. Large-scale and repeated efforts to deceive would be treated by dismissal or demotion as the participants depend on trust to get their work done, it being impossible, even in those days, up through the 1950s, to study most claims firsthand. Now that budgetary stringency has become severe, as a consequence of deficits and a general attack on spending, however, the use of gimmicks has reached major proportions. The difference is that gimmicks are now used by participants who once opposed them. As gimmickry becomes more like the rule and less like the exception, it is no longer so funny.

[24]James D. Thompson and Arthur Tuden, "Strategies, Structures, and Processes of Organizational Decision," in J. D. Thompson et al., eds., *Comparative Studies in Administration* (University of Pittsburgh Press, 1959), p. 202.

Cuts may be used as sanctions against legislators opposed to spending programs. Senator Pete Domenici, chair of the Senate Budget Committee until 1987, was compelled to vote for certain projects in his district so as to show that in this respect he was "one of the boys." When Senator James Buckley attempted to remove 44 public works projects at the committee stage, members of the Public Works Committee ostentatiously voted for 43, all except the one in his state.[25]

A former OMB official, Bo Cutter, tells an instructive story:

> In 1978, HEW Secretary Joseph Califano offered Jimmy Carter a deal. If the President would increase certain discretionary programs in the "restrained" 1980 budget by a few hundred million dollars, he would return to the President more than that amount in savings—by proposing a number of sensible and small reductions in Social Security. Secretary Califano's offer, in the larger scheme of things, made a great deal of sense. But he was offering to trade uncontrollables for discretionary dollars. The President agreed. Secretary Califano got his budget increases for 1980. Congress never gave the President his savings.[26]

Congress may appear to meet spending targets in budget resolutions by voting only eleven months of funds, knowing the rest will have to be restored. The food stamp program received this treatment several times. Paydays may be moved forward or back so they don't count toward the deficit for the fiscal year in question. A similar feat is accomplished by failing to provide essential spending authority. The Commodity Credit Corporation is financed by authority to borrow in order to provide farm price supports. By refusing some hundreds of millions of CCC's request, thereby seemingly cutting the budget, Congress fails to provide funds that will have to be restored later.[27]

Gimmicks are chosen for a purpose. Congress needs to meet a certain figure for reducing the deficit. One way to help accomplish this purpose, while still not savaging programs, is to do what consumers do, that is, "buy now and pay later." The deficit figure may be met by choosing the

[25]Reported in David Mayhew, *Congress: The Electoral Connection* (New Haven: Yale University Press, 1974), pp. 91–92, footnote 32.

[26]Cutter, "The Battle of the Budget," pp. 61–67; quote on page 65.

[27]Jerome A. Miles, "The Congressional Budget and Impoundment Control Act: A Departmental Budget Officer's View," *The Bureaucrat*, Vol. 5, No. 4 (January 1977).

House outlay number for defense, which is lower, and the Senate authority, which is higher but can be paid out over a number of years.

"Hypocrisy," La Rochefoucauld observed, "is an homage vice pays to virtue." This maxim comes to life in light of the current budget quandry. There would be no reason to vote both for a lower budget resolution and for higher individual expenditures if the appearance were not seen as serving virtue. "In effect," Senator Hatfield complained, "we're talking out of both sides of our mouth. We want everyone else's project reduced." No one wants to make what have come to be mostly painful choices. But occasionally Congress resists. The fiscal 1986 appropriations bill for the Department of Housing and Urban Development and seventeen independent agencies shows the Senate tempted but resisting.

> . . . spending would exceed targets by about $800 million. Sen. Jake Garn, R-Utah, the chairman of the Appropriations Subcommittee on HUD-Independent Agencies, offered a package of further cuts to the bill, worked out by the Appropriations Committee, to bring it within the budget. The Senate agreed to the package but then went on to add spending, pushing the bill back over the limit. Domenici responded with an amendment cutting the bill back to the target; the Senate adopted that and then once again agreed to amendments adding spending back. Garn admonished the Senate, "Let's stop having it both ways"; after some private discussions, the Senate finally agreed to cuts that stuck.[28]

Fiddling with the fiscal year—either to put expenditure in an earlier or later accounting period, depending on which will help the most—is a pure (if that word may be used) gimmick. Defense salaries may be paid a day earlier or later, thus "saving" billions for the next fiscal year. Medicare miraculously lived an eleven-month year in 1980 and a thirteen-month year in 1981.[29] In order to make the 1986 deficit look smaller than it was so as to meet Gramm–Rudman–Hollings targets, Congress moved a big $680 million revenue-sharing payment forward by five days so the Balanced Budget and Deficit Reduction Act would not

[28]Jonathan Rauch, "Senate Budget Panel Leaders Wage War on 'Budget-Busting' Appropriations Bills," *National Journal,* November 30, 1985, p. 2705.

[29]See Allen Schick, "Controlling the 'Uncontrollables': Budgeting for Health Care in an Age of Mega-Deficits." Paper prepared for AEI Pew Fellows Conference, November 1985, pp. 25–26.

officially take notice of it. Noting that the advance payment would entail borrowing costs, Representative Jack Brooks said "Isn't it ironic that we are wasting a half a million dollars trying to fool the taxpayer into believing that we are getting the deficit down, when in fact we are actually increasing it?"[30] A *Wall Street Journal* headline—"Administration Expected to Use More Gimmicks in Effort to Reduce . . . Deficit"—suggests that the day of the gimmick is not yet over.[31]

During Dwight David Eisenhower's presidency, every dollar reduction in outlays was matched by a three-dollar reduction in authority. Since budget authority extends over time, while outlays are confined to a single year, the behavior of the Eisenhower administration signified its genuine commitment to expenditure reduction. Not so with President Lyndon Baines Johnson. He initiated a tradeoff between outlays and authority that guaranteed larger future spending while temporarily cutting existing expenditure. When the combination of the Great Society programs with the war in Vietnam left funds short, LBJ got new domestic programs started with small early outlays, his version of the wedge or camel's nose strategy. Agencies also found it more palatable to accept small current losses in outlays for future gains.[32]

There is a different, task-oriented reason for budgetary side payments—giving agencies more authority to spend over time in exchange for lesser immediate cuts in outlays. Under the Employment Act of 1946, the president is given responsibility for economic management. This management, called fiscal policy, requires fixing the level of outlays and revenues so as to affect the economy. "From this perspective," Kamlet and Mowery remark perspicaciously, "the goal of macroeconomic stabilization may be viewed as yet another competing interest, supported by the White House, which gives rise to the possibility of trading. . . ."[33]

There are other unacceptable reasons for the use of gimmicks. One is the reverse gimmick, a real spending cut, but one that actually reduces

---

[30]*National Journal*, October 11, 1986, p. 2415.

[31]*Wall Street Journal*, November 18, 1986, p. 68.

[32]Mark S. Kamlet and David C. Mowery, "Budgetary Side Payments and Government Growth: 1953–1968," *American Journal of Political Science*, Vol. 27, No. 4 (November 1983), pp. 636–64.

[33]*Ibid.*, p. 662.

quality while increasing future costs. In making across-the-board cuts, for example, the first things to go are such "unessential" items as travel and staff training. These may be false economies, however, when the lack of necessary information or training produces poor performance, more expensive medical treatment, and the like. After the closing of public health hospitals, to take another example, the Indian Health Service had to dismiss a number of its lower-paid professionals in order to make room for higher-paid people from public health who had more seniority.[34]

What is gained by making genuine economies if the result is only further reductions? Padding the budget to leave room for OMB and Congress to cut makes sense in the face of formula cuts. Donna Shalala, a political scientist, now chancellor of the University of Wisconsin at Madison, then Assistant Secretary of the Department of Housing and Urban Development, tells a familiar tale:

> If you want to maintain your budget in an agency at a certain level, there's no incentive for coming and suggesting ways of delivering those precise services in different ways. Cost-conscious budget managers for the President will take advantage of your initiative, and they'll simply take the rest of the money off to someone else who didn't show that ingenuity.
>
> I went to the Hill this year without an increase in my budget. . . . And I told the Secretary I didn't want an increase, and everybody yelled and screamed and jumped up and down and said, "You've got to take an increase the way everybody does, 'cause when you get to the Hill you've got to take a cut." The Hill paid no attention to the fact that I went up without an increase; they just gave me the same cut they gave everybody else. And I went up and I argued that I hadn't asked for an increase. And they said that was just dumb.[35]

Gimmickry has spawned criticism of the post-1974 process inside and outside of Congress. Citing evidence that "the reconciliation process has run amok," for instance, Richard Cohen of the *National Journal*— noting that the 1985 bill ran to 198 pages in small print—provided this

[34]An article by Joseph S. Wholey contains examples of both true and false economies: "Executive Agency Retrenchment," in Mills and Palmer, *Federal Budget Policy*, pp. 295–332.

[35]Quoted in David Broder, *Changing of the Guard: Power and Leadership in America* (New York: Simon and Schuster, 1980), p. 434.

list of what he (and most observers) considered extraneous matters, a bill so complex that 30 subconferences were required to negotiate Senate–House differences.

- routine extension of several housing programs;
- a requirement that the Transportation Secretary withhold 10 percent of highway funds starting in fiscal 1989 from states that have not set their minimum drinking age at 21;
- an instruction to build three highway bridges over the Ohio River between designated points in Ohio and Kentucky;
- a plan to allocate to Gulf Coast states billions of dollars from oil and gas drilling on the Outer Continental Shelf;
- extensive overhaul of medicare, including changes in the 1983 law that set up a new prospective reimbursement system for hospital fees to limit costs;
- extension of the right to social security benefits to children adopted by and living with their great-grandparents;
- eligibility of Connecticut state police for social security;
- an increase in the federal excise tax on domestically minded coal to finance the black lung disability trust fund and a waiver for five years of interest payments on the fund's indebtedness.[36]

Cohen concluded that "members would do well to stop criticizing his [President Reagan's] shortcomings and take their own role more seriously."[37]

Congressmen themselves, now that the reform act of 1974 makes them responsible for their own budget resolutions, have become aware that gimmickry is institutionally destructive. Members can now ring all the changes on devices to make spending fit within resolutions or to have them appear lower than they actually are. Committees report savings

[36]Richard E. Cohen, "Unreconciled," *National Journal*, January 11, 1986, p. 110.
[37]*Ibid.*

that actually are only temporary. Votes are forced on cuts so as to make it difficult to approve them. Payments for medicare are pushed into the next fiscal year. That is why SBC and OMB try to get multiyear reconciliations for appropriations and authorizations.[38] The lack of connection between appearance in the resolution and reality in spending fools no one but does contribute to low morale and self-doubt in Congress.

Padding in the exception of cuts is part of playing the game. As Senator James Abdnor argued, "While this figure [the 7.5 percent figure for real growth in defense spending] is entirely responsible and defensible in its own right, the truth of the matter, as we all realize, is that whatever number we settle on will be our starting point when we go to conference with the House. The House approved only a 2.3 percent increase." Similarly, Representative David Obey, desiring to ameliorate cuts in social programs, suggested that "I simply don't think you should lead with your bottom line. It's like selling your soul to the devil before you're tempted."[39] Later, Representative Obey let it all hang out: "The only kind of budget resolution," said he sadly, "that can pass this place is a dishonest one. I think that degrades the entire congressional process."[40]

Gimmickry was a precursor of Gramm–Rudman–Hollings. If Congress is so out of control, if it is in disrepute with its own members, then maybe they cannot trust themselves. Why not, then, force themselves to do the right thing, namely, balance the budget in such a fashion that they cannot reverse the process by playing the usual games? GRH, to be sure, is itself only part of a larger game in which legislators gain electoral protection against arguments that they are unbalancing the budget by saying they have already arranged to do that very thing. Such a demanding posture would not have been adopted, however, if rampant gimmickry had not convinced enough legislators that they were being too clever.

[38]Robert D. Reischauer, "The Congressional Budget Process," in Mills and Palmer, *Federal Budget Policy*, pp. 385–413, especially pp. 397–98.

[39]Reischauer, "Mickey Mouse," p. 33.

[40]Quoted in Richard E. Cohen, "House Braces for Showdown Over How It Should Package Its Annual Budget," *National Journal*, November 27, 1982, pp. 2024–26.

WHY GRH PASSED

The Gramm–Rudman–Hollings bill (formally known as the Balanced Budget and Deficit Reduction Act of 1985), which essentially requires five yearly sequential across-the-board reductions in federal spending until the deficit has been reduced to zero, is proof positive of mistrust. (Of course, these sequential reductions were required only if prior agreement on reductions was not forthcoming; but it was the sequences that were normal, the hoped-for agreement, abnormal.) Here we have a procedure that almost every member of Congress believes is foolish, if not stupid; that everyone who knows anything about it thinks could be improved upon in five minutes; yet it received majority support in both houses of Congress and was signed by the president. The act, which dramatically affects the future of numerous government programs and congressional budget procedures, was passed without public hearings, without debate by any House or Senate standing committee, and without any substantive debate on the House floor. When everyone says that something is not right, and yet they keep doing it, there is a puzzle that should excite our interest.

Year after year Congress has advertised its disabilities by taking longer and longer to reach agreement; few can remember the last year all appropriations bills were passed on time. Congress is tired of budgeting to no purpose, tired of budgeting, budgeting, and nothing but budgeting. Its members despaired sufficiently of accommodation to wish to cover over their disagreements by a formula, all the while expecting, even hoping, that the balancing mechanism had been made so onerous (After all, who wants to reduce the number of aircraft controllers?) that it would collapse of its own weight. Crash! This is no way to run a ship, especially not the ship of state, unless you regard the wreckage the lesser evil compared to giving in to the other side.

Gramm–Rudman–Hollings is as (or more) important for what it symbolizes as for what it does. The imposition of a formula for replacing the power of the purse, the most important congressional power, is an abdication of power. Congress is saying that it is out of control. It cannot help itself. Faced with difficult decisions, the one thing Congress knows is that it won't be able to decide wisely. Therefore, guarding against its own worst tendencies in advance, Congress anticipates its collective unwisdom by taking away its discretion.

Binding oneself against one's worst inclinations may appear strange, but it has precedent. Fearing continual scandal, Congress took away its power to appoint local postmasters. Observing as well the unfortunate consequences of the Smoot–Hawley Tariff, Congress also created a buffer, a tariff commission between it and temptation so that it could no longer, as an ordinary matter, set tariff rates on individual items. At least since Ulysses and the Sirens, attempting to protect oneself against self-destructive tendencies has been a well-known strategy. Why did Congress agree to limit its most important power, the power that humbled tyrants and brought about representative government, a power, moreover, on which other legislative powers depend?

The rise of the Gramm–Rudman–Hollings Act took place in an environment of disarray, dismay at the ever-rising deficits, and concern by legislators with their own inability to govern. The opportunity was ripe for an outsider, Phil Gramm of Texas (who, upon being read out of the Democratic party in the House, won a seat as a Republican senator), to ally himself with a Democratic outsider, Senator Fritz Hollings of South Carolina, and with a dedicated budget balancer, Republican Warren Rudman of New Hampshire. The three offered the radical proposal as a rider to the annual misery of raising the debt ceiling, this time to a previously unheard of level of $2 trillion. They believed, as did many other legislators, that unless Congress was faced with something much worse than business as usual, it would continue to avoid balancing the budget.

Ronald Reagan felt (partly rightly, partly wrongly, but with conviction) that every time he compromised by raising taxes, he did not get in return promised cuts in domestic spending. Though he preferred tax reductions to lower deficits, he did want balance if (and only if) it could be achieved solely by spending cuts. The GRH formula looked like it might make that possible. The president did not want to cut defense, but that was happening anyway.[41] So he supported GRH.

[41]This summary is taken from a book by Joseph White and Aaron Wildavsky entitled *The Deficit and the Public Interest: The Search for Responsible Budgeting in the 1980s* (Berkeley: University of California Press, 1990).

But why did Democratic liberals, Republican moderates, and otherwise sane and sensible legislators (there were a few, such as Republican Senator Nancy Kassebaum and Democrat Pat Moynihan, who opposed GRH to the end) go along? Fearful of rising deficits, frustrated by inability to get agreement on taxing and spending, unwilling to say "no" to any plan for balance, realizing that they could change their minds later when the crunch came, they went along.

Liberals have another story to tell. They wanted to pin the deficit tag on Reagan and not allow him to do that to them. Led by Speaker O'Neill, they insisted on changes in the original conception, where everything, except possibly social security, was subject to proportional cuts, and succeeded in getting the most important entitlements for low-income and elderly people either excluded or subject only to modest reductions of 1 to 2 percent. By doing this, congressional liberals hoped not only to protect the poor and elderly but also, by making defense bear a disproportionate share, encourage the president to compromise with them so as not to invoke the dreaded sequestration procedure.

Opinions understandably vary as to whether the Balanced Budget and Emergency Deficit Control Act of 1985 (Public Law 99-172) is meant to be workable. If (as in the phrase Senator Rudman made famous, "it's so bad it's good") the idea is to scare legislators into reducing the deficit, the consequences must be horrendous. And, if followed for the full course, so they would be, wiping out half of general government. Anticipating this havoc, legislators may be motivated to settle on a more variegated and hence more sensible deficit-reduction package than across-the-board cuts. Unfortunately, being sensible requires being able to choose among the entire panoply of governmental programs. But the act exempts 48 percent of these (mostly entitlements and debt interest) from across-the-board cuts, with an additional 24 percent available only for very limited reductions. Only 27 percent of the budget, mostly in defense, is fully available for sequestration—that is, the withholding of budget authority up to the amount required to be cut to meet the deficit target. The *National Journal* table, "Where the Ax Would Fall," tells the story: You cannot get 100 percent of the deficit reduction you need from 27 percent of the budget (Table 6-1).

TABLE 6-1
Where the Ax Would Fall

It may be that Congress will act to avoid the triggering of automatic spending cuts of any great magnitude. If it does not, however, a small portion of the federal budget would be cut to the core.

By the time Congress was through exempting some major programs and writing special rules for others, not much was left. Of almost $1 trillion in federal spending, about 27 per cent—of which two-thirds is defense spending and the rest domestic—would bear almost all of any major automatic cut. After subtraction of some $3 billion in cuts from health programs and from the cancellation of cost-of-living adjustments (COLAs), half of the total amount of any automatic spending cut—which could be tens of billions of dollars—would have to come out of less than $100 billion in domestic spending.

Not by accident, virtually every major domestic program providing direct payments or benefits to individuals is exempt or exposed to only limited automatic cuts. The programs left to be cut heavily are those providing more generalized benefits and services: transportation, aid to state and local governments, housing, education, infrastructure, energy, environmental quality and general government.

According to an unofficial House analysis, here's the breakdown of which programs would be exempt, which would take limited cuts, and which would bear the brunt of automatic spending cuts (spending shows outlays in billions of dollars; percentages may not add to totals because of rounding):

	Fiscal 1986 spending	*Percent of budget*
Exempt programs		
Social security	$202	21%
Interest on the national debt	142	15
Nondefense spending obligated in prior years	78	8
Major low-income programs*	61	6
Unemployment compensation	20	2
Veterans' pensions and compensation	14	1
Offsetting receipts	−52	−5
Total exempt	$465	48%

*Medicaid, aid to families with dependent children, special supplemental feeding program for women, infants and children, supplemental security income, food stamps and child nutrition.

(continued)

TABLE 6-1

(continued)

	Fiscal 1986 spending	Percent of budget
Programs taking limited reductions		
Defense spending obligated in prior years (contracts)*	$100	10%
Medicare, veterans' health, other health programs**	86	9
Retirement programs with COLAs***	48	5
Total taking limited reductions	$234	24%

*Contracts can be cut or modified at President's discretion.
**Cannot be automatically cut more than 1 percent in fiscal 1986 and 2 percent thereafter.
***Only COLAs can be automatically cut; rest of spending exempt.

	Fiscal 1986 spending	Percent of budget
Programs bearing the brunt		
Domestic: discretionary spending (newly budgeted only)	$ 74	8%
Domestic: minor entitlements	11	1
Domestic: other	6	1
Defense: new spending	164	17
Defense: unspent from prior years	10	1
Total bearing the brunt	$265	27%

Source: *National Journal*, January 4, 1986, p. 21.

In this game of budgetary chicken, one side assumes that as automatic defense cuts are triggered, the Republicans will blink by raising taxes while the other hopes that as meat-ax cuts in domestic spending grow near, Democrats will blink by making the policy decisions needed for domestic reductions. Each side hopes to prevail by making the budgetary process unworkable. This political Ludditism does not bode well for the ability to govern.

HOW GRH WAS SUPPOSED TO WORK

The Gramm–Rudman–Hollings process is invoked if (and only if) the preexisting process fails to meet the annual deficit reduction targets— from $171.9 billion in 1986 to $144.0 billion in 1987 to zero in 1991. Except in the first and last years, a $10 billion cushion is allowed above the target figure before the sequestration procedure is invoked.

To invoke GRH, the first thing that must happen is a determination that the maximum deficit amount (MDA) has been exceeded. Were there mutual trust, this calculation could have been left to OMB, the agency in charge of making requests for expenditure to Congress. Then, again, mutual trust would imply the ability to work out an accommodation so that everyone would be spared sequestration. The convoluted procedure for calculating MDA, together with the reductions necessary to reach the target figures, is the very manifestation of distrust.

The president is required to submit a budget that does not exceed the annual target figure. In January, however, his budget is only his opinion. Congressional budget resolutions also must conform to the targets for cutting the deficit. But resolutions do not raise revenue or reduce spending any better than most New Year's resolutions predict our behavior.

Snapshot day is August 15. (See Table 6-2 for timetable.) OMB and CBO issue a joint report estimating revenue, expenditures, and, therefore, the gap between them at that moment in time for the fiscal year beginning October 1. This early warning is designed to alert all players to the fact that the rules of the budget game are about to be altered. For the month that follows is supposed to be budgetary show-and-tell time. I say "supposed" because no piece of paper, even a law, can make Congress do what it doesn't want to do. Congress can still ignore GRH or make believe, by various gimmicks, that it has done what is required.

On the 20th of August, according to the original legislation, the directors of OMB and CBO must submit a joint report, not to Congress

TABLE 6-2

Revised Budget and Deficit Reduction Process under
Gramm–Rudman–Hollings

Action	To Be Completed By
President submits budget	Monday after January 3
CBO report to Congress	February 15
Committees submit views and estimates to budget committees	February 25
Senate Budget Committee reports budget resolution	April 1
Congress passes budget resolution	April 15
House Appropriations Committee reports appropriations bills	June 10
Congress passes reconciliation bill	June 15
House passes all appropriations bills	June 30
Initial economic, revenue, outlay and deficit projections made by OMB and CBO	August 15
OMB and CBO report tentative contents of sequester order to GAO	August 20
GAO issues deficit and sequester report to the president	August 25
President issues sequester order	September 1
Fiscal year begins and sequester order takes effect	October 1
OMB and CBO issues revised projections based on subsequent congressional action	October 5
GAO issues revised sequester report to president	October 10
Final sequester order becomes effective	October 15
GAO issues compliance report on sequester order	November 15

Source: Balanced Budget and Emergency Deficit Control Act of 1985.

or the president but to the Comptroller General. This CBO–OMB report estimates revenues and expenditures (income and outlays) for the fiscal year. After comparing the two figures, the report states for the record whether the difference plus the allowable $10 billion is larger than the MDA. If the amount is smaller, and the Comptroller General concurs, the GRH process stops there. If the target figure has been breached, the joint report specifies the reductions necessary to reach that level.

Before describing how that is to be done, a word about the role of the General Accounting Office is in order. The Comptroller General was supposed to review joint OMB–CBO calculations, explain differences between their report and his, and issue his own independent calculation of the deficit and of the required sequestration order. In other words, after CBO and OMB check each other, they can be overruled by the GAO whose recommendations are binding on the president. It was this binding character that led the Reagan administration to support the challenge to the constitutionality of the provision, a challenge upheld by the Supreme Court. For us, it is not constitutionality but rather the political theory behind this tripartite device—OMB, and the president for whom it stands, is not trusted to faithfully execute this law—that is revealing.

On the 15th of August, in addition to estimating the size of the deficit, GRH requires OMB and CBO to estimate economic growth for each quarter of the existing year as well as the last two quarters of the preceding year. The purpose is to tell Congress whether there have been two consecutive quarters of negative growth, in which case sequestration procedures are suspended. Depression, though obviously undesirable, is one way out of the deficit-reduction process.

At this point, CBO and OMB recommend, and GAO was supposed to decide upon, a base from which sequestration is to occur. The calculation of this base is no simple matter. The spending budget itself is complex. Specific priorities are embedded within GRH, requiring numerous exceptions and adjustments. And congressional desire to limit presidential discretion, especially on defense, led to extraordinary arrangements. The president is not to achieve by sleight-of-calculation what he has not won by legislative majorities.

Step one reduces the base for sequestration by the total of exempt programs. Step two deducts from the base the cost of living increases in the rest of government that can be cut. These available COLAs are divided in half and then subtracted from domestic and defense programs, respectively. The reason for this rather strange 50–50 split is that defense and domestic programs have come to be seen as competitors. Where defense lost out in step one (because it is eligible for sequestration while the bulk of domestic spending is not), it gained a bit back in the second stage: Though defense represents more than half of the cutable base, some 60 percent, it takes just half the hit. By strict proportionality, on the other hand, defense should get credit for 60 percent of the sequestered COLAs. Such are the odd outcomes of political bargaining.

The defense sequestration is designed not merely to lower spending but to make sure that, after the first year, the president has as little discretion as possible.

To begin to understand defense sequestration (the amount required not to be spent, by being withheld at the source), it is useful to review the sources of spending. In any year, the defense function (Number 050) has at its disposal new budget authority and old budget authority that is partly obligated and partly unobligated. The outlay base consists of outlays from new budget authority due to be spent that year, plus outlays generated from prior years' obligated balances. What is sequestered (or, better still, sequesterable) is called budgetary resources—that is, the total of new budget authority together with unobligated balances. The use of the composite term *budgetary resources* has led to talk about "blending" rates of spending by mixing its two components. The percentage reduction for outlays is calculated as the amount needed divided by the definition of the outlay base. That exact percentage then is applied to the budgetary resources (which are what is sequestered). For example, in a personnel account, maybe $1.03 billion in budgetary resources exists with $1 billion in projected outlays. If a 10 percent outlay cut is needed, $103 million in resources will be cut. Complexity is the price paid because of congressional concern that the administration would provide the wrong kind of defense or would act outside the spirit of the law to favor defense over domestic policy.

The president issues an initial sequestration report on September 1 telling Congress he has followed the rules (the 50–50 defense-domestic split, the exempt and partially exempt categories, the deficit reduction). At the same time, the president is allowed to suggest an alternative budget quite outside these rules, providing it meets the MDA. As long as GRH is in force, however, presidential sequestration must be done by uniform percentage reductions in defense and domestic categories.

The immediate significance of this uniformity is that, in order to control presidential behavior, it trades off flexibility for rigidity. The president cannot, on his own, eliminate programs or make transfers among categories. For fear of breaking ranks, he can move only in lock-step. Thus the president cannot move to protect programs he deems vital or to advantage new ones, with small bases, compared to large ones with large bases that can better withstand cuts. After sequestration, however, presidents retain whatever reprogramming authority they have been able to exercise in the past.

To continue with the close monitoring of presidential performance, on September 5th he submits a list of proposed changes in contracts to the Armed Services and Appropriations committees. At the end of that month, GAO certifies that the savings stemming from sequestration of contracts are correct.

Starting in mid-August, Congress and the president have had the chance to come up with an alternative to sequestration. If they do not, sequestration takes place automatically on October 15th. But that was before the Supreme Court declared sequestration unconstitutional.

THE SUPREME COURT AND THE SEPARATION OF POWERS: THE COMPTROLLER GENERAL'S ROLE IN SEQUESTRATION RULED UNCONSTITUTIONAL

A lawsuit brought by Representative Michael L. Synar (D-Okla.) and other congressmen, joined by the Public Citizen Litigation Group affiliated with activist Ralph Nader, argued that "Gramm–Rudman tried to insulate Congress from the hard choices our Founding Fathers gave us and expected us to make."[42] Instead of relying upon the concept of

[42]*Congressional Quarterly*, July 12, 1986, p. 1559.

excessive delegation—that Congress could not delegate its powers to one of its chambers or officers, a principle that might have threatened the legality of independent regulatory commissions—the Supreme Court held that while the delegation might be proper it was unconstitutional to give final authority for making cuts to the Comptroller General who could conceivably be dismissed by joint resolution of Congress. Asserting that the Framers had provided not merely a separate but a "wholly independent executive branch" (a big surprise to scholars who follow Richard Neustadt's celebrated formulation of "separated institutions sharing powers"), the Supreme Court, by a seven to two majority on July 7, "held that the powers vested in the Comptroller General . . . violate the command of the Constitution that the Congress play no direct role in the execution of the laws."[43]

Dissents by Justices Byron White and Harry Blackmun sharpened the issues. Reacting against what he considered the majority's "distressingly formalistic view of separation of powers," White argued that in fact the Comptroller General was "one of the most independent officers in the entire federal establishment." He saw no "genuine threat to the basic division between the lawmaking power and the power to execute the law" but a real loss in depriving the president and the Congress of their effort "to counteract ever-mounting deficits." Blackmun thought that the old provision for removing the Comptroller General "pales in importance beside . . . an extraordinary, far-reaching response to a deficit problem of unprecedented proportions." Wise or foolish, Blackmun continued, GRH was among the most important laws of recent decades. "I cannot," he concluded, "see the sense of invalidating legislation of this magnitude in order to preserve a cumbersome, 65-year-old removal power that has never been exercised and appears to have been forgotten until this litigation."[44]

Congress could have decided to reinstate some constitutionally permissible form of the automatic sequester procedure. At first there was talk of altering the provisions for firing the Comptroller General by making GAO an independent agency whose head could be dismissed by

---

[43]"Supreme Court's Gramm-Rudman Opinion," *Congressional Quarterly*, July 12, 1986, p. 1581.

[44]*Congressional Quarterly*, July 12, 1986, p. 1561.

the president but only for wrongdoing. But congressional leaders did not want to lose the valuable services of GAO. That left OMB. But "OMB," as House Majority Whip Foley put it, "was not trusted to avoid politically motivated cooking of the books and skewing of the figures."[45] Accusing OMB of becoming "a rogue elephant in this Administration," Senator Gary Hart quoted the Republican Senate Governmental Affairs Committee as finding that "budgeting at OMB has become a partisan political process."[46] The dilemma is straightforward: The more OMB acts as a nonpartisan career service, as it used to be, the broader its bipartisan support but the less able it would be to satisfy presidential demands for responsiveness.

Senators Gramm, Rudman, and Hollings introduced an amendment on July 23, 1986, that would have given OMB final say in determining how the sequester procedure would be carried out. Immediately it became apparent that distrust of OMB was too great to permit passage. Senator Moynihan claimed that an OMB director could decide whether to hit defense or domestic harder and could distort the actual size of the deficit. The publication of former Budget Director David Stockman's book describing how he had done just that in 1981 did not help OMB's cause. "Do not use David Stockman as a reason against this particular measure," Senator Hollings pleaded, damning with faint praise, "because I do not believe you will find that kind of artful dodger activity in the Office of Management and Budget again."[47] The bill failed in the House.

AVOIDING SEQUESTRATION

Since its authors suspected the role of the GAO might be invalidated by the Supreme Court, thus rendering automatic sequestration null and void, they wrote in a backup procedure. The CBO–OMB joint report

[45]*New York Times*, July 17, 1986, p. D6.
[46]Senator Gary Hart, "What Should Be Done about Gramm-Rudman? Get Rid of the Monster," *New York Times*, July 22, 1986, p. A25.
[47]Elizabeth Wehr, "Gramm-Rudman Repair Effort Stumbles on Mistrust of OMB," *Congressional Quarterly*, July 26, 1986, p. 1682.

of the budget snapshot is now sent to a Temporary Joint Committee on Deficit Reduction, which is made up of the entire membership of the House and Senate Budget Committees. Within five days the Temporary Joint Committee is supposed to report to both houses a joint resolution of sequester based on the arithmetic average of the OMB and CBO reports. The full House and Senate have five days to act on the Joint Resolution. Debate is limited to two hours—easily done by special rule in the House, but requiring unanimous consent in the Senate. A determined senator, therefore, could hold up a vote or force separate votes on individual program restrictions. In addition, and most important, joint committee reports having the force of legislation are subject to presidential veto.

In 1986 the joint report of OMB and CBO was sent to Congress and referred to the Temporary Joint Committee on Deficit Reduction. But a sequestration proposal was never passed because Congress decided it had met the $154 billion reduction target. Informed observers doubt it. By estimating revenue far higher and expenditure far lower than expected, GRH's formal conditions were met. Overlooking gimmicks was widely believed preferable to damaging many desirable programs.

Between the rock of sequestration and the hard place of reductions in the deficit, all that was left were appearances. "Given the choices, which are none," Representative Mike Lowery, a Democratic member of the House Budget Committee, said plaintively, "it's better to do this, given the ridiculous situation we are in." The near $15 billion required to reach the $154 billion deficit figure necessary to avoid sequestration was not exactly nothing; neither was it much of anything as far as making long-lasting inroads on the deficit. The largest category, tentatively agreed to by House, Senate, and OMB negotiators, were estimated asset sales of around $7 billion, especially rural housing and development loans. Aside from the uncertainty of how much would be realized, selling assets would reduce future income, thus leaving future deficits untouched. While asset sales might be desirable as a form of privatization, receiving the discounted future value today does not constitute a deficit reduction tomorrow. Next came some $4 billion plus in revenues, more than half of which were due to increased tax enforcement. A billion or so was to come from a variety of user fees and a third of a billion from increasing the charges on banks to obtain Federal Deposit Insurance. A final billion and a half or so would arise out of accelerating excise tax collections due in fiscal 1988 and moving back the last payment for general revenue sharing so it applied to the fiscal 1986 budget, which was about over.[48] Not too much to be proud of in these accounting gimmicks. The most acute comment came from Representative Leon Panetta: "This place is reflective of the American people: they don't want taxes, they don't want cuts, and they don't want a deficit."[49]

The best that congressional leaders could do was to use humor to ward off depression. Among the kindest was Senator William Armstrong's (R-Colo.) "A package of golden gimmicks, a package of smoke and mirrors." Harsher was Senator James Exon's (D-Nebr.) characterization of the measure as "perverted, phony, unrealistic." Responding to Senate consideration of this purported deficit reduction, Senator Lawton Chiles (D-Fla.) bespoke the common understanding: "It's midway between the best we could do and the worst that could happen." Others, like Representative Martin Leath (D-Tex.), a member of the House Budget Committee, felt that "We're about to pull the ultimate scam, and everybody's included."[50]

UNDESIRABLE YET UNAVOIDABLE

The main lesson of the Gramm–Rudman–Hollings process may well be that while total trust is hard to come by, total mistrust makes budgeting impossible. Why not, then, dispense with GRH altogether? The nub of the matter is that political polarization prevents successful direct annual bargaining on the budget. Since the conservatives think of enhanced defense as essential to protect against external threats to liberty, and the liberals believe that defense growth takes away from domestic welfare

[48]*Federal Budget Report,* September 9, 1986, pp. 3–4; *New York Times,* September 19, 1986, p. A30.

[49]*New York Times,* September 23, 1986, p. B8.

[50]*New York Times,* September 20, 1986, pp. 1 and 50; *Oakland Tribune,* September 10, 1986.

spending, the twain have trouble meeting. Only moderate Republicans and Democrats, who see their devotion to stability threatened by un-balanced budgets, are ready to raise taxes and cut defense and domestic spending. But they are not in the majority.

At every stage of the GRH process, there will be alternatives that appear more intelligent than going through the proportional cut. But polarization will prevent agreement. When no cohesive majority exists, GRH is all that is left. "There is no confidence," Leon Panetta said, "that Congress can pass an alternative."[51] At every stage, therefore, GRH may continue to be both unsatisfactory and unavoidable. That is why GRH may surprise us by surviving.

WHY DOESN'T GRH WORK?

Following regular budget procedure, failure to make changes merely sustains the status quo. The deficit might rise or fall because of external events, such as the condition of the economy, but not by deliberate governmental action. In order to bring the deficit center stage, the Gramm–Rudman–Hollings Act transforms inaction into a form of ac-tion: When Congress and the president do not work together to reach five annual deficit reduction targets, GRH would mandate spending cuts.

GRH establishes a fast track for the regular budget process even before its new procedures, if applicable, take over. Congress is supposed to pass its yearly budget resolution by April 15th, its reconciliation instructions by June 15th, and the House appropriations by June 30th. Moreover, there is a provision stating that the House cannot recess (for Independence Day festivities) until it has passed appropriations. In 1986 none of these deadlines was met. A rule to suspend the rule prohibiting adjournment whizzed by in two minutes flat. The June 15th deadline for reconciliation was missed and spending bills were delayed beyond the June 30 deadline. Budget decisions were finally made in late-night ses-sions in early October, after the beginning of the fiscal year. Why won't Congress follow its own procedures?

[51]*New York Times*, July 17, 1986, p. D6.

No one has reason to play along with the Gramm–Rudman–Hollings procedure unless and until they know whether their favorite programs will do better or worse in negotiation than in sequestration. Until two things happen, no player can know how this comparison would work out. These are (1) negotiations are tried and an agreement reached, and (2) the actual extent of sequestration is determined by estimating the size of the deficit in mid-August. William H. Grey (chair of the House Budget Committee), who opposed GRH, was right on the mark: "I see Gramm-Rudman as a disincentive for making the hard choices. What happens if your favorite programs are slated for elimination or you see the consensus moving to cut them 50–75 percent? It is not in your interest to have a budget."[52]

The incentives all work to promote delay. The speeded up schedule provided in the act is not adhered to because no one wants to bargain without knowing what the terms are. Would you?

The very same severity of GRH that is supposed to spur negotiation is bound to raise doubts about its workability. If all the consequences are so catastrophic, maybe no one will want to play. Table 6-3 reveals how drastic sequestration would have to have been in 1987 to make 1988's deficit reduction level. To scare others is also to scare oneself. When such a time was reached, actual 1987 (fiscal 1988), the ability of the parties to come to a consensus was again tested. The old familiar songs—entitlements, defense, taxes—was sung again because these "C" notes are where the money is. And, in fact, no one has played that game.

Despite its apparently mindless across-the-board cuts, GRH reflects a very strong sense of national policy priorities. That which cannot be touched is holy—social security, Unemployment Compensation, WIC (Women, Infants and Children), child nutrition, medicaid, veterans' pensions and compensation, food stamps, AFDC (Aid to Families with Dependent Children). Programs from which large numbers of people receive cash or equivalent value are exempt from cuts. Children, pregnant women, and veterans are favored. So are programs, such as payments to doctors and other providers under medicare, that under seques-

---

[52]Jonathan Rauch, "Politics of Deficit Reduction Remain Deadlocked Despite Balanced Budget Act," *National Journal*, January 4, 1986, p. 15.

TABLE 6-3

Shrinking Government

(Projected changes in federal spending during the next three years if
Gramm-Rudman forces automatic reductions in the budget)

	1985	*1988*
Defense	$273 bil.	$250 bil.
Commodity Credit Corp.	19 bil.	11 bil.
NASA	5.2 bil.	3.0 bil.
Farmers Home Adm.	3.6 bil.	2.1 bil.
IRS	3.2 bil.	1.9 bil.
Federal Aviation Adm.	2.9 bil.	1.7 bil.
Institutes of Health	2.6 bil.	1.5 bil.
Coast Guard	1.5 bil.	892 mil.
College, student aid	1.4 bil.	800 mil.
EPA	1.1 bil.	661 mil.
FBI	1.0 bil.	613 mil.
Congress	1.4 bil.	598 mil.
Aid to schools	814 mil.	477 mil.
Customs Service	796 mil.	466 mil.
National Park Service	595 mil.	348 mil.
Amtrak	588 mil.	344 mil.
Prisons	531 mil.	311 mil.
Food and Drug Adm.	369 mil.	216 mil.
White House	95 mil.	55 mil.
Supreme Court	13 mil.	7 mil.

Source: Jeffrey L. Sheler, "Budget Skirmishing Begins," *U.S. News & World
Report*, February 3, 1986, p. 21.

tration can be cut no more than 1 percent the first year or 2 percent
over the remaining four years.

The trouble is that negative agreement on what cannot be cut overwhelms positive agreement on what can be cut. Getting all cuts essentially out of defense and general government (a category that goes by

the bloodless title of "non-defense discretionary") is too tough and too foolhardy. Given the technical difference between fast-spending and slow-spending accounts of budget authority, moreover, a difference that has nothing to do with the desirability of programs, an awful lot of budget authority would have to be sequestered to meet GRH's outlay targets. Reduction is one thing; destruction is another.

Apparent agreement on Gramm–Rudman–Hollings obscures the built-in disagreement that it embodied. What has happened, I shall be telling you, is that growing polarization among political elites has produced agreement on extremism, that is, that Congress should make fundamental choices on total spending and revenues every year. But these self-same elites disagree over what these levels should be, or how burdens and benefits should be divided. On the one hand, there is agreement that we should stand up like men and women and say our piece: "Yes, this is what the size of the budget should be, this is what the level of taxes should be, this is how spending and taxing burdens and benefits should be divided." The only problem is that while each of us could make a wonderful budget alone, together we cannot agree on how to make a budget for the rest of us. Thus, there is agreement over the desirability of having budget resolutions, but disagreement about their contents. The ability to govern depends ultimately on the capacity to agree; if Gramm–Rudman–Hollings has taught us anything, it is that no formula can substitute for political consensus. But a formula might help enforce consensus if there is one.

THE IMPORTANCE OF CONSIDERING OTHERS: ENFORCING LIMITS THROUGH OFFSETS

Lost in the fascination with Gramm–Rudman–Holling's budgetary formulas were procedural changes of potential importance. Representatives Obey, Beilenson, and others sought to make the economic principle of opportunity costs—the value of a good is what one has to give up to get it[53]—effective in the politics of budgeting by writing procedural

---

[53]See Bruce Wallin and Aaron Wildavsky, "Opportunity Costs and Merit Wants," in *Speaking Truth to Power* (Boston: Little, Brown, 1979), pp. 155–83.

changes into the law. Each decision—a *giving to* someone requires a *taking from* someone else—is made painful.

Spending control in the Senate is subject to a point of order to enforce the 302(b) provisions of the 1974 budget act, which are enforceable at the subcommittee level for budget authority, credit authority, and entitlement authority. In the House, following the Fazio Rule, subcommittees cannot be subject to points of order if their proposals lie within the total spending for the entire Appropriations Committee under the 302(a) allocations of new budget authority. Therefore, if an appropriations subcommittee spends beyond the amount allocated to it by the House Budget resolution, there is no way of stopping it until total approved spending goes beyond the ceiling specified. Control comes too late.

In the Senate, each subcommittee can be kept within its own allocation by a point of order. This is a vital difference. Section 302(d) limits amendments to reconciliation bills and resolutions by requiring "reduction in other . . . outlays [and/or increases in] . . . revenues equivalent to . . ." the amount of spending being added or the amount of revenue being decreased. Spending cannot go beyond the resolution without offsets at the crucial time, when spending is being approved in the committee or on the floor—not after the process is almost over. While an offset provision existed in the 1974 Budget Act, Gramm–Rudman–Hollings gave the rule some teeth: Three-fifths (rather than majority) must vote to waive the offset rules.

The offset rule has made itself felt. In May 1987 a point of order was raised against the Senate's continuing its debate on the fiscal 1987 supplemental appropriation because the bill would increase total spending above the level for that year. The required 60 votes to override the point of order could not be found and the bill was taken off the agenda.

Expenditure does not involve choice unless those resources are in competition for alternative uses. If one good cause does not take from another, there is resource addition, not resource allocation. Here, in GRH Section 310(d), we have the great desideratum of budgeting: More of one good means less of another. Every measure that increases budget authority or outlay beyond an appropriations subcommittee's 302(b) allocation in the budget resolution (GRH formalizes the fact that there is only one resolution per year) is out of order.

This is the point of order: If only two-fifths of the Senate is willing to live by the law it has supported, by upholding a single member's point of order, it can enforce budget discipline. No process can be stronger than this: to require offsets for increases.

OFFSETS IN ACTION

In the winter and spring of 1986, the United States Senate backed up its Budget Committee's invocation of a 310(d) point of order. Thus we have the rare opportunity of previewing a budget process as it might play out under rules that establish spending limits.

"Gramm–Rudman–Hollings is not a 4.3 percent," a lobbyist for public higher education said, referring to the proportional reductions required in 1986. "It's a new way of thinking, a new mentality."[54] Exactly so. And a chorus of senatorial voices affirmed Senator Domenici's observation: "I see less demand by special interest groups for increases than I have ever seen in my five years of being Budget chairman and in 14 years of serving as a senator."[55] What brought about this remarkable reversal? "The zero-sum provision [add-ons require take-outs or new revenues] in Gramm-Rudman-Hollings," according to Richard N. Brandon (Democratic party staff director of the Senate Budget Committee), "was the most significant change in the lobbying process." He referred to the rule of order that could be invoked against any legislation breaking a subcommittee ceiling unless compensatory action was taken. That is why state and local governments, in a failing effort to save revenue sharing, recommended tax increases.[56]

"Basically, if you want to change something," as Martin A. Corry,

[54]Jonathan Rauch, "Zero-Sum Budget Game," *National Journal*, May 10, 1986, p. 1099.
[55]*Ibid.*, p. 1097
[56]*Ibid.*

who lobbies Congress for the American Association of Retired Persons (AARP) noted, "you have to come up with something else to make it neutral. It establishes a substantial amount of discipline."[57] Since creating such discipline has been the unachievable objective of budget reformers through the ages, it is worth having several participants tell us how it works.

By common account, the AARP is one of the nation's powerful lobbies. Its operatives have done well in Congress. Yet its executive director, Cyril Brickfield, had to remind its lobbyist that "This year [unlike other years] we just can't say don't cut this and don't cut that." Indeed, Brickfield continued, "If we don't want $5 billion cut from medicare, we have to say there should be a slowdown of that size in defense." "Or as bad as we don't like taxes," lobbyist Corry chimes in, "a revenue increase might not be so bad if we compare it to decimating medicare."[58]

The new term in town was "offsets." When the National Rural Housing Coalition needed a tiny $1.5 million supplemental to rescue a low-income program, the Senate Subcommittee on Agriculture, Rural Development and Related Agencies was sympathetic but not forthcoming. So the interest group's legislative director, Robert A. Rapoza, felt he had to compensate for the increase by proposing to cut a program involving home repair. "In another year, Rapoza would simply have requested the increase."[59]

The demand for offsets was the "amazing turn around" seen by Susan J. White of the National Association of Counties. In previous years, White recalled, these conservative county officials "didn't even want to discuss" tax increases or defense cuts.[60]

Enforcing the notion of opportunity costs in budgeting—more for one program means less for another—calls for the intervention of those who stand to lose. In this way, a true conflict of priorities takes place.

---

[57] *Ibid.*
[58] Monica Langley, "Changing pitch . . . Gramm–Rudman Cuts Have Retirees Pushing Taxes, Less Spending for Defense," *Wall Street Journal*, March 27, 1986, p. 1.
[59] Rauch, "Zero-Sum Budget Game," p. 1096.
[60] *Ibid.*

Although Senator Dale Bumper's (D-Ark.) proposal to increase funds for immunization programs by $25 million was popular, for instance, his proposed offset—cutting foreign aid—drew such fierce opposition from the chair of the Foreign Relations Committee, Senator Richard Lugar (R-Ind.), that it narrowly lost.[61]

Crossing to the other side of the street, United Technologies Corporation usually works with Pentagon documents specifying increases and decreases in the defense budget. In the winter of 1986, a similar stack of documents was delivered; but this time they concerned cuts in nutrition and housing programs. Why this change? According to a company lobbyist, "It's sure as hell not because we see them as business opportunities. We're just in a panic trying to figure out how to lobby this monster."[62]

When the executive director of the American Hospital Association says that "It makes sense for hospital lobbyists to get involved in other areas of the budget, such as defense spending," and the Edison Electric Institute thinks of asking Congress to allow it to contribute more to a fund for the disposal of nuclear waste,[63] one of the great objectives of budget reform has been fulfilled: The entire budget, not just parts of special interest, have become relevant to all the participants. And while not everyone would like what happens to their prized part of the budget, the concept of tradeoffs has moved from a forlorn hope to an everyday reality.

Why is the phone of the chair of the Senate Budget Committee "ringing off the hook with calls from people I've never heard of before"?[64] As the implications of Gramm–Rudman–Hollings became apparent to corporate representatives, who had been caught off guard, *Business Week* reports, "Instead of concentrating on their own narrow interests, they are gathering every shred of information they can find on the budget as a whole."

Before Gramm–Rudman–Hollings, groups were interested in appro-

[61]*Ibid.*, p. 1099.
[62]*Business Week*, February 17, 1986, p. 37.
[63]*Ibid.*, p. 33.
[64]*Ibid.*

priations and authorizing committees that affected them specifically, not in the budget process as a whole, and certainly not in such remote matters as budget resolutions. Why should they attend to something that was either irrelevant or unfathomable in its effects on their piece of the pie?

In the past, a lobbyist of the American Association of Colleges and Universities reports, "[We] tended to say the budget process was irrelevant"; in 1986 "We're working to try to get them to pass a budget resolution, and quickly."[65] Why the hurry? "We see the passage of an actual budget this year as being much more important than in the past," the legislative director of the National Association of Retired Federal Employees stated. "If there's not a budget, we're standing out there to get hurt again."[66]

Interest in resolutions has risen so high that lobbies now urge the budget committee to propose and Congress to pass them. Going back to AARP's well-informed lobbyist, Martin Corry, GRH's offset provisions "clearly gives the Budget Committee much more leverage" for "once a package is put together [by the committee], it's much harder to lobby against it." Moreover, "It's going to be much harder for groups to get amendments offered on the floor to use against people in elections."[67] Not so easy anymore to offer amendments increasing popular programs now that another senator can offer a point of order requiring the sponsor to come up with offsets, that is, other programs popular with other legislators.

Now we know what it takes to make agencies and interest groups care about the entire budget, not just their small corner. We also know how to arrange a political process in which the values of disparate expenditures are related each to the other. All that is necessary is a firm ceiling on total spending and a rule requiring offsets. Given the willingness to abide by these two conditions, implementation of budget reform becomes easier because the participants will enforce it upon one another. Because spending interests will call attention to any perceived weakness

---

[65]*National Journal*, May 10, 1986, p. 1098.
[66]*Ibid.*
[67]Rauch, "Zero-Sum Budget Game," p. 1097.

in program or political support for competing programs, there is less reason for controllers to be ever-present. Mutual dependence leads to mutual control.

A word of caution is in order. Strictly speaking, the effect of the offset provision is to reduce the power of the legislators who use floor amendments in favor of giving greater power to the committees. Similarly, committee majorities are given power over committee minorities. How well this works over time depends on whether the idea of offsets gathers moral force, that is, that it is seen to be right that Congress work within totals laid down by majorities. The specter of huge deficits now supplies that moral force. Whether the zero-sum provision will, in the words of Alice Rivlin, former head of the CBO, "establish a rule or a tradition of deficit neutrality,"[68] cannot yet be determined. Mandating offsets might well provide a way for those who wish to get together to solidify their union, but no procedure will yoke together what fundamental political differences have rent asunder. With egalitarian Democrats desiring to balance the budget by higher rates of taxation on people with higher incomes plus reductions in defense spending, and with Republican individualist and hierarchists desiring to balance the budget by holding down taxes while substantially reducing domestic spending, agreement on the objective of balance will not necessarily produce agreement on how balance should be achieved.

Before going on to consider a variety of proposals to remedy the defects, real and alleged, of the existing budgetary process, we shall pause to examine more closely spending on entitlements and defense. There are two chapters on entitlements because they amount to something under half the budget. There is a chapter on defense because it adds up to over a quarter of all spending. Clearly, no one can claim to know about the federal budget who does not know something about how and why most of the money in it is spent.

---

[68]Jonathan Rauch, *National Journal*, January 31, 1987, p. 248.

THE POLITICS OF
THE ENTITLEMENT
PROCESS

7

THE OLD POLTIICS REMAINS a good description of 12 percent of the budget. Aside from defense (which now makes up 21 percent of the total) and the 15 percent devoted to interest on the debt, some 52 percent—more than half the budget—is devoted to entitlements, mostly payments to individuals, leaving that catchall category—nondefense discretionary—to cover most of what we think of as domestic government—the Weather Bureau, the Forest Service, the State Department, the Labor and Commerce departments, and the rest.

Entitlements are legal obligations created through legislation that require the payment of benefits to any person or unit of government that meets the eligibility requirements established by law. Budget authority for such payments may be but is not necessarily provided in advance. Thus some entitlement legislation, such as food stamps, requires the subsequent enactment of appropriations. Examples of entitlements are social security, revenue sharing (now abolished), and Unemployment Compensation. Entitlements comprise the largest single part of the

272

budget. Yet the phenomenon of entitlements (the only generic study is an excellent article by Kent Weaver[1]) languishes in neglect. Obviously any contemporary account of budgeting cannot only be about the appropriations process, but must also cover the politics of the entitlement process.

GRAND POLITICS

Before we go into description and analysis, we want to know why it is worthwhile making an effort to understand entitlements, and why their larger significance should be appraised first as a phenomenon radically altering the character of budgeting and thereby, second, changing its political significance.

Budgeting and entitlement are incompatible concepts. Budgeting refers (or used to refer) to the allocation of limited resources for financing competing purposes. But if budgeting is supposed to be resource allocation, then entitlement is mandatory resource segregation. Nothing can be taken away; every person or entity who qualifies for payment—by meeting conditions for Unemployment Compensation, for agricultural subsidies, and so on—is entitled to receive the amount stipulated by the formulas in the authorizing statutes, no matter what is happening elsewhere or to other people. Basically, entitlements are about budgeting by addition—each sum for every program added to the others—not budgeting by subtraction, in which programs are eliminated or reduced, or where more for one means less for another.

Entitlement is, well, entitlement; these programs shall not be moved. For if the sums provided are seen to be not merely a matter of judgment of comparative merits, but also of singular moral virtue (this must be provided because a class of people is entitled to receive it), then allocation, priorities, and similarly relative terms are inappropriate when absolute judgments must be made. So where budgets are understood to be

[1] R. Kent Weaver, "Controlling Entitlements," in John E. Chubb and Paul E. Peterson, eds., *The New Direction in American Politics* (Washington, D.C.: Brookings, 1985).

integrative, relating one part to another, entitlements forbid comparisons, allowing consideration only of the program, or activity in and of itself. Budgeting is about balancing commitments; if something is an "entitlement" then it is not to be compared to anything else. While it is true, of course, that relating parts of the budget to the whole was an aspiration not an accomplishment, it was universally considered proper conduct.

Entitlements completely change the direction of budgeting. Classical budgeting was concerned largely with internal relationships between central recommenders and allocators (president and Congress), and spenders (the executive agencies). To control spending, the central units sought to control agencies. Nowadays that control apparatus is obsolete (not the drastic changes to come in OMB) because agencies (bureaus and departments) no longer do most of the spending. In the past, most government spending activity was composed of its own purchases of goods and performance of services; now, the era of entitlements has changed all that. Today government spends most of its money by writing checks to individuals. Whereas in earlier times government faced inward, doing and controlling its own programs, in our time government faces outward to the people it must support. Aiding pregnant women to eat nutritious foods, or the elderly to put aside money for retirement, or the poor to use medical services are but a few examples of governmental efforts to alter citizen behavior.

If one asks a grand question about political life—Who will bear the costs of change?—entitlements provide a markedly new answer. The old one—"we the people"—has been changed to "all of us except the entitled." When the entitled are few in number and their entitlements are relatively small, the vast majority pays for a small minority. But when entitlements grow large (covering not only poor but rich, not only the elderly but the young), the budgetary system becomes loaded with many constants and few variables. Put plainly, the prevalence of entitlements means that but a minority of programs and agencies remain to absorb the vast majority of cuts. Resource allocation becomes a lot harder when you have to take three-fifths of total spending (entitlements plus interest) off the table. Bottom-up budgeting (by adding programs together) works just fine for entitlements; but it does not suit budgeting from above (trying to fit spending within a given total) because the cuts that have to be apportioned over the remainder of the budget are necessarily severe. It is obviously difficult, if not nearly impossible, for example, to apportion tens of billions of cuts on 40 percent of the budget, as required by the Gramm–Rudman–Hollings procedure. Where classical budgeting is mostly about modifications of the budgetary base (increments up or down), entitlements guarantee a permanent base, thus foregoing flexibility. The entitlement *is* the base, and a base that can go only one way—up—unless a deliberate and difficult decision is made to alter the natural course of spending. Moreover, entitlements hold the size of the base hostage to external events—to price increases (if payments are indexed to inflation), to demographic changes (if the entitled group increases in size), to the weather, to the economy, and more.

The external focus that entitlements have imparted to budgeting has profound implications for the political lives of participants in the budgetary process. The lives of the beneficiaries may become more stable but relationships among budgeters become more hostile as agreement on what constitutes "fair shares" breaks down. Once the program base is guaranteed, with additions to it coming from formulas tied to external events, no one can say how much is too much. Internal conflict over budgeting rises. Bad enough, but there is worse to come.

As entitlements grew, congressmen grew nervous; more and more spending was controlled by appropriations committees. And if spending was out of control, so were legislators and the Congress from which their authority stemmed.

Now if higher spending on entitlements was so desirable that sacrifices could be justified in the form of higher taxes, well and good. But if taxes were not to be raised, and if spending increases came under question, what would Congress' answer be? If the norm of balance were totally gone, the answer could be further deficits. But as that norm has survived, albeit in weakened form, there was no answer. Entitlements posed the grim possibility that Congress would not be deemed responsible enough to hold the purse strings, the main fact and symbol of its power.

Congressional control of public policy was thus under challenge. In pursuing entitlement programs, Congress subjected itself and the budget to great uncertainty. With other programs, legislators would give an agency some money for a project and, if it cost a little more than expected, Congress had a real choice about what to do next: build a smaller building, change some schedules, allocate more money, or just tell the agency to do its best with the funds it had. If the agency incorrectly estimated a project, it could be forced to give up some other part of its budget, (e.g., travel expenses). Relations were largely between congressmen and the agency, and Congress could displace a lot of the burden of error onto bureaucrats. If Congress misestimated entitlement costs, by contrast, it had no opportunity for second thoughts; the money just poured out from the Treasury.

Arguments about uncontrollability or fiscal policy were also weapons, wielded in a battle royal over the size and purposes of the American government. They were used by one side or the other to appeal to neutrals. Conservatives argued that liberal programs created deficits, or inflation, (i.e., bad things), so as to upset people who thought the programs were good. When they were not stressing social justice, liberals would invoke Congress's right to make fiscal policy—to counter the president's claim that his program preferences served a higher purpose of economic management.

Who would solve the problem? The budget system laid that burden on the president and the appropriations committees. But neither could touch entitlements. Authorizing committees alone could change entitlement law; neither appropriation bills nor presidential vetoes could change that. If the president and appropriations committees focused on what they were able to do, all the burden of deficit reduction would fall on one part of the budget; interests funded by entitlements would escape scot-free. The appropriations committees naturally did not like that.

With the adoption by Congress of a unified budget in 1969, whereby trust funds were included in the same budget as non-trust fund entitlements and annual appropriations, the tensions between entitlements and appropriations were exacerbated. The new form of the budget structured tradeoffs in a more direct and, hence, conflictual way. Entitlements and appropriations were increasingly forced to fight over the same pie, often to the detriment of the more controllable expenditures—appropriations.[2]

With the arrival of budget committees in 1974, a new alternative presented itself; these super budget committees (see Chapters 4 and 5) could require the legislative committees to cut entitlements by such measures as reducing eligibility or increasing payments by individuals. Procedural possibility did not, however, mean political ease. As long as the principle of entitlement remained and the big ones had overwhelming political support, they had the effect I have just outlined.

The growth of entitlements heightened long-standing tensions between appropriations and tax-writing committees. There had always been jealousies because Ways and Means and Finance were the chief beneficiaries of Appropriations' efforts: If the latter cut spending, taking blame, the former could cut taxes, taking credit. Or it could work in reverse: If Appropriations was lax, the tax committees got the bill. Now as entitlements burgeoned, Ways and Means could take credit for expanding programs, but Appropriations took the blame for the deficit. When Appropriations blamed Ways and Means or Finance, the tax writers replied that entitlements were fully funded by their own taxes; that is, since social security itself was in balance, it could not be blamed for the deficit; true as far as it went, but a bit of the story had been left out. Since social insurance taxes were going up, but the public did not want to pay more in taxes (and half of these taxes were charged to business), Congress had to keep reducing other taxes, particularly the corporate income tax; thus the total tax burden remained a nearly constant proportion of the economy. In other words, entitlements "paid for themselves" by the reduced taxes paid for everything else; the appropriations committees indeed had a legitimate gripe. If revenues remained, say, at 18 percent of GNP but an ever-larger proportion went to social security, much less was left to fund the rest of government.

Thus entitlements squeezed the old budget process (1) directly by

[2]Allen Schick, *Congress and Money* (Washington, D.C.: The Urban Institute, 1980).

increasing spending, (2) indirectly by siphoning off revenues from other programs, and (3) institutionally by pitting appropriations committees against tax committees. The guaranteed certainty of entitlement funding creates so much uncertainty for budgeters that it reduces the capacity of public officials to govern. Entitlements place a sizable burden on budgetary actors: They must find a way to support large numbers of individuals while still helping manage the economy and control the deficit, all this with most of the budget "committed" or essential. Government must be simultaneously firm (for entitlements) and flexible (for appropriations) while still trying to govern. It is as if government were a giant centipede on its back in space with innumerable little feet holding up innumerable little people, with scant attention being paid to what holds up the creature who holds everyone else up. More tax money or fewer entitlements—either would solve the problem. But our legislators and presidents so far have not been able to see eye to eye. They agree that entitlements make a big difference, but not on what to do about them.

But the squeeze of entitlements on the budget is not the end of the story. A new player has entered the game in the name of trust fund surpluses. Social security, which is supported by a self-financed trust fund, has begun to generate surpluses (which are projected to approach $75 billion by 1992). The result: These surpluses may be used to create the appearance that deficits are declining (see Table 7-1).

TABLE 7-1
Social Security and the Deficit

	1987	1988	1989	1990	1991	1992
Revenue minus spending:						
For all but social security	−$193	−$205	−$208	−$192	−$176	−$160
For social security	19	36	46	58	67	75
Total (deficit)	−174	−169	−162	−134	−109	−85

Source: Congressional Budget Office. Cited in *National Journal*, February 14, 1987, p. 363.

In fact, Congress has recognized the value of these social security surpluses. As Jonathan Rauch noted, "The 1985 Balanced Budget Act removed social security from the unified budget for all purposes *except* calculating the size of the deficit. In other words, lawmakers explicitly said the social security trust fund surpluses will count toward reducing the deficit."[3]

Is there anything wrong with this sort of action? The danger is that we will be deluding ourselves into believing that actual deficit reductions are being made by counting money in one pocket that will later have to be paid out to another. Surpluses in the social security trust fund are there for a purpose: to pay for future costs. The existence of trust fund surpluses, therefore, may serve to decrease the urgency of solutions to the rapid rise of entitlements.

ENTITLEMENTS: LEGAL, MORAL, AND BUDGETARY

Entitlements stand somewhere between a privilege—which need not be given or, once granted, may be withdrawn—and a right that cannot be denied. Because entitlements have not been held to comprise fundamental rights, the Supreme Court so far has not expanded its interpretation of the due-process clause of the Fourteenth Amendment to include constitutional guarantees to a specified level of food, clothing, shelter, education, or income. As yet, Congress has not been deemed by the Constitution to be required to provide funds for a variety of welfare programs. By statute, applicants for benefits that Congress has chosen to provide are guaranteed an appeal for review of denial of their applications. And recipients of benefits are held to be constitutionally guaranteed a hearing before benefits authorized by statute are reduced.[4] Proce-

[3]Jonathan Rauch, *National Journal*, February 14, 1987, p. 365, italics in original.

[4]Relevant cases include *Goldberg* v. *Kelly*, holding that a person receiving welfare benefits under statutory and administrative standards defining eligibility for them has an interest in continued receipt of those benefits that is safeguarded by procedural due process (397 U.S. 254, 90 S. Ct. 1011, 25 L. Ed. 2d 287, 1970); *Board of Regents* v. *Roth*, holding that a professor hired by annual renewable contract was not entitled to a hearing before dismissal under Fourteenth Amendment due process, absent a showing of sufficient cause

dural guarantees, however, are not substantive rights. A welfare applicant may be denied, or a recipient's payments cut, providing the courts find that the relevant administrative agency acted in a reasonable manner. Thus at present there is no constitutional barrier to diminishing or eliminating entitlements.[5] To do this, of course, is an entirely different matter.[6]

"Entitled to" may suggest "deserving of." Without touching on questions the courts have sought to avoid—namely, whether entitlements constitute what Charles Reich called "the new property"[7]—one's picture of the just society may include a view of what individuals are entitled to, of what they should give to others, and of what part government should play in making such provisions. Who should give or take how much from whom is a fundamental political question. For entitlements are not only benefits to some people, but also represent costs to others. Transfers of income from taxpayers to recipients require moral justification as well as political clout. Should poverty be the criterion? What about the well-off elderly? Should the criterion be financial loss? If there is an entitlement for beekeepers (yes, there is, read on), why not for anyone else in danger of losing income or going out of business? Why are certain farmers who raise particular crops given price supports, but

for reasonable expectation of renewal (408 U.S. 566, 92 S. Ct. 2701, 1972); *Shapiro* v. *Thompson,* holding unconstitutional state and federal provision denying welfare benefits to individuals who had resided in administering jurisdictions less than one year as violative of the constitutional guarantee of all citizens to be free to travel throughout the U.S. (394 U.S. 618, 1969); and *Rodriguez* v. *San Antonio Independent School District,* sustaining against equal protection attack on public school finance schemes using local property taxation as a base and thereby forcing districts with lower property values to make more effort than others in order to raise the same amount of money per pupil for educational purposes (411 U.S. 1, 1973).

[5] I am indebted to Maureen Young for an illuminating paper on the legal status of housing entitlements.

[6] For a critique of entitlements as vitiating "the distinction essential to liberal constitutionalism, between the rights the government exists to protect and the exercise of those rights by private individuals, or between state and society. For an entitlement is a right whose exercise is guaranteed to a certain degree by the government—a right that is therefore exercised to that degree by the government," see Harvey C. Mansfield, Jr., "The American Election: Entitlements Versus Opportunity," *Government and Opposition,* Vol. 20, No. 1 (Winter 1985), pp. 3–17, quote on pp. 13–14.

[7] Charles Reich, "The New Property," *Yale Law Journal,* Vol. 73 (April 1964), pp. 733–87.

not others? Should anyone who is already a farmer or anyone who wishes to become one be entitled? Actually, it is not so much who is entitled, important though this question is, but rather the priority given to entitlement over nearly all other claims that has occasioned the most controversy.

The status of entitlements is both accepted (no one expects much change in the largest ones) and disputed, due to the budgetary bind into which their cumulative impact has led government. Because entitlements stand as prior claims that must be paid before others, they achieve certainty at the expense of all other residual claimants on government. It is the "non-entitled" who must change. When revenues rise as fast or faster than expenditures, this conflict among classes of claimants— the entitled versus general government programs (justice, information, regulation, etc.) and defense—is muted. When deficits rise, however, and spending levels are considered too high while entitlements have risen to half or more of the total, the desirability of entitlements does come into question. One sign of this questioning is the Budget Act of 1974, subsequently strengthened, that requires special notice of and procedures for new entitlements—which may help explain why there haven't been any.

Entitlements represent a protean subject: At the edges, it is not easy to say exactly what is in or out; and one can say virtually nothing that is true of everything. The reason is that entitlements are a product of history, not logic—of evolution, not design. The features one wishes to stress depend on the kind of analysis one wishes to make. Some entitlements, like social security, are permanent (sometimes called "no-year") and run on in perpetuity unless changed. Others, like commodity credit-price supports and food stamps, receive annual appropriations, though, in effect, they are treated as full entitlements because shortfalls are made up by supplemental appropriations. Some entitlements, such as medicaid for the poor, are means-tested; that is, eligibility depends on income and other assets. By contrast, unemployment compensation has no means test at the entry stage, but benefits are subject to taxation above a specified level of income. Retirement programs (for civilian and military federal employees but also for others) are financed in part by trust

funds based on employer and employee contributions. Some entitlements serve narrow clienteles (e.g., black lung, student loans) and others
(e.g., medicare) are broadly based. Railroad retirement and veterans'
pensions are tied (or indexed) to the consumer price index (so as to
protect recipients against inflation), while the kidney dialysis entitlement is not. Merely to describe the characteristics of these programs
would be like reading the telephone directory—helpful when you need
a bit of data, but not recommended reading. As students of budgeting,
what we want to know is how entitlements grow compared to one
another and to appropriations and why. How does the struggle over
entitlements differ, if at all, from the conflict over appropriations? And
what does the rise of entitlements portend for the ability of our political
institutions to make effective budgets?

THE TREND IS UP

Why is there concern over entitlements? Because (see Table 7-2) entitlements are not merely growing twice as fast as the rest of the budget
(outside of interest on the debt) but also two-and-a-half times faster than
GNP; consequently, all sides of the political spectrum are troubled.
Conservatives fear much higher taxes and/or deficits; liberals fear that
entitlements will squeeze out other programs and, if they keep growing,
use up future revenue increases. Taking only those composed of payments to individuals, entitlements went from 33.5 percent in 1970 to
49.9 percent (leaving out interest) of the budget in 1985.[8] Spending
classified by OMB as "relatively uncontrollable" (not counting outlays
authorized in previous years) rose from 34.5 percent of federal outlays
in fiscal 1967 to 52.6 percent in 1974, and 54.8 percent in 1980.[9] Which
programs accounted for most of the increase?

Taken together, social security and medicare (see Figure 7-1)
amounted to $242.2 billion in 1984, making up 60.6 percent of all

[8]See Weaver, "Controlling Entitlements," Table 11-1 on p. 319.
[9]OMB, *Budget of the U.S. Government, 1968–1985.*

TABLE 7-2
Growth in Entitlement Spending from 1970 to 1984 Outpaces Both the
Federal Budget and GNP

	1970 (billions)	*1984 (est.) (billions)*	*Growth 1970–1984 (annual constant $)*
´ Entitlement outlays	$ 64.6	$ 400.0	6.3 %
Federal budget outlays	195.7	853.8	3.7
Nonentitlement outlays	131.7	453.8	2.0
GNP	968.8	3558.7	2.4

Source: OMB, Budget of the U.S. Government, 1968–1985.

entitlement outlays and 28.4 percent of total government spending. Social security ranks first, followed by health (medicare and medicaid), federal employee retirement, and Unemployment Compensation. The "Other" category includes a multitude of different programs. Entitlements are driven by a few programs concerned with retirement, health, and welfare. Thus whatever drives these programs (see the next chapter) propels the largest part of the budget.

There are legitimate policy reasons—of efficiency, or the political difficulty of alternatives, or the desire to keep promises that are made— for entitlement funding. There are also good policy reasons for protecting government from adversity by enabling it to limit demands on its resources. When good reasons conflict, difficult choices among policies become necessary.

Do all entitlement programs grow at the same pace or do some leap ahead while others lag behind? Two useful benchmarks are the growth over time of the nonentitlement budget and the Consumer Price Index. One side of Table 7-3 (p. 286) groups programs that exceed both benchmarks; the middle column, those that equal or exceed the CPI; and in the last column, those that did not even keep up with inflation. Immediately we see that the largest programs show the fastest growth. There are indeed slow-growing programs, but these are small. Our initial conclusion must be (1) that there is nothing magic in entitlements per se

FIGURE 7-1

Entitlement Payments for Individuals as a Percentage of Gross National Product, Fiscal Years 1965–1986[a].

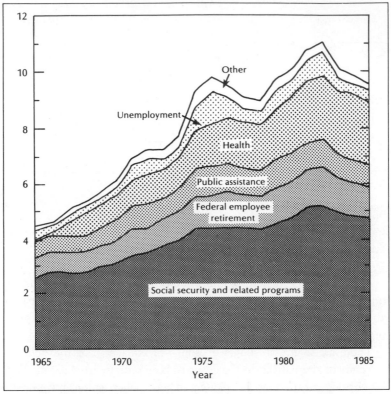

[a] *Social security and related programs* includes old age and survivor's insurance, social security disability insurance, and railroad retirement. *Federal employee retirement* includes military and Coast Guard retirement pay, civil service and foreign service retirement and disability, and compensation paid to veterans and their survivors as a result of service-related death or disability. *Public assistance* includes supplemental security income, grants to the states for aid to families with dependent children, food stamps, the earned income tax credit, and veterans' pensions. *Health* includes medicare hospital insurance, medicare supplementary medical insurance, and grants to the states for medicaid. *Unemployment* includes unemployment compensation, trade adjustment assistance, and federal employee unemployment benefits. *Other* includes child nutrition programs, the special milk program, guaranteed student loans, veterans' readjustment and education benefits, coal miners' (black lung) disability benefits, special workers' compensation expenses, Veterans Administration burial benefits, and the national service and U.S. government life insurance fund for veterans.

Source: Kent Weaver, "Controlling Entitlements," in John E. Chubb and Paul E. Peterson, eds., *The New Direction in American Politics* (Washington, D.C.: Brookings, 1985), p. 313.

because many individual programs do less well than appropriations but that (2) the largest and fastest growing entitlements continue to increase. Why?

The political climate of the late 1970s and the first half of the 1980s, running from the decline of the Carter administration to the ascendancy of President Reagan, was less favorable to domestic spending in general and to certain (but not all) entitlement programs in particular. In an incisive analysis of entitlements, Kent Weaver concludes that

> (1) Income maintenance programs have continued to increase their share of GNP, but their share of the federal budget has ended its secular growth and now responds primarily to swings of the business cycle. (2) Health care entitlements have continued to increase their budget share, although at a reduced pace. (3) Statutory changes in individual programs (policy choices) have been largely in the form of cutbacks, with most of those cuts occurring under the Reagan administration. (4) Means-tested programs have been cut more than social insurance programs, especially for beneficiaries at the higher end of eligibility scales (the "working poor"). (5) Program changes have generally been marginal, rather than comprehensive reforms.[10]

Universal entitlements that apply to very large numbers of people, that are not means-tested, and that go for pensions or health have done well. The combination of growth in numbers of beneficiaries, political potency (many people in most places), and sense of being well-deserved have given these entitlements first-class status. Yet there are others (compare the three columns) with a clientele that is elderly or sick or numerous (though not as numerous) and yet have declined or grown more slowly. Before turning to studies of individual entitlements and comparing them to appropriations, as we will in the next chapter, we should first examine the more general factors that help determine the growth or decline of entitlements.

Entitlements are too varied, and historical contingency is too important, to permit universal generalization. Federal Civil Service Retirement has long fared well, for instance, because its highly mobilized members cared more about their benefits than scattered and inattentive

---

[10]Weaver, "Controlling Entitlements," p. 318.

TABLE 7-3
Entitlements Grouped by Growth Rates, 1977–1986[11]

Exceeded the growth in CPI, GNP, and nonentitlements	Exceeded growth in CPI	Less than growth in CPI
Social Security	Military Retirement	Railroad Retirement
Medicare	Supplemental Security Income	AFDC
Medicaid	Veterans' Compensation	General Revenue Sharing
Guaranteed Student Loans		Veterans' Pensions
Federal Civilian Retirement		G.I. Bill
Food Stamps		Benefits for Disabled Miners
Farm Price Supports		Unemployment Compensation
		Social Services
$353.9 billion (1986 outlays)	$38.1 billion (1986 outlays)	$43.4 billion (1986 outlays)

Data Sources:
Budget outlays: The Budget of the United States Government, FY78–87. Outlays for the Guaranteed Student Loan Program for FY77–79, were taken from The Budget of the United States Government, FY79–81 (Appendix).
Nonentitlement budget outlays consist of national defense and nondefense discretionary spending as defined in Congressional Budget Office, "The Economic and Budget Outlook: Fiscal Years 1987–1991," pp. 74, 141.
GNP: The Budget of the United States Government, FY87.
CPI: Computed from figures in U.S. Department of Labor, *Monthly Labor Review* for September 1977 and September 1986.
[11]Compiled by Walter Wong.

taxpayers about the small amount per person required to finance the program. In 1982, however, despite the strong opposition of civil service unions, members were required to contribute to social security, which was subtracted from their pensions. The unions did everything right politically; they launched a major campaign against inclusion. The trouble was that their little juggernaut was overwhelmed by a much bigger one, the gripping concern that social security retirement might become insolvent. There is a lot to learn about entitlements as a general phenomenon, but without a detailed knowledge of their history we are bound to be mistaken in some respect.

THE IMPORTANCE OF BEING ENTITLED

The place to begin is with the protection given to a program by virtue of the fact that it stands as an entitlement and, therefore, is not subject to the pressures of the annual appropriations process. It is not easy for Congress to consider reneging on obligations it already has incurred, or intervening to deprive beneficiaries of something to which the law says they are entitled. Entitlement means not having to say you're sorry, the money has run out.

Like other decision-making bodies, Congress does not necessarily spend its time on what is most important but rather on what it can change. Often this means neglecting the much larger entitlements in favor of the much smaller but more readily changeable appropriations. A typical debate occurred over the fiscal consequences of a $25 million supplemental for the Head Start program after the House of Representatives had left unscathed a 40-times larger increase for Aid to Dependent Children. In seeking to silence protest over this disparity, Representative Holland explained that "We thought this $1,150 million required for welfare funds for the States, and the $28 million required to pay veterans' and unemployment compensation for Federal employees, were important enough items that we should not permit them to go into default any longer."[12]

[12]*Congressional Record*, 1968, Vol. 114, Part 8, p. 9483.

Entitlements alter the prevailing conception of the budgetary base. From a concept formerly tied to individual programs, the base emerges here as a function of the type of financing: Entitlements become the base that is expected to continue much as before while appropriations become the increments that are subject to dispute and negotiation.

While the expansion of entitlements has not eliminated legislators' interest in distributing projects geographically, the public-works pork barrel has nonetheless been dwarfed by payments to individuals. Now it is not departments that control most federal spending but the Treasury that writes checks.

As entitlements come to dominate much of public spending, they act so as to place the budget on automatic pilot. Far more than before, the budget is determined by prior authorizations. And, as what might be termed "maximal entitlements" (universal, no-year, fully indexed, financed in part by their own trust funds) come to take up a larger share of the total, the scope for change is reduced still further.

In recognition of the necessary tradeoff between collective and individual security, Congress has begun to challenge the notion of entitlement as total or forever. Beginning in 1980 and continuing sporadically thereafter, Congress, through its budget committees, began to use the reconciliation procedure to chip away at some entitlements. What happens is that in issuing reconciliation instructions under a budget resolution approved by each house, the budget committees direct other committees to reduce budget authority and outlays by set amounts. While not specifically stating where cuts should be made, the selection of committees to make changes (What else does Ways and Means have?) and a strong norm (violated only in 1981) against changing authorizations on programs the Appropriations Committee can control serve to focus reconciliation reductions on entitlements. The committees are half compelled and half given political cover to modify promises by such things as delaying or diminishing COLAs (cost of living adjustments), restricting access, or reducing the scope of the service offered.

At the present time, in sum, it can be said that we are living in a twilight zone of "quasi" or "near" entitlements. Whether political support will be mobilized to increase the number of people entitled and the amounts they receive (requiring higher levels of taxation or deficits), or whether the scope and size of entitlements diminish (thus lowering taxes or deficits), will in large measure determine the kind of government Americans will have.

TRUST FUNDS

Reliance on trust funds deserves further comment because this device has become part of new budgetary strategies. By no mere chance do the two fastest growing types of entitlements, social insurance and federal retirement, share trust-fund financing. Obviously, the large number of beneficiaries and the accepted position that recipients are paying their way help these entitlements prosper. Slightly less obvious is the tendency of trust-fund financing to create vast un- or under-financed liabilities by sweeping costs under the rug of the future. "Over the years," Andrew Ruddock of the Civil Service Commission observed, "all efforts to strengthen retirement financing have been tempered by concurrent searches for ways to postpone the budgetary burden to some future Administration."[13] On the one hand, trust-fund managers (backed up as they are by the credit of the United States), knowing they will not be allowed to default, need only keep funds sufficient to pay for the current year plus a small margin for error. This is quite different from the usual insurance practice of trying to retain enough to pay also for future benefits. On the other hand, accumulations of surplus in the early years, while people are paying in but not taking out, does tempt presidents and Congresses to increase benefits. Surpluses may also be artificially created, as was true of social security, by unrealistic assumptions about the level of earnings or the life span of affected individuals. Eventually, of course, these benefits have to be paid for by increased payroll taxes, now the largest tax many people pay.[14]

[13]Andrew E. Ruddock, "A Critique of Various Study Documents," in Dan McGill, ed., *Financing the Civil Service Retirement System* (Homewood, Ill.: Richard D. Irwin, 1979), p. 134.

[14]See Martha Derthick, *Policymaking for Social Security* (Washington, D.C.: The Brookings Institution, 1979); and James Tobin, "The Future of Social Security: One Economist's Assessment," Working Paper #4, Project on the Federal Social Role, National Conference on Social Welfare, Washington, D.C., 1985.

In the entitlement business there are many ways of making present spending appear less than it is likely to be later on. Underestimating costs is epidemic. So is the strategy of the receding increment. Small increases to beneficiaries, which also cumulate into large future sums, may be obtained because their full future impact is not evident. Thus a pension benefit to be obtained in five years, or slowly phased in, may seem almost as good as one obtained right now, since most recipients will not retire until then. The present cost is at or close to zero, though future costs may be large. In 1966, for instance, the 5 percent annuity reduction for retiring at age 55 (with 30 years of federal service) was eliminated. A colloquy at a 1965 hearing tells the story:

> Mr. Daniels: Can you give the Committee any cost figures as to the Government if such a recommendation was enacted?
> Mr. McCart: . . . Let me simply point out, Mr. Chairman, that the cost is not going to be very high, because what this represents at the most is a 5 percent increase in the annuity that an individual can secure if he retires.[15]

At each step, the costs look small; the overall change since 1942, however, was a 50 percent increase in the annuity of 55/30 retirees. The liberalizations also encourage greater use of early retirement, further increasing costs. Given the vast size of the largest entitlements, the logic of incrementalism is inexorable: A tiny proportion of a huge number, compounding over time, gets to be pretty big itself.

The games played with social security have become notorious. Tens of billions of surplus are projected through the 1990s. Keeping social security on budget during this time helps reduce the size of the overall deficit. In Senator John Heinz's apt phrase, these surpluses provide "spending encouragement that Congress doesn't need."[16]

The opposite of the surplus strategy is to artificially create a deficit, which has to be repaid. Every year, for example, the president's budget request includes an amount to reimburse the Commodity Credit Corpo-

[15] Joseph White, "The Budgeting of the Civil Service Retirement 'Entitlement,'" typescript, 1983, p. 19.

[16] Nina Bonnelycke, "Social Security: Understanding Our Biggest Entitlement Program," student paper, 1985.

ration (CCC) for losses on price supports so it can retain its full borrowing authority. This is an example of appropriations chasing entitlement spending. Congress can estimate that the entire borrowing authority will not be needed, thereby shifting elsewhere some funds needed to pay for prior years' losses. This strategy helps Congress get out from under its own spending ceilings. In the fiscal 1984 budget, for example, the Reagan administration requested $10.2 billion for the CCC while Congress, led by Representative Jamie Whitten, the wily chairman of the Appropriations Committee and an advocate of agricultural interests, appropriated $9.7 billion. The $500 million difference was used to fund soil conservation programs that had been cut out by the administration.[17]

THE ECONOMY, DEMOGRAPHY, AND UPTAKE

The size of entitlements depends on how many qualify and how much they are paid. Both eligibility and payment depend in turn on the state of the economy, trends in population dynamics, and provisions for protection against inflation. These three variables are considered together because they show how the size of entitlements may be influenced by external forces. However, I do not want to leave the impression that Congress is helpless in the face of forces it cannot control. Congress could limit expenditures by eliminating or reducing indexing, changing eligibility rules, or even eliminating programs.

Changes in the economy reverberate throughout the realm of entitlements. A decline in employment increases unemployment compensation. If prolonged, it may well encourage more people to retire, thereby raising pension costs. As people drop below the poverty line, they become eligible for medicaid, food stamps, and other programs. For those programs linked to the price level through COLAs, inflation can dramatically increase expenditure. A 1 percent decrease in unemployment, for instance, can lead to a $600 million reduction in food stamp

[17]From Michael Sieverts, a student paper on agricultural price supports.

costs. Even in the midst of general prosperity, a decline in farm income, spurred, perhaps, by increased foreign competition or a debt crisis, will increase payments by the Commodity Credit Corporation (CCC).

Demography defeats policy, at least some of the time. Different age distributions have large effects not only on pensions but also on medical care and poverty. Often, demographic trends work in contrary directions. People are healthier than they have been, thus decreasing costs at comparable ages, but they live longer, thereby increasing them. Through the end of the 1940s, early retirement was virtually unknown; almost all men worked to age 64; and half of those over 65 still worked. Therefore they did not receive pensions. Nowadays, retirement by age 65 is the rule, and one-third of men 55–64 retire early.

Sometimes demographic change works in tandem with changes in entitlements. Much improved social security income in the 1970s and 1980s facilitated early retirement, but then total payments grew accordingly.

Levels of entitlement spending were sometimes unintended. Costs were underestimated. Costs of health care programs in particular— whether well known (as medicare) or less familiar, such as end-stage renal disease (dialysis) support—were far greater than anticipated. In part the underestimates were failures of calculation, but they resulted also from failures to calculate at all—the committees of jurisdiction having little reason to make costs visible, and no other institution picking up the slack. Let me put it this way: If you are worried about spending too much, you take measures against that possibility; but if your main concern is not to do too little, you don't worry about the total cost. The fast growth of entitlement spending would not have been possible without the prevailing view that government's task was to use public money to alleviate private distress, the more the better.

While demographic and program changes may offset each other—the rise in working wives increases equality while the rise in female-headed households decreases it—occasionally programs do what they are supposed to. Whereas 35 percent of the elderly were below the poverty line in 1959 (compared to 21 percent for the rest of the population), by the mid-1980s elderly income, thanks to social security, had risen considerably faster than that of younger people; 14.1 percent of the elderly were deemed poor, a percentage point below the general population. Naturally, this increase in cost led to concern about government's ability to pay social security in the future.[18] There is also concern with intergenerational equity; fewer younger people will be paying to support more older people. But the program did work.

The "uptake," the degree to which eligible people take advantage of entitlements, depends in part on how morally acceptable this use becomes and in part on how advantageous it is. As Aid to Families with Dependent Children declined by a quarter in real terms from 1976 to 1983, for example, the proportion of eligible families who chose to participate declined.[19]

Controlling the costs of entitlements has proven to be quite difficult. In medical care, for example, once the decision is made to reimburse patients for costs as incurred in the private sector, it becomes impossible to limit spending in advance. Every administration has looked for ways to control medicare costs, but the focus has been on regulating use or prices, while praying for an effect on totals.

In food stamps, the government under Carter did submit the program to the appropriations process and a total expense is mandated each year in the agriculture appropriation. But, since the law sets rules for payment of benefits and the USDA follows those rules, when the money is nearly used up the USDA just asks Congress for more. Rather than kill the program in June, Congress obliges. The alternative approach, holding to a cap (or ceiling), has two disadvantages: It would not assure nutritional aid adjusted to financial need, and it would require giving administrators massive discretion as to who gets what benefits.

INDEXING: TRYING TO TRANSFER UNCERTAINTY

When the dollars individuals receive from entitlements are tied to a measure of price changes, such as the Consumer Price Index (CPI), the

---

[18]See Frank Levy, "Families, Households and the Government," in *Dollars and Dreams: The Changing American Income Distribution*, Russell Sage Foundation, transcript, 1987.

[19]*Ibid.*, p. 175.

benefit is said to be "indexed." At set intervals, a change in the price index beyond a specified degree triggers a change in the dollars received by beneficiaries. About 30 percent of federal spending now is indexed, as are nearly 90 percent of payments received by individuals.[20] And the cost is high. The GAO estimates that provisions for indexing accounted for half of the rapid increase of social security in the 1970s and 42 percent of medicare spending.[21]

More is indexed than meets the eye. Since government pay is linked to private sector pay, for instance, and since wages in the private sector are related to inflation, ". . . this may be thought of," the GAO correctly informs us, "as an implicit form of indexing."[22] (The linkage is weak, however, because government did not follow recommendations to assure comparability.) Although medicaid and medicare are not indexed to price changes, they do promise to provide a fixed volume of services, so that as these increase in price, so does the cost of programs. When high levels of inflation coincide with high levels of unemployment, programs not indexed for price changes may nevertheless rise, because they are triggered by economic changes. The GAO calls this "indexed eligibility."[23] When federal payments respond to a certain level of state funding, increases by states operate as indexing mechanisms to generate federal spending increases. It is hard to isolate major programs from economic developments. Indexed entitlements (see Table 7-4 for illustration) offer a fertile field for the interconnection of spending programs.

Hard as it may be to believe, indexation was once adopted as a way to save the government money. In 1972, buoyed by false predictions of future surpluses and perhaps by hopes of electoral rewards, Congress voted to raise social security benefits by 20 percent while raising taxes hardly at all. In 1973, to prevent a recurrence of this episode, Congress, in an act designed to "take Social Security out of politics," adopted

[20]General Accounting Office, Report to the Congress by the Comptroller General of the United States, "What Can Be Done to Check the Growth of Federal Entitlement and Indexed Spending?" PAD-81-21, March 3, 1981.
[21]GAO, "An Analysis of the Effects of Indexing for Inflation on Federal Expenditures," PAD-79-22, August 15, 1979.
[22]Report to Congress, "What Can Be Done?" p. 13.
[23]*Ibid.*

TABLE 7-4
Indexing Status of Selected Major Entitlement Programs 1980

	Outlays (billions)	Indexed	Index used	Indexing frequency
Social Security—Old Age Survivors	$101.8	Yes	CPI[a]	Annually
Medicare	35.0	No[b]		
Federal Employees' Retirement and Insurance	27.3	Yes	CPI	Semiannually
Unemployment Assis.	18.0	No		
Social Security—Disability	15.3	Yes	CPI	Annually
Medicaid	14.0	No		
Veterans Compensation and Pensions	11.0	Yes	CPI	Annually
Food Stamps[c]	9.1	Yes	CPI	Annually
Aid to Families with Dependent Children	7.3	No[d]		
Revenue Sharing	6.8	No		
Supplemental Security Income	6.4	Yes	CPI	Annually
Railroad Retirement	4.7	Yes	CPI	Annually
Commodity Credit Corp. (price supports)	2.9	Yes	Parity prices, etc.	Varies, part annually
Social Service Grants	2.8	No		
Veterans Readjustment Benefits	2.4	No		
Benefits for Disabled Miners	1.8	Yes	CPI, indirectly	Annually

[a]Consumer Price Index (CPI).

[b]Some parts of the medicare and medicaid programs—physicians' payments, for example—are explicitly indexed but not to a general price index.

[c]The entitlement status of the Food Stamp program is questionable. The Food and Agriculture Act of 1977 capped the overall funding level of the program and required that the program be funded through advance appropriations, thus removing the entitlement status. However, the Congress has continued to fund the program at the full level needed to provide stamps to all eligible people who apply; therefore the Congress still treats the program as a mandatory expenditure.

[d]Since Aid to Families with Dependent Children is an open-ended federal commitment to pay a fixed percentage of state costs, increases in payment levels by states affect the federal budget in a manner similar to automatic indexing.

Source: GAO, Report to Congress, "What Can Be Done?" p. 12.

TABLE 7-5
Wage Gains Contrasted to CPI Increases[24]

Year	CPI (% adjustment to yearly base)	Wage index gain
1976	6.4	5.7
1979	9.9	6.8
1980	14.3	6.8

automatic indexation. Retirees would not have to wait to catch up with inflation and politicians would have less reason to provide their regular election-time increase. Tax rates were set on the assumption that wages would grow at the rate for the Consumer Price Index (CPI) plus an additional amount of productivity. The plan backfired; although in the past price increases had lagged behind wage growth, starting in the 1970s, inflation began to outstrip wages. (See Table 7-5.)

But it is hard to outguess the future. A friend of social security, economist James Tobin, tells us what went wrong.

> In retrospect it is easy to see that indexation by the CPI is not a good idea, even in less turbulent economic times than the 1970s. Such indexation immunizes the favored group from inescapable national losses—in 1973/74 and 1979/80 the big rise in the cost of imported oil—and throws their costs onto unprotected fellow-citizens. Likewise indexation in effect exempts its beneficiaries from paying increased taxes embodied in the prices that compose the index; others must bear the burdens of the public programs financed by those taxes.[25]

When only a favored few are indexed, little harm is done. The selected few may well need more protection than the rest of us. But when indexation covers tens of millions of people, the few begin to protect the many and the social contract of mutual support in society is weakened.

Pity the poor taxpayer. Maybe not. In 1981, as part of the Kemp–

[24]Table in Bonnelycke, "Social Security." Table adapted from Timothy Clark, "Time Running out on Moves To Ensure Social Security's Financial Solvency," *National Journal,* October 9, 1982.
[25]Tobin, "The Future of Social Security," p. 10.

Roth across-the-board tax cuts, tax brackets were indexed to inflation. Thus ended the infamous "bracket creep," under which taxpayers were pushed into higher brackets by inflation even though they had no more real purchasing power. The government that under a progressive rate structure used to get 1.6 times the revenue for each percentage point increase in the price level now gets no inflation bonus.

Taking the two forms of indexing together—continuance of expenditure indexing, which pushes spending up, and discontinuance of tax indexing, which keeps revenue down—adds up to a foolproof formula for producing deficits. Unless taxes are raised, or spending is cut, or economic growth rises way beyond prior levels, maintaining the status quo results in deficits.

There is no end of suggestions for diminishing or eliminating the effects of indexing. OMB, CBO, and GAO variously referred to the possibility of abolishing indexing altogether, making the index less generous, delaying COLAs or adjusting them less frequently, and giving the president the right to propose changes in the formula unless Congress chooses to override. Were the law changed, say, to limit indexing to 85 percent of the expected rise in the CPI in social security, CBO under one inflation assumption calculated a cumulative savings of $43.9 billion over five years.[26] For recipients, of course, the income would be lost not saved.

The difficulty lies not in devising measures to limit the effects of indexing but in doing so while (1) maintaining the objectives of the program involved and (2) gaining the necessary political support. After all, if retirees are meant to receive financial protection or poor people to gain access to medical care or farmers to get more income, it is not helpful to have these gains eroded by inflation. Security is not aided by economic uncertainty. The same, however, may be said of those who must pay taxes to provide these entitlements or compete with the federal government for credit. Whether the security of parts of the population can be improved through the insecurity of other parts is the question.

[26]Report to Congress, "What Can Be Done?" p. 29.

POLITICS: THE "OUGHT" AND "IS" OF ENTITLEMENTS

Moral power—the shared beliefs about who is entitled to what in society—is a necessary though not a sufficient condition for an entitlement program not only to exist on a minimal level but to grow. In the beginning of the American republic, the concept of entitlement did not exist and there were no such programs. After the Civil War, pensions were provided for veterans and their widows. The era of modern entitlements begins with railroad retirement in 1934, a combination of influence and of grievance no more easy to disentangle than the general question of where moral norms begin and political power ends.

Suffice it to say now that at one level, individuals appear to be more deserving of entitlements than do governments (viz. the demise of revenue sharing). Affirmative action in regard to employment has not yet been matched by entitlements based on race or gender (except for women's roles as mothers). The elderly, especially, the poor, children, the sick are now favored, but inconsistencies in the categories—some sick, say, black lung sufferers, but not others, say, lung cancer victims—suggest special historical considerations.

The moral force of entitlements has varied with the degree to which beneficiaries are deemed responsible for their condition. The more the individual is considered responsible for poverty, for instance, the less likely is governmental provision. The more government or society is held responsible, the more appropriate an entitlement would be. Two views on civil service retirement illustrate the difference. The conservative position, emphasizing individual responsibility and fearful of government "handouts," was expressed in a 1956 hearing by Tom Murray, chairman of the House Committee on Post Office and Civil Service:

> In this day and time you never hear of the philosophy of saving for a rainy day, or practicing thrift; it looks like everybody wants to depend, or so many want to be dependent, on the Government to keep on supporting them for the rest of their lives after they retire. I cannot go along with that

philosophy. I am interested in getting a retirement bill, but I want a sound actuarial fund.[27]

The liberal position, emphasizing adequacy, won out, as is expressed in a House report in 1969:

> Federal staff retirement systems represent a mixture of insurance and humanitarian principles. In the matter of adjusting annuities after retirement, insurance practice would guarantee that whatever annuity an employee had earned at the time of retirement should be preserved without change. On the other hand, humanitarian considerations would argue that the welfare of the retired person is the major concern, and that annuities should be adjusted to changing needs. The latter theory has prevailed through congressional action.[28]

Differences of opinion on who is responsible for poverty, and therefore entitled to what, remain great as Verba and Orren's survey shows. (See Table 7-6.) As entitlements rose, the balance swung away from individual and toward social (i.e., governmental) responsibility.

In John Mortimer's television series, "Rumpole of the Bailey," the irascible Rumpole refers to his long-suffering wife as "she who must be obeyed." Apparently, she has acquired entitlement status. The importance of moral force may be seen by returning to the classical notion of a budgetary base—that which ought not be moved. As a policy claim, entitlement is a way of guaranteeing a base. The program may go up but not down; she shall not be cut. This resistance is not only a matter of keeping old conflicts closed, but of a shared sense of justice. The base thus becomes the politically shared belief about "who is entitled to what" and is therefore bolstered and contested by arguments about equity and fairness.

A crucial factor in arguments about entitlements, therefore, is the socially constructed definition of equity or fairness. Should employees get what they paid for? Get what (somehow comparable) employees get?

[27]House Committee on Post Office and Civil Service, *Hearings on S.2875 and Related Matters*, June 18, 19, 21, 26 and July 3, 10, 12, 1956, p. 78.

[28]House Committee on Post Office and Civil Service, U.S. House of Representatives Report 91-158, *Civil Service Retirement Financing and Benefits*, p. 14.

TABLE 7-6
Poverty in America[29]

Group	Fault of poor	Fault of system
Business	57%	9%
Labor	15	56
Farm	52	19
Intellectuals	23	44
Media	21	50
Republicans	55	13
Democrats	5	68
Blacks	5	86
Feminists	9	76
Youth	16	61

Not lose (to inflation)? Keep pace with society (retiree gets increases in line with increases in the standard of living)? Be guaranteed some "adequate" level of benefit? Any of these may legitimate an increase, but a package that reduces benefits overall can be justified on the ground that beneficiaries are already doing better than they should.

Even the prevailing sense of fairness—people should not be deprived of benefits—has variations. Is it fair to change the benefits for someone already retired, that is, reduce benefits currently received? If that is unfair, what about a change in benefits promised to those already working? Is it more fair to change the promise to younger employees than to older? The notion is that certain obligations are more obligating than others, in part because the ability of recipients to compensate for changes, and the degree to which they may have relied on the old system, varies.

Comparisons are crucial, but they cut both ways. In fiscal 1981, federal outlays for affordable housing came to some $7.5 billion, yet only a small proportion of those eligible were served. In fiscal 1982, however,

[29]Taken from Sidney Verba and Gary R. Orren, *Equality in America: The View from the Top* (Cambridge, Mass.: Harvard University Press, 1985), p.74.

tax preferences for mostly middle-class homeowners amounted to some $35.5 billion. These, too, can be considered entitlements. Is it that these politically untouchable but indirect tax expenditures should be reduced (they escaped the 1986 tax reform unscathed) or that the housing entitlements be increased?

Only the naive think that political power plays no role in entitlements; only the foolish think that politicians' perceptions of who is deserving play no part in determining who receives entitlements. Indeed, the two conceptions are related; perception that a clientele is powerful makes it easier to think they are deserving and belief that a clientele is worthy makes it easier to justify mobilizing resources on their behalf. Widespread belief that a class of citizens ought to be helped makes it harder to deny them entitlements just as the opposite belief in their unworthiness makes it harder to keep giving them this priority claim on our collective resources. In the nature of human affairs where mixed motives prevail, it is difficult to disentangle them; yet we can still recognize reciprocal influence between the "is" and "ought" of entitlements.

Anyone affected by a program may be among its clientele. This clientele includes not only the direct beneficiaries—wheat growers or schoolchildren who also eat subsidized lunches—but also the service providers—fertilizer and tractor companies, cooks and bottle washers, administrators and interest groups—who live off of the recipients. Also included are the politicians and publicists who claim credit or bask in the glow of having not only done well but good. Clients comprise, to use Hugh Heclo's term, the issue networks of people not only in the federal but at all levels of government who are regularly concerned with operating, defending, criticizing, and altering entitlements.

The conditions for constituency influence are well known: the broader-based the group, the larger its numbers, the wider its geographic spread, the more intense its feelings (a joint product of the perceived importance of the benefits and beliefs about their rightness—I have fought for my country or worked all my life), the better its organization, the more resources (votes, money, intelligence, ability to appeal to shared values) it can mobilize, the more politically powerful it will be. So far so obvious. The size of a constituency depends not only on those affected now but those who expect to be affected later, not only on those directly involved but on those who care about them. The political potency of social security depends, to be sure, on the many millions of retired people. But it also is a consequence of those who contribute now and hope to benefit later, their families who will have to provide less support, and providers, like nursing homes, who service them.

The size of the direct beneficiaries is not a given factor, out there in nature like a fruit waiting to be plucked, but rather is socially and politically constructed. Who is or is not physically or mentally handicapped to what degree, requiring what sort of assistance, as in the Supplemental Security Income Program (SSI), changes with the standards of the time.[30] While the extremes are usually clear enough, programs can be altered to allow in more or fewer people. Major efforts may be made, as with food stamps, to actively encourage more people to apply. Here social mores figure prominently: Whether programs are seen as stigmatizing or whether recipients are exercising a too-long delayed right makes a considerable difference in "take-up" rates and hence in costs. Potential recipients have both to know about the availability of benefits and to feel the moral desirability of applying before their numbers will rise.

Similarly, a combination of a change in statutes, together with the rise of judicial activism in an egalitarian direction, have led to much greater court intervention on behalf of program expansion than in the past. When the Department of Agriculture failed to comply fully with the 1971 outreach amendment of the food stamp act to inform poor families of the benefits available to them, class-action suits compelled much greater compliance. Even more striking, the department's slowness in implementing the Special Supplemental Food Program for Women, Infants, and Children led to a class-action suit in 1976 requiring it to spend all the budget authority for the program accumulated since 1972.[31] The courts substituted their judgment for that of the Executive

[30]See Deborah Stone, *The Disabled State* (Philadelphia: Temple University Press, 1984).
[31]Report to Congress, "What Can Be Done?" p. 24.

branch as to the pace and sum of spending. Thus changes in values among elites, in the judiciary, the media, and sources of opinion formation have their effect on entitlements.

While it is true that political forces create and alter entitlements, it is also true that entitlements help create political forces. Whether or not interest groups are influential in creating entitlements—often they are not[32]—the very existence of these benefits creates incentives for interest groups to organize.[33]

Since size is such an important resource in obtaining political support, strong clients with weak claims, to use David Stockman's apt phrase,[34] or with insufficient influence are motivated to form coalitions. The survival of price supports in Congress is largely due to coalition building: Representatives from farm states, already advantaged by the rule that gives states with sparse population equal representation in the Senate, trade votes with each other; cotton is added to wheat and other commodities, farm and urban representatives trade votes on price supports in return for food stamps, nutrition programs, and so on. "It was the height of cynicism," so Robert Bauman, Republican from Maryland, felt, "to marry the food stamp program to the agricultural bill . . . it was done for purposes of political logrolling to gain votes for both bills."[35]

Logrolling may be limited by imposing a limit under which spending must fit, thereby trying to force tradeoffs among programs. Budget Director Stockman hoped to break the practice of budgeting by addition by coming "in with a plan that's unacceptable to the farm guys so that the whole thing begins to splinter."[36] At that time he succeeded; as a farm lobbyist said "It used to be that everybody could get their piece

---

[32]See Aaron Wildavsky, *Speaking Truth to Power* (Boston: Little, Brown, 1979), Chapter 3, "Policy as Its Own Cause," pp. 62–85.

[33]*Ibid.*

[34]David Stockman, "The Social Pork Barrel," *The Public Interest*, No. 39 (Spring 1975), pp. 3–30.

[35]John A. Ferejohn, "Logrolling in an Institutional Context: A Case Study of Food Stamps Legislation," *Working Papers in Political Science*, P-5-85 (Palo Alto, Calif.: Hoover Institute, October 1985), p. 19.

[36]William Greider, "The Education of David Stockman," *The Atlantic*, December 1981, p. 35.

of the pie, and if the pie was too small [Congress] would just make it bigger."[37] An acute observer pictured the situation as a pond where "the water level is going down and the fish are flopping and sticking each other and biting."[38] But the story was not over. By disregarding its own advice not to outguess markets, a combination of external factors—good weather with bad international markets—and internal misjudgment— target prices went up much faster than inflation—spending on price supports soared far more under Reagan and Stockman than under the allegedly profligate Carter administration.

But how, if changing values matter, the reader may wonder, have tobacco supports survived? By compromise and by craft. The bad name given to smoking by the massive evidence of its connection to lung cancer, emphysema, heart disease, and other health dangers has naturally raised questions about why government should subsidize the production of the noxious weed. Then, again, counterbalancing this concern is the plight of the family farmer in the South. On one side, this clash of values led to compromise: Without going into the very technical details, a complex scheme was devised through which it could be said that tobacco farmers were paying for their own support. On the other side, strategies were followed making it difficult to single out tobacco for special (and, therefore, hostile) treatment. At various times, under the aegis of Senator Jesse Helms, Republican of North Carolina, tobacco supports have been combined with wheat and dairy programs or held hostage by southern senators to other dearly desired programs. By reducing the visible budgetary cost and by making opposition politically expensive, tobacco support has been maintained, albeit at a reduced level.

BEEKEEPERS AND (PUBLIC) PURSE SNATCHERS: GIVING ENTITLEMENTS A BAD NAME

Though there are good reasons for entitlements (government may wish to keep promises and provide income and services regardless of its own

[37]From Sieverts, on agricultural price supports.
[38]*Ibid.*

circumstances), their rapid growth began to give them a bad name. Entitlements as a class were held to blame for deficits. Entitlements were balls and chains that kept Congress from running to the rescue of an economy in distress. (Actually, some of them, by going up while the economy went down, may have helped.) While hardly anyone dared to oppose the programs that made up the bulk of entitlements, or that spoke to important values, such as alleviating hunger and providing pensions for the elderly, abuses in less-favored ones were regularly cited. The message was that entitlements were being misused, that charitable impulses had turned into commercial ventures with only government sure to lose. The beekeepers' entitlement is far from typical; but it raises the question of who is getting stung by entitlements in an extreme form. Seeing the worst will help us appreciate the moral force behind other entitlement programs.

Why is the United States federal government the sweetest touch in the world? The answer—because it stores and subsidizes the most honey—tells us something about why entitlements have become suspect. It may be small but the honey entitlement carries a big message.

The rationing of sugar and the need for beeswax to waterproof ammunition in World War II led to an increase in the production of honey. Prices dropped after the war, so the industry requested assistance. The Agricultural Act of 1949 required the Secretary of Agriculture to support the price of honey. The rationale given was that bees are essential in pollinating a number of crops and that this service either would be insufficient due to a shortage of bees or, in any event, farmers could not afford to pay. Naturally, like the World War II buildings that still dot our college campuses, the honey price support was supposed to be temporary. As usual, it was the government that got stung.

A price support level for honey is set. Beekeepers then obtain loans using honey stored with the government as collateral. If the market price rises, the keepers sell the honey and pay the government the principal plus a low rate of interest. If the market price declines, producers may default on their loans (without paying interest), leaving the government holding bags of honey.

Sweet stuff can lull you to sleep. From 1970 to 1979, no loans were in default. Then the usual combination of life (external forces) and government (internal legislation specifying conditions for entitlements) took hold. The inflation of the mid-70s, tied to an index for farm products, doubled the support price from 32.7 cents per pound in 1977 to 65.8 cents in 1984. Around the same time, foreign suppliers increased production and the world price of honey dropped. The rising value of the dollar, which made foreign goods cheaper, led imports to double between 1979 and 1984.

The combination of high support and low market prices had the expected results: Honey loans increased almost three times, honey left to the government increased twenty times (from 5.3 to 106 million pounds); the defaults cost Uncle Sam $133 million, and administrative costs for managing the honey rose from very little to $33 million. Essentially, honey was being produced to serve as collateral on which beekeepers could default. In the 1983 crop year, for example, 113.6 million pounds of honey were used as loan collateral but only about 7 million pounds were redeemed. A little more than half (52 percent) of all honey produced in the United States was defaulted to its government.

Nor is that all. Investigation by the General Accounting Office revealed that it is easy to adulterate bee honey with much cheaper corn syrup; even experts would have difficulty distinguishing by taste or appearance as much as 40 percent corn syrup mixed with honey. Yet the Department of Agriculture does not require tests of honey stored as collateral to see if it has been adulterated. "Some beekeepers told us," the GAO reports, "that they feed corn syrup to their bees during the winter or off-season. One of the beekeepers we talked with was installing a 30,000-gallon tank to store corn syrup at the time of our visit."[39]

Among the population of beekeepers—hobbyists, part-timers, and business—only 1 percent were classified as commercial, yet they operated around half of the honeybee colonies and made 60 percent of the honey. For some reason, only 1 percent of the nation's beekeepers take part in the price support program. It may well be that the entire commercial

[39]Report to the Congress by the Comptroller General, "Federal Price Support for Honey Should Be Phased Out," GAO/RCED-85-107, August 19, 1985, p. 36.

industry produces essentially for government storage. Departing from its usual staid and cautious approach, GAO leads its report with the headline "Federal Price Supports for Honey Should Be Phased Out."[40]

Funny-honey no more justifies condemnation of all entitlements than evidence of fraud is sufficient to reject welfare programs or "goldplating" (see Chapter 9) should lead us to abandon national defense. Like GAO, I suspect most of us would choose to satisfy our sweet tooth another way. It is not that any single entitlement broke the bank. It is, rather, that entitlements, taken together, without a corresponding willingness to raise taxes, broke the back of classical budgeting.

America, it is said, is promises. In that case, entitlements are very American. But it is also said that promises are made to be broken. Insofar as an old promise is a good promise, because of its long acceptance, we might expect new ones to be more readily subject to cutbacks. Insofar as notions of "fair shares" guide decision makers, those programs that have done well in the past or that have increased rapidly would be subject to cuts. Unfortunately, the record contains examples of "all of the above" without guidelines as to when they are applicable.

Consider the most common explanation: Congressmen cut in the most politically vulnerable areas. According to Kent Weaver

> Policymakers obviously wish to minimize political costs to themselves [in the distribution of cutbacks]. This gives clientele groups that are large (social security recipients), well-organized to mobilize recipients (veterans), and have a wide geographic base an advantage over those that are poorly organized and have a low voter turnout (AFDC recipients). Programs with a narrow geographic base (black lung disability) are also likely to fare poorly unless they can form logrolling coalitions with other programs, or policy control is monopolized by program supporters. Many of the program cuts were indeed directed at groups least able to resist them.[41]

It is true that in 1981 and 1982, the first two years of the Reagan administration, means-tested entitlements were hit hardest. The near-poor lost the most. In 1986, however, payment of approximately $120 billion in tax preferences were shifted from individuals, with a decided

[40]*Ibid.*, p. 1.
[41]Weaver, "Controlling Entitlements," pp. 328–29.

emphasis on the near-poor, to corporations. And in 1984, 1985, and 1986, very large amounts were cut from the defense budget, not everyone's idea of a bastion of budgetary vulnerability. It does appear, if only by definition, that the groups and functions that had benefits reduced must have been weak, for if they had been strong this could not have happened to them. Since these targets of opportunity varied considerably over a short time, however, we are no wiser.

Much has been written that attempts to link the size and distribution of expenditures with such factors as party composition of Congress and party affiliation of the president. Hibbs and Dennis, for example, have sought to identify how shifts in party control of the presidency and Congress have affected the distribution of government spending. They suggest that "the strength of the Democrats in Congress is the main political source of increases in the share of transfers in gross personal income," whereas "shifts in party control of the presidency had negligible direct influence."[42]

There is evidence, however, that party control may be rivaled in importance by economic factors (inflation, unemployment) and program-specific spending desires, such as coal mine disasters. Given a large deficit, increases in big ticket items, from defense to medicare, may create pressure to pare down other programs.[43]

To obtain a better understanding of why some entitlements flourish while others wither, it will be informative to take a closer look at the budgetary history of specific entitlements. I have selected them to show rapid, moderate, and slow growth. The perceptive reader, who begins to wonder whether scholars are asking for too much—a key to political change—may be on the right track.

---

[42]Douglas A. Hibbs, Jr., and Christopher Dennis, "The Politics and Economics of Income Distribution Outcomes in the Postwar United States," transcript, 1986, p. 16.

[43]See Mark S. Kamlet and David C. Mowery, "Influences on Executive and Congressional Budgetary Priorities, 1953–1981," *American Political Science Review*, Vol. 81, No. 1 (March 1987), pp. 155–78.

THE RISE AND FALL
OF ENTITLEMENTS

8

I HAVE DISCUSSED SOME FACTORS that purport to explain the growth of entitlements. Entitlements escape annual review through the appropriations process. Entitlements with strong constituency influence and moral power fare better than programs lacking these attributes. Entitlements grow also because of external factors, such as changes in population, inflation, or unemployment. If that were all there was to it, however, programs with entitlement status would keep growing; none would become smaller; and all would fare better than programs in similar policy areas funded by appropriations. But the facts belie such easy generalizations. Appropriations sometimes grow faster than entitlements, which, in turn, do actually decline, or even are abolished. Understanding the growth or decline of an entitlement calls for a closer examination of the history of particular programs.

All entitlements are not created equal. Entitlements (see Table 8-1) follow three trajectories: those that are growing quickly, those that have stayed about the same (adjusting for inflation), and those programs that have been terminated or have declined significantly. Obviously, entitlements are not an automatic ticket to financial paradise (although entitlement status greatly helps) and being funded through annual appropriations is not necessarily a death knell.

TABLE 8-1
Selected Entitlement Programs
(in constant FY86 $ billions)

	Actual 1977 outlays	*Estimated 1986 outlays*	*Annual growth 1977–1986*
Farm Price Supports	$ 6.7	$ 20.4	13.20%
Medicare	37.8	66.7	6.86
Medicaid	17.3	24.7	4.02
Social Security	147.1	200.1	3.48
Food Stamps	9.5	12.6	3.18
Military Retirements	14.4	17.4	2.15
Supplemental Security Income	9.3	10.2	1.00
Veterans' Compensation	10.0	10.5	0.47
Black Lung	1.7	1.7	−0.41
AFDC	11.1	9.7	−1.48
Social Services	4.5	2.6	−5.84
General Revenue Sharing	11.9	4.4	−10.34
G.I. Bill	6.5	0.9	−19.63

HIGH RISERS

Medicare

Medicare for the elderly and medicaid for the poor represent rapidly rising entitlements. In FY67, medicare enrolled 19 million eligible beneficiaries and had expenditures of $4 billion.[1] By FY82, medicare had 29 million eligible beneficiaries and almost $50 billion in expenditures. Those figures reflect a less than 3 percent annual increase in the eligible population, but an 8 percent annual growth rate for expenditures. Over

[1]This account is drawn from student papers by Walter Wong and Marc de la Vergne.

that same period, this last figure outpaced such stiff competition as the rise in the Consumer Price Index and expansion of the federal budget.

The medicare program has two components: Part A provides hospital insurance, and Part B, the supplementary Medical Insurance Program (SMI), covers physician services and other health care services. Under Part A, funds (raised by a 2.6 percent tax on payrolls) are placed in the Hospital Insurance Trust Fund, administered by the Department of Health and Human Services. Anyone over the age of 65 who has contributed wages to social security may have part of their medical costs paid for through Part A. Part A therefore represents a genuine entitlement. Elegible beneficiaries are automatically enrolled in Part A. Part B, however, is voluntary and requires participants (96 percent of eligibles are enrolled) to pay a monthly premium ($12 to $20 monthly).

Together, these two eligibility criteria create a strong political base for the medicare program. Aside from the 29 million people currently eligible for payments, medicare also draws support from family members who are protected against possible financial responsibility for the illness of a parent or relative, and of active members of the work force who are current contributors and future beneficiaries of the trust fund. Since medical care for the elderly has come to be recognized by society as the morally correct course to follow, politicians talk about cutting medicare only at the risk of sounding uncaring toward the aged.

The age and social security criteria have served to define the boundaries for expansion of the beneficiary base. In 1972, for instance, disabled individuals younger than 65 became entitled to monthly disability benefits under the social security retirement program; and individuals under 65 suffering from kidney failure were made eligible for the social security or retirement program or the spouse or dependent child of such an insured individual became entitled to hospital insurance benefits. Each of these groups was in some way a contributor to the trust fund and, accordingly, had some type of claim to payments from the trust. Yet other groups, such as the unemployed, have been unable thus far to work their way onto the medicare rolls.

Between 1966 and 1982, the taxable wage base rose from $6,600 to

$32,400, almost a fivefold increase. Over that same period the medicare tax rate increased from 0.7 to 2.6 percent.[2] An individual with no change in income would have incurred a 270 percent increase in his medicare contribution over that period. And a person whose income matched or exceeded the wage base would have seen her annual contribution increase from $23.10 ($6,600 × .0035) to $421.20 ($32,400 × .013), an increase of over 1,700 percent. Contributions by employers increased in a corresponding manner, though in greater total amounts, since they were required to match the contributions of each employee.

Medicare is shielded through its relationship with social security. Social security, approximately four times greater and longer in existence, takes a much larger share of the pie. Individuals tend to identify the payroll tax as "the social security tax," and many are more or less unaware of the portion being taken to finance medicare. The relative attention paid to each of these programs shows up at higher levels as well. Congress usually considers social security funding problems to be much more important than medicare's woes.

The history of the medicare trust fund demonstrates that incremental changes can and do produce significant results. Or, as Martha Derthick would say, "incremental enlargements" are capable of "obscuring their long-term consequences."[3] Looking down Table 8-2, notice the relatively large total increases that occur over the five-year period and compare those figures to the relatively small changes that occur in any particular year. The maximum tax contribution, for example, climbed from $148.50 in 1977 to $421.20 in 1982, a compound annual growth rate of 23 percent and a total increase of 184 percent over that period. These figures would apply only to individuals whose incomes matched or exceeded the taxable wage base in each year. Nevertheless, for any individual, the annual increments in the tax contribution will appear small relative to the total change occurring over the five-year period.

Like the Part A payroll tax, the SMI (Part B) premium gives enrollees

---

[2]U.S. Senate Committee on Finance (Staff REport), *Staff Data and Materials Related to Social Security Financing* (Washington: GPO, 1982).

[3]Martha Derthick, *Policymaking for Social Security* (Washington, D.C.: The Brookings Institution, 1979), p. 290.

TABLE 8-2

Annual Changes Add Up in Big Ways: Tax Base and Tax Rate, 1977–1982

Year	Taxable wage base		Individual's tax rate		Maximum tax contribution	
1977	$16,500		0.90		$148.50	
1978	17,700	7%	1.00	11%	177.00	19%
1979	22,900	29	1.05	5	240.45	35
1980	25,900	13	1.05	0	271.95	13
1981	29,700	15	1.30	24	386.10	42
1982	32,400	9	1.30	0	421.20	9
	Total	96%		44%		184%

Source: Figures for the taxable wage base and the tax rate are from U.S. Senate Committee on Finance (Staff Report), *Staff Data and Materials Related to Social Security Financing.* Percentages and tax contribution amounts were calculated from those two columns. Yearly percentages reflect change from the previous year. Total percentages represent total change from 1977 to 1982.

the impression that they are paying for their benefits. For SMI, however, general revenues are a significant funding source. When medicare was enacted, it was expected that enrollees and the government would make equal contributions to the SMI trust fund. Premium rates were to be set annually by the Secretary of Health, Education and Welfare. This aspect was unique because it was the only instance at that time allowing action by someone other than Congress to change financing conditions under the Social Security Act.[4] The Treasury and enrollees did make equal contributions until 1972 when Congress placed a limit on the extent to which SMI premiums could be increased. By this method any increase in the SMI premium was limited to the rate of increase in social security cash benefits; and Congress also made the federal treasury responsible for differences between the funds necessary to make SMI benefit payments and the size of SMI premiums.

Then crisis came. Medicare and medicaid's share of the budget virtually doubled from 4.6 percent in 1970 to 9.1 percent in 1985. Though

[4]Robert J. Myers, *Medicare* (Bryn Mawr: McCahan Foundation, 1970), p. 164.

medicaid spending slowed down by the end of the 1970s, however, medicare kept rising, from $6 billion in 1970 to $66 billion in 1985 (medicaid came to "only" $20 billion). Before long, fears were voiced that the medicare trust fund Part A would be depleted. In hearings before the House Select Committee on Aging's Subcommittee on Health and Long-Term Care, Representative Vandergriff of Texas set an urgent tone for the debate:

> I believe that we in the United States face a crisis of potentially cata-strophic proportions. . . . All too few Americans realize that the catastrophe is near at hand. . . . Medicare is the fastest-growing expenditure in the Federal Budget. The Hospital Insurance Trust Fund will be depleted by 1986 or 1987. . . . Skyrocketing health care costs push the Medicare bill even higher.[5]

At the same time, medical care inflation, part quality, part profit, outpaced the general increase in prices (as it does to this very day) by a large margin. Analysts and politicians alike attributed this inflation to the ability of patients and providers to pass on cost increases to others. "The problem," then-Representative Phil Gramm said, "is that nobody has a bottom line interest . . . under our current system in making rational decisions on the basis of cost."[6] In his testimony before the Task Force on Entitlements and Uncontrollables, Representative Wirth tes-tified that "If we don't break into this cycle, the cost of medical care as a percentage of the budget, and as demand on the gross national product, is going to get so great that it is going to make that Social Security issue . . . look like nickels and dimes . . . in comparison."[7] Republicans and Democrats alike sang that song.[8]

The Board of Directors of the Hospital Insurance Fund reported in 1982 that funds would be depleted by 1987. And the Supplementary Insurance fund, which supported doctors' fees, was not in much better shape.[9]

---

[5]Hearings, 98th Congress, Senate Committee on the Budget, Task Force on Entitle-ments, Uncontrollables, and Indexing, "The Administration's FY 1984 Medicare and Medicaid Budget Proposals," February 1983, p. 2.
[6]*Ibid.*, p. 35.
[7]*Ibid.*, p. 30.
[8]*Ibid.*, p. 2.
[9]See *National Journal*, April 16, 1983.

Two billion dollars in savings were realized under the first-ever use of the reconciliation procedure in 1980 through such devices as lowering rates that could be charged by skilled nurses. In addition to raising the deductibles paid by patients under medicare, Congress slightly reduced payments to states in the 1981 Omnibus Budget Reconciliation Act, allowed states to set up rules that gave patients the ability to choose their source of medical care and, among other things, repealed the "reasonable cost" provision for reimbursing hospitals and other providers. In the 1982 reconciliation law, the Tax Equity and Fiscal Responsibility Act (TEFRA), Congress further reduced hospital reimbursement for medicare, cut government's contribution to medicaid to states with high error rates (i.e., providing services to unauthorized persons) and allowed (but did not compel) states to charge small fees for certain services, in an effort to discourage frivolous use.

Within a month after President Reagan proposed prospective reimbursement in March 1983, Congress approved. No longer, it was thought, would hospitals and doctors pass on costs after they were incurred (i.e., retrospectively); rather they would be paid a fixed price for patients who fit any one of the 467 "diagnosis related groups."[10] Yet costs continued to escalate.

Why have cost-sharing rules been unable to control demand? One reason is that medicare's primary goal is to improve access. Consequently, rather than designing cost-sharing schedules to ensure that beneficiaries don't overuse services, schedules have been designed to ensure that no one who needs services hesitates to seek help merely because of cost-sharing arrangements. Another is that both providers and intermediaries have strong incentives not to control costs. For providers, like hospitals, lower costs would mean lower revenues. For intermediaries, such as insurance companies, the incentive is somewhat different. Their interest is to promote good relationships with providers, for insurers have to deal with providers to process their own claims. By facilitating medicare reimbursement requests, intermediaries maintain positive relationships. Intermediaries certainly have no incentive to

---

[10]Allen Schick, "Controlling the 'Uncontrollables': Budgeting for Health Care in an Age of Mega-Deficits." Paper prepared for AEI Pew Fellows Conference, November 1985, pp. 1–2.

lower costs, since the government is paying the bills. Finally, medicare payments often subsidize private insurance payments. If providers garner higher revenues from medicare patients, they can afford to charge lower rates to privately insured patients. These incentives add fuel to the high rate of inflation in the health care sector, which, ironically, had been an early impetus for medicare legislation.

While food stamp recipients or mothers on AFDC have been the targets of administrative efforts to reduce "fraud and abuse" in those programs, providers have been the targets (and on occasion the perpetrators) in medicare. In the old days, as I know from personal experience, some doctors provided care to poor people at much lower rates (in my case, $2 for what the same doctor charged $10 at his Park Avenue office). It was good for rich doctors to help poor patients. Nowadays, the same logic is used to condemn doctors. As a result of disagreement over reimbursement rates, many providers, especially physicians, have left the medicare program (or in medicare terminology, they refuse to accept assignment). The result has been higher costs for beneficiaries.

Meanwhile, back in the Treasury, what happened to the crisis? Under the rubric of "Buy time, pay later," Allen Schick contends

> The pattern of medicare cutbacks shows that Congress has been unwilling to directly face up to the prognostications that demographic and other trends will compel drastic structural changes in the program. Instead, Congress has skillfully postponed the day of reckoning in the hope that it might never arrive. The evidence is that Congress has been successful thus far. While 1983 forecasts gave medicare only four years until bankruptcy, 1985 projections suggest that the trust funds might make it until the mid-1990s. Success begets repetition; the fact that the bad news has been postponed reinforces the tendency of Congress to behave in this manner.[11]

My own view is that Congress is looking at the wrong things—wicked providers and other bad actors—instead of probing its own system of financing. So long as huge flows of money continue to wash over the medical care system, costs are going to rise. Attempting to monitor trillions of transactions is futile. Will not hospitals diagnose patients into higher-cost categories? Won't workers choose higher-cost medicine (or

[11]*Ibid.*, pp. 30–31.

pay no attention to cost) so long as insurance is "free"? It would be better to place limits on financial resources. With less money around, fewer or less expensive services would result. Those who dislike this prospect, whatever their other virtues, do not wish to control costs.[12] True, one step has been taken; tax deductions for medical care, used by middle- and upper-income groups, were substantially diminished during the Reagan administration. But fringe benefits, including comprehensive policies, were not.

Medicaid

The discovery of "Medicaid Mills" that provide bad or overpriced medicine, as well as the belief that while poor people are sicker than richer ones and should have more medical care, they do not need as much as they are getting, have made medicaid an unpopular system. So it is necessary to begin by observing that many people, otherwise unable to afford adequate medical care, are getting services through medicaid. For students of budgeting, the point is to ask why the relative unpopularity of medicaid is not translated into comparable cuts. The answer, to prefigure the story, is twofold: The alternatives for the states (i.e., paying a larger share) are worse, and the federal government wants to shift the blame (to providers, preferably, or to the states, reluctantly) rather than limit the amount of money that can be spent.

Medicaid's enactment was an outgrowth of a slow but orderly involvement of government in health care spanning decades. As early as 1798, the federal government funded the delivery of medical services to merchant seamen in special hospitals.[13] Later, the federal government provided hospitalization and other types of medical care for members of the armed forces, veterans, Indians, and certain other groups. The Federal Emergency Relief Act of 1933 constituted the first federal legislation to provide health care for the needy. Under this act, the Federal Emer-

[12]See my "Doing Better and Feeling Worse: The Political Pathology of Health Policy," *Daedalus* (Winter 1976), pp. 105–23.
[13]Anthony Jong, *Dental Public Health and Community Dentistry* (St. Louis: C.V. Mosby, 1981).

gency Relief Administration (FERA) was set up to make funds available to states for paying medical-care costs of the unemployed needy.

The FERA program lasted only two-and-a-half years. Although it was not uniform throughout all the states, did not cover some essential services, and had many serious shortcomings,[14] the program did exercise great influence on subsequent medical-care programs. FERA, for example, emphasized the role of governmental agencies as purchasers of medical care in contrast with previous reliance on volunteer services of physicians and hospitals, and set a precedent for increased participation of the federal and state governments in financing medical care for the indigent.[15]

Medicaid is one of several federal-state social welfare programs in which benefits are made available to eligible groups of citizens. The benefits are medical services; the eligibles are welfare recipients and poor people; the mechanism is public payments to vendors of services. This vendor-payment mechanism operates as third-party coverage. In other words, state programs pay bills for services rendered to recipients by health providers. Payment is made directly to providers rather than to eligibles. Once eligible, recipients are entitled to receive services for which they are covered.

Like Aid to Families with Dependent Children, medicaid is a means-tested, residual welfare program. As a residual program, it is intended to pick up the slack when the market and the family do not meet the need. Medicaid requires individual applicants for benefits to demonstrate not only that they are poor but also that they meet certain other requirements (which vary with the state).

Medicaid also can be characterized as a grant-in-aid program by which the federal government pays a portion of the cost incurred by states in providing medical care to the poor, the aged, the blind, and the disabled. The program is financed by payroll taxes and general revenues. Medicaid is a bifurcated program; that is, the federal government pays half or more of the money but leaves development and administration of the program to the states. In actuality, medicaid is not a single program but fifty,

[14]See Margaret Greenfield, *Medicare and Medicaid: The 1965 and 1967 Social Security Amendments* (Westport, Conn.: Greenwood, 1968).
[15]*Ibid.*

since the decisions that states make within the federally established framework of laws and regulations determine the character of the program.

Because of the open-ended nature of medicaid, new fiscal controls cannot be applied through budget limits. States can assert fiscal control only by changing their programs—eligibility standards, services covered, and the like. The federal government asserts fiscal control indirectly by enacting laws and promulgating regulations that increase or restrict states' options in designing and administering their programs. How have states reduced medicaid spending?

Unemployed adults who still had financial resources were more likely to be targeted for cuts than individuals who were poor enough to have been eligible for welfare if they had applied. States were reluctant to cut welfare eligibles because such an action would have forced those individuals to apply for assistance, thus increasing costs for which states were entirely responsible.

In general, taking direct action affecting existing beneficiaries was less popular than relying on inflation to effect cuts, though a few states did change eligibility standards. The most important argument against eligibility reductions was the fact that many of the medically needy are aged and institutionalized. Consequently, elimination of eligibility was extremely unpopular. The cost of treating such individuals (at least under medicaid the "feds" pay their half) would have been shifted to county-run hospitals and facilities and ultimately to local taxpayers.

There are two main ways to affect eligibility: (1) reduce eligibility for AFDC or SSI recipients, or (2) restrict groups covered specifically and optionally under medicaid itself. Some states restricted the number of AFDC recipients by lowering the income level and allowable assets people could retain while receiving AFDC. Many states filed to raise welfare standards to keep pace with general inflation. As poor people's incomes and assets rose and surpassed the unindexed eligibility ceilings, they were cut from AFDC and hence lost medicaid eligibility. Automatic medicaid eligibility for SSI recipients occurs at the state's option. Thus some states decided to place SSI recipients in the optional category of medically needy rather than cover them as medically eligible.

States have an incentive to obtain federal matching dollars. If they choose not to, there is an increased financial burden on states, counties, and cities. The need for government assistance in providing or paying for medical care for the poor would not disappear if medicaid eligibility were constrained. Experience showed that broad medicaid eligibility standards (and higher federal assistance) actually reduced overall medical spending by states, counties, and cities instead of increasing it.[16]

When President Reagan took office, his interest in reducing federal spending carried over to medicaid. In 1981 he proposed to end medicaid's status as an entitlement program. Under this proposal, federal medicaid expenditures would be capped. Most governors opposed the cap and lobbied against it in Congress. With the federal cap, each marginal dollar would have come entirely from state revenues, creating intense pressure to cut their programs. The states argued that it was

> unfair for them to bear the entire fiscal burden when national economic policy had caused the recession that had virtually eliminated earlier state surpluses by raising expenses and lowering revenue. Moreover . . . past and continuing federal policies have contributed to the medical cost inflation that the national government was not taking action to curb.[17]

Both the Senate and the House rejected the proposal; Congress took a different tack. It acted indirectly to promote cost containment strategies by giving the states more flexibility to make many types of targeted cuts in their programs. In doing so, however, Congress did not impose any cuts on the program, nor did it drop mandatory or optional services from federal assistance. Rather, it transferred from the mandatory to the optional eligibility category coverage for those under 21 years of age who do not receive AFDC payments but who would be eligible for AFDC if they attended school. In addition, Congress gave states the freedom to offer varying amounts of services to different categories of individuals in the medically needy programs, although certain restrictions still existed.

Asked to tell Congress how it might lower medicaid spending, CBO bit the bullet; it suggested that

[16]Randall R. Bovbjerg and John Holahan, *Medicaid in the Reagan Era: Federal Policy and State Choices* (Washington: Urban Institute, 1982).

[17]*Ibid.*, p. 8.

Federal outlays could be reduced if the current formulas for calculating Federal support for Medicaid and AFDC were modified or new formulas were adopted. One possible modification would be to remove the statutory 50 percent minimum Federal share from Medicaid and AFDC. This would lower outlays by $3.3 billion. Under this option, the decline of the Federal share of State Medicaid and AFDC expenditures in 13 affected States would range from about 2 percentage points to about 33 percentage points. An alternative proposal, one that would affect all States rather than just those with the highest per capita incomes, would be to reduce the Federal share under the Medicaid formula by 3 percentage points. This would save roughly the same total amount as removing the 50 percent Federal minimum.[18]

Such embarrassing directness would put Congress in the position of being seen to cut benefits. Caught between conflicting desires—less spending and more benefits—Congress never directly removed medical services. Rather it cracked down on hospitals or doctors (the providers), or let inflation eat away the benefits through freezes on payments or slightly increased payments by beneficiaries. While its expenditures continue to rise, the rate of increase in medicare has been reduced by 6.8 percent, despite its public popularity, but only 2.8 percent in the more unpopular medicaid. Why? Allen Schick provides a cogent response:

(1) A dollar cutback in medicare reduces federal costs by $1; the same cutback in medicaid saves the federal government only about 50 cents. (2) Medicaid is seen by many members of Congress as a vital part of the safety net for low-income Americans. Moreover, as pressure has grown to curtail entitlements, there has been greater willingness to differentiate between means-tested and other benefits. (3) Medicare cutbacks have been spurred by financial crises in the HI and SMI funds. Since it is financed out of general revenues, medicaid is affected only by the overall deficit. (4) States have been effective lobbyists against federal cutbacks in medicaid. Their efforts have been motivated by concern that reduced federal assistance would compel them to pick up a larger share of medicaid costs.[19]

[18]CBO, "Reducing the Federal Budget: Strategies and Examples, Fiscal Years 1982–1986," p. 118, quoted in Report to the Congress by the Comptroller General of the United States, "What Can Be Done to Check the Growth of Federal Entitlement and Indexed Spending," p. 36.

[19]Schick, "Controlling the 'Uncontrollables,'" pp. 27–28.

TABLE 8-3

Federal Health Outlays

(billions of dollars)[20]

	1978	1980	1983	Percent change (constant dollars)*
Medicare	25.2	35.0	52.5	−56
Medicaid	10.7	14.0	17.0	+01
Discretionary	7.7	9.1	8.6	−36

*Adjusted using medical CPI as reported in Statistical Abstracts through May 1983.
Source: *Budget of the United States,* Fiscal Years 1975–1985.

In sum, under certain circumstances, strength can be weakness. Since medicare is about three times larger than medicaid, moreover, every time there is a felt need to reduce the deficit, medicare is the more tempting target.

With all this furor about the impact of medicaid and medicare on the budget, what has been happening to the discretionary (i.e., nonentitlement) health programs (community centers, preventive medicine, high blood pressure control, etc.) of the federal government? Table 8-3 tells the tale. While medicaid has just kept even with inflation and medicare jumped by 52.5 percent in just six years from 1978 to 1983, the purchasing power of discretionary programs has eroded by 36 percent. Again we see that one of the hidden effects of entitlements in times of stringency is to squeeze out appropriations, not necessarily because they are undesirable but rather because they are more readily controllable.

HOLDING THEIR OWN

Saving the food stamp program for a later comparison of entitlements to appropriations in the same field, I have chosen the Black Lung and End-Stage Renal Disease programs to illustrate entitlements that just keep up with the cost of living. Though their budgetary outcomes are

[20]From David Blumenthal, "Right Turns, Wrong Turns and Road Untaken: The Discretionary Federal Health Budget," in *Health Care: How to Inprove It and Pay for It,* Alternatives for the 1980s, No. 17, Center for National Policy, Washington, D.C., p.61.

stable, their trajectories—slow beginning, fast rising, abrupt halt—are not. How did we the people of the United States get into the rather unusual business of helping people with these two, rather than many other, health problems? And what factors explain the budgetary histories of these programs?

Black Lung[21]

On November 20, 1968, a coal mine explosion at Farmington, West Virginia, killed seventy-eight miners and sparked a nationwide outcry over working conditions in the mines. The television pictures of smoke, rescuers, and weeping families made such a powerful impression that the federal government was called to redress the miners' plight with regulation and compensation. It was intended, however, that federal participation would be temporary and limited in scope so as to function while the states and the coal mining industry were negotiating a compensatory mechanism for on-the-job disability and coal-dust pneumoconiosis. Once these arrangements were settled, it was thought, the federal government would withdraw its administrative and financial involvement. Sixteen years later, the government has contributed (and still does) nearly $1.8 billion a year to support disability payments to miners.[22]

Black lung disease (or pneumoconiosis) refers to the pathological process of inhaled coal dust lining the airways of the lung. The disease, to a very significant degree, increasingly restricts the person's activities. In extreme cases, fibrotic changes can be so overwhelming as to inhibit blood flow from the heart to the lungs, resulting in heart failure and eventual death. For the great majority of pneumoconiosis cases, even in coal miners, the result is dust retention with no visible pathology. These "category 1" people may or may not progress to the disabling manifestations of the disease. Since other factors (smoking, lifestyle, and the gender of the individual) may be involved, there is no predictive correlation between the presence of category 1 pneumoconiosis and disability.

The black lung issue became a passion when, by early 1969, spontane-

---

[21]This section is based on a paper by Jack Chow.
[22]Budget of the United States Government, FY 1983 (Appendix), Executive Office of the President: Office of Management and Budget, I-014-15.

ous walkouts at various mines exploded into a series of "black lung strikes" involving over 45,000 miners in West Virginia, Pennsylvania, and Ohio. Miners besieged the State House in Charleston to clamor for inclusion of black lung as a compensable occupational illness. A bill before the West Virginia legislature included a "presumptive diagnosis" clause that would award benefits to a miner on the basis of (1) the number of years worked in the miners, and (2) the presence of a "lung disease." The coal companies unsurprisingly opposed the bill and called for a series of diagnostic procedures beyond merely x-rays to firmly establish presence of pneumoconiosis. A compromise bill was arranged whereby a liberal definition of black lung was adopted along with acceptance of an array of diagnostic criteria to be considered as evidence of disability. West Virginia governor Arch Moore signed the bill in March 1969 and effectively ended the strikes.[23]

The West Virginia law took on greater influence in Washington because it established a black lung entitlement framework that miners took to be a central tenet of their health care interests. As federal policy on the black lung issue evolved, a broad definition of black lung as adopted by West Virginia became a lever by which miners could establish and increase their federal benefits. The fervent demonstration of militancy by the miners, furthermore, instilled a popular notion of moral obligation by the federal government to ensure safety and compensation. The public image of the miner as an economic instrument of the coal companies put that industry, and the expenditure-control groups in Congress, on the defensive for the coming decade.

Soon Congress crafted the landmark Federal Coal Mine Health and Safety Act of 1969, the forerunner to the Occupational Safety and Health Act (OSHA) of 1970. Title IV of the coal mine act, entitled "Black Lung Benefits," mandated that the disease be compensable with general revenue funds. The black lung provisions entitle two main groups of people: coal miners totally disabled from pneumoconiosis derived from underground mines, and widows of underground coal miners who died from pneumoconiosis. Basic benefit amounts are linked

[23]Alan Derickson, "The Origins of the Black Lung Insurgency," *Journal of Public Health Policy*, Vol. 4, No. 1 (March 1983), pp. 32–33.

to Federal Civil Service disability benefit levels that increase as federal salaries rise with adjustments.[24]

To simplify the verification of occupational causality of black lung disease and presence of total disability, there are three key "presumptive" clauses in the law that automatically qualify the applicant to benefits. One clause assumes that pneumoconiosis is derived from mining if the worker spent ten or more years in an underground mine. Another assumes that the miner is totally disabled if the prevailing pneumoconiosis is "complicated" (classified as category A, B, or C in the International Classification of Radiographs of Pneumoconiosis). The remaining clause entitles a widow to benefits if the miner had "complicated" pneumoconiosis or had already been drawing benefits. This clause included the presumption that pneumoconiosis was derived from mining if the miner had worked ten years in an underground mine and had died of a "chronic lung disease."[25]

For those miners and widows not covered by the clauses of irrefutability, the presentation of medical evidence of disability caused by pneumoconiosis from working in an underground mine is necessary for evaluation by the Social Security Administration (SSA). Applicants who are rejected by the SSA are empowered with the right to an administrative review; if they are still denied, they may seek a hearing before a hearings examiner, the appeals council, and the federal judiciary system.[26]

Since it was anticipated that many people applying for coal miner benefits were also receiving or applying for social security or state workmen's compensation benefits, both the Social Security and Coal Mine Act contain clauses to reduce overlapping and duplication of benefits. On the social security side, the law limits the amount of combined income from social security disability benefits and workmen's compensation to 80 percent of the worker's current earnings. If the combined amount exceeded that amount, the social security benefit would be

---

[24]Bernard Popick, "The Social Security Disability Program. III. The Black Lung Benefits—an Administrative Case Study," *Journal of Occupational Medicine*, Vol. 13, No. 7 (July 1971), p. 335.
[25]*Ibid.*, pp. 334–36.
[26]*Ibid.*, p. 337.

reduced. The Coal Mine Health and Safety Act ordains a dollar for dollar reduction of federal coal mine benefits if the miner is also receiving money from a state disability program.[27]

It was expected that by mid-1970 over 165,000 applications would be filed. In reality, over 183,000 were filed by June and 250,000 by the beginning of 1971.[28] The backlog of claims created innumerable delays for thousands of miners and their dependents as well as frustration for many who were otherwise qualified but could not produce x-rays showing dust opacities in their lungs.[29]

Overall, several aspects of the entitlement make for future growth. First, the clauses of irrefutability (the cause of pneumoconiosis is defined by law as related to the amount of time spent in the mine), and the assumption of total disability upon demonstration of "complicated" pneumoconiosis makes it hard for government to deny claims. Second, unlike most workmen's compensation programs (where there is an inherent adversarial relationship between worker and company), the black lung entitlement neutralizes antagonism by forcing the government to pay out benefits without assessing responsibility upon the coal-mine operators. Although government reserves the right to recover from the operator responsible monies paid to workers, the lengthy and costly appeals process available to the operators makes such recovery a very expensive enterprise. Third, the appeals process available to unsuccessful applicants incurs additional legal and administrative expenses. Backlogs of cases add to the frustration of both worthy miners and claims adjusters and fuel political pressure to simplify the process by liberalizing eligibility criteria. Fourth, the very specificity of the entitlement— pneumoconiosis and disability derived from underground coal mining— entails substantial effort to document, review, and assess medical criteria (often incomplete) relevant to the benefit.

The first expansion of the black lung entitlement occurred in May 1972 when President Nixon signed PL 92-303 specifying that incon-

[27]*Ibid.*
[28]*Ibid.*
[29]L. E. Kerr, "Black Lung," *Journal of Public Health Policy*, Vol. 1, No. 1 (March 1980), p. 50.

clusive or negative x-rays could not be the basis for denial of benefits. The 1972 amendment also declared that surface miners would be eligible for benefits. In addition, the amendment strengthened the government's authority to specify the "last responsible operator" as being liable for benefits the government already had disbursed to an individual miner. The federal government would honor claims presented to it up to December 31, 1973; thereafter, claims would be paid by operators via state worker's compensation laws (or federal laws if state laws were inadequate). If no operator could be charged, benefits would be paid by the government. The operator's right to appeal remained intact.[30]

The 1972 amendment's liberalization of medical criteria needed to establish eligibility foretold a key development in expanding the entitlement. By accepting the eligibility of some miners who could not demonstrate radiographic evidence of coal workers' pneumoconiosis, the amendment effectively expanded the definition of "black lung" to include dust-induced bronchitis and emphysema.[31] Expanding the number of compensable diseases under a generic category not only added financial responsibility for the government, but—through looser standards of medical criteria and administrative review—also greatly enhanced applicants' accessibility to the entitlement. How did this change take place?

Action on eligibility standards by House and Senate authorization committees effectively bypassed the more conservative Appropriations Committee. In the Senate, eligibility provisions fell under the aegis of the Human Resources Committee while trust fund details were the responsibility of the Finance Committee. Splitting the two key elements of the entitlement proposal among separate committees allowed for little leverage by expenditure control groups to limit fiscal obligations. Limitations imposed in one committee could be negated by the liberalizations passed by another.

As time passed, and costs rose, words of warning were heard. Repre-

[30]*1975 Congressional Quarterly Almanac*, p. 494.
[31]Kerr, "Black Lung," p. 57.

sentative John Erlenborn aroused nagging doubts about congressional intentions by stating that "The main issue . . . is whether Congress should turn what was originally a one-shot disability benefit program into a permanent pension program, partially funded by taxpayers, for one class of workers—the coal miners. I say 'pension program' because there is no other way to describe benefits that are automatically awarded to workers solely on the criteria of years of service."[32] Congress dropped automatic eligibility, but passed more lenient standards of disability and restricted governmental review of x-rays in 1978. A new Black Lung Disability Trust Fund was to be financed through a federal excise tax on coal—50 cents a ton on underground coal and 25 cents a ton on surface coal. Congress also gave tax preferences to companies that established their own fund to cover obligations towards miners. The industry-wide trust fund was to pay miners for whom the government could not find an individual operator responsible.[33]

Another key provision committed the Treasury to cover deficits produced by the trust fund. Unfortunately, the trust fund began to bleed almost immediately, committing the government to pay nearly $420 million after FY79, $1 billion after FY80,[34] and $1.5 billion after FY81, with projections of a $9 billion deficit by FY95.[35] Lagging coal sales reduced income for the fund as operators continued to contest a high percentage of claims, thus transferring more cases to the trust fund's responsibility. The number of cases financed by the trust fund nearly doubled: from 69,500 in 1979 to 138,000 in 1980.[36]

With the advent of the Reagan administration, the focus changed from one of increased federal participation to a desire to shift costs to other parties. Reagan's FY82 budget proposals called for restricting benefits to the "truly medically disabled" and increasing the coal tax for the trust fund. The president's budget stated that "Lax statutory and

[32]Statement to Subcommittee on Labor of Committee on Human Resources. Hearings on the Administration of the Black Lung Program, April 4, 1977, p. 2.

[33]*1977 Congressional Quarterly Almanac*, p. 267.

[34]Richard Corrigan, "Miners Rally to Block Black Lung Benefit Cuts," *National Journal*, March 28, 1981.

[35]*1981 Congressional Quarterly Almanac*, p. 115.

[36]Kerr, "Black Lung," p. 59.

administrative procedures have expanded the program from its original purpose—to compensate people who are medically disabled because of black lung disease—into a general coal miner's benefit program that approaches an automatic pension."

In exchange for a sharp reversal in benefit and eligibility standards, Congress transferred 10,200 unresolved cases to the fund, more than offsetting savings from benefits changes for the next five years. The bill doubled the coal tax until such time as the trust fund had fully repaid the government for monies paid from general revenues. The change in eligibility standards was even more striking: It ended the presumption that miners with 15 years in the mines and totally disabled due to respiratory impairment were indeed disabled from black lung disease; and it allowed the Labor Department to seek a second opinion in determining whether an x-ray showed pneumoconiosis.[37] Survivor benefits were limited to cases in which the miner died specifically from black lung disease, and black lung benefits were reduced for those who had earnings above the social security limit.[38]

The entry of black lung disease on the roster of federal entitlements is partly explained by the mood of the time. It felt so good to help those in need in the late 1960s; money appeared not to be an object. The wish was father to the thought. The usual financial myopia led legislators to believe the initial cost would be small and, anyway, that it would be paid by the coal companies. Nevertheless, Congress pledged its general revenues. In the first decade, attention to black lung came from interested parties—the miners and their relatives who wanted to get on the rolls, and the owners who were happy to support their workers provided the federal government paid. Talk of medical procedures introduced notions of bureaucracy and miserliness into what many legislators thought should be concern for human suffering. Only with evidence of cascading costs and the appearance of a new administration did a question, sidestepped in the past, rise to the fore—namely, why the federal government was operating essentially another retirement program. From the

---

[37]"Plan to Wipe Out Deficit in Black Lung Trust Fund Is Approved by Congress," *Congressional Quarterly*, December 26, 1981, p. 2569.
[38]*Ibid.*

joy-through-giving that dominated the early days of the black lung program, the mood by the mid-1980s had changed to one of "How do we get out of this?"

End-Stage Renal Disease

End-stage renal disease (ESRD) describes the kidney as it is in its dying moments, unable to filter and process the body's metabolic wastes and allowing the waste to accumulate to fatal levels in the blood. Only medical and surgical intervention can save the person's life. Two methods prevail today—hemodialysis and transplantation. Hemodialysis filters the patient's blood after it has been diverted from the body to an outside machine. The process takes six to eight hours per session and requires the patient's return to the machine three or four times a week. Transplantation is the surgical grafting of a new kidney from a volunteer or cadaver. The successful transplant often results in permanent restoration of kidney function, but the patient must face all of the attendant risks of such surgery—infection, immunological rejection, and other physiological complications.

As early as 1963, the federal government had established a small ESRD entitlement program for veterans eligible for medical benefits. The Veterans Administration had provided for ESRD treatment with the concurrence of the Bureau of the Budget (BOB). By 1972, dialysis units were established in 30 VA hospitals and maintained nearly 15 percent of all dialysis patients in the United States.[39]

The VA ESRD entitlement was significant because it catalyzed discussion between BOB and the Office of Science and Technology (OST) over the cost implications of sustaining the units. BOB and OST drew together a panel of experts known as the Gottschalk Committee to make recommendations on government dialysis and transplantation and therapy policy. In 1967 the Gottschalk group endorsed the VA use of dialysis and transplantation and also urged use of home dialysis, a much cheaper mode of treatment. More significantly, the Gottschalk Committee rec-

[39]R. A. Rettig, "The Policy Debate on Patient Care Financing for Victims of End-Stage Renal Disease," *Law and Contemporary Problems,* Vol. 40, No. 4 (Autumn 1976), p. 217.

ommended patient care financing for renal disease through medicare.[40] The committee thus linked the Johnson administration disability-benefits recommendation with the matter of treating end-stage renal disease—a linkage that provided the impetus for conferring medicare benefits on the severely disabled.

In terms of expanding access to renal dialysis and transplantation, the appropriations committees moved cautiously by providing only limited support to the first 14 community dialysis centers administered by the Public Health Service (PHS). The Senate Appropriations Committee in 1964 explicitly limited the PHS's use of appropriated monies in renal treatment to "demonstration and training programs" and not toward patient care financing. The overriding concern was costs:

> The Federal Government has borne the cost of treatment for its legal beneficiaries and shared these treatment costs when it has been in connection with research investigation or demonstration. Traditionally, payment for illness has been the responsibility of the patient or the local community. If the Federal Government were to share the full costs of lifetime treatment for all who suffer from these chronic diseases and conditions, the financial burden would be excessive.[41]

If this was the voice of the classic budgeter, new budgeters were more concerned with alleviating individual suffering and less with collective financial burdens.

The general discussion of federal support for medical care rested upon the quality-of-life and inability-to-pay issues. Each of these issues influenced the chairs of key congressional authorization committees to favor ESRD as an entitlement. Senator Russell Long, chairman of the Senate Finance Committee and long-time advocate of health insurance for financially catastrophic illnesses, viewed kidney disease not only as a disability but also as a disease whose cure or amelioration few people could finance on their own. He favored including kidney benefits under medicare not only to protect people financially from kidney-engendered disability but also to serve as a forerunner of catastrophic health insurance to be funded by medicare.

The plight of people who must undergo dialysis became highly publi-

[40]*Ibid.*, pp. 217–18.
[41]*Ibid.*, pp. 203–204.

cized and introduced an emotional element to the issue. A demonstration of dialysis before a hearing of the House Ways and Means Committee apparently convinced the chairman, Wilbur Mills, to favor inclusion of benefits under medicare.[42]

In 1970 community-based dialysis centers, threatened with termination by the Health Services and Mental Health Administration, were transferred through legislation from the Public Health Service (PHS) to the Regional Medical Programs Service (RMPS). This transfer separated the dialysis and transplantation program from the restrictive, research orientation of the PHS and the appropriations committees, to locate it instead within the capacity-building, patient-oriented RMPS. This transfer allowed decentralized funding through the established regions of the service, though patient-care financing continued to be excluded.[43]

Another significant factor favoring ESRD entitlement benefits was the growing number of clinically oriented renal physicians. As opposed to research physicians, the clinicians' primary concern was the advancement of therapy for their patients. As the efficacy of renal therapy improved, the clinicians advocated a stronger federal role in ESRD[44] and became increasingly frustrated by what they considered the denial of patient-care financing.

An existing entitlement framework (VA benefits), a growing cohort of clinically oriented renal physicians, and expanded capacity for dialysis and transplantation brought federal kidney programs to the brink of entitlement. What was needed was a new framework for ESRD to garner legitimacy as therapy and thus eligibility for patient-care financing. The vehicle chosen was to entitle people with kidney failure to medical benefits.[45]

As Allen Schick tells the story:

> On the next to last day of its 1972 session, Congress completed action on an omnibus social security bill that (among its many provisions) entitled

[42]*Ibid.*, p. 220.
[43]*Ibid.*, p. 216.
[44]*Ibid.*, pp. 210–11.
[45]*Ibid.*, p. 219.

victims of kidney failure to medicare benefits. The provision was added to the bill by a Senate floor amendment, without prior committee hearings or review and without any consideration of the issue in the House. When it adopted the amendment by an overwhelming margin, the Senate had no reliable cost estimates and only a fuzzy notion of how expanded medicare coverage would affect future budgets. During brief floor debate, Senator Vance Hartke, the amendment's sponsor, implored the Senate to put health care ahead of budgetary concerns: "How do we explain," he asked, "that the difference between life and death is a matter of dollars." Hartke estimated that the new benefits would cost $75 million in the first year and perhaps $250 million in the fourth. Annual expenditures turned out to be much higher—about one billion dollars by the end of the 1970s. By then, however, the entitlement of kidney patients to medicare was inscribed in law and the budget routinely labeled these expenditures as "uncontrollable."[46]

Financing for ESRD is derived from the medicare drawing account that is built up by payroll taxes, premiums, and other federal funds. The drawing account is overseen by the Health Care Financing Administration (HCFA) of the Department of Health and Human Services. HCFA administers the medicare program, setting its policies and contracts with intermediaries and carriers that process claims from medical providers. HCFA then disburses funds from the medicare drawing account to certified providers and suppliers of ESRD services.[47]

To be eligible for ESRD benefits, a person must be over 65, disabled, have worked under the social security or railroad retirement system, or be the spouse or dependent child of an employee with enough social security or railroad retirement work credits. This covers nearly 93 percent of all patients needing kidney treatment. The others are covered by the Veterans Administration, Department of Defense, and other agencies. Medicare's Part A covers hospital expenses incurred during in-patient dialysis or surgical transplantation, after the patient assumes a deductible and any costs during a waiting period. Part B covers physician services, outpatient hospital services, outpatient maintenance

[46]Schick, "Controlling the 'Uncontrollables,' " p. 1.
[47]R. T. Ney, "The ESRD Medicare Program—A Clarification," *Dialysis and Transplantation,* Vol. 10, No. 3 (March 1981), p. 227.

dialysis, durable medical equipment, and most items necessary for home dialysis.[48]

With its enactment, ESRD enrollment grew from 11,000 at the start of the program to 63,200 at the end of 1980. More spectacularly, the total cost of ESRD rose from $283 million in fiscal 1974 to $1.8 billion in fiscal 1982.[49] In 1986 the federal government paid over $3 billion for 87,000 kidney patients. How did this happen?

While entitlements are generally thought of as benefits conferred upon individuals or families who meet certain eligibility critera, the reimbursement mechanism of payment to enterprises and institutions that secure the promised benefit becomes a form of entitlement for the providers. In ESRD, as long as they deliver treatment to the designated beneficiaries, the providers are guaranteed reimbursement for their service. Often more vocal in promoting the entitlement than the beneficiaries, providers themselves then become a vested interest group.

The National Medical Care Corporation (NMC) grew phenomenally after the 1972 enactment of ESRD. By keeping its costs low and opening centers in populous areas, NMC was able to reap substantial profits with government reimbursements. By 1980, NMC earned over $20 million on revenues of $245.5 million, while its 120 dialysis centers treated nearly a fifth of the nation's dialysis patients.[50]

The medical and technical expertise of NMC also translated into increased political influence. In the early years, NMC members were able to use their medical credentials and network of peers at the Harvard Medical School to establish support for their pioneering company. As NMC expanded into new regions, renal physicians from the top medical schools were recruited to run local NMC centers. This strategy effectively lessened opposition to NMC from area doctors because of the prominent renal physicians who stood behind it.[51] Thus NMC became

[48]C. L. Fortnier-Frazier, *Social Work and Dialysis* (University of California Press, 1981), pp. 120–23.
[49]J. K. Iglehart, "Funding the End-Stage Renal Disease Program," *The New England Journal of Medicine*, Vol. 306, No. 8 (February 25, 1982), p. 492.
[50]G. B. Kolata, "NMC Thrives Selling Dialysis," *Science*, Vol. 208 (April 25, 1980), p. 380.
[51]*Ibid.*, p. 381.

a potent lobbying force, able to call upon the most prestigious names in nephrology (the study of kidney disease) to testify about ESRD.

Entitlements that are enacted on the coattails of a larger initiative and that have not been subjected to legislative scrutiny often can generate unanticipated costs in later years.[52] Then again, vast cost underestimation is a feature of almost all entitlements.

The sharp drop of patients using home dialysis, a much cheaper mode of treatment than dialysis at a hospital or proprietary clinic, raised costs to the government. The ESRD amendment, while liberalizing provisions for care in a hospital or outpatient dialysis, did not provide economic incentives, such as full coverage for medical supplies, supportive services, and reimbursement to facilities providing equipment and supervision for home dialysis. As a result, many patients who might otherwise have considered home dialysis continued to depend on hospital or proprietary-center dialysis.

When ESRD was enacted, there was hope that a cure for renal disease would arise. The entitlement then could justify itself as a temporary, life-sustaining measure (I am tiny, I am cheap) until a cure could be found. But as of today no medical or surgical breakthrough has come about to free patients on dialysis. Such stagnation in scientific progress allows a steady increase in the patient pool and continued rise in federal spending.

Another therapy that did not live up to the optimistic expectations was transplantation. A successful transplant restores the recipient to an independent life with only regular immunosuppressant therapy needed to maintain the new kidney. It is the general rule in surgery that as a procedure is carried out more often, the success rate increases. But for transplantation there has been a slight decrease in the success rate— down from a high of 54 percent to nearly 45 percent.[53] Thus a greater percentage of patients who have unsuccessfully tried transplantation will return to dialysis.

[52]Aaron Wildavsky, *Speaking Truth to Power* (Boston: Little, Brown, 1979), pp. 101–102.

[53]R. A. Rettig, "End-Stage Renal Disease and the 'Cost' of Medical Technology," in *Medical Technology: The Culprit Behind Health Care Costs?* (U.S. DHHS, 1979), p. 103.

In order to stem the tide of rising costs, a bill introduced by Representatives Rostenkowski and Vanik included incentives for home self-dialysis and additional support for transplantation. The bill also called for a national quota (50 percent) of all ESRD patients in renal disease networks to be on home dialysis or in self-dialysis training. All major groups who testified on behalf of eliminating disincentives, however, opposed the establishment of quotas.[54]

Fierce opposition to the home dialysis quotas came from the National Medical Care Corporation. Ostensibly, a federal mandate of a 50 percent home-dialysis rate would substantially cut into NMC's patient load, revenues, and profit margin. NMC's strategy was to oppose quotas on the ground that home dialysis patients' survival rates were lower than those of center dialysis patients, a controversial medical point at that time. "After careful analysis," stated Dr. Edmund Lowrie, a prominent Harvard nephrologist testifying on behalf of NMC, "the only obvious reason for this inferior patient survival that we can think of is the indiscriminate use of home dialysis therapy."[55]

Even a national goal was unacceptable. NMC successfully lobbied Senator Herman Talmadge, chair of the Senate Finance Health Subcommittee, to reject quotas altogether in the final bill. In its place was the statement, "It is the intent of Congress that the maximum practical number of patients who are medically, socially and psychologically suitable candidates for home dialysis or transplantation should be so treated."[56] President Carter signed the watered-down bill on June 13, 1978.

NMC's strategy was successful; it prevented a quota and enhanced its own revenues by getting 100 percent (instead of the previous 80 percent) reimbursement for home dialysis supplies and equipment purchased for their patients. There also arose the politically interesting question of whether all providers should get the same rate. Hospitals vehemently opposed this, although HCFA felt a single rate would force

[54]R. A. Rettig, "The Politics of Health Cost Containment: ESRD," *Bulletin of New York Academy of Medicine*, Vol. 56, No. 1 (January/February 1980), p. 131.

[55]*Ibid.*, p. 133.

[56]D. Greenberg, "Renal Politics," *New England Journal of Medicine*, Vol. 298, No. 25 (June 22, 1978), p. 1428.

more efficient operation from providers. Hospital spokespersons, however, claimed that their overhead for specialized personnel costs was higher, and that hospitals care for sicker patients than do proprietary centers. The hospitals thus strenuously argued for a dual rate (with the higher rate for themselves). Otherwise, they warned, the single rate would force many hospitals to close down units and leave many patients without convenient access to dialysis.

Proprietary dialysis centers, particularly National Medical Care, strongly preferred a single rate. Aside from their usual pro-competition, pro-efficiency stand, NMC argued that a dual rate would draw more patients to specialized medical centers even if those patients did not need such highly technical care. Such a trend would reduce NMC's patient load and cut revenues. Conversely, a single rate would enhance NMC's competitive standing and thus draw more patients to NMC even at the expense of the hospital centers. NMC chairman Constantine Hampers argued also that there was no demonstrable difference in overhead or caseload between hospitals and NMC, since the main cost of ESRD is in labor and supplies. "Overhead is not the major difference," Hampers said, "it's a question of efficiency, and the hospitals just don't focus on that."[57] NMC went on to threaten closing sixty of its centers if a dual rate were adopted.[58]

The Carter administration could not agree on the rate question; and though President Reagan proposed retaining a single rate, the hospitals successfully lobbied Congress to adopt a dual rate. The 1981 Omnibus Reconciliation Act directed HCFA to craft separate reimbursement rates—not only for hospital and proprietary centers but for home-dialysis patients of each group as well. The home-dialysis rate was designed to boost home dialysis use by both hospitals and for-profit centers. Since home care is substantially cheaper, hospital and proprietary centers would make money from the higher rate of federal payment for each patient they trained to perform dialysis at home.[59] Such a provision was most likely meant to ameliorate NMC's opposition to the multiple-rate

[57]L. E. Demkovich, "Kidney Dialysis Payments May Be Test of Reagan's Commitment to Competition," *National Journal* (December 5, 1981), p. 2162.
[58]Iglehart, "Funding the End-Stage Renal Disease Program," p. 496.
[59]Demkovich, "Kidney Dialysis Payments," pp. 2162–63.

structure, because NMC would profit by encouraging home care. HHS Secretary Schweiker, in setting the basic dual rate only $5 within each other ($133 for hospitals, $128 for proprietary) signaled the administration's sympathy for price competition.[60]

The Department of Health and Human Services also sought to revamp the reimbursement mechanism for physicians. Originally there were two methods of reimbursement: the initial and the alternative reimbursement method (ARM). Essentially, the initial method pays the doctor on a fee-for-service basis for work done either in a center or at the patient's home. ARM paid doctors a fixed, monthly, per-capita fee regardless of the mix of medical services provided. Also the doctor would receive less for home care under ARM than under the initial method.[61] Secretary Schweiker eliminated the initial method of payment in favor of a consolidated prospective payment under ARM for home and center care ($184.60 per month for each patient).[62] The intention was to engender a greater incentive for physicians to shift patients to home dialysis if medically allowable. The Reagan administration strategy was clear: Use prospective reimbursement for both institutions and physicians, rather than reducing benefits, to foster the cheapest mode of treatment.

When costs rose very quickly after the ESRD entitlement was enacted, the two main authorization committees (House Ways and Means and Senate Finance) used the strategy of liberalizing the provisions surrounding the cheapest mode of therapy to encourage higher demand from home-dialysis patients. Administrative agencies such as HCFA and HHS preferred the strategy of enticing providers of care to have their patients use home dialysis by offering prepayment for services. Spending has slowed but is still high.

Kidney patients themselves were never a particularly active or powerful force in the ESRD debate. This may be because eligibility was never questioned by politicians and policymakers, and entitlement seemed

[60]Iglehart, "Funding the End-Stage Renal Disease Program," p. 495.
[61]*Ibid.*
[62]R. J. Pristave and J. B. Riley, "HCFA Publishes Final ESRD Prospective Reimbursement Regulations," *Dialysis and Transplantation,* Vol. 12, No. 6 (June 1983), p. 452.

assured. Or perhaps there were not enough patients to be a potent force.

Whether prospective payment slows the growth of the ESRD entitlement to the satisfaction of present and future political administrations remains to be seen. But ESRD beneficiary enrollment is growing by an average of 12,000 cases a year, while dialysis and transplantation keep their cohorts alive; total costs thus will continue to rise. There may come a time when policymakers will have to grapple with reexamination of the eligibility standards themselves. Americans might have to ration dialysis capacity and funds (as is done in Great Britain under their National Health Service) by denying treatment to the elderly. How much is a life worth?

RIDING FOR A FALL: SOCIAL SERVICES AND REVENUE SHARING

Since it is so commonly believed that entitlement status favors programs, it is especially useful to examine programs that belie this common understanding. In this way we can seek to discover conditions that limit the advantages that entitlement status usually confers on programs.

First a word about a program from which I personally benefited, the G.I. (or government issue, as soldiers' equipment, and then soldiers, in the Second World War, were known) Bill that provided education and offered benefits to facilitate adjustment to civilian life. Annual outlays fell rapidly. The reasons are demographic (the number of World War II and Korean War veterans declined) and legislative (in 1976 Congress limited eligibility to ten years after separation from the service). Following Sherlock Holmes's dictum to search for the dog that didn't bark, the exceptional thing about the G.I. Bill is that it followed the path specified: It came, blossomed, and faded away just as old soldiers are supposed to do.

Another example, considered briefly, will help us understand the importance of administrative discretion when used in a determined and consistent way. Trade Adjustment Assistance is provided to workers in communities deemed to be hard hit by competition from imports.

Spending for this grew more than fivefold between 1978 and 1979—from $269 million to $1.5 billion. But by 1982, trade assistance had slimmed down to $45 million. Two things happened to bring costs down: The 1981 budget reconciliation act emphasized job search and reduced benefits, postponing eligibility until Unemployment Compensation had been used up; and the Reagan administration used its discretion to deny that imports were a major cause of unemployment (denials went up to 84 percent in 1981). Without a favorable Labor Department ruling, trade adjustment assistance cannot be paid.[63]

SOCIAL SERVICES GRANTS[64]

Title XX of the Social Security Act gives the federal government authority to mete out grants to states for the provision of social services. For each dollar spent on certain social services, as defined by the legislation and in subsequent regulations, the federal government would provide $3 in matching funds to the state. The states give money to local governments, which give money to agencies that provide services to individuals. Many things can happen along this road.

Through 1969, there were no great increases in spending from year to year. Suddenly, expenditures grew rapidly from 1969 to 1972. How come? A few participants learned that certain provisions of the Social Security Act permitted the federal government to pay up to 75 percent of various services that heretofore had been borne by state and local governments. A few federal departments and administrators actually encouraged states to exploit the program.

States were in financial difficulty. Welfare provision was being cut. A creative California administrator-cum-welfare advocate, Tom Joe, thought he saw an opening. Soon the word was out. It was Illinois that opened the door to huge increases in social services expenditures. As Schick notes:

[63]Weaver, "Controlling Entitlements," p. 323.
[64]This section is based on a paper by David Gamson.

Illinois in the early 1970s had a $100 million overrun on welfare programs. The Governor rejected cutbacks in welfare assistance, and he and his budget aides turned instead to the Federal government in an effort to gain Federal funding of various social programs. After months of intensive political pressure, Illinois won the additional Federal assistance it sought.[65]

Once Illinois gained this foot in the door, other states followed suit. Creative financing was in order: "An example of how the states took advantage of the program would be an alcohol or drug abuse prevention program that the state had previously financed itself. By purchasing the same services from a private agency, the state would qualify for 75 percent Federal financing."[66] In this manner, the federal government was asked to "buy" Mississippi; in 1972 that state submitted claims for social services grants totaling over half of its state budget.[67]

When the cost of the program was estimated to skyrocket to $4.7 billion in 1973, Congress took action. Media attention made social services into a case of government ineffectiveness in controlling spending. Budget deficits of $20 to $30 billion (that seemed large at the time) caused worry about a program that was out of control. The states were seen as greedy for expecting such huge expenditure growth under such dubious legal conditions. Politics entered as well: "As more Republican governors successfully pressured a Republican administration into granting more funds, more Democrats developed an interest in limiting the volume of funds."[68]

HEW in 1973 proposed restrictive regulations. This upset many of the traditional social services interest groups. Within two months after the proposed regulations were published, HEW received 200,000 letters of protest from private agencies and supporters. In the face of such public outcry, HEW softened the regulations to some extent and Congress kept postponing the new regulations. Provisions were added that

[65] Allen Schick, "Budgetary Adaptations to Resource Scarcity," in Charles H. Levine and Irene Ruben, eds., *Fiscal Stress and Public Policy* (Beverly Hills: Sage Publications, 1980).

[66] "'67 Law Is Giving States Windfall in Federal Funds," *New York Times,* August 7, 1972, p. 1.

[67] "How the Government 'Bought' Mississippi," *Washington Post,* June 8, 1972, p. 1.

[68] Martha Derthick, *Uncontrollable Spending for Social Services Grants* (Washington, D.C.: Brookings, 1975), p. 7.

required a "maintenance of effort" on the part of states. This meant that federal matching funds could be used only to supplement but not to supplant existing state programs. Finding that out, however, would not be easy.

A consensus had developed that limits were necessary. Ultimately, the State and Local Fiscal Assistance Act of 1972 placed a $2.5 billion annual ceiling on social services grants and limited states' shares to their percentage of the national population.[69] Yet the ceiling was set higher than the previous year's expenditures. This was done both to ensure higher funding levels and to "grandfather" in the existing elements of services provided. Benefits once granted, it appears, are not to be taken away.

In enacting the cap, Congress first established spending limits and then developed a formula for allocating funds among the beneficiaries. While this action suggests that Congress is both able and willing to control spending, part of the price for obtaining support for the social services cap was passage of the revenue sharing program that created over $4 billion in new benefits for state and local governments and corresponding new costs for the federal government.

THE ENTITLEMENT THAT FAILED[70]

On October 20, 1972, in Independence Hall in Philadelphia, President Nixon signed into law the State and Local Fiscal Assistance Act of 1972 (better known as general revenue sharing). Basically, the General Revenue Sharing (GRS) program consisted of federal grants to state and local (city and county) governments with virtually no strings attached to the funds.[71] A publication from the Office of Revenue Sharing labeled GRS an automatic entitlement, meaning that "no application is necessary to receive funds. . . . To be eligible, governments must return a simple form

[69]PL 92-7.

[70]This section is based on student papers by Carol Lazzarotto and Ron Mester.

[71]David T. Irwin, "Evaluating Municipal Revenue Sources," *Government Finance*, Vol. 5 (February 1976), p. 11.

which they automatically receive, certifying that funds will be spent in accordance with the law."[72] In total, approximately 39,000 state and local governments received GRS funds.[73]

Unlike most entitlements, the GRS program did not grow. After eight years of a slightly declining budget in real terms, the GRS program suffered a severe cutback in 1980; it was terminated in 1986. For GRS, entitlement status did not lead to budget increases, or even budget maintenance. The question, of course, is why? The answers can best be found by tracing the program's political history.

A distinguishing feature of revenue sharing is that its enabling legislation established annual budget ceilings first, and only afterwards determined individual benefits as a proportion of that ceiling. Entitlement expenditures, in this case, are not the sum of a set of relatively unforecastable individual benefits, but were established through legislated expenditure appropriations that did act effectively as expenditure caps.

When GRS was enacted in 1972, different people assigned different purposes to it. The Nixon administration claimed its primary aim to be the return of power to state and local governments.[74] While many Republicans agreed with this goal, they hoped GRS would also bring about the consolidation of other federal grant programs, thus reducing their cost.[75] Still others felt that GRS would allow citizens more opportunities to affect the way their tax money was spent.[76] Many Democrats hoped that GRS would be a particular help to financially strapped cities. As John Tomer wrote in the *Public Finance Quarterly* in 1972, "General Revenue Sharing in a sense meant 'all things to all people.' "[77]

Originally, there were only three restrictions on state governments' use of GRS funds: (1) to avoid discriminatory practices, (2) to avoid

---

[72]"Controversy Over Federal Revenue Sharing," *Congressional Digest*, Vol. 59 (June–July 1980), p. 165.

[73]Joel Havemann, "Last Minute Extension of Revenue Sharing Expected," *National Journal Reports*, Vol. 7 (August 9, 1975), p. 1141.

[74]Joel Havemann, "Revenue Sharing Plan Likely to Be Extended, Changed," *National Journal Reports*, Vol. 6 (July 20, 1974), p. 1074.

[75]Irwin, "Evaluating Municipal Revenue Sources," p. 13.

[76]Havemann, "Revenue Sharing Plan," p. 1080.

[77]John F. Tomer, "Revenue Sharing and the Intrastate Fiscal Mismatch," *Public Finance Quarterly*, Vol. 5 (October 1977), p. 446.

using the money as matching funds for federal categorical grants, and (3) to use the grants only for capital expenditures in certain broad programmatic areas.[78] Amendments in 1976 strengthened the civil-rights and citizen-participation provisions of GRS, while removing all other restrictions on both state and local governments.[79] The biggest changes in the program, however, occurred in 1980, when the state-grant portion of the GRS program was eliminated. From 1980 until GRS expired, only local governments received GRS funds.[80]

The major controversy surrounding GRS in 1972 concerned its entitlement status. Congressional proponents of GRS argued that entitlement status was necessary because that would be the only way to provide states and cities with budgetary stability (which, they claimed, was necessary for government efficiency). George Mahon (D-Tex.), chairman of the House Appropriations Committee, felt differently: "The bill represents an indefensible abrogation . . . of the power of the House for a five-year period. Think of it—writing ourselves out of the action for a five-year period."[81] Exactly that, however, writing Congress out so as to write individuals in is the purpose of entitlements.

Early in 1973 Nixon submitted his 1974 budget proposing the reduction or termination of over 100 programs. Further, he stated his intention to renew his request for special revenue sharing. Although Nixon claimed that the programs were being eliminated because they had failed, several places in the budget mentioned that state and local governments might use revenue sharing funds for these general purposes.[82] State and local governments quickly felt deceived by revenue sharing. After Nixon's proposed budget of 1974, economist Walter Heller claimed that "the birth of general revenue sharing is being used to justify the homicide of selected social programs."[83] Liberal support began to wane in Congress. As the date for renewal approached and opposition

---

[78]Havemann, "Revenue Sharing Plan," p. 1075.

[79]"Controversy over Federal Revenue Sharing," p. 164.

[80]Jerry Hagstron and Neal R. Peirce, "The Cities, not the States, May Bear the Brunt of Revenue Sharing Cutbacks," *National Journal Reports*, Vol. 12 (April 19, 1980), p. 637.

[81]"Congress Clears Nixon's Revenue-Sharing Plan," *Congressional Quarterly Almanac*, Vol. 28 (1972), p. 642.

[82]Quoted in Carol Lazzarotto, student paper on "Revenue Sharing."

[83]*Ibid.*

grew, supporters (namely, state and local government organizations) increased their lobbying efforts.

If GRS could be had only as a replacement for, rather than a complement of, categorical grants, then liberals wanted no part of it. They preferred categorical grants because these gave the federal government, where they were stronger, a greater degree of control over the spending of funds than state and local governments, where liberals were weaker. Democrats were also disappointed with "the allegedly poor record of the program in the civil rights and citizen participation areas."[84] With a majority in both the House and Senate in 1976, Democrats voiced growing doubts about the desirability and effectiveness of the GRS Program, putting it in jeopardy. GRS became an even better candidate for cutting once congressmen discovered that states were enjoying fiscal surpluses. Many agreed with the House Government Operations chairman, Jack Brooks (D-Tex.) when he stated, "It [GRS] is a wasteful, illogical giveaway to the states when they're rolling in money."

When the GRS program was enacted in 1972, Representative George Mahon predicted that "the passage of the revenue sharing bill will organize and galvanize the most powerful lobby group this country has ever known." Yet, in 1975, just a year before the program would come up for extension, Senator Edmund Muskie commented, "For the life of me, I can't understand how any program that is supported by thirty-eight thousand state and local governments could conceivably be in trouble in the Congress."[85] Muskie's comments represent the frustration felt by GRS supporters with the weakness of the "Big Six" coalition of state and local organizations supporting GRS, a coalition once thought to be virtually invincible. (The "Big Six" were the National Governors' Association, the Council of State Governments, National Association of Counties, U.S. Conference of Mayors, National League of Cities, and the International City Managers' Association.)[86] While it is true that most state and local officials supported GRS, they stood

---

[84]"Congress Clears Revenue Sharing Extension," *Congressional Quarterly Almanac*, Vol. 32 (1976), p. 75.

[85]Joel Havemann, "Most Powerful' Lobby Faces First Test—Revenue Sharing," *National Journal Reports*, Vol. 7 (December 27, 1975), pp. 1718–20.

[86]Paul L. Leventhal, "Revenue Sharing Gains in Senate as Drive for Welfare Reform Falters," *National Journal*, Vol. 4 (August 5, 1972), pp. 1250–51.

alone. Ordinary citizens, perhaps the most important potential support group, largely ignored GRS, and they are the ones who vote.

A second reason for the Big Six coalition's vulnerability was its fragility. If Congress changed the distribution formula so that it favored cities over rural areas, for instance, the rural areas would begin to fight cities in attempting to secure a more favorable formula.[87] In fact, during the debate before the 1976 extension, precisely this type of splintering over a formula change began to occur.[88] In 1980 a different type of splintering resulted from the GRS extension debate. "The Carter Administration," noted the *National Journal*, "has attempted to ease the cities' pain—and perhaps to divide the intergovernmental lobbying coalition— by proposing an additional $500 million in local revenue sharing for fiscal 1981 and a gain for fiscal 1982."[89] With money up for grabs, disagreement surfaced over who was to spend it. The League of Women Voters, the National Urban Coalition, Americans for Democratic Action, the United Automobile Workers, the National Association for the Advancement of Colored People, the National Urban League, and the AFL–CIO joined in the fight against GRS.[90] In addition, Hagstron and Peirce have identified a very special coalition against GRS: ". . . the famed 'iron triangle'—Members of Congress, federal agencies, and interest groups that have a stake in special-purpose [categorical grant] aid."[91] They further argue that "Congress has never been very enthusiastic about the program; one reason is that members receive little or no credit when the money is spent." That is, it is difficult for House members, who represent local districts, to claim credit for state action financed with federal money.[92]

By the 1980s many Republicans believed that GRS was actually strengthening the federal government relative to state and local govern-

[87]Joel Havemann, "Ford to Recommend Few Changes in Revenue Sharing," *National Journal Reports*, Vol. 7 (January 18, 1975), p. 92.

[88]"Controversy over Federal Revenue Sharing," p. 163.

[89]Hagstron and Peirce, "The Cities, Not the States," p. 637.

[90]Joel Havemann, "It Will Be 'No-Holds-Barred' When House Takes up Revenue Sharing," *National Journal Reports*, Vol. 8 (June 5, 1976), p. 783; "Last Minute Extension," p. 1143; "Ford to Recommend," p. 86.

[91]Hagstron and Peirce, "The Cities, not the States," p. 639.

[92]*Ibid.*, p. 636.

ments, rather than increasing the independence of these governments. It became clear that many local governments had become dependent on GRS funds for their basic programs. In their view, this money was not all discretionary. Clearly, dependency does not fit with the Republican espousal of decentralization.

Social services and general revenue sharing spending slowed way down or were abolished: Their progress, limited by caps, then was whittled down even further. The two programs suffered both from moral doubts and inability to identify constituents—the one flaw compounding the other. None of this was inevitable. Congress could have seen an opportunity in the ability to spend in previously unsuspected ways. Once deficit spending became marked as the culprit, however, to enable some states to do better than others became suspect. There's the rub: If benefits are widely spread, costs escalate; if costs are contained, it is difficult to find acceptable rationales for providing some states with more and others with less. The Big Six were wrongly regarded as powerful because a crucial condition for the exercise of that power—agreement among themselves—was omitted. Their potential, if agreed, was much higher than their actual influence when disagreed.

ENTITLEMENTS VERSUS APPROPRIATIONS

While the view that entitlement programs always expand faster than appropriations (here I agree with Kent Weaver) is simplistic,[93] it is true more often than not. Would you prefer to have programs you favor funded through entitlements or through appropriations? This is the same as asking whether you would like more or less. Once we decide not to argue with the obvious, we can concentrate on the special conditions that might lead appropriations to do as well as if not better than entitlements. Since a comparison of entitlements with appropriations would require a separate volume, we must be content with a couple of comparisons—deliberately designed to point in opposite directions so as to make

[93]Weaver, "Controlling Entitlements," p. 310.

it hard to draw easy conclusions. Relating the popular Head Start Program (HSP) to the less popular Aid to Families with Dependent Children (AFDC) entitlement primes us to ask why, despite its difficulties, AFDC has grown faster. If the entitlement wins out over the appropriation in that pairing, the appropriation for Women, Infants and Children (WIC) has done better budetarily than the food stamp entitlement. For sure, there is a lot of explaining to do.

NOT BY POLITICS ALONE: HEAD START AND AID TO DEPENDENT CHILDREN

A striking difference between Head Start and AFDC is that while Head Start's allocation formula is used to determine what share of already established program funds a state will receive, the AFDC formula determines how much of a state's benefits the federal government must pay. Head Start allocation is a top-down process, while AFDC allocation proceeds from the bottom up.

Prior to 1965, the most important federal program to help children was AFDC, which sought to alleviate the poverty of fatherless children by providing them and their mothers with cash grants. In the 1960s, however, a new analysis of the problem of poverty suggested that the way to eradicate poverty was to treat its causes rather than its symptoms. The idea of a self-perpetuating culture of poverty was gaining currency among intellectuals. In response to these new ideas, the Johnson administration inaugurated a War on Poverty that would seek to compensate for the social disadvantages of those trapped in what came to be called the culture of poverty.

Project Head Start was the component of the War on Poverty that provided a comprehensive preschool development program. Head Start targeted a subset of the population served by AFDC, and, like AFDC, it is federally funded but locally administered. Yet Head Start provides services rather than cash benefits. Thus, even though both programs address the problem of childhood poverty, they differ in the solutions proposed. This difference has been responsible for very different attitudes toward the two programs. Since the Johnson administration, every president has attempted to reform the welfare system. Liberals and conservatives have united in unrelenting criticism of both the premises and the outcomes of AFDC. Head Start, by contrast, has been deemed a success by both Democrats and Republicans.

A glance at the budgetary history of the two programs shows that the AFDC program has served a much larger proportion of those entitled to its benefits. Neither program has seen much real growth in spending, but over the years Head Start has served less than 20 percent of the eligible children.[94] Given that Head Start has enjoyed bipartisan support while AFDC has received bipartisan condemnation, this budgetary pattern suggests that it is not politics alone that determines the success of a program.

AFDC grew at an annual compound rate of 3.8 percent from 1978 to 1984; but in terms of constant dollars, the program experienced an annual decrease in outlays of 3.5 percent during this period. Thus, rather than an entitlement, Angela Browne calls AFDC the children's "disentitlement."[95] Nevertheless, operating under similar conditions of fiscal stringency, AFDC outperformed Head Start. Benefit levels for AFDC declined by 15 percent from 1973 to 1985, while Head Start expenditures per child declined by over 33 percent.[96]

When Sargent Shriver took his proposal for Head Start to President Johnson, Johnson responded, "That's such a magnificent idea, triple it."[97] Shriver did not need to make much effort in order to expand the program. In March, OEO requested funding proposals from local communities and received such a massive response that it decided to fund

[94]Hearings before the Subcommittee on the Departments of Labor, HHS, and Education of the House Appropriations Committee, 98th Congress, 1st Session, No. 4, Part 5, p. 24.

[95]From Angela Browne, student paper on AFDC.

[96]Data are the result of calculations based on information provided in Appendix to the Budget of the U.S. Government, FY67-84; Administration for Children, Youth and Families, Department of Health and Human Services Statistical Fact Sheet, 1985; Committee on Ways and Means, U.S. House of Representatives, Background Material and Data on Programs within the Jurisdiction of the Committee on Ways and Means, 1985, House Committee on Ways and Means, 99th Congress, 1st Session, pp. 329–80.

[97]Quoted in Edward Zigler and Jeanette Valentine, eds., *Project Head Start: A Legacy of the War on Poverty* (New York: Free Press, 1979), p. 90.

2,500 applications which proposed to serve 530,000 children. By the end
of the summer, Head Start had in fact served 561,000.

"In our society," Shriver explained, "there is a bias against helping
adults . . . but there's a contrary bias in favor of helping children."[98] So
he decided to launch a nationwide program of OEO-sponsored preschool education as a way to "overcome a lot of hostility in our society
against the poor in general and against black people who are poor in
particular, by going at the children."[99] Community Action Program
(CAP) organizers considered Head Start an opportunity to receive favorable publicity. They recruited Lady Bird Johnson to spearhead the
publicity drive in hopes that by receiving favorable coverage on the
society pages CAP would seem more respectable.[100]

The program began so rapidly because OEO had a major incentive
to spend money. In the spring of 1965, OEO officials realized they had
several hundred million dollars to spend before the end of the fiscal year
on June 30th. They could hardly expect much support for further appropriations in Congress if they had failed to spend their 1965 appropriation. Head Start provided an opportunity to spend money and at the
same time win favor in the nation's communities.[101] As Shriver gleefully
explained his use of those funds previously designated for other purposes,

> That illustrates one of the fantastic aspects of OEO. I increased the
> funding by myself! I didn't have to go to Congress; I didn't have to go to
> the president; I didn't have to go to the Bureau of the Budget. Congress
> had appropriated the money, and if I wanted to spend it on Head Start,
> I could spend it on Head Start. . . . I felt we had a gigantic breakthrough,
> so I pumped in the money as fast as we could intelligently use it. It was
> really quite spectacular.[102]

By initiating such a program as part of OEO, Shriver set a precedent
that prevented Head Start from achieving the entitlement status im-

[98]Interview with Sargent Shriver by Jeanette Valentine in Zigler and Valentine,
Project Head Start, p. 52.
[99]*Ibid.*
[100]Jule M. Sugarman, in Zigler and Valentine, *Project Head Start*, p. 117.
[101]*Ibid.*, p. 116.
[102]Shriver interview, in Zigler and Valentine, *Project Head Start*, p. 56.

plicit in its rationale. Head Start was conceived of as a compensatory education program that, like an entitlement, had both social utility and moral legitimacy. Head Start regulations required that 90 percent of its participants be children of families who were below the official poverty line; it therefore shared the eligibility criteria of entitlement programs. Yet despite concerted efforts during the late 1960s and early 1970s to establish an entitlement for child development services, Head Start was never able to overcome its origins.

Now AFDC began, as Daniel P. Moynihan writes, "almost as an afterthought."[103] It was tacked onto higher priority components of the Social Security Act and the need for it was expected to fade out. As with many depression era programs, AFDC was not designed for the poorest of the poor but rather for the temporarily submerged working and middle classes, such as the wife and children of a factory worker killed on the job. The legislative record indicates Congress's expectation that the program would wither away as the economy improved and as such programs as social security (which was a contributory social insurance program rather than a poverty program) became established.[104]

By the early 1960s, it was clear that AFDC was serving a different constituency—the broken families of blacks and whites who had migrated out of agriculture into urban areas. And despite the fact that the economy was steadily improving, the AFDC rolls were steadily growing—from 803,000 families in 1960 to 1.1 million families in 1965. Though this growth was disturbing,[105] it paled against what came next: Between 1967 and 1971, the number of AFDC cases literally doubled, reaching 3.2 million families by 1974. State and local officials (who had to pay much of the bill) were shaken and angry.

Between the mid-1960s and 1976, the cost of all antipoverty programs tripled to $81 billion (in 1983 dollars) and then grew more slowly,

[103]Daniel P. Moynihan, *The Politics of Guaranteed Income* (New York: Random House, 1973), p. 42.
[104]*Ibid.*, p. 197.
[105]See Frank Levy, *Dollars and Dreams: The Changing American Income Distribution,* Russell Sage Foundation, typescript, 1987, Chapter 8, "Households, Families, and the Government."

reaching $102 billion in 1984.[106] The proportion of the population in poverty traced a less optimistic path. Over the 1960s and early 1970s, it fell more or less steadily, reaching 11.1 percent in 1973. It then remained constant through 1979 when it began rising again, and by 1983 it exceeded 15 percent. This contradiction—a rising poverty rate in the face of rising antipoverty expenditures—led to the argument that the expenditures themselves had caused poverty by fostering dependence.[107] As chairman of the Ways and Means Committee, Wilbur Mills (D-Ark.) asked, "Is it in the public interest for welfare to become a way of life?"[108]

Why, despite substantial reductions in its funding, has AFDC been maintained at a steady if reduced rate? AFDC is a "matching" program; costs are shared with state and local governments, which have considerable flexibility in establishing eligibility and benefit guidelines. Cutting AFDC is not so attractive as it otherwise might be because the states and the federal government would pay in other program categories, such as general welfare and food stamps, for further declines.

Food Stamp Program (FSP) outlays are sensitive to changes in other programs; benefits in one may affect benefits in another. Attempts to reduce expenditures in a program such as AFDC will actually lead to increased food stamp expenditures. It was estimated in 1984 that roughly 82 percent of AFDC households received food stamps, a third received housing assistance, and 95 percent took medicaid. Provisions in one program that confer "categorical eligibility" to participants in other programs create financial connectedness.[109] For these people ap-

---

[106]Gary Burtless, "Public Spending for the Poor: Trends, Prospects, and Economic Limits." Paper presented at the Institute for Research on Poverty conference on Poverty and politics: Retrospect and Prospects, Williamsburg, VA, December 6–8, 1984. In Levy, *Dollars and Dreams.*

[107]Charles Murray, *Losing Ground: American Social Policy, 1950–1980* (New York: Basic Books, 1984).

[108]Cited in Angela Browne, "Welfare Legislation," *Congress and the Nation, 1965–1968,* p. 772.

[109]U.S. Bureau of Census, Current Population Reports, Series P-70, No. 4, *Economic Characteristics of Households in the United States: Second Quarter 1984* (U.S. Government Printing Office, 1985).

proximately one-third of any cut in AFDC benefits will be offset by increased food stamp benefits.[110]

Head Start takes a larger share of cuts because reductions there do not increase other programs. Adding a few children to a class, moreover, is not as visible as a reduction in AFDC payments. Better one way—in accomplishment—is not necessrily better in another—holding the line of spending without raising too much fuss. AFDC has to be attacked directly; Head Start can be eroded indirectly by inflation. Whether AFDC is an entitlement because it is considered necessary or necessary because it is an entitlement, either way its budgetary status has protected it against a worse fate.

WOMEN, INFANTS AND CHILDREN PROGRAM VERSUS FOOD STAMP PROGRAM

Over the past 25 years, the United States government has greatly increased its investment in attacking domestic hunger. New programs have been added and old programs significantly expanded. Expenditures for food and nutrition programs have increased multifold as the number of benefits, value of benefits, and number of recipients have risen. Today federal antihunger programs are offered in all jurisdictions in every state, and benefits also are available in U.S. territories. There is widespread agreement that the United States has committed itself to putting "an end to hunger in America for all time," in the words of President Nixon in 1969,[111] only the parties still differ about how much it takes to end hunger.

What makes these programs particularly worthy of attention is that (1) some fit into the category of entitlements—that is, programs whose authorizing legislation obligates spending funds on behalf of people who

[110]Reuben Snipper, "Interactions among Programs Providing Benefits to Individuals: Secondary Effects of the Budget," *Congressional Budget Office Report*, May 1982, p. xii.
[111]Maurice MacDonald, *Food Stamps and Income Maintenance* (New York, 1977), p. 10.

meet certain criteria, and are not bound by the appropriations process;
(2) some follow the traditional pattern—having appropriation committees determine the level of funding within the guidelines of authorizing
legislation; and (3) some are hybrids. These differences offer the possibility of making a comparative analysis of programs that have similar aims
but different structural characteristics.

The Food Stamp Program (FSP) and the Special Supplemental Food
Programs for Women, Infants and Children, more commonly referred
to as the Women, Infants and Children Program (WIC), share some
important characteristics. Both are specifically intended to help prevent
the occurrence of problems associated with undernutrition and malnu-
trition by helping low-income people obtain an adequate diet. Both
programs are administered at the federal level by the Office of Food and
Nutrition Services within the USDA. Both provide 100 percent federal
funding of actual benefits provided to recipients (in the FSP, however,
states share in the cost of administration). Both provide benefits in the
form of vouchers that are exchanged for food. These similarities reduce
the number of factors that might be expected to result in differences in
growth rates, such as differences in state funding commitments.

FSP is the largest federal food program, with a total outlay of about
$11 billion in fiscal year 1982.[112] It is intended to fill the gap between
the amount of money low-income households are expected to use for
buying food, based on a standard share of total income (currently 30
percent), and the amount of funds USDA determines is necessary to
purchase an adequate diet.[113] Food stamp benefits and eligibility are
principally determined by household size, countable monthly income,
assets such as real property, and the cost of the USDA Thrifty Food
Plan. Food stamp benefits are generally not restricted on the basis of
demographic characteristics, such as people's ages, though certain people are deemed ineligible (e.g., illegal aliens). Households may receive

---

[112]U.S. Congressional Budget Office, "Major Legislative Changes in Human Resources
Programs Since January, 1981," August 1983, p. 34.

[113]U.S. House of Representatives, Committee on Ways and Means, "Background
Material and Data on Major Programs within the Jurisdiction of the Committee on Ways
and Means," February 18, 1982, p. 309.

benefits from other federal programs; approximately 34 percent of recipients, for example, also receive AFDC.[114] The current national caseload is about 22 million, and the average benefits per recipient per month is about $43.[115]

From 1969 to 1971 several changes were made in the FSP. The significant features of these changes were (1) lowering the amount families had to spend to obtain food stamps (known as the "purchase requirement"); (2) increasing the food stamp allotment, which, with the first change, had the effect of more than doubling benefits for the poorest recipients; (3) adding a benefit indexing provision; (4) directing USDA to develop nationwide eligibility standards; (5) turning FSP into an open-ended entitlement program; and (6) making the program available in U.S. territories.[116] In 1973 further amendments to the Food Stamp Act required that FSP be offered in all localities by July of 1974.[117] All these changes greatly expanded the number of beneficiaries and program expenditures.

The next significant program change came in 1977 when, with the support of President Carter, legislation was enacted that eliminated the purchase requirement and effectively terminated eligibility for some relatively high-income recipients. The aim of these changes was to better target benefits to those most in need, since the purchase requirement was thought to be especially burdensome for those with very low incomes who are unlikely to be able to accumulate the cash necessary to obtain the coupons. The administration claimed that the cost of the proposed changes would offset each other. Congress remained concerned about the program's rising costs, however, and included yearly authorization ceilings.[118] Two years later, the Carter administration

[114]*Ibid.*, p. 375.

[115]Elizabeth Wehr, "Congress, Administration Debate Need for More Help to Fight Hunger in America," *Congressional Quarterly Weekly Report,* Vol. 41 (May 7, 1983), p. 881.

[116]See MacDonald, *Food Stamps and Income Maintenance,* pp. 10–12; and U.S. Congressional Budget Office, "The Food Stamp Program: Income or Food Supplementation?" January 1977, pp. 4–11, 17–18, 31, and 34.

[117]MacDonald, *Food Stamps and Income Maintenance,* p. 10.

[118]Kathryn Waters Gest, "Major Food Stamp Overhaul Near Approval," *Congressional Quarterly Weekly Report,* Vol. 34 (August 6, 1977), pp. 1642–47.

acknowledged that eliminating the purchase requirement had resulted in a bigger caseload and indicated that large increases in food costs were driving the program over the authorization limits. The administration asked for and received an increase in these limits.[119]

In 1981 and 1982, as part of a general effort to reduce domestic expenditures, President Reagan requested major cutbacks in the FSP. The Congressional Budget Office estimated the cumulative impact of the 1981–1982 legislation to be a 13 percent cut in FSP expenditures relative to the projected "base," and a 4 percent decline in the number of recipients (representing about a million people).[120]

Additionally, in 1980 Congress created a sanction system that held states financially responsible for providing benefits to ineligible recipients above an established error rate. In 1982 Congress made the error-rate targets more stringent. This move suggests that the attitude of Congress is shifting from a belief that all who are entitled to food stamps should get them to a view that those who are not entitled should not get them. The change in perception is important. In administering any large program, there will be an error rate or "waste." A tradeoff exists, however: As emphasis is placed on reducing the number of ineligibles, the chance increases that some eligibles may also be cut from the program. While Congress does not wish for the deserving to be cut from the program, the point is clear: Food stamps are now under scrutiny.

A smaller ($1.2 billion in total expenditures in fiscal 1982) and more narrowly targeted program than the FSP, WIC is designed to provide both supplemental food and nutrition information for low-income pregnant, postpartum, and breast-feeding women, and for children up to the age of five who are determined to be at special health risk because of inadequate nutrition. The determination of nutritional risk is made by a health official such as a nutritionist or public health nurse. The program is administered regionally by state and health departments that distribute funds to local public and private, nonprofit agencies (e.g., clinics, local health departments), which in turn supply the actual benefits to recipients These benefits consist of food vouchers for items tai-

---

[119]"The Food Stamp Controversy," *The Congressional Digest,* Vol. 60 (January 1981).
[120]U.S. Congressional Budget Office, "Major Legislative Changes in Human Resources Programs Since January 1981," August 1983, p. 41.

lored to the particular family's needs, such as infant formula, as well as nutritional counseling and pamphlets. The average monthly value of the coupons per recipient is about $29, and the total national caseload is about 2.2 million.[121]

WIC grew out of a special commodity distribution effort begun in 1968. The program was first authorized for two years in 1972 with an annual ceiling of $20 million. No funds were actually expended until 1974 when USDA was forced to do so by court action. Then the program took off.[122]

According to Jonathan Rauch in the *National Journal,*

> WIC . . . has done better than stand untouched; it has gained ground. After more than quadrupling in size during the late 1970s, the program has grown by more than 40 per cent during the Reagan years. The growth gives every sign of continuing.
>
> In theory, WIC is part of the so-called discretionary budget that Congress can easily fiddle with from year to year. In practice, however, it is politically off limits.
>
> To the delight of its supporters, WIC has slipped out of Reagan's reach. What worries some conservatives is that, as they see it, WIC's growth may have slipped out of everyone's reach.[123]

During the Reagan years, several unsuccessful efforts were made to reduce WIC expenditures. In 1982 Reagan proposed combining WIC with an existing maternal and child health block grant, and reducing the total level of funding by $356 million. Congress rejected this proposal, actually adding $100 million in extra funds for WIC as part of the 1983 employment and emergency poverty relief legislation. As a result, WIC grew during the Reagan administration. Indeed, the Congressional Budget Office noted (in its study of the effects of 1981 and 1982 legislation on 26 domestic programs) that WIC was one of only two such programs to have increased expenditures as the result of laws enacted over this time.[124]

---

[121]U.S. Senate, Committee on Agriculture, Nutrition, and Forestry, "Child Nutrition Programs: Description, History, Issues and Options," January 1983, pp. 60–65.

[122]*Ibid.,* pp. 69–72.

[123]Jonathan Rauch, "Women and Children's Food Program is 'Off Limits' to Reagan Budget Cutbacks," *National Journal,* November 17, 1984, p. 2197.

[124]U.S. Congressional Budget Office, "Major Legislative Changes," pp. vii–viii.

WIC has benefited from very strong general congressional support. In conversations with legislative staff members, program administrators, and interest group activists, it was clear that all emphasized the program's "great popularity" with members "on both sides of the aisle." Why is WIC not merely popular but expanding in a restrictive environment?

Favorable implementation reports apparently have been important in congressional support for WIC. Based on analysis of WIC recipients vis-à-vis a control group consisting of a similar population not receiving program benefits, these reports have concluded that WIC leads to such desirable results as increases in childbirth weight, fewer problematic pregnancies, and reduced health care costs. One study showed $3 in health care savings for every $1 invested in WIC. Some of the claims made on behalf of WIC have been challenged, but the bulk of literature and professional opinions available to policymakers remain highly supportive of the program.[125] The GAO reported that "the information is insufficient for making any general or conclusive judgments about whether the WIC program is effective or ineffective over all."[126]

Interest group activity has been instrumental in the growth of FSP and WIC. Support for both programs has been led by a few nonprofit organizations dedicated to antipoverty advocacy, such as the Food Research and Action Center; liberal church organizations, such as Bread for the World; and also by recipient organizations. None of these groups can offer support to legislators in the form of campaign contributions or ready-made campaign workers. Activists for these groups, however, can help to highlight issues and inform legislators (this may be particularly important to sympathetic representatives and senators in need of "ammunition"); generate support or opposition to particular policies; and indicate to their own members and the press which legislators have "good" or "bad" records in the area of hunger programs. Legislators have at times paid backhanded compliments to the political effectiveness of these groups, as did Senator Carl Curtis of Nebraska who com-

[125]U.S. Senate, Hearing before the Subcommittee on Nutrition of the Committee on Agriculture, Nutrition, and Forestry, February 23, 1982.
[126]Rauch, "Women and Children's Food Program," p. 2198.

plained on the Senate floor about the pressure they brought to bear for eliminating the FSP purchase requirement.[127]

Contrary to common opinion, there is little evidence that farm organizations have played an important role in advancing the cause of either FSP or WIC. In the early 1960s, farmers were divided in support for FSP, with the National Farmers Union favoring FSP, while the American Farm Bureau Federation and some other agricultural producers supporting the then-existing system of direct distribution of surplus commodities.[128] Since that time, farming organizations have seldom been actively involved in hunger program issues.

An advantage of WIC, according to Marc Bendick of the Urban Institute, is that "You're linked into two very powerful communities: the food manufacturing community and the health community. . . . You can believe that the infant formula manufacturers, the milk producers and the cereal manufacturers like it." Producers of sugary cereals and chocolate flavored milk, however, were unable to get their products included in WIC food packages.[129] So popular is WIC that Representative George S. Miller, chairman of the Select Committee on Children, Youth and Families and a member of the Budget Committee, wanted the program to become an entitlement.

Does it make a difference that FSP has generally been treated as an entitlement and WIC as a traditional appropriation? The answer appears to be "no." Although WIC is not an entitlement, its benefits do go directly to people who are eligible if they meet certain qualifications. From the outside, the entitlement to food stamps and WIC vouchers must look very much alike.

The entitlement status of FSP becomes especially important in what happens after legislative guidelines are established. Because funding is not fixed, but is a function of the indexed benefit level, and because of the number and characteristics of recipients, expenditures may vary

[127]Kathryn Waters Gest, "Senate Votes Food Stamp Overhaul," *Congressional Quarterly Weekly Report,* Vol. 35 (May 28, 1977), p. 1039.
[128]U.S. House of Representatives, Hearings before the Committee on Agriculture, June 10–12, 1963.
[129]*Ibid.,* p. 2198.

from what is actually "appropriated." The factors behind this variance may be labeled as "automatic" and "non-automatic" forces.

By automatic forces, I mean factors that do not require changes in behavior of recipients, potential recipients, or other significant actors. These include indexing of benefits and interactive effects of changes in different programs. The FSP benefit levels and income eligibility standards are tied to the cost of a "nutritionally adequate diet," now adjusted annually (in earlier years it was adjusted semiannually). The result is that program expenditures rise when food prices increase, an effect particularly evident at times of dramatically rising food costs. In January of 1974, for example, coupon allotments for a family of four were raised from $116 to $142 as a result of indexing, a 22.4 percent increase.[130] In early 1979, with estimates of food stamp obligations running well over $1 billion higher than had been anticipated (the eventual total would be still higher), CBO estimated that $760 million of the overrun could be attributed to higher than expected food costs.[131]

One area in which we might expect to find differences between FSP and WIC on the basis of entitlement status is in the actions of appropriations committees, even though the rules as to who receives benefits are set by the authorizing committees. The FSP is the type of entitlement that requires appropriations committees to actually provide funding. Nevertheless, the role of appropriations is more technical than substantive, suggesting that it considers the program to be an entitlement. As a result, hearings focus on administrative issues such as eligibility error rates and fraud prevention.

With regard to WIC, it would be possible for appropriation committees to play an active role in reducing spending. Thus far, however, they have not shown the inclination to do so. In 1982, for example, both House and Senate appropriation committees rejected the administration's block grant proposal, and both committee reports praised the program's "effectiveness."[132] Congressional staff members indicate that

[130]U.S. Congressional Budget Office, "The Food Stamp Program," p. 12.

[131]U.S. House of Representatives, Hearings before the Subcommittee on Domestic Marketing, Consumer Relations, and Nutrition of the Committee on Agriculture, May 9, 1979.

[132]"34 Billion Voted for Farm/Food Programs," *1982 Congressional Quarterly Almanac* (Washington, 1983), pp. 255–62.

there is a tendency for the appropriations committees to provide enough funding to maintain a certain caseload level, such as the year-end level, which means that this program is moving toward something of a hybrid status: Appropriation committees retain formal control but base their decisions on caseload considerations. It's how you are treated not what you're supposed to be that matters.

WIC has evolved so that it is actually treated as a medical rather than a poverty program. Its bureaucracy is small. Because it is admired, WIC administrators are able to practice classical budgetary strategy. "Running the thing through the medical system," Bendick said, "gave the program more an aura of 'true necessity,' with large quotes around 'true necessity.' "[133]

WIC shows that if commanding majorities treat a program like an entitlement, it will, in effect, become one. AFDC shows that if shifting majorities believe people are not entirely entitled, they will treat the program as more variable. Though some may think Head Start is in some way better, deep down they believe that AFDC is more important. Put another way, public officials do not have to come up with an immediate substitute for Head Start but they could not leave so many AFDC families destitute, especially since they would have to be dumped onto other programs or levels of government.

There are many factors other than size or political organization that contribute to the fate of entitlements. The ways in which entitlements are connected to other programs help determine how public officials will regard them. It is not only the merits of the entitlement itself but which level of government has to pay for it that matters. Comparisons made at certain times—poor states, rich federal government—may be invalid at other times—huge federal deficits, state surpluses. Developments in knowledge may make some programs more and others less expensive. Taken together with economic and demographic changes, entitlements as a class are buffeted by so large a variety of factors that it is vain to search for a common denominator.

When I suggested earlier that we might be asking for too much, this is what I meant: A full explanation-cum-prediction of the trajectory of

[133]Rauch, "Women and Children's Food Program," p. 2198.

entitlements, including comparison with appropriations in similar fields, would be equivalent to comprehending most of American national public policy. Since entitlements make up a good half of noninterest spending, and related appropriations add to the proportion, explaining entitlements is like asking for an explanation of domestic spending. A tall order.

Yet we have learned a few things worth knowing. One of these is that despite their image of being inviolable, entitlements are modified all the time: What else have we been discussing? Another, not quite contradictory thing, is that despite the fact that entitlements as a class are continuously being modified, the people through their government mean to keep these promises. Consequently, control mostly means preventing entitlements from rising too fast, not abolishing or severely diminishing them. Since the largest entitlements, especially the family of programs under social security, are the most sacrosanct, their growth overwhelms efforts to control their poorer cousins.

It is true that being funded through appropriations does not guarantee that a program will grow more slowly than an entitlement; WIC shows us that. The fact is, however, that we would be hard put to come up with many other exceptional programs. And that is the point: Entitlements can afford to be ordinary; programs funded by appropriations have to be extraordinary in order to do well.

Entitlements are meant to be stronger promises (cross my heart three times) than mere appropriations. When promises conflict, however, someone is bound to be disappointed. A promise to pay implies a willingness to tax. Even where trust funds for retirement and medical care are now adequate, they constitute, in effect, a base above which taxpayers are reluctant to go. Certain citizens may be entitled to payments and services, but they cannot be entitled to a balanced budget at the same time. On the one hand, multi-billion-dollar surpluses in retirement trust funds will tempt public officials to use them to meet other promises, thus creating worse financial problems in the future. On the other hand, it looks as if social security and medicare taxes would have to rise substantially in order to meet promises by the first quarter of the next century. No matter how often the problem of social security is supposed to have been solved "once and for all," it will keep coming back because (1) that is where the money is, and (2) other policy promises cannot be kept if it is kept whole. The concept of entitlement sits uneasily with the concepts of resource allocation and budgetary control.

To anticipate, changes made by the Omnibus Budget Reconciliation Act of 1990 (see Chapter 12) simultaneously increased and decreased congressional control over entitlements. Should expenditures increase in other portions of the budget, entitlements will not be affected. In a parallel manner, increases in expenditures within the entitlement category that go beyond the deficit target specified by OBRA must be paid for by cutting other spending or raising other revenues involving entitlements. If not, the sequestration procedure reduces all entitlement accounts across the board. This is not easy to say but it is a lot easier to say than it will be to do. For the entitlement sequestration strongly suggests that these are not mandatory expenditures, dependent only on who qualifies, but are subject to control on an annual basis by Congress. Whether the affected constituencies will allow these reductions to take place or Congress can take the flack or whether Congress will choose to cut "administrative" expenses in an unreal manner cannot yet be determined. Should there be external events, like an economic downturn or a war that raises spending, however, entitlements and their legislative committees do not have to pay for what they did not do. Perhaps presidents, wishing not to recommend cuts in entitlements, will always find "external" reasons that the targets have to be changed. For students of budgeting, the future is likely to be every bit as or more interesting than the recent past.

BUDGETING
FOR DEFENSE

9

UNDERSTANDING DEFENSE BUDGETING, even at a relatively simple level, is a lot like finding your way through a maze blindfolded. Defense is huge; its procurement alone could qualify as the largest business in the world. It plans and funds the largest organization in the free world. The Department of Defense (DOD) employs more than 2 million active uniformed-service personnel, and another 1 million civilian employees.[1] More than 80 percent of federal employees work for DOD or on defense projects. At least 1.2 million private sector jobs (some say over 2 million) are created directly by DOD procurement, contract projects, and overseas military bases.[2]

The defense budget represents an enormous amount of money. In fiscal 1985 the national defense budget was $296 billion, the largest defense budget in both real and nominal terms since 1945.[3] While comprising 26.5 percent of federal outlays in 1985, defense spending amounted to 73.9 percent of federal purchases of goods and serv-

[1]William W. Kaufmann, *A Reasonable Defense* (Washington, DC: The Brookings Institution, 1986), p. 42.
[2]Lawrence J. Korb, "The Process and Problems of Linking Policy and Force Structure through the Defense Budget Process," in Robert Harkavy and Edward Kolodziej, eds., *American Security Policy and Policy Making* (Lexington: Lexington Books, 1980), p. 186.
[3]Kaufmann, *A Reasonable Defense,* p. 39.

ices.[4] (The reason for the disparity is that domestic spending is composed largely of entitlements, mostly payments to individuals.)

THE INTERNAL BUDGETING PROCESS

Before attempting to understand the relationship between defense and other governmental actors, most notably Congress, it will be helpful to examine the internal workings of the Department of Defense.

Formal preparation of the defense budget is divided into three phases. The *planning phase,* which begins more than two years before the fiscal year in which funds will be spent initially, establishes defense objectives and indicates the resources needed to meet these objectives. The *programming phase* centers on the development of programs to meet these goals. In the *budgeting phase,* program cost and efficacy are reviewed and defense spending is combined with the rest of the federal budget for submission to Congress.

The planning phase begins with the drafting of the defense guidance by the Secretary of Defense. This defense guidance outlines the Secretary's perceptions of threats to American security, assesses the ability of U.S. forces to counter threats, and suggests actions in response to a changing environment. Each service is given goals to meet and preliminary levels of spending. These goals and spending levels are planned for the five following years. The defense guidance is preceded by submission to the Secretary of the Joint Services Planning Document (JSPD), which is drafted by the Joint Chiefs of Staff (JCS) and assesses threats to national security and the optimal military response, with no regard given to budgetary considerations. Review of the previous year's guidance is also undertaken by the Undersecretary of Defense for policy, Office of the Secretary of Defense (OSD) officials, the services, JCS, and various military commanders. Major changes in strategy and the global situation, as well as congressional action to date on the previous submitted budget, are discussed.

[4]*Ibid.,* p. 25.

The JSPD is passed on by the Secretary of Defense to an executive budget committee, the Defense Resources Board (DRB). (Everybody talks about Defense in initials because there are so many organizations dealing with each other, if they didn't use initials, all the time would be spent naming the participants.) The DRB consists of the top DOD civilian staff, the service secretaries, the chair of the Joint Chiefs, and a representative from OMB. The DRB circulates drafts of the defense guidance to various DOD offices and integrates the feedback it receives. Major decisions on defense policy and spending are made and the JSPD's pie-in-the-sky estimates are brought into line with spending limits.

In the programming phase, the services and defense agencies develop and propose programs designed to meet the five-year objectives of the defense guidance and the fiscal objectives of the projected DOD budget. These proposed programs, presented as program objective memoranda (POMs), are reviewed by the OSD, JCS, and service staffs in a group led by the comptroller and the program analysis and evaluation directorate. The focus of the review is on the relationship of proposed programs to overall goals and fiscal guidelines. Attempts are made to examine the programs across service categories to avoid duplication and to locate efficiencies. The key issues in the POMs are discussed by the DRB and final decisions are relayed through program decision memoranda (PDMs).

In the budgeting phase, PDMs serve as the basis for cost estimates to be submitted by DOD elements to the DOD comptroller. The comptroller, with other OSD staffs and the OMB, review the budget for accuracy in cost estimates, feasibility, scheduling, and consistency with established priorities.

The comptroller then develops a "final" budget. Unresolved issues between the OSD and the OMB are discussed, and the latest economic assumptions are incorporated into the budget estimates (usually causing adjustments in hundreds of budget items). The budget is submitted to the president for approval. After this, the OMB incorporates the defense budget with the rest of the federal budget for submission to Congress. In total, 27 months of planning and debating occur before the defense budget is finally adopted. This includes an 18-month planning process within the Defense Department and 9 months of congressional review.

Does the Department of Defense actually use a Planning Programming Budgeting System (PPBS), as it claims? In the sense that DOD provides a breakdown of its spending proposals by broad strategic functions (see Table 9-1), this is true. But in the sense that DOD makes spending decisions by comparing alternatives for achieving strategic objectives, I find no supporting evidence. The form is there but not the incentive. Since each branch of the service loses no resources by pushing for its favored programs, the exercise remains sterile. In the words of a knowledgeable defense official, "People are running around looking for what was left out and should be in there." In the budget phase, these new programs are winnowed down but by no means eliminated. As this defense official goes on to observe, "I used to say, in the Summer they put it in with shovels; then during Budget we take it out with tweezers." Worse, the PPBS exercise is confusing because it suggests a procedure is in place that really is not followed.

If confirmation were needed, the joint DOD–GAO Study Group came up with the same conclusions as past studies of PPBS.[5] A mission-oriented budget, which is what program budgeting is supposed to be, requires corresponding organizational procedures. "However, the current organization of DOD is not along strictly combat mission lines."[6] A whole host of essential activities are difficult to accommodate within PPBS—recruiting, medical care, housing, food, repairs, provisions, on and on. They amount to more than 30 percent of service budgets. "It is not clear how those support activities could be related to missions."[7] Even those programs that could be related to missions suffer from inadequate linkages between funding and outcomes. In a separate study, the GAO "found no accountability systems linking military capability and rising or falling program funding levels. . . . Since funding is not

---

[5]See Aaron Wildavsky, "Rescuing Policy Analysis from PPBS," *Public Administration Review*, Vol. 29, No. 2 (March/April 1969), pp. 189–202; and "The Political Economy of Efficiency: Cost-Benefit Analysis, Systems Analysis, and Program Budgeting," *Public Administration Review*, Vol. 26, No. 4 (December 1966), pp. 292–310.

[6]Joint DOD-GAO Study Group, pp. 119–20.

[7]*Ibid.*, p. 121.

TABLE 9-1
Principal Defense Budget Formats, Fiscal Year 1985
(billions of dollars)

Item	Budget Authority
Appropriation title	
Military personnel*	68.9
Operation and maintenance	78.2
Procurement	96.8
Research, development, test, and evaluation	31.5
Military construction	5.5
Military family housing	2.9
Revolving and management funds	1.7
Receipts and deductions	−0.6
Total	284.7
Component	
Department of the Army	74.4
Department of the Navy	96.5
Department of the Air Force	99.9
Defense agencies, OSD, JCS	13.0
Defense-wide	1.0
Total	284.7
Program	
Strategic forces	27.8
General purpose forces	120.6
Intelligence and communications	25.1
Airlift and sealift	7.0
National Guard and Reserve	15.7
Research and development	24.6
Central supply and maintenance	24.4
Training, medical, and other general personnel activities	33.1
Administration and association activities	5.9
Support of other nations	0.5
Total	284.7

*This category now includes funds for the military retired pay actual account.
Source: *Budget of the United States Government, Fiscal Year 1986*, pp. 5–5, 5–6; and *Department of Defense Annual Report to the Congress, Fiscal Year 1986*, p. 294. Numbers are rounded. Table in William W. Kaufmann, *A Reasonable Defense* (Washington, D.C.: The Brookings Institution, 1986), p. 13.

linked to intermediate outputs, such as increased proficiency or mission capable weapon systems, or to ultimate outputs, such as increased readiness, there is no way of determining if the services could achieve the same goals with fewer dollars."[8] In the end as at the beginning, the joint study group was preoccupied with the same subject: "This theme is the difficulty in relating the output orientation of decision making, so necessary for broad policy making at the national level, to the input orientation used for purposes of management and control at the budget level."[9]

The combination of secrecy and complexity surrounding weapons systems, the immense detail involved, the networks of relationships within the services and between the branches and their contractors and the communities in which they are located make defense budgeting exceedingly difficult to comprehend. Distinguishing between self-serving arguments and defense achievements is difficult for civilian and military defense personnel alike. No one can be certain of the threats that will be faced, or how their choices of weapons and personnel policies will turn out. Mix vast uncertainty with immense complexity and it is not clear that anyone, no matter what position is taken, can have but a small grip on the future.

The combination of huge size and long lead times for weapons systems makes the defense budget prey to all sorts of accounting manipulation. In the late 1960s and the 1970s, defense spending was hurt by low estimates of inflation. In the first half of the 1980s, DOD estimated inflation too high (to the tune of $35 billion from FY82 to FY85).[10] What should happen to this money—a rainy day reserve, compensation for past insufficiency, return to the Treasury—has been subject to much dispute that has not helped build trust between DOD and the appropriations committees. Other matters only aficionados would think of, from foreign currency fluctuations to what year should be the basis of comparison for long-lived projects, can amount to hundreds of millions of dollars

[8]Report to the Congress by the Comptroller General of the United States, "The Defense Budget: A Look at Budgetary Resources, Accomplishments, and Problems," GAO/PLRD-83-62, April 27, 1983, p. 24.

[9]*Ibid.*, p. 113.

[10]Gordon Adams and Jeffrey Colman, "Gramm–Rudman–Hollings and the FY 1986 Defense Budget," Center on Budget and Policy Priorities, January 6, 1986, p. 2.

and more. Let us just say that this chapter is defense budgeting for beginners, not the advanced course.[11]

Rivalry

Competition between agencies within a department for resources and prestige is a commonplace event in all bureaucratic institutions. No other federal department has the intensity of competition or the stakes as high as in the DOD budget. Former Chairman of the JCS General David Jones described the defense budget as an "intramural scramble for resources."[12] The primary level of conflict is between the services: army versus navy versus air force.

Each service is a separate organizational entity. There is no such thing as a "military officer." An officer is a member of either the army, air force, navy, or marines. The services maintain separate facilities, training programs, and budgets. Each service has its own distinct traditions, service academies, and uniforms. Organizational boundaries are clearly marked and well understood by all participants. A particular service is the source of individual identification and serves "as the predominant source of sanctions, rewards, and focus of organizational loyalty."[13]

Competition is a mixed bag; on the downside, there is plenty of evidence for lack of essential battlefield coordination, even in such a tiny place as Grenada. Services may seek programs because the programs are beneficial to the particular branch—its size, importance, promotions—while claiming (or believing) the programs are good for the nation.[14] The navy fought the Polaris missile submarine program because it believed Polaris was "not a traditional navy mission and therefore should not be financed out of the navy's share of the defense budget."[15] The

---

[11]See David Morrison, "Defense Focus," *National Journal*, March 29, 1986, p. 794; GAO, "DOD Financial Management—Improper Use of Foreign Currency Fluctuations Account." Report to Senator David H. Pryor, July 1986.

[12]Glenn Pascall, *The Trillion Dollar Budget* (Seattle: University of Washington Press, 1985), p. 6.

[13]Arnold Kanter, *Defense Politics* (Chicago: University of Chicago Press, 1975), p. 17.

[14]See Mark Rovner, *Defense Dollars and Sense* (Washington, D.C.: Common Cause, 1983), p. 36.

[15]Alain C. Enthoven and Wayne K. Smith, *How Much Is Enough?* (New York: Harper & Row, 1971), p. 17.

air force has not been enthusiastic about the A-10 ground attack aircraft. The A-10 is designed specifically to destroy tanks and other ground targets while flying above the battlefield at the slow speeds necessary for accurate aiming. Destroying tanks, in the air force mindset, is a job for the army. Air force officers like supersonic aircraft with state-of-the-art technology. One of the few programs the air force voluntarily cut, the simple, slow A-10 was just not their idea of what the air force is about. Defense analyst William W. Kaufmann lays it on the line:

> . . . all three services are trying simultaneously to expand their capabilities, upgrade older weapons, and replace them as rapidly as possible with new and more costly models. Furthermore, [each service] is investing in weapons that will enable it to operate independently of the others. The Army is buying expensive attack helicopters and air defense weapons because it does not expect to be given the necessary support by the Air Force. The Air Force, which could acquire more close air support aircraft and short-range air defense interceptors, prefers to invest in long-range fighter-attack aircraft that can attack targets deep in the enemy's rear and conduct an interdiction campaign in the hope of winning the war regardless of what happens to the Army. The Navy, asserting its independence of everyone else, prepares to fight its own small wars with amphibious forces and carrier-based tactical aircraft, more than half the cost of which goes into protecting this power-projection capability.[16]

On the upside of service independence, all innovation requires advocates. A fine study of naval aviation, for instance, shows that the success of the United States and Japan and the failure of Britain before the Second World War were due to the institutionalization of advocacy. Britain turned naval aviation over to central command, which always had other priorities. It never came up with enough money or promotions to create a cadre of people able to push the cause against other competitors.[17]

President Eisenhower made creative use of interservice rivalry. By setting down a spending ceiling in advance, he encouraged the service chiefs to come to him when they could not agree on how to divide that

[16]Kaufmann, *A Reasonable Defense,* pp. 101–102.
[17]Thomas C. Hove and Mark D. Mandeles, "Interwar Innovation in Three Navies: USN, RN, IJN," sponsored by the Office of Net Assessment, DOD, 1982.

sum.[18] The Packard Commission believed that reinstituting this practice—"the President would issue provisional five-year budget levels to
the Secretary of Defense reflecting competing demands on the federal
budget"[19]—would create incentives for the services to resolve their
differences earlier and would diminish the practice of putting in wish
lists while waiting until the last minute to engage in serious negotiations.[20]

In an effort to improve coordination among the services, Congress has
passed the Goldwater–Nichols Reorganization Act. The act seeks to
increase the authority of the chairman of JCS by making him the
principal military adviser to the president and the Secretary of Defense.
Previously, the Joint Chiefs advised the president as a group. Whether
more will be gained through central control than is lost through uniformity remains to be seen.

Better Weapons

The services constantly strive for greater performance from military
hardware. The search for superior performance requires expensive research into new fields at the cutting edge of science and engineering.
The services promote the production of sophisticated, and therefore
costly, weapons systems. The air force paid $7 billion (1983 dollars) for
6,300 airplanes in 1951. In 1983, for $11 billion, the air force bought
322 fighter aircraft.[21]

The drive to acquire the most sophisticated weaponry available is
dramatically revealed in cost differences for weapons between the
Carter and Reagan administrations. According to a Congressional
Budget Office study, in his first term, Reagan bought 6.4 percent more
missiles than Carter, but it cost 91.2 percent more in constant dollars.
Reagan funded 30 percent more tanks, but paid 147.4 percent more

[18]Kanter, *Defense Politics*.

[19]President's Blue Ribbon Commission, "National Security," p. 4.

[20]President's Blue Ribbon Commission on Defense Management, "A Formula for
Action." A Report to the President on Defense Acquisition, April 1986.

[21]J. Ronald Fox, "Revamping the Business of National Defense," *Harvard Business
Review*, Vol. 62, No. 5 (September/October 1985), p. 63.

for them;[22] 8.8 percent more aircraft cost 75.4 percent more; and 36.1 percent more ships were acquired at a cost that was 53 percent higher.[23]

All soldiers understandably want the best weapons they can get. As General Tooey Spatz said, "A second-best airplane is like a second-best poker hand. No damn good."[24] The services know that expensive equipment will lead to fewer units being purchased, but they are willing to accept fewer weapons in order to have the highest possible quality. Weapons development takes years and cannot easily be quickened. Since each service only gets a new generation of weapons every ten years or so, moreover, each seeks to incorporate all conceivable capabilities in every upgrade. The services know from experience that in times of war or heightened tension Congress will make available the funds to expand forces and increase production of weapons. However, congressional action cannot instantly create the advanced technology the services believe will be needed. It takes a long time so they try to stick everything on each weapon, so it takes longer, so a vicious cycle ensues.

Some observers believe that the desire for enhanced performance goes beyond reason and is derided as "goldplating." In recent years, a chorus of voices has called for a larger number of simpler weapons. Others rely on the adage of fewer but better. In this war of the proverbs—many heads are better than one but too many cooks spoil the broth—where no one specifies conditions of applicability, it is not easy to discern where wisdom lies.

Cost Overruns

The history of weapons procurement cost overruns is long and inglorious. On March 27, 1794, Congress approved the creation of a sea-going

[22]Jacques S. Gansler, "How to Improve the Acquisition of Weapons," in Robert J. Art et al., eds., *Reorganizing America's Defense* (Washington, D.C.: Pergamon Brassey, 1985), p. 384.

[23]Kaufmann, *A Reasonable Defense*, p. 43.

[24]Robert J. Art, "Restructuring the Military-Industrial Complex: Arms Control in an Institutional Perspective," *Public Policy*, Vol. 21, No. 4 (Fall 1974), pp. 429–30.

navy by appropriating funds to build six frigates. The work was contracted to six private shipyards geographically spread in order to distribute the benefits of federal spending and to garner political support for the program. War in Europe prevented the purchase of necessary supplies and the keels were not laid until the end of 1795. Shortly thereafter, due to mismanagement, delays, and cost overruns, the number of frigates to be purchased was cut to three.[25]

On average, weapons systems' costs (including inflation) increased 100 percent over the initial cost estimate given to Congress by the services for the first appropriation.[26] A recent example of this problem occurred with the B-1 bomber. The initial cost for 100 aircraft was estimated by Rockwell International, the prime contractor, as $11.9 billion in 1981 dollars. This estimate was given to the House Appropriations Subcommittee in January of 1981. Fifteen months later the air force estimated the cost at $25 billion (excluding inflation).[27] No doubt there are reasons (redesign, reductions in quantities, etc.), but the result is the same.

Defense contractors want to stay in business; this means winning DOD contracts. In competitive bidding, contracts are awarded to the lowest bidder. When contracts are not put out to bid because there is only a sole source, or because of a desire to keep firms in the business so there can be competition in the future, both the Pentagon and the contractors have an incentive to look good by coming in low. Once a service selects a contractor, there is little chance that the contractor will lose the job. Contracts are initially given for relatively low cost research and development. The firm that does the research and development almost always is assured of performing production as well (thus eliminating price competition during the production phase). Contractors, therefore, are willing, and the system demands, that the initial bid be unrealistically low. Contractors know or hope they can recoup research losses

[25]Charles Hitch, *Decision-Making for Defense* (Berkeley: University of California Press, 1970), p. 6.
[26]Rovner, *Defense Dollars and Sense*, p. 42.
[27]*Ibid.*, p. 44.

on production overhead. Consequently, contractors often give unrealistically low bids to get a project started thus placing the force of bureaucratic inertia on their side, a process called "buying in."

The services have incentives to play along with the "buy-in" game. They want to fund as many programs as possible, even though many receive less than optimal resources. It is more difficult to launch a program than to keep it going once it is started. It is also easier to launch an inexpensive program than an expensive one. In such circumstances, the services have strong incentives to accept the most optimistic cost estimates.

Costs can be underestimated any number of ways. An unrealistically low inflation rate may be used. Particular resource costs may not be fully accounted for. Additionally, necessary components may not be included in the estimate, either deliberately or because of changes in specifications or the addition of features.

The time horizon for defense budgeting also contributes to cost overruns. Since each defense program must receive annual appropriations (and most must receive annual authorizations), neither the Defense Department nor defense contractors can safely commit resources for more than one year. This short-run view of defense budgeting is further aggravated by congressional concern with reelection and the short time defense officials usually spend at any one job (about two years). "Because of the short-term focus of the congressional and defense officials, problem areas in the defense industry often get a 'quick fix'— more fixed-price contracts, more incentive contracts . . . more reporting requirements—rather than the basic reforms needed for lasting improvements."[28]

A final factor that contributes to overruns is that military managers are trained primarily in field operations and not in the complex business of procurement and program management. Because the job is so difficult and the chances of failure are high, promising officials avoid careers in this field. Additionally, field command experience is usually necessary for

[28]Fox, "Revamping the Business of National Defense," p. 65.

promotion above lieutenant colonel (army and air force) or commander (navy). Thus far, only the air force has sought to create alternative careers in program management.[29]

Cost overruns are not unique to the Defense Department. Basing its conclusions on Rand Corporation studies, the Packard Commission shows that large cost overruns are common in the domestic public sector; in matters of innovative technology almost all big projects are woefully underestimated. (See Figure 9-1.) Comparing the best examples of private domestic research and development (the Hughes Communication Satellite, the IBM 360 computer, the Boeing 767 transport) with defense programs done under streamlined procedures (the Polaris and Minuteman missiles), the good results were comparable.[30] Unfortunately, the conditions judged necessary for superior achievement in private industry and public service, from financial stability to clear channels of command to communication with users who are willing to trade lesser performance for lower cost, are the ones so far absent from defense.

The causes of cost overruns are well known without our knowing how to correct them. Taking old technology off the shelf is a lot cheaper but not necessarily more effective. It is not only costs that change but also technology; the desire to have the best leads to new specifications and retrofitting all along the line, which is very expensive. Dropping projects prematurely is as bad as carrying them on way past their time. Contractors do take advantage, but forcing them out of business leaves DOD without sufficient variety in the future. According to Rand, the corporations, too, suffer from uncertainty: "In virtually every program we surveyed, neither the total volume of demand for a system, nor the rate of that demand, matched what had been projected at the outset of the program."[31] What is most needed, that elusive yet vital quality called good judgment, is hard to find. What is most wanted from the political authorities, a steady hand, is hardest to obtain.

[29]*Ibid.*
[30]President's Blue Ribbon Commission, "A Formula for Action," p. 11.
[31]Andrew Mayer, "Erosion of the Defense Industrial Base at the Subcontractor Level," typescript, n.d., p. 4.

FIGURE 9-1
Cost Growth in Major Projects (Rand).

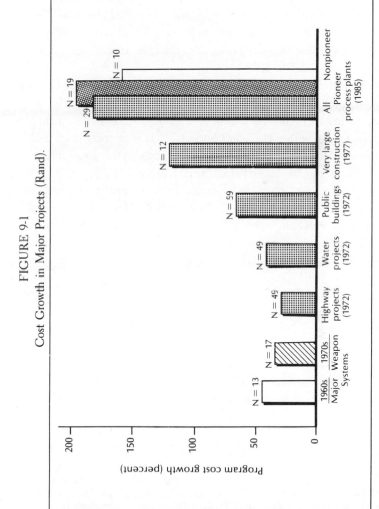

Source: President's Blue Ribbon Commission on Defense Management, June 1986, p. 61.

Waste

In past years there have been charges of waste and mismanagement leveled against government. Some of the worst horror stories depicted the Defense Department as composed of bumbling bureaucrats being ripped off by dishonest contractors. Stories circulated about the Pentagon paying $91 for a 3-cent screw, $110 for a 4-cent diode, and $9,609 for a 12-cent Allen wrench. These stories may be true, though it is not easy for an outsider to tell.[32]

Some waste can also be traced to the budget process. "Annual Appropriations cycles often waste money, since weapons systems and spare parts, for instance, may have to be ordered in uneconomical quantities in order to stay within the year's budget."[33] It is in spare parts, not in setting priorities, that the DOD prefers to absorb cuts. In an interview on Public Radio on January 13, 1987, I heard Secretary of Defense Caspar Weinberger agree that ordering larger quantities (he had criticized the Carter administration for not doing that) would cost a lot less per item. Senator Sam Nunn of Georgia, also being interviewed, chimed in that procuring too few weapons was vastly more expensive than all the "horror stories" put together. True. Yet Weinberger was recommending the same sort of "stretch outs" as his predecessor had done for the same reason: Given that Congress would not provide enough both to increase the quantities procured and to provide other things the secretary believed desirable, he would take a smaller number of items to get more diverse weapons. By over-committing at the start of programs, the Defense Department makes stretch-outs more likely.

Despite the implications of reports on waste, the Defense Department does review equipment costs. When a contractor submits designs

---

[32]Steve Kellman argues that many of the stories were exaggerated. The $91 screw and the $110 diode were not indicative of waste, he says, but of accounting procedures. Often contractors will allocate overhead on an "item" basis rather than a "value" basis. For example, if there is an overhead total of $1 million to be allotted over 10,000 parts, some contractors will allocate $100 to each item regardless of its proportionate cost. Thus a $15,000 item will appear at a cost of $15,100 and a 4-cent item as $100.04 [Steve Kellman, "The Grace Commission: How Much Waste in Government?" *The Public Interest*, No. 78 (Winter 1985), p. 64]. Unfortunately, it is not certain that such procedures exist.

[33]*Ibid.*, pp. 80–81.

for spare parts for the original weapon, for example, a Defense Department contracting officer will review the designs and make suggestions about substituting common-use for custom-designed parts where appropriate. An independent evaluation by DOD value engineers is undertaken at a later stage to analyze whether custom-designed items are necessary. In the case of the $9,609 Allen wrench, the system worked. Value engineers in the DOD found that an ordinary wrench should be substituted for a proposed custom-designed one.[34]

This is not to say that waste does not occur. For example, $1,118 was paid for a custom-designed plastic cap for a navigator's seat, even though the cap could have been purchased commercially. At the heart of the problem of waste is the tendency for the Pentagon, motivated by congressional micro-management as well as bureaucratic tendency, to spell out detailed specifications (as is done for major procurements) for everyday items. It hopes to avoid blame by proceeding according to the rules. The need for a whistle resulted in 16 pages of military specifications, including the requirement that the item should "make an audible characteristic sound when blown by the mouth with medium or high pressure." There are similarly thorough specifications for taco shells and fruitcakes.[35]

Concern also has been expressed about misdirection of funding from higher to lower priority items. A sample of what a GAO study found includes: The army resurfaced tennis courts and installed swimming pool filters at a cost of $443,000, while fire alarms at the same installation that would have cost $163,000 were not funded; a navy boathouse was repaired and painted only to be demolished less than six months later; the air force used funds to refurbish officers' clubs and replace sprinkler systems on golf courses, even though this money could have been used for unfunded backlogs of runway repaving and roofing projects.[36]

My own amateur judgment is that the most serious waste occurs because of incessant program and product changes. Without a greater

[34]*Ibid.*, p. 65.
[35]"In Wake of Foul-Ups, the Pentagon Is Pressured to Shop Around for Bargains on Everyday Goods," *Wall Street Journal*, October 3, 1986, p. 50.
[36]Report to the Congress, "Defense Budget: A Look at Budgetary Resources."

understanding of why there are so many "add-ons" or "enhance-ments"—keeping up with opponents, technological advances, discover-ies of weakness along the production path, self-protection by managers, criticism from Congress, etc.—we will not get to the root of the matter.

It is easy to find examples of waste and abuse in any large program. In the Defense Department, which signs 52,000 contract actions every working day, even if a 99.9 percent purity in contract actions were achieved, 15,000 actions would still be defective.[37] It is difficult to argue that defense spending cannot be made more efficient. But in military spending, as well as in social programs, the price of achieving a worth-while objective is often to fund some unworthy items. As we have seen in the discussion of the food stamp program, what is important to decide is where the line will be drawn between waste and getting things done.

DEFENSE VERSUS DOMESTIC BUDGETING

Before delving deeper into the intricacies of funding for the armed forces, it will be informative to compare defense budgeting with its domestic counterparts. Since pejorative comparisons are often made as if one or the other were not getting its due, we need to know more about how domestic relates to defense budgeting.

The defense budget has a highly symbolic value. The amount of spending for defense is believed by some observers to be an indicator to foreign countries, and to the home front, of American resolve to assert our national interests.[38] What the money is spent for, in this regard, is less important than how much is being spent: If budget levels are thought to affect the behavior of potential foreign threats, budget totals then become an instrument of foreign policy.

Defense differs from domestic budgeting in other crucial ways. One I have already described: The defense budget process does not begin with a ceiling (as it did in Truman and Eisenhower's time), but rather

[37]Report of the Secretary of Defense Caspar W. Weinberger to the Congress, Fiscal Year 1987, February 5, 1986.
[38]Kanter, *Defense Politics*, p. 5.

with estimates of all the military might that would be necessary to defend against the worst imaginable threat. This "no resource limit" approach began in the early 1960s under former Secretary of Defense Robert McNamara and President John F. Kennedy, on the grounds that whatever was required should be provided. The result of trying planning without budgeting, that is, without resource constraints, is that important decisions get put off until the last possible minute because every participant wants to know what the real restraints are like. While it is true that fiscal pressures do affect spending on defense, these constraints come close to the end, not the beginning of the process.

A second difference is that defense, which represents a little over one-quarter of the budget, makes up over half of the "relatively controllable" expenditures in the federal budget. But this is a gross comparison, based only on the proportion of funds passing through the annual appropriations process; it would be seriously misleading if it were used to suggest that all or most of defense spending is up for grabs at any one time. Just as the high proportion of goods and services in the defense bill guarantee, as Representative Jim Courter of the House Armed Services Committee observed, that "it's going to attract a lot of flies," the fact is that the bill also contains something like 70 percent of controllable outlays. Committee member Patricia Schroeder of Colorado pointed out that " 'If you want anything for your district, you're not going to get it in housing or any other place.' The Balanced Budget Act 'and the deficits have knocked that out, [and so] the only place there is any money at all is the Armed Services Committee bill.' "[39]

Since the defense budget is considered "must legislation" and usually "veto proof," the temptation to attach unrelated legislation (called "riders") has grown as well. Moreover, as numbers of congressional players in defense rise—there is now a bipartisan Military Reform Caucus with over a hundred of its 133 members unrelated to a defense-oversight committee—it has become more difficult to tell what is, or is not, germane to national defense. The great increase in legislative staff

[39]David C. Morrison, "Chaos on Capital Hill," *National Journal*, September 27, 1986, p. 2305.

is helping to make this interest more than cursory. "The downside," Gordon Adams, director of the Defense Budget Project in Washington added, "is that you do get this phenomenon of everybody looking for their issues and having the staff to exploit it: a combination of micro-management and flagwaving."[40]

A third and substantial difference between defense and domestic budgeting is procedural: Owing its origins to Robert McNamara, who presumably knew what the defense budget ought to be, the OMB does not play the same adversarial role as it does in regard to domestic programs. Leaving out entitlements, which do not go through the appropriations process at all, federal agencies usually submit their requests to OMB in September. In recent years, these requests have been preceded by OMB "guidance," telling the agencies how much they might expect will be cut or how high they can go. The director's review panel at OMB makes its recommendation to the president and domestic agencies can appeal to him for a restoration of funds. Not so in defense.

Instead of providing an independent review, OMB works as part of a DOD team to come up with a joint recommendation to the president. Under presidents Kennedy and Johnson, it became a matter of tradition that the budget director would have to appeal budgetary decisions of the Secretary of Defense to the president—a direct reversal of the relationship between the other department heads and the budget director. Budget Director David Stockman tried to restore the traditional relationship—the onus is on agencies to carry appeals—but President Reagan supported his Secretary of Defense.[41] OMB scorekeepers on appropriations action send a letter detailing objections to each act on a domestic bill in subcommittee vote, full committee, etc. But on defense, one reported, "We just say 'it's too little; the Pentagon will send the details later.' " The OMB role became even weaker under the Reagan presidency—staff left because their role was short-circuited. It may be that growing congressional cuts and criticism of defense programs are rooted in part in OMB's abandonment of its adversary position.

---

[40]*Ibid.*, p. 2305.
[41]David Stockman, *The Triumph of Politics* (New York: Harper & Row, 1986).

There are also alleged differences between the domestic and defense budgets that are widely believed but are contrary to fact. Numerous opinion polls reveal that large proportions of people believe that defense is as large as or larger than domestic spending and that nuclear weapons take the lion's share of the defense budget.[42] Not so. In order to present the truth to the incredulous, I will present different aspects of the same domestic/defense relationships. Outlays refer to total federal spending. "Human resources" is a traditional classification (see Table 9-2) for getting at social welfare spending. By using these classifications, we can see how defense and welfare have fared from 1950 to the present. The trend is clear: After stabilizing at around half of total spending in the late 1950s, defense expenditure declined proportionately (but not absolutely) to a bit more than one-quarter in the mid-1980s. In the same time period, human resources rose from a little over a quarter to half—as neat a reversal as one could find. Viewed as a proportion of gross national product (GNP), human resources doubled from around 5 percent in the late 1950s to over 10 percent today. Defense had declined by half from the late 1950s to the late 1970s (10 percent to 5 percent) but picked up to over 6 percent of GNP as a result of the big push begun by President Carter in 1980 and accelerated by the Reagan administration.

From a time when conventional forces were small compared to nuclear, in 1961, general (i.e., nonnuclear) military expenditure has risen today to over 80 percent of the total. (See Table 9-3.) Even if large cuts

---

[42]The President's Blue Ribbon Commission on Defense Management found that:

> Americans considerably overestimate the amount of money that the U.S. spends on the military. On the average, Americans believe that 46 percent of the total federal budget goes to military spending. Since 1986 outlays include only 27 percent for the military (32% of the total if Social Security is not included), Americans believe *almost twice as much* is spent on the military as actually is. Only 7 percent of all Americans correctly apportion 25 percent to 29 percent of the federal budget to the military. Eleven percent . . . admit they *don't know* what proportion of the federal budget is spent on the military.
>
> Women think more is spent on the military (49% of the federal budget) than do men (43%). Blacks have the highest average estimate of defense spending (53% of the federal budget), and people in the high income group have the lowest estimate (42%). However, all groups significantly overestimate the proportion spent for defense (June 1986, p. 197).

TABLE 9-2

National Defense and Human Resources as a Percentage of Federal Outlays
and Gross National Product (GNP) and National Defense Outlays as a
Percentage of Human Resource Outlays, 1950–1986

| | *Percent of Outlays* | | *Percent of GNP* | | |
Year	Defense	Human Resources[a]	Defense	Human Resources	Defense Resources
1950	32.2	33.4	5.1	5.3	.96
1951	51.8	24.2	7.5	3.5	2.14
1952	68.1	17.4	13.5	3.4	3.97
1953	69.4	15.6	14.5	3.2	4.53
1954	69.5	18.5	13.3	3.5	3.80
1955	62.4	21.8	11.0	3.8	2.89
1956	60.2	22.7	10.2	3.8	2.68
1957	59.3	23.7	10.3	4.1	2.51
1958	56.8	27.0	10.4	5.0	2.08
1959	53.2	27.0	10.2	5.2	1.96
1960	52.2	28.4	9.5	5.2	1.83
1961	50.8	30.5	9.6	5.7	1.68
1962	49.0	29.6	9.4	5.7	1.65
1963	48.6	30.1	9.1	5.7	1.60
1964	46.2	29.8	8.7	5.6	1.55
1965	42.8	30.9	7.5	5.4	1.39
1966	43.2	32.2	7.8	5.8	1.34
1967	45.4	33.0	9.0	6.5	1.38
1968	46.0	33.3	9.6	7.0	1.37
1969	44.9	35.8	8.9	7.1	1.25
1970	41.8	38.5	8.2	7.6	1.08
1971	37.5	43.7	7.5	8.7	.86
1972	34.3	46.5	6.9	9.3	.74
1973	31.2	46.5	9.3	9.3	.65

TABLE 9-2
(continued)

1974	29.5	50.4	5.6	9.6	.58
1975	26.0	52.1	5.7	11.4	.50
1976	24.1	54.2	5.3	12.0	.44
1977[b]	23.2	54.2	5.0	11.5	.43
1978	23.8	52.8	5.0	11.1	.45
1979	22.8	53.1	4.8	10.9	.44
1980	23.1	53.0	4.7	11.7	.40
1981	23.2	53.4	5.3	12.1	.44
1982	24.9	52.1	5.9	12.1	.48
1983	26.0	52.7	6.3	12.8	.49
1984	26.7	50.7	6.2	11.7	.53
1985	26.7	49.9	6.4	12.0	.53
1986	27.1	49.0	6.3	11.4	.55

[a]Human resources includes money spent on education, training, employment and social services, health, medicare, income security programs (off and on budget), and veterans benefits and services.
[b]Does not include transition quarter
Sources: Executive Office of the President Office of Management and Budget, *Historical Tables, Budget of the United States Government Fiscal Year 1987* (Washington, D.C.: Government Printing Office, 1986), pp. 3.1(2)–(6).

were made in spending on nuclear weapons, therefore, only modest changes in overall defense expenditure would result.

A lot of defense money (see Table 9-1) goes into the care and feeding of personnel. Defense is a people-oriented activity. It follows ineluctably, therefore, that major reductions in the defense budget would have to come from reducing the size of the armed forces and its conventional equipment. And in order to do that (see Table 9-4), it is necessary to decide what program accompanying which missions (say, airlift and sealift for the conventional defense of central Europe or the Persian Gulf) should be eliminated or curtailed. Relating commitments to re-

TABLE 9-3

Allocation between Nuclear and Conventional Forces and
Percentage of Nuclear Forces to General Forces, Selected
Fiscal Years (figures in billions of 1986 dollars)

| Year | Total Obligational Authority | | Percent |
	Nuclear	General	
1948	9.4	38.2	25
1952	60.4	151.1	40
1956	46.5	80.9	57
1961	53.2	77.1	69
1971	20.6	82.8	25
1979	13.0	87.7	15
1981	15.3	102.8	15
1985	27.8	143.3	19

Source: 1948–1981 data from Kaufmann, *A Reasonable Defense*,
Table 3-3, p. 21. 1985 data calculated from Kaufmann, Table 2-4, p. 13.
Percentages are author's calculations.

sources remains the crucial problem of budgeting, whether for defense
or for anything else.

Displayed in a different way (see Figures 9-2 and 9-3 on p. 388), we
see a relationship that might otherwise have eluded us: Starting soon
after the Second World War, domestic spending (essentially human
resources, especially entitlements) soared upward, pausing slightly but
never turning back. Defense spending, by contrast, is more a matter of
peaks and valleys, going upward in real dollars by fits and starts, but
declining as a proportion of total spending.

There is one area in which everyone knows that defense differs from
domestic spending: Secret activities appear (or don't appear) in the
budget process either as generally appropriated funds with undisclosed
purposes (confidential funds) or as completely covert funds where everything, including the appropriations, is kept secret (secret funds). Sometimes the activities funded by secret or confidential funds are called

TABLE 9-4

The Fiscal 1986 Defense Budget by Major Mission[a]

(billions of dollars)

Mission	Budget Authority[b]
Strategic nuclear retaliation	51.5
Theater nuclear retaliation	3.2
Conventional defense of:	
Central Europe	80.2
North Norway	17.2
Greece and Turkey	9.8
Atlantic and Caribbean[c]	25.8
Persian Gulf states	20.9
Republic of Korea	12.9
Pacific and Indian oceans	21.7
Continental United States, Alaska, and Panama[c]	16.2
Intelligence and communications	36.5
Subtotal	295.9
Retired pay accrual	17.8
Total budget authority	313.7

[a]The missions and their costs reflect the main contingencies for which the United States plans and the forces associated with those planning contingencies. Reality and the planning contingencies may never coincide.

[b]Totals include indirect as well as direct costs of the forces. Consequently, they are higher than the totals shown in the program budget.

[c]These totals are so high because they include the costs of forces unable to deploy overseas in a timely fashion or undergoing maintenance and training.

Source: *Budget of the United States Government, Fiscal Year 1986,* pp. 5–6, and Kaufmann's estimates in *A Reasonable Defense,* p. 14.

"black programs." Secret funds have been with us since the early days of our republic.[43] In 1811 Congress secretly provided President Madison with $100,000 to take temporary possession of some territory south

[43]Louis Fisher, *Constitutional Conflicts between Congress and the President* (Princeton: Princeton University Press, 1985), pp. 244–47.

FIGURE 9-2

Defense Budget as a Percentage of Federal Outlays and Percentage of GNP.

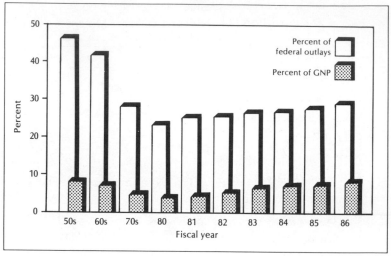

FIGURE 9-3

Defense Budget in Comparison to Total Federal Outlays (in 1986 dollars).

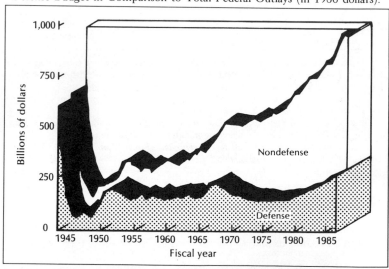

Source: In *Defense,* U.S. Government Printing Office (April 1985), p. 22.

of Georgia out of fear that the land would pass from Spain to another foreign power. During World War II, $1.6 billion was secretly provided to fund the development of the atomic bomb.[44]

Billions of secret funds are expended on weapons systems. While there is little doubt among legislators that "black" budget programs are necessary for national security, Congress has become increasingly concerned with the significant rise of such requests from an estimated $5.5 billion in fiscal 1981 to $24.3 billion in the fiscal 1988 request.[45] What concerns Congress is that the Defense Department has a tendency, according to the House Armed Services Committee's ranking Republican, William Dickinson (R-Ala.), "to put things into the black unnecessarily or to prolong them in the black world unnecessarily, probably because it is easiest to do work without somebody looking over your shoulder."[46] Because "black" budget items go through much less review, having to deal only with the defense oversight committees, there is a suspicion that the "black" budget may be getting an easy ride.

It is estimated that the Central Intelligence Agency's (CIA) piece of the "black" budget is $1.5 billion.[47] The Central Intelligence Act of 1949 provided that funds for the CIA "may be expended without regard to the provisions of law and regulations relating to the expenditure of Government funds. . . ."[48] Rather than Congress directly appropriating funds to the CIA, the agency was authorized to transfer funds to and receive funds from other agencies to perform functions authorized by the National Security Act of 1947. Intelligence funds, estimated in 1971 to be $6 billion per year, are initially appropriated to the Defense Department and then transferred (with the approval of the OMB) to the CIA.[49]

Acknowledging the occasional need for secrecy, annual appropriations acts for defense, following the provisions of 10, United States Code 140,

---

[44]Louis Fisher, *Presidential Spending Power* (Princeton: Princeton University Press, 1975), p. 214.
[45]David Morrison, *National Journal*, April 1, 1987, p. 867.
[46]*Ibid.*
[47]*Ibid.*, p. 871.
[48]Fisher, *Presidential Spending Power*, p. 214.
[49]*Ibid.*, pp. 214–15.

give authority to the services to use their operations and maintenance money for Emergency and Extraordinary (E&E) expenses. These come in two categories: One for extending official courtesies to guests of the United States (hardly an emergency), and the other "when the use of normal funding channels would compromise the security of operations, jeopardize the safety of personnel and sources involved, or result in losing an investigative or intelligence opportunity."[50] The amounts are tiny, coming to about $25 million a year.[51] Their importance is that, subject to DOD regulation, they can be used for any purpose the Secretary of Defense or the service secretaries deem proper. Thus official representation funds cannot be used for personal items and a certain ratio of authorized guests to defense personnel must be maintained. Of the total of $601,465 of such expenditures for 1983 and 1984 reviewed by GAO, 81 percent were within the guidelines and 19 percent were not. A small sample of deviant items include stag dinners for the Brigadier General Selection Board, a hospitality tent at the Army–Navy game, and a tie for an official who won an award.[52] The fault there probably lies in undue parsimony in providing for modest entertainment expenses.[53]

Of far greater interest is the question of whether E&E funds may be used to violate the law. Executive Order 12333 on United States Intelligence Activity asserts that the collection of information must be in accord with the Constitution and must not involve assassinations and unauthorized electronic eavesdropping. Otherwise, the field of legality–illegality is muddy. A GAO report states that

> We asked Defense officials whether E&E funds could be used in violation of law and found that their views varied. An OSD general counsel official would not say whether the funds could be used illegally, but told us that

[50]U.S. General Accounting Office, "Internal Controls: Defense's Use of Emergency and Extraordinary Funds," Report to the Chairman Legislation and National Security Subcommittee, Committee on Government Operations, House of Representatives, GAO/AFMD-86-44, June 1986, p. 2.

[51]*Ibid.* "E&E expenses in fiscal years 1984 and 1985 were about $24 million and $25 million respectively. In both fiscal years, approximately 86 percent of the E&E expenses were for confidential purposes."

[52]*Ibid.*, pp. 1–7.

[53]See GAO, *Review of Unvouchered Expenditures at the Department of State,* AFMD 82-57, March 23, 1982, for emergency spending not due to emergencies.

the purpose of the emergency and extraordinary authority was to make funds available for uses which would otherwise be unauthorized. An Army general counsel official advised us that he interpreted the OSD view to be that the funds could be used for any purpose unless specifically prohibited by statute. The official explained that if a statute does not specifically state that E&E funds cannot be used, then these funds could be used in contravention of that statute.[54]

Presumably, then, diverting funds from one purpose to another might be legal unless specifically prohibited in the authorizing statute. Should anyone get the idea that DOD can do anything it wants with appropriations, however, a brief study of internal reprogramming of funds should suggest otherwise.

REPROGRAMMING: DEFENSE VERSUS DOMESTIC

The stringency of congressional control is undoubtedly an indicator of distrust. Congress simultaneously wants defense to be done well and worries that appropriations may be excessive. Because defense is by far the largest purchaser of goods and services, Congress is also concerned with defense as a continuation of constituency policy. Where military bases are located, what DOD buys from whom, according to which criteria, subjects defense to all sorts of social, economic, and ultimately political judgments. Now that most domestic spending is in the form of payments to individuals (entitlements), the defense budget becomes a candidate for the "new pork barrel." Of course it is more than that—the debate over defense spending is still largely concerned with national security—but a lot of money still remains to aid localities, and many other worthies.

"Reprogramming," to use the GAO definition, "is the use of funds for purposes other than those originally contemplated at the time of appropriation."[55] In the five years from 1981 to 1986, requests to use defense funds already appropriated for other purposes came to some $29

---

[54]GAO, "Internal Controls," p. 4.

[55]CAO, "Budget Reprogramming: Department of Defense Process for Reprogramming Funds." Briefing Report to the Honorable David Pryor, United States Senate, GAO/NSIAD-86-164BR, July 1986, p. 1.

billion or 2.7 percent of the total. A small proportion of a huge amount can still be pretty big.

Reprogramming is not the same as the *transfer* of funds. Transfers move money from one appropriations account to another; reprogramming moves money from one item to another within the same account. Transfers can be undertaken only with specific formal authority while reprogramming is based on informal understandings. Taking money from maintenance to give to personnel, for instance, is a transfer, while providing more money for certain items and less for others within the maintenance account constitutes reprogramming.

Always there are exceptions. When defense appropriations accounts are very large and very controversial, and when Congress has created statutory subdivisions—as with army missile procurement and navy shipbuilding and conversion—the rules for transfer apply. And while reprogramming ordinarily takes place at the request of the military services, Congress may decide to fund certain items by directing that they be taken from others, such as a pay raise subtracted from air force procurement. This tactic leaves the military unhappy[56] but not as unhappy as if they had to determine where what are called "undistributed adjustments" will come from. For if Congress says to find the money within the defense budget but does not specify where, the services may have to struggle over whose hide it will come from.[57]

There are four types of reprogramming. Congressional Prior Approval Reprogramming occurs when it is known that the legislature is especially interested, when the DOD uses its general transfer authority (you can do it, apparently, but you have to ask), and when there is increased procurement for an item already approved. When the agreed-upon dollar amounts in the appropriation law are exceeded, or new programs or items are undertaken that would lead to continuing costs, congressional Notification Reprogrammings are supposed to take place. Both Prior Approval and Notification Reprogramming require approval by the Secretary or Assistant Secretary of Defense. Internal Reprogramming,

[56]*Ibid.*, pp. 6–7.
[57]*Ibid.*, p. 6.

which has to be approved by the DOD comptroller, involves accounting changes that reclassify dollar amounts between and within appropriations accounts. The purpose is to leave an audit trail so Congress can see what went where. Finally, Below-Threshold Reprogramming, as its name implies, does not require prior approval but can be handled within a service. Nevertheless, a semiannual report of cumulative changes in line-items goes to Congress so it can maintain its oversight responsibilities. In case of doubt, say a new program begun by a small amount, Congress expects advance notification by mail.

How large is large enough to require that Congress be notified? It depends (see Table 9-5).

The objectives of reprogramming are to prevent DOD from undertaking new programs or items under the guise of old activities, while

TABLE 9-5

Criteria for Notification by Appropriation Account[58]

Appropriation Account	*Criteria*
Military Personnel	Increases a budget activity by $10 million or more
Operation & Maintenance	Increases a budget activity by $5 million or more
Procurement	Increases an existing line item by $10 million or more
	Adds a line item of $2 million or more
Research, Development, Test and Evaluation	Increases an existing program element in an account by $4 million or more
	Adds a new program of $2 million or more
	Adds a new program estimated to cost $10 million or more within a 3-year period

[58]*Ibid.*, p. 10.

permitting flexibility where merited. Four congressional committees—the House and Senate appropriations subcommittees on defense and the Armed Services committees (secret matters bring in the two intelligence committees)—decide what is merited. Since all this oversight is carried on without a statutory basis, reprogramming requirements are not legally binding, but are rather, as GAO says, a matter of "keeping faith."[59] Since all four committees must approve requests for Prior Approval, any one can turn it down. The result is negotiation and differentiation. The Subcommittee on Defense of the Senate Appropriations Committee turns Notification Reprogrammings into Prior Approval Reprogrammings by demanding that it give approval. In 1985, 92 congressmen (57 House and 35 Senate), nearly a fifth of the members, were involved in reviewing requests for reprogramming.

Reprogramming reviews are carried out a bit differently by the various committees. Upon receipt of a request for reprogramming, the staff of the Senate Armed Services Committee sends copies to the legislative assistants of all members and to the professional staff members. All professional staff must sign off. If, in ten days, no objection is received, a favorable response for submission to DOD is prepared. This draft response is then circulated to the committee general counsel and the party majority and minority staff directors for approval. A single senatorial objection is sufficient to deny reprogramming, though this could be overridden by a vote of the full committee. No such vote has yet been held.

The staff of the Senate Appropriations Subcommittee reviews the requests, shows them to the chairman and ranking minority members and anyone else especially interested, and prepares a letter containing a decision. The staff may request a subcommittee vote in five to seven days. Though formal hearings are not usually held, reprogramming may be discussed at other hearings or at sessions where appropriations bills are being marked up prior to decision. Whether or not Congress is in session, the committee expects DOD to wait for a response letter before proceeding with reprogramming.

In the House Committee on Armed Services, Prior Approval Repro-

[59]*Ibid.*, p. 19.

gramming is given a full-dress discussion during regular business meetings. Notifications of reprogramming are sent only to staff who take up objections with the chair. A letter of objection stops the reprogramming.

Following its receipt of reprogramming request forms, the Subcommittee on Defense of the House Appropriations Committee holds hearings at which the comptrollers of the services testify. Committee action is taken at markup sessions. The subcommittee is especially interested in anything it sees as new; it responds by phone or letter and has procedures for expediting decisions. Even internal reprogramming may be brought up if the staff or a member wishes to intervene.

The major differences between defense and civilian reprogramming procedures is that Congress watches the military more closely, as GAO concludes from a study of several domestic agencies.

> DOD waits for a written affirmative response before proceeding with certain reprogramming actions. At the civilian agencies, the general concept is that if no response is received, it means approval is granted. One agency official said that his agency can proceed with a reprogramming action even if objections are made. He said that the normal response from the congressional committee, though, is "Thank you for keeping us informed."[60]

These civilian agencies write simple letters describing their proposed action and keep no statistics on their cumulative effect. It appears that each agency has worked out a somewhat different agreement with its appropriations subcommittees concerning the amounts that trigger a reprogramming request, the degree of latitude involved, and whether approval must be in written form. In the Department of Housing and Urban Development, for instance, the trigger amount is 10 percent of a program or $250,000. Since HUD officials feel that its detailed budget justification is "a type of contract between the agency and the Congress . . . all significant changes are reported."[61]

OMB, as in almost all budgetary matters, is involved in establishing the criteria for reprogramming and in approval of transfers. Most matters are routine, but, if dissatisfied, OMB can hold up a request.

With all these fingers in the budget pie, the question has naturally

[60]*Ibid.*, p. 24.
[61]*Ibid.*, p. 26.

arisen as to whether the reprogramming process might be a wee bit too cumbersome. If managers in business were thought to require such close supervision, they would more likely be fired.[62] The unique aura of the governmental milieu comes across as committee staff uniformly respond that "cumbersome is desirable" because it assures that only high priority requests will be brought up.

The point of giving the reader such a heavy dose of procedure is that practices like these fill the lives of agency and congressional budgeters, who live, perforce, in each other's pockets. Trust is essential, for without it the wheels would turn ever so slowly. Should it happen that differences over policy were translated into distrust of motives, budgeting in defense would be like walking through tar.

DISSENSUS ON DEFENSE

Whether one listens to advocates of higher or lower spending, they all agree that the defense effort should be apportioned to estimates of the perceived threat from abroad. While there is some agreement—it is a dangerous world and the Soviet Union's armament does have to be countered—there is considerable disagreement over how much and exactly what the United States ought to do. The best argument in favor of spending on national defense remains the straightforward one: The nation will better be able to defend itself. Unfortunately, without being able to try different types and amounts of defense, we cannot know whether more or less or different would have been better.

There are different approaches that an administration can take toward defense spending. It may believe that continued levels of defense expenditures are no longer necessary, as after the Persian Gulf War, and seek a cut in defense on its own. Or the administration may attempt to work out a long-term agreement with Congress, as the Bush administration has done, that would provide steady funding and allow for long-range planning. The reality of defense funding, as we have seen, is

[62]So experience on the boards of three companies, including two audit committees, tells me.

typified by peaks and valleys. Operating in this feast or famine environment, the Reagan administration sought to get as much as it could as fast as it could for as long as it could. Defense Secretary Caspar Weinberger noted, "When we began our program in 1981, we sought to avoid the future inefficiencies and high costs that are caused by the 'surge and starve' approach to defense funding." Even when it became apparent that the rapid buildup would not continue, few attempts were made to relate future plans to cost realities. Lawrence Korb, assistant defense secretary for Manpower, Installations and Logistics from 1981–1985, complained that every time anyone suggested preparing for sparser times, "it was said, 'we can't do that because it will become a self-fulfilling prophecy.' All of the effort then went into trying to get these marginal increases."[63] Asking for a lot more does have its advantages; those who do not ask usually do not receive.

No one can say that filling the pipeline with projects left defense worse off than it otherwise might have been. Since World War II, the longest period of real annual increases for defense was three years. President Reagan entered office with two years of real military growth created by the Carter administration. Reagan was able to extend that increase for four more years (a total of six consecutive years). Now it is believed by many members of Congress that the Pentagon, in the words of Vic Fazio (D-Calif.), chairman of the House Budget Committee's defense and international affairs task force, will "attempt to get as many things crammed into the budget as possible and to lock future Congresses, administrations and budget directors into the priorities this Administration is advocating."[64] DOD does this for many reasons, as we have seen, including the fact that there is no mechanism for making restraint pay in the form of a steady stream of future appropriations. But this time President Bush and Secretary of Defense Cheney decided to anticipate cuts while locking the remaining funds for five years into the 1990 OBRA.

Combined with efforts to diminish domestic spending and lower taxes, however, the strategy of maximizing defense dollars both reflected

---

[63]David Morrison, *National Journal,* February 21, 1987, p. 412.
[64]*Ibid.,* p. 413.

and deepened the dissensus among public officials on public policy. Domestic policy became defense policy in that slimming the former became the way to fatten the latter. Defense policy became domestic policy in that more for defense became less for domestic, mostly welfare programs. As defense was divorced from whatever was intrinsic to it, more for defense came to be viewed as an inegalitarian taking from the worst-off elements in the population. As the parties polarized over issues of equality, defense spending became more partisan and more ideological and became part and parcel of broader issues in which human resources were pitted against military hardware.

Where had the nation been in defense spending? Between 1963 and 1969, the combination of a missile buildup and the Vietnam War led to a 23 percent (or $34.1 billion) increase in real purchasing power; between 1970 and 1979, due to a combination of the end of the war in Vietnam and concentration on welfare policy, defense spending declined by 25 percent (or $58 billion) in real terms. By 1983, after four years of substantial increases, the defense budget had risen by $62 billion since 1979.[65] The defense rollercoaster (see Table 9-6) was in full swing. What has been happening since then depends on how one wishes to interpret it.

The Reagan administration's view, as presented by Secretary of Defense Caspar Weinberger, was that what DOD expected in March 1981 (the Reagan revision of the Carter budget) was $148.7 billion short in promised budget authority in 1986.[66] Taken from 1986 onwards, it appears (see Table 9-6) that budget authority will barely keep up with price increases or will decline. Perhaps the best indicator is a headline in a budget newsletter—"Wall Street Warns Investors to Steer Clear of Defense Contractor Stocks."[67]

Symptomatic of rising dissensus is the inability of governmental actors

[65]Study by the Staff of the U.S. General Accounting Office, "Defense Spending and Its Relationship to the Federal Budget," GAO/PLRD-83-80, June 9, 1983, p. 5.

[66]Caspar W. Weinberger, Statement of the Secretary of Defense before the House Appropriations Defense Subcommittee, in Connection with the Fiscal Year 1986 Budget for the DOD, 2/27/85, p. 4.

[67]*Inside the Administration,* November 27, 1986, p. 12.

TABLE 9-6

Going Up, Coming Down[68] (in billions)

Fiscal Year	Current $	FY86 Constant $	Annual Real Change
1978	117	196	−1.5%
1979	126	195	−0.7
1980	144	199	1.8
1981	180	224	12.7
1982	217	252	12.6
1983	245	274	8.7
1984	265	287	4.8
1985	292	303	6.0
1986	284	284	−6.3
1987	284	272	−4.2

to agree on what constitutes a proper budgetary base. As Congress has made increasingly greater cuts in presidential requests, DOD has tried to choose the highest base from which to seek the president's standard request of 3 percent above inflation. Instead of choosing a low figure, usually what Congress actually provided the previous year, DOD has gone either for the prior year's presidential proposal or the amount in the resolution recommended by the Senate Budget Committee.

An example of controversy over the base will help illuminate what is at stake in this debate. The 1987 defense budget was originally built on an August 1985 resolution calling for no real increase for defense in fiscal 1986 (equaling $302.4 billion), followed by two years of 3 percent real growth. But, with the adoption of the Balanced Budget Act, the baseline for 1986 was reduced to $286.1 billion. On February 4, 1986, Secretary Weinberger continued to argue for a $320.3 billion 1987 budget, suggesting that this request represented a 3 percent real increase over the base (now $286.1 billion). The secretary brushed aside a difference over

[68]*National Journal,* January 11, 1986, p.93.

the defense budget baseline by saying "We're not talking about 'actual.' This budget is 3 per cent real growth over what would have been zero this year."[69] Needless to say, this selective choice of a base was hotly disputed. Over the years, the White House staff discovered that the political price of adopting a higher base than Congress would use or approve was to reduce the acceptability of the president's proposed budget as a starting point for discussing spending.

Except to say that their suspicion has now become reality, I could not do better on "atmospherics" than to quote a joint DOD–GAO study team:

> At the height of the controversy over the war in Vietnam and the debate over the War Powers Act, there appeared to be precious little trust and a great deal of suspicion among many on Capitol Hill. During World War II, on the other hand, there was precious little suspicion and a great deal of trust. Today, the balance appears to be fairly even between trust and suspicion, and, as a result, the balance between flexibility and control seems fairly even. However, some observers have begun to suspect an erosion in the level of trust.[70]

Micro-Management

The congressional politics of defense budgeting has changed, in the words of James Lindsay, from the "inside game" in the 1960s to the "outside game" in the 1980s. Defense deliberations in both the Armed Services Committees and the Defense Appropriations subcommittees were at one time dominated by senior congressional leaders. Representative Carl Vinson (D-Ga.) and his successor, Representative L. Mendel Rivers (D-S.C.), committee chairman of the House Armed Services

---

[69]David Morrison, "Old Pentagon Script," *National Journal*, February 8, 1986, pp. 320–21.

[70]Joint DOD–GAO Working Group on PPBS, "The Department of Defense's Planning, Programming, and Budgeting System," GAO/OACG-84-5, September 1983, pp. 70–71.

Committees through the 1960s, "ran the committees as their personal baronies."[71] The four standing committees had no formal jurisdiction; hearings and markups of the annual defense authorization bills were completed in full committee, which were controlled by Vinson and Rivers. While less autocratic than the chair of the House Armed Services Committee, Representative George Mahon (D-Tex.), chairman of the House Appropriations Defense subcommittee, dominated deliberations (along with the most senior members of the subcommittee). Similarly, in the Senate defense committees, "The norms of apprenticeship and deference to the committee chair were strong, and the chair possessed a wide range of formal powers to direct the committee's operations."[72]

In the 1970s Congress saw a rise in influence of junior members of the defense committees and subcommittees. This more dispersed power can be attributed to several reforms adopted in the 1970s, including the Subcommittee Bill of Rights, which provided subcommittees with formal jurisdictions, budgets, authorization to hold hearings, staff selected by the subcommittee chair, and which stripped committee chairmen of their power to make subcommittee assignments. While power was wielded less autocratically during the 1970s, influence remained primarily within the defense committees. In the early 1970s, there was a rise in floor activity precipitated largely by congressional dissatisfaction with the conduct of the Vietnam War. This heightened interest in defense issues was reflected in criticisms of defense programs (particularly the Anti-Ballistic Missile) and major weapons systems (especially the C-5 transport plane). With the end of the war, though, this interest tapered off.[73]

In the 1980s, the locus of defense discussion shifted from the committees to the much broader community of interested members. The rise of the House Democratic Caucus exemplifies the new influence of

[71]James M. Lindsay, "Congress and Defense Policy: 1961 to 1986," *Armed Forces & Society*, Vol. 13, No. 3 (Spring 1987), p. 377.
[72]*Ibid.*
[73]*Ibid.*, p. 381.

outsiders. In May 1983 the caucus was able to force the House Democratic leadership to oppose the production of the MX missile. In 1984 the caucus forced the House Armed Services Committee to accept dozens of delegates to the House–Senate conference on the defense authorization bill in addition to the regular House–Senate conferees. This action was prompted by a fear among the Democratic leadership that the regular conferees would be unable to defend controversial amendments added by the House. The caucus was also able to replace Melvin Price with Les Aspin as chair of the House Armed Services Committee. Aspin, who was the seventh-ranking Democrat on the committee, was selected over five more senior (and more conservative) Democrats.[74]

The caucus is not the only example of how the defense committees' powers have been circumscribed. Pressure to limit anti-satellite testing and the push to reform the defense procurement process (in response to stories on defense waste in spare parts acquisition) originated outside the defense committees. The defense committees have also found their recommendations challenged more frequently on the floor. Decreased success on the floor has, in turn, created a fear by committees that their legislation would be defeated unless crafted to anticipate the reactions of floor members.[75]

Rivalry (called "turf wars") between the Armed Services and Defense Appropriations Subcommittees, whose budget jurisdictions have become nearly equivalent, has reached pandemic proportions. As one observer noted, "The Defense Appropriations Subcommittees are doing more legislating; the Armed Services Committees are doing more 'budgeteering.' "[76] Whereas only 3 percent of the defense budget was subject to annual legislative authorization in 1947, today 70 percent of it is so treated.[77] Whether this expansion of authorization is due to

[74]*Ibid.*, p. 383.
[75]*Ibid.*, p. 387.
[76]Robert J. Art, "Congress and the Defense Budget: Enhancing Policy Overnight," *Political Science Quarterly*, Vol. 100, No. 2 (Summer 1985), pp. 227–48; quote on 228.
[77]Les Aspin, "Congress vs. Department of Defense," in Thomas M. Franck, *The Tethered Presidency* (New York: New York University Press, 1981), p. 251; Rovner, *Defense Dollars and Sense*, p. 28.

ideological differences (Armed Services has been more favorable to higher spending than Appropriations in the House), disputes over arms control and how much should be devoted to conventional readiness versus new weapons, distrust of each other and the executive, or patronage and district benefits, the consequence has been growing uncertainty.

The politization on defense issues is also evidenced in the proliferation of committees involved in defense. Ten Senate committees and 11 House committees have formal jurisdiction over one aspect or another of defense policy. And other committees without formal jurisdiction now hold hearings on particular defense matters.[78]

The three-tiered layers of consideration, from budget resolutions on totals to Armed Services on authorizations to Appropriations subcommittees on budget authority, each of which has to occur in sequence, leads to compounding delays. The extension of annual authorization resulted in closer scrutiny of the budget by the Armed Services Committees. This, in turn, required the Appropriations Subcommittees to examine a larger number of line items. The reaction by Congress against the "imperial presidency" and against Vietnam in the 1970s caused Congress to even more closely scrutinize the defense budget. And the expansion of congressional staff provided the committees with the capability to examine the budget in detail. As more members have become involved in decisions on a politically volatile defense budget, budgeting delays have compounded.

Indicative of this increased scrutiny, the total number of pages in Appropriation Committees' reports on the defense budget has increased from 138 in 1968 to 593 in 1984. The Armed Services Committees' reports increased from 80 pages in 1968 to 858 in 1984.[79] The length of the annual reports issued by both Armed Services committees and Defense Appropriations subcommittees rose from an average of 231 pages between 1961 and 1969 to 829 pages in the 1970s and then to 1,186 pages between 1980 and 1985.[80] Where in 1962 the Senate and House Armed Services Committees held 17 hearings that produced

---

[78]Lindsay, "Congress and Defense Policy," p. 389.
[79]In Rovner, *Defense Dollars and Sense.*
[80]Lindsay, "Congress and Defense Policy," p. 373.

1,400 pages of testimony, in 1985 the separate hearings rose to 80 and the testimony amounted to 11,246 pages. The GAO reports that from 1982 to 1986, 1,420 hours were spent by 1,306 DOD witnesses at hearings before 84 committees and subcommittees.[81]

Because of the rise in committee activity and floor debate, Congress has become increasingly involved in revising defense budget details. In 1969 Congress made 180 changes to the defense authorization bill and 650 revisions to the appropriations bill. These numbers increased to 222 and 1,032, respectively, in 1975 and skyrocketed by 1985 to 1,145 authorization adjustments and 2,156 appropriations adjustments.[82] Out of 2,600 line-items in procurement for weapons and munitions alone in 1986, for example, the Armed Services Committees made 1,000 changes in authorizations.

The result has been a defense budget that has been passed on time for the fiscal year only three times in the past 15 years. On average, defense bills have been 80 days late after the start of the fiscal year.[83] The Appropriations subcommittees recommend funds for programs never authorized and the Armed Services committees make funding changes at the line-item level.[84] With fiscal 1987 half over, disagreements between the committees left $6 billion in expenditures in limbo. There are so many changes in toto—over 1,800 in 1985 alone, together with 458 required studies—that it is difficult for defense officials to know where they are.[85] "If I am going to be responsible to make certain that I have done a good job in trying to prioritize defense systems," Donald A. Hicks, then Defense undersecretary for research and engineering, admonished the Senate Appropriations Subcommittee on Defense in 1985, "I can hardly be held responsible if in one-third of my programs I am told by Congress what to do, not to kill a program or to add this or subtract that."[86]

[81]Morrison, "Chaos on Capital Hill," p. 2302.
[82]Lindsay, "Congress and Defense Policy," p. 373.
[83]Morrison, "Chaos on Capital Hill," p. 2303.
[84]*Ibid.*, pp. 2303–2306.
[85]Report to the President by the President's Blue Ribbon Commission on Defense Management, "National Security Planning and Budgeting," June 1986, pp. 15–16.
[86]Morrison, "Chaos on Capital Hill," p. 2303.

There are numerous instances of projects being forced on DOD in order to maintain local employment. Unlike the 1960s, when it could only be acquired by cultivating support of committee members (a lengthy and uncertain process), "pork" has now been democratized. The barrel has been placed out in the street. Now everyone, junior committee members as well as other legislators, has a chance to use defense to benefit their constituents. As the New York State delegation fought to maintain funds for the T-46 jet trainer, which the air force wanted to cancel because of poor performance, for instance, the ranking Republican on the House Armed Services Committee, William M. Dickinson of Alabama, told his colleagues off: "Many of the very people who voted to cut the defense budget Friday led the fight to stuff the T-46 into the budget Monday. The T-46 is a $3 billion program of airborne pork . . . a program that wasn't even included in the $320 billion budget request these same people call bloated."[87] Most members agree with Representative Jim Courter of New Jersey: "We can't reform the Pentagon until we've reformed ourselves."[88] Both sides play this game: The navy pushed two new carriers in 1987 with district-by-district job breakdowns.

Comments by Frank Carlucci, a veteran government administrator, former President Reagan's National Security adviser, who had been in command of DOD, but at the time was a business executive, express common frustration with the instability of the defense budget. He objects to congressmen who call for economy and then prevent DOD from opening the M-1 tank engine to competition and require it to ship expensive American coal to Germany. He is unhappy about Congress telling DOD the prices it can charge in the Secretary's mess or whether officers' clubs should use margarine or butter. Mindful of stories on the subject, Carlucci provided a relevant colloquy:

> Not long ago I was riding with the chief financial officer of a major company. "Can't we do something about waste in defense?" he asked. I said, "Mike imagine that it took four years to produce your product. Then let's say I give you a budget at six month intervals, that is to say, a six month

[87]*Ibid.*, p. 2305.
[88]*Ibid.*, p. 2302.

budget punctuated by six month intervals of no budget, at the end of which 50 percent of the budget items are changed. How well would your company run?" "It wouldn't," he responded.[89]

The complaint of the Packard Commission was that late in the calendar year, as DOD is trying to firm up its budget proposal for the coming year, the previous year's budget is still being debated. Whenever Congress acts on the past year, DOD, at the last minute, has to revamp its submission for the coming year.[90] ". . . Unfailingly," Carlucci reports from personal experience, despite the joint DOD–OMB review, "after you have put the budget together, OMB will make a run on Christmas Day [the ghost of Stockman past?], and then you have to redo it overnight." Can this be true? Carlucci claims that there are as many as 900 late line-item changes. "As late as December, based on issues raised by the OMB review," the Packard Commission revealed, "the President has directed changes to the Secretary's budget plan that have affected thousands of line items and that have required major revisions to the Five-Year Defense Program." Obviously, DOD does not have much time to calculate the consequences of these changes or to appeal for reconsideration (a "reclama") by the president. Since DOD, like other departments operating under OMB's quarterly apportionment rules, is not allowed to spend more than 20 percent of its funds in the last quarter, it has to do a lot of guessing on its huge (say, $90 billion) procurement budget. Afterwards, DOD has to go back to Congress if it wishes to reprogram its funds.[91] While the executive branch is changing the defense budget as it is being made, Congress, for added emphasis, is doing the same.

If, as Senator Stevens of Alaska said, "You're dealing with a govern-

[89]Frank C. Carlucci, "Management in Government," text of a talk, December 6, 1985, George Washington University, School of Government and Business Administration Alumni Breakfast Meeting, Washington, D.C., p. 8.

[90]President's Blue Ribbon Commission, "National Security Planning and Budgeting," p. 16.

[91]Frank Carlucci, "A Private Sector and National Perspective," The State of American Public Service, Occasional Papers, National Academy of Public Administration, sixth in a series of reports on American government, p. 7.

ment that's run by continuing resolution"[92] (resolutions to provide funding in the absence of regular appropriations measures), the political context of CRs is bound to affect a department whose budget passes through the appropriations process. CRs are used to pressure the president or other legislators into giving in on a matter in dispute. Thus CRs are often written for irregular periods, which may fit the rhythm of legislative bargaining but create additional uncertainty for administrators. Without a definite accounting period, DOD has to operate under the prior year's funding.[93] "The timing and scope of these changes," the Packard Commission concluded, "prevent the DOD from making coherent linkages among the three defense budgets that it manages at any one time—the budget being executed, the budget under review by the Congress, and the budget that DOD is developing for the upcoming fiscal year."[94]

Unfortunately, the close attention Congress pays to the military budget does not translate into discussions of the overall direction of military spending, a task that arguably would be a more fruitful use of congressional resources. Senator William Roth, commenting on congressional micro-management, points out that "Congress has become mesmerized with the budget process to the detriment of other responsibilities and considerations. It spends so much time on budget matters that we really fail to adequately provide the kind of oversight that I think is necessary. We have failed to have the kind of debates that are essential on national issues such as foreign policy and defense."[95]

While congressmen wish to influence the defense budget, they often do not want to take responsibility for specific decisions terminating programs. According to Representative Les Aspin, chair of the House Armed Services Committee, "Congress almost never cuts a major weapons procurement request from the Administration's defense budget. It

---

[92]Morrison, "Chaos on Capital Hill," p. 2302.
[93]Joint DOD–GAO Working Group on PPBS, p. 84.
[94]President's Blue Ribbon Commission, "National Security Planning and Budgeting," p. 16.
[95]Art, "Congress and the Defense Budget," p. 235.

usually approves those systems requested though not always the amount sought."[96] What accounts for the practice of stretching out procurement when everyone pays lip service to its undesirability?

Stretch-Outs

One reason for this practice of partial funding (and the corresponding unwillingness to eliminate a defense program) stems from the development of entrenched interests. Large defense contractors gather congressional support for purchasing their products by distributing production facilities and subcontracts over a wide geographic area, thereby maximizing the number of representatives having constituents with a direct economic interest in securing a contract for a weapons system. North American Rockwell has exercised this strategy close to the absolute limit in producing the controversial B-1 bomber. Parts of the B-1 are made in 48 states and 400 congressional districts. In 1985, $8.2 billion was spent to purchase 32 aircraft.[97] The services and DOD civilians attempt to cultivate political support by creating programs with large and dispersed constituencies. When former Secretary of the Navy John Lehman recently won a measure of Senate support for a $791 million plan to build twelve new homeports for 60 navy vessels in thirteen states, Senator Barry Goldwater, well known for his pro-defense views, commented that: "It was a brilliant political idea. . . . I thought about having one in Arizona. . . . The plan is a terrific waste of money . . . it is going to cost $10 billion before you're through fooling around."[98]

Congress is probably the worst offender of all. In 1980, an estimated 300 bases were unnecessary, but could not be closed. If domestic support is essential, however, the money may well bolster defense or at least spending on defense.

Presidents can cancel programs that would bust the budget or are no longer militarily useful due to changing conditions. President Jimmy

[96]Art, "Restructuring the Military-Industrial Complex," pp. 429–30.
[97]Pascall, *Trillion Dollar Budget*, p. 104.
[98]John Felton, "While Senate Blunts Most Arms Challenges," *Congressional Quarterly Weekly Report*, Vol. 44, No. 32, p. 1789.

Carter campaigned on a pledge to cancel the B-1 bomber, arguing it was too expensive, Soviet air defenses had grown too dangerous, and the cruise missile had rendered the B-1 obsolete. Despite a House and Senate controlled by his own party, Carter barely killed the program in the House with a majority of three votes.[99] Ronald Reagan picked it up.

Once a service, contractors, Congress, and labor groups have committed themselves to a program, it is difficult to stop procurement and deployment. Representative Michael Harrington, former member of the House Armed Services Committee, described this situation: By the time a weapons program reaches the stage at which it becomes a prominent issue of debate, the battle is lost. The defense department's near monopoly on relevant information together with the vested bureaucratic and economic interests which propel the high-budget high-prestige weapons programs conspire to give such programs an unstoppable momentum."[100] Were this often-expressed view the only truth—programs get in but never out—the defense budget would be larger than the gross national product. The truth is programs are canceled or underfunded, leading to eventual abandonment or "stretching out."

Other reasons help to explain this reluctance to eliminate defense programs. Congressmen may not feel qualified and they may not wish to take the heat if whatever they advocate turns out badly or if something they eliminate turns out to have been necessary. They are well aware that, in the event of actual hostilities, public opinion may shift from thinking too much has been done for defense to not enough was done to give the fighting forces the best of everything, especially if opponents have something advanced that the United States lacks.

When Congress must make cuts, they are made along the path of least resistance. Traditionally, this means that when defense is cut the burden falls on the readiness and manpower accounts of the services. Manpower is the number of people employed by the services and readi-

[99]Norman J. Ornstein and Shirley Elder, "The B-1 Bomber: Organizing at the Grassroots," in Eston White, *Studies in Defense* (Washington, D.C.: National Defense University Press, 1983), p. 46.

[100]Michael Harrington, "Building Arms Control into the National Security Process," *Arms Control Today* (February 1975), p. 4.

ness comprises repairs, maintenance of equipment, and the expenses needed to keep the service's equipment in working order. Both the services and Congress have incentives to cut (more accurately to "cap") these accounts first. Congress prefers manpower caps because the effects are not concentrated in any one district. Additionally, as Table 9-7 indicates, manpower and readiness cuts are "quick" money, resulting in an immediate decrease in outlays. Outlay rates for procurements, on the other hand, are distributed over several years, so an identical cut in procurement budget authority would result in a much smaller annual decrease in outlays. When Congress is looking for an immediate way to cut a budget, these fast spend-out accounts produce quick results. In the environment of defense budgeting, famine is expected to follow feast. When the famine hits, defense will most likely cut readiness and manpower, knowing that funds for these categories are easiest to restore and quicker to rebuild than major procurements. Manpower and readiness cuts thus spare procurement contracts. As a bonus to Congress and the military, manpower and readiness cuts can be spread to preserve the force structure.

Congress also will often make cuts in general but not in particular or make additions without stating specifically what programs are to be reduced. DOD may be told to absorb part of the annual pay raise when that supplemental comes up late in the fiscal year. Budget requests may be cut with DOD being told to make up for them by "undistributed adjustments."[101] In the fiscal 1985 budget, for example, Congress cut the president's request by $20.5 billion, yet only half a billion, or 2 percent, involved termination of procurement or cancellation of programs. The rest was made up of stretching out procurement, reducing the level of effort, and accounting changes.[102] So what? "Large annual contracts may be deobligated and renegotiated monthly," the joint DOD–GAO Study Group observed, "resulting in higher costs and severe disruption to those programs involved. Delays in contract award for combat readiness and other initiatives and delay or cancellation of com-

---

[101]Joint DOD–GAO Working Group on PPBS, p. 73.
[102]President's Blue Ribbon Commission, "National Security Planning and Budgeting," p. 16.

TABLE 9-7

Defense Outlay Rates by Appropriation Title

(percent of first-year budget authority)

	Year					
Appropriation Title	*1st*	*2nd*	*3rd*	*4th*	*5th*	*6th**
Military personnel	97.79	1.49	0.05	0	0	0
Operation and maintenance	73.02	21.03	2.69	0	0	0
Procurement	14.64	31.32	26.69	13.35	6.73	0.42
Research, development, test, and evaluation	46.62	40.33	7.96	1.74	0	0
Military construction	12.91	36.09	25.96	10.35	7.71	2.61
Family housing	46.36	29.56	13.49	3.57	1.80	0.82

*Sixth-year spendout rates are not given for the current fiscal year in the *Financial Summary Tables*, though they are given for the preceding year. For fiscal 1987 procurement, military construction, and family housing, the sixth-year outlay rates are estimated assuming the same six-year total lapsed-funding percentage (cents on the dollar not spent) as exhibited by the six-year outlay rates beginning in fiscal 1986, which are given in the *Financial Summary Tables* for fiscal 1987.

Source: Department of Defense, *Financial Summary Tables, Fiscal Year 1987*, tab M. Not shown are outlay rates for special foreign currency program and Defense-wide contingencies. In Joshua M. Epstein, *The 1987 Defense Budget*, (Washington D.C.: The Brookings Institution, 1986), p. 5.

bat training exercises are common."[103] Once weapons procurement or combat readiness is stretched out, moreover, the unit costs of these endeavors change, resulting in "reconsidering previously discarded alternatives that a stretch-out now makes cost effective."[104] Instability feeds on itself.

One hears complaints to the effect that only the military make decisions about weapons systems. As Les Aspin once said,

The real battles over weapons and defense policy are not fought out in Congress, the public arena, but in the Pentagon itself. It is in the Puzzle Palace of the Potomac, as the career military dubs the Pentagon, that the

[103]Joint DOD–GAO Working Group on PPBS, p. 85.
[104]*Ibid.*, p. 47.

decision is made as to whether a new helicopter takes precedence over a new tank. It is in that Disneyland East that the decision is taken whether investment for conventional warfare should take precedence over investment for strategic warfare.[105]

Hyperbole aside, the question arises as to who ought to initiate and promote weapons programs. Presumably, congressmen and their staffs, fascinated as they are with individual weapons systems, lack the expertise and the time. While they cannot replace contracting officers, however, congressmen can hamstring their authority.[106] The problem is that they want to do what they can't—choose weapons—and do not wish to do what they might—contribute to overall defense policy. "If they would just concentrate on new policy," Appropriations Subcommittee Chairmen Ted Stevens said of the Armed Services Committees, "we would get along a lot better. They want not only to devise the programs, they want to say how many nuts we have that fit certain kinds of bolts [and dictate] that they only be made in one state."[107] In the end, if Congress cannot get its act together on defense, Congress may be unable to defend one of its sacred cows—the division between authorizing and appropriations committees.[108]

Amid these competing certainties—spending is unstable; no, it is unstoppable—students of the procurement process have reached certain conclusions. They would like a variety of concepts and systems to be developed at an early stage when programs are easier to stop. With two or three prototypes in existence, and a vigorous and impartial testing program (hopefully, in place), choices would be more intelligent. Then, with that added assurance, procurement of sufficient quantities would be efficient. The trouble with the story is that it "front loads" the costs.

[105]Aspin, "Congress vs. Department of Defense," p. 247.

[106]See the Packard Commission's section on "Determination of the Contracting Officer's Authority," President's Blue Ribbon Commission on Defense Management, June 1986, pp. 347–48.

[107]*National Journal*, September 27, 1986 pp. 2305–2306.

[108]An October 1985 study on the organization of DOD, by the staff of the Armed Services Committee, also criticizes congressional budgeting as being conducted at the wrong level.

Design and testing become separate and expensive items. Most of what is done is deliberately designed to be discarded. But Congress has thus far shown no disposition for such forward funding. Rejected prototypes are counted as failures. In these circumstances, DOD tries to hitch its wagon to rising weapons systems whose financial future depends on overselling from the very beginning because that is what Congress will support.

The United States is the only nation, so far as I know, that budgets for defense on an annual basis. This is said to be too short and too frequent. The annual appropriations and authorization process has been blamed for what the Senate leader on defense, Democratic Senator Sam Nunn of Georgia, often refers to as "the trivialization of Congress' responsibilities for oversight . . . and excessive micromanagement." I think this criticism puts the cart of stability before the horse of policy and hence political agreement. What Nunn desires, discussions of broad defense issues, presumes basic consensus about the amount of resources that should be committed to the military and the types of weapons systems that should be pursued.

If one has to choose between the old days when DOD had much freer rein (Pentagon witnesses routinely used to submit questions in advance at hearings until in 1969 "a committee member read both the prepared question and its answer"[109]) and the present adversarial climate, chaos is preferable to order. No doubt it would be better if skepticism was saved for larger questions of defense policy. If the political leadership cannot agree on the largest questions—the "how muches" and "what fors"—either DOD will get to choose by default or no one will be able to make intelligent choices.

The Gramm–Rudman–Hollings Act creates a severe cumulative impact on defense. Recall that deficits are calculated in terms of outlays, while budget authority may be spent out over a period of years. Given a weighted average of spend-out rates for different types of expenditure, it can take a lot of authority to achieve a lesser degree of outlay reduc-

---

[109]D. Ronald Fox, *Arming America: How the U.S. Busy Weapons* (Harvard University Press, 1974), quoted in Morrison, "Chaos on Capital Hill," p. 2303.

tion.[110] The Packard Commission estimated that in 1986 DOD was compelled to achieve a $5.2 billion reduction in outlays covering 4,000 programs and activities by making a $13.6 billion cut in budget authority.[111] There were no program cuts resulting from this process: Existing contracts were protected, military personnel were exempted, and the Strategic Defense Initiative and Stealth bomber were fully protected. More of the same medicine, however, would either require cuts everywhere or decimate what was left. Even if defense totals have to be cut, there has to be a better way. But that way won't be found so long as there is budgetary dissensus. As things stand, both Congress and the DOD engage in practices they claim are deleterious, like stretch-outs, because it is better for them. Telling them less is more won't work.

But a war easily won, demonstrating that high- and medium-tech weapons really work, will undoubtedly drive the defense budget somewhat higher than it otherwise would have been. Those who appear to be arguing that defense contractors produce only shoddy goods will have greater difficulty making their case. Those who understood that the military gets to fight wars only with what is on the shelf will have that sentiment reinforced. Personnel costs, in light of high unemployment as well as national gratitude for a job well done, will probably be higher than expected. Over all, however, I expect defense spending to decline over time as long as there are no probable and substantial external threats. Which is as it should be. One reason for the expected decline is that six years of cuts in budget authority will continue to take their toll. Another reason is the general disinclination of Americans to support higher defense totals in the presence of disturbing domestic difficulties. Finally, it would take a lot of bad news to make increased defense spending more important than reducing the deficit. The Persian Gulf War is likely to be barely a blip on the screen of defense totals declining in absolute amount and even more steeply as a proportion of the total budget and of gross national product.

---

[110]An excellent study of the intricacies is Glenn A. Gotz, "Notes on the Gramm–Rudman–Hollings Deficit Reduction Plan," Rand Publication Series N-2426-FMP/RA, March 1986.

[111]President's Blue Ribbon Commission, p. 17.

REFORM

10

There's nothing wrong with the process, it's those who are in the process.
—Senator Phil Gramm

That process has gone all to hell.
—Representative Leon Panetta

I can't imagine anybody wanting to go back to a time when we had no
budget process, to inform you as to what the situation is and . . . what
the choices are.
—Representative Anthony Beilenson

BUDGETING HAS BECOME THE MAJOR ISSUE of American political life
because it brings to a head questions about what kind of a government
we will have and, therefore, what kind of a people we will be. In the first
section of this chapter, we shall see how disagreement over public policy
leads to the disintegration of classical budgetary norms—how the very
weakness of these premises of decision contributes to budgetary dissensus. If there is to be a new consensus, I shall ask, what norms will take
their place?

In order to provide a thorough review, I will then consider the efficacy
of all the known methods of budgeting, from the top down to the
bottom up and in between, under different conditions. Since budgets
must serve diverse purposes, it is not surprising that most methods are
not good for all seasons. I will finish the chapter by describing and

415

evaluating current major proposals for reform: the item veto, constitutional taxing and spending limits, and the "offset" provisions of Gramm–Rudman–Hollings (every increase in spending to be balanced by a decrease or a tax hike) now in operation in the Senate. Along the way, I shall also give brief consideration to lesser but still important measures: a capital budget, a two-year budget, reduction of tax expenditures, and control of credit.

This seems like (and is) a lot. If, when readers think "reform," they also think about changes in "what kind of government" and "what kind of people," they will be on the right track.

NORMS OF BUDGETARY BEHAVIOR

There is no better way to understand what has happened to budgeting in our time than to consider the radical changes in the norms of desirable behavior that used to guide budgeters, for all current reforms are efforts to devise formal replacements for what used to work reasonably well informally. The legacy of centuries of budgetary reform upon which expenditure control is still based—the norms of balance, annualarity, and comprehensiveness—have been shattered beyond recognition. What is more, the assumptions behind these norms—accepted limits on taxes and spending, predictability for a year, and departmental control of spending—no longer hold.

The norm of balance established an equilibrium between spending and taxing. Strong feelings about the limits of taxation (modified at the margin by raising or lowering tax rates) established effective ceilings for government spending. Everyone concerned, consequently, had a pretty good idea of allowable spending for years to come. Bids by departments to increase their shares beyond the level of expected increases, if any, would be resisted by other departments and program advocates who knew that much more for some department meant much less for others. Spending thus was inhibited at the source; bids to "break the bank" were not put in because everyone knew that also meant breaking social solidarity among departments. The interests entrusted to the care of these spending departments would expect to suffer. Along with budget balance, then, went the widely shared assumption that requests for funds would be made in the context of fairly firm spending limits. Budgets would not merely bubble up from below but would be shaped by pressure from above, pressure that affected the perception of departments about what was reasonable to ask for as well as what they might get.

Balance as a desirable norm, however, began to be weakened by near-universal acceptance of Keynesian economic precepts: Don't balance the budget, dummy, balance the economy at some hypothetical equilibrium point that would bring full employment. Because of disagreements about its proper level, the norm of balance has eroded even further; it lacks operational guidance. One side wants higher taxing and spending; the other, the reverse. So both swear fealty to the idea of balance while clinging to their opposite preferences as to the level and distribution of taxing and spending.

The norm of comprehensiveness stipulated the ideal that all revenues go to the central Treasury and that all expenditures be made within a comprehensive set of accounts. This ideal, though never wholly realized, of course, was appointed; although there were some special funds, the vast bulk of revenue did go to the Treasury. Today no one needs to be told that direct loans, loan guarantees, tax preferences, off-budget corporations, regulations that increase costs in the private sector, open-ended entitlements, and other such devices have made a hash out of comprehensiveness.

Comprehensive accounting once meant accounting by departments; governmental expenditure, except for a special fund here and there, meant departmental expenditure. If you controlled departments, the understanding was, you controlled expenditure. Today, when spending by departments on goods and services in industrial democracies accounts for only a third of spending, the inescapable conclusion is that traditional norms do not cover the bulk of expenditure. Most money is spent to affect citizen behavior rather than to support direct government actions. Since most spending is done by individuals who receive payments or loans, and by subnational governments, the irrelevance of department control is clear.[1]

Control of spending has declined along with the norm of comprehensiveness because one cannot simultaneously maximize in opposing directions. Varying the level of spending to help modulate swings in the economy is not compatible with keeping departmental spending constant. The more interest a government has in influencing citizen behavior, say by encouraging use of medical facilities, the less such a government is able to control its own spending.

Nor can it be said, following the norm of comprehensiveness, that there is a house of budgeting whose conceptual rooms are comparable. Accounting is in a shambles: Money borrowed one way ends up entirely in the budget; another way, partially; and a third way, not at all. Because there is no common budgetary currency, it is not possible to reallocate resources from loans to tax preferences to entitlements to departmental spending to government corporations (not, at least, in the sense of being intended).

A phenomenon that used to be confined to poor countries—repetitive budgeting, remaking the budget several times a year[2]—has now become standard practice in relatively rich nations as well. Whether the budget is formally redrawn or not, its underlying premises, financial assumptions, and actual allocations are subject to rapid change measured in months rather than years. Because governments cannot control large proportions of their budgets, they lack the reserves to cope with short-run economic fluctuations. Therefore, they reconfigure allowable spending several times a year. Annualarity, the one budgetary norm thought to be unassailable (because so simple and so uncontroversial), has been gravely weakened.

So what? Does it matter if some old-fashioned norms—derived from an era in which industrialization had hardly begun—have outlived their

---

[1]See the important paper by Allen Schick, "Off-Budget Expenditure: An Economic and Political Framework." Paper prepared for the Organisation for Economic Co-Operation and Development, Pairs, August 1981.

[2]Naomi Caiden and Aaron Wildavsky, *Planning and Budgeting in Poor Countries* (New York, 1974). Paperback edition by Transaction, Inc. (New Brunswick, N.J., 1980).

usefulness? Not necessarily, a prudent person would reply, providing such norms have been replaced by something better or, at least not noticeably worse. For, if one set of norms no longer applies and another is not yet in sight, budgeting is adrift, without rudder or compass. This means that the main governmental process for reconciling differences and setting directions—for consent and for steering—creates problems instead of solutions.

Let us look first at what happens when traditional norms no longer guide behavior. Annualarity signifies predictability; the budget *will* last a year. With this common expectation, agencies are impelled to make accommodation with central controllers, the Office of Management and Budget. Though not spelled out, this is the mutual understanding: Because the Treasury promises to pay the amount passed in the budget, agencies will exercise restraint in requests and try to stay within allotted amounts. To break that implied contract is to court a number of consequences. When the Treasury cannot guarantee payment of the allotted amount, agency political activity increases—not merely to get all that it asked for but also to keep what it has. Early accommodation is unwise if the budget sends a signal to "get it if you can"; this in turn results in delayed decisions.

Rather than remain within the appropriations process and absorb the inescapable uncertainty, program advocates seek to escape by making direct drafts on the Treasury (called "backdoor spending," or entitlements); by loans or loan guarantees; through shifting functions to "off-budget" entities; through special funds and "earmarked taxes"; and by imposing regulations on private parties, which then must bear the cost even though these amounts do not appear in agency budgets.

We see where we are: The decline of predictability worsens the Treasury's ability to maintain comprehensiveness. Revenues are diverted through increasing use of tax preferences (called tax expenditures by those who dislike them)[3] and special funds. The numerous devices for

---

[3]See John F. Witte, "Tax Philosophy and Income Equity," in Robert A. Solo and Charles Anderson, eds., *Value Judgment and Income Distribution* (New York: Praeger, 1981), pp. 340–78; and Ronald King, "Tax Expenditures and Systematic Public Policy."

getting around the appropriations process make it impossible to compare expenditures. No one can compare an appropriation to a direct loan, to a guarantee, or to any of a number of other spending devices.

The decline of comprehensiveness weakens control. Confused about how much is being spent, central budget offices are less able to say that any specific amount (in which account, please?) is too much. Looking good, as opposed to doing well, becomes tempting for guardians as well as advocates. Treasurers, who tend to be judged by the degree of budget imbalance, can improve their position by shifting spending to accounts such as loan guarantees that, except for a small amount for defaults, do not show up in the budget. Or they can trade lower spending outlays in one year for larger budget authority in future years.[4] Without rules that equate all major forms of spending, accounting sleight-of-hand substitutes for (but does not achieve) spending control.

There is a supportive relationship between classic budgetary norms, so that a decline in one reinforces a contraction in the others. Nowhere is this more apparent than in the deleterious effect the decay of budget balance has had upon annualarity and comprehensiveness. Budget balance comprises two kinds of equivalencies: accepted limits on revenue and expenditure, and the desire for these totals to come close together. Such limits fostered a sense of mutual dependence because all faced similar constraints. The norm of balance engendered a sense of self-sacrifice because each of the parts had to limit their wants to achieve the broader goal of balance. In a word, limits enhanced predictability by narrowing the scope of what was attainable. Participants knew that their individual adherence to the provisions of the budget contract would be rewarded by the contract being kept by all other parties. This anticipatory coordination was facilitated by pouring streams of revenue into a single reservoir out of which all (well, most) spending flowed. Everyone knew the size of the pipe and the size of the pieces.

Paper prepared for delivery at the Annual Meeting of the American Political Science Association, Denver, Colorado, September 2–5, 1982.
[4]David C. Mowery, Mark S. Kamlet, and John P. Crecine, "Presidential Management of Budgetary and Fiscal Policymaking," *Political Science Quarterly*, Vol. 95 (Fall 1980), pp. 395–425.

In the absence of restraints imposed by the norm of budget balance, all was up for grabs. Without agreement on limits, estimates about what constitutes a fair share of the budget could not be made. Consequently, all participants were encouraged to go their own way—to continue to ask for more. With no widespread agreement on either taxing or spending, the inner restraint that used to keep the budget battle within tolerable limits has eroded. Anything goes; end-runs are made to get around even the weak restraint of the existing process. Budget control gives way to a free-for-all.

Basic to the classical process is a division of roles between spending advocates and guardians of the Treasury. This separation cannot continue to exist, however, if the budgetary process is geared to expanding rather than limiting spending. When "budgeting by addition" replaces "budgeting by subtraction" (from an accepted total), who will take on the role of guardianship? After all, if program advocates can be satisfied by adding the costs of their proposals together, there is no need for anyone to undertake the painful task of cutting by subtraction. With advocacy less restrained, relationships that rely on trust between agencies and congressional committees become more variable: Either the two sides join to push pet programs or they do not trust each other at all, because common understandings are lacking. Congressional guardianship is gravely weakened because the decline in interdependence among agencies and programs makes such oversight seem less worthwhile. If a rise in certain programs does not imply a fall in others, or if cuts do not make larger savings, because there are many other additions, why take the heat for turning people down?

The Office of Management and Budget is hard put to play the role of guardian consistently. For one thing, OMB acts for the president— and not every Chief Executive wants to be known as a nay-sayer. Ronald Reagan, for instance, was intent on rapidly raising the defense budget. Other presidents may wish to increase spending on social welfare or in some other area of public policy. For another, budget examiners are too few, spending programs too many and too diverse, to permit detailed scrutiny of most agency requests. Only agency people know what is happening, to the extent anyone does; clearly it is not in their interest (given the lack of protection OMB can afford them) to tell. After all, if OMB is attacking the heart and muscle of agency operations, it cannot be expected that people identified with these activities will help in their own demise.

It is possible that the Senate and House budget committees will take over the role of guardianship. But at a price—the decline of guardianship in the appropriations committees, which are a lot closer to the sources of spending. Aside from the relative weakness of the House Budget Committee, because of rotating terms of office, HBC tends to raise its domestic spending bids in order to bargain with a somewhat more parsimonious and defense-minded Senate. It is difficult to be a guardian when one is simultaneously an advocate. Unless the House of Representatives accepts and the Senate maintains something like an offset system—i.e., a willingness to set global spending limits accompanied by a requirement that additions be made up by subtractions—budget committees will remain ineffective guardians. That is why Republican Representatives Michel and Lott (see their letter in the Preface) want to abolish the Fazio Rule and institute the Senate offset practice instead.

Central control makes most sense against a historical background of agreement, so that only small proportions of the budget remain in dispute. The old *Politics of the Budgetary Process* could focus on incremental differences because the base was largely agreed. When there is disagreement about the starting point as well as the desirable outcome of budgetary negotiation, as there is now, incremental change is in trouble.

There are, to be sure, other explanations for the demise of the traditional budgetary process characterized by incrementalism, fair shares, mutual confidence, a division of roles, including legislative guardianship, and the rest of the classical budgetary practices. The main alternative explanation, in the period from the end of World War II to the present, is economic growth—its presence until the mid-1970s and its lessening or absence thereafter. It is easy to reach agreements, the growth theory holds, when everyone is getting more. Incrementalism, Schick says, is based on the expectation of continued plenty. Now that prosperity has declined, incrementalism has gone with it.[5]

Doubtless, the decline of expected revenues does make things harder all the way around. The question I wish to raise is whether it is economic growth (or its absence) that regulates budgetary behavior, or whether it is the prevailing budgetary norms that determine what happens when growth goes up or down.

Had the parties agreed, a slowdown in spending accompanied by an increase in taxation could have balanced the budget. But one side wanted to maintain spending levels and the other to cut income taxes. Budget imbalance means more than a gap between spending and revenue; imbalance also signifies that the major political parties are too far apart to agree on how the budget should be balanced—by tax increases or spending cuts. This is dissensus.

Consider the consequences of economic growth, which makes it possible to raise revenue without reducing personal income. Budget balance would be easier, not harder to maintain. Tax rates could remain stable or even decline while spending rose, thus raising budget balance to a higher level. Precisely because there is more to go around, comprehensive accounts could be facilitated. There could be less objection to maintaining the regular appropriations process. Why use backdoor spending when the front door is wide open?

Yet that—the proliferation of spending sources during a time of plenty, from the mid-1960s through the mid-1970s—is exactly what did happen. Today both parties claim they want substantial spending increases to support a program of public works for rebuilding state and local infrastructure—sewers, bridges, waterworks, tunnels. Why, then, we may ask, during that time of plenty, was the substructure on which we stand allowed to deteriorate? And why, when economic conditions improved, didn't that inattention to essential maintenance recur? To me it seems more reasonable to suppose that a widespread desire to

[5]Allen Schick, "The Politics of Budgeting: Can Incrementalism Survive in a Decremental Age?" Paper prepared for the 1982 Annual Meeting of the American Political Science Association, Denver, Colorado, September 2–5, 1982.

increase spending (no matter what the state of the economy) lies behind the weakening of budgetary norms. Once one believes that government spending is laudatory (the more the better), at least in regard to certain objects, it follows that balance and comprehensiveness become obstacles, because they restrict opportunity; and annualarity is an impediment, because the money must be voted every year rather than pouring from the Treasury in a continuous stream. In this view, open-ended, "no-year" entitlements, loans, regulations, off-budget entities, and tax expenditures enable government to do good by spending more.

Which comes first, we may well ask, the change in budgetary norms, or the change in spending practices? Did the practices change the norms or vice versa? My view is that both change together. The purpose of norms is to justify practices. When there is a strong desire to change behavior, as in the New Deal America of the 1930s in regard to government spending, there is also a search for new norms to rationalize that conduct. It is not only that John Maynard Keynes found answers for America but also that influential Americans were actively looking for a theory to justify greater government spending—so they found him.[6] And later on, we observe that many new spigots were being opened in the 1960s and 1970s, spending that coincided with the civil rights and environmental movements, seeking enhanced equality and concern for ecology through governmental action. There is a struggle over theory as well as over practice; each influences the other so that one cannot say which came first but only that ideas and actions go together.

The implications of a practice depend on how it works within the pattern of norms that provide the structure of the budgetary process at any given time. Incremental budgeting is a good example. During the period when budget balance (and, hence, a sense of limits on totals) was the norm, incrementalism referred to small, regular modifications of an agency's accepted level of spending, a level known as its budgetary base. Spending was also limited by a sense of what the country could afford, tied to observations of economic performance. Alter the norms, how-

---

[6]Felix Frankfurter, later a Justice of the Supreme Court, played such a role. See H. N. Hirsch, *The Enigma of Felix Frankfurter* (New York: Basic Books, 1981).

ever, and the practice that seems the same takes on a different significance. Without agreement on balance, and therefore a sense of limits, spending grows through small but regular increases without regard for corresponding capacities in economic growth or revenue. When continuous increases fall short of aspirations, new sources of spending arise that also grow regularly. The result is that public spending grows faster than the private economy. Thus we see that incrementalism is a neutral concept; it permits slow or rapid or zero growth of government spending depending on the structure of budgetary norms within which it is employed.

The importance of these budgetary norms can be seen indirectly in new practices and proposals for reform that are meant to make up for what used to be. Budget resolutions, constitutional spending limits, and other budget methods, such as the presidential item veto, which we will discuss in this chapter, are all efforts to do by law what once was done by custom—namely, provide accepted premises under which conflict over the budget could be negotiated so as to resolve disagreements while still imparting stability to government. Once, the norms of balance, annualarity, and comprehensiveness performed that task. Let us, by reviewing different proposals, appraise to what extent the genie of agreement can be put back into the bottle of budgeting.

FORMS OF BUDGETING[7]

So far as I know, existing forms of budgeting have never been compared systematically, characteristic for characteristic, with the leading alternatives.[8] By doing so, we can see better which characteristics of budgetary processes suit different purposes under a variety of conditions.

What purpose should any form of budgeting be expected to serve? Control over public money and accountability to public authority were

[7]This section is a revised version of "A Budget for All Seasons? Why the Traditional Budget Lasts," in *The Public Administration Review,* No. 6 (November/December 1978), pp. 501–509.

[8]But, for a beginning, see Allen Schick, "The Road to PPB: The Stages of Budget Reform," in *Public Administration Review* (December 1966), pp. 243–58.

among the earliest purposes. Predictability and planning—knowing what there will be to spend over time—were not far behind. From the beginning, relating expenditure to revenue was of prime importance. In our day we have added macroeconomic management, intended to moderate inflation and unemployment. Spending is supposed to be varied to suit the economy. In time, the need for money came to be used as a lever to enhance the efficiency or effectiveness of policies. Here we have it: Budgeting is supposed to contribute to continuity (for planning), to change (for policy evaluation), to flexibility (for the economy), to rigidity (for limiting spending), and to openness (for accountability).

These different and (to some extent) opposed purposes contain a clue to the perennial dissatisfaction with budgeting. Obviously no single form can simultaneously provide continuity and change, rigidity and flexibility. And no one should be surprised that those who concentrate on one purpose or the other should find budgeting unsatisfactory; or that, as purposes change, these criticisms should become constant.

The ability of a budgetary form to score high on one criterion may increase the likelihood of its scoring low on another. Planning requires predictability, and economic management requires reversibility. Thus, there may well be no ideal mode of budgeting. If so, this is the question: Do we compromise by choosing a budgetary process that does splendidly on one criterion but terribly on others? Or, do we opt for a process that satisfies all these demands even though it does not score brilliantly on any single one?

A public-sector budget is supposed to ensure accountability. By associating government publicly with certain expenditures, opponents can ask questions or contribute criticisms. Here the clarity of the budget presentation—linking expenditures to activities and to responsible officials—is crucial. As a purpose, accountability is closely followed by control: Are the authorized and appropriated funds being spent for the designated activities? Control (or its antonym "out of control") can be used in several senses: Are expenditures within the limits (1) stipulated or (2) desired? While a budget (or item) might be "out of control" to a critic who desires it to be different, in this nomenclature control is lacking only when limits are stipulated and exceeded.

Budgets may be mechanisms of efficiency—doing whatever is done at least cost, or getting the most out of a given level of expenditure—and/or of effectiveness—achieving certain results in public policy, such as improving child health or reducing crime. An efficient program may still be ineffective.

In modern times, budgeting also has become an instrument of economic management and of planning. With the advent of Keynesian economics, efforts have been made to vary the rate of spending so as to increase employment in slack times or to reduce inflation when prices are deemed to be rising too quickly. Here (leaving aside alternative tax policies) the ability to increase and decrease spending in the short run is of paramount importance. For budgeting to serve planning, however, predictability (not variability) is critical. The ability to maintain a course of behavior over time is essential.

Budgeting is not only an economic but also a political instrument. Since inability to implement decisions nullifies them, the ability to mobilize support is as important as making the right choice. So, too, is the capacity to figure out what to do, that is, to make choices. Thus the effect of budgeting on conflict and calculation—the capacity to make and support decisions—must also be considered. When conflict overwhelms calculation (that is, when there is dissensus), subterfuge, either to permit some sort of agreement or to carry on the struggle, may overwhelm the more desirable qualities of budgeting.

Classical budgeting is annual (repeated yearly) and incremental (departing marginally from the year before). It is conducted on a cash basis (in nominal currency). Its content comes in the form of line-items (such as personnel or maintenance). Alternatives to all these characteristics have been developed and tried, though never, as far as I know, with success. Why this should be so, despite the obvious and admitted defects of tradition, will emerge as we consider the criteria each type of budgetary process has to meet.

REFORM WITHOUT CONFLICT

A large part of the literature on budgeting in the United States is concerned with reform. The goals of proposed reforms are couched in similar language—economy, efficiency, improvement, or just better budgeting. The president, the Congress and its committees, administrative agencies, even the interested citizenry all stand to gain by some change in the way the budget is formulated, presented, or evaluated. For a long time there was little or no realization among the reformers that effective change in budgetary relationships must necessarily alter the outcomes of the budgetary process. Today this is widely recognized. Far from being a neutral matter of "better budgeting," proposed reforms inevitably contain important implications for the political system, that is, for the "who gets what" and the "who ought to get," and even the "who ought to decide what is worth getting" of governmental decisions. What are some of the major political implications of budgetary reform? I begin with the noblest vision of reform: development of a normative theory of budgeting (stating what ought to be) that would provide the basis for allocating funds among competing activities.

In 1940, in what is still the best discussion of the subject, V. O. Key lamented "The Lack of a Budgetary Theory." He called for a theory that would help answer the basic question of budgeting on the expenditure side: "On what basis shall it be decided to allocate X dollars to Activity A instead of Activity B?"[9] Although several attempts have been made to meet this challenge,[10] not one has come close to succeeding—and for an excellent reason: The task, as posed, is impossible to fulfill.

For a normative theory of budgeting to be more than an exercise, to have any practical effect, it must actually guide the making of governmental decisions. Expenditures that are passed by Congress, enacted into law, and spent must in large measure conform to the theory, which is tantamount to prescribing that virtually all government activities be carried on accordingly.

The budget (for whatever the government does must be paid for from public funds) is the financial reflection of what the government does or

---

[9]V. O. Key, Jr., "The Lack of a Budgetary Theory," *The American Political Science Review,* Vol. 34 (December 1940), pp. 1137–44.

[10]Verne B. Lewis, "Toward a Theory of Budgeting," *Public Administration Review,* Vol. 12 (Winter 1952), pp. 42–54; "Symposium on Budget Theory," *Public Administration Review,* Vol. 10 (Winter 1950), pp. 20–31; Arthur Smithies, *The Budgetary Process in the United States* (New York: McGraw-Hill, 1955).

intends to do. A theory that contains criteria for determining what ought to be in the budget, therefore, is nothing less than a theory stating what government ought to do. If we substitute the words "what the government ought to do" for the words "ought to be in the budget," it becomes clear that a normative theory of budgeting would be a comprehensive and specific political theory detailing what the government's activities ought to be at a particular time. Given that the budget represents the outcome of political struggle, a normative theory of budgeting suggests the elimination of any such conflict over the government's role in society. Such a theory, therefore, is utopian in the fullest sense of the word: Its creation and acceptance would mean the end of politics.

By suppressing dissent, dictatorial regimes do enforce their normative theories of budgeting on others. Presumably, we reject this solution to the problem of conflict in society and insist on democratic procedures. How then arrive at a theory of budgeting that is something more than one person's preferences?

Two crucial aspects of budgeting are "how much?" and "what for?" • The problem is not only "how shall budgetary benefits be maximized?" as if it made no difference who received or paid for them, but also "who shall pay for and who shall receive how much in the way of budgetary benefits?" One may purport to solve the problem of budgeting by proposing a normative theory that specifies a method for maximizing returns for budgetary expenditures. If it is impossible to impose a set of preferred policies on others, however, this solution breaks down. It amounts to no more than saying that if you can persuade others to agree with you, then you will have achieved agreement. Yet such a state of universal agreement hardly has arisen.

Another approach is to treat society as a single organism with a consistent set of desires. Instead of revenue being raised and the budget being spent by and for many individuals who no doubt have varied preferences, these processes would be regarded, in effect, as if only a single individual were concerned. This approach sidesteps the central problem of social conflict, of the need somehow to aggregate different preferences so that a decision may emerge. (After all, the grave difficulties we experience in agreeing on annual budgets today is not a result of individual incapacity; any number of congressmen and presidents could make a coherent budget; it is gaining the consent of others that is difficult.) How can we compare the worth of expenditures for irrigation to certain farmers with that of widening a highway to motorists, or weigh the desirability of aiding old people to pay medical bills against the degree of safety provided by an expanded defense program?

In the real world, the process Americans have developed for dealing with interpersonal comparisons in government is not economic but political. Conflicts are resolved (under agreed-upon rules) through the political system by translating different preferences into units called votes or into such types of authority as veto power. There need not be (and there is not) full agreement on goals or the preferential weights to be accorded to different goals. Participants directly threaten, compromise, and trade favors in regard to policies in which values are implicitly weighted, and then agree to register the results according to the rules for tallying votes.

Bargaining takes place among many dispersed centers of influence, and favors are swapped as in the case of logrolling public-works appropriations. Since no single group can impose its preferences upon others within the American political system, special coalitions are formed to support or oppose specific policies. In this system of fragmented power, support is sought at numerous centers of influence—congressional committees, congressional leadership, the president, the Office of Management and Budget, interdepartmental committees, departments, bureaus, private groups, on and on. Nowhere does a single authority have power to determine what is going to be in the budget.

THE POLITICS IN BUDGET REFORM

The seeming irrationalities of a political system that does not provide for formal consideration of the budget as a whole (except by the president, who cannot control the final result) have led to many attacks and proposals for reform. But such reforms are aimed at the wrong target. If the present budgetary process rightly or wrongly is deemed unsatisfactory, then one must alter in some respect the political system of which the budget is but an expression. It makes no sense to speak as if one could make drastic changes in budgeting without also altering the distribution of influence. This task, however, is inevitably so formidable that most reformers prefer to speak only of changing the budgetary process (as with the Congressional Budget and Control Act of 1974 or Gramm–Rudman–Hollings), as if by some subtle alchemy the intractable political element also could be transformed into a more malleable substance.

In actuality, it is the other way around. The budget is inextricably linked to the political system; by far the most significant way of influencing the budget, therefore, would be to introduce basic political changes. Give presidents powers enabling them to control the votes of their party in Congress; enable a small group of congressmen to command a majority of votes on all occasions so they can push their program through (now that would be a budget committee!); then you will have exerted a profound influence on the content of the budget.

Further, no significant change can be made in the budgetary process without also affecting the political process. There would be no point in tinkering with the budgetary machinery if, at the end, the pattern of outcomes was precisely the same as before. On the contrary, budget reform has little justification unless it results in different kinds of decisions and, when and if this has been accomplished, the play of political forces has necessarily been altered.

Since the budget represents conflicts over whose preferences shall prevail, moreover, one cannot speak of "better budgeting" without considering who benefits and who loses or by demonstrating that no one loses. Just as the supposedly objective criterion of "efficiency" has been shown to have normative implications,[11] so a "better budget" may well be a cloak for someone's hidden policy preferences. To propose that the president be given an item veto, for example, is an attempt to increase the influence of those particular interests that have superior access to the Chief Executive (rather than, say, to the Congress).

[11]Dwight Waldo, *The Administrative State* (New York: Ronald Press, 1948); Herbert A. Simon, "The Criterion of Efficiency," in *Administrative Behavior*, 2nd ed. (New York: Macmillan, 1957), pp. 172–97.

Unit of Measurement: Cash or Volume

Budgeting can be done not only in terms of cash but also in terms of volume. Instead of promising to pay so much over the next year or years, the commitment can be made in terms of operations to be performed or services to be provided. The usual way of guaranteeing a volume of activity is indexing the program against inflation so its purchasing power is kept constant. Why might someone want to budget in terms of volume (or in currency held constant as to purchasing power)? To aid planning: If public agencies know that they can count not on variable currency but rather on what that currency actually can buy (i.e., on a volume of activity), they can plan ahead as far as the budget runs. Indeed, if one wishes to make decisions now instead of at future periods, so as to help assure consistency over time, then estimates based on stability in the unit of effort (so many applications processed or such a level of services provided) are the very way to go about it.

So long as purchasing power remains constant, the distinction between budgeting in cash or by volume makes no difference. But should the value of money fluctuate (and, in our time, this has meant inflation), the public budget must expand available funds so as to provide the designated volume of activity. Budgeters then lose control of money because they have to supply whatever is needed. Given large and unexpected changes in prices, the size of the budget in cash terms obviously would fluctuate wildly. But it is equally obvious that no government could permit itself to be so far out of control. Hence, the very type of stable environment that budgeting by volume is designed to achieve turns out to be its major unarticulated premise.

Given an irreducible amount of uncertainty in the system, not every element can be stabilized at the same time. Who, then, will enjoy stability? And who will bear the costs of change? The private sector and the central budget office pay the price for budgeting by volume. What budgeting by volume says, in effect, is that the public sector will be protected against inflation by getting its agreed level of services before other needs are met. The real resources necessary to make up the gap between projected and current prices must come from the private sector in the form of taxation or borrowing. In other words, for the public sector, volume budgeting is a form of indexing against inflation.

The sensitivity of budgetary forms to inflation is a crucial consideration. It follows that budgeting by volume is counterproductive in fighting inflation because it accommodates price increases rather than encouraging the struggle against them. Indexing benefits against price increases also is counterproductive because the beneficiaries have less reason to be concerned about inflation.[12]

Time Span: Months, One Year, Many Years

Multiyear budgeting, that is, viewing resource allocation in a long-term perspective, has long been proposed as a reform to enhance rational choice. Considering one year at a time, it has been argued, leads to short-sightedness (only next year's expenditures are reviewed), overspending (because huge future disbursements are hidden), conservatism (incremental changes do not open up larger future vistas), and parochialism (programs tend to be viewed in isolation rather than by comparison to future costs in relation to expected revenue). Extending the budget time span to two, three, or even five years, it is argued, would enable long-range planning to overtake short-term reaction, and to substitute financial planning for merely muddling through. The old tactic of the camel's nose—beginning with small expenditures while hiding larger ones that will arise later on—is rendered more difficult. Moreover, the practice of stepped-up spending to use up resources before the end of the budgetary year would decline in frequency.

A two-year budget would not change much. There is no reason to believe it would facilitate agreement or encourage better understanding. But it might be approved as a sort of budget officers' humane act. Instead of working 80 hours a week every year, participants in budgeting

[12]See Hugh Heclo and Aaron Wildavsky, *The Private Government of Public Money: Community and Policy inside British Political Administration,* 2nd ed. (London: Macmillan, 1981).

might get a breather every other year. Being less tired, they just might decide more wisely. In any event, no great harm is likely to be done and a bit of good might be accomplished.

A multiyear budget would work well for certain parts of the budget, like military procurements, which take years to complete. But benefit, salary, and operating expense categories are ill-suited to long-term budgeting. The size of these items is significantly influenced by external factors, such as inflation, that are difficult to predict. The problem of prediction appears more formidable when it is recalled that preparation of the budget begins almost a year before the budget is implemented. A two-year budget cycle, consequently, would have to forecast economic changes almost three years into the future. The result may be that budgeters would "spend more time tinkering with the assumptions over the 33-month period and, even assuming good faith, making some decisions on longer-term assumptions that would have to be altered even more dramatically later on."[13]

Much depends, to be sure, on how long budgetary commitments last. The seemingly arcane question of whether budgeting should be done on a cash or volume basis will assume importance if a nation adopts multiyear budgeting. The longer the term of the budget, the more significant becomes inflation. To the extent that price changes are automatically absorbed into budgets (volume budgeting), a certain amount of activity is guaranteed. But to the extent that agencies thus must absorb inflation, the real scope of activity will decline. Multiyear budgeting in cash terms, without indexing, diminishes the relative size of the public sector and leaves the private sector larger. Not always up front in discussing the time span of the budget, but very important, is the debate over the relative shares of the public and private sectors—which sector will be asked to absorb inflation and which will be allowed to expand into the other.

A similar issue of relative shares is created within government by proposals to budget in some sectors for several years, and in others,

[13]Symposium on Budget Balance, p. IV-30.

for only one year. Entitlements, for example, can be perpetual. To operate in different time spans poses the question of which sectors of policy are to be exposed to the vicissitudes of life in the short term and which are to be protected from them. Like any other device, multiyear budgeting is not neutral but distributes indulgences differently among the affected interests. Although being treated as an entitlement, until basic legislation changes, is no guarantee of future success, it is better for beneficiaries. But entitlements, if they grow large, are not necessarily better for government because they reduce legislative discretion.

Another potential downside to multiyear budgeting is the increased permanence of programs. Just as some programs may have a more difficult time getting into the budget, so "hard in" often implies an even "harder out." Once an expenditure gets included in a multiyear projection, it is likely to remain because it has become part of an interrelated set of proposals that might be expensive to disrupt. Thus control in a single year may have to be sacrificed to the maintenance of limits over the multiyear period. And, should there be a call for cuts, promised reductions in future years (which are always "iffy") are easily traded for maintenance of spending in the all-important present.

Suppose, however, that it were deemed desirable to reduce some expenditures significantly in order to increase others. Due to the built-in pressure of continuing committments, what could be done in a single year is extremely limited. But, making arrangements over a 2–5 year period would permit larger changes in spending to be effected in a more orderly way. This is true; other things, however—prices, priorities, politics—seldom remain equal. At a time when maintaining the annual budget has become problematical, so that the budget may have to be remade several times a year, lengthening the cycle possibly will just compound uncertainty. As Robert Hartman put it, "There is no absolutely right way to devise a long-run budget strategy."[14]

[14]Robert A. Hartman, "Multiyear Budget Planning," in Joseph A. Pechman, ed., *Setting National Priorities: The 1979 Budget* (Washington, D.C.: The Brookings Institution, 1978), p. 312.

Calculation: Incremental or Comprehensive

Just as the annual budget on a cash basis is integral to the traditional process, so also is the budgetary base; normally, only small increases or decreases to the existing base are considered in any one period. If such budgetary practices may be described as incremental, the main alternative to the traditional budget is one that emphasizes comprehensive calculation. The main modern forms of the latter are planning, programming, and budgeting (PPB) and zero-base budgeting (ZBB).

Think of PPB as embodying horizontal comprehensiveness—comparing alternative expenditure packages to decide which of them best contributes to large programmatic objectives. ZBB, by contrast, might be thought of as manifesting vertical comprehensiveness: Every year alternative expenditures from base zero are considered, with all governmental activities or objectives being treated as discrete entities. In short, PPB compares programs, while ZBB compares alternative funding levels for the same program.

The strength of PPB lies in its emphasis on policy analysis to increase effectiveness: Programs are evaluated, found wanting, and presumably replaced by alternatives designed to produce superior results. Unfortunately, PPB engenders a conflict between error recognition and error correction. Now there would be little point in designing better policies so as to minimize their prospects of implementation. But why should a process devoted to policy evaluation end up stultifying policy execution? Answer: because PPB's policy rationality is countered by its organizational irrationality.

For an error to be altered, it must be relatively easy to correct; but PPB makes this hard. The "systems" in PPB are characterized by their proponents as highly differentiated and tightly linked. The rationale for program budgeting lies in its connectedness: Like groups are grouped together. Program structures are meant to replace the confused concatenations of line-items with clearly differentiated, nonoverlapping boundaries—that is, only one set of programs to a structure. Hence a change in one element or structure necessarily reverberates throughout every element in the same system. Instead of alerting only neighboring units or central control units, which would make change feasible, all are, so to speak, wired together so that the choice is, in effect, all or none.

Imagine one of us deciding whether to buy a tie or a kerchief. A simple task, one might think. Suppose, however, that organizational rules require us to keep our entire wardrobe as a unit. In those circumstances, if everything must be rearranged when one item is altered, the probability that we will do anything is low. The more tightly linked and the more highly differentiated the elements concerned, the greater the probability of error (because tolerances are very small) and the less the likelihood that error will in fact be corrected (because, with change, every element has to be recalibrated with every other that had been previously adjusted). To be caught between revolution (change in everything) and resignation (change in nothing) has little to recommend it.

Program budgeting increases rather than decreases the cost of correcting error. The great complaint about bureaucracies is their rigidity. Viewed from the standpoint of bureau interests, to some extent programs are negotiable: Some can be increased, others decreased, while keeping the agency on an even keel, or if necessary, adjusting agency programs to less happy times without calling into question the agency's very existence. Line-item budgeting, precisely because its categories (personnel, maintenance, supplies) do not relate directly to programs, is easier to change. Budgeting by programs, precisely because money flows to objectives, makes it difficult to abandon objectives without also abandoning the very organization that gets its money for those activities. It is better, I think, to use nonprogrammatic rubrics as formal budget categories, permitting a diversity of analytical perspectives, than to transform a temporary analytic insight into a permanent perspective through which to funnel money.

The cutting edge of dealing with competition among programs lies in postulating a range of policy objectives small enough to be encompassed and large enough to overlap so that there can be choices (tradeoffs) among them. Instead, PPB tends to generate a tendency either toward only a few generalized objectives (so anything and everything can fit under them), or such a multitude of objectives that each organizational unit has its own home and does not have to compete with any other.[15] Participants learn how to play any game.

Despite the force of these objectives, there is an even greater defect: PPB operates without global spending limits. Now PPB is avowedly based on an analogy to economic markets where competition facilitates choice of the most productive alternative. Competitive markets perform feats of calculation. And they also create incentives for the most productive economic choice to be made. Without a global limit on spending, however—where more for one program leaves less for others—participants in PPB lack this incentive. The principle of opportunity costs— the value of an expenditure is what you have to give up to get it—does not apply. And neither does economic theory, because it is based on exchange, and exchange cannot be used to estimate equivalent values if things are no longer worth whatever is given up for them. Since nothing is lost by trying harder, no participant has reason to stop lobbying for more. Program budgeting might operate effectively if the people involved had to work within known limits on resources. Yet it is precisely these limits that are under stress as the norm of balance has collapsed without an agreed standard to take its place.

The ideal a-historical information system is zero-base budgeting. The past, as reflected in the budgetary base, is explicitly rejected: There is no yesterday; nothing will be taken for granted; everything at every period is subject to searching scrutiny. As a result, calculations become unmanageable.

To say that a budgetary process is a-historical is to conclude that the sources of error multiply while the chances of correcting mistakes decrease: If history is abolished, nothing is ever settled. Old quarrels resurface as new conflicts. Both calculation and conflict increase exponentially, the former complicating selection and the latter obstructing error correction. As mistrust grows with conflict, willingness to admit (and hence to correct) error diminishes. Doing without history is a little

[15]See Jeanne Nienaber and Aaron Wildavsky, *The Budgeting and Evaluation of Federal Recreation Programs, or Money Doesn't Grow on Trees* (New York: Basic Books, 1973).

like abolishing memory—momentarily convenient, perhaps, but ultimately embarrassing.

Nowhere does a true zero-base budget practice exist. Everywhere the "zero" is ignored and the base gets larger, amounting, in the end, to 80 to 90 percent of the prior year; this, of course, is a reversion to classical budgeting. What is worse, ZBB cannot give expression to the main reason for most activities, namely, to support some other activity. By building the budget entirely from the bottom up, the justification for expenditures is divorced from their connections to other activities and purposes. This does not make sense.[16] It does explain why ZBB has declined in use. But why do people keep resurrecting it? Because ZBB holds out the hope of liberation from restraints of the past, as if they could be willed away.

ZBB and PPB share an emphasis on the virtue of objectives. Program budgeting seeks to relate larger to smaller objectives among different programs, and zero-base budgeting promises to do the same within a single program. The policy implications of these budgeting methods, which distinguish them from existing approaches, derive from their overwhelming, shared concern with ranking objectives. Thinking about objectives is one thing, however; making budget categories out of them is quite another. Of course, if one wants the objectives of today to be the objectives of tomorrow, if one wants no change, then it is a brilliant idea to build the budget around objectives. Conversely, if one wishes to alter existing objectives radically, it may be appropriate to highlight the struggle over them. But if one desires flexibility (sometimes known as learning from experience), it must be possible to change objectives without simultaneously destroying the organization by withdrawing financial support.

Both PPB and ZBB are expressions of a view in which ranking objectives is rendered tantamount to reason. Alas! An efficient mode of presenting results in research papers—find objectives, order them, choose the highest valued—has been confused with proper processes of

[16]See Thomas H. Hammond and Jack H. Knott, A *Zero-Based Look at Zero-Base Budgeting* (New Brunswick, N.J.: Transaction, 1979).

social inquiry. For purposes of resource allocation, which is what budgeting is about, it is irrational to rank objectives without considering resources. The question cannot be "What do you want?"—as if there were no limits—but should be "What do you want compared to what you can get?" After all, an agency with a billion would not only do more than it would with a million but might well wish to do something quite different. Resources affect objectives as well as vice versa. Budgeting should not separate what reason tells us belongs together.

There is a critical difference between the financial form in which the budget is voted in the legislature and the different ways of thinking about budgeting. It is possible to analyze expenditures in terms of programs, over long periods of time, and in many other ways, without requiring that the form of analysis be the same as the form of appropriation. All this can be summarized: The more neutral the form of presenting appropriations, the easier to translate other changes—in program, direction, organizational structure—into the desired amount without increasing the rigidity in categories, and thus erecting barriers to future changes.

The forms of budgeting that once occupied center stage (PPB, ZBB, and similar reforms) have lost their allure. Now what matters is the level and distribution of spending. Size replaces efficiency as the criterion of a good budget. In a time of growing budgetary dissensus, a concern with radical changes in process replaces concern with modest alteration in technique.

APPROPRIATIONS OR TREASURY BUDGETING

A classical budget depends on classical practice—authorization and appropriation followed by expenditure, and postaudited by external auditors. But in many countries, classical budgeting does not in fact control most public spending. Rather than appropriations budgeting, nearly half of public spending takes the form of "treasury budgeting," so called because it bypasses the appropriations process in favor of automatic disbursement of funds through the treasury.

For present purposes, the two forms of treasury budgeting that constitute alternatives to classical appropriations are tax preferences and entitlements. Concessions granted in the form of tax reductions for home ownership or college tuition or medical expenses are equivalent to budgetary expenditures, except that the money is deflected at the source. In one sense, this is a way of avoiding budgeting before the budget comes into being. Whether one accepts this view or not is a matter of philosophy. It is said, for instance, that our government has a progressive income tax. Is that the real tax system? Or is it a would-be progressive tax as modified by innumerable exceptions? The budgetary process is usually described as resource allocation by governing authorities. Is that the real budgetary process? Or is it that process, plus numerous provisions for tax preferences, low-interest loans, and other such devices? From a behavioral or descriptive point of view, actual practices constitute the real system. Exceptions are part of the rule. Indeed, since less than half of the budget now passes through the appropriations process, the exceptions indeed are greater than the rule.

Obviously, treasury budgeting leaves a great deal to be desired in controlling costs of programs, since these depend on such variables as levels of benefits set in prior years, rate of application, demographic changes, and severity of administration. If the guiding principle is that no one who is eligible should be denied, at the cost of including some who are ineligible, expenditures will rise. They will decline if the opposite principle—no ineligibles even if some eligibles suffer—prevails.[17]

Treasury budgeting is popular because of its antibudgetary character—it allows spending to rise without calling attention to it. Conflict is reduced, for the time being at least, because no explicit decisions (giving more to this group and less to another) are necessary. Ultimately, of course, there comes a day of reckoning in the form of a loss of flexibility due to the implicit preprogramming of so large a proportion of available funds.

For the purposes of economic management, treasury budgeting is a

[17]The importance of these principles is discussed in my *Speaking Truth to Power: The Art and Craft of Policy Analysis* (Boston: Little, Brown, 1979).

mixed bag. It is useful in providing what are called automatic stabilizers. When it is deemed desirable not to make new decisions every time conditions change (unemployment benefits, for example), an entitlement enables funds to flow according to the size of the problem. The difficulty is that not all entitlements are countercyclical (child benefits, for example, may rise independently of economic conditions), and the loss in financial flexibility generated by entitlements may hurt when the time comes to do less. Nevertheless, treasury budgeting has one significant advantage over appropriations budgeting—timing. Changes in conditions are manifested quickly in changes in spending.

The recalcitrance of all forms of budgeting to economic management is not surprising; after all, spending programs and economic management cannot both be made more predictable if one must vary in order to serve the other. Every way one turns, it appears, budgetary devices are good for some purposes and bad for others.

Capital Budgeting

An idea that is receiving a great deal of attention lately is separating capital expenditures from the current budget. Two budgets would exist: an operations budget and a capital budget. The capital budget would include investment in assets as balanced against debt acquired through purchase of these assets.

Economically, the idea has a great deal of merit. A separate capital budget would help focus on national investment needs. Under current practices, financing for capital assets (which produce long-term benefits) is lumped with expenses. Since short-term factors weigh heavily in budgeting decisions, capital assets, whose benefits may not be immediately apparent, may be sacrificed to more immediately pressing needs.

Yet the distinction between capital expenses and other expenses is not clear-cut. For example, is education a current expense that is payable immediately (yes), or does it represent an investment in human capital (also yes)? Experience in nations around the world shows that it is not possible to separate the political aspects of budgeting—who wants and gets what—from technical definitions. Since a capital budget appears to be good (i.e., an investment), expenditures in its budget would surely rise.[18] Besides, capital goods, being considered as assets, are often not included in the deficit.

A good idea can take many bad turns when put into practice. The immediate response of budgeters, once provided with an operating and a capital budget, would in all likelihood be to transfer as many expenditures as possible from the operating to the capital budget. The announced deficit would consequently appear significantly smaller. All participants could claim victory in holding the line on deficits even though spending had actually increased. The danger is that expenditures would escalate as attention is turned from deficit reduction. To add insult to injury, the capital budget

> is quite likely to unpredictably disrupt the existing budget process. A dual budget would more than likely require some changes in institutional structure, shifts in responsibility, and modifications of the budget cycle's timing. The need to relate aggregate debt, tax, and spending limits to two separate budgets—capital and operating—would introduce greater complexity into the already complicated budget process.[19]

Far better, I think, to include an appendix in the president's budget proposal attempting a breakdown between capital and recurrent expenditure, subject to criticism and refinement over time, than to make matters worse in the guise of making them better.

Why is it necessary to settle for second or third best? Why not combine the best features of the various forms of budgeting, specifically selected to work under prevailing conditions? Observation reveals that a number of different processes do in fact coexist right now. Some programs are single-year while others are multiyear; some have cash limits while others are open-ended or even indexed; some are analyzed in increments while others (where repetitive operations are involved) receive, in effect, a zero-base review. Thus, beneath the facade of unity there is in fact diversity.

[18]See Caiden and Wildavsky, *Planning and Budgeting in Poor Countries.*

[19]Report to the Committee on Environment and Public Works, U.S. Senate by the Comptroller General of the United States, "Pros and Cons of a Separate Capital Budget for the Federal Government," GAO/PAD-83-1, September, 22, 1983, p. 8.

THREE DIRECTIONS FOR BUDGETING: BOTTOM-UP, TOP-DOWN, AND IN-BETWEEN

The classical method of federal budgeting may justly be called decentralized or "bottom-up." Within Congress where, with two-thirds majorities, the power of the purse still resides, consideration of spending was divided between authorizing and appropriations committees and subcommittees, with important aspects of spending—especially entitlements, as well as tax preferences—under the aegis of the House Ways and Means and the Senate Finance committees. On the executive side, in various combinations, bureaus and departments proposed, under different degrees of constraint, and the president and the OMB disposed of, requests that eventually became the president's budget.

The advantages of this extreme decentralization are well known.[20] By factoring the budget into relatively small components, calculation was simplified; the budget as a whole, as its critics never tired of saying, was not formally considered. There were few disputes over the budget in its entirety because the process was organized (critics would say disorganized) to prevent exactly that sort of confrontation. And since the budget was, in effect, factored out to numerous bureaus, departments, OMB examiners, House and Senate substantive appropriations and finance committees, conflicts were limited not only to these smaller subsets but to the increments of these amounts—the differences between the prior year and what was proposed for the next—that participants felt it worthwhile to consider. Calculations were made, conflict diffused, and yet, wonder of wonders, budgets were passed on time while revenues and expenditures stayed within hailing distance.

A bottom-up decentralized process, as we know, required widespread agreement on the norms of balance and comprehensiveness.[21] A commitment to budget balance meant acceptance of a de facto spending limit: Big-ticket items could rise only so far without taking funds from

---

[20]See Aaron Wildavsky, *The Politics of the Budgetary Process* (Boston: Little, Brown, first published in 1964; revised fourth edition, 1984).

[21]Aaron Wildavsky, "The Transformation of Budgetary Norms," *Australian Journal of Public Administration,* Vol. XLII, No. 4 (December 1983), pp. 421–32.

other programs. Playing the game of balance meant agreeing to anticipatory restraints on spending demands. Adherence to the norm of comprehensiveness meant that almost everything was in the same pot. When restraints had to be exercised in the name of balance, therefore, neither substantial revenues nor expenditures were outside the purview of the political authorities for ratcheting up or down.

Economic growth was a facilitating factor. So long as revenues rose, politically painless increases in spending were possible. If the demand for spending went up while growth failed to keep pace, however, there were other informal devices to maintain balance. Congresses could vote more spending expecting that, if things got worse, presidents would come to the rescue by impounding funds. And if visible tax increases proved difficult, the same result might be obtained by reducing tax preferences, and by "bracket creep" as inflation moved taxpayers into higher brackets.

If all these protective devices failed, our politicians would be reduced to the most basic assumption of all: agreement on the division of sacrifices, at least among the major programs—defense, social security, and other entitlements. If all these giant programs were regarded as contributing to the national interest, accommodations among them might be arranged. By contrast, if "welfare" and "warfare" were considered to be at odds, this polarization of opinion would make agreement difficult if (or, rather, when) a decline in the rate of economic growth rendered this conflict visible.

What happened to bring bottom-up budgeting into disrepute was that every one of these assumptions, understandings, and agreements was undermined. Government became spending. Whether it was defense to bolster America's position as the leader of the West, or social welfare to make long deferred payments on social justice, positive government became the order of the day. Balance withered away. Republicans grumbled but did little, and Democrats took satisfaction in ignoring another shibboleth from olden times that stood in the way of social progress.

Watergate gravely weakened presidential power over impoundment of funds already appropriated. The growth of entitlements, coupled with automatic cost of living increases, substantially reduced the proportion of the budget controllable through annual appropriations and thus through across-the-board reductions. The Reagan administration applied the coup de grâce in 1981 when it cut income taxes across the board by 23 percent, thus negating equivalent but silent tax increases in social security, bracket creep, and energy that had been in place at the end of the Carter administration. Congress also indexed tax brackets beginning in 1985. Consequently, the proportion of national income derived from federal taxation failed to rise enough to cover higher spending. As deficits soared to unprecedented levels, participants in budgeting discovered that they had lost their traditional devices for accommodating disagreement—their piecemeal approach had been overtaken by budget resolutions and reconciliation, and impoundment and bracket creep were mostly gone—while disrespect for the president's budget, which once had at least provided a starting point, symbolized the fact that budgeters no longer agreed on the priorities between welfare and defense.

The opposite end of the budgetary spectrum can be called centralized, top-down budgeting. Global levels are set by limits on revenues or expenditures or deficits—the difference between them. A formula exists, say across-the-board cuts, for bringing spending down or revenues up to these limits. This top-down method depends on certain understandings and assumptions. One of these is that enough be thrown up for grabs to make a difference. If, as in a number of European nations, for instance, social welfare entitlements (preeminently payments to individuals) are left out—these programs comprising a half to two-thirds of total spending, with interest on debt making up another fifth—the remainder is not large enough to do the job. So the United States also discovered in the Gramm–Rudman–Hollings process. The attraction of this across-the-board method, however, is precisely its severity: Agreement on innumerable separate items is rendered unnecessary by a formula. Yet the very lack of analysis about individual programs is bound to lead to foolish actions as less and more important matters receive similar treatment.

If both bottom-up and top-down budgeting are unsatisfactory, what else is there? A combination of the top-down and bottom-up methods may avoid the worst excess of each; alternatively, it may bring out the worst of both. The budgetary process is centralized to the extent that there is a global limit but decentralized to the degree that, within such a prescribed total, participants are allowed to work out disagreements, as before, on a case-by-case basis. Indeed, this combination lay behind the Budget Reform Act of 1974, whose budget resolutions were designed to set totals in a top-down fashion so as to structure the work of the committee system. As things turned out, bottom-up penetrated top-down. Totals were set on top with a view to accommodating demands down below. What resulted was the worse of both worlds—disagreement was exacerbated by the need to decide the largest questions of total expenditures and revenues, thus giving up the advantages of decentralization, while the totals were too flexible to exert the necessary downward pressure on demands so as to produce lower levels of spending. Is there any way out of this trap?

LIMITS

The idea of budgeting from above—either by limiting revenue and requiring expenditure to fit within it, or limiting spending and forbidding revenue to exceed that level—would revolutionize resource mobilization and resource allocation. Budgeting by addition would no longer be possible; adding requests together would not work because exceeding a prearranged total would be ruled out. More for one program or agency, consequently, would mean less for another. Budgeting by subtraction—tradeoffs among good things that could not all be funded—would usher in a new budgetary order. Budgeting would become more like the 1981 Reagan–Stockman reconciliation procedure than anything before or since.

The spending-and-revenue limit plus budget balance amendment is designed to do just that. By embodying limits in a more permanent form in the Constitution and specifying their total—last year's outlays times the percentage increase in national income—without predetermining priorities within this total, an effort is made to combine centralization with decentralization.

The amendment's supporters believe the existing budgetary process is biased in favor of higher spending because it focuses attention on individual programs rather than totals. They believe that by placing programs in competition, within a limited total, the public's desire for less total spending can be made compatible with its support for many of the programs that make up public expenditure.

The amendment encapsulates a macro- and micro-political theory. The macro theory expresses a political preference: The public sector should not expand into the private sector. This philosophy is supported by the provision that spending cannot exceed the percentage growth in national income. The micro theory seeks to create incentives for limiting expenditure by motivating program advocates to restrain their demands. Imposing a global limit means that increases for one program or agency above the percentage increase in national income must be accompanied by equivalent decreases in others. Budgeting by addition, in which program costs are piled on top of each other to be paid for by tax increases or debt, would be replaced by budgeting by subtraction, in which desired increases would have to compete within the limits of economic growth.

The political result of constitutional revenue-and-expenditure limitation, according to its advocates, would be to increase cooperation in society and conflict within government. As things stand, so the amendment's supporters contend, program advocates within government, by increasing their total share of national income, have every incentive to raise their spending while reducing their internal differences. Why fight among their public selves if private persons will pay? Thus conflict is transferred from government to society.

Once limits are enacted, however, the amendment's advocates believe, the direction of incentives would be reversed: There would be increasing cooperation in society and rising conflict in government. Citizens in society would have a common interest whereas the sectors of policy—housing, welfare, environment, defense—would be plunged into conflict. Organizations interested in income redistribution to favor poorer people would come to understand that the greater the increase in real national income, the more there would be for government to spend on their purposes. Instead of acting as if it didn't matter where the money came from, such groups would have to consider how they might contribute to enhanced productivity. Management and labor, majorities and minorities, would be thinking about common objectives, about how to get more out of one another rather than about how to take more from the other.

Make no mistake, the amendment would radically alter the character of contemporary budgeting. For one thing, there would have to be grave concern about exceeding allowed totals. Hence money would have to be kept back in the form of large contingency funds. For another, entitlements could not be guaranteed at full value; if the total were about to be breached, payments might have to be reduced, say from 100 to 97 percent of the guarantee. The amendment, that is, would modify open-ended promises to citizens—you will get yours no matter what—with only the promise (by their collective expression, the government) that beneficiaries would get something close to what they expected.

Since constitutional spending limits have so far failed to gather the necessary support, attention has turned either to legislative remedies— the Gramm–Rudman–Hollings offset procedure—or to narrow constitutional changes—the presidential item veto. None of these proposed reforms, I shall argue, does away with the need for prior agreement on the scope and distribution of taxing and spending. Put plainly, the federal government could control spending if it could only agree on how much for what purpose and who is to pay.

THE LINE-ITEM VETO

With the 1988 election coming up, facing the unpleasant task of explaining away historically unprecedented deficits, unwilling to talk of raising taxes, and unable to reduce domestic spending—it was understandable that Republicans spoke favorably of the line-item veto. So long as the Democrats resisted, blame for continuing deficits could be placed on them. And, focusing entirely on the immediate future, Republicans could indulge themselves in fantasies of their leader cutting and slashing, slashing and cutting, until big government was vetoed out root and branch. But that is all it was—a fantasy.

Experience of States with the Item Veto

Experience in state governments has been cited to support the efficacy of the item veto. The argument for the item veto rests on a combination of alleged cuts made by states, together with a version of the marginal fallacy. On the surface it does appear that under certain governors in some states, such as Ronald Reagan in California, the item veto eliminated 1 or 2 percent of spending, which, if cumulated over a number of years, adds up to significant reductions. I say "alleged" savings because it is well known that legislators pad their requests in anticipation of vetoes.

Apparently, it is possible to interweave items so that they are not separable, thereby nullifying the intent of the item veto. At least, Roy D. Morey, writing about Arizona, says that "A major reason why the governor has not used the item veto more frequently is that the legislature has deliberately constructed appropriation bills in such a way as to stymie its use. Those items which the legislature feels have questionable gubernatorial support are rearranged or lumped with those items the governor is forced, either by conviction or necessity, to approve."[22] For this reason, Morey concludes that "this device has proved to be of little value to Arizona governors."[23] It appears that the item veto is more powerful in Pennsylvania where governors do use it a good deal. But this conclusion must be modified by interaction effects: "When a legislator, even though opposed in principle to an appropriation, is reasonably certain that the governor will slice it down to more moderate size," M. Nelson McGeary states in his study of Pennsylvania, "he is tempted to bolster himself politically by voting large sums of money to a popular

---

[22]Roy D. Morey, "The Executive Veto in Arizona: Its Use and Limitations," *The Western Political Quarterly*, Vol. 19, No. 3 (September 1966), quote on p. 512.
[23]*Ibid.*, p. 515.

cause."[24] Where there is no item veto, as in North Carolina, Coleman B. Ransome, Jr., reports that "the legislature seems to have developed some sense of responsibility; there can be no buckpassing of undesirable legislation to the governor with the knowledge that he will veto the bill in question and thus take the burden from the legislature."[25]

A fatal impediment to a federal line-item veto shows up in the detailed and separable character of state budgets, which makes it relatively easy for most governors to select out the parts they wish to reject. At the federal level, however, budget items are far larger and more aggregated. Thus there would normally be no way for a president to veto individual public works projects, since the budget lists only general totals, while individual projects are found in committee reports. Hence the president would have to veto all public works spending and not just the projects to which he objected.[26]

A Little Tool for a Big Job

It takes little imagination to realize that presidents far different from Ronald Reagan or George Bush are going to occupy the White House. Would a Mario Cuomo or an Edward Kennedy (to mention just two well-known liberal Democrats) use the item veto to increase defense and decrease domestic spending, or might not it be just the other way around? Might not a president interested in increasing domestic spending hold defense spending ransom to achieve that very purpose?

Even granting proponents the best of their possible worlds—their president in the White House ready to throttle the expenditure machine does not rescue the item veto from the charge of inappropriateness. Presidents do not usually wish to cut defense, which amounts to around 21 percent of the budget. Without the item veto, President Reagan

[24]M. Nelson McGeary, "The Governor's Veto in Pennsylvania," *American Political Science Review*, Vol. 41, No. 5 (October 1974), p. 943.

[25]Coleman B. Ransome, Jr., *The American Governorship* (Westport, Conn.: Greenwood Press, 1982), p. 159.

[26]See Louis Fisher, "The Item Veto: The Risks of Emulating the States." Prepared for delivery at the 1985 Annual Meeting of the American Political Science Association, New Orleans, August 29–31, 1985.

helped reduce small, means-tested entitlements; and his inability and/or unwillingness to cut the large universal entitlements, especially social security, in view of the political price, would, in any event, have remained unaffected by the item veto. Nor is this all. Together these social welfare programs amount to about 52 percent of the budget. Allowing approximately 15 percent (and rising!) for interest on the debt, this leaves little more than a small number (12 percent) on which to try the item veto.

Even there, in the midst of what is left of general government, there is much that will prove resistant to the item veto. There is misadventure. Rejecting smaller items may increase support for overriding vetos on larger ones. There is politics. Perhaps the president's people think he will use the item veto to eliminate or reduce politically important expenditures on which there has long been a negative professional consensus. I refer to agricultural and maritime subsidies, way-below-market prices for grazing rights on federal land, water for irrigation in the west, all sorts of river and harbor projects, and the like. In any event, though there are, as always, tempting targets for elimination, there is not enough to make a big difference in that 12 percent of the federal budget which in part has already been severely pruned.

There is misconception. The item veto cannot quell the widespread will to spend. What it does is convey an image of presidents valiantly trying to stem the tide of spending but, for want of this one weapon, being overwhelmed by hordes of congressional spenders. There is no truth in this. Presidents have been in the forefront of spending. In this respect, think not only of Democrat Lyndon Johnson but of Republican Richard Nixon, in whose administration, and in service to his vaunted flexibility, huge increases took place in social security, loan guarantees, and other prospending developments too numerous to mention. There also are other misconceptions about political systems in general and American politics in particular that lie behind belief in the efficacy of the item veto.

First the general, then the particular: The general case against the sufficiency of the item veto is overwhelming. Line up the world leaders favoring public expenditure as a proportion of GNP among democracies:

In all of these countries, cabinets have the power to determine the entire spending budget, item by item. These governments do not need an item veto because nothing gets into the budget without their approval. Why, then, do the budgets grow? Part of the reason (in some but by no means all of these spending leaders) is that most have coalition governments or corporatist arrangements in which the cost of consent is side payments to partners, thus increasing the size of the budget. To the extent that the United States shares this characteristic of divided government—either because the presidency and all or part of Congress are held by different parties or because, though ostensibly of the same party, their policy preferences differ—there is no reason to believe the item veto will do what total formal control of the budget cannot.

It is not that most of these governments do not have periodic budget-cutting drives, but that these campaigns are never (that's right, never) successful.[27] Hence the essential nature of the problem is clarified: governmental self-control. Governments must (1) want to reduce spending and (2) have an effective technology for doing so. The item veto does not qualify as an effective instrument of spending control because it locks the Treasury doors after the spending bids have already been proposed. The trick is to inhibit the presentation of expenditure demands, not to engage in the futile task of rejecting a small proportion after they have been made. Nor is this relationship—prevention is preferable to cure—unique to budgeting. Once participants in the budgetary process assume that it is desirable to ask for more or that end-runs around the process (loans, guarantees, entitlements, regulations) pay off, the game is lost. For no central controller has the time to examine so many programs or the capacity to understand them. Where information is a prerequisite of control, the numerous people on the spot are bound to prevail over the few who are far away. Just as criminals should be deterred before crimes are committed, spending agencies must be persuaded to limit their demands at the

---

[27]See Daniel L. Tarschys, "Curbing Public Expenditures: A Survey of Current Trends." Paper prepared for the Joint Activity on Public Management Improvement of the Organisation for Economic Co-Operation and Development, Paris (Technical Co-Operation Service), April 1982.

source. Where governments spend increasing proportions of GNP because that is what citizens want, they will not fix spending because they believe it isn't broken. Under such conditions, the item veto is irrelevant because the idea is to include expenditures in, not exclude them out.

To consider the United States by itself, there is a good chance that the item veto, instead of merely being limited or ineffective, would be positively counterproductive. Understanding why this might well happen requires a brief excursion into the separation of powers. The legislative function is shared between Congress and the president. Every schoolchild knows that. Presidents may veto proposed legislation and Congress may pass it into law by a two-thirds vote. That is also understood. What is not stated, because it is taken for granted, is that Congress may act irresponsibly, that is, pass a law and not be accountable for it. For then the branches of government really would not be separated—each one responsible within its sphere, cooperating when possible, conflicting when necessary—but joined together. But not openly.

Voting on the understanding that a bill may become law is not quite the same as expecting part of the proposal to be taken out even though the rest will remain. The responsibility of the president has been clarified and strengthened: He is responsible for every part of an appropriation or a law he does not veto. Whereas before he had to make a judgment about whether to accept or to reject the bill as a whole, now he can pick and choose. Thus the old excuse that the president did not want a particular appropriation but had to accept it as part of a package would no longer be acceptable. Instead of putting the onus on Congress to moderate its expenditure proposals, the item veto, by giving presidents more formal power, also places the onus on them.

How tempting! Weakening the formal powers of Congress would make it more irresponsible. Congress would have less reason to consider the collective consequences of its acts. Why should it? After all, presidents can (soon legislators will think "should") veto every item proposing spending of which they do not approve. Why not just throw in whatever is at hand and leave it to the president to get rid of the worst? Certainly, the efforts of congressmen to convince constituents that a particular item was of low priority (every bit of spending helps somebody, or so they think, or they would not want it) is gravely weakened by the retort: Let the president worry about that. With proposals for spending becoming entirely a sign of good will rather than of collective responsibility, who will refuse? How helping Congress avoid responsibility will reduce the growth of spending is not self-evident.

An argument used in favor of the item veto is that it would interfere with the normal practice of logrolling in Congress. Here is legislation (in this example, items of appropriation) whose passage depends on spreading benefits broadly. If A gets a project but B does not, then A's project is also in jeopardy. At first blush, it appears that withdrawing a log (or logs) from the roll will mean fewer agreements and hence lower spending. QED: The item veto will reduce spending. Or will it? A linear argument suggests a one-way result; bringing in circular interaction effects can lead to the opposite conclusion. As a perceptive congressman put it, in a confidential interview,

> Where Congress has appropriated for A and for B, Congress means to say that it gives to each, conditioned upon the gift to the other, and that it gives to neither unless it gives to both. . . . The new veto power proposed would give the President the right by the veto of one and the approval of the other, to exercise the function of giving to one an appropriation independent of the other, when Congress has only given it conditioned upon the appropriation to the other.[28]

Congress is a highly interactive and tightly linked system. Alter one element and the others are also likely to change. When Congress is faced with the perpetual problem of overriding vetoes, the structure of incentives will change to favor much larger (and, therefore, aggregatively more expensive) logrolls. The ultimate size of unrepentant logrolling, the making of bargains that cumulate into ever-larger aggregates, cannot be reduced by cutting the number of small bargains because that only increases the incentive to make bigger bargains. What is necessary is to begin at the end, that is, to start by fixing the total permissible size of all bargains so that all expenditure logs must fit within a preexisting size.

[28]House Resolution No. 1879, 49th Congress, 1st Session, 3.

Then logrolls would compete with each other, thereby ending their upward spiral.

According to Lord Bryce, the item veto is one of those practices that "is desired by enlightened opinion."[29] The executive would be strengthened (doubly so in Bryce's day, since at the end of the nineteenth century the executive budget was not yet a reality) and responsibility more clearly identified and located in a centralized place. Indeed, the origin of the item veto in the United States lies in the Constitution of the Confederate States. The rationale there and then was avowedly to bring in some of the advantages of the British way. As we know, this hypothesis was never put to the test because the political system in which it was embedded was overthrown.

Without a global spending limit, the line-item veto would be both weak and perverse. It would be weak because the veto would apply only to a small proportion of the budget that is, like general government, either already under severe attack or, like maritime subsidies, has so far proved politically invulnerable. It would be perverse because pro-expenditure presidents could use the veto (or, more accurately, the threat of veto) to increase total spending, and because legislators would use the existence of a veto to increase spending bids on the grounds that presidents could always veto them if they were deemed unsound. Thus a measure designed to reduce spending and increase responsibility for budgetary totals probably would have exactly the opposite effects—increasing irresponsibility as well as the size of the budget.

But I have not yet considered how a line-item veto might work in the presence rather than the absence of global spending limits. Let us suppose that, by congressional or by constitutional action, budget outlays for any year are forbidden to exceed the prior year's totals times the percentage increase in GNP. Everyone would know that spending could not exceed a given sum for years to come. Let us suppose, further, that the usual incentives operated and spending reached this global limit. No

---

[29]Quoted in John F. Wolf, "The Item Veto in the American Constitutional System," *Georgetown Law Journal*, Vol. 25 (1936), p. 113.

doubt such a situation would reduce the demand for an item veto on the grounds that the end in view (i.e., control over spending) had been achieved by far more stringent and effective means. Nevertheless, I believe it will be instructive to consider how the veto would work under these much-altered circumstances.

Presidents so disposed could not use the threat of vetoing an item desired by many in Congress simply in order to increase an item they preferred. For, if more for one item means less for another (recall that everyone is operating at the margin of the global limit), presidents would have to match substantial increases with proposed cuts or leave it to congressmen to cut where they wanted. Such a strategy would be self-defeating.

Nor would congressional spenders be disposed to pad old items or slip in new ones on the supposition that presidents would be responsible for vetoing them. Under the new rules imposed by global spending limits, Congress could not act so as to exceed the global total. Congress itself would have to cut some items to make up for increases in others. Now this is what I understand about taking responsibility for the consequences of one's own actions. If Congress proposed a budget exceeding the limit (and even if it stayed within the limit), presidents could use their veto to cut at will, a process that would leave Congress in the weakest possible position.

With limits in place, therefore, the item veto would be restricted to two uses: (1) reducing the size of the budget below the global total, or (2) enhancing the bargaining power of presidents, vis-à-vis a congressional majority in regard to which items should be included in the budget at what level. Assuming that presidents, over a range of vetoes, have reasonable prospects of support from a little over one-third of the House or Senate, they can eliminate (or, in prior bargaining, reduce the amount of) spending items in dispute. This would spell enormous power for presidents who, with only minority support, could impose their will. Perhaps that threat would suffice to enhance the prospects of items presidents prefer over those desired by an ordinary majority of Congress. Perhaps Congress, mindful of being at a disadvantage, would word items so as to make them difficult to veto. In any event, we see that under global limits the item veto would actually work in the ways its sponsors desire by sometimes decreasing but never increasing the size of spending and by giving presidents greater power to make marginal adjustments in the budget. But if an item veto would work only in the presence of preexisting limits, we must turn to the question of limits for further instruction.

RESPONSIBILITY, MAYBE

If the item veto won't work, if Gramm–Rudman–Hollings is unworkable, if the balanced budget amendment is unpopular, what hope is there for responsible budgeting—that is, for paying for what you spend?

There is a glimmer of hope. In the letter from the House Republican leadership quoted in the Preface there was concern expressed about the absence of a point of order in the House against an appropriations bill that breaches the outlay total in the budget resolution. This concern is justified. Recently, the Committee for a Responsible Budget sounded the alarm. (See their letter on p. 460.)

Wonder of wonders, the House voted to cut the supplemental by $2 billion across-the-board to keep the appropriation within the total allocation. Responsibility lives. Maybe.

In some ways, OBRA is the epitome of responsibility; it raises a lot of revenues, cuts some spending, and bids to reduce the deficit substantially. Without an underlying consensus on taxing and spending, however, all manner of events may alter the situation. Should Democrats follow Senator Moynihan in reducing payroll taxes, making up the difference by large increases for upper-income taxpayers, all bets would be off. Should Republicans react to victory in the Persian Gulf War by keeping defense spending much higher than contemplated in the Budget Summit or OBRA, that would break the original understanding. Should there develop a variety of loopholes through which members of Congress of various stripes could push additional spending, the same result would ensue. Democrats wrote provisions into OBRA that might loosen its provisions should one of their party become president, a consideration considerably weaker since President Bush's popularity has risen so sharply. The best thing OBRA has going for it is that it is something. Should OBRA collapse, however, Gramm–Rudman is still on the books where its virtue is also that it is better than nothing. Better than something awful, however, is not the usual recommendation when the people involved are agreed on a course of action. The volatility of budgeting is not only a mirror of the world outside government to which it must adapt; it is also a product of disagreement over the fundamental dimensions of taxing and spending.

OVERLOADING BUDGETING

In the period of classical budgeting, there was an effective, albeit informal, ceiling beyond which spending could not go. Nowadays there are basic disagreements about the size and composition of the public sector. Bringing back the good old ways implies something that can no longer be achieved, namely, summoning up agreement on the underlying beliefs that once made them work.

Indeed, budget resolutions, automatic spending reductions to achieve balance, item vetos, balanced budget amendments, and offsets are all formal substitutes for what used to be done informally. If (and when) congressional majorities do wish to control spending, we have seen that spending ceilings safeguarded by requiring that additions be balanced by subtractions (or by new revenues) work powerfully well. There's a way if there's a will. Suppose, however, that not one, but several wills are incompatible? Then perhaps the budgetary stalemate of the early to mid-1980s may be seen not as an aberration but as a sign of continuing dissensus. What, then, can be hoped for from budgeting?

The budgetary process is an arena in which the struggle for power over public policy is worked out. Budgeting is a forum for the exercise of political power, not a substitute for that power. By itself, budgeting cannot form majorities and enforce their will. While the rules for voting on spending and taxing may make agreement marginally easier or harder, they cannot close unbridgeable gaps. It is more reasonable to

RESPONSIBLE BUDGET ACTION GROUP

220 1/2 "E" STREET, N.E.
WASHINGTON, D.C. 20002

(202) 547-4484

April 9, 1987

Members of the 100th Congress
U.S. House of Representatives
Washington, DC 20515

Dear Congressman:

Do you think the supplemental appropriations bill is just business as usual? If so, maybe you ought to consider what the final results on the Gramm–Rudman–Hollings FY87 deficit target will be. The FY87 Spring Supplemental Appropriations Bill (H.R. 1827) is as clear a vote as you ever will face on fiscal responsibility.

The simple fact is: there is no money to pay for this bill. The CBO current status shows that even if Congress does not pass another spending bill this year, outlays will exceed the FY87 budget total by $13.4 billion.

We recognize there may be high priority items for which you must pass a supplemental appropriations bill. This is not an argument for or against the specific spending items in this bill. Congress, however, should find off-sets to pay for those increases—given the fact that you already are over the budget.

In the House, there is no point of order against an appropriations bill which breaches the outlay total in the budget. The Appropriations Committee will argue they are within the budget authority ceiling, and budget authority is all the Appropriations Committee really can control, so there should be no budget argument about this bill.

But outlays do matter. We determine the deficit by subtracting revenues from outlays. The outlay overages which would result from enactment of H.R. 1827 are not assumed in the baseline for FY88. Enactment of this bill without off-sets would increase the deficit both this year and next.

Early last year, the first and only sequester under G-R-H cut FY86 outlays by $11.4 billion. That action had an added benefit. It reduced this year's deficit by $16.3 billion. This supplemental, by contrast, would make the deficit problem worse next year. H.R. 1827 as reported would eat up nearly half the spending cuts contained in the Budget Resolution the House just adopted for FY88.

If you care about the size of next year's deficit, if you care about trying to live within the budget this year, you cannot ignore the impact of this bill. The amounts involved are not large in the context of total Federal spending: less than 1% of total outlays controllable through appropriations actions; but they are significant as a measure of Congress' commitment to spending restraint. If reducing the deficit remains a high priority on your agenda, surely you can find off-sets for spending you believe to be necessary.

Sincerely,

Robert N. Giaimo   John J. Rhodes

RNG/JJR:mfh

suppose that general political processes shape budgeting than that budgeting determines political alignments.

It is one thing to translate decisions and choices on defense and domestic policy into budgetary categories; it is quite another to use the budgetary process itself to decide who shall pay and who shall receive. Only a political system so polarized that it cannot make these choices through the usual legislative, executive, and party mechanisms, I submit, would arrive at a general formula (e.g., GRH) for maximizing discontent rather than trying to agree, case by case, on reasonable choices. To saddle budgeting with a formula for decision making that is nearly as broad as government itself is to make budgeting equivalent to government. I bring up this truism—budgeting is a subsystem of politics, not vice versa—because of the current tendency to overload budgeting. As much as I respect the importance of budgeting and the talents of budgeters, to substitute budgeting for governing will not work. No better illustration can be found of budgeting as politicking than the struggles over how and how much to reduce the deficit.

THE DEFICIT

11

WHY DO STUDENTS OF BUDGETING and of American politics need to understand the deficit? Two reasons are paramount: One is that the federal deficit has become part of the language of budgeting; to understand what is said and done about budgeting, therefore, it is necessary to understand the deficit. The other and perhaps more important reason is that the deficit has become the leading issue of our time. As Joseph White and I put it,

> Political time is counted not in years but in issues; a political era is defined by the concerns that dominate debate and action, so that about other issues we ask: How does that affect _____? . . . The budget has been to our era what civil rights, communism, the depression, industrialization, and slavery were at other times. Nor does the day of the budget show signs of ending. . . . Year after year the key question has been, What will the president and Congress do about the deficit?[1]

I deliberately do not refer to the impact of the deficit on the economy because the importance of that impact is part of the controversy.

In this chapter I ask and attempt to answer the following questions: Where did the deficit come from? What were its causes and what are its consequences? Are its consequences so bad as to require a drastic solution? Who or what was to blame for the creation of an annual $200 billion (or without Social Security surpluses but with the savings and loan bailout, $300 billion) deficit? And what size should the deficit be?

---

[1] Joseph White and Aaron Wildavsky, *The Deficit and the Public Interest* (Berkeley: University of California Press, 1990), pp. xv–xvi.

462

WHO DONE IT?[2]

In February 1983 the Congressional Budget Office (CBO) projected $200 billion deficits far into the future. It explained that "to a great extent" the 1983 and 1984

> deficits are attributable to the economic recession, which has reduced federal revenues and increased federal outlays for unemployment compensation and other income maintenance programs. But even as these cyclical crises wither as economic recovery proceeds, the proposed deficits remain . . . high. . . . This indicates a long-term mismatch between federal spending and taxing.[3]

CBO projected a deficit in the mid-1980s that would consume considerably more GNP than in the late 1970s, even though unemployment in those years would be similar.

This long-term mismatch was what economists called the "structural deficit." This structural deficit amounted to 3.6 percent of GNP difference between income and outgo, consisting of a rise in outlays of 1 percent of GNP, and a drop in revenues of 2.6 percent. By this standard, the major source of the deficit problem was the reduction in revenues, though there was also a lack of spending restraint.

Any analysis was flawed, however, if it assumed that 1981's 20.9 percent of GNP was a politically acceptable base level for federal taxes. The pattern of the 1970s was to let inflation increase the tax burden and then have a tax cut. In 1978, revenues had been 19.1 percent of GNP, but bracket creep, payroll tax increases for social security, the windfall-profits tax on oil, and the effects (from 1977 to 1979) of a progressive income tax on increasing real incomes had increased the tax burden.

The trend in federal government tax burdens from 1961 to 1981 (see Table 11-1) showed that taxes, including higher income taxes, were a lot higher than had been customary. The 1981 tax burden was higher than

---

[2]This chapter is a revised version of work done with Joseph White, *The Deficit and the Public Interest* (Berkeley: University of California Press, 1990); and "How to Fix the Deficit—Really," *The Public Interest*, No. 94 (Winter 1989), pp. 3–24.

[3]Congressional Budget Office, "Reducing the Deficit: Spending and Revenue Options," A Report to the Senate and House Committees on the Budget—Part III, February 1983, p. 1.

TABLE 11-1

Federal Taxes as a Percent of GNP

FY1961–1965	FY1966–1970	FY1971–1975	FY1976–1980	FY1981
19.2%	19.2%	18.6%	19.2%	20.8%

Source: Gregory B. Mills and John L. Palmer, *The Deficit Dilemma* (Washington, D.C.: Urban Institute, 1983), pp. 8–10.

most people or politicians desired.[4] While it is clear that Carter was willing to use bracket creep to narrow the deficit, most observers in Washington in 1980 assumed there would be a tax cut in the early 1980s no matter who got elected.

If a normal level of revenues is roughly 19 percent of GNP, not roughly 21 percent, then the long-term budget problem was not simply an artifact of the Reagan tax cuts. (The reason the tax level did not decrease was that the Carter administration had left behind an equivalent amount of tax increases, such as the social security payroll tax.) We must, therefore, turn our attention to the outlay side.

1. In 1979—a pretty good year for the economy—outlays at 20.8 percent of GNP were 1.2 percent of GNP above revenues.

2. Spending growth from 1979–1985, roughly 2.4 percent of GNP, can be entirely explained by increases in defense, social security, medicare, and debt interest. The real growth in social spending was entirely a product of the bad economy; it disguised the significant reductions made in domestic discretionary programs and in means-tested entitlements during this period.[5]

3. During the same period, social security got into trouble. Its difficulty stemmed from the recession's effect on GNP, and from stagflation in the last half of the 1970s. The recession slowed production, and thus revenue collection, while not slowing the

[4]Gregory B. Mills and John L. Palmer, *The Deficit Dilemma* (Washington, D.C.: Urban Institute, 1983), pp. 8–10, give a short summary of the tax increases.

[5]For extensive discussion, see Jack A. Meyer, "Budget Cuts in the Reagan Administration: A Question of Fairness," in D. Lee Bauden, ed., *The Social Contract Revisited* (Washington, D.C.: Urban Institute, 1984), pp. 33–64.

growth in program recipients or the delayed effects of their COLAs (cost of living adjustments). Stagflation caused benefits, linked to prices, to grow faster than either the economy or contributions to the social security fund, which increased more slowly than wages. These combined effects threw the social security system into crisis as payments to recipients grew faster than collections from workers. Medicare, meanwhile, grew mainly because of the tremendous cost inflation in the medical business, a trend with which Congress had been wrestling for years.[6] Given underlying demographic trends (more old people), only an optimist could predict even a stabilization of this medicare increase.

4. Net interest costs increased drastically because the government had to borrow more as deficits increased; then borrowing and interest began to feed on themselves, generating higher deficits, more borrowing, and, it was argued, higher interest rates. The economy's troubles—inflation and then unemployment, creating first an insistence by lenders for higher rates and then a great need to borrow to make up for lower incomes—were the major cause of the government's interest-rate problems.

5. The defense buildup began under the Democrats; not until 1983 did the Reagan budgets significantly increase outlays.[7] Still, a substantial part of the increase in the "structural deficit" was due to Reagan administration plans to raise defense spending.

These upward trends in entitlements, in interest costs, and in defense suggest that given the behavior of the economy, any president and any Congress would have faced a serious deficit problem by 1983. They suggest also that only part of the problem was avoidable. The Democrats lost the 1980 election in part, they believed, because they had let taxes rise to their highest level since World War II.

Where could the government have found 3.6 percent of GNP in budget savings to close the gap created by the structural deficit? Keep

[6]See CBO, "Reducing the Deficit," pp. 98–99.
[7]See CBO, "The Economic and Budget Outlook," p. 153.

taxes at 20.9 percent? That would be a big chunk, but then there might not be a recovery in 1983 or a president in office to support it. Have a slower defense buildup? Worth a try but it would be very hard, given first the Soviet invasion of Afghanistan and then the backlog of budget authority from the last year of Carter and the first two years of the Reagan administration. Reduce interest costs? It was too late and not really subject to discretionary action.

How about domestic programs? Reductions actually began under Carter. Then, as David Stockman explained, at the beginning of 1984,

> The Great Society programs . . . peaked out at a cost of $140 billion in 1984 dollars in 1979–1980. That cost will be down to $110 billion this year, no matter what Congress does. We have not succeeded in challenging the premise of the Great Society, but the level has been adjusted downward. . . . Aside from defense, interest, and social security, we have shrunk the government by 15 percent.[8]

Unfortunately for budget balancers, the big money was in the accounts Stockman couldn't reach.

From 1962 to 1979, nondefense spending increased its share of GNP from 9.9 to 15.9 percent, yet total spending rose only from 19.5 to 20.8 percent. Growth in domestic spending was financed not by taxes or deficits but by a lower defense share of total outlays.

Spending grew because of past decisions made about entitlements for the elderly: They grew because the eligible population grew—people were living longer, and more and more of them were fully vested in the social security system; there were also big, multiple legislated hikes in social security in the 1969–1972 period with the support of Republican President Richard Nixon. In 1962 the Old Age and Disability funds had 16.8 million beneficiaries; in 1972, 25.2 million; in 1982, 31.9 million.[9] Spending grew in medicare because virtually nobody anticipated the costs of coverage; Congress began struggling with medical inflation soon

[8]Peter W. Bernstein, "David Stockman: No More Big Budget Cuts," _Fortune,_ February 6, 1984, pp. 53–56.

[9]Committee on Ways and Means, U.S. House of Representatives, _Background Material and Data on Programs Within the Jurisdiction of the Committee on Ways and Means,_ Committee Print, 99th Congress, 1st Session, 99-2, February 22, 1985 (U.S. Government Printing Office), pp. 55–56.

after the program began. Costs grew, finally, because politicians kept benefits in line with rising prosperity (but out of line with contributions by recipients), eager to please a powerful group of voters and confident that continuing economic growth would enable current workers to pay the bill. The last big increase in social security coverage in 1972 tells both sides of the story: Democrats and Republicans competed to woo the elderly; the resulting increase "was financed largely by a change in actuarial assumptions" that politicians had little reason to reject.[10] But the economy did not behave as expected, and almost everybody was asking the wrong question.

With the first OPEC oil shock in 1973, the economy went into a "quiet depression,"[11] and social security got into deep trouble. Revenues for the trust fund would not cover the outlays. Social security had to be "rescued" twice. Whether social security's taxes could fund the system's expenses was important. But throughout the program's history, *no one asked* a second question: *If social security taxes increased, would those be new taxes or replace old ones?* (Tax aficionados speak of "fiscal cannibalism" where one tax eats up another.) Government raised the social security payroll tax from 3.1 percent of GNP in 1962 to 6.6 percent in 1982.[12] And it was scheduled by legislation to go higher. When these new taxes took effect, the government usually cut other taxes to compensate. This strategy worked because either the economy grew so strongly that other programs could live with a smaller share, or because spending (and thus revenues) was diverted from the shrinking defense budget to domestic (mostly welfare) programs. But it never had to make that choice—higher taxes on social security in addition to or in subtraction from income and other taxes—in advance. The repetition of what appears to be a truism—social security is self-financing—by Ronald Reagan, his congressional opponents, and spokesmen for the elderly, though true as far as it goes, left the profoundly mistaken

[10]Martha Derthick, *Policymaking for Social Security* (Washington, D.C.: Brookings Institution, 1979), p. 357.

[11]The term is Frank Levy's. See his *Dollars and Dreams: The Changing American Income Distribution* (New York: Russell Sage Foundation, 1987).

[12]CBO, "The Economic and Budget Outlook," p. 162.

impression that by far the biggest domestic program did not affect the rest of government. Nonsense. Individuals and businesses feel taxation from all sources, so government eventually had to face the consequences of social security expansion either in deficits, higher taxes, or lower spending later on other things.

Here's the catch: Maybe the government *could not* have chosen in advance. No one could foresee the size of future problems; perhaps they would be small, for economic growth heals many ills. Perhaps it was for people in the future to choose whether they wanted higher taxes or fewer programs, or even (gasp!) higher deficits. Even if politicians in 1962 had decided that other programs would have to be cut by the same amount by 1972, for instance, how could they have done so? All right, one might say: If you can't plan, don't make the commitment. Don't have a national retirement plan, or policies with long-term, increasing costs. Toss out civil service pensions and medicare while you're at it. But that inaction would be intolerable. People in real life make long-term commitments like buying a house (even with an adjustable-rate mortgage). They marry, have children, plan to send them to college; they will figure out later what to sacrifice to that end. The government, with heavy public support, committed itself to social security. There is little evidence that people, on the whole, dispute that commitment or its necessity. Some problems come with the territory.

Is there, then, no room for choice? Yes, there is; one can always exercise prudence. Increases in payments to recipients, for example, could have been smaller. Many provisions, such as early retirement, could have been less generous. When bad times come, the nation must decide who will bear the costs of change. But choice is politically circumscribed by the difficulty of breaking promises on which millions have planned their lives. Because old commitments did not match the new economy, huge deficits would have occurred even without Ronald Reagan—unless you think taxes were going well above the level that helped defeat Jimmy Carter. The Democrats' response would have been that they would have cut taxes by less than Reagan did and accelerate defense less. If true, that would have made a modest difference.

What could the politicians have done about the coming tidal wave of deficits? The Reagan administration assumed away the problem, hoping, as Reagan's Budget Director David Stockman wrote, that "the transition from rising to falling inflation and from low real growth to rapid output expansion would occur immediately and simultaneously, and without intervening financial and economic disturbance."[13] If everything had worked, spending would have stabilized between 19 and 20 percent of GNP, that is, at roughly the same level as expected revenues, and the budget would have been balanced. Neither they nor their opponents anticipated that inflation would be bridled so quickly as to slash revenues, nor the size of the economic slump that increased the deficit even more.

The Federal Reserve and the administration were only too successful in fighting inflation with a monetary squeeze. In addition to the increased expenditure and lower revenue due to recession, receipts plunged far below estimates because no one, neither the Reagan administration nor its opponents nor any one of the private forecasters, expected so fast a drop in inflation.

Not only were higher deficits likely given the course of the economy, but it is also hard to argue that the first two installments of Reagan's individual income tax cut in 1981 and 1982 were excessive either in prospect (when they seemed smaller because people anticipated more inflation) or in effect (for they responded to a much bigger recession than was anticipated). As for business tax cuts, Democratic tax leaders accepted the basic size of the administration's package, for Democratic economists were also pushing "capital formation." Given what economists were saying in 1981, as well as the actual course of the economy, it is hard to argue that tax policy as of the beginning of 1983 could have been much different.[14] To say that the nation would have stood for still higher taxes in 1981 and 1982 is not only to go against historical experience but also to imply that Democrats would not have cut taxes. The evidence is that they would have, albeit not as much.[15]

The difference between the two parties was essentially the third year

[13]David A. Stockman, *The Triumph of Politics: How the Reagan Revolution Failed* (New York: Harper & Row, 1986), p. 399.

[14]Mills and Palmer, *Deficit Dilemma*, p. 22.

[15]See Joseph White and Aaron Wildavsky, *The Deficit and the Public Interest* (University of California Press, 1990).

of the tax cut. For that Reagan is responsible. By 1982 he knew that large deficits were in store. He chose to err on the optimistic side, toward higher rather than lower rates of economic growth and thus bigger rather than smaller deficits. Once the tax package was enacted, he protected the third year with his veto, because he cared more about lower taxes than deficits, arguing that Congress would just spend the extra money anyway. Although Reagan did not start the defense buildup, he pushed it farther and faster than a more fiscally prudent president might have. That part of the deficit, by no means the largest part but a part, is fairly attributable to him.

The president could not be blamed for the stagflation of the 1970s or the recession of his first term, save to the extent that he supported Federal Reserve Chairman Paul Volcker's monetary squeeze. Possibly another Fed chairman might have brought the economy in with a softer landing. But citizens were so distraught over inflation that "too tough" would have been judged far better than "too weak" by market and populace. Credit for the good face of deflation has to go with blame for its bad side in reducing revenues. The blame for commitments past might also seem like credit to supporters of social security.

A reasonable conclusion would be that all who govern now and in the past half century share some of the blame for the deficit, some more than others, but few guiltless. Hardly anyone anticipated the relatively poor economic performance of the 1970s. Much of this slowdown may be due to international oil increases or to vast numbers of new entrants (especially women) into the labor market or the emergence of new economic powers on the world scene or too high taxes or insufficient demand or too little saving, some of which government could affect and much of which it could not.[16]

It has been alleged that Reagan engineered the large deficit in order to keep down domestic spending. Not so.[17] He hoped that his policies would be successful; that is, the nation would avoid a recession and lower

---

[16]See Frank Levy, *Dollars and Dreams* (Russell Sage Foundation, 1987), for a splendid analysis of how demographic changes affect spending outcomes.

[17]This judgment is based on numerous interviews and a perusal of virtually all of the documentary record. See White and Wildavsky, *The Deficit and the Public Interest.*

tax rates would bring in higher revenues. Once faced with a big deficit, however, he did choose to accept it rather than raise income taxes substantially.

THE DEFICIT PANIC

The most obvious result of both President Reagan's choices and the policies he inherited, however, was the deficit panic of the 1980s. The deficit became the dominant policy problem, an issue that shaped consideration of all other issues. It was blamed for every economic ill, from inflation to unemployment to high interest rates to the large trade imbalance, from the strong dollar to the weak dollar. Strife over the deficit spilled over from policy into procedure, hogging the congressional agenda, encouraging paralyzing legislation, such as Gramm–Rudman, frustrating legislators, and stalemating the government. Otherwise, it was benign.

All political factions, hamstrung by the deficit, increased the pressure on themselves by using the deficit to attack each other. Liberals, blocked from responding to their definition of social needs by a lack of money, claimed prosperity under Ronald Reagan was bought on the credit card, to be charged to our grandchildren. Conservatives blamed ills like high taxes on the legacy of liberal overspending. Centrists, hating the deficit for its own sake as a sign of the government's inability to control itself, accused everyone, including themselves, of cowering before "special interests." Moderates, exemplified by people like Pete Peterson, former head of Lehman Brothers investment house and former Secretary of Commerce, excoriated the existing political system for failing to balance the budget. Whereas the economic conservatives want liberty and growth and the egalitarian liberals want equality and growth, these social conservatives want balanced growth. Their Cassandra cries are heard on radio, television, newspapers, magazines, wherever people listen. And they invoke the public interest over and over as if there was only a single interest and they were the only ones who knew exactly what it was.

Propagated by so many factions for so many different reasons, the anti-deficit clamor has persisted for so long that it has taken on a life of its own. The deficit has become a self-fulfilling crisis. The deficit is a difficulty, I contend, but it is not a disaster next to which all else is insignificant.

When the deficit panic began in 1980, it was supposedly due to the deficit's inflationary effect. Jimmy Carter was excoriated for a proposed deficit of $15.6 billion! When the deficit burgeoned and inflation shrank, however, the panic did not decline accordingly. As Herbert Stein expressed the common syllogism, budget deficits cause bad things, so whatever bad things were happening to us were blamed on deficits. The evolution of its supposed evils, from inflation to recession to strong dollar to weak dollar, and more, suggests that the massive disapproval of deficits has been supported by no consistent logic of cause and effect. The cause is constant but the supposed effects keep changing.

Economic arguments about the deficit have been inconsistent. By economic arguments I mean those made in the public sphere of policy debate. When *Time* and *Newsweek* do a cover article on the deficit, or report that a market crash requires deficit reduction, it is part of the process of political debate that shapes notions of how to manage the economy. Since that debate is a process of persuasion, even otherwise trustworthy economists sometimes shade their arguments for effect in order to push the policy they desire. Excessive condemnation of the deficit has proceeded, in part, from such experts putting matters too strongly for fear of otherwise being ignored by politicians, or in order to counter the minority of economists who dismiss the deficit's importance. Where the press presents majority economic wisdom, the schools of economists make arguments that fit into wider politico-economic agendas.

My own views on deficits are well-expressed in Guess and Koford's study of OECD countries: "The U.S. results, taken by themselves, imply that deficits do not cause, but are themselves caused by, inflation and reduced national product. If the United States continues to enjoy rapid economic growth and reduced inflation, we expect that the budget deficits should shrink from current projections. However, the broader seventeen-country results show that any definite relationship is difficult to pinpoint. We conclude that the macroeconomic harmfulness of budget deficits has not been shown, certainly for deficits within historical experience."[18]

Although the deficit need not cause inflation or recession, a weak dollar or a strong dollar, reasons for concern remain. The deficit feeds the interest costs of the federal government. More and more of the federal dollar goes to debt service. From an economically conservative point of view, this may be desirable. From an economically liberal view, this restriction is doubly undesirable: Debt creates economic opportunities for the well-off and limits new social programs for poor people. Net interest payments roughly equaled the size of the deficit in fiscal year 1988. Many Democrats have been concerned that the deficit crowds out social program initiatives, now and in the future. Giving up programs now, however, for programs they might not get later is sure to seem to them like a bad bargain. Their ideal is higher revenues without reductions in their favored domestic programs.

A second argument says the budget must be balanced, or more, so as to increase national savings. Productivity has grown slowly; more productivity requires more investment; investment requires more savings; the United States saves less than its major competitors, particularly Japan; government deficits, by definition, reduce national savings; since our growth was too slow even before the era of big deficits, we therefore have to raise saving above the level of that time. Therefore, the federal government needs to bring its budget into balance or even surplus.

This savings argument has become the major reason academic economists object to the deficit. Savings, surely, is a Good Thing (though at other times it has appeared too much of a Good Thing), but I have a few questions. If investment is so strongly related to productivity growth, why did growth decrease steadily through the 1970s, while investment remained steady? Growth is a long-term problem, not a short-term crisis: Why is it to be treated as requiring immediate drastic changes in the entire federal government, rather than a slow movement

[18]George Guess and Kenneth Koford, "Inflation, Recession and the Federal Budget Deficit (or, Blaming Economic Problems on a Statistical Mirage)," *Policy Sciences*, Vol. 17 (1984), pp. 385–402; quote on p. 400.

toward less consumption and more investment throughout our economy? That would require attention to the composition of outlays, the type of taxes, and many other complicated matters that have only begun to be addressed in the 1990 deficit reduction legislation discussed in the next chapter. Would it be morally right for government to force individuals to save more? The counterargument goes that it is precisely because we seem unable to shift the long-term pattern of individual saving that the net dissaving of the federal government (that is, the deficit) becomes so important. Could a fall-off in savings be due to other factors, such as changes in the life cycle (e.g., baby boomers spending more on education, housing, and children, therefore temporarily saving less)? Could it be that Americans only appear to be saving less because equity in mortgages and a significant part of pensions are not counted as savings?

It bothers some people to discover foreigners are taking up the slack and investing more in the United States. I consider that an act of confidence. Now if there were capital flight, that would be a reason to worry. Why does it matter to us where the money comes from? In the nineteenth century, a great deal of development in the United States took place with foreign money. Why shouldn't they share our risks?

Even if all other things are not quite equal, I would like the nation's investment to increase. That is a very long-term concern; it makes little difference whether the budget reaches some desired state in five or eight or ten years. The savings argument therefore does not justify a demand that the federal budget be balanced soon. It does argue for lower deficits, while telling us little about how much lower, how quickly.

The argument that the deficit must be reduced to guarantee market confidence is ubiquitous. Yet it presumes falsely that we can both know and influence what the financial markets "expect." Certainly we cannot assume that markets think (if they do) like an economist. For example, the dollar's steady increase in Reagan's first term cannot simply be ascribed to high U.S. interest rates. The United States was running high trade deficits, exchanging paper for goods, which ought to produce a countervailing trend for the paper (the dollar) to depreciate. If large budget and trade deficits increase the value of a currency, the dollar should be riding high, which it is not. Perhaps investors put their money where they trust the government. They fled the franc when socialist François Mitterand was elected president of France, then bought dollars when America was governed by the hypercapitalist Reagan. This may be rational, but has nothing to do with inflation, interest rates, or other measurable variables.

Nobody knows why markets, whether in stocks or bonds or currencies or hog bellies, go in any particular direction, at any time. If they did, they would be rich. There are tendencies and explanations that look obvious in retrospect, but markets are panicky, neurotic, swayed by a million forces we don't understand, and thus unpredictable. And they don't behave the way their "experts" claim.

Market gurus told the politicians in 1980 that a $15 billion deficit would create hyperinflation; then when the government ran deficits of more than that per month, the markets threw a massive party (the stock market boom), but kept claiming the deficit was terrible. Would you have much confidence in such experts' judgment?

There is a whole lot of dollars controlled by nervous international investors. In recent years, a substantial portion of our national consumption and investment—roughly the same as our budget and trade deficits—has been loaned to us by foreigners. If they were suddenly to withdraw that funding, our interest rates might spiral (to attract the money back); the dollar might plummet (thereby increasing inflation through the price of imports, perhaps even driving the OPEC cartel back together); any number of nasty scenarios could unravel. We therefore want to be able to intervene to prevent small panics from becoming big ones. To do so, the United States needs cooperation from the governments and central banks of our major allies. They naturally do not desire a doomsday scenario, but they don't want to be alone in fighting it, and they cannot buy dollars forever if nobody else in their countries wants them. They want, at least, to believe that the U.S. government is doing what it can to reduce the trade deficit.

In order to deal with these allies, therefore, there was a strong case to be made for taking action to reduce the deficit to a level they would consider responsible—the Japanese and German norm of about 1 to 2 percent of GNP. That is what the 1990 budget package (probably) does.

Economists are hardly alone in thinking politicians have not done enough about the deficit. In giving talks on the deficit, I ask the audience whether they believe Congress and the president have done a little, a fair amount, or a lot to reduce the deficit. In every instance an overwhelming proportion signifies that the politicians have done very little. The audience mistakes the apparent lack of progress in reducing the deficit, especially to balance the budget, for failure to take corrective action. Not true.

As Rodney Dangerfield gets no respect, politicians neither get nor give themselves credit. From 1982 on, Congress has gored a series of special interests, ranging from doctors to defense contractors. You don't take on the AMA (freezing physician payments on medicare), or Wall Street (many of the provisions of the 1984 tax bill), or the armed services and arms makers (cutting defense in the past six years), unless you really care about the deficit. Through 1986, according to the most careful analysis of policy changes, the politicians had reduced the fiscal year 1986 deficit by an estimated $162 billion, or 3.9 percent of gross national product, from what it would have been if past policies had been left in place.[19] Why, then, did these efforts not show up in absolutely smaller deficits?

Perhaps these analyses give Congress a bit too much credit. Policy in 1981 included a projected defense buildup of 7 percent real growth per year. You can save a lot of money by scaling down such an increase; it hurts less than cutting from what people already have. Yet the defense buildup was stopped because moderate Republicans and conservative Democrats who supported it in 1980 and 1981 decided that reducing the deficit was more important. (No one then imagined that the cold war would be won, thus allowing even bigger cuts in 1990.) Nevertheless, despite persistent and positive congressional efforts, the deficit did not decline.

---

[19]Joseph J Minarik and Rudolph G. Penner, "Fiscal Choices," in Isabel V. Sawhilll, ed., *Challenge to Leadership* (Washington, D.C.: Urban Institute, 1988), pp. 279–316; John Palmer did his calculations for "Should We Worry About the Deficit?" by John Palmer and Stephanie Gould, *The Washington Monthly*, May 1986, pp. 43–46.

Unfortunately for our politicians, the deficit problem was too big, always bigger than it seemed. Going back through summaries of each year's efforts, we can see Congress swimming upstream. Each year's policy change was balanced by revisions in the economic assumptions, namely, worse than projected, so the deficit kept ending up around $200 billion. Since they were not getting anywhere, politicians came to believe they were not doing anything.

Dealing with the huge budget shortfall was made even more difficult by political dissensus. Many of us can think of ways to reduce the deficit substantially. Ronald Reagan would have eliminated much of the domestic government. Jesse Jackson would lop off much of the military and soak the rich. Any reader could no doubt craft a more coherent deficit-reduction package than Congress did in the years between 1982 and 1989 or than it did in 1990. So (I hope this is not too surprising) could any legislator. Yet the problem of budgeting is not for any one of us to create a budget alone but to do it together. Assembling a majority behind any scheme is difficult, because anything substantial we do will change the size, shape, and role in society of our government. You might say that the participants in budgeting agree on everything except how much revenue should be raised and who should pay, how much should be spent and on which programs. The budget is about the future shape of government and society, not just balance; balance at low or high levels of spending would make a difference for our future.

American political activists and citizens agree that the deficit is a bad thing. Yet the budget deficit is a no-win issue. The presidential nominating process of 1988 showed that any candidate who proposed a real solution would lose more votes than he would gain. On the Democratic side, former Arizona governor Bruce Babbitt challenged his opponents to stand up for a tax hike. His opponents stayed in their chairs, yet applause from journalists and commentators couldn't keep Babbitt in the race. Among the Republicans, Vice President Bush bounced back from his Iowa defeat by charging that Senator Dole opposed tax increases less than he did. Bush promised to attack the deficit with vetoes (ignoring the fact that most spending is in entitlements, interest on debt, and other fixed commitments that cannot be vetoed) and a "flexible freeze" (a nice self-canceling phrase) on domestic, discretionary spending, that is, a whole 11 percent of the budget.

Perhaps the candidates were just hiding their budget plans until after the election. Therefore, deficit-cutting strategists wished for a fairy godmother to give politicians some magic deficit-reducing potion. They even created such a creature—the National Economic Commission (NEC). The NEC was a bipartisan group modeled on the Greenspan Commission that supposedly fixed social security.[20] Sometime between December 1988 and March 1989, this group of (politically) wise men was supposed to propose a budget solution free from the political considerations that it was believed made it impossible for elected officials to do so. The NEC had first-rate staff and much political experience. Yet the same conflicts that invaded Congress and stultified its decision-making processes also invaded the NEC. It ended its time without producing an agreed report or a plan for budget balance.

Politicians could not balance the budget because the policy costs of doing so would have been huge. Before the costs of the savings and loan bailout ballooned, making the task obviously impossible, Joseph White and I asked what kind of deficit reduction in the first year of a new government, elected in 1988, would give a balanced budget, as Gramm–Rudman promised, by fiscal year 1992? Allowing for complexities of implementation, we estimated that the new government could meet the Gramm–Rudman target if it changed policy by $100 billion on taking office. How much is that in policy terms?

One hundred billion dollars roughly equals the U.S. navy. Not a smaller navy but no navy. One hundred billion dollars is larger than medicaid, the Department of Education, National Institutes of Health (including cancer and AIDS research), Department of Justice, Department of State, and Federal Highway Administration *combined.* That is the scale of policy change—no navy or any six domestic departments of your choice—required to eliminate the deficit through spending cuts.

How could we have found our $100 billion from taxes? Individual

---

[20]See Joseph White and Aaron Wildavsky, *The Deficit and the Public Interest,* Chapter 22, pp. 530–61.

income taxes would have to be raised by 21 percent, almost completely reversing the 1981 tax cut. Or we could have raised individual income taxes by 10 percent, corporate taxes by 20 percent, and doubled excise taxes. Even the most dedicated fan of the public sector can imagine the political difficulty of such tax hikes. Instead one might try a "balanced" package, say raising income taxes by 10 percent, cutting the navy 20 percent (pick a fleet!), and abolishing medicaid. That sounds no easier.

Even more narrow options for deficit reduction had difficulties: Small does not mean harmless. For example, determining eligibility or benefit levels for Aid to Dependent Children and food stamps by counting as income payments under the Low-Income Home Energy Assistance program (LIHEAP) would have saved $225 million in FY90. It would eliminate duplication as well as a situation in which some recipients of LIHEAP are better off monetarily than nonrecipients who actually earn more. But the change would penalize families whose energy bills are particularly high, exactly the large families the program is supposed to help. What are they to do, shower in the dark? Move south?

These examples should put common calls for "tough choices" in perspective. Choices are tough because the consequences either way are unpalatable. Often people hide these choices by talking about cutting the deficit in stages: $30 billion one year, $20 billion the next year, and so on. It may well be desirable to cut spending incrementally. But that does not change the huge amounts of reductions required to approach a balanced budget. Gramm–Rudman is another version of the same (self-)deception. Cutting in stages doesn't change the policy stakes. Indeed, what you would have to do if you did it all at once is the *smallest* measure of the stakes, for that approach would maximize the savings from lower interest payments. There is no "free lunch" of harmless deficit reductions. Politicians who do not want to slash medicaid or education or infrastructure or defense or raise income taxes by more than they have ever been raised in peacetime are not showing a lack of courage; they are making a reasonable choice about the national interest.

Budgeting is a process of discovering and enforcing preferences. The most basic difficulty is matching preferences about programs and totals. In the 1980s, panic about the deficit led both elites and the public to claim a breakdown of governance, for the total, the deficit, was too big. Yet it is fair to argue that, facing tough choices, Congress and the president have bargained responsibly, balancing the costs and benefits of both lower deficits and the policy choices to get there. The macroeconomic logic of balancing the budget is, at best, confused; balancing the budget would have serious policy costs. These costs are not simply "politics" or "special interests." Social Security is in the special interest of the elderly; the navy is in the special interest of the people who serve in and sell to it. They are also policies that define the nation; a nation that at least tries to guarantee to all citizens a financially decent old age, and one that is the world's dominant sea power. Whether the national interest is served by cutting such programs to eliminate the deficit is an open question. Politics is about debating such questions, not assuming they have only one answer.

I have taken an uncommon approach to the deficit by viewing it as a policy problem like any other. Looking at the deficit this way, I have reached the following conclusions:

1. There is no economic necessity to balance the budget within the next five years. Mainstream economics provides no reason why deficits of 2–3 percent of GNP should cause panic, and smaller deficits, say 1 percent of GNP, are surely acceptable.

2. The deficit persists not because of a lack of political "courage" but because politicians and the public judge, correctly, that serious efforts to reduce it—whether tax hikes or cuts in domestic or defense spending—themselves have serious consequences for the general welfare.

3. The 1990 budget agreement is, therefore, in terms of size, an adequate response to the deficit "crisis." Barring a severe and prolonged depression, and despite its optimistic economic assumptions, it should reduce the government's borrowing so that the national debt as a share of the economy, which reflects the debt burden on both citizens and the government, decreases.

If citizens were to look at the federal government's actual accomplishments in holding down the size of the deficit, they might be optimistic about further progress. Were these same citizens to look at the ideological divisions over how to reduce the deficit, they might well be more pessimistic. There were grounds in the 1990 legislation—to cut the deficit and alter once more the process of budgeting—for both feelings. As congressional Democrats in 1991 wanted to meet the recession with increased spending, they discovered that the new legistation prevented them from doing so. What will happen when the general public discovers they are being forced to save by artificially inflating the size of the deficit is anybody's guess. This part of the deficit story comes next.

THE SOLUTION?

12

THE HOPE WAS THAT IF THE prospect of a balanced budget were dangled before the American electorate by an agreement from on-high, the bane of tax increases and spending cuts would be overawed by the glow of a leadership willing to sacrifice itself for the public interest. How could the president and his advisers believe this fairy tale? How could they not when every source of responsible opinion kept telling them that all that was required to make big dents in the deficit was political courage. Skeptics like political scientist Donald Kettl pointed out the obvious difficulty: "The president," Kettl said, "has little incentive to take strong action to reduce the deficit when the consequences are that the Democrats would make hay out of it."[1] Well, the president did screw up his courage and the Democratic party did make hay out of it, thus explaining why such action had not been forthcoming earlier.

Before we plunge into this serpentine tale of budget agreements won, lost, and superseded, however, we should ask whether this trip is necessary. Why add complexity by describing the new legislation? That's easy, for it is not possible to understand budgeting without these substantial new changes in the process. No new rules, no current comprehension. For another, the journey from GRH to the Budget Summit to OBRA evokes the grand themes of budgeting in our time—ideological dissensus

[1] Donald Kettl, "The Great Budget Debate," Vanderbilt Institute for Public Policy Studies, *VIPPS News*, Vol. 4, No. 2 (Summer 1990), pp. 1–2.

so deep the opposing sides make minute measurements of outcomes, a deficit octopus so entangling that its grip can be loosened but not cut through, and a temporary truce based on the common desire of politicians to create a process that will not automatically stigmatize them as failures. Thus they move from budget balance, which they cannot often achieve, to expenditure control, which they have a fighting chance to attain. The deadlock over the budgetary base—the levels of revenue and expenditure and, within them, different proportions for different programs and taxpayers—remains and may eventually undermine all hopes. By legislating agreement on the base, politicians hope that action will focus on staying within stipulated targets, that is, on increments. Whether incrementalism can be restored by fiat, without the precondition of consensus on the base, is now being tested.

THE BUDGET SUMMIT

The Budget Summit of 1990 held between representatives of President Bush and top party leaders in both houses of Congress agreed on an approximately $500 billion deficit reduction package over a five-year period, only to have it defeated by a bipartisan majority in the House of Representatives. From the start of the Summit, indeed from the beginning of the Bush administration, the question of how to reduce the deficit was complicated by an argument over not just whether to raise some taxes but whether to cut others, namely, taxation of capital gains. Ronald Reagan followed the strategy of across-the-board reductions in tax rates. In the 1986 tax reform, he accepted capital gains rates equal to those of wage income, reversing historic Republican policy, not because Reagan would not have liked to see them lower but because his free-market principles and advisers argued that all sources of revenue should be treated the same. Moreover, as long as attention was focused on flat, across-the-board tax rate reductions, it was difficult for liberals to raise the question of class conflict. While it was true that the major tax reform of 1986 lowered taxes for higher-income individuals, for instance, it also took some six or seven million of the poorest taxpayers off the tax rolls. Most everyone could see a stake in this reduction for themselves.[2]

By contrast, when President Bush sought to lower capital gains rates, he unhinged the implicit social contract in which lower rates were traded for fewer and/or lower tax preferences, the famous "loopholes" or "gimmicks" that enabled some taxpayers greatly to reduce their burdens. Since Bush's proposal mostly favored the better off, the Democrats were able to raise the rich-versus-poor issue of tax equity. The sanctity of the 1986 agreement having been broken by the president, Democrats could attack the rates themselves, especially the infamous "bubble."

In final negotiations over the 1986 tax reform, scorekeepers discovered their agreed-on two brackets, 15 and 28 percent, would not raise enough money. They felt committed to a low top rate, so they got around the difficulty by redefining it. With a top marginal rate of 28 percent, no one actually pays that high a rate on the average dollar earned, because a portion of each individual's income is not taxed, and another part is taxed at 15 percent. This left upper-middle-income people paying less than 28 percent on their taxable income. Since revenue is hard to come by when cutting rates, the lawmakers had their technicians invent a device called "the bubble." The lawmakers decided to reduce deductions and exemptions so that upper-middle-income people would effectively pay 33 percent at the margin of their incomes, until their overall rate reached 28 percent. Actual tax rates, therefore, rose through the income brackets from zero to 28 percent. But the very richest people were paying a lower marginal rate (28 percent) than the merely quite comfortable (33 percent) below them. To the tax technician that was treating all income the same; to the politicians that 33 percent "bubble" would be very difficult to explain.

[2] An account of this story can be found in White and Wildavsky, *The Deficit and the Public Interest.* For the fuller account, see Jeffrey H. Birnbaum and Alan S. Murray, *Showdown at Gucci Gulch: Lawmakers, Lobbyists, and the Unlikely Triumph of Tax Reform* (New York: Random House, 1987).

There was also new reason for hope that budget balance was within reach. Those who argue against the more excitable that tough issues should be postponed have one thing in their favor; sometimes conditions actually change. The incredibly swift collapse of communism in Eastern Europe and the Soviet Union, together with the latter's widely believed more peaceable intent, opened up possibilities of greater reductions in the defense budget. At the same time, there was less need for the Republican administration to defend as sacrosanct the previous pattern of spending. The election of George Bush as president signified the replacement of a hard-nosed ideologue, Ronald Reagan, with a flexible and more moderate conservative. Bush had a history of conveniently changing his mind; unfortunately, to get an agreement he would have to switch on the major promise of his election campaign and a paramount concern of many of his constituents—his pledge not to raise taxes.

Though John Sununu, the president's Chief of Staff, was leery of putting that message in a presidential address—"Read my lips," taken from he-man, strong man Clint Eastwood—Peggy Noonan, the brilliant speech writer who put that phrase in, said it would help the campaign. Probably it did, especially in keeping committed conservatives on the Bush side, but sufficient thought wasn't given to whether this pledge could be maintained in the fullness of time. One of Bush's opponents in the Republican party primaries, Robert Dole, for instance, refused to take the pledge. The best person to have understood this was President Bush himself, because his desire for the United States to play a bountiful, healing role in international affairs, as well to create a cleaner environment and better educational outcomes, meant that more money would be needed. Nevertheless, the phrase was inserted, the president said it in public, it took hold, it was not easy to abandon . . . it just kept hanging there.

The administration finessed the deficit with optimistic economic assumptions in its 1991 budget. By the spring, those assumptions looked even less plausible and there was a need to come clean on the large costs of the savings and loan bailout; some of the president's advisers thought that if the deficit were to be addressed they had better do it soon, not anytime close to the 1992 elections. Meanwhile, back in the rarified atmosphere of international negotiations, President Bush had been asking all sorts of leaders of all sorts of countries—China, Japan, Germany—to make sacrifices for the common international good. After a while they naturally turned to him and said when are you doing to deal with your problems, especially the deficit. So the president attempted to show his bonafides by negotiating substantial deficit reduction. As so often in the past decade, a key move was technical. Putting pressure, he hoped, on both Congress and his own administration, Budget Director Richard Darman drastically revised his forecast, predicting a deficit so large as to require a $100 billion Gramm–Rudman sequester, enough to devastate the government. Once Darman did that, the president was committed to the high-risk strategy of a deal or a huge sequester.

Democrats, in turn, insisted that the president publicly rescind his no-tax pledge. After much negotiation, the president's men tried to do so with as little fanfare as possible. Richard Darman wrote a short announcement in which the president agreed to support revenue increases provided they were accompanied by expenditure reductions and reform of the entitlement expenditure processes. The statement was worded to provide some wiggle-room, but when the Democrats and the press immediately declared the president had recanted, and he did not disagree, that flexibility disappeared.

The president's backsliding had immediate political consequences. Even some who liked the policy change attacked the president on moral grounds. His reversal was seen as proof of deceit, and thus brought the political process into exactly the kind of disrepute his actions were designed to protect against.

In his own eyes, no doubt, the president believed he had done the right thing. Were not leaders taught that they must sometimes discomfort their followers in order to serve the larger public interest? These thoughts fell on deaf ears, either because people no longer wanted this behavior from their leaders—or not in contradiction to such a clear, precise, and forceful pledge—or because the president did next to nothing to explain to the people why he had done what he did. He did try to explain to reporters who covered the White House[3] but they did not convey his message perhaps because they didn't believe him.

The major mover on the administration side of the summit was Budget Director Darman, who not only knew the most but wanted to show that he could do what others, especially his friend David Stockman, had been unable to do, namely, engineer a massive deficit-reduction package. The collapse of parts of the savings and loan industry added impetus to the negotiations because of its high cost and the doubt it left in the minds of many people whether their government was operating in their interests or even operating at all. In consultation with the president and the other important summit figures, Chief of Staff John Sununu, Secretary of the Treasury Nicholas Brady, and Darman set the strategy. They proposed extreme budget process reforms, such as an item veto, knowing the Democrats would never accept them, so the White House could blame Congress if the negotiations collapsed.

---

[3] This paragraph is based on large numbers of news stories in *The New York Times, The Los Angeles Times,* the *Washington Post,* the *Washington Times,* and the *Oakland Tribune.* Whereas it was done only irregularly before, it has become standard practice in the Bush admininstration for top officials, under a pledge of anonymity, to try to put a better spin on the story. When all most people really know is the headlines or the lead paragraph, this is understandable, but the kinds of stories thus produced have become so self-serving and so contrary to common sense that they need to be exposed. In the first year of his administration, President Bush tried very hard to get a capital gains tax passed. He had the votes but procedural hurdles in the Senate, enforced by majority leader George Mitchell, defeated him. Instead of reconsidering whether capital gains were a good idea, or accepting the generous Democratic offer to index capital gains in the future, the Bush admininstration put out anonymous stories to the effect that this was really a victory, explaining how Democrats had been put on the defensive on discovering that many if not most Americans still thought they might one day hit it rich. When defeat is victory and victory is defeat, we have entered another era. More recently, we have the ubiquitous "senior White House official" informing exceedingly credulous readers that, from the beginning, the Republican strategy had been to "create congressional vulnerability" on the deficit issue, as David Lauter, the reporter put it, "even if that might weaken GOP incumbents." This interpretation is unfortunate. Put yourself in the shoes of any number of Republican candidates, say Claudine Schneider, who gave up a relatively safe seat as representative in order to try to defeat elderly Senator Claiborne Pell, on discovering that the opportunity she had been assured she would have had been denied by an action of the president himself. Such dissimulation only serves to increase the denigration of political institutions against which President Bush has set himself over a lifetime of public service. For another, in addition to saying that defeat is victory, early defeats now become the harbingers of later triumphs. (The quotations are from the *Oakland Tribune,* October 26, 1990, p. A3. Lauter is a reporter for *The Los Angeles Times.*)

They also used these proposals as a palliative for their right wing, as a promise that the hated tax increases would not simply give more money to the liberal spenders. The Bush administration's priorities were very different from the Democrats' but, unlike President Reagan and his wing of their party, it did not simply identify the deficit with spending.

The leading members of the Bush administration believed that the deficit was a great blight on the country because it showed that government could not control itself. Responsibility, to them, meant supporting governmental institutions by showing that they worked. Part of their view of the deficit problem, shared by any number of businesspeople and editorialists, was that the American people were consuming too much and producing too little. They bought the economic argument that, other things not intervening too much, a lesser rate of savings would mean a lower rate of investment. If the people's representatives were unwilling to reduce expenditure to the lower level desired by the Bush administration, the people would have to support their government at the level to which it had, for better or worse, become accustomed: with new taxes.

The Republican negotiators also knew that there were other problems of great magnitude just beneath the surface. In addition to increasing national savings, therefore, they wanted to use the deficit problem to avoid a crisis everyone could see coming in the financing of medicare. Their ideal agreement would be one that taxed consumption most heavily, especially consumption of undesirable commodities such as liquor and tobacco. The wanted to charge the elderly more for consumption of health services. In return for the unpalatability of taxes in general, the Bush administration wanted to reduce taxes on business by cutting capital gains substantially and subsidizing small businesses. Their hope was that a large increase in consumption taxes would pave the way for easier credit, higher exports, and capital spending, and thus not dampen economic activity, a position in accord with that of many economists.

The Democratic notables in Congress who attended the Budget Summit were led by Richard Gephardt, the majority leader; the chairs of the House and Senate budget committees, Representative Leon Panetta and Senator Jim Sasser; the chairs of the appropriations committees, Senator Robert Byrd and Representative Jamie Whitten; the chairs of the tax committees, Senator Lloyd Bentsen and Representative Dan Rostenkowski; and Senator Wyche Fowler, who represented Majority Leader George Mitchell and House Majority Whip William Gray, former chair of the House Budget Committee and a member of the House Black Caucus. Republican representatives included the usual suspects, the minority leaders in the House and Senate, Robert Michel and Robert Dole; the ranking minority members of the tax, spending, and budget committees respectively; Senators Bob Packwood, Mark Hatfield, and Pete Domenici, as well as Representatives William Archer, Silvio Conte, and Bill Frenzel; and House Minority Whip Newt Gingrich and Senator Phil Gramm.

Early on, Ways and Means Committee staff devised a format, and CBO and Joint Committee on Taxation staff provided support, so congressional participants could cost out, overnight, any proposals and, for the Democratic party members at least, the distributional consequences of revenue measures among richer, poorer, and middle-class individuals. Quickly, as faxes arrived from Andrews Airforce Base, where the later stages of the Summit were held (to avoid, so they said, the distractions of Washington and to keep the meetings down in size), estimates came back. This was a gain in calculating ability but not necessarily in agreement. Allegations that certain parts of proposed packages were unfair (i.e., inegalitarian) brought heated denials on the Republican side. Nevertheless, equality was an important value from beginning to end, institutionalized, as it was, in Democratic demands and available formulas.

The most obvious decision was the target: How much deficit reduction was enough? Virtually all players agreed that they should focus on a long-term package. Four years of Gramm–Rudman created near-consensus that attention to just one year guarantees fraud.[4] Recall the wonderworking devices: shifting a month's heavy payroll to the previous year or

---

[4] Robert W. Hartman, "Budget Summit 1990: The Role of Economic and Budget Analysis," paper prepared for the Association of Schools of Public Policy and Management Reserach Conference, October 18–20, 1990.

not counting spending after the formal Gramm–Rudman deadline, to make the deficit look technically smaller so as to avoid the ultimate ignominy of sequestration. Nobody wanted to allow such dishonest devices to color their proceedings. Well, mostly not! For the short term, the extreme-moderate view that $100 billion was the only deficit reduction worth making quickly went out the window. Very early on, CBO was asked how much of a hit in higher taxes and lower spending the economy could take in 1991 without going into recession; the organization came up with a ballpark figure that would have been agreed to by most economists, namely, around $50 billion, roughly 1 percent of GNP. If one could achieve this in FY1990 (actually 1991), the total amount of cumulative reduction for the five-year planning period the Summit adopted would be more than five times $50 billion or $250 billion but some further savings in later years, plus savings on interest payments that otherwise would have been paid to finance the previously anticipated higher deficits. The total was about $450 billion. However, Democrats pushed for a $600 billion total and Republicans for $400 billion. Their agreement in the spring of 1990 on $500 billion, which sounded euphorious at least ("50/500"), helped force Bush's hand.

But what were the participants to do about the midsummer outbreak of aggression as Iraq conquered Kuwait? The price of oil began to skyrocket and the costs of military assistance would undoubtedly be large but were incalculable. Aside from lowering the first year's deficit-reduction target from $50 to $40 billion, the conferees, correctly in my opinion, decided to ignore the whole thing. Rather than stultify the enterprise by bringing in a variable that could not be calculated, or artificially raising the military budget for future years, they decided to see what happened and to proceed as if the Persian Gulf wasn't there.

Now we come to a subject of great intrinsic interest for budget aficionados: the more detailed the instructions of the Budget Summit, the greater the potential for conflict with congressional committees. If programs are to be grouped, the obvious place to start is with the thirteen appropriations subcommittees and then the authorizing committees with substantial authority over entitlements. But this is exactly what experience shows must be avoided. For one thing, save for the chairs of the full appropriations and tax committees, committee chairs were not at the Summit and would not look kindly on being told what they must do. For another, the negotiators would be more likely to make mistakes the more they engaged the details. For a third, smaller categories left less room for change while still adhering to the deal. Fortunately, David Stockman had originated and CBO had developed for another high-level negotiating enterprise just five categories—taxes, entitlements and mandatory items, offsetting receipts and net interest, national defense, and nondefense discretionary. These were small in number and, except for defense, did not appear to be concerned with substance, yet matched mechanisms of control (nondefense discretionary and defense, for instance, were annual appropriations, while changes in entitlements and other mandatory programs were covered in the reconciliation process). Moreover, given the ideological-policy differences between largely egalitarian Democrats and the economically and socially conservative Republicans, the divide between defense, thought of as taking money otherwise available for welfare payments, and nondefense discretionary, which basically covered what we think of as the entire domestic government outside of entitlements, facilitated large-scale negotiations. The Democratic party idea was to cut defense as much as possible while keeping domestic cuts down.

How much would each category contribute to the deal? The easiest category was the savings to be achieved by compounding the interest that otherwise would be necessary to service the high level of debt that would be incurred if there were no deficit reduction. To get $500 billion total, they could expect $70 billion in interest savings and thus need "only" $430 billion from everything else. Next there were discretionary programs, both defense and nondefense. (The reader is reminded that the term "discretionary" means the item is within the annual control of the appropriations committees in Congress while "entitlement" or "mandatory" signifies that the expenditure is required by prior legislation, not that it must last forever or that Congress and the president could not cut or eliminate the program were they so inclined.)

Not usually thought of as the budget-cutting party, the Democratic representatives initially came up with a target of nearly $200 billion in discretionary programs, while the Republicans wanted a lower amount, approximately $160 billion. Both numbers were large by historical standards; both parties were assuming the big cuts in defense made possible by the end of the cold war. The Republicans wanted to do less cutting on defense, so their total was lower.

Rather early it was agreed to split the difference so total discretionary spending would be cut—from the baseline—about $180 billion. But thereby hangs a tale.

Some Republican negotiators wanted cuts in discretionary domestic spending. The Democrats, especially the appropriators, wanted increases. They argued that the domestic sector under the appropriations process had been paying for deficit reduction for years; that vital national needs had been neglected; and that small increases for them were diddly-squat compared to getting a fair contribution from entitlements. In this they had a quiet ally in Budget Director Darman. The administration had lots of initiatives, such as space exploration and other scientific research—all of them discretionary. The appropriators' goal could be viewed as paying for those initiatives (which the committees might otherwise deep-six) by cuts in entitlements. That doesn't sound so bad. Darman told the appropriators he would give them their increases but in order to avoid flack from his right, they would have to let him manipulate the baseline so it would look like there were no growth, which he did. In fact, the Summit deal allowed at least a 4 percent and perhaps as much as a 6 percent real increase in outlays from FY1991–1993. The bulk of the increase was in FY1992, the first year to be fully debated after the Summit.

The real disagreement was whether the Democrats could try for bigger domestic increases by cutting defense even more. Democrats wanted "caps" for discretionary spending in total; to protect its priorities, the administration wanted separate figures for defense, international affairs, and domestic spending. In the Summit agreement, as well as the final package, they compromised on separate caps for 1990–1992 and combined caps for 1993–1994. The reason for this division was to give whoever won the 1992 presidential election a chance to make changes.

There would be lots of little disputes, but the basic framework on discretionary spending was clear in mid-September: Cuts that would be called $180 billion and were likely to be $10 to $20 billion less. That left the hard cases, entitlements, which Democrats wanted to protect, and taxes, where Republicans hoped to hold down the damage.

What would be a "fair" or "acceptable" outcome? Presumably, $125 billion in new taxes and $125 billion in entitlement cuts would split the differences down the middle. Almost. At the last moment the sum-miteers, reduced to the three main Democratic leaders and the Bush administration, came up with a $134 billion increase in revenues and $119 billion reduction in entitlements.

Here, as everywhere, however, there were technical questions that quickly became strategic. Consider the question of user fees. These fees covered such things as a $25 sticker required on boats (that presumably benefited from Coast Guard services), animal inspection, and a lot more. Negotiators agreed to try to raise some $14 billion in additional revenues from fees. Not easy, but also only part of the story: Where should these revenues be counted? Republicans wanted them counted toward reve-nues, thus reducing the total hit with relatively noncontroversial items. By contrast, Democrats wanted fees to count toward domestic programs so as to hold down the amount they would have to cut. In the end, fees were counted under "Entitlements and Mandatory," which helped the Democrats but not the Republicans.

Then there were taxes on capital gains. The president had made cutting capital gains a major priority. The Democrats, presenting the bubble as a self-evident example of unfairness (why should the rich be taxed at a lower rate, 28 percent, than the upper-middle class, 33 per-cent?), responded by proposing to eliminate the bubble through elimi-nating the fourth marginal tax bracket, so brackets would just go 15/28/33 instead of 15/28/33/28. They then proceeded gleefully to beat up the president on both issues, while hinting they might give him something on capital gains if he would make it fair by agreeing to burst the bubble. As the negotiations neared their end, congressional Republi-cans, namely minority leaders Dole and Michel, decided they would be better off if both issues were taken off the table, and by saying so ended the capital gains fight.

Was there nothing on which both parties agreed? Yes, there was:

excise (essentially sales) taxes on tobacco, alcohol, gasoline, and what they considered luxuries. This widespread agreement, however, hid a disagreement: Yes, these excise taxes should be substantially increased but, the Democrats countered, if poorer and middle-income people paid more of their income proportionately, that would have to be offset by hitting richer people harder. In the end, Democrats won a covert increase in income taxes on the better off in terms of a reduction in allowed itemized deductions (one solution to disagreement is complexity and confusion). But their leaders also accepted a series of subsidies for small-business investment, which Bush could call "growth oriented" tax provisions, but were greeted with scorn by tax professionals.[5]

Therefore, the final deal, agreed to by Speaker Foley and majority leaders Mitchell and Gephardt early on September 30, was, by Democratic lights, regressive. And that quickly became evident as Congress members scanned the distributional tables, conveniently prepared by Ways and Means Committee staff on the basis of calculations provided by CBO and the Joint Committee on Taxation, showing how the income of each fifth of the population would be affected by the total agreement. This calculation included the effects of generally regressive consumption taxes but did not include the effects of large reductions in defense spending. In the midst of much argument, the tables showed that the top 20 percent of high-income individuals had their taxes increase by 0.9 percent, while the lowest 20 percent had theirs increased by 2 percent. To a budgeteer, such as Robert Hartman of CBO, imagining a conversation with a wavering Congress member, such regressivity was small:

> I'd have to tell my undecided Congressman that he does have to apply a sense of proportion to these numbers. If the average family in the lowest quintile's tax burden could have been reduced by about $60 a year, there would have been no grounds to proclaim this as a regressive change. Is this a sufficient sum to cause you to fall on your sword? (To the sharp Congressman's rebuttal—"OK, then put the $60 in the package and I'll be happy"

[5]Richard Kasten and Frank Sammartino, "Who Pays For Federal Deficit Reduction?" CBO, paper presented at the APPAM research conference, October 18–20, 1990.

or "$60 is a lot of money if you don't have it"—I confess to having little to say!)[6]

But many liberals who believed that the time had come for progressive changes were not convinced by such arguments. Nor did they much like the cuts in entitlements.

The one that raised the most anger would have made recipients wait two weeks for unemployment benefits.[7] By far the two largest cuts were $13 billion in farm support and $60 billion in medicare over five years, the reductions being divided between lower fees to hospitals and providers and higher fees and deductibles for medicare recipients. Location of these cuts tells us that budgeters were looking both for big cuts and for programs that were vulnerable for specific reasons (because farm supports were to be negotiated down in international agreements and because medicare was running out of money). So far, so sensible; but how it was done, in the case of medicare, turned out to be crucial.

When the agreed-on deficit-reduction plan was presented in the House of Representatives early in October 1990, the unexpected result—at least unexpected to the Bush administration—was instantaneous and total defeat. Democratic party liberals might have gone along with their leadership—angrily!—providing the Republicans had supplied the necessary minimum, to wit, more than half their members supporting the package. But the Democrats got lucky. Economically conservative Republicans vehemently rejected the plan. Led by Minority Whip Newt Gingrich of Georgia, they felt left out of the whole process, alone and set adrift to face likely defeat in the midterm elections. They had not yet reconciled themselves to the president's abandonment of his no-new-tax pledge. Besides, a lot of Republicans had no more interest than Democrats in a plan that would get $30 billion in medicare savings (around half of the total) from the pockets of the most

[6]Hartman, "Budget Summit 1990 . . . ," p. 15.
[7]It could be justified as inhibiting people going on and off the rolls systematically. Construction workers are accused of doing so; some policy analysts argue that being able to go on unemployment enables them to demand higher wages, which in turn reduces construction activity, all partly subsidized by the government.

powerful group in America, the elderly. Their reaction makes it easier to understand that a lawmaker's budget savings may be a lot of citizens' higher spending.

Once Republicans would not provide the minimum level of support, Democrats felt free to vote against the plan as well. Since all concerned recognized that deficit reduction, or at least Gramm–Rudman avoidance, still remained a task to be accomplished, negotiations continued.

Defeat of the Summit agreement was a double disaster for the president. Not only was it embarrassing, it also put him on the defensive in the next round of negotiations. And it put the conservative (mostly House) Republicans on the outside looking in. Consequently, he would have to rely mostly on Democratic votes to get it passed. As a result, the package would be more "Democratic" than the defeated agreement.

On the theories that anything was better than Gramm–Rudman and that some agreement was necessary to show they could govern, Speaker Foley and majority leaders Mitchell and Gephardt had accepted a package far less progressive, particularly due to gasoline taxes, than their troops could buy. When they did so, it made some sense. If the talks broke down, and Democrats had to offer their own plan, it would be progressive—at least by raising the top rate. They could hope voters understood that the increase hit only a very small percentage of households. But class jealousy on taxes rarely works in a vacuum. Middle-class voters think they might be rich themselves one day—or the politicians might tax them next. A Democratic package without the Summit would have given the Republicans a chance to exploit these suspicions, while themselves being vague about alternatives.

Instead, the president went on television to endorse the Summit package, identifying himself with its provisions. Once House Republicans torpedoed the deal, Democrats could sell their package as an alternative to the Summit, particularly to its fuel taxes and medicare costs. That made more egalitarian taxes a much more attractive proposition. From the moment the Summit package was defeated, the issue was not whether but how and by how much the next package would be more progressive. When pain is to be distributed, it doesn't pay to go first.

Unfortunately for the Democrats, they could not be sure of support in the Senate, where their own troops were more conservative. Further, they had no more interest than the president in allowing a sequester; if he played chicken, they could not just wait him out. They needed to get home to campaign. Finally, political advantage was in the battle, not the peace treaty. They therefore stretched out the fight as long as they could and, when Bush had taken a heavy pounding for such politically dubious but budgetarily insignificant positions as resisting a surtax on millionaires, settled for a moderately progressive settlement.

THE SUMMIT VERSUS OBRA

At 1 A.M. on October 27, 1990, the staff of The Committee of Conference issued a "Summary of Reconciliation Conference Report" on what was to become the Omnibus Budget Reconciliation Act of 1990, which is especially useful for our purposes because it lists the expected revenue gains and losses that, after approval by Congress and signature by the president, became the law of the land. (See Table 12-1.) Items 1 and 5 are relatively straightforward: They increase the top rate from 28 to 31 percent, begin taxing the top rate at $82,000, and increase the alternative minimum tax rate (what a person pays despite the value of deductions) from 21 to 24 percent. They also increase excise taxes on luxuries. So far, so simple. Then come the complications. Raising the top rate to 31 percent replaced the old 33 percent as well. But that reduced revenue and gave a tax cut to families with incomes in the $80,000 to $150,000 range. So items 2, 3, and 4 are disguised income tax increases of roughly 1 percent each, whether due to raising taxable payroll on medicare to $125,000 or phasing out personal exemptions or limiting itemized deductions.

Amidst the revenue-raising measures are others deliberately designed to reduce governmental income in the substantial amount of $27.5 billion. Other revenue-losing propositions, which are hardly known to the general public, such as credits for orphan drugs, add up to over $9 billion. What would be the rationale for an item that reads strangely to most eyes: "eliminate appreciation of certain donated property (e.g.,

TABLE 12-1

Summary of Reconciliation Conference Report*

Major changes primarily affecting high-income taxpayers:

1. Increase top statutory tax rate from 28 to 31 percent
   (beginning at a taxable income of $82,200 for a joint return)
   and increase the individual alternative minimum tax rate from
   21 to 24 percent. Maximum capital gains rate is 28 percent.   +11.2

2. High-income "floor disallowance of itemized deductions" equal
   to 3 percent times the extent to which adjusted gross income
   exceeds $100,000.   +18.2

3. New high-income "phase-out" of the tax benefit from personal
   exemptions (beginning at a taxable income of $150,000 for a
   joint return and extending for approximately $125,000).   +10.8

4. Increase cap on wages taxable for Medicare to $125,000.   +26.9

5. Ten percent luxury excise taxes on amount of price over
   $30,000 for autos, $100,000 for boats, $250,000 for airplanes,
   and $10,000 for furs.   +1.5

Major excise tax changes:

6. Increase motor fuels taxes by 5 cents a gallon; one-half of
   revenues to trust funds.   +25.4

7. Tobacco and alcoholic beverages: Raise tax on a pack of
   cigarettes by 8 cents for 1993. Raise tax on liquor by $1.00 to
   $13.50 per "proof gallon." Raise tax on beer from 16 to 32
   cents per six-pack. Raise tax on table wine from 3 cents per
   bottle to 21 cents.   +14.6

8. Extend Airport and Airway Trust Fund excise taxes and
   increase by 25 percent compared to 1990 rates.   +11.9

9. Extend 3 percent excise on telephone service.   +13.1

Regressivity offset and childrens' credits:

10. Expand Earned Income Tax Credit and adjust for family size.
    Create a low-income credit for the premium costs of health
    insurance that includes coverage for children.   -18.3

TABLE 12-1

(continued)

Other changes:

11. Extend Social Security taxes to state/local employees without other pension coverage.   +9.1

12. Raise interest rate charged corporations on late tax payments.   +1.8

13. Supplemental 0.2% unemployment insurance surtax.   +5.4

14. Insurance companies must amortize a portion of "policy acquisition costs."   +8.0

15. Other: permit transfers from "overfunded" pension plans for retiree health. Add chemicals subject to ozone-depleting chemicals tax. Reimpose Leaking Underground Storage Tank Trust Fund tax. Reduce loss deductions by property and casualty insurance companies. Improve IRS ability to obtain information from foreign corporations. Increase harbor maintenance tax. Reduce business income tax loopholes.   +6.4

Revenue-losing provisions:

16. One-year extension of R&E, low-income housing, business energy, targeted jobs and orphan drug credits, tax exemption for mortgage revenue and small issue bonds, exclusions for employer-provided legal and educational assistance, and 25 percent health insurance deduction for the self-employed.   −5.9

17. Energy producer tax benefits: extend nonconventional fuels credits and tax incentives for ethanol production; new credit for enhanced oil recovery costs; amend percentage depletion; reduce alternative minimum tax (AMT) preference treatment of energy items.   −2.5

18. Small-business oriented credit for accommodations for disabled persons. Modify estate "freeze" rules. Eliminate appreciation of certain donated property (e.g., paintings) as a minimum tax preference item.   −0.8

*The right column of the table gives five-year total revenue gains and losses in billions of dollars.

paintings) as a minimum tax preference item." Of course, the very rich get deductions, but their benefits are incidental. The culprit is the nefarious special interest called your local museum, which finds it more difficult to get valuable paintings donated to it if the person who does so has to pay more taxes on the paintings' current rather than their purchase values. The credits for children are part of an unannounced, children-oriented family policy, as is the credit for health insurance for people of low income, insurance that includes children.

The seemingly straightforward income tax rate increase would bring in only $8.2 billion—partly because for some people it's a cut. That is small compared to the $18.2 billion reduction in allowable deductions, almost equal to the phasing out of benefits in personal exemptions for people of high income, and tiny compared to raising wages taxable for medicare, which weighs in at a hefty $26.9 billion. The moral of the story is to pay attention not only to what is affected but by how much.

There are little, itty-bitty changes, barely noticeable except to those directly involved, and so-called "other changes" that sum to over $24 billion, by altering what is taxable (the unemployment insurance surtax) or who is taxable (extending social security taxes to state and local employees without other pension coverage) or how much is taxable (upping interest rates for late corporate tax payments) or changing the rules (viz. insurance company amortization) so that more income is taxable. Amid a very simple political battle over distribution, tax policy remains as complicated as ever.

"Saving" is a nice term because it fudges the difference between an actual reduction in prior years' outlays and money projected to be spent but that wasn't. It is like a story we kids used to tell each other—I stopped a candy store from being robbed today. How did you do that? I decided not to.

This strategy, which Allen Schick calls "Cutting Back and Spending More," is known in the trade as "baseline budgeting." As Schick explains,

> The baseline assumes that existing programs will continue without policy change. It adjusts projected expenditures for estimated inflation and man-

dated workload changes. A simple example will show how a baseline is constructed and used. A program spending $100 million a year and projected to have an annual 5 percent increase in participants and a 5 percent inflation rate would have approximately a $110 million baseline for the next year, a $121 million baseline for the second year, and a $133 million baseline for the third. . . . Suppose that a . . . program with the spending profile outlined above receives a $105 million appropriation for the next year. Using their "old math," the appropriations committees would record this as a $5 million increase. This traditional way of keeping score has one big advantage. It does not require any assumptions about future behavior or conditions but is based solely on past action. There is no place in it for supposition about what might happen in the future, no need to speculate about what next year's inflation rate might be. When the baseline is used, the same $105 million appropriation is scored as a cutback even though it is above the previous level. The political advantage of transforming an increase into a reduction is enormous because it enables the appropriations committees to continue their historic role of cutting the budget and financing programs.[8]

There can be good reasons for baseline budgeting: If inputs do cost more and are related to outputs, as they usually are, the unadjusted figures hide the program impacts of the budget. Put differently, as in Britain, a practice of assuming increases in efficiency, thereby reducing the amount of the budgetary base, places the onus on the spending departments. But baseline adjustments also let the players hide their actions, which disguised increased domestic discretionary spending.[9]

As a consequence of mutual accommodation on budgetary baselines, Schick comments, "Anything goes in federal budgeting these days, as long as it is agreed to by the White House and congressional leaders."[10] In regard to estimating the size of expenditure cuts or additions, Schick believes, honesty requires rules for keeping score that count only reductions in outlays.[11] The basic fault of the baseline approach, Schick says

[8]Allen Schick, *The Capacity to Budget* (Washington, D.C.: Urban Institute, 1990), p. 96.

[9]Reality is a little more complicated than this. For discretionary programs, the CBO baseline adjusts only for inflation, so the $105 million would be scored as no gain/no loss from baseline. Liberals can argue that more participants mean a real cut. Conservatives can say $105 million is bigger than $100 million.

[10]*Ibid.*, p. 204.

[11]*Ibid.*

and I agree, is that it concedes what must be fought for if there is to be expenditure control. By giving program advocates protection against inflation, they start from a protected base when it is that base they should have to defend.[12]

The biggest difference from Summit to OBRA was in medicare, for which the Summit's $60 billion saving became $42.46 billion over five years, $32.4 billion in reductions to providers of medical care and $10.7 billion in increases that beneficiaries would have to pay. The differences all came by reducing the Summit's planned charges to beneficiaries.

Congress kept looking for ways to cut without hurting anyone. In medicare they simply added $1.25 billion for mammography screening (which in the long run might save money). Savings on medicaid, which is designed to help people of low income afford medical care, comprised $2.9 billion over five years and are made up by getting discounts on pharmaceutical items and by using private insurance where that costs less. Again, it appears that the providers do the saving, not the beneficiaries. Given the proven ability of providers to shift costs to beneficiaries or to withhold services, however, one could question whether this is a costless saving. There is also an expansion of coverage for the most vulnerable elements in the population—children, the mentally ill, and the frail elderly.

Consider the student loan program as described in a paper prepared by the staff of the House Budget Committee on October 27, 1990:

The conference agreement assumes the following savings:

Stafford Student Loan Program:

- Requires 30 day delay in disbursement of loans to all first-time borrowers;

- Requires borrowers without a high school diploma or GED to take and pass an independently administered test;

- Eliminates from all student loan programs any school with a calculated default rate over the last three years in excess of 35 percent

---

[12]*Ibid.*, p. 210. For a more substantial discussion of just this point under earlier British circumstances, see Hugh Heclo and Aaron Wildavsky, *The Private Government of Public Money,* 2nd ed. (Macmillan 1981). See especially "The Politics of Projection or Rashomon Revisited," pp. 216–26.

for 1991 and 1992 and 30 percent or more for 1993 and beyond (does not apply to Historically Black Colleges or Universities or Tribally Controlled Community Colleges until July 1, 1994);

* Extends the current limitation on SLS loan limits in short-term programs;

* Extends the current limitation on SLS loan program eligibility for borrowers attending schools with a calculated default rate in excess of 30 percent.

* Prohibits eligibility of a school filing bankruptcy.

* Amends the Bankruptcy Code to tighten laws as they relate to student borrowers; and

* Mandates supplemental pre-claims assistance on all delinquent loans and reimburse guarantee agencies for successfully preventing a default claim through early intervention.

The first thing to look at is what is not there, namely, increases in the costs of student loans. Instead, there is a variety of stringent procedures that are supposed to make it more difficult for educational institutions whose students do not repay loans to qualify in the future. And this holds true, too, of amending the bankruptcy law to make it easier for the government to get its money back. Thus the onus is not on all students or on all educational institutions but only on those judged to be at risk of default. None of these provisions affects Historically Black Colleges or Universities or Tribally Controlled Community Colleges until July 1, 1994, an extension of the egalitarian character of these antideficit provisions. Again, there are savings ostensibly without depriving clients.

Another way in which policy preferences enter is shown by the five to seven times increase in penalties for violations of laws regarding safety:

OSHA/MSHA Revenues:

* Increases by seven times the maximum civil penalties that can be imposed by the Occupational Safety and Health Administration (OSHA) for violations of OSHA laws with a mandatory minimum penalty of $5,000 for a willful violation.

- Increases by five times the maximum civil penalties that can be imposed by the Mine Safety and Health Administration (MSHA) for violations of MSHA laws, with no minimum penalty.

It is doubtful that these fines will amount to a great deal. But they are a way of slipping into deficit-reduction provisions desired on other grounds. Always there are wheels within wheels within wheels turning in large-scale budget legislation. If a big budget bill is the only train in town, those who want to reach their policy destination will have to find a way to get on board.

Did Congress write a more equitable set of tax increases than did the Budget Summit? That depends on how you look at it. If you adopt the usual definition of progressive taxation in which individuals with higher income have to pay not only larger absolute amounts, which they would anyway, but a larger proportion of their income, then the Omnbus Budget Reconciliation Act of 1990 (OBRA) is far more progressive. But if you focus not on who pays proportionately more or less of their income but rather on who pays what proportion of total taxes paid, then you come to a diametrically different conclusion. Consider Table 12-2, adapted from one by Warren Brookes, an economic columnist. From this table we see that the rich, defined as those receiving the top 1 percent of income, paid an increasingly larger share of the total tax take in the 1980s. And so did the top 5 and 10 percent in income. The bottom half in terms of income as well as the middle masses paid a decreasing share.[13] What is at issue is truly ideological in that the question revolves around which definition of what is just—higher proportions of income or of taxes paid—should prevail.

As the House Budget Committee explained it to House Democrats:

> When *all* tax changes are considered, the increases for the middle class are less than 2½ percent, while the average increase for those with over

[13]Warren Brookes, "Blowing Up the Bubble of Envy," the *Washington Times*, October 12, 1990, pp. F1, F4. Another capitalistically inclined columnist, Paul Craig Roberts, argues from IRS figures that "Upper-income tax payers pay the bulk of the income tax and have paid a rising percentage throughout the 1980s." the *Washington Times*, October 18, 1990, pp. F1, F4.

TABLE 12-2

Comparison of Income Tax Paid (by Percentile) in 1981 and 1987*

	1981		1987		Change	
	Amount	Share	Amount	Share	Amount	Share
Top 1 Percent	$ 51.7	17.6%	$ 77.1	24.6%	49.1%	39.8%
Top 5 Percent	$ 94.6	35.1%	$134.9	43.1%	42.6%	22.8%
Top 10 Percent	$144.4	48.0%	$173.7	55.5%	20.3%	15.6%
Middle 50–90%	$132.9	44.3%	$120.4	38.5%	−9.4%	−13.1%
Bottom 50%	$ 22.4	7.5%	$ 19.1	6.1%	−14.7%	−18.7%
Total	$300.3	—	$313.0	—	4.3%	—

*Amounts are in billions of 1982 dollars using GNP deflator.

Sources: Data from the Internal Revenue Service, Statistics on Income; table adapted from Warren Brookes, "Blowing Up the Bubble of Envy," *Washington Times,* October 12, 1990, p. F1.

$200,000 incomes is about 6 percent. The poor are shielded from tax increases by expanding the earned-income and other tax credits; on average, their taxes are *reduced.*[14]

Conservatives claimed this calculation was unfair because the rich were already paying a larger share of the total tax take than they had in 1981. This was true but their share of the income had increased even more. Which is it, then, paying a larger share of total taxes or a smaller share of income that was more just? The two sides differ not only on how much each income class should pay but also about which criterion to apply.

[14]U.S. House of Representatives, Committee on the Budget, "Fiscal Year 1991 Budget Agreement Summary Materials," October 27, 1990, p. 24.

Table 12-3, adapted from a chart by *The New York Times,* contrasts spending cuts from four plans—the Summit, the Senate, the House (with its big Democratic majority), and the compromise (OBRA) that became law. The largest by far, as we know, is medicare. The Summit wanted $60 billion shared between providers and beneficiaries with providers paying somewhat more. The Senate reduced that by $10 billion while creating the opposite disparity in which providers pay the bulk of the cost. House Democrats cut $6 billion from the size of the total plan while making the cost to providers more than three times larger than that of the beneficiaries, whereas in the Senate plan the difference had been somewhat less than two to one. And the House won. In short, with each stage in the development of OBRA there was stronger egalitarian sentiment.

In an effort to save OBRA from what he considered undeserved abuse (he called it a "five hundred billion dollar orphan," because Republican candidates ran so fast from it), Budget Director Richard Darman asked

TABLE 12-3
Proposed Spending Cuts Based on Four Plans*

	Summit	*Senate*	*House Democrats*	*Compromise*
Medicare				
Cost to beneficiaries	$ 27.8	$ 17.1	$ 10.0	$ 10.0
Cost to providers	32.2	32.1	33.0	33.0
Total Savings	60.0	49.2	43.0	43.0
Agriculture				
Savings	13.0	15.1	16.3	13.4
Medicaid				
Savings	1.6	0.9	0.3	—
Military				
Savings	$182.4	$182.4	$182.4	$182.4

*Amounts are in billions of dollars for cuts over a five-year period beginning October 1, 1990.
Source: Adapted from *The New York Times,* October 26, 1990, p. A10.

for credit where it was due. "Our political system," he told the *Wall Street Journal*, "has shown many times that it can raise taxes, but it has been very rare, perhaps unprecedented, that it has shown the capacity to reform a broad range of middle-class entitlement programs. That's what's unique here."[15] Even so, Republicans would have done far better if they had passed Darman's Summit package. Let's see how these "reforms" (really, reductions) work out.

There are those who believe that the spending cuts, especially those on entitlements (the largest by far), are illusory. Other budget professionals claim that providers' attempts to evade the medicare cuts have already been accommodated in the scorekeeping. For example, only half of the reduction in doctors' fees is credited as savings. Still, it is unwise to assume that all the savings will come true.

OBRA's cuts in commodity support programs are roughly at the Summit level. Costs could balloon, of course, because of weather and international prices (a big increase in the price of oil would mean much less money available to buy American agricultural products). That would be true without OBRA. More relevant, about half the savings disappear if there is no GATT (the General Agreement on Tariffs and Trade) agreement by mid-1992. Defense cuts should hold firm unless there is a drastic change in the international security environment. Nevertheless, costs for intervention in the Persian Gulf will erode some savings.

The package, in short, is subject to uncertainty under its own terms (like the agriculture provisions and the magic baseline for domestic and defense discretionary) and because, as always, bad news (perhaps the savings and loan bailout will require more funds) would raise the deficit. Of course, a recession or war would raise the deficit, and the uncertainties in the legislation itself should still leave about $450 billion in savings—enough to reduce the deficit, by 1995, to a moderate level. If the agreement holds.

But will it hold? Enter the Budget Enforcement Act (BEA) of 1990, Title XIII of OBRA. Once more, complexity increases. Think of it; where before there was only one sequester, in the era of budget balance,

---

[15] *The Wall Street Journal*, November 5, 1990, p. 1.

there are three and, believe it or not, five subsequesters within the categories.

THE BUDGET ENFORCEMENT ACT OF 1990

Before new procedures can take place, it is necessary to do something about the old way. The first thing done by the BEA, therefore, was to raise the fiscal year 1991 GRH deficit target (actual 1990) way up to $327 billion (and these figures were adjusted upward in fiscal 1991 by the Bush administration, as the law allows). Why are these targets so large? The short answer is (a) recession, (b) the savings and loan bailout, and (c) surpluses in the social security trust funds no longer count toward reducing the deficit. That recessions increase deficits by lowering revenues and increasing spending we know, but why do something voluntarily to make the deficit look much larger?

Veterans of the budget wars know that the economic effects of greater or lesser spending or borrowing do not depend on the locus where they are incurred. A surplus in state trust funds and in social security can offset a deficit in the federal budget without so much as a by-your-leave. Yet, unlike the British who routinely refer to the Public Sector Borrowing Requirement to sum up the total effects of borrowing at all levels of government, the U.S. federal government does not do so, even though this move is justified in economic terms and would lower the deficit by $50 to $100 billion a year over the next two decades. Why make the government look worse?

Proponents of balance believe that Congress and the president (the politicians) will not do enough unless they feel threatened. The larger the deficit, presumably, the greater the threat. This antipolitician sentiment also explains why they refuse to publicize the deficit in terms of proportions of GNP but insist on absolute numbers. Some $200+ billions is enough to frighten anyone, whereas under 3 percent of GNP sounds (and, in my opinion, is) a modest amount. The politicians also wanted to reassure retirees that social security was safe from budget cuts.

As a matter of economics, there are two currently popular ways to analyze the budget. The first economic approach emphasizes aggregate demand. By borrowing and spending the proceeds, the government increases demand for goods, thereby raising employment (good) or prices (bad). The second approach emphasizes savings: Government borrowing reduces total national savings, leaving less money to be invested; if we borrowed less we could invest more, the theory is, and hence the economy would grow more.

Neither approach would count the savings and loan bailout, which will supposedly cost more than $100 billion in 1991, fall to $21 billion by 1992, and then, as the government starts selling more assets than it buys (we hope!), generate income of nearly $50 billion per year in 1993–1994.[16] The bailout, much as we may resent it, is necessary to preserve our financial system. Not spending the money would hardly increase savings, because bank failures don't increase investment. Spending the money doesn't increase demand; instead it preserves the values people already have in their accounts. The S&L bailout, prayerfully, is a one-time thing. Usual accounting practice, as followed in regard to sending forces into the Persian Gulf, is to keep these off-budget. Since money is to be returned in part to the federal government in later years, deficits would be artificially diminished in return for making deficits artificially larger in the first few years. Why is this being done?

Over the next five years, social security will spend $1.5 trillion and collect $300 billion in surplus taxes. Demand managers say the social security surplus has an immediate economic effect, and should not be ignored. Those who focus on savings, however, want to increase the social security surplus. They say we should treat the surplus not as income this year, but as savings for later social security expenses, when the baby-boom generation retires.

If Congress and the president had adopted the demand managers' perspective, they would have kept savings and loans out and social security surpluses in the totals. Then, even with a more plausible (lower) economic forecast, the deficit would fall to around 1 percent of GNP,

---

[16]House Budget Committee Summary, October 27, 1990, p. 52.

comparable to that of Germany or Japan, by 1994. It would indeed balance by 1996 if not before. But they adopted the savers' perspective on social security, taking its surpluses out, while keeping the S&L bailout in the deficit calculation. The S&L costs balloon immediate deficits, on top of which the social security decision raised the 1994 deficit by $87 billion.[17] At baseball games, the hawkers say you can't tell the players without a scorecard. How much more true this is for the deficit!

This paroxysm of accounting "responsibility" created two problems. First, opponents of removing social security from the deficit feared that it would create an inviting target for those who wish to appropriate social security surpluses for their own preferred policy purposes. The House and Senate, therefore, adopted an array of provisions to try to prevent such raids.

More important, they had to find some way around the optimistic economic forecast, which they had adopted to make up for their social security scorekeeping but which, by not coming true, would put them right back in sequester land. For both Bush and congressional leaders, 1990's pain would be worthless if it did not at least result in peace through the 1992 election.

Therefore the president is legally required to alter the hoped-for deficit target each year in order to account for changes in the economy, changes in budgetary terms, and changes in estimates of the cost of federal credit programs. That is, the targets are not really targets— thereby abolishing, at least for 1990–1992, the deficit sequester, though it remains in the law and might return in fiscal 1994–1995 if the president doesn't exercise his option to continue to make adjustments.

In reality, the old Gramm–Rudman sequester, designed to force action to reduce the deficit, is replaced by two much more sensible sequesters designed (a) to keep Congress from increasing the deficit, thereby enforcing the new package, and (b) to maintain the status quo by making proposers pay for spending increases and revenue decreases.

There are discretionary funds in defense, the international arena, and

---

[17]These comments are adapted from Joseph White, "Better News Than They Think," published in the *San Diego Union* on October 7, 1990.

for domestic purposes. There are separate limits for outlays and for new budget authority for these three types of discretionary spending for the years between 1990 and 1992, after which these merge to a single category called total discretionary spending.

Now comes the first new sequester, which would occur only within one of the three discretionary programs or, in 1994 and 1995, within total discretionary programs. Should expenditures within the relevant category be deemed, after the end of session, to exceed their target, the accounts for that category in the following fiscal year would be reduced across-the-board to make up the difference. There are further complications, but that is the basic idea: The offending category pays the fine.

The second new sequester applies to decreases in revenue or increases in entitlement expenditure enacted into law. This PAYASYOUGO sequestration must occur within fifteen calendar days of congressional adjournment and on the same day as enforcement of limits on discretionary spending and overall deficit targets. Thus there is one sequestration for deficit targets (which won't happen, as I will explain), another for discretionary spending, and a third for new entitlement spending or revenue reduction. All of these provisions are further buttressed by elaborating on previous Gramm–Rudman points of order, designed to prevent offending legislation from being passed in the first place. It should also be noted that the entitlement sequester follows the GRH pattern in that the exemptions from sequestration for poor people's programs are still in place. The "cap" on medicare reductions, however, has been raised from 2 percent to 4 percent.

As part of a long process of change that will undoubtedly continue, the Budget Enforcement Act contains provisions on federal credit reform. It not only calls on the federal government to state the cost of loans and loan guarantees but requires that, except for entitlements and the credit programs of agricultural price supports, there must be appropriations to cover outlays defined as "the long-term costs . . . on the net present value basis. . . ."[18] This requires calculating the cost to the federal government of borrowing to acquire the funds that are being lent

[18]*Ibid.*, p. 8.

in guaranteed loans in relation to the amount the borrower pays back. This is a positive and important change.[19]

Government sponsored enterprises (GSEs), which are established by the federal government but operated and owned by private individuals, have long been the object of suspicion. Such entities include the Federal Home Loan Bank system, the Student Loan Marketing Association, the Farm Credit System, the Federal National Mortgage Association, and the Federal Home Loan Mortgage Corporation. By the end of April 1991, the Treasury Department and CBO are required to report to Congress on the GSEs' financial soundness. The savings and loan debacle has made everyone more cautious, thus giving force to concern over the last several decades about the exposure of federal finances to failures of GSEs. From now on, as is true of federal credit activities, a report on GSEs will be included in the president's budget.

These substantial changes in the budgetary process, partially eliminating but mostly adding new procedures on top of the old, as has become customary, are the product of experience under GRH. This experience has made its impact on observers as well as on members of the executive and legislative branches. Believing that general sequesters do not work, both because these tend to be too large and because the penalty does not fit the crime, they have made them more numerous, more precise, and more responsible.

The legislative package I have described restores budgeting's long-term focus and substitutes real policy change for Gramm–Rudman's hostage game. It uses, rather than fights against, our political system's designed difficulty of action. It tries to limit scorekeeping games, and it extends oversight to areas such as credit and GSEs.

What the package does *not* do is prevent the economy from destabilizing the budget. Entitlement spending that rises because of changes in the economy, or because of aging of the population or other demographic reasons, or for anything and everything outside of legislative enactment is not covered. Subjecting any change in entitlements to PAYASYOUGO principles would be much more powerful. But this

---

[19]In the general spirit of protecting the appropriators from things they don't control, the discretionary targets are "held harmless" by being adjusted for the calculations that will be made to translate previous loan levels into BA levels for fiscal 1994–1995.

would mean that entitlements would not be total entitlements but only quasi-entitlements, in that full payment could not be guaranteed. And it might be economically perverse. On the one hand, new benefits will be more difficult to establish; on the other hand, the growth of costs under existing guidelines will not be touched at all. And there you have the essential compromise.

On the political level there is not so much compromise as unspoken agreement to resolve the main charge against all politicians—that they cannot govern because they cannot balance the budget—in the two ways intractable problems are usually solved: (1) by doing something about them, that is, reducing the deficit and (2) by redefining them so they become solvable. Essentially the politicians moved away from a deficit-reduction enforcement process to a spending control enforcement process. Inasmuch as objectives may be inferred from legislation, the current goal of the budgetary process is to keep spending down to current policy, liberally defined, rather than to specific dollar limits. OBRA switches from deficit to expenditure control.

I ask in conclusion, is it true, as frequently alleged, that the Budget Summit was a disaster for the Bush administration? No doubt the decline in Republican morale is traceable to rescinding the president's vow not to raise taxes. Comparing the Budget Summit to OBRA, however, makes it clear that the president's chief negotiators, Budget Director Richard Darman and Chief of Staff John Sununu, did well by their president and party. Were they suckered, for instance, into changes in medicare larger than Congress could take so their agreement would collapse? I doubt it. Only if one judged that, even if supported by House Republicans, the Summit package would have failed to pass, would they be culpable. I would also have to agree with Representative Howard Berman (D-Calif.) that "It's [OBRA] far more progressive, less onerous on the middle class and it is not trying to reduce the deficit on the backs of the elderly."[20] So we can say that the Democrats did a lot better than the Republicans but we must postpone judgment on whether the country has done better.

In explaining why the president went along with OBRA, John

[20]*Oakland Tribune,* October 26, 1990, p. A12.

Sununu stated that "The Democrats held the economy hostage to an increase in taxes. . . . If he'd had more Republicans there [in Congress], he wouldn't have had to pay the ransom."[21] Of course, the idea that the Democratic devils made the president do this didn't travel well. But the essential point is really not disputed by anyone: Democrats generally want more ample social welfare programs to aid those less well-off, and want to raise taxes on the better-off in order to do so. The accompanying bar graph produced by the House Budget Committee shows that while the bottom 20 percent of the population in income would actually benefit from OBRA, the top 10 percent (in white) paid by far the most (Figure 12-1). The comparison with the Summit package reveals that people of high income paid correspondingly less and those of middle and lower income correspondingly more. Whether one thinks it desirable that people of lower income should pay virtually no taxes is not a matter to be discussed here. Always, however, the middle classes pay more absolutely because there are so many more of them and they have most of the income.[22]

The one tax on which President Bush drew the line was a surtax on millionaires. As columnist Mona Charen expressed it, "Republicans have not been this depressed since Watergate." Bush ended up supporting virtually every kind of tax except on the richest. And, "That," she wrote, "is Republican hari-kari."[23] Why did the president and his advisers commit so obvious a political blunder? Only they know for sure. But the accounts of the negotiations suggest they were outraged because they knew that the Democrats knew there were too few millionaires to be worth taxing. The administration also did not want to set a precedent for beating down on people who made it financially. Perhaps these Republicans are now better able to empathize with Democrats who felt the facts were on their side when Ronald Reagan berated them over deficits, but he had the better talking points.

Do not suppose that tinkering with the budget process is now over

[21] *The Wall Street Journal,* October 29, 1990, p. A3.

[22] House Budget Committee, "Fiscal Year 1990 Budget Agreement Summary Materials," October 27, 1990.

[23] *Washington Times,* November 1, 1990, p. G4.

FIGURE 12-1

Administration-Supported Budget Summit Package Compared to Final
Budget (Shares of Deficit Reduction Compared to Shares of Income).

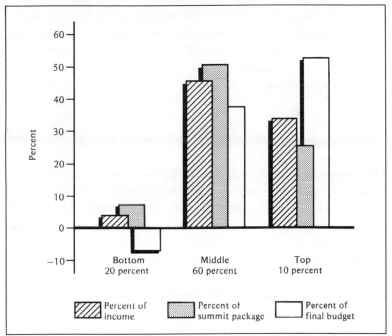

Source: "Fiscal Year 1991 Budget Agreement Summary Materials," House Budget Committee, October 27, 1990, p. 25.

for awhile. After all, OBRA was created in a short time. There are bound
to be errors and misconceptions. Suppose an entitlement is not changed
by a piece of legislation but by a new administrative rule that opens it
up to many more people. Is that covered or not? As exceptions are duly
noted and inserted, the most confident prediction that can be made is
that future versions will be even more complex than this one.

Nevertheless, the driving force will continue to be the will of the
people as reflected in who gets elected and defeated. With Congress
largely moving in an egalitarian direction and the presidency becoming
more individualist, the twain did not meet in Reagan's time. Therefore,

there was stalemate punctuated by modest advances, depending on what could be agreed on. When Reagan was succeeded unpredictably not by someone who followed his preferences but by a vice-president who loved him but not his major policies, the die was cast for a different outcome. With a president who felt deficit reduction was more important than keeping taxes down, and with House Republicans who could not tolerate violating their no-tax pledge, the way was opened for Democrats to get more of what they wanted.

GRH VERSUS OBRA

The procedural changes under OBRA, as we have seen, are many and varied. Because GRH only recently was the last word in budgetary process, it is important to consider how the new process modifies the old.

What is left of GRH? The patient reader should suspect by now that it has not been superseded, so it no longer need be considered, but has been left partly in place, the new rising somewhat shakily atop the old. Conditions differ as between 1991 to 1993 and 1994 to 1995. In the earlier period, GRH's deficit targets, and therefore its sequestration procedures, are effectively nullified. After all, there is now PAYASYOUGO sequestration to guard against legislation decreasing revenue or increasing entitlements, and there is discretionary sequestration to guard against increases in domestic, international, and defense spending. So what? A skeptic might be excused for believing that revenues might still decline because of economic slowdown and entitlements might go up because more people take advantage of existing provisions. True, as Alice might say, but not true in OBRA's budgetary wonderland. The ramparts of the maximally allowed deficit for 1991 to 1993 cannot be scaled, because external forces like changes in the economy or war are not allowed to count against the deficit. And the players are the ones who will make up the rules for what counts as they go along.

Some parts of GRH still matter. Suppose there arises legislation that does reduce revenues or increase the cost of entitlements; the

PAYASYOUGO sequester would apply only to those entitlements subject to the old GRH sequester, namely, medicare and price supports by way of the Commodity Credit Corporation.

There being no specific time when budget balance has to be achieved, it will not be possible to fail to accomplish that legally nonexistent goal. Moreover, the limit on the size of the deficit and the spending caps must be adjusted in the fiscal 1992 and 1993 presidential budgets so they take account of the latest economic, technical, and conceptual changes. No one can say exactly what might be included under "conceptual" other than that the concept of failing in deficit reduction is not one that is likely to survive. Though the language is more general, the president appears to be able to make similar adjustments in fiscal 1994 and 1995, the end of OBRA's five-year reign, when the party of the occupant of the White House might have changed or by which time the budget targets may be amended. Whether the nation will benefit because presidents can declare such phenomena as the savings and loan bailout or operations in the Persian Gulf to be emergencies, not to be offset by mandatory sequesters, depends on what the politicians choose to call emergencies.

In policy terms, under OBRA more children were made eligible for medicaid up to age 18 and child care provisions were substantially expanded. Though medicare premiums were raised somewhat, there are, depending on how one separates provisions, somewhere between fifteen and twenty expansions of services. It is difficult to count all the changes made to Aid to Dependent Children (AFDC), Supplemental Security Income (SSI), social security itself (OASDI), and more. Furthermore, the conflict over defense spending that occurred during the two terms of the Reagan administration has been postponed for the rest of President Bush's first term by fixing limits on all discretionary spending. OBRA allows this conflict to be reinstituted under conditions that, though less than two years away, no one can now predict. By changing the rules beginning in 1993, Democrats get a chance to cut defense even further, and the Bush administration does not have to face the issue until it can see what the international situation looks like.

THE REVENGE OF THE APPROPRIATORS

Whereas in the bad old days, members of appropriations committees felt they were either required to make deeper cuts or falsely criticized for actions over which they had no control, such as failures of authorizing committees to reduce entitlements as required in reconciliation instructions or because events pushed entitlement spending up, now they have given themselves what they believe (though they may be mistaken) are fairly generous spending caps, and protected these against all comers, whether external (e.g., the economy) or internal (e.g., direct spending).

Perhaps OBRA should be called the revenge of the appropriators. They have accomplished this purpose by putting as much of the budget total as possible under preset, automatic controls. Like the economic stabilizers that kick in when unemployment grows large, these protections for appropriations are designed to create lulls in the budget battles so that the appropriators do not have to refight the same battles over and over and over again. The onus is against changing priorities by saying so through direct legislation. Having gotten everybody else off their backs, maybe they will be able to return, in their part of the budget, to the relatively simple process I described in the original *Politics of the Budgetary Process* over a quarter century ago!

It is one thing to say that one ought to be free and another to be able to act free of powerful forces. All the appropriations committees have got is a couple of years to satisfy the rest of Congress that the new rules are in everyone's institutional interests.[24] If not, OBRA will be but a temporary hiatus in long-standing institutional struggles.

Other informed observers express amazement that a Democratic Congress allowed OMB to gain so much power over the budget by deciding such seemingly arcane but vital matters as what item of expenditure fits under which spending cap, or how much program costs have

---

[24]See Lawrence J. Haas, "New Rules of the Game," *National Journal,* November 17, 1990, pp. 2793–97.

risen due to factors out of Congress's control.[25] As we know, this power was granted because it is essential to budgetary control and the courts have ruled that only an executive agency can perform this function. And the Democratic budget professionals are not, in private, concerned.[26] The rules as we have discussed them apply in full only for two years. Why would OMB choose to discomfort Democratically controlled Congresses when it knows that its authority will be up for grabs again in a couple of years? The considerable attention devoted to scoring cuts and increases in the last decade has created a Washington community view of what is tolerable and appropriate so that on most issues, the technicians are near a consensus. Nevertheless, distrust is rampant, so a fight is likely over whether OMB should be allowed to make these judgments.

Both the House and Senate Budget Committees issued long descriptions and analyses of the process changes. The rules have changed so much and so often that making them has become part of budgeting. To get the feeling, here is one such process change.

> *Estimating adjustments.* There is a very small BA allowance and a larger outlay allowance provided on an "as used" basis. They differ from the other "as used" adjustments in that they are not intended to be used under congressional scorekeeping. . . . Imagine that appropriation bills meet their caps using congressional scorekeeping but breach them using OMB scorekeeping; if the breach is within the allowance, there would be no sequester.[27]

Technicalities include a series of "estimating adjustments" to bridge the inevitable small differences between congressional and OMB scorekeeping. Note also that while Senate and House do not follow precisely the same rules, the thrust of the major proposals in OBRA, especially the three sequesters, is expected to compel similar behavior.

[25]Susan F. Rasky, "Substantial Power on Spending Is Shifted from Congress to Bush," *The New York Times,* National Edition, October 30, 1990, pp. 1A, 13.

[26]Joe White, conversations with Appropriations, Ways and Means, and Budget staff.

[27]Richard Kogan, "The Budget Enforcement Act of 1990: A Technical Explanation," November 1, 1990, typescript, pp. 6–7. Senate Budget's typescript on the "Budget Enforcement Act of 1990" is supplemented by CRS Report 90-520 GOV: "Budget Enforcement Act of 1990: Brief Summary," by Edward Davis and Robert Keith, November 5, 1990.

Those who suspect that this tranquility-in-budgeting act is not for this world may have experience on their side. Starting in 1993, coterminous with the new presidential administration, spending cuts from defense can be transferred to other discretionary purposes. By this time, perhaps, there may well be general agreement on how large these defense cuts should be and what programs should be beefed up or started anew. That seems a lot to ask for.

Stanley Collender has the winners and losers straight:

For a number of reasons, the House and Senate Appropriations Committees are also clear winners.

First, because of the appropriations caps, the committees now know how much they will have to spend for both fiscal 1992 and 1993. Therefore, they no longer have to endure the often interminable wait for the budget resolution to be passed before they find out what they can do.

Second, the creation of the appropriations caps by category means that the appropriations committees do not have to determine the split between military and domestic programs, traditionally one of the most contentious budget issues that has to be decided each year.

Third, under the new GRH rules, if the budget resolution is not adopted by April 15, the appropriations committees will receive their section 302(a) allocations based on the amounts requested by the president in his budget. These allocations tell appropriations committees how much they have to spend and so is a critical element in their work. Therefore, this will also allow the committees to move ahead without having to wait for the budget resolution to be passed.

Fourth, because there is little chance of the excess-deficit type of sequester, the only way that a sequester can occur in appropriated programs is if the appropriations committees themselves propose legislation that causes the discretionary caps to be breached. Since this is unlikely, there is very little chance that any sequester will occur.

This means the appropriations committees can move ahead with their bills without having to worry about any across-the-board cuts changing the amounts they have provided. This, in turn, makes it more likely that most fiscal 1992 and 1993 appropriations will be enacted by the start of the fiscal year and so will take some of the political heat off the appropriations committees that has occurred over the last decade when their bills were generally not passed on time. . . .

It is hard to find larger losers in the budget debate than the two budget committees, which now have little more to do than explain the new budget process to their colleagues. There are no priorities to be determined, no deficit reduction packages to be compiled, and it will be OMB's estimates that are likely to hold the most weight.

Furthermore, although the formal requirement remains, there really is no need for Congress to pass a budget resolution, at least for 1992 and 1993. Virtually all of the decisions that are usually not made until the budget resolution is adopted have now already been made by both this year's deficit reduction agreement or by the budget process changes. In addition, the appropriations committees no longer have to wait for the budget committees to draft the budget resolution and for the resolution to be adopted before finding out how much they will have to spend.[28]

A TRUCE, NOT A TREATY

OBRA is real, OBRA is earnest, and it just might foreshadow a permanent change in national priorities. It might also represent the continuation of ideologically divisive budget wars under new rules.

My guess is that these changes in process will have different effects depending on how power over the budget is arrayed. If there is a Democratic president and Democratic majorities in both houses, albeit a small majority in the Senate, Democratic party cohesiveness will be at a maximum. This presidential and congressional majority will have to moderate its views to suit a more conservative Senate. In producing more liberal-egalitarian policies, somewhat higher levels of taxes on higher incomes, and somewhat greater benefits in social programs, they will find the new rules starting in 1993 exceedingly useful. They will be able to shift funds from defense to domestic and otherwise rearrange priorities at a modest but steady pace. Should there be a Republican president with large Democratic majorities in the House and a substantial Democratic majority in the Senate, however, the new rules will exacerbate already high levels of conflict. They will disagree about the rules for scoring, for sequesters, for the division between direct legislation and appropriations, whether OMB should do the scoring, and so forth.

[28]*Federal Budget Report*, Vol. IX, No. 23 (November 12, 1990), pp. 10–11.

Because the new provisions are more complex, and there are many of them, there will be more grounds for dispute and hence enmity. Should there be overwhelming majorities of the same party in Congress and the presidency, neither these provisions nor anything that has gone before would matter. The primacy of politics in a democracy means that when majorities are sufficiently strong and agreed they get their way.

THE PARTS VERSUS THE WHOLE

Through the thicket of budget provisions, piled helter-skelter atop one another, there comes the recognizable outline of disputes that have pitted institutions in the budgetary process against each other as far back as anyone can remember. If one were to ask the members and chairs of the House and Senate appropriations committees how they feel about their part in the budgetary process, they would undoubtedly answer "Hard done by." Why? Because, they would reply in classical tones, their authority is not commensurate with their responsibility, especially because presidents have gone too far away to share responsibility and budget committees have come too close for the appropriators to exercise what they feel is their rightful autonomy, the budgetary process has come into deserved disrepute. In the classical process of the 1950s and earlier decades, presidents submitted budgets that accorded with their policy preferences, adding a gaming factor to allow the House Appropriations Committee, through its subcommittees, to cut at the margins, knowing full well the Senate Appropriations Committee would act as an appeals court, making selective additions so that in the end almost all the players got most of what they wanted. That is, the appropriators were second-guessers, marking up or down the bids proposed by the president and the authorizing committees. However, this budget minuet depended on the participants being close enough to begin with so they could play their appointed roles: There cannot be a second guess without a first. In an age of budgetary dissensus, by contrast, presidents have maintained responsibility to their party and their own preferences but have behaved irresponsibly, as appropriators in both parties see it, by presenting budgets that are so far from what is likely to pass muster in Congress that they are pronounced (as we know) dead on arrival. Understanding as well the sense of the medieval dictum that one prince nearby is worse than many princes far away, the appropriators have not taken kindly to the efforts of budget committees to control their operations. Members of appropriations committees would rather be constrained, if they must, by a president concerned mostly with the size of spending than by many representatives and senators with detailed changes they wish to enforce. Little as the appropriators liked to observe the outlays of entitlement programs grow ever larger ("Look ma, no hands!"), they liked even less being told by budget committees through reconciliation orders (yes, instructions are orders) that they must make up for entitlements out of control by cutting their own appropriations authority far more than they thought desirable. Nor were the appropriators enthralled to observe deeply divisive ideological debates over budget resolutions, which may have sounded fine to those who like abstract discussions, but which, in their view, brought Congress into disrepute by forbidding the bargains and compromises that might have added up to the appearance of responsible budgeting.

OBRA tries to change all of this. While it cannot create ideological and policy agreement where it does not exist, it does take away the necessity of making believe there is such agreement, thereby demonstrating once more that Congress is not what it was never supposed to be, a unified body. To begin with, presidents are now required to submit a budget that is within the ball park of existing past agreements as memorialized in multiyear instructions about levels of taxing and spending. Therefore, for the next five years the appropriators can look forward to the ancient pleasure of working off presidential budgets, marking them up here, marking them down there, as they used to do in what they think of as better days. Moreover, the appropriators succeeded in getting an additional $37 billion to spread around their part of the budget so as to lubricate the joints and ease the pain of making adjustments as they were wont to do in days of old. Nor can budget committees tell appropriators what to do. For one thing, the appropriators themselves have worked out agreements on what they are supposed to do, thus usurping the place taken in the bad old days by budget resolutions. For another, problems that arise from shortfalls in revenue or overages in entitlements would be dealt with where they occurred; only where appropriations themselves have departed from agreed-on guidelines would there be points of order and sequestration provisions to restrain them by passing out the pain within their balliwick, a principle they accept provided it is accepted by others. Oh yes, this nonsense about meeting some artificial deficit target regardless of whether the world is at war or at peace and the economy is booming or busting has been done away with. In the future, the appropriators devoutly hope, each part of the process will be held responsible for what it does or does not do and the rest of the world will have to take care of itself.

In order to make presidents play their assigned parts, especially in view of the decision of the Supreme Court in *Synar* v. *The United States,* presidents, through the OMB, are given stronger procedural powers. It is they who must submit a certain kind of budget according to their own calculations; who must alter their budget proposals according to the state of the economy; and whose findings must or must not trigger sequestrations of various kinds. This is a lot of procedural clout. It could be that some farseeing budget director will attempt to use these procedural powers to bargain with the appropriations committees at every stage of the process, not just the stage of formulating the budget or of certifying sequestration. Indeed, David Stockman, who was President Reagan's first director of the budget, started to do exactly this with his corps of bill trackers and his practice of preemptive intervention. Now, his latest successor and friend, Richard Darman, has the tools to do even more. Will he use them, assuming he remains in office? I think so. Will they be effective? A little, yes, but a lot, no. My reason is that Congress has the means, namely, the power of the purse, to compel OMB and through it the president to back down.[29] In following the thrust and

[29]For a somewhat different view, see Stanley Collender's *Federal Budget Report,* "A Primer on the New Budget Process," and "Political Winners and Losers Under GRH Number 3" [by which is meant OBRA], Vol. 9, No. 23, November 12, 1990, pp. 1–12. Collender writes: "It is also not hard to imagine that OMB could be remarkably successful in this sort of effort. While it would clearly make Democratic leaders unhappy or worse to find OMB continually threatening sequester throughout the year, this might be one

maneuver of budgeting, it is all too easy to imagine that skill is all (or most) that matters. Skill counts but votes count more, especially in an age of ideological dissensus. That is why OBRA and not the Budget Summit is now the law of the land.

THE POLITICS OF OBRA FROM A MACROPOLITICAL PERSPECTIVE

OBRA is intended to do two things that have largely escaped public notice. By taking social security out of the deficit calculation and by putting the savings and loan bailout in the deficit calculation, the size of the deficit has been artificially enlarged so as to create huge forced savings down the road. I will explain. Social security is being taken out of the deficit calculation while it is generating large surpluses; in five or six years its surplus should amount to something like $100 billion annually. (Of course, this surplus will eventually become a shortage, but not for a decade or two.) At the same time, the monies devoted to buying savings and loans should begin to come back to the federal treasury in the form of repaid loans amounting to some $20 billion a year for five or six years. Combining the two numbers, we get an actual surplus in the unified budget of something like $120 billion while the federal deficit alone would either be balanced or show a small (within 1 percent of GNP) deficit.

What's wrong with this? If the great problem with the American economy is that the American people do not save enough, as political leaders on both sides now agree, then government will have to borrow much less, thereby making much more available for investment; this should raise GNP per capita far above what it otherwise would have been, thus preparing the nation for a time when it has a much higher proportion of older people. Should the real economic problem not be lack of investment but monetary deflation, however, as a few economists

of the few tactics that is available to the administration to influence legislation in light of the election losses it suffered this year, especially in the House." I think those losses and the already large Democratic majorities will prove effective.

fear, then these hidden savings will lead to the very slow economic growth they were designed to prevent.

OBRA also relieves the president and Congress of the necessity of responding to external events that cause downward perturbations in revenue or upward alternations in expenditure, thus bringing the budget way out of balance. Held more tightly responsible for the effects they cause directly, the appropriators are relieved from responsibility for what they cannot help immediately. If we assume that the balance of political responsibility has been shifted too far toward government and not enough toward the citizenry, holding government harmless is a good idea. If we think that government should bear its burden of the cost of change, or that everyone has to deal with forces they cannot control, then these hold-harmless provisions are a bad idea.

OBRA also can perform a scorekeeping function for us if we will allow it to do so. The problem, I said before, was not balance but what kind of balance—high tax, high spending versus lower tax and less service—to move toward. If that general statement sums up the differences between the parties, then we are now in a position to make an accounting: (1) The hidden savings favor the high-tax, high-service state because they raise taxes beyond what would otherwise be necessary to achieve balance, thereby placing much less pressure on reduced spending; (2) the hold-harmless provisions, bolstered by giving extra funds to general government, make it easier to raise spending (and, therefore, justify higher taxes) by divorcing those parts that government does not control directly from those that it does, though all add up to spending just the same. Moving to the ideological side of OBRA, it does a great deal more to raise taxes than to reduce spending, the increased revenues being far more certain and larger and the decreased spending being far less certain and far smaller. If the high-service, high-tax state lost under Ronald Reagan, it is winning so far under George Bush. Of course, it may be far too small for others. A politics of budgetary dissensus means that anyway the budget goes—upward, downward, or sideways—there will be a lot of dissatisfaction.

GLOSSARY*

APPROPRIATED ENTITLEMENTS: Budget authority provided in annual appropriations, although payment must be made to all eligible people who apply. Examples of appropriated entitlements are medicaid, Supplemental Security Income, Aid to Families with Dependent Children, and veterans compensation.

APPROPRIATION: An act of Congress that permits federal agencies to incur obligations and to make payments out of the Treasury for specified purposes. Appropriations are one form of budget authority.

APPROPRIATION ACT: A statute that provides funds for federal programs. An appropriation act generally follows enactment of authorizing legislation unless the authorizing legislation itself provides the budget authority.

AUTHORIZATION (AUTHORIZING LEGISLATION): Substantive legislation enacted by Congress that sets up or continues legal operation of a federal program or agency either indefinitely or for a specific period of time or sanctions a particular type of obligation or expenditure within a program. Authorizing legislation is usually a prerequisite for subsequent appropriations or other kinds of budget authority to be contained in appropriation acts. Such legislation may limit the amount of budget authority to be provided subsequently or may authorize the appropriation of "such sums as may be necessary." Budget authority may be provided in the authorization (see Backdoor authority) which eliminates the need for subsequent appropriations or requires only an appropriation to liquidate contract authority or reduce outstanding debt.

BACKDOOR AUTHORITY: Budget authority provided in legislation outside the appropriations process. The most common forms of backdoor authority are authority to borrow (borrowing authority), contract authority, and entitle-

---

*Most of the definitions of these terms are taken verbatim or adapted from *A Glossary of Terms Used in the Federal Budget Process and Related Accounting, Economic, and Tax Terms*, U.S. General Accounting Office, March 1981, Third Edition, PAD-81-27. Terms of more recent origin have been defined by Dean Hammer.

ments. In some cases (e.g., interest on the public debt), a permanent appropriation is provided that becomes available without any current actions by the Congress.

BACKDOOR SPENDING: Authority of federal agencies to spend money through the Treasury rather than going through the appropriations process.

BORROWING AUTHORITY: Statutory authority (substantive or appropriation) that permits a federal agency to incur obligations and to make payments for specified purposes out of borrowed monies. Section 401 of the Congressional Budget Act of 1974 limits new borrowing authority (except for certain instances) to such extent or in such amounts as are provided in appropriation acts.

BUDGET AMENDMENT: A formal request submitted to the Congress by the president, after his formal budget transmittal but prior to completion of appropriation action by the Congress, that revises previous requests, such as the amount of budget authority.

BUDGET AUTHORITY: Authority provided by law to enter into obligations that will result in immediate or future outlays involving federal government funds. Budget authority does not include authority to insure or guarantee the repayment of indebtedness incurred by another person or government. The basic forms of budget authority are <u>appropriations, authority to borrow, and conract authority</u>. Budget authority may be classified by the period of availability (one-year, multiyear, no-year), by the timing of congressional action (current or permanent), or by the manner of determining the amount available (definite or indefinite).

CAPITAL BUDGET: A divided budget with investment in capital assets excluded from calculations of the budget surplus or deficit. A capital budget provides for separating financing of capital or investment expenditures from current or operating expenditures.

CONCURRENT RESOLUTION ON THE BUDGET: Under the Congressional Budget Act of 1974, a resolution passed by both houses of Congress, but not requiring the signature of the president, which sets forth, reaffirms, or revises the congressional budget for the United States government for a fiscal year. There were two such resolutions required preceding each fiscal year. The first required concurrent resolution, due by May 15, established the congressional budget. The second required concurrent resolution, due by September 15, reaffirmed or revised it. Other concurrent resolutions for a fiscal year could be adopted at any time following the first required concurrent resolution for that fiscal year.

The Balanced Budget Act of 1985 revised this process. Only one annual budget resolution is required, with action by both houses scheduled to be completed by April 15.

CONTINUING RESOLUTION: Legislation enacted by the Congress to provide budget authority for specific ongoing activities in cases where the regular fiscal year appropriations for such activities have not been enacted by the beginning of the fiscal year. The continuing resolution usually specifies a maximum rate at which the agency may incur obligations, based on the rate of the prior year, the president's budget request, or an appropriation bill passed by either or both houses of the Congress.

CONTRACT AUTHORITY: A form of budget authority under which contracts or other obligations may be entered into in advance of an appropriation or in excess of amounts otherwise available in a revolving fund. Contract authority must be funded by a subsequent appropriation or the use of revolving fund collections to liquidate the obligations. Appropriations to liquidate contract authority are not classified as budget authority since they are not available for obligation. Section 401 of the Congressional Budget Act of 1974 limits new contract authority, with few exceptions, to such extent or in such amounts as are provided in appropriation acts.

CURRENT POLICY BUDGET: Projections of the estimated budget authority and outlays for the upcoming fiscal year to operate federal programs at the level implied by enacted appropriations and authorizations of the current fiscal year without policy changes, but adjusted for inflation, changes in the numbers and kinds of beneficiaries, and in some instances to reflect the continuation of certain programs scheduled to terminate.

CURRENT SERVICES ESTIMATES: Estimated budget authority and outlays for the upcoming fiscal year based on continuation of existing levels of service, that is, assuming that all programs and activities will be carried on at the same level as in the fiscal year in progress and without policy changes in such programs and activities. These estimates of budget authority and outlays, accompanied by the underlying economic and programmatic assumptions on which they are based (such as the rate of inflation, the rate of real economic growth, the unemployment rate, program caseloads, and pay increases), are transmitted by the president to the Congress when the budget is submitted.

DEFERRAL OF BUDGET AUTHORITY: Any action or inaction by an officer or employee of the United States government that temporarily withholds, delays, or effectively precludes the obligation or expenditure of budget authority, including authority to obligate by contract in advance of appropriations as specifically authorized by law and including the establishment of reserves under the Antideficiency Act as amended by the Impoundment Control Act.

The president must provide a special message to Congress reporting a proposed deferral of budget authority. Deferrals may not extend beyond the end of the fiscal year in which the message reporting the deferral is transmitted. Deferrals can be overturned only by Congress passing a law, which the president must sign.

ENTITLEMENTS: Legislation that requires the payment of benefits to any person or unit of government that meets the eligibility requirements established by such law. Authorizations for entitlements constitute a binding obligation on the part of the federal government, and eligible recipients have legal recourse if the obligation is not fulfilled.

EXPENDITURES: See OUTLAYS.

FAZIO RULE: House procedure whereby appropriation subcommittees cannot be subject to points of order under Section 302(a) for total spending if their spending proposals are within their allocations for discretionary (not mandatory) budget authority from the Appropriations Committee's 302(b) process.

FISCAL POLICY: Federal government policies with respect to taxes, spending, and debt management, intended to promote the nation's macroeconomic goals, particularly with respect to employment, gross national product, price level stability, and equilibrium in balance of payments. The budget process is a major vehicle for determining and implementing federal fiscal policy. The other major component of federal economic policy is monetary policy.

FISCAL YEAR: Any yearly accounting period, without regard to its relationship to a calendar year. The fiscal year for the federal government begins on October 1 and ends on September 30. The fiscal year is designated by the calendar year in which it ends (e.g., fiscal year 1992 is the fiscal year ending September 30, 1992).

IMPOUNDMENT: Any action or inaction by an officer or employee of the United States government that precludes the obligation or expenditure of budget authority provided by Congress. Two kinds of impoundment are rescission and deferral.

LOAN GUARANTEE: A loan guarantee is an agreement by which the government pledges to pay part or all of the loan principal and interest to a lender or holder of a security, in the event of default by a third-party borrower. If it becomes necessary for the government to pay part or all of the loan principal or interest, the payment is a direct outlay and is counted toward the deficit. Otherwise, the guarantee does not directly affect federal budget outlays and is not counted toward the deficit.

MULTIYEAR BUDGETING: A budget planning process designed to make sure that the long-range consequences of budget decisions are identified and reflected in the budget totals.

OBLIGATIONAL AUTHORITY: The sum of budget authority provided for a given fiscal year, balance of amounts brought forward from prior years that remain available for obligation, and amounts authorized to be credited to a specific fund or account during that year, including transfers between funds or accounts.

OFF-BUDGET OUTLAYS: Outlays of off-budget federal entities whose transactions have been excluded from the budget totals under provisions of law, even though these outlays are part of total government spending.

OFFSETS: Requirement that an appropriation subcommittee's spending that exceeds the amount allocated to it by the Budget Resolution under Section 302(b) be matched by a reduction in other outlays and/or an increase in revenues equivalent to the amount of spending being added. Offsets may also apply to making up decreases in revenue proposed in tax legislation.

OFFSETTING RECEIPTS: All collections deposited into receipt accounts that are offset against budget authority and outlays rather than reflected as budget receipts in computing budget totals. Under current budgetary usage, cash collections not deposited into receipt accounts (such as revolving fund receipts and reimbursements) are deducted from outlays at the account level. These transactions are offsetting collections but are not classified as "offsetting receipts."

OUTLAYS: The amount of checks issued, interest accrued on most public debt, or other payments, net of refunds and reimbursements. Total budget outlays consist of the sum of the outlays from appropriations and funds included in the unified budget, less offsetting receipts. The outlays of off-budget federal entities are excluded from the unified budget under provisions of law, even though these outlays are part of total government spending.

PAYASYOUGO: A process for keeping expenditures within major elements of the budget by requiring that additions to outlays above amounts set by budget resolutions or in law be made up by new sources of revenue or by reductions elsewhere within (and only within) that category. See also OFFSETS.

PERMANENT APPROPRIATIONS: Authority to spend provided in authorizing legislation without the need for subsequent annual appropriations. Examples include medicare, social security, and interest on the public debt.

PLANNING PROGRAM BUDGETING SYSTEM (PPBS): A budgetary process that initially sets out goals (the planning phase), develops and approves programs for reaching these objectives (the programming phase), and prices and allocates inputs required for reaching these objectives (the budgetary phase).

PRESIDENT'S BUDGET: A proposed budget for a particular fiscal year transmitted to the Congress by the president in accordance with the Budget and Accounting Act of 1921, as amended. Some elements of the budget, such as the estimates for the legislative branch and the judiciary, are required to be included without review by the Office of Management and Budget or approval of the president.

RECONCILIATION PROCESS: A process used by Congress to reconcile amounts determined by tax, spending, and debt legislation for a given fiscal year with the ceilings enacted in the required concurrent resolution on the budget for that year. Section 310 of the Congressional Budget Act of 1974 as amended provides that the required concurrent resolution on the budget, which sets binding totals for the budget, may direct committees to determine and recommend changes to laws, bills, and resolutions, as required to conform with the binding totals for budget authority, revenues, and the public debt. Such changes are incorporated into either a reconciliation resolution or a reconciliation bill.

REPROGRAMMING: Utilization of funds in an appropriation account for purposes other than those contemplated at the time of the appropriation. Reprogramming is generally preceded by consultation between federal agencies and the appropriate congressional committees. It involves formal notification and, in some instances, opportunity for disapproval by congressional committees.

RESCISSION: A bill or joint resolution that cancels, in whole or in part, budget authority previously granted by Congress. Rescissions proposed by the president must be transmitted in a special message to Congress. Under Section 1012 of the Congressional Budget and Impoundment Control Act of 1974, unless both houses of Congress complete action on a rescission bill within 45 days of continuous session after receipt of the proposal, the budget authority must be made available for obligation.

SEQUESTRATION: Under the Balanced Budget Act of 1985, the withholding of budget authority, according to an established formula, up to the amount required to be cut to meet the deficit target.

SUPPLEMENTAL APPROPRIATION: An act appropriating funds in addition to those in an annual appropriation act. Supplemental appropriations provide additional budget authority beyond original estimates for programs or activities (including new programs authorized after the date of the original appropriation act).

TRANSFER OF FUNDS: When specifically authorized in law, all or part of the budget authority in one account may be transferred to another account.

TRUST FUND: Funds collected and used by the federal government for carrying out specific purposes and programs according to terms of a trust agreement or statute, such as the social security trust fund.

UNIFIED BUDGET: The current form of the budget of the federal government (beginning with the 1969 budget) in which receipts and outlays from federal funds and trust funds are consolidated. When these fund groups are consolidated to display budget totals, transactions that are outlays of one fund group for payment to the other fund group (i.e., interfund transactions) are deducted to avoid double-counting. Transactions of off-budget federal entities are not included in the unified budget.

ZERO-BASE BUDGETING: Zero-base budgeting provides for analysis of alternative methods of operation at various levels of effort, including the possibility that the activity in question will not be funded at all.

GUIDE TO ACRONYMS

AFDC	Aid to Families with Dependent Children
BEA	Budget Enforcement Act of 1990 (Title XIII)
BOB	Bureau of the Budget
CBO	Congressional Budget Office
CCC	Commodity Credit Corporation
CEA	Council of Economic Advisors
CETA	Comprehensive Employee Training Administration
COLAs	cost-of-living adjustments
CR	continuing resolution
CRS	Congressional Research Service
DOD	Department of Defense
DRB	Defense Resources Board
E&E	Emergency and Extraordinary
EOP	Executive Office of the President
EPA	Environmental Protection Agency
FAA	Federal Aviation Administration
FFB	Federal Financing Bank
GAO	Government Accounting Office
GATT	General Agreement on Tariffs and Trade
GNP	gross national product
GRH	Gramm–Rudman–Hollings Deficit Reduction Act
GSEs	government-sponsored enterprises
HBC	House Budget Committee
JCS	Joint Chiefs of Staff
JSPD	Joint Services Planning Document
LIHEAP	Low-Income Home Energy Assistance Program

MDA	maximum deficit amount
NASA	National Aeronautics and Space Administration
NEC	National Economic Commission
OBRA	Omnibus Budget Reconciliation Act of 1990
OECD	Organization for Economic Co-Operation and Development
OMB	Office of Management and Budget
OSD	Office of the Secretary of Defense
OSHA	Occupational Health and Safety Administration
PDMs	program decision memoranda
POMs	program objective memoranda
PPB	planning, programming, and budgeting
RFC	Reconstruction Finance Corporation
RIF	reduction in force
SBC	Senate Budget Committee
WIC	Women, Infants, and Children
ZBB	zero-base budgeting

BIBLIOGRAPHY

Adams, Gordon. *The Politics of Defense Contracting: The Iron Triangle.* New Brunswick, N.J.: Transaction Press, 1982.

Art, Robert J. "Congress and the Defense Budget: Enhancing Policy Oversight." *Political Science Quarterly*, Vol. 100, No. 2 (Summer 1985), pp. 227–48.

Asbell, Bernard. *The Senate Nobody Knows.* Garden City, N.Y.: Doubleday, 1978.

Aspin, Les. "Congress vs. Department of Defense." In Thomas M. Franck, ed. *The Tethered Presidency.* New York: New York University, 1981.

Berman, Larry. *The Office of Management and Budget and the Presidency.* Princeton, N.J.: Princeton University Press, 1979.

Bernstein, Peter W. "David Stockman: No More Big Budget Cuts." *Fortune* (February 6, 1984), pp. 53–56.

Bickley, James M. "The Federal Financing Bank: Assessments of Its Effectiveness and Budgetary Status." *Public Budgeting and Finance*, Vol. 5, No. 4 (Winter 1985), pp. 51–63.

Birnbaum, Jeffrey H., and Alan S. Murray. *Showdown at Gucci Gulch: Lawmakers, Lobbyists, and the Unlikely Triumph of Tax Reform.* New York: Random House, 1987.

Bolles, Albert S. *A Financial History of the United States, 1774–89.* New York: Appleton, 1879.

———. *The Financial History of the United States from 1861 to 1885.* New York: Appleton, 1886.

Borcherding, Thomas. "A Hundred Years of Public Spending, 1870–1970." In Thomas Borcherding, ed. *Budgets and Bureaucrats: The Sources of Government Growth.* Durham, N.C.: Duke University Press, 1977.

Borg, Sten G., and Francis G. Castles. "The Influence of the Political Right on Public Income Maintenance Expenditure and Equality." *Political Studies*, Vol. XXIX (December 1981), pp. 604–21.

Bovbjerg, Randall R., and John Holahan. *Medicaid in the Reagan Era: Federal Policy and State Choices.* Washington, D.C.: Urban Institute, 1982.

Braybrooke, David, and Charles E. Lindblom. *A Strategy of Decision.* New York: Free Press, 1963.

Brookes, Warren. "Blowing Up the Bubble of Envy." *The Washington Times,* October 12, 1990.

Bruner, Jerome S., Jacqueline J. Goodnow, and George A. Austin. *A Study of Thinking.* New York: Wiley, 1956.

Buchanan, James M., and Richard E. Wagner. *Democracy in Deficit: The Political Legacy of Keynes.* New York: Academic Press, 1977.

——. *Fiscal Responsibility in Constitutional Democracy.* Leiden and Boston: Martinus Nijhoff Social Sciences Division, 1978.

Buck, A. E. "The Development of the Budget Idea in the United States." *Annals of the American Academy of Political and Social Science,* Vol. LXIII (May 1924).

——. *Public Budgeting.* New York: Harper, 1929.

Bullock, Charles. "The Finances of the United States from 1775–1789 with Special Reference to the Budget." In Frederick Turner, ed. *Bulletin of the University of Wisconsin,* Vol. 1, 1894–1896. Madison: University of Wisconsin Press, 1897.

Burkhead, Jesse. *Government Budgeting.* New York: Wiley, 1956.

Caiden, Naomi, and Aaron Wildavsky. *Planning and Budgeting in Poor Countries.* New York: Wiley, 1974. Paperback edition by Transaction, Inc. New Brunswick, N.J., 1980.

Christensen, Jorgen Gronnegard. "Growth by Exception: Or the Vain Attempt to Impose Resource Scarcity on the Danish Public Sector." *Journal of Public Policy,* Vol. 2 (May 1982).

Cleveland, Frederick A. "Leadership and Criticism." *Proceedings of the Academy of Political Science,* Vol. 8 (1918–20).

Cleveland, Frederick A., and Arthur E. Buck. *The Budget and Responsible Government.* New York: Macmillan, 1920.

Collender, Stanley E. *The Guide to the Federal Budget: Fiscal 1987.* Washington, D.C.: The Urban Institute Press, 1986.

——. "A Primer on the New Budget Process" and "Political Winners and Losers Under GRH Number 3." *Federal Budget Report,* Vol. 9, No. 23 (November 12, 1990), pp. 1–12.

Crocker, Royce. "Federal Government Spending and Public Opinion." *Public Budgeting and Finance,* Vol. 1 (August 1981), pp. 25–35.

Cutter, W. Bowman. "The Battle of the Budget." *The Atlantic Monthly,* Vol. 247, No. 3 (March 1981).

Davis, Otto A., M. A. H. Dempster, and Aaron Wildavsky. "On the Process of Budgeting II: An Empirical Study of Congressional Appropriations." In R. F. Byrne, A. Charnes, W. W. Cooper, A. A. Davis, and Dorothy Gilford, eds. *Studies in Budgeting.* Amsterdam: North Holland, 1971, pp. 292–375.

————. "Toward a Predictive Theory of the Federal Budgetary Process." *The British Journal of Political Science,* Vol. 4, Part 4 (October 1974), pp. 419–52.

Dawes, Charles G. *The First Year of the Budget of the United States.* New York: Harper, 1923.

Dempster, M. A. H., and Aaron Wildavsky. "On Change: Or, There Is No Magic Size for an Increment." *Political Studies,* Vol. XXVII (September 1979), pp. 371–89.

Derickson, Alan. "The Origins of the Black Lung Insurgency." *Journal of Public Health Policy,* Vol. 4, No. 1 (March 1983).

Derthick, Martha. *Uncontrollable Spending for Social Services Grants.* Washington, D.C.: The Brookings Institution, 1975.

————. *Policymaking for Social Security.* Washington, D.C.: The Brookings Institution, 1979.

Dobell, Rod. "Pressing the Envelope: The Significance of the New, Top-Down System of Expenditure Management in Ottawa." *Policy Options,* November/December 1981, pp. 13–18.

Dorfman, Joseph. *The Economic Mind in American Civilization 1918–1933.* New York: Viking Press, 1959.

Downs, Anthony. "Why the Government Budget Is Too Small in a Democracy." *World Politics,* Vol. XII (July 1960), pp. 541–63.

Eisner, Robert. *How Real Is the Federal Deficit?* New York: Free Press, 1986.

Ellwood, John W., ed. *Reductions in U.S. Domestic Spending: How They Affect State and Local Governments.* New Brunswick, N.J.: Transaction Books, 1982.

————. "The Great Exception: The Congressional Budget Process in an Age of Decentralization." In Lawrence Dodd and Bruce Oppenheimer, eds. *Congress Reconsidered,* 3rd ed. Washington, D.C.: CQ Press, 1985.

Ellwood, John W., and James A. Thurber. "The New Congressional Budget

Process: The Hows and Why of House–Senate Differences." In Lawrence
Dodd and Bruce Oppenheimer, eds. *Congress Reconsidered.* New York:
Praeger, 1977, pp. 163–92.

Enthoven, Alain C., and Wayne K. Smith. *How Much Is Enough?* New York:
Harper & Row, 1971.

Feldman, Paul, and James Jandrow. "Congressional Elections and Local Federal
Spending." *American Journal of Political Science,* Vol. 28, No. 1 (February
1984), pp. 147–64.

Fenno, Richard F., Jr. "The House Appropriations Committee as a Political
System: The Problem of Integration." *The American Political Science Review,* Vol. 56 (June 1962), pp. 310–24.

———. *The Power of the Purse: Appropriations Politics in Congress.* Boston:
Little, Brown, 1966.

Ferejohn, John A. "Logrolling in an Institutional Context: A Case Study of
Food Stamps Legislation." *Working Papers in Political Science,* P-5-85. Palo
Alto, Calif.: Hoover Institute, 1985.

Fiorina, Morris. *Congress—Keystone of the Washington Establishment.* New
Haven, Conn.: Yale University Press, 1977.

Fisher, Louis. *President and Congress.* New York: Free Press, 1972.

———. *Presidential Spending Power.* Princeton: Princeton University Press,
1975.

———. "The Authorization-Appropriation Process in Congress: Formal Rules
and Informal Practices." *Catholic University Law Review,* Vol. 29, No. 5
(1979), pp. 52–105.

———. "In Dubious Battle? Congress and the Budget." *The Brookings Bulletin,* Vol. 17 (Spring 1981), pp. 6–10.

———. "The Budget Act of 1974: A Further Loss of Spending Control." In
Thomas Wander et al., eds. *Congressional Budgeting.* Baltimore: Johns Hopkins University Press, 1984, pp. 170–89.

———. *Constitutional Conflicts Between Congress and the President.* Princeton: Princeton University Press, 1985.

Fisher, Louis, and Neal Devins. "How Successfully Can the States' Item Veto
Be Transferred to the President?" *Georgetown Law Journal,* Vol. 75, No. 1
(October 1986), pp. 159–97.

Fitzpatrick, Edward Augustus. *Budget Making in a Democracy.* New York:
Macmillan, 1918.

Forsythe, Dall W. *Taxation and Political Change in the Young Nation 1781–1833*. New York: Columbia University Press, 1977.

Fox, Ronald J. *Arming America: How the U.S. Buys Weapons*. Cambridge: Harvard University Press, 1974.

———. "Revamping the Business of National Defense." *Harvard Business Review*, Vol. 62, No. 5 (September/October 1985).

Gansler, Jacques S. "How to Improve the Acquisition of Weapons." In Robert J. Art et al., eds. *Reorganizing America's Defense*. Washington, D.C.: Pergamon Brassey, 1985.

Gilmour, Robert. "Central Legislative Clearance: A Revised Perspective." *Public Administration Review*, Vol. XXXI (March/April 1971), pp. 150–58.

Greenberg, D. "Renal Politics." *New England Journal of Medicine*, Vol. 298, No. 25 (June 22, 1978).

Greenfield, Margaret. *Medicare and Medicaid: The 1965 and 1967 Social Security Amendments*. Westport, Conn.: Greenwood, 1968.

Greider, William. "The Education of David Stockman." *The Atlantic Monthly*, December 1981, pp. 27–54.

Guess, George, and Kenneth Koford. "Inflation, Recession and the Federal Budget Deficit (or, Blaming Economic Problems on a Statistical Mirage)." *Policy Sciences*, Vol. 17 (1984), pp. 385–402.

Haas, Lawrence J. "New Rules of the Game." *National Journal*, November 17, 1990, pp. 2793–97.

Hammond, Thomas H., and Jack H. Knott. *A Zero-Based Look at Zero-Base Budgeting*. New Brunswick, N.J.: Transaction, 1979.

Hardin, Clifford M., and Arthur T. Denzau. "Closing the Back Door on Federal Spending: Better Management of Federal Credit." Formal Publication #64, September 1984, Center for the Study of American Business, Washington University, St. Louis, Missouri.

Harper, Edwin L., Fred A. Kramer, and Andrew M. Rouse. "Implementation and the Use of PPB in Sixteen Federal Agencies." *Public Administration Review*, Vol. XXIX (November/December 1969).

Harrington, Michael. "Building Arms Control into the National Security Process." *Arms Control Today*, February 1975.

Hartman, Robert W. "Multiyear Budget Planning." In Joseph A. Pechman, ed. *Setting National Priorities: The 1979 Budget*. Washington, D.C.: The Brookings Institution, 1978.

————. "Congress and Budget-Making," *Political Science Quarterly,* Vol. 97, No. 3 (Fall 1982), pp. 381–402.

————. "Making Budget Decisions." In Joseph A. Pechman, ed. *Setting National Priorities: The 1983 Budget.* Washington, D.C.: The Brookings Institution, 1982.

————. "Budget Summit 1990: The Role of Economic and Budget Analysis." Paper prepared for the Association for Public Policy Analysis and Management Conference, October 18–20, 1990.

Heclo, Hugh. "Executive Budget Making." In Gregory B. Mills and John L. Palmer, eds. *Federal Budget Policy in the 1980s.* Washington, D.C.: The Urban Institute, 1984.

Heclo, Hugh, and Aaron Wildavsky. *The Private Government of Public Money: Community and Policy inside British Political Administration,* 2nd ed. London: Macmillan, 1981.

Hibbs, Douglas A., Jr., and Christopher Dennis. "The Politics and Economics of Income Distribution Outcomes in the Postwar United States." Transcript, 1986.

Hitch, Charles. *Decision-Making for Defense.* Berkeley: University of California Press, 1970.

Huntington, Samuel P. *The Common Defense.* New York: Columbia University Press, 1961.

Iglehart, J. K. "Funding the End-Stage Renal Disease Program." *The New England Journal of Medicine,* Vol. 306, No. 8 (February 25, 1982).

Ippolito, Dennis S. *Hidden Spending: The Politics of Federal Credit Programs.* Chapel Hill: University of North Carolina Press, 1984.

Irwin, David T. "Evaluating Municipal Revenue Sources." *Government Finance,* Vol. 5 (February 1976).

Johnson, Bruce. "From Analyst to Negotiator: The OMB's New Role." *Journal of Policy Analysis and Management,* Vol. 3, No. 4 (1984).

Kamlet, Mark S., and David C. Mowery. "The Budgetary Base in Federal Resource Allocation." *American Journal of Political Science,* Vol. 24, No. 4 (November 1980), pp. 806–21.

————. "Budgetary Side Payments and Government Growth: 1953–1968." *American Journal of Political Science,* Vol. 27, No. 4 (November 1983), pp. 636–64.

————. "Contradictions of Congressional Budget Reform: Problem of Congressional Emulation of Executive Branch." Typescript, 1984.

————. "The First Decade of the Congressional Budget Act: Legislative Imitation and Adaptation in Budgeting." *Policy Sciences,* Vol. 18, No. 4 (December 1985), pp. 313–34.

————. "Influences on Executive and Congressional Budgetary Priorities, 1953–1981." *American Political Science Review,* Vol. 81, No. 1 (March 1987), pp. 155–73.

Kamlet, Mark S., David C. Mowery, and Tsai-Tsu Su. "Whom Do You Trust? An Analysis of Executive and Congressional Economic Forecasts." *Journal of Policy Analysis and Management,* Vol. 6, No. 3 (1987), pp. 365–84.

Kanter, Arnold. *Defense Politics.* Chicago: University of Chicago Press, 1975.

Kasten, Richard, and Frank Sammartino. "Who Pays for Federal Deficit Reduction?" Paper prepared for the Association for Public Policy Analysis and Management Conference, October 18–20, 1990.

Kaufmann, William W. *A Reasonable Defense.* Washington, D.C.: The Brookings Institution, 1986.

Keith, Robert, and Edward Davis. "Congress and Continuing Appropriations: New Variations on an Old Theme." *Public Budgeting and Finance,* Vol. 5 (Spring 1985).

Kellman, Steve. "The Grace Commission: How Much Waste in Government?" *The Public Interest,* No. 78 (Winter 1985).

Kerr, L. E. "Black Lung." *Journal of Public Health Policy,* Vol. 1, No. 1 (March 1980).

Kettl, Donald. "The Great Budget Debate." *VIPPS News,* Vanderbilt Institute for Public Policy Studies, Vol. 4, No. 2 (Summer 1990), pp. 1–2.

Key, V. O., Jr. "The Lack of Budgetary Theory." *The American Political Science Review,* Vol. 34 (December 1940), pp. 1137–44.

Kim, Sun Kil. "The Politics of a Congressional Budgetary Process 'Backdoor Spending.'" *Western Political Quarterly,* Vol. 21 (December 1968), pp. 606–23.

Kimmel, Lewis H. *Federal Budget and Fiscal Policy 1789–1958.* Washington, D.C.: The Brookings Institution, 1959.

King, Ronald. "Tax Expenditures and Systematic Public Policy." Paper presented for delivery at the Annual Meeting of the American Political Science Association, Denver, Colorado, September 2–5, 1982.

Kogan, Richard. "The Budget Enforcement Act of 1990: A Technical Explanation." November 1, 1990, unpublished.

Korb, Lawrence. "The Budget Process in the Department of Defense 1947–77:

The Strengths and Weaknesses of Three Systems." *Public Administration Review*, Vol. XXXVII (July/August 1977), pp. 334–36.

————. "The Process and Problems of Linking Policy and Force Structure through the Defense Budget Process." In Robert Harkavy and Edward Kolodziej, eds. *American Security Policy and Policy Making*. Lexington, Mass.: Lexington Books, 1980.

Kolata, G. B. "NMC Thrives Selling Dialysis." *Science*, Vol. 208 (April 25, 1980).

Kristensen, Ole P. "The Logic of Bureaucratic Decision-Making as a Cause of Governmental Growth." *European Journal of Political Research*, Vol. 8 (1980), pp. 249–64.

Ladd, Carl. "Americans' Hate Affair with Deficits." *Fortune*, June 14, 1982, pp. 77–84.

Larkey, P. D., C. Stolp, and M. Winer. "Theorizing about the Growth of Government: A Research Assessment." *Journal of Public Policy*, Vol. I (1981), pp. 157–220.

Lawton, Frederick J. "Legislative-Executive Relationships in Budgeting as Viewed by the Executive." *Public Administration Review*, Vol. 13 (Summer 1953), pp. 169–76.

Lekachman, Robert. *The Age of Keynes*. New York: McGraw-Hill, 1966.

LeLoup, Lance. "Discretion in National Budgeting: Controlling the Controllables." *Policy Analysis*, Vol. 4, No. 4 (Fall 1978), pp. 455–75.

LeLoup, Lance, Barbara Luck Graham, and Stacey Barwick. "Deficit Politics and Constitutional Government: The Impact of Gramm–Rudman–Hollings." *Public Budgeting & Finance*, Vol. 7, No. 1 (Spring 1987), pp. 83–104.

Leonard, Herman B. *Checks Unbalanced: The Quiet Side of Public Spending*. New York: Basic Books, 1986.

Levine, Charles H., and Paul L. Posner. "The Centralizing Effects of Austerity on the Intergovernmental System." *Political Science Quarterly*, Vol. 96 (Spring 1981), pp. 67–85.

Levine, Charles H., and Irene Rubin, eds. *Fiscal Stress and Public Policy*. Beverly Hills: Sage Publications, 1980.

Levy, Frank. *Dollars and Dreams: The Changing American Income Distribution*, New York: Russell Sage Foundation, 1987.

Lewis, Verne B. "Toward a Theory of Budgeting." *Public Administration Review*, Vol. 12 (Winter 1952), pp. 42–54.

Lindblom, Charles E. "Decision-Making in Taxation and Expenditure." In *Public Finances: Needs, Sources and Utilization*, National Bureau of Economic Research. Princeton: Princeton University Press, 1961, pp. 295–336.

————. "The Science of 'Muddling Through.' " *Public Administration Review,* Vol. XIX (Spring 1959), pp. 79–88.

Lindsay, James M. "Congress and Defense Policy: 1961 to 1986." *Armed Forces & Society,* Vol. 13, No. 3 (Spring 1987).

Maas, Arthur. "In Accord with the Program of the President?" In Carl Friedrich and Kenneth Galbraith, eds. *Public Policy,* Vol. 4. Cambridge, Mass.: Graduate School of Public Administration, 1954, pp. 77–93.

MacDonald, Maurice. *Food Stamps and Income Maintenance.* New York: Academic Press, 1977.

McGeary, M. Nelson. "The Governor's Veto in Pennsylvania." *American Political Science Review,* Vol. 41, No. 5 (October 1947).

MacMahon, Arthur. "Congressional Oversight of Administration." *Political Science Quarterly,* Vol. LVIII (June and September 1943), pp. 161–90, 380–414.

————. "Woodrow Wilson: Political Leader and Administrator." In Earl Latham, ed. *The Philosophy and Policies of Woodrow Wilson.* Chicago: University of Chicago Press, 1958, pp. 100–22.

Manley, John F. "The Conservative Coalition in Congress." *American Behavioral Scientist,* Vol. 17, No. 2 (November/December 1973), pp. 223–48.

Mansfield, Harvey C., Jr. "The American Election: Entitlements Versus Opportunity." *Government and Opposition,* Vol. 20, No. 1 (Winter 1985), pp. 3–17.

Marvick, L. Dwaine. *Congressional Appropriation Politics.* Ph.D. Dissertation, Columbia University, 1952.

Marx, Fritz Morstein. "The Bureau of the Budget: Its Evolution and Present Role." *American Political Science Review,* Vol. 39, No. 4 (August 1945), pp. 653–84.

————. "The Bureau of the Budget: Its Evolution and Present Role, II." *American Political Science Review,* Vol. 39 (October 1945), pp. 869–98.

Mayhew, David. *Congress: The Electoral Connection.* New Haven: Yale University Press, 1974.

Meyer, Jack A. "Budget Cuts in the Reagan Administration: A Question of Fairness." In D. Lee Bauden, ed. *The Social Contract Revisited.* Washington, D.C.: Urban Institute, 1984, pp. 33–64.

Miles, Jerome A. "The Congressional Budget and Impoundment Control Act: A Departmental Budget Officer's View." *The Bureaucrat,* Vol. 5, No. 4 (January 1977).

Mills, Gregory B., and John L. Palmer. *The Deficit Dilemma.* Washington, D.C.: Urban Institute, 1983.

Minarik, Joseph J., and Rudolph G. Penner. "Fiscal Choices." In Isabel V

Sawhill, ed. *Challenge to Leadership.* Washington, D.C.: Urban Institute, 1988.

Morey, Roy D. "The Executive Veto in Arizona: Its Use and Limitations." *The Western Political Quarterly,* Vol. 19, No. 3 (September 1966).

Mosher, Frederick C. *Program Budgeting: Theory and Practice, with Particular Reference to the U.S. Department of the Army.* Chicago: Public Administration Service, 1954.

————. *The GAO: The Quest for Accountability in American Government.* Boulder, Colo.: Westview Press, 1979.

————. *A Tale of Two Agencies: A Comparative Analysis of the General Accounting Office and the Office of Management and Budget.* Baton Rouge: Louisiana State University Press, 1984.

Mowery, David S., Mark S. Kamlet, and John P. Crecine. "Presidential Management of Budgetary and Fiscal Policymaking." *Political Science Quarterly,* Vol. 95, No. 1 (Fall 1980), pp. 395–425.

Moynihan, Daniel P. *The Politics of a Guaranteed Income.* New York: Random House, 1973.

Myers, Margaret G. *A Financial History of the United States.* New York: Columbia University Press, 1970.

Myers, Robert J. *Medicare.* Bryn Mawr, Penn.: McCahan Foundation, 1970.

Naylor, E. E. *The Federal Budget System in Operation.* Washington, D.C.: Hayworth Printing, 1941.

Nelson, Dalmas H. "The Omnibus Appropriations Act of 1950." *Journal of Politics,* Vol. XV (May 1953), pp. 274–88.

Newstadt, Richard. "Presidency and Legislation: The Growth of Central Clearance." *American Political Science Review,* Vol. 48 (September 1954), pp. 641–71.

————. "Presidency and Legislation: Planning the President's Program." *American Political Science Review,* Vol. XLIX (December 1955), pp. 980–1021.

Ney, R. T. "The ESRD Medicare Program—A Clarification." *Dialysis and Transplantation,* Vol. 10, No. 3 (March 1981).

Niskanen, William A. *Bureaucracy and Representative Government.* Chicago: University of Chicago Press, 1971.

————. "Deficits, Government Spending and Inflation: What Is the Evidence?" *Journal of Monetary Economics,* Vol. 4 (August 1978), pp. 591–602.

Ornstein, Norman J., and Shirley Elder. "The B-1 Bomber: Organizing at the

Grassroots." In Eston White, ed. *Studies in Defense.* Washington, D.C.: National Defense University Press, 1983.

Palmer, John, and Stephanie Gould. "Should We Worry About the Deficit?" *The Washington Monthly* (May 1986), pp. 43–46.

Pascall, Glenn. *The Trillion Dollar Budget.* Seattle: University of Washington Press, 1985.

Payne, James L. "Voters Aren't So Greedy After All." *Fortune,* August 18, 1986, pp. 91–92.

Penner, Rudolph G. "Forecasting Budget Totals: Why Can't We Get It Right?" In Michael J. Boskin and Aaron Wildavsky, eds. *The Federal Budget: Economics and Politics.* San Francisco: Institute for Contemporary Studies, 1982, pp. 89–110.

Perloff, Harvey Stephen. *Modern Budget Policies: A Study of the Budget Process in Present-Day Society.* Ph.D. Dissertation submitted to the Departments of Government and Economics, Harvard University, December 1, 1939.

Peters, Jean. "Reconciliation 1982: What Happened?" *PS,* Vol. 14, No. 4 (Fall 1981), pp. 732–36.

Phaup, Marvin. "Accounting for Federal Credit: A Better Way." *Public Budgeting and Finance,* Vol. 5, No. 3 (Autumn 1985), pp. 29–39.

Pocock, J. G. *The Political Works of James Harrington.* Cambridge, Mass.: Cambridge University Press, 1977.

Popick, Bernard. "The Social Security Disability Program. III. The Black Lung Benefits—an Administrative Case Study." *Journal of Occupational Medicine,* Vol. 13, No. 7 (July 1971).

Potter, Jim. *The American Economy between the World Wars.* New York: Wiley, 1974.

Pristave, R. J., and J. B. Riley. "HCFA Publishers Final ESRD Prospective Reimbursement Regulations." *Dialysis and Transplantation,* Vol. 12, No. 6 (June 1983).

Ransome, Coleman B., Jr. *The American Governorship.* Westport, Conn.: Greenwood Press, 1982.

Rasky, Susan F. "Substantial Power on Spending Is Shifted from Congress to Bush." *The New York Times,* October 30, 1990, pp. 1A, 13.

Reischauer, Robert. "Mickey Mouse or Superman? The Congressional Budget Process during the Reagan Administration." Paper presented to APPAM, Philadelphia, October 20–22, 1983.

Rettig, R. A. "The Policy Debate on Patient Care Financing for Victims of

End-Stage Renal Disease." *Law and Contemporary Problems,* Vol. 40, No. 4 (Autumn 1976).

———. "End-Stage Renal Disease and the 'Cost' of Medical Technology." In *Medical Technology: The Culprit behind Health Care Costs?* U.S. DHHS, 1979.

———. "The Politics of Health Cost Containment: ESRD." *Bulletin of New York Academy of Medicine,* Vol. 56, No. 1 (January/February 1980).

Rivlin, Alice M. "The Political Economy of Budget Choices: A View from Congress." Paper presented at AEA meeting, December 29, 1981.

———. "Reform of the Budget Process." *The American Economic Review,* Vol. 74, No. 2 (May 1984), pp. 133–37.

Rovner, Mark. *Defense Dollars and Sense.* Washington, D.C.: Common Cause, 1983.

Rubin, Irene. *Shrinking the Federal Government: The Effect of Cutbacks on Five Federal Agencies.* New York: Longman, 1985.

Ruddock, Andrew E. "A Critique of Various Study Documents." In Dan M. McGill, ed. *Financing the Civil Service Retirement System.* Homewood, Ill.: Richard D. Irwin, 1979.

Sanders, Arthur. "Public Attitudes on Public Spending." Paper prepared for the 1984 Annual Meeting of the American Political Science Association, Washington, D.C., August 30–September 2, 1984.

Shanks, J. Merrill, and Warren Miller. "Policy Direction and Performance Evaluation: Complementary Explanations of the Reagan Elections." Presented to the Annual Meeting of the American Political Science Association, New Orleans, August 29–September 1, 1985.

Schelling, Thomas C. *The Strategy of Conflict.* Cambridge: Harvard University Press, 1960.

Schick, Allen. "The Road to PPB: The Stages of Budget Reform." In *Public Administration Review,* December 1966, pp. 243–58.

———. "The Budget Bureau That Was: Thoughts on the Rise, Decline, and Future of a Presidential Agency." *Law and Contemporary Problems,* Vol. XXXV (Summer 1970), pp. 519–39.

———. "Budgetary Adaptations to Resource Scarcity." In Charles H. Levine and Irene Rubin, eds. *Fiscal Stress and Public Policy.* Beverly Hills: Sage Publications, 1980.

———. *Congress and Money.* Washington, D.C.: Urban Institute, 1980.

———, ed. *Perspectives on Budgeting.* American Society for Public Administration, 1980.

———. "Controlling the Budget by Statute: An Imperfect but Workable Process." In Alvin Rabushka and William Craig Stubblebine, eds. *Constraining Federal Taxing and Spending.* Stanford, Calif.: Hoover Institution, 1982.

———. "Controlling the 'Uncontrollables': Budgeting for Health Care in an Age of Mega-Deficits." Paper prepared for AEI Pew Fellows Conference, November 1985.

———. "The Evolution of Congressional Budgeting." In Allen Schick, ed. *Crisis in the Budget Process.* Washington, D.C.: American Enterprise Institute, 1986.

———. *The Capacity to Budget.* Washington, D.C.: Urban Institute, 1990.

Schier, Steven E. "Thinking about the Macroeconomy: The House and Senate Budget Committees in the 1980s." Paper prepared for 1985 Annual Meeting of APSA, New Orleans, August 29–September 1, 1985.

Shultz, George P., and Kenneth W. Dam. *Economic Policy beyond the Headlines.* New York: W. W. Norton and Co., 1977.

Shultz, William J., and M. R. Caine. *Financial Development of the United States.* New York: Prentice-Hall, 1937.

Seligman, Edwin R. A. *The Income Tax.* New York: Macmillan, 1921.

Simon, Herbert A. "The Criterion of Efficiency." In *Administrative Behavior,* 2nd ed. New York, Macmillan, 1957.

———. *Models of Man.* New York: Wiley, 1957.

Simon, Herbert A., Donald Smithburg, and Victor Thompson. "The Struggle for Existence." In *Public Administration.* New York: Knopf, 1950, pp. 381–422.

Smithies, Arthur. *The Budgetary Process in the United States.* New York: McGraw-Hill, 1955.

Snipper, Reuben. "Interactions among Programs Providing Benefits to Individuals: Secondary Effects of the Budget." Congressional Budget Office Report, May 1982.

Stein, Herbert. *The Fiscal Revolution in America.* Chicago: University of Chicago Press, 1969.

Stewart, Charles Haines, III. *The Politics of Structural Reform: Reforming Budgetary Structure in the House, 1865–1921.* Dissertation submitted to Stanford University, August 1985.

Stockman, David. "The Social Pork Barrel." *The Public Interest*, No. 39 (Spring 1975), pp. 3–30.

———. *The Triumph of Politics*. New York: Harper & Row, 1986.

Stone, Deborah. *The Disabled State*. Philadelphia: Temple University Press, 1984.

Straussman, Jeffrey D. "Spending More and Enjoying It Less." *Comparative Politics*, January 1981, pp. 235–51.

Tarschys, Daniel L. "The Growth of Public Expenditures: Nine Modes of Explanation." *Scandinavian Political Studies*. Vol. 10 (1975), pp. 9–31.

———. "Curbing Public Expenditures: Current Trends." *Journal of Public Policy*, Vol. 5 (1985), pp. 23–67.

Thompson, James D., and Arthur Tuden. "Strategies, Structures, and Processes of Organizational Decision." In J. D. Thompson, et al., eds. *Comparative Studies in Administration*. Pittsburgh: University of Pittsburgh Press, 1959.

Tobin, James. "The Future of Social Security: One Economist's Assessment." Working Paper #4, Project on the Federal Social Role, National Conference on Social Welfare, Washington, D.C., 1985.

Tomer, John F. "Revenue Sharing and the Intrastate Fiscal Mismatch." *Public Finance Quarterly*, Vol. 5 (October 1977).

Van Gunsteren, Herman R. *The Quest for Control*. New York: Wiley, 1976.

Verba, Sidney, and Gary R. Orren. *Equality in America: The View from the Top*. Cambridge, Mass.: Harvard University Press, 1985.

Waldo, Dwight. *The Administrative State*. New York: Ronald Press, 1948.

Walker, Robert. "William A. Jump: The Staff Officer As a Personality." *Public Administration Review*, Vol. XIV (Autumn 1954), pp. 233–46.

Walker, Wallace Earl. *Changing Organizational Culture: Strategy, Structure, and Professionalism in the U.S. General Accounting Office*. Knoxville: University of Tennessee Press, 1986.

Weaver, R. Kent. "Controlling Entitlements." In John E. Chubb and Paul E. Peterson, eds. *The New Direction in American Politics*. Washington, D.C.: The Brookings Institution, 1985.

Webber, Carolyn, and Aaron Wildavsky. *A History of Taxation and Expenditure in the Western World*. New York: Simon and Schuster, 1986.

White, Joseph. "What Budgeting Cannot Do: Lessons of Reagan's and Other Years." In Irene Rubin, ed. *New Directions in Budget Theory*. Albany: SUNY Press, 1988, pp. 165–202.

———. "Better News Than They Think." *San Diego Union*, October 7, 1990.

White, Joseph, and Aaron Wildavsky. *The Deficit and the Public Interest.* Berkeley: University of California Press, 1990.

―――. "How to Fix the Deficit—Really." *The Public Interest,* No. 94 (Winter 1989), pp. 3–24.

White, Leonard D. *The Jeffersonians: A Study in Administration History, 1801– 1829.* New York: Macmillan, 1951.

―――. *The Jacksonians: A Study in Administrative History, 1829–1861.* New York: Macmillan, 1954.

―――. *The Federalists: A Study in Administrative History.* New York: Macmillan, 1961.

Wildavsky, Aaron. *Dixon-Yates: A Study in Power Politics.* New Haven: Yale University Press, 1962.

―――. *The Politics of the Budgetary Process.* Boston: Little, Brown, 1964; revised 4th ed., 1984.

―――. "The Political Economy of Efficiency: Cost-Benefit Analysis, Systems Analysis, and Program Budgeting." *Public Administration Review,* Vol. 26, No. 4 (December 1966), pp. 292–310.

―――. "Rescuing Policy Analysis from PPBS." *Public Administration Review,* Vol. 29, No. 2 (March/April 1969), pp. 189–202.

―――. *The Budgeting and Evaluation of Federal Recreation Programs, or Money Doesn't Grow on Trees.* With Jeanne Nienaber. New York: Basic Books, 1973.

―――. *Budgeting: A Comparative Theory of Budgetary Processes.* Boston: Little, Brown, 1975; revised 2nd ed., Transaction Publishers, 1986.

―――. "Doing Better and Feeling Worse: The Political Pathology of Health Policy." *Daedalus,* Winter 1976, pp. 105–23.

―――. "Ask Not What Budgeting Does to Society but What Society Does to Budgeting." Introduction to the second edition of *National Journal Reprints.* Washington, D.C., 1977.

―――. "A Budget for All Seasons? Why the Traditional Budget Lasts." *The Public Administration Review,* No. 6 (November/December 1978), pp. 501– 509. Also in B. Geist, ed. *State Audit: Developments in Public Accountability.* London & Basingstoke: Macmillan, 1981, pp. 253–68.

―――. *Speaking Truth to Power.* Boston: Little, Brown, 1979.

―――. *How to Limit Government Spending.* Los Angeles and Berkeley: University of California Press, 1980.

―――. "Budgets as Compromises among Social Orders." In Michael J. Boskin and Aaron Wildavsky, eds. *The Federal Budget: Economics and Politics.* San Francisco, 1982, pp. 21–38.

――――. "Modelling the U.S. Federal Spending Process: Overview and Implications." With Michael Dempster. In R. C. O. Matthews and G. B. Stafford, eds. *The Grants Economy and Collective Consumption.* London & Basingstoke: Macmillan, 1983, pp. 267–309.

――――. "The Transformation of Budgetary Norms." *Australian Journal of Public Administration,* Vol. XLII, No. 4 (December 1983), pp. 421–32.

――――. "The Unanticipated Consequences of the 1984 Presidential Election." *Tax Notes,* Vol. 24, No. 2 (July 9, 1984), pp. 193–200.

――――. "Budgets as Social Orders." *Research in Urban Policy,* Vol. 1 (1985), pp. 183–97.

――――. "A Cultural Theory of Expenditure Growth and (Un)Balanced Budgets." *Journal of Public Economics,* Vol. 28 (1985), pp. 349–57.

――――. "Item Veto without a Global Spending Limit: Locking the Treasury after the Dollars Have Fled." *Notre Dame Journal of Law, Ethics and Public Policy,* Vol. 1, No. 2 (1985), pp. 165–76.

――――. "The Logic of Public Sector Growth." In Jan-Erik Lane, ed. *State and Market.* London: Sage Publications, Ltd., 1985, pp. 231–70.

Willoughby, William Franklin. *The National Budget System with Suggestions for Its Improvement.* Baltimore: Johns Hopkins, 1927.

Wilmerding, Lucius W., Jr. *The Spending Power: A History of the Efforts of Congress to Control Expenditures.* New Haven: Yale University Press, 1943.

Wilson, Woodrow. *Congressional Government: A Study in American Politics.* Boston: Houghton Mifflin, 1895.

Witte, John F. "Tax Philosophy and Income Equality." In Robert A. Solo and Charles Anderson, eds. *Value Judgment and Income Distribution.* New York: Praeger, 1981, pp. 340–78.

――――. *The Politics and Development of the Federal Income Tax.* Madison: University of Wisconsin Press, 1985.

Wolf, John F. "The Item Veto in the American Constitutional System." *Georgetown Law Journal,* Vol. 25 (1936).

Young, James Sterling. *The Washington Community, 1802–1828.* New York: Columbia University Press, 1966.

CREDITS

Margulies cartoon, p. xxxii: Reprinted by permission of United Feature Syndicate, Inc.

Chapter 2, pp. 36–73: This chapter incorporates much of the material from Chapter 7, "Balanced Regimes, Balanced Budgets: Why America Was So Different," in *A History of Taxation and Expenditure in the Western World* by Carolyn Webber and Aaron Wildavsky (New York: Simon & Schuster, 1986). Copyright © 1986 by Carolyn Webber and Aaron Wildavsky. By permission.

Excerpt, p. 70: From *The New York Times,* December 27, 1938. Copyright © 1938 by The New York Times Company. Reprinted by permission.

Figure 4-1, p. 147: From *Fortune,* June 14, 1982. Copyright © 1982 Time Inc. All rights reserved.

Excerpts, pp. 179–180, 183–184: From Bruce Johnson, "The Increasing Role of the Office of Management and Budget in the Congressional Budget Process." Paper prepared for the 5th Annual Conference of the Association for Public Policy Analysis and Management, Philadelphia, October 21–22, 1983, pp. 6, 7–8. This paper later appeared, in revised form, under the title "From Analyst to Negotiator: The OMB's New Role," in *Journal of Policy Analysis and Management,* copyright © 1984 by the Association for Public Policy Analysis and Management. 3, no. 4 (1984), pp. 501–515. Reprinted by permission.

Excerpt, p. 200: From *Shrinking the Federal Government,* by Irene S. Rubin. Reprinted by permission of Irene S. Rubin.

Excerpt, pp. 217–218: From *Thinking about the Macroeconomy: The House and Senate Budget Committees in the 1980s,* American Academy of Higher Education Monograph Series, no. 12 (Washington, DC: AAHE, 1986), pp. 15, 21, 22. Reprinted by permission.

List, p. 246: From *National Journal,* January 11, 1986. Reprinted by permission.

Table 6-1, pp. 251–252: From *National Journal,* January 4, 1986. Reprinted by permission.

INDEX